The

Probation Directory 2013

Incorporating Offender Management and Interventions

Consultant Editor Owen Wells

Introduction

The Probation Directory is compiled each October. Wherever possible, changes that occur after October are included in the text up to 19th November. The very short time between compilation and publication means that the Probation Directory is probably the most up-to-date book of its kind published anywhere. If you wish to supply updated information for the next edition, please contact Sweet and Maxwell:

Email: probation.directory@thomsonreuters.com or sweetandmaxwell.customer.services@thomson.com

Owen Wells is the Consultant Editor of The Probation Directory 2013

Acknowledgement

Without the help of the Chief Officers and their administrative staff, NOMS and Prison Department, and many others this directory could not have been produced. The consultant editor and publisher wish to thank them all.

Abbreviations

Where a person has no designation after their name, they can be presumed to be a Probation Officer.

ACO	Assistant Chief Officer
CCLO	Crown Court Liaison Officer
CO	Chief Officer
JS	Job-sharing
P	Part-time
PAO	Principal Administrative Officer
PSA	Probation Service Assistant
PSO	Probation Service Officer
QA Mgr	Quality Assurance Manager
SPO	Senior Probation Officer
SSW	Senior Social Worker
SW	Social Worker
VLO	Victim Liaison Officer

Other job titles are explained in the text. In general, job titles in the Probation Service are becoming ever longer and more obscure. In the text they are usually abbreviated, but hopefully in a manner that will allow the reader to make an intelligent guess as to what they mean.

CONTENTS

PROFESSIONAL ORGANISATIONS

Napo

4 Chivalry Road, London SW11 1HT
Tel: 020 7223 4887 Fax: 020 7223 3503
Email: initiallastname@napo.org.uk
www.napo.org.uk

General Secretary: Jonathan Ledger
Asst Gen Sec (Campaign & PR): Harry
Fletcher
Asst Gen Sec (Conditions of Service): Ian
Lawrence
National Official (Health & Safety): Mike
McClelland
National Official (TUO / Equality &
Diversity): Ranjit Singh
National Official (Professional, Training,
Family Court): Sarah Friday
HR & Office Manager: Keith Waldron
Finance Officer: Theresa Boorman

Administration
Gen Sec, Neg & St: Annoesjka Valent
Resources & Information, TUO: Margaret
Pearce
Ags, Conditions of Service: Cynthia Griffith
Ags, Cam & PR: Kath Falcon
Equality & Diversity, Professional, Training:
Shireena Suleman
Membership: Anne Burbidge, Taytula Burke
NEC & Officers: Alison Bonner
Reception, Family Court: Jacqueline Paryag
(p)

Chair: Lisa Robinson / Tom Rendon (job
share)

Vice Chairs
Probation: Megan Elliott; Nick Smith; Eve
Chester/Caroline Bewley (job share)
Cafcass: Tony Mercer

Treasurer: Keith Stokeld

Probation Association

The Probation Association is the national
voice of the Trusts which employ the
service's 20,000 members of staff. We
represent the interests of Trusts to
Government, the Ministry of Justice and a
range of stakeholders.
29 Great Peter Street, London SW1P 3LW
Tel: 020 7340 0970
Email: association@probationassociation.co.uk
www.probationassociation.co.uk

Chief Executive: Mark Ormerod
Employment and HR Manager: Norma
Beechey
Governance Services Mgr: Mike Caldwell
Employment and Reward Mgr: Lynne Last
Accountant: Duncan Gaskell
PR & Communications Mgr: Neil Lampert
Sec to the Council & Board of Directors: Jo
Whyte
Office Administrator: Yasmin Jankowski-Doyle
Office Mgr: Liz Hogan

Probation Chiefs Association

The PCA is the independent leadership voice
of probation in England and Wales. It
represents the views of current probation
leaders, promoting confidence in and
increased understanding of the work
probation does to protect the public and cut
crime through reducing re-offending and
encouraging rehabilitation.

First Floor, 151 Buckingham Palace Road,
London, SW1W 9SZ
Tel: 0300 0480 229 or 0300 0480228
www.probationchiefs.org

Chair: Sue Hall (CEO West Yorkshire
Probation Trust)
Business Director: Savas Hadjipavlou Email:
savas.hadjipavlou@probationchiefs.org
Administrator and Director's PA: Jenny
Seaton Ulliott Email:
pcaadmin@probationchiefs.org

National Approved Premises Association

NAPA, PO Box 502 Newton Abbot TQ12 9GW
Tel: 07967 821776
Email: duncan.moss@napa-uk.org
www.napa-uk.org

National organisation working to support and
promote all approved premises (hostels) both
within probation and the independent
managed sector. The Association works in
partnership with other bodies concerned with
residential facilities for offenders and tackling
crime.
Director: Duncan Moss
Chair: Neville Thompson

Association of Black Probation Officers

The Association's definition of black is a
political one, which emphasises the common
experiences and determination of people of

African, African-Caribbean and Asian origin to oppose the effects of racism.

2nd Floor, Mitre House, 223/237 Borough High Street, London SE1 1JD
Tel: 020 7740 8537 Fax: 020 7740 8450
Chair: Abdallah Nagib-Ali 01753 537516
Vice Chair: Earl Smith 01443 494571
National Coordinator: Susan Roye 020 7740 8537
Treasurer: Trevor Bernard 0161 226 1179
Information Officer: Derek Rhoden 03000 478350
Midlands Region Convenor:
Northern Regional Convenor: Delpherine Blair 03000 478350 & Chinchin Oyolu-Barker 0191 584 3109
South Regional Convenor: Cheryl St. Luce 01992 504444, Patrick Jumbe 020 8472 5412 & Steve Oko 01273 810332

National Association of Asian Probation Staff

Encourages and maintains a support group of members promoting an Asian perspective on professional issues. Initiates and campaigns for changes within the CJ system to adjust the imbalance of disadvantage suffered by all minority ethnic groups.

Room 102a, 1st Floor, Mitre House, 223/237 Borough High Street, London SE1 1JD
Tel: 020 7740 8563; 07970 650360 Fax: 020 7740 8450

National Coordinator: Sarah Garg
Co-Chairs:
Azra Sharif 01274 704500
Dalvinder Singh 0161 620 4421
Vice Chair: Pervez Sadiq 07970 650360
Treasurer: Anita Dhokia 0116 299 5830
Membership Secretary: Sudeep Bone 0116 254 9059

Regional Coordinators:
London: Navinder Subherwal 020 7740 8455
Midlands: Intiaz Khan
East Midlands: Kiran Patel 01476 583153; Ranjna Sharma 01623 468850
North: Elizabeth Jan 01274 704565; Ishtiaq Ramzan 01274 704503
South: Sheetal Moore

LAGIP—Lesbians, Gay Men, Bisexual and Transgendered Individuals working in probation & family courts

Chair: Margaret Sinclair, West Mercia

Acting Vice Chair: Claire Saunders, Hampshire
National Coordinator: Richard Beavis, Norfolk & Suffolk
Regnl Coord East: Ann Rowe, Bedfordshire
Regnl Coord London: Sean Chapman, London
Regnl Coord Midlands and Wales: Margaret Sinclair, West Mercia
Regnl Coord North East: Vacant – please contact chair or vice chair
Regnl Coord North West: Janet Holton, Greater Manchester
Regnl Coord South-and West: Clare Saunders, Hampshire
Trans Lead: Helen Dale, Greater Manchester

Email: firstname.lastname@(trust name).probation.gsi.gov.uk
General Enquiries: admin@lagip.org.uk, telephone 01603 302180
Website: www.lagip.com

National Disabled Staff Network

Working to identify and remove institutional barriers and to empower disabled staff and service users in the Probation Service, MoJ, NOMS and Cafcass.

Chair Northumbria: Barbara Randall Tel: 01670 840871; 07812 347851 Email: Barbara.randall@northumbria.probation.gsi.gov.uk

Regional Coordinators
East of England: Vacancy
South East: Peter Wade Tel: 023 9272 8445; 07952 474903 Email: peter.wade@hampshire.probation.gsi.gov.uk
South West: Alyson Mannion alyson.mannion@devon-cornwall.probation.gsi.gov.uk
London: Charron Culnane Email: charron.culnane@london.probation.gsi.gov.uk
East Midlands: Theresa Lapidge Tel: 01456 614645 Email: theresa.lapidge@leicestershire.probation.gsi.gov.uk
West of Midlands: Ami Grewal Tel: 0121 248 6460 Email: ami.grewal@west-midlands.probation.gsi.gov.uk
Yorkshire & Humberside: Vacancy
North West: Vacancy
North East: Julie McShane Email: julie.mcshane@dtv.probation.gsi.gov.uk
Wales: Alistair Jinks Tel: 029 2078 5140; Fax: 029 2022 0042
Coordinator Cafcass: Vacancy

The Edridge Fund

The Edridge Fund of Napo is a registered charity that gives financial help to those in need. All members of the Probation Service, or CAFCASS, who are members of Napo, or are eligible to be members of Napo, can benefit as can retired staff and bereaved partners and dependants of either of the above. Each Napo branch has its own Edridge representative. Applications are generally made direct to the Fund, but can be made through these representatives and passed on to the trustees. Further details are available on the Edridge Fund website www.edridgefund.org, where application forms can be downloaded.

The Edridge Fund is in the process of a major reorganisation, with office functions performed in various locations. A modern telephone facility is being arranged, and details will be available on the website. In the meantime telephone enquiries should be made to David Cox – Treasurer & Business Manager on 01453 836119 Mobile 0775 3608917.

All postal communications should be sent to

The Secretary,

4, Chivalry Road, London, SW11 1HT.
Email: office@edridgefund.org
Website: www.edridgefund.org

Respect

4th Floor, Development House, 56–64 Leonard Street, London EC2A 4LT
Tel: 020 75490 578 Fax: 020 75490 352
Respect Phoneline: 0800 802 4040
Email: info@respect.uk.net
www.respect.uk.net
UK-wide membership organisation which promotes effective interventions with perpetrators of domestic violence to reduce the risk posed to victims and others. Respect sets service standards for organisations working with perpetrators of domestic violence and provides an accreditation for organisations against this standard.
Respect phoneline: 0808 802 4040; an information and advice line for domestic violence perpetrators and their (ex)partners as well as frontline workers
Email: phoneline@respect.uk.net
Men's Advice Line tel: 0808 801 0327; a helpline for male victims of domestic violence

www.mensadviceline.org.uk or info@mensadviceline.org.uk

Social Care Councils

The General Social Care Council is the regulatory body for the social work profession in England. Similar organisations exist in Northern Ireland, Scotland, and Wales (see below). It issues codes of practice, registers social workers and regulates social work education and training. On 31 July 2012, the Health Professions Council will take over the regulation of social workers in England, subject to Royal Assent of the Health and Social Care Bill.

England

General Social Care Council Goldings House 21 Bloomsbury Street, London WC1B 3HF
Tel: 020 7397 5100 Fax: 020 7397 5101
Helpline: 0845 070 0630
Email: info@gscc.org.uk
www.gscc.org.uk

General Social Care Council Myson House, Railway Terrace, Rugby CV21 3HT
Tel: 01788 572119 Fax: 01788 532474

Northern Ireland

Northern Ireland Social Care Council, 7th Floor, Millennium House, 19–25 Great Victoria Street, Belfast BT2 7AQ
Tel: 028 9041 7600
Email: info@niscc.hscni.net
www.niscc.info

Scotland

Scottish Social Services Council
Compass House, 11 Riverside Drive, Dundee DD1 4NY
Tel: 01382 207101 Fax: 01382 207215
Registration enquiries: 0845 603 0891
Email: enquiries@sssc.uk.com
www.sssc.uk.com

Wales

Care Council for Wales, 6th Floor, West Wing, South Gate House, Wood Street Cardiff CF10 1EW
Tel: 029 2022 6257 Fax: 029 2038 4764
Email: info@ccwales.org.uk
www.ccwales.org.uk

Care Council for Wales, Unit 19, St Asaph Business Park, Glascoed Road St Asaph LL17 0LJ
Tel: 01745 586850 Fax: 01745 584357

The National Organisation for Practice Teaching

NOPT, PO Box 145, Glossop, Derbyshire SK13 9AF
Email: admin@nopt.org
www.nopt.org

NOPT is a voluntary organisation promoting quality practice education in social work, offering membership to both individuals and organisations. NOPT provides members for several national committees and influences social work training and education and holds an annual Conference.

OFFENDER MANAGEMENT & PUBLIC PROTECTION GROUP

London: Room G.07A Clive House 70 Petty France London SW1H 9HD
London: Ground and 2nd Floor Grenadier House 99–105 Horseferry Road London SW1P 2DD

Public protection out of hours contact no: 0300 047 5000

Email: firstname.lastname@noms.gsi.gov.uk (some email addresses may also contain a figure; please check with recipient)
Head of OMPPG: Gordon Davison 0300 0474544
Personal Secretary: Brenda Tewson 0300 0474544
Senior Statistical Officer: Adam Spriggs 0300 0476241

NOS DIRECTORATE CORPORATE SERVICES HUB TEAM

Email: NOScorrespondence.omppg@noms.gsi.gov.uk
Email: TranscriptPublicProtection@noms.gsi.gov.uk
Ground and 2nd Floor Grenadier House 99–105 Horseferry Road London SW1P 2DD
Business Manager: Jennifer Lawrence Wynne 0300 047 4487
Business Administrator Manager: Mark Lee 0300 047 4489
Business Administrator Manager (Mon/Tues/Weds/Thurs): Linda Doran 0300 047 4441
Business Administrative: Kolawole Solanke 0300 047 4539

DANGEROUS OFFENDERS SECTION

Head of Dangerous Offenders Section: Al Reid 0300 047 4524

CENTRAL PROJECTS SECTION
Room G.07A Clive House
Email: cpt@noms.gsi.gov.uk
Officer Mgr: Daniella Parascandolo 0300 047 6070
Admin Support: James Keen 0300 047 6069

Extremism
Head of Extremism: Maxwell Beatson 0300 047 TBC

Critical Public Protection Casework
Email: cppc@noms.gsi.gov.uk
Head of Critical Public Protection Casework: Nichola Whiley 03000 474528
Section Senior Casework Mgr: Janet Gregory 0300 0474 466
Section Casework Mgr & Policy Development: Archana Sturge 0300 047 4514

Serious Further Offences (SFOs) Team
Email: sfo@noms.gsi.gov.uk
Head of SFOs Team: Matthew Ryder 0300 047 4526
Senior Probation Officer: Deanne Francis 0300 047 4550
Senior Policy Advisor: Victoria Quinn 0300 047 4521
Policy Mgr: Lee Quinn 0300 047 4522
Admin Support: Philip Cogram 0300 047 4427

PUBLIC POTECTION PARTNERSHIP, SAFEGUARDING VICTIMS SECTION
Ground Floor Grenadier House
Head of Public Protection Partnership, Safeguarding & Victim Section: Claire Wiggins 0300 047 4551

MAPPA Team
Email: mappa@noms.gsi.gov.uk
Joint Head of MAPPA Team: Becky Hart 0300 047 4377
Joint Head of MAPPA Team: Roy Ledingham 0300 047 4488
Policy Adviser: Paul Walsh 0300 047 5882
Admin Support: Eugenia Agyei 0300 047 4403

Domestic Abuse
Domestic Abuse Lead: Andrea King 0300 047 4263

Sex Offender Team
Head of Sex Offender Team: Joan Scott 0300 047 4530
Senior Probation Officer: Phil Jarvis 0300 047 4240
Policy Mgr: Maria Duraes 0300 047 4443

ViSOR
Email: mappa@noms.gsi.gov.uk

ViSOR Lead: Susan Fiddler 0300 047 4494
Approved Premises/Custodial

Public Protection/Safeguarding Team
Email: approvedpremises@noms.gsi.gov.uk
Head of Approved Premises/Custodial Public Protection/Safeguarding Team: Sean Langley 0300 047 4486
Custodial Public Protection: Khyati Parmar 0300 0474 513
Licence Conditions Policy Lead: Brian Chapman 0300 047 4424
Indeterminate Sentence Prisoners Policy Lead: Polly Churcher 0300 047 4426
Safeguarding Policy Mgr: Angela Colyer 0300 047 4431

Victims Team
Head of Victims Team: Laura Toze 0300 047 4228
Senior Policy Advisor: Vacancy 0300 047 4471
Policy Mgr: Julie Dennis 0300 047 4438

OFFENDER ASSESSMENT & MANAGEMENT
2nd Floor Grenadier House
Head of Offender Assessment & Management Section: Catriona Laing 0300 047 TBC

Offender Management Probation Qualifying
Probation Qualifying Framework/Community Order Specification Lead: Richard Pearce 0300 047 4266

Court Work/Bail Specification
Court Work/Bail Specification Lead: Roz Evenden 03000 475596
Court Work/Bail Specification Policy Manger Robin Dickens 0300 047 5595

Offender Management Custody Specification
Email: OMPPG.IPP.Queries@noms.gsi.gov.uk
Offender Management Custody Specification/ISP Co-ordination Lead: Gareth Mercer 0300 047 5601
Indeterminate Sentence Prisoners Policy Lead: Polly Churcher 0300 047 4426
Support Officer: Robert Hatch 0300 047 5582

Offender Management Specification Project Manager
Offender Management Specification Project Manager/Licence Conditions Policy Lead: Miranda Wilkinson 0300 047 5580
Licence Conditions Senior Policy Manager: Brian Chapman 0300 047 4424

OASys Operational Management
OASys Operational Manager Lead: Charlie Baker 0300 047 4374
OASys Operational Implementation Support Manager: Sharifa Mohamed 0300 047 4375
OASys Operational Implementation Support Manager: Joseph Sugden 0300 047 5585

Offender Management Change Programme
Head of Offender Mangement Change Programme: Paul Martin 0300 047 4373
Deputy Head of Offender Mangement Change Programme: Ian Hird 0300 047 TBC

PUBLIC PROTECTION CASEWORK SECTION
Ground and 2nd Floors Grenadier House

Head of Public Protection Casework Section: Russell A'Court 03000 474557

Pre-Release Casework Teams B, C, D, E
Desktop Fax: 0870 336 9209
Head of Casework Teams B-E: Clare Pope 03000 474518
Dep Head of Casework Teams B-E: Lisa Burrell 03000 474418

Pre-Release Casework Teams A, F, G, H, I, J
Head of Casework Teams A & F-J: Susan Gambling 03000 474461
Dep Head of Casework Teams A & F-J: Kerry Adams 03000 474401

Pre-Release Team A – Initial Action and Guittard applications
Desktop Fax: 0870 336 9213
Email: pre-releaseteama@noms.gsi.gov.uk
Team Ldr: James Hough 0300 047 4475
(Responsible for tariff casework & determinate compassionate release applications)
Jennifer Stoke 0300 047 4278
(Responsible for prisons beginning A-D)
Shahida Ali 0300 047 4404
(Responsible for prisons beginning E-NOR)
Rita Shah 0300 047 4533
(Responsible for prisons beginning NOS-Z)
Anne Gibbons 03000 474462

Pre-Release Team B – Dossier Team (indeterminate sentenced prisoners only). Dossiers, pre-tariff sifts, re-release life licences, cancellation life licence
Desktop Fax: 0870 336 9200
Email: pre-releaseteamb@noms.gsi.gov.uk

Team Ldr: Aaron Hiscox 0300 047 4474
Dossier Mgrs:
Frances Gregory 0300 047 4497

Azi Eniasoro 0300 047 4445
Susan Falola 0300 047 4447
Noor-Siraj Din 03000 474439
Karron Lovatt-Fraser 0300 047 4201
Claudia Busby 0300 047 6023
Dossier Support: Vacancy
Cheryl Anson-McAndrew 0300 047 4406
Lillian Onu 0300 047 4376

Pre-Release Team C (indeterminate sentenced prisoners only)
Desktop Fax: 0870 336 9209
Email: prereleaseteamc@noms.gsi.gov.uk

Team Ldr: Vacancy
Caseworker Mgrs:
Richard Walden 0300 047 4549
(Responsible for HMPs Chelmsford, Holloway, Latchmere House, Littlehey & Lowdham Grange (surname N–Z))
Neil Goodson 0300 047 4464
(Responsible for for HMPs Blundeston, Brixton, Highpoint, Hollesley Bay, Norwich and Warren Hill)
Anu Mojid 0300 047 4501
(Responsible for HMPs Bronzefield, Bure, Feltham and Wayland)
Valerie Henry 0300 047 4473
(Responsible for HMPs Belmarsh, Rye Hill & Whitemoor)
Irum Syed 0300 047 4543
(Responsible for HMPs Bedford, Lowdham Grange (surname A–M), The Mount & Peterborough)
Caseworker Support: Mark Ferrigan 0300 047 4448

Pre-Release Team D (indeterminate sentenced prisoners only)
Desktop Fax: 0870 336 9206
Email: pre-releaseteamd@noms.gsi.gov.uk
Team Ldr: Joanna Lindley 0300 047 4476
Caseworker Mgrs:
Christopher Hatzar 0300 047 4472
(Responsible for HMPs Isle Of Wight (Albany), Standford Hill and Wellingborough)
Marsha Spence 0300 047 4540
(Responsible for HMPs Blantyre House, Bullingdon, Lewes and Maidstone)
Vacancy
(Responsible for HMPs Elmley, Ford and Isle Of Wight (Parkhurst))
Gita Ladva 0300 047 4485
(Responsible for HMPs Cookham Wood, Coldingley, Downview, East Sutton Park, Huntercombe and Rochester)
Vacancy

(Responsible for HMPs Grendon, Isle Of Wight (Camp Hill), Ranby and Spring Hill)
Caseworker Support: Philippa Muir 03000 474503

Pre-Release Team E (indeterminate sentenced prisoners only)
Fax: 03000 474379
Email: pre-releaseteame@noms.gsi.gov.uk
Team Ldr: Philip Ransom 03000 474523
(Interim referall of HMPs Only, Swaleside (surnames L–Z) and Woodhill)
Caseworker Mgrs:
Baljit Khangura 0300 047 4483
(Responsible for HMPs Gartree (A–K), HMYOI Reading, and Whatton)
Vacancy
(Responsible for HMP Stocken and Swaleside (surnames A-K))
Kisha Broomfield 0300 047 4415
(Responsible for HMP Onley, Swaleside (surnames G-Z) and Woodhill)
Louise Chambers 03000 474423
(Responsible for HMPs HMYOI Aylesbury, High Down, Kingston, Leicester, North Sea Camp and Sudbury)
Fiona Mcghie 03000 474204
(Responsible for HMPs Foston Hall, Gartree (surnames L-Z), HMYOI Glen Parva, Lincoln, Morton Hall, Nottingham, Send and Winchester)
Prisoner Casework Team 1

Prisoner Casework Team 1
Email: BCU.Casework@noms.gsi.gov.uk
Fax: 0300 047 4379
Team Leader: Patricia O'Neill 0300 047 6047
Casework Managers:
Deborah Burke 0300 047 6037
Paul Lanham 0300 047 6036
Maria Tiramani 0300 047 6061
John White 0300 047 6062
Casework Support: Hoolsy Pattar 0300 047 6048

Prisoner Casework Team 2
Email: BCU.Casework@noms.gsi.gov.uk
Fax: 0300 047 4379
Team Leader: David HEALY 0300 047 6033
Casework Managers:
Soheli HOSSAIN 0300 047 6034
Jesha SUNDARESAN 0300 047 6058
Darren BUTLER 0300 047 4419
Jane DAWS 0300 047 4436
Administrative Support:
Manjinder NANDRA 0300 047 6045
Pravin SHAH 0300 047 6054

Pre-Release Team F – West Midlands (indeterminate sentenced prisoners only)
Fax: 03000 474394
Email: prereleaseteamf@noms.gsi.gov.uk
Team Ldr: Richard Modelly 03000 474500
Caseworker Mgrs:
Vacancy
(*Responsible for HMPs Birmingham & Full Sutton*)
Michele Bent 0300 047 4410
(*Responsible for HMPs Brinsford, Hewell and Swinfen Hall*)
Tony Cole 0300 047 4428
(*Responsible for HMPs Featherstone and Stafford*)
Hansha Deenoo-Bagchi 0300 047 4437
(Responsible for HMPs Drake Hall, Long Lartin and HMYOI Werrington)
Bill John 0300 047 4479
(Responsible for HMPs Dovegate, Shrewsbury and Stoke Heath)
Casework Support: Christine Amoako 03000 474405

Pre-Release Team G – North West (indeterminate sentenced prisoners only)
Desktop Fax: 0870 336 9206
Email: pre-releaseteamg@noms.gsi.gov.uk

Team Ldr: Jackie Cummins 0300 047 4547
Caseworker Mgrs:
Sherifat Idris 0300 047 4477
(*Responsible for HMPs Altcourse, Buckley Hall, Kennet & Manchester – Monday to Thursday*)
Anne Carter *0300 047 4422*
(*Responsible for HMP* Havering (A-H), Kirkham, Lancaster Farms and Styal)
Sangeeta Sachdeva 03000 474527
(*Responsible for HMPs* Forest Bank, Hindley, Preston and Risley)
Nadia Mujtaba 0300 047 4504
(*Responsible for HMPs* Garth, Havering (I-Z) and Thorne Cross)
Casework Support: Kevin Hampton 0300 047 4470

Pre-Release Team H – London, North East, Yorkshire (indeterminate sentenced prisoners only). Extremism, deport & MHCS cases, restricted transfers
Fax: 03000 474394
Email: pre-releaseteamh@noms.gsi.gov.uk

Team Ldr: Nicola Halse 03000 474468
Caseworker Mgrs:
Deborah Piper *0300 047 4517*
(Restricted Transfers Scottish and Northern Ireland cases and also responsible for HMPs Durham, Deerbolt and Frankland A-L)

Ajay Mungur 03000 474505
(Responsible for HMP Low Newton and for all PPCS FNP cases)
Shanelle Mccalla 03000 474495
(Responsible for HMPs Guy Marsh, Hull, Kirklevington Grange, Northumberland and Wetherby)
Joanne Chapman 0300 047 4496
(Responsible for Extremism, MHCS and also responsible for HMPs Frankland M-Z and Wandsworth)
Marcel Hawker 0300 047 4474
(Responsible for HMPs Holme House, Lindholme, Pentonville and Wormwood Scrubs)
Casework Support: Nicola Corbin 0300 047 4432

Pre-Release Team I – South West & Wales (indeterminate sentenced prisoners only)
Fax: 03000 474394
Email: pre-releaseteami@noms.gsi.gov.uk
Team Ldr: Samuel Asiedu 0300 047 4407
Caseworker Mgrs:
Laura Picton 0300 047 4516
(*Responsible for HMPs Bristol, Cardiff, Leyhill, Portland and Swansea*)
Carol Parke 0300 047 4512
(Responsible for HMPs Ashfield, Eastwood Park, Erlestoke, Exeter, Gloucester and Usk)
Omolara Ochei 03000 474508
(*Responsible for HMPs Channings Wood and The Verne*)
Naresh Kailayanathan 0300 047 4481
(*Responsible for HMPs Dartmoor, Dorchester and Shepton Mallet*)
Vacancy 0300 047 TBC
(*Responsible for HMPs Liverpool, Parc and Wymott*)
Casework Support: Keith Miller 03000 474498

Pre-Release Team J – Yorkshire & Humber (indeterminate sentenced prisoners only)
Fax: 0300 047 4394
Email: pre-releaseteamj@noms.gsi.gov.uk

Team Ldr: Kevin Breame 0300 047 4412
Caseworker Mgrs:
Leena Sajeev 0300 047 4245
(*Responsible for HMPs Everthorpe, Wakefield (A-P)*)
Daniel Bainbridge 0300 047 4246
(*Responsible for HMPs Askham Grange, Wakefield (Q-Z) and Wolds*)
Agnes John 0300 047 4248

(Responsible for HMPs Doncaster, Leeds, Moorland, New Hall, Northallerton and Wealstun)
Casework Support: Sindu Vaithiyanathan 0300 047 TBC – Maternity Leave

Public Protection Representatives
Ground and 2nd Floor Grenadier House
Representative Officers:
Amanda Smith 0300 047 4537 / 07894 489659
Darryl Burns 0300 047 4417 / 07889 600709
Anne Murphy 0300 047 4506 / 07889 600704
Penny Britton 0300 047 4413 / 07889 600706
Joanna Cain 0300 047 4420 / 07889 600710

HDC Breach Team – home detention curfew, all recalls of offenders on HDC
Email:
HDCBreachteamnoms@noms.gsi.gov.uk
Senior Office Manager HDC and Electronic Monitoring Breach Team and Pre-Tariff Sifts:
Peter Charlesworth: 0300 047 4425

HDC Mgr: Simon Brock 0300 047 4414
HDC Caseworkers:
Marcio Grana 03000 474465
Thomas Joseph 03000 474480
Umar Patel 0300 047 TBC

Quality Assurance, Operational Policy & Training Team
2nd Floor Grenadier House
Fax: 0300 047 4397
Email: Pre-Release
SPPU4PS@noms.gsi.gov.uk
Email: Post-Release
Performanceteam@noms.gsi.gov.uk
Email: PPCScomms@noms.gsi.gov.uk
Email: PPCS.Policy@noms.gsi.gov.uk
Head of Quality Assurance and Operational Policy: Christopher Kemp 0300 047 4482
Parole Hub Project Manager: Andrew Sansom 0300 047 4219 mobile 07887 745481
Deputy Head of Quality Assurance: Khatija Seedat 0300 047 4532
PPUD & Statistical Information Officer: Paul Wyatt 0300 047 4556

Operational Policy
Operational Policy Manager: Carly Jeffrey 0300 047 4247
Operational Policy Officer: Akil Esmail 0300 047 4446

Quality Assurance Team – Recall
Post Release Statisitical Information Manager: Sarah Odds 0300 047 4509
Post Release Statistical Information Officer: Sarah Wood 0300 047 4554

Quality Assurance & Training Team – Pre-Release
Training Manager: Neil Corry 0300 047 4433
Quality Assurance and Parole Helpdesk: Bukie Awomolo0300 047 4510
Quality Assurance Officer: Angela Fitzsimons 0300 047 4066
Training Officers:
Neil Wright 0300 047 4555
Rachel Wheatley 0300 047 4294
Joss Mistry (Mon/Weds) 0300 047 4499

Post Release Casework & Review Teams

Head of Post-Release Casework & Review: Ian York 0300 047 4330
Deputy Head of Post Release Casework: Nuzhat Razvi 0300 047 4331
Deputy Head of Recall Review Teams Sajjda Zafar 0300 047 4559
Review and Re-Release Team & Judicial Reviews Casework Manager (Tues/Weds): Kim Fitzgerald 0300 047 4332
Annual Review and OralHearing – Email: ppacasework@noms.gsi.gov.uk

Recall Team 1 – London, Durham & Teesside, Northumbria, Bedfordshire, Cambridgeshire, Essex, Hertfordshire, Norfolk, Suffolk, South Wales and North Wales
Email: recall1@noms.gsi.gov.uk
Casework Mgr Team 1: Gareth Hunter 020 8774 0267
Duty Officer: Nicola Priestley 0300 047 4304
Senior Caseworkers:
Aneeta Nahar 0300 047 4402
Ayodele Adeosun 0300 047 4402
Caseworkers:
Sagar Ravalia 0300 047 4301
Susan Theedam 0300 047 4307
Laura Watts 0300 047 4299
Fatima Reddiar 0300 047 4303
Margaret Billingsley 0300 047 4296
Haroon Baig 0300 047 4298
Hayley Turner 0300 047 4295
Fiona Corcoran 0300 047 4302

Recall Team 2 – Hampshire, Kent, Surrey, Sussex, Thames Valley, Avon Somerset, Devon Cornwall, Dorset, Gloucestershire, Wiltshire, Cheshire, Cumbria, Great Manchester, Lancashire, Merseyside, Gwent and Dyfed-Powys
Email: recall2@noms.gsi.gov.uk
Casework Mgr Team 2: Gareth Hunter 0300 047 4306
Duty Officer: Anu Kelmendi 0300 047 4309

Senior Caseworkers:
Lilly Brown 0300 047 4308
Diana Plummer 0300 047 4313
Phyllis Ofoha 0300 047 4317
Claire Owens 0300 047 4338
Sean Medford 0300 047 4311

Joanna Taylor 020 8774 0291
Yasmine Behardien 0300 047 4315
Sophie Lacey 0300 047 4316

Recall Team 3 – Staffordshire, West Midlands, Warwickshire, West Mercia, North Yorkshire, South Yorkshire, West Yorkshire, Derbyshire, Leicestershire Rutland, Lincolnshire, Northamptonshire, Nottinghamshire and Humberside
Email: recall3@noms.gsi.gov.uk
Casework Mgr Team 3: Conroy Barnett 0300 047 4318
Duty Officer: Ayesha Jassat 0300 047 4320

Senior Caseworkers:
Jacqueline King 0300 047 4484
Richard Jackson 0300 047 4323
Caseworkers:
Joshna Solanki 0300 047 4326
Norma O'Reilly 0300 047 4321
Benham Nelson 0300 047 4324
Menaka Ravindran-Sivapalan 0300 047 4325
Paul Mokuolo 0300 047 4334
Bushra Suleman 0300 047 4327
Rebecca Almond 0300 047 4328
Nikhil Rawell 0300 047 4322
Sonia Khan 0300 047 4319
Tally Heer 0300 047 TBC

Review Team 1 – London, Durham & Teesside, Northumbria, Bedfordshire, Cambridgeshire, Essex, Hertfordshire, Norfolk, Suffolk, South Wales and North Wales
Casework Mgr Review Team 1: Tracey Liston 0300 047 4490
Probation Officer: Heather Foster 0300 047 4290
Senior Caseworkers:
Sean Coles 0300 047 4429
Natalie Pang 0300 047 4291
Rebekah Weeks 0300 047 4081
Caseworkers:
Barbara Dow 0300 047 4292
Sarah Cortesi 0300 047 4289
James Gillam 0300 047 4293
Ian Barton 0300 047 TBC
Admin Support for Review Teams: Karen Duke 0300 047 4442

Review Team 2 – Hampshire, Kent, Surrey, Sussex, Thames Valley, Avon Somerset, Devon Cornwall, Dorset, Gloucestershire, Wiltshire, Cheshire, Cumbria, Great Manchester, Lancashire, Merseyside, Gwent and Dyfed-Powys
Casework Mgr Review Team 2: Emma McMaster 0300 047 4276

Probation Officer: Natalie Duncan 0300 047 TBC

Senior Caseworkers:
Claire Johnson 0300 047 4273
Daniel Martin 0300 047 4275
Lisa Madisson 0300 047 4492
Jennifer Dyer 0300 047 4444
Ambreen Ahmed 0300 047 4277

Caseworkers:
Zahida Brown 0300 047 4288
Moneka Bains 0300 047 4274
Lauren Brothwood 0300 047 TBC
Lakshmi Sreenivasan 0300 047 TBC

Review Team 3 – Staffordshire, West Midlands, Warwickshire, West Mercia, North Yorkshire, South Yorkshire, West Yorkshire, Derbyshire, Leicestershire Rutland, Lincolnshire, Northamptonshire, Nottinghamshire and Humberside
Casework Mgr Review Team 3: Emma Thompson 0300 047 4280
Probation Officer: Kauser Mukhtar 0300 047 4284

Senior Caseworkers:
Jennifer Hall 0300 047 4282
David White 0300 047 4286
Nazima Baubony 0300 047 4409

Caseworkers:
Glenda Dennis 0300 047 4285
Gavin Henry 0300 047 4281
Dean Shergold 0300 047 4279
Michael Strange 0300 047 4542

MENTAL HEALTH CASEWORK SECTION
Email: public_enquiry.mhu@noms.gsi.gov.uk
Faxes: 03000 474387 and 0300 047 4395

Head of Mental Health Casework Section:
Lindsay McKean 0300 047 4205

Quality Assurance & Casework Systems Team
Head of Quality Assurance & Casework Systems Team: Tish Jennings 0300 047 4230

Deputy Head of Quality Assurance & Casework Systems Team: Nigel Battson 0300 047 4180
Quality Assurance Officers:
Kalpna Verma 03000 474233
Lyndel Grover 03000 474193
Casework Systems Team Support Manager:
Ayesha Kalama 0300 047 4196
Casework Systems Support Administration:
Matt Noise 0300 047 4213
Casework Systems Team Support Assistants:
Nick Channell 0300 047 4182
Ray Mckennon 0300 047 4206
Stephen Curtis 0300 047 4185
Joanne Wong 0300 047 4235

Casework Team 1 – Patient Surname A-Gile
Fax: 0300 047 4387
CD reports desktop fax: 0870 336 9163
Email: cdreportsfax@noms.gsi.gov.uk
Email: MHCSTeam1@noms.gsi.gov.uk
Head of Casework Team 1: Mark Clark 0300 047 TBC
Casework Mgr: Michael Turner 0300 047 4229
Caseworkers:
Surname AA-Arn: Sophia Mir 0300 047 4208
Surname AA-Arn: Melati Flint 0300 047 4191
Surname Aro-Bec: Elizabeth Bamigboye 0300 047 4179
Surname Bed-Brax: Maria Madsen 0300 047 4202
Surname Bray-Care: Jenny Etienne 0300 047 4190
Surname Carf-Colel: Dharmarajen Valydon 0300 047 4232
Surname Colem-David: Salathiel Leboho 0300 047 4197
Surname Davie-Dunl: Graham Copeland 0300 047 4184
Surname Dunm-Fir: Martin Redman 0300 047 4217
Surname Fis-Gile: Rita Jayapal-Rajiah 0300 047 4242
Casework Support:
Surname AA-Brax: Abraham Ilori 0300 047 4195
Surname Bray-David Chen: Christopher Eseigbe 0300 047 4189
Surname Davie-Gile: Derek Tansill 0300 047 4227

Casework Team 2 – Patient Surname Gilf-Nev
Fax: 0300 047 4395
CD reports desktop fax: 0870 336 9163
Email: cdreportsfax@noms.gsi.gov.uk
Email: MHCSTeam2@noms.gsi.gov.uk

Head Of Casework Team 2: David Elliott 0300 047 4186
Casework Mgr: Stewart Mead 0300 047 4207
Caseworkers:
Surname Gilf-Hale: Stephen Lee 0300 047 4198
Surname Half-Herr: Dawn Anderson 0300 047 4178
Surname Hers-If: Sarah Pocknell 0300 047 4216
Surname Ig-Jor: Arlene Munir 0300 047 4210
Surname Jos-K: Gopalan Srinivasan 0300 047 4226
Surname La-Low: Michelle Shippie 0300 047 4535
Surname Lox-Mccalk Vacancy
Surname Mccall-Mitr: Seema Vishram 0300 047 4238
Surname Mits-Nev: Christian Secondis 03000 474220
Casework Support
Surname Gilf-If: Ravi Sond 0300 047 4225
Surname Ig-Low: Richard Roberts 0300 047 4218
Surname Lox-Nev: Sheba Sohail 0300 047 4224

Casework Team 3 – Patient Surname New-Z
Fax: 0300 047 4395
CD reports desktop fax: 0870 336 9163
Email: cdreportsfax@noms.gsi.gov.uk
Email: MHCSTeam3@noms.gsi.gov.uk

Head of Casework Team 3: John Buckle 0300 047 4181
Casework Mgr: Geraldine Marsh 0300 047 4203
Caseworkers:
Surname New-Parker P: Martine Green 0300 047 4192
Surname Parker Q-Q: Colin Napper 0300 047 4212
Surname Ra-Rog: Matthew Picot 0300 047 4215
Surname Roh-Shaw: Kerry Dougan 0300 047 4187
Surname Shax-Stai: Vincent Hardy 0300 047 4187
Surname Staj-Thomas K Sara Nall 0300 047 4211
Surname Thomas L-Walk: Hainsley Hinds 0300 047 4194
Surname Wall-Williams A: Shah Monjur 0300 047 4209
Surname Williams B-Z: Stephen Lott 0300 047 4199
Casework Support:

Surname New-Rog: Sue Loughran 0300 047 4200
Surname Roh-Thomas K: Graham Shuter 0300 047 4221
Surname Thomas L-Z: Harjeet Singh 0300 047 4223

ASSISTED PRISON VISITS UNIT
Head of Unit: Philip Creighton
Email: philip.creighton@noms.gsi.gov.uk

1. Assisted Prison Visits Scheme
Members of the public on a low income claim assistance with the costs of prison visits.
APVS, PO Box 2152, Birmingham, B15 1SD
Tel: 0300 063 2100, 09.00 to 17.00, Monday to Friday
(except Bank Holidays)
Email: assisted.prison.visits@noms.gsi.gov.uk
Fax: 0121 626 3474

2. Prisoner Location Service
To locate a prisoner in England and Wales.
PLS, PO Box 2152, Birmingham B15 1SD
Email: prisoner.location.service@noms.gsi.gov.uk
Fax: 0121 626 3474

3. NOMS Victim Helpline
Victims of crime and their relatives who have received unwanted contact from a prisoner or are worried about their release from prison can contact the NOMS Victim Helpline.

NOMS Victim Helpline, PO Box 4278, Birmingham B15 1SA
Tel: 0845 7585 112
Email: Victim.Helpline@noms.gsi.gov.uk

4. West Midlands Visit Booking
Visit booking service for West Midlands prisons.
Telephone service open 09.00 to 18.00, Monday to Friday (except Bank Holidays).

Brinsford: 0300 060 6500
Email: legalvisits.brinsford@hmps.gsi.gov.uk
Drake Hall: 0300 060 6501
Email: legalvisits.drakehall@hmps.gsi.gov.uk
Featherstone: 0300 060 6502
Email: legalvisits.featherstone@hmps.gsi.gov.uk
Hewell: 0300 060 6503
Email: legalvisits.hewell@hmps.gsi.gov.uk
Shrewsbury: 0300 060 6504

Email: legalvisits.shrewsbury@hmps.gsi.gov.uk
Stafford: 0300 060 6505
Email: legalvisits.stafford@hmps.gsi.gov.uk
Stoke Heath: 0300 060 6506
Email: legalvisits.stokeheath@hmps.gsi.gov.uk
Swinfen Hall: 0300 060 6507
Email: legalvisits.swinfenhall@hmps.gsi.gov.uk
Werrington: 0300 060 6508
Email: legalvisits.werrington@hmps.gsi.gov.uk

ENGLAND AND WALES MAPPA AREAS

Lists all key MAPPA Co-ordinators and Managers for each area of England and Wales; includes the MAPPA Administrators of London by borough. Information displayed in this section has been provided by the National MAPPA team and verified by each area.

Avon and Somerset
Liz Spencer – Interim MAPPA Coordinator
Public Protection Unit, Avon and Somerset Constabulary, Police HQ, Po Box 37, Valley Road, Portishead BS20 8QJ
Tel: 01275 816949
Mobile: 07803 008 893
Fax: 01275 816187

Bedfordshire
Chris De Souza – MAPPA Co-ordinator
Bedfordshire Probation Area, Saxon Centre, 1st Floor, 230 Bedford Road, Kempston, Bedford MK42 8PP
Tel: 01234 844287
Fax: 01234 844289
Email: chris.desouza@bedfordshire.probation.gsi.gov.uk

Cambridgeshire and Peterborough
Andy Jarvis – MAPPA Coordinator
Cambridgeshire Police Authority, Copse Court, Thorpe Wood, Peterborough, PE3 6SF
Tel: 01733 863 116
Mobile: 07736 617911
Fax: 01733 868585
Email: andy.jarvis@cppt.probation.gsi.gov.uk

Cheshire
Ian Smith – MAPPA Coordinator

NPS Cheshire Probation Trust, Marshall
Memorial Hall , Woodford Lane, Winsford
CW7 2JS
Tel: 01606 551166
Mobile: 07894 510146
Fax: 01606 861267
Email:
ian.smith@cheshire.probation.gsi.gov.uk

County Durham

Hugh Storey – MAPPA Co-ordinator
Forest House, Aykley Heads Business Centre,
Durham City DH1 5TS
Tel: 0191 383 9083
Mobile: 07825 008 901
Fax: 0191 383 7979
Email: hugh.storey@dtv.probation.gsi.gov.uk
Durham MAPPA mailbox:
durhammappa@dtv.probation.gsi.gov.uk

Cumbria

Andrea Balderstone – MAPPA Co-ordinator
Cumbria Police Headquarters, Carleton Hall,
Penrith, Cumbria CA10 2AU
Tel: 01768 217648
Mobile: 07967 572249
Fax: 01768 217611
Email:
andrea.balderstone@cumbria.pnn.police.uk

Derbyshire

Brian Nuttall – MAPPA Co-ordination
Manager
Derbyshire Constabulary HQ, Public
Protection Co-ordination Unit, Butterley Hall,
Ripley, Derbyshire, DE5 3RS
Tel: 01773 573601
Mobile: 07786 190491
Fax: 01773 572976
Email:
brian.nuttall.9177@derbyshire.pnn.police.uk

Paul Taylor – Deputy MAPPA Co-ordination
Manager
Derbyshire Constabulary HQ, Public
Protection Co-ordination Unit, Butterley Hall,
Ripley, Derbyshire, DE5 3RS
Tel: 01773 573602
Email:
paul.taylor.4935@derbyshire.pnn.police.uk

Devon & Cornwall

Alex Jones – MAPPA Coordinator
Public Protection Unit, Devon and Cornwall
Police Headquarters, Middlemoor, Exeter
EX2 7HQ
Tel: 01392 452 865

Mobile: 07855 267 939
Email:
alexandra.jones@devonandcornwall.pnn.
police.uk

Dorset

Kristy Middleton-Roberts – MAPPA
Coordinator
Bournemouth Probation Office, 7 Madeira
Road, Bournemouth, BH1 1QL
Tel: 01202 200239
Mobile: 07867452195
Email:
kristy.middleton-roberts@dorset.probation.gsi.
gov.uk

Durham Tees Valley

Andrew Bake – MAPPA Co-ordinator
(Teesside)
160 Albert Road, Middlesbrough TS1 2PZ
Tel: 01642 247438
Fax: 01642 24465
Email: andrew.bake@dtv.probation.gsi.gov.uk

Dyfed Powys

Andrew Edwards – MAPPA Co-ordinator
Dyfed Powys Police HQ, PO Box 99,
Llangunnor, Carmarthen, SA31 2PF
Tel: 01267 226 153
Mobile: 07980 726242
Fax: 01267 221620
Email:
andrew.edwards.mappa@dyfed-powys.pnn.
police.uk;
andrew.edwards@wales.probation.gsi.gov.uk

Essex

Allan Taplin – MAPPA Manager
MAPPA, Dangerous Offender Management,
PO Box 2, Springfield, Chelmsford, Essex,
CM2 6DA
Tel: 01245 452767
Mobile: 07866 540 346
Fax: 01245 452749
Email: Allan.Taplin@essex.pnn.police.uk

Gloucestershire

Mark Scully – MAPPA Co-ordinator
Public Protection Bureau, Gloucestershire
Police Constabulary, Wilton House, 63
Lansdown Road, Cheltenham GL51 6QD
Tel: 01242 247 974
Mobile: 078336 56997
Fax: 01242 276879
Email:
mark.scully@gloucestershire.probation.gsi.
gov.uk

Kirsty Ridge - MAPPA Administrator
Public Protection Bureau, Gloucestershire
Police Constabulary, Wilton House, 63
Lansdown Road, Cheltenham GL51 6QD
Tel: 01242 247980

Gwent

Gareth Hale – MAPPA Co-ordinator
Probation Office, Torfaen House, Station
Road, Sebastopol, Pontypool. NP4 5ES
Tel: 01495 745 031
Mobile: 07980 277459
Fax: 01495 763233
Email:
Gareth.Hale@wales.probation.gsi.gov.uk

Hampshire

Jackie Rowland – MAPPA Co-ordinator
Palmerston Building, Police Southern Support
and Training, Hamble Lane, Hamble,
Southampton SO31 4TS
Tel: 02380 604761
Mobile: 07780 958 812
Email:
jacqueline.rowlands.14536@hampshire.pnn.
police.uk

Julia Watt – Deputy MAPPA Co-ordinator
Palmerston Building, Police Southern Support
and Training, Hamble Lane, Hamble,
Southampton SO31 4TS
Tel: 02380 604762
Email: Julia.watt@hampshire.pnn.police.uk

Hertfordshire

Morris Johnson – MAPPA Manager
Police HQ, Dacorum Building, Stanborough
Road, Wewyn Garden City, AL8 6XF
Tel: 01707 354858
Mobile: 07534 526060
Fax: 01438 765206
Email:
morris.johnson@hertfordshire.probation.gsi.
gov.uk

Humberside

Chris Brookes – MAPPA Co-ordinator
Priory Road Police Station, Priory Road, Hull,
HU5 5SF
Tel: 01482 220687
Fax: 01482 220689
Email:
chris.brookes@humberside.probation.gsi.gov.
uk

Kate Munson – MAPPA Co-ordinator

Director of Probation and SMB Chair,
Humberside Probation Trust, Head Office
Floor, Liberty House West, Liberty House,
Hull HU1 1RS
Tel: 01482 480000
Fax: 01482 398063
Email:
kate.munson@humberside.probation.gsi.gov.
uk

Kent

Paula Ratledge – MAPPA Manager
Kent Police Headquarters, Public Protection,
Unit, Sutton Road, Maidstone, Kent, ME15
9BZ
Tel: 01622 650457
Mobile: 07595 006176
Fax: 01622 654749
Email:
paula.ratledge@kent.probation.gsi.gov.uk

Lancashire

Susan Boydell-Cupitt – MAPPA Co-ordinator
Keasden Block, Force Major Investigation
Team, Lancashire Police Headquarters,
Hutton, Preston, Lancashire, PR4 5SB
Tel: 01772 412391
Fax: 01772 416189
Email:
Susan.Boydell-Cupitt@lancashire.probation.
gsi.gov.uk

Leicester, Leicestershire and Rutland

Andy Gullick – MAPPA Manager
Mansfield House Police Station, Belgrave
Gate, Leicester, LE1 3GG
Tel: 0116 2486606
Mobile: 07920 835 584
Fax: 0116 248 6608
Email:
andy.gullick@leicestershire.probation.gsi.gov.
uk

Lincolnshire

Nicole Hilton – MAPPA Co-ordinator
Lincs Police HQ, Deepdale Lane, Nettleham,
Lincoln LN2 2LT
Tel: 01522 558 255
Mobile: 07979 700 327
Fax: 01522 558299
Email:
nicole.hilton@lincolnshire.probation.gsi.gov.
uk

London

Charles Hayward – Business Director, London
MAPPA Executive Office

151 Buckingham Palace Road, Victoria,
SW1W 9SZ
Tel: 0300 048 0092
Mobile: 07798 831 720
Email:
charles.hayward@london.probation.gsi.gov.uk

Kim Dormer – MAPPA Manager and ViSOR
Lead
21 Harper Road, London SE1 6AW
Tel: 020 7407 7333
Mobile: 07957 362083
Email:
kim.dormer@london.probation.gsi.gov.uk

In addition to the two Business Managers of
London MAPPA listed here, each London
Borough has a MAPPA Administrators.

**MAPPA Administrators by London
Borough
Barking & Dagenham**

Donna Rose – MAPPA Administrator
1 Regarth Avenue, Romford, RM1 1TJ
Tel: 01708 742 453

Barnet

Madeleine Skinner – MAPPA Administrator
Denmark House, West Hendon Broadway
NW9 7BW
Tel: 0208 457 6820

Bexley

Kathleen Clegg – MAPPA Administrator
Norwich Place, Bexleyheath, Kent, DA6 7ND
Tel: 0208 304 5521

Brent

Donna O'Brien – MAPPA Administrator
440 High Road, Willesden, NW10 2DW
Tel: 0208 451 6212

Bromley

Ann Willins – MAPPA Administrator
6 Church Hill, Orpington, BR6 0HE
Tel: 01689 806695

Camden

Helen Thompson and Vicky Mawas – MAPPA
Administrators
401 St John Street, EC1V 4RQW
Tel: 0207 014 9800

City of London

Margaret Zebedee – MAPPA Administrator
Reed House, 1–4 Rectory Road N16 7QS
Tel: 020 7923 4656

Croydon

Jade Bess – Acting MAPPA Administrator
Church House, Old Palace Road, Croydon,
Surrey, CR0 1AX
Tel: 0208 253 4737

Ealing

Diana Stevens – MAPPA Administrator
4 Birkbeck Road, Acton, W3 6BG
Tel: 0208 752 8377

Enfield

Sean Davis – MAPPA Administrator
The Old Court House, Windmill Hill, Enfield,
EN2 6SA
Tel: 0208 366 6376 / 0208 884 7365

Greenwich

Dolly Olaleye – MAPPA Administrator
Riverside House West, Beresford Road,
Woolwich, SE18 6DH
Tel: 0208 855 5691

Hackney

Margaret Zebedee – MAPPA Administrator
Reed House, 1–4 Rectory Road N16 7QS
Tel: Switchboard: 020 7923 4656 Direct: 020
7014 7948

Hammersmith & Fulham

David Jefford – Acting MAPPA Administrator
191A Askew Road W12 9AX
Tel: 020 8811 2025

Haringey

Gillian Williams – Acting MAPPA
Administrator
Telfer House, Church Road, Highgate N6 4QJ
Tel: 0208 341 9060

Harrow

Darren Brooker – MAPPA Administrator
Rosslyn Crescent, Harrow, Middlesex, HA1
2SU
Tel: 020 8427 7246

Havering

Ross Martin – MAPPA Administrator
1 Regarth Avenue, Romford, RM1 1TP
Tel: 01708 742453

Hillingdon

Debbie Collins – MAPPA Administrator
The Court House, Harefield Road, Uxbridge,
UB8 1PQ
Tel: 01895 231972

Hounslow

Pippa Fogg – MAPPA Administrator
Banklabs House, 41a Cross Lances Road,
Middx, TW3 2AD
Tel: 0208 570 0626

Islington

Tunde Philbert and Robert Kedge – MAPPA
Administrators
401 St John Street EC1V 4RW
Tel: 020 7014 9800

Kensington & Chelsea

Jessica Stephen – MAPPA Administrator
1–5 Dorset Close, Marylebone, NW1 5AN
Tel: 0207 563 3600

Kingston

Robert Kedge – MAPPA Administrator
45 High Street, Kingston-Upon-Thames, KT1
1LQ
Tel: 0208 939 4114

Lambeth

Michael Emmett – MAPPA Administrator
Harpenden House, 248–250 Norwood Road,
SE27 9AW
Tel: 0208 766 5700

Lewisham

Janet Gray – MAPPA Administrator
208 Lewisham High Street, Lewisham SE13
6JL
Tel: 0208 297 7300

Merton

Julia Friend – MAPPA Administrator
103 Westmead Road, Sutton, SM1 4JD
Tel: 0208 652 6942

Newham

Debi Vernall – MAPPA Administrator
Plaistow Police Station, 44 Barking Road E13
8HJ
Tel: 0207 275 5765

Redbridge

Louise Potgieter – MAPPA Administrator
1b Farnham Ave, Walthamstow E17 4TT
Tel: 0208 478 8500

Richmond

Robert Kedge – MAPPA Administrator
45 High Street, Kingston-Upon-Thames, KT1
1LQ
Tel: 0208 939 4114

Southwark

Alexandra Prew – MAPPA Administrator
2 Great Dover Street, SE1 4XW
Tel: 0207 740 8483

Sutton

Julia Friend – MAPPA Administrator
103 Westmead Road, Sutton, SM1 4JD
Tel: 020 8652 9670

Tower Hamlets

Matthew Narbrough – MAPPA Administrator
50 Mornington Grove Bow E3 4NS
Tel: 0208 980 1818

Waltham Forest

Louise Potgieter – cover MAPPA
Administrator
1b Farnham Ave, Walthamstow E17 4TT
Tel: 0208 531 3311

Wandsworth

Rita Douglas – MAPPA Administrator
79 East Hill, Wandsworth, London, SW18 2QE
Tel: 0208 704 0200

Westminster

Nina Dukes – MAPPA Administrator
1–5 Dorset Close, Marylebone, London, NW1
5AN
Tel: 0207 563 3600

Greater Manchester

Angela Cope – MAPPA Co-ordinator
MAPPA Support Unit Manager, 3rd Floor
Nexus House, Alexandra Drive, Ashton under
Lyne, OL7 0QP
Tel: 0161 856 7817
Mobile: 07775 938 222
Email:
angela.cope@manchester.probation.gsi.gov.uk

Merseyside

Jayne Philips – MAPPA Co-ordinator
222 Mather Avenue, Police Training Centre,
Liverpool L18 9TJ
Tel: 0151 777 1358 or 0151 2576362
Mobile: 07894 177 013
Fax: 0151 777 4528
Email:
Jayne.phillips@merseyside.probation.gsi.gov.
uk;
mrs.mappa.unit@merseyside.probation.gsi.
gov.uk

Norfolk

Donna Monk – MAPPA Co-ordinator
Public Protection Unit, Norfolk constabulary,
OCC, Jubilee House, Falconers Chase,
Wymondham, NR18 0WW
Tel: 01603 276344
Mobile: 07500 125 927
Fax: 01603 276 343
Email: monkd@norfolk.pnn.police.uk

North Wales

Carolyn Clark – MAPPA Co-ordinator
Crime Services, North Wales Police, William
Morgan Road, St Asaph, Denbighshire LL17
0HQ
Tel: 01745 588649
Mobile: 07795 127 963
Fax: 01745 588498
Email:
carolyn.clark@wales.probation.gsi.gov.uk

North Yorkshire

Gina Griffiths – MAPPA Co-ordinator
York & North Yorkshire Probation Trust,
Pavilion 2000, Amy Johnson Way, York YO30
4XT
Tel: 01904 698 920
Mobile: 07889 702504
Fax: 01904 698929
Email:
Gina.griffiths@north-yorkshire.probation.gsi.
gov.uk

Northamptonshire

Mike Chantler – MAPPA Co-ordinator
MAPPA Office, 2nd Floor, Criminal Justice
Centre, 700 Pavilion Drive, Brackmills
Industrial Estate, Northampton NN4 7FL
Tel: 101 Ext 343521
Mobile: 07795 051 109
Fax: 01604 888639
Email:
mike.chantler@northants.pnn.police.uk

Northumbria

Susan Tauk – MAPPA Co-ordinator
Protecting Vulnerable People Unit, MAPPA,
North Tyneside Area Command, Middle
Engine Lane, Wallsend, Tyne & Wear NE28
9NT
Tel: 0191 295 7229
Fax: 0191 295 7229
Email:
susan.tauk.8390@northumbria.pnn.police.uk

Nottinghamshire

Ian Williams – MAPPA Policy & Strategy
Officer
Holmes House, Ratcliffe Gate, Mansfield,
NG18 2JW
Tel: 0300 300 9999 ext 817 1470
Mobile: 07879 486848
Fax: 01623 483052
Email:
ian.williams@nottinghamshire.pnn.police.uk

Jane Hilton – MAPPA Co-ordinator
Holmes House, Ratcliffe Gate, Mansfield,
NG18 2JW
Tel: 0300 300 9999 ext 817 1479
Mobile: 07894 971441
Fax: 01623 483052
Email:
jane.hilton11336@nottinghamshire.pnn.police.
uk

Staffordshire

Mark White – MAPPA Co-ordinator
PO Box 3167, Stafford ST16 9JZ
Mobile: 07921 094 880
Fax: 01785 235172
Email: Mark.white@swm.probation.gsi.gov.uk

Suffolk

Tim Sykes – MAPPA Co-ordinator
11–13 Lower Brook Street, Ipswich IP4 1AQ
Tel: 01473 282 308
Mobile: 07872 678 099
Fax: 01473 232506
Email: tim.sykes@nspt.probation.gsi.gov.uk

Surrey and Sussex

Mark Bamford – MAPPA Co-ordinator
Invicta House, 4th Floor, Trafalgar Street,
Brighton, East Sussex BN1 4FR
Tel: 01483 863 512
Fax: 01273 625 207
Email:
mark.bamford@sspt.probation.gsi.gov.uk
Kim Gray – Deputy MAPPA Co-ordinator
Hillside Cottage, Ferry Lane, Guildford GU2
4EE
Email: kim.gray@sspt.probation.gsi.gov.uk

Thames Valley

Bob Stirling – MAPPA Coordinator
Thames Valley Police, Fountain Court, Spires
Business Park, Kidlington OX5 1NZ
Tel: 01865 293101
Fax: 01865 293292
Email:
Bob.Stirling@thamesvalley.pnn.police.uk

Andrew Taylor – MAPPA Co-ordinator
Thames Valley Police, Police Headquarters,
Oxford Road, Kidlington, Oxon OX5 2NX
Tel: 01865 293 501
Email:
andy.taylor@thamesvalley.pnn.police.uk

South Wales

Nigel Rees – MAPPA Co-ordinator
MAPPA Unit, Public Protection Department,
South Wales Police Headquarters, Cowbridge
Road, Bridgend CF 31 3SU
Tel: 01656 306043
Mobile: 07810 854211
Fax: 01656 303464
Email: nigel.rees@south-wales.pnn.police.uk

Des Grant – Deputy MAPPA Co-ordinator
MAPPA Unit, Public Protection Department,
South Wales Police Headquarters, Cowbridge
Road, Bridgend CF 31 3SU
Mobile: 07794201463
Email: des.grant@south-wales.pnn.police.uk

Warwickshire

Derek Ridgway – MAPPA Co-ordinator
Warwickshire Justice Centre, Newbold
Terrace, Leamington Spa, CV32 4EL
Tel: 01926 684477
Mobile: 07788 100864
Email:
derek.ridgway@warwickshire.pnn.police.uk

West Mercia

Neil Slater – MAPPA Co-ordinator
West Mercia Constabulary HQ, Hindlip Hall,
PO Box 55, Worcester, WR3 8SP
Tel: 01905 332252
Mobile: 07977 218493
Email: neil.slater@westmercia.pnn.police.uk

Pete Clark – MAPPA Co-ordinator
West Mercia Police HQ, CID Block, Hindlip
Hall, PO Box 55, Worcester WR3 8TA
Tel: 01905 747014
Mobile: 07973 753006
Fax: 01905 747044
Email: mappa@westmercia.pnn.police.uk

Esther Vaughan – MAPPA Co-ordinator
West Mercia Constabulary HQ, Hindlip Hall,
PO Box 55, Worcester, WR3 8TA
Tel: 01905 332252 Ex 252
Fax: 01905 747044
Email:
esther.vaughan@westmercia.pnn.police.uk

West Midlands

Angie Batham – MAPPA Co-ordinator
Room 710A, Lloyd House, Colmore Circus
Queensway, Birmingham B4 6NQ
Tel: 0121 609 6954
Mobile: 07834 696 521
Email:
angie.batham@swm.probation.gsi.gov.uk

Wiltshire

Alan Hemming – MAPPA Co-ordinator
MAPPA Office, Room 54 Police Station, New
Park Street, Devizes, Wiltshire, SN10 1DZ
Tel: Nat Police phone no 101 Wiltshire Ext
737579
Mobile: 07736 617979
Fax: 01380 731465

South Yorkshire

Dean Clarke – MAPPA Co-ordinator
South Yorkshire Police HQ, Snig Hill,
Sheffield, S3 8LY
Tel: 0114 252 3703
Mobile: 0773 939 9673
Email:
dean.clarke@south-yorkshire.probation.gsi.
gov.uk

West Yorkshire

Chris Maxwell – MAPPA Co-ordinator
West Yorkshire Probation Trust, 3 Sandy
Walk, Wakefield WF1 2DJ
Tel: 03000 487103
Fax: 03000 487152
Email:
Chris.Maxwell@west-yorkshire.probation.gsi.
gov.uk

HER MAJESTY'S INSPECTORATE OF PROBATION

Functions

HM Inspectorate of Probation is an independent inspectorate funded by the Ministry of Justice and reporting directly to the Secretary of State. HM Inspectorate of Probation's purpose is to report to the Secretary of State on the effectiveness of work with adults, children and young people who have offended, or who are likely to offend, aimed at reducing offending and protecting the public, whoever undertakes this work; to report on the effectiveness of the arrangements for this work, working with other inspectorates as necessary; to contribute to improved performance by the organisations whose work we inspect; to contribute to sound policy and effective service delivery, especially in public protection, by providing advice and disseminating good practice based on inspection findings, to Ministers, officials, managers and practitioners; to promote actively race equality and wider diversity issues, especially in the organisations whose work we inspect; and to contribute to the overall effectiveness of the Criminal Justice System, particularly through joint work with other inspectorates.

HM Inspectorate of Probation is based in Manchester (main office) and London, at the addresses indicated below.

Manchester
6th Floor, Trafford House, Chester Road, Stretford, Manchester M32 0RS

London
2nd Floor, Ashley House, 2 Monck Street, London SW1P 2BQ

General enquiries
Tel: 0161 869 1300
Fax: 0161 869 1350
Email:
HMIP.enquiries@hmiprobation.gsi.gov.uk
Website:
www.justice.gov.uk/about/hmi-probation

Staff
HM Chief Inspector of Probation:
Liz Calderbank Tel: 0161 869 1301

HM Assistant Chief Inspectors of Probation
Julie Fox Tel: 0161 869 1300
Sally Lester Tel: 0161 869 1300
Alan MacDonald Tel: 0161 869 1300

Andy Smith Tel: 020 7035 2215
Head of Support Services:
Andy Bonny Tel: 0161 869 1300

NATIONAL OFFENDER MANAGEMENT SERVICE

Tel: 0300 047 6325
Email: public.enquiries@noms.gsi.gov.uk
Website: www.justice.gov.uk/about/hmps

Chief Executive Officer: Michael Spurr
Director of Finance and Analysis: Andrew Emmett
Director of High Security: Phil Copple
Director of Human Resources: Robin Wilkinson
Director of Offender Health: Richard Bradshaw
Director of Change & IT: Martin Bellamy
Director of Commissioning and Commercial: Ian Poree
Director of Probation & Contracted Services: Colin Allars
Directory of Public Sector Prisons: Steve Wagstaffe
Director of National Operational Services: Digby Griffith

CIRCLES OF SUPPORT AND ACCOUNTABILITY

Circles of Support and Accountability (Circles) is a highly effective community contribution to reducing re-offending by medium to high-risk sex offenders living in the community. Volunteers are recruited, trained and supervised to monitor and support these men and women, helping to reduce emotional loneliness and isolation thus reducing the risks of re-offending. Working in partnership with probation, police, the prison service and other statutory and voluntary agencies, a number of Circles Projects have been established in England, Wales and Scotland. The umbrella organisation, Circles UK, is an authorised service provider to the Ministry of Justice supporting the development of local projects and working to ensure consistency of national standards across England and Wales.

National Office
Circles UK
Abbey House
Abbey Square
Reading RG1 3BE
Tel: 0118 950 0068 Fax: 0118 950 0064

Email: info@circles-uk.org.uk
www.circles-uk.org.uk
Email: firstname.lastname@circles-uk.org.uk

Hanvey, Stephen (Chief Executive Officer)
Wilson, Chris (National Development
Manager)
Earnshaw, Kerry (National Support Officer)
Curnow, Heather (Office Manager)

CROPT
Magistrates Court
Rickergate, Carlisle, Cumbria CA3 8XP
Tel: 0777 501 0443
Mob: 07824 350227

O'Brien, Margaret (Circles Coordinator)
Email:
Email: cumbriacircles@gmx.com

East of England Circles
c/o North Hertfordshire Probation Centre
Argyle House, Argyle Way
Stevenage SG1 2AD
Tel: 0777 501 0443

Francis, Annabel (Coordinator)
Email:
annabel.francis@hertfordshire.probation.gsi.
gov.uk

Greater Manchester Circles
MAPPA Support Unit
3rd Floor Nexus House
Alexandria Drive
Ashton under Lynne L7 0QP
Tel: 0161 8563636

Circles South East (part of HTV Circles)
Ridgeway House, 1A Hagbourne Road
Didcot OX11 8ER
Tel: 01235 816050 Fax: 01235 810779

Saunders, Becky (Chief Executive)
Williams, Dominic (Senior Coordinator)
Webb, Carrie (Hampshire Coordinator)
Macrae, Ron (Thames Valley Coordinator)
Mill, Ian (Kent Coordinator)
Ringsell, Keith (Mentoring Coordinator)
Email: info@htvcircles.org.uk

Leicestershire & Rutland Circles
Leicestershire & Rutland Probation Trust
38 Friar Lane, Leicester LE1 5RA
Tel: 0116 262 0440 ext 2118
Wain, Stuart (Volunteer/COSA Coordinator)
Email:
stuart.wain@leicestershire.probation.gsi.gov.
uk

Lucy Faithfull Foundation Circles
Nightingale House, 46–48 East Street
Epsom, Surrey KT17 1HB
Tel: 01372 847160

Sauze, Simon (Programme Manager)
Email: ssauze@lucyfaithfull.org.uk
Shonk, Tracy (London)
TShonk@lucyfaithfull.org.uk
Davies, Steve (West Midlands)
SDavies@lucyfaithfull.org.uk

Circles North East
Barnardos, 75 Osborne Road
Jesmond, Newcastle-upon-Tyne NE2 2AN
Tel: 0191 212 0237
Mob: 07554 333513

Dale, Wendy (Circles Coordinator)
Email: wendy.dale@barnardos.org.uk

North Wales Circles
c/o Wales Probation Trust
Plas y Wern (Approved Premises)
Llangollen Road, Ruabon
Wrexham LL14 6RN
Tel: 01978 814949 Fax: 01978 810435

Ennis, Juliet (Project Dev Manager)
Email: juliet.ennis@wales.probation.gsi.gov.uk
Gibson, Neil (Volunteer Coordinator)
Email: neil.gibson@wales.probation.gsi.gov.uk

Circles South West
Dorset Probation Trust
7 Maderia Road
Bournemouth
Dorset, BH1 1QL
Tel: 07786 729746

Rousseau, Pauline (Regional Coordinator)
Email: paulinerousseau.circlessw@gmail.com

Yorkshire and Humberside Circles
Priory Centre
Priory Street
York YO1 6ET
Tel: 01904 630 0911
www.yhcosa.or.uk
Burton,Melva (Director)
E Mail: melva.burton@yhcosa.org.uk

ANALYTICAL SERVICES DIRECTORATE

Director: Rebecca Endean

OFFENDER MANAGEMENT & SENTENCING ANALYTICAL SERVICE (OMSAS)

102 Petty France, 7th Floor, Zone B, London SW1H 9AJ
Head of Unit: Cressy MacDonald 020 3334 6865

Youth Justice Analysis Programme (YJAP)
Programme Director: Alana Diamond 020 3334 2864

Heads of Sections/Teams:
Juvenile Cohort Study (JCS) & Criminal Careers Analysis: Sarah Fisher (nee Hansbury) 020 3334 5781
Youth PbR Approaches & Youth Justice Evidence: *Jess Sondhi* 020 3334 5079
Youth Remand & Youth Secure Estate: *Rob Crawford* 020 3334 5991
Youth Justice Effective Practice Research at the YJB: *Jorgen Lovbakke* 020 3334 5940

Reducing Adult Reoffending
Programme Director: Post vacant (Alana Diamond temporarily covering the role: 020 3334 2864)

Heads of Sections/Teams:
Probation Research Team: Anna Upson 020 3334 4981
Prisoner Survey and Public Protection Research Teams: Kathryn Hopkins 020 3334 5097
What Works in Reducing Offending: Robyn Polisano 020 3334 5248

PbR, LJR & Working Prisons
Programme Director: Ben Warner 020 3334 5575
Heads of Sections/Teams:
PbR Evaluation: Andy Healey 020 3334 5095
PBR Roll out strategy: Tessa Fairman 020 3334 3459
PbR Roll out strategy: Cris Coxon 020 3334 4263
MI and Payment Mechanisms : Richard Field 020 3334 3453

Sentencing Analysis & Research
Programme Director: Gareth Harper 020 3334 5551
Heads of Sections/Teams
IPP Analysis: Paul Cowell 020 3334 4997 & Paul Allen 020 3334 3072
Sentencing Research & Evidence Base: Sarah Hansbury 020 3334 5781

Legal Aid, Sentencing & Punishment of Offenders Bill Analytical Support: Jon Roberts 020 3334 4972
Criminal Law Policy Analytical Support & Sentencing Council Support: Bindi Shah 020 3334 3462

JUSTICE STATISTICS ANALYTICAL SERVICES (JSAS)

102 Petty France, 7th Floor, Zone B, London SW1H 9AJ
Chief Statistician: Mike Elkins

JSAS Prison, Probation & Re-offending Statistics
Programme Director: Jo Peacock 020 3334 5066

Heads of Sections/Teams:
Prison Statistics: Chandni Lakhani 020 3334 3882
Re-offending Statistics: Nick Mavron 020 3334 3972
Probation, IT & Outputs: Bridgette Miles 020 3334 4571

Data, Improvement, Analysis and Linking
Programme Director: Ben Coleman 020 3334 4984
Heads of Sections/Teams:
PNC & Criminal Histories: Catherine Cousins 020 334 4949
Statistical Methods & Development: Aidan Mews 020 3334 3083
Data Improvement Project: Melissa Cox 020 3334 3081
Justice Data Lab: Nicola Abrams 020 334 4396

Criminal Justice System Statistics
Programme Director: John Marais 020 3334 4960
Heads of Sections/Teams:
Criminal Justice Statistics: David Jagger 020 3334 4980
CJS Development & Sentencing Statistics: Nicola Owen 020 3334 4960
Criminal Court Statistics: Lisa Vine 020 3334

Court Statistics and Information
Programme Director: Miguel Goncalves 020 3334 5091
Heads of Sections/Teams:
Civil Justice Statistics: Adrian Shepherd 020 3334 2483
Family Justice Statistics: Wincen Lowe 020 3334 3080
Freedom of Information, Coroners and GIS: Mark Edwardes 020 3334 3077

Judicial and Tribunal Statistics: Tracie Kilbey
0121 681 3139
Information and Rights: Lisa Davy 020 3334
3169

PRISONS AND PROBATION OMBUDSMAN

Ashley House, 2 Monck Street, London SW1P
2BQ
Tel: 020 7035 2876; 0845 010 7938 Fax: 020
7035 2860
Email: mail@ppo.gsi.gov.uk
Website: www.ppo.gov.uk

The Prisons and Probation Ombudsman
investigates: complaints from prisoners,
people on probation and immigration
detainees held at immigration removal
centres; deaths of prisoners, residents of
probation service approved premises, and
those held in immigration removal centres.

The Ombudsman is appointed by the
Secretary of State for Justice and is
completely independent of the Prison Service,
the Probation Service and the Border and
Immigration Agency.

Acting Prisons & Probation Ombudsman: Jane
Webb
Acting Deputy Ombudsman – Fatal Incidents:
Thea Walton
Deputy Ombudsman – Complaints: Elizabeth
Moody
*Deputy Ombudsman – Business Dev & Corp
Services:* Tony Hall

Assistant Ombudsmen:
Karen Cracknell
John Cullinane
Kate Eves
Wendy Martin
Gordon Morrison
Olivia Morrison-Lyons
Colleen Munro
Louise O'Sullivan
Dionne Spence
Thea Walton
Nick Woodhead

PAROLE AND LIFE SENTENCE REVIEW DIVISION

2nd Floor Rear, St Andrew's House, Regent
Road, Edinburgh EH1 3DG
0131 244 8524/8530 *Fax 0131 244 8794*

Functions Administration of the release and
sentence management of offenders under the
Prisoners and Criminal Proceedings
(Scotland) Act 1993. Sentence management
policy. Managing children sentenced to
custody under the Criminal Procedure
(Scotland) Act 1995. Sponsorship of the
Parole Board for Scotland and the Risk
Management Authority. Prisons Commission
Secretariat. There are three casework teams
and a policy team.
Casework teams deal with the release,
supervision and recall of life, determinate and
extended sentence prisoners: set licence
conditions for short-term (sentences of 6
months to under 4 years) sex offenders;
present Scottish Ministers' views at Tribunals
on suitability for release on licence of life
sentence prisoners and recalled extended
sentence prisoners. Work distributed on an
alphabetical basis.
Prisoners' surnames A-Ge
0131 244 8543
Prisoners' surnames Gf-Mac/Mc
0131 244 8529
Prisoners' surnames M-Z
0131 244 8535
Sentenced Children
0131–244 8524

PAROLE BOARD OF ENGLAND AND WALES

The Parole Board for England and Wales
Grenadier House, 99–105 Horseferry Road,
London SW1P 2DX
Tel: 0300 047 4600 Fax: 0300 047 4714 or 4716
DX: 155620 Victoria 17

Senior Management Team
Fax: 020 7217 0454

David Calvert-Smith (Chairman)
Tel: 0300 047 4601
Email:
david.calvert-smith@paroleboard.gsi.gov.uk

Claire Bassett (Chief Exec)
Tel: 0300 047 4651
Email: claire.bassett@paroleboard.gsi.gov.uk

Nadine Abbott (Exec Asst to Chair & CEO)
Tel: 0300 047 4601
Email: nadine.abbott@paroleboard.gsi.gov.uk

Chitra Karve (Director of Performance &
Dev)
Tel: 0300 047 4649
Email: chitra.karve@paroleboard.gsi.gov.uk

Martha Blom-Cooper (Director of Business Development)
Tel: 0300 047 4734
Email: martha.blom-cooper@homeoffice.gsi.gov.uk

Terry McCarthy (Head of Litigation)
Tel: 0300 047 4656
Email: terry.mccarthy12@paroleboard.gsi.gov.uk
Tim Morris (Head of Corporate Affairs)
Tel: 0300 047 4659
Email: tim.morris5@paroleboard.gsi.gov.uk

Ray Phillips (Head of Learning and Development)
Tel: 0300 047 4668
Email: ray.phillips@homeoffice.gsi.gov.uk

Andy Cobbett (Head of Finance)
Tel: 0300 047 4623
Email: andy.cobbett3@paroleboard.gsi.gov.uk
Kay Fielding (Head of Quality Unit)
Kay.fielding@homeoffice.gsi.gov.uk
Tel: 0300 047 4633

CASEWORK TEAMS
Oral Hearings Team
Responsible for all casework relating to oral hearings for life sentence prisoners, including representations against recall.
Jonny Twidle (Senior Operations Manager)
Tel: 0300 047 4684
Email: Jonathan.Twidle2@paroleboard.gsi.gov.uk
Andrew Humphrey (Manager Team A)
Tel: 0300 047 4267
Email: andrew.humphrey@paroleboard.gsi.gov.uk
Tim Byrom (Manager Team B)
Tel: 0300 047 4619
Email: tim.byrom4@paroleboard.gsi.gov.uk
Rebecca Bayley (Manager Team C)
Tel: 0300 047 4384
Email: rebecca.bayley@paroleboard.gsi.gov.uk
Tanina Langdon (Admin Team Manager)
Tel: 0300 047 4666
Email: tanina.langdon@paroleboard.gsi.gov.uk

Recalls

Responsible for arranging oral hearings to consider representations against recall from determinate sentence prisoners, as well as recalls decided on the papers.
Imran Inamdar (Team Mgr)
Tel: 0300 047 4643
Fax: 0300 047 4714 or 4716
Email: imran.inamdar@paroleboard.gsi.gov.uk

Litigation Team
Responsible for pre-action correspondence related to Parole Board procedures, decisions and recommendations.
Vince Peters (Team Mgr)
Tel: 0300 047 4667
Email: vincent.peters10@paroleboard.gsi.gov.uk

SUPPORT TEAMS
Human Resources Team
Responsible for all human resources issues including secretariat staff recruitment but not member recruitment.
Jo Gillibrand (Head of HR and Change Management)
Tel: 0300 047 4637
Email: joanne.gillibrand@paroleboard.gsi.gov.uk

Finance Team
Responsible for financial management, including the payment of invoices, fees and expenses claims.

Andy Cobbett (Head of Finance)
Tel: 0300 047 4632
Email: andy.cobbett3@paroleboard.gsi.gov.uk

IT Team
Responsible for maintaining the Parole Board website, maintaining all databases and providing IT support to members and staff.

Jacob Asare (Team Mgr)
Tel: 0300 047 4607
Email: jacob.asare4@paroleboard.gsi.gov.uk

Corporate Affairs Team

Responsible for communications, corporate governance issues, supporting the management board, producing performance statistics and dealing with complaints.
Tim Morris (Head of Corp Affairs)
Tel: 0300 047 4659
Email: Tim.Morris5@paroleboard.gsi.gov.uk

THE OFFENDER HEALTH RESEARCH NETWORK

Jean McFarlane Building (2nd Floor), University of Manchester, Oxford Road, Manchester M13 9PL
A Department of Health funded initiative, led by the University of Manchester. The OHRN provides a focal point for the research and best practice agenda underpinning the cross-sector partnerships working to improve health services and opportunities for

offenders. It aims to ensure that research in this field is of high quality; targeted to address the particular needs of this population; contributes to addressing identified gaps in current knowledge and practice. The OHRN focuses on health care work streams pertinent to offenders, including primary care, public health, mental health and substance abuse. Research is also being carried out into workforce planning and management, and issues of staff culture. This research will contribute to the growing knowledge base upon which cross-agency partnerships can draw to meet common goals from different organisational perspectives.

OHRN:
• is a multi-disciplinary, multi-agency network focused on offender health care innovation, evaluation and knowledge dissemination
• works with regional networks to promote offender health care research and development locally
• encourages clinical and criminal justice agency staff to become actively involved in research in their workplace
• hosts workshops for clinical, criminal justice and academic staff
• works toward developing the frequency and quality of service user involvement in offender health care provision and research
• works with NHS and criminal justice agencies to develop pathways to research in terms of securing funding, research ethics and governance requirements and practical information
• hosts an annual international conference highlighting innovative research findings and best clinical practice examples in offender health care from the UK and worldwide.

Contacts
Jenny Shaw (Academic Lead)
Email: jen@jenshaw.net

Jane Senior (Research Project Manager)
Email: jane.senior@manchester.ac.uk
Tel: 0161 275 0730

Charlotte Lennox (Research Associate)
Email: charlotte.lennox@manchester.ac.uk
Tel: 0161 306 8014

CHILDREN AND FAMILY COURT ADVISORY & SUPPORT SERVICE—CAFCASS

Cafcass National Office

6th Floor Sanctuary Buildings
Great Smith Street London SW1P 3BT
Tel: 0844 353 3350 Fax: 0844 353 3351
Email: webenquiries@cafcass.gov.uk
www.cafcass.gov.uk

Local Offices
Tyneside, Northumbria and Cumbria

Newcastle Office
3rd Floor, Parkview House
Front Street
Benton
Newcastle upon Tyne
NE7 7TZ
Office Telephone Number: 0844 353 3630
Office Fax Number: 0844 353 3631

Carlisle Office
Capital Building
Hilltop Heights
Carlisle, Cumbria
CA1 2NS
Office Telephone Number: 0844 353 2130
Office Fax Number: 0844 353 2131

Durham, Teesside and North Yorkshire

Durham (Alport House) Office
Alport House, 35 Old Elvet
Durham DH1 3HN
Office Telephone Number: 0844 353 2520
Office Fax Number: 0844 353 2521
DX Cafcass (North) 60205 DURHAM

Durham (Saddler St.) Office
Please note this office is not a service office.
Please contact the Alport House office for queries regarding your case.
38 Saddler Street, Durham DH1 3NU
DX Cafcass (North) 60201 DURHAM

Middlesbrough Office
2nd Floor, Prudential House
31–33 Albert Road
Middlesbrough TS1 1PE
Office Telephone Number: 0844 353 3550
Office Fax Number: 0844 353 3551
DX Cafcass (North) 60528
MIDDLESBROUGH

York Office
James House, James Street
York YO10 3YZ
Office Telephone Number: 0844 353 4860
Office Fax Number: 0844 353 4861

Scarborough Office
First Floor, Pavilion House
Valley Bridge Road, Scarborough
YO11 2JR
Office Telephone Number: 01723 343270
Office Fax Number: 01723 343275
DX Cafcass (North) 61804
SCARBOROUGH

West Yorkshire

Bradford Office
PO Box 92, Kenburgh House, 28a Manor
Row
Bradford, West Yorkshire BD1 4WR
Office Telephone Number: 01274 386 100
Office Fax Number: 01274 735 019
DX Cafcass 11732 BRADFORD

Leeds Office
1 Park Cross Mews,Park Cross Street
Leeds LS1 2QS
Office Telephone Number: 0844 353 2960
Office Fax Number: 0113 247 0989
DX Cafcass (North) 26429 LEEDS

Wakefield Office
Bull Ring House, 3rd Floor, 23 Northgate
Wakefield, West Yorkshire WF1 3BJ
Office Telephone Number: 0844 353 4670
Office Fax Number: 0844 353 4671
DX Cafcass (North) 15023 WAKEFIELD

South Yorkshire & Humberside

Doncaster Office
Kings Mews, 1 Frances Street
Doncaster South Yorkshire
DN1 1JB
Office Telephone Number: 0844 353 2440
Office Fax Number: 0844 353 2441
DX Cafcass 711892 DONCASTER 2

Hull Office
The Deep Business Centre
Hull HU1 4SA
Office Telephone Number: 0844 353 2790
Office Fax Number: 0844 353 2791

Sheffield Office
3 Dragoon Court Hillsborough Barracks
Penistone Road Sheffield
South Yorkshire S6 2GZ

Office Telephone Number: 0844 353 4220
Office Fax Number: 0844 353 4221

Greater Manchester

Manchester Office
6th Floor, Byrom House
Quay Street Manchester M3 3JD
Office Telephone Number: 0844 353 3440
Office Fax Number: 0844 353 3441

Cheshire, Merseyside and Lancashire

Blackburn Office
St John's Court, Ainsworth Street
Blackburn, Lancashire
BB1 6AR
Office Telephone Number: 0844 353 1830
Office Fax Number: 0844 353 1831
DX Cafcass (North) 15259 BLACKBURN
2

Lancaster Office
711 Cameron House, White Cross
South Road Lancaster
LA1 4XQ
Office Telephone Number: 0844 353 2940
Office Fax Number: 0844 353 2941
DX Cafcass (North) 63507 LANCASTER

Runcorn Office
Ground Floor, Area B
Castle View House, East Lane
Runcorn
Cheshire WA7 2GJ
Office Telephone Number: 0844 353 3220
Office Fax Number: 0844 353 3221
DX Cafcass 15205 RUNCORN 2

**Cambridge, Derbyshire, Leicestershire,
Lincolnshire and Nottinghamshire**

Chesterfield Office
Hayfield House, Devonshire Street
Chesterfield
Derbyshire S41 7ST
Office Telephone Number: 0844 353 2240
Office Fax Number: 0844 353 2241
DX Cafcass (Central) 12357
CHESTERFIELD

Derby Office
New Enterprise House, St Helen's Street
Derby Derbyshire DE1 3GY
Office Telephone Number: 0844 353 2380
Office Fax Number: 0844 353 2381
DX Cafcass (Central) 700891 DERBY 4

Leicester Office
Riverside House, 49 Western Boulevard
Leicester LE2 7HN
Office Telephone Number: 0844 353 3120
Office Fax Number: 0844 353 3121
DX Cafcass (Central) 10802 LEICESTER

Nottingham Office
2A Castlebridge Office Village
Castle Marina Road
Nottingham NG7 1TN
Office Telephone Number:0844 353 3780
Office Fax Number: 0844 353 3781
DX 745130 Nottingham 53

Lincoln Office
2nd Floor, Hamilton House, 1–3
Claskegate
Lincoln, Lincolnshire LN2 1JG
Office Telephone Number:01522 580 750
Office Fax Number: 01522 580 751
DX 716717 LINCOLN 9

Peterborough Office
71 London Road, Peterborough
Cambridgeshire PE2 9BB
Office Telephone Number:0844 353 3860
Office Fax Number: 0844 353 3861
DX 745140 PETERBOROUGH 26

National Business Centre, Warwickshire and Northamptonshire

National Business Centre
Milburn Hill Road
University of Warwick Science Park
Coventry CV4 7JJ
Office Telephone numbers:
Coventry and Northampton teams: 0844 353 1651
Central Team: 0844 353 4971
North Team: 0844 353 4973
South Team: 0844 353 4974
Central EIT: 0844 353 4972
Main fax number: 0844 353 2271
DX 744940 Coventry 29

Shropshire, Staffordshire, Herefordshire and Worcestershire

Stafford Office
University Court, Stafford Technology Park,
Beaconside, Stafford
ST18 0GE
Office Telephone Number: 0844 353 4430
Office Fax Number: 0844 353 4431
DX Cafcass 745120 Stafford 9

Worcester Office
Virginia House, The Butts
Worcester WR1 3PA
Office Telephone Number: 0844 353 4820
Office Fax Number: 0844 353 4821
DX Cafcass 715232 WORCESTER

Birmingham, Black Country, Lincolnshire and Cambridgeshire

Birmingham Office
1st Floor, The Citadel
190 Corporation Street
Birmingham B4 6QD
Office Telephone Number: 0844 353 1740
Office Fax Number: 0844 353 1741
DX Cafcass (Central) 744840
BIRMINGHAM 82

Essex, Suffolk, Norfolk, Hertfordshire, Bedfordshire and Buckinghamshire

Chelmsford Office
2nd Floor, Redwing House
Hedgerows Business Park
Colchester Road
Chelmsford CM2 5PB
Office Telephone Number: 0844 353 2170
Office Fax Number: 0844 353 2171
DX Cafcass 161310 Chelmsford 21

Ipswich Office
6 Merchants Court, 74 Foundation Street
Ipswich Suffolk
IP4 1BN
Office Telephone Number: 0844 353 2870
Office Fax Number: 0844 353 2871
DX Cafcass (Central) 3205 IPSWICH

Luton Office
1st Floor Cresta House
Alma Street
Luton LU1 2PU
Office Telephone Number: 0844 353 3270
Office Fax Number: 0844 353 3271
DX Cafcass 97763 LUTON 4

Milton Keynes Office
Clyde House, 10 Milburn Avenue
Oldbrook, Milton Keynes
Buckinghamshire MK6 2WA
Office Telephone Number 0844 353 3620
Office Fax Number 0844 353 3621
DX Cafcass (South) 31425 MILTON
KEYNES

Norwich Office
Rosebery Court. St Andrews Business
Park

Norwich NR7 0HS
Office Telephone Number: 0844 353 3750
Office Fax Number: 0844 353 3751
DX 745380 NORWICH 29

Avon, Gloucestershire, Wiltshire and Thames Valley

Bristol Office
Unit 9, York Court
Wilder Street Bristol
BS2 8QH
Office Telephone Number 0844 353 2048
Office Fax Number 0844 353 2051
DX Cafcass (South) 122078 BRISTOL 11

Gloucester Office
Northgate House, 19 London Road
Gloucester GL1 3HB
Office Telephone Number: 0844 353 2650
Office Fax Number: 01452 386 474
DX 745080 Gloucester 26

Oxford Office
1st Floor, 2 Cambridge Terrace
Oxford OX1 1TP
Office Telephone Number: 01865 728421
Office Fax Number: 01865 245938
DX Cafcass (South) 4315 OXFORD

Swindon Office
Units 1a & 1b York House, Edison Way
Swindon, Wiltshire SN3 3RB
Office Telephone Number: 0844 353 4560
Office Fax Number: 0844 353 4561
DX Cafcass 745110 Swindon 32

Reading Office
Glasson Centre, 319 Oxford Road
Reading, Berkshire
RG30 1AU
Office Telephone Number: 0844 353 4019
Office Fax Number: 0844 353 4021

Greater London

Croydon Office
3rd Floor, Carolyn House
22–26 Dingwall Road
Croydon, Surrey CR0 9XF
Office Telephone Number: 0844 353 2320
Office Fax Number: 0844 353 2321
DX Cafcass 148004 CROYDON 31

Holborn Office
5th Floor, First Avenue, 42 – 49 High
Holborn
London WC1V 6NP
Office Telephone Number: 0844 353 3990
Office Fax Number: 0844 353 3991

Ilford Office
2nd Floor, Charter House
450 High Road
Illford, Essex IG1 1UF
Office Telephone Number: 0844 353 2830
Office Fax Number: 0844 353 2831
DX Cafcass 97514 ILFORD 3

Slough Office
Early Intervention Service – London
1st Floor, Regal Court
42–44 High Street Slough
Berkshire SL1 1EL
Office Telephone Number: 0844 353 4320
Office Fax Number: 0844 353 4321
DX 42262 Sough (West)

Wells Street Office
First Floor, 59–65 Wells St
London W1A 3AE
Office Telephone Number: 0844 353 2620
Office Fax Number: 0844 353 2621

Kent

Canterbury Office
3rd Floor, Charter House
St George's Place
Canterbury, Kent
CT1 1UQ
Office Telephone Number: 0844 353 2110
Office Fax Number: 0844 353 2101
DX 161020 Canterbury 7

Chatham Office
Suite B, 3rd Floor,
Prince Regent House, Quayside,
Chatham Maritime, Kent ME4 4QZ
Office TelephoneNumber: 0844 353 2140
Office Fax Number: 0844 353 2141
DX Cafcass 131397 ROCHESTER 2

Sussex & Surrey

Guildford Office
2nd Floor, Blenheim House
1–2 Bridge Street Guildford
Surrey GU1 4RY
Office Telephone Number: 0844 353 2710
Office Fax Number: 0844 353 2701
DX Cafcass (South) 97869 GUILDFORD 5

Brighton Office
1st Floor Crown House
11 Regent Hill
Brighton
BN1 3ED
Office Telephone Number: 0844 353 2540
Office Fax Number: 0844 353 2541

Hampshire and Isle of Wight

Basingstoke Office
Priestley House, Priestley Road
Basingstoke Hampshire RG24 9NW
Office Telephone Number: 0844 3531620
Office Fax Number: 0844 3531621

Newport Office
30 Quay Street, Newport,
Isle of Wight PO30 5BA
Office Telephone Number: 01983 528 867
Office Fax Number: 01983 528 771

Portsmouth Office
Ground Floor, Peninsula House
Wharf Road Portsmouth
Hampshire PO2 8HB
Office Telephone Number: 0844 353 3930
Office Fax Number: 0844 353 3931
DX 159050 Cafcass South Basingstoke 25

Cornwall, Devon, Somerset and Dorset

Exeter Office
Minerva House, Pynes Hill,
Exeter EX2 5JL
Office Telephone Number: 0844 353 2590
Office Fax Number: 0844 353 2591

Poole Office
Bourne Gate, Bourne Valley Road,
Poole BH12 1DR
Office Telephone Number: 0844 353 4770
Office Fax Number: 0844 353 4771

Plymouth Office
8 Ford Park Lane,
Plymouth PL4 6RR
Office Telephone Number: 0844 353 3920
Office Fax Number: 0844 353 3291
DX 120157 MUTLEY PLAIN PLYMOUTH

St Austell Office
2 Southview House,
St Austell Enterprise Park,
PL25 4EJ
Office Telephone Number: 0844 3534920
/ 01726 626 810
Office Fax Number: 0844 3534921

Taunton Office
6 Mendip House,
High Street, Taunton
TA1 3SX
Office Telephone Number: 0844 353 4590
Office Fax Number: 0844 353 4591
DX Cafcass 744920 TAUNTON 11

Wales

The functions of Cafcass in Wales are
functions of the Welsh Assembly.

TRAINING & CONSULTANCY ORGANISATIONS

Organisations that feel they should be included in this section are invited to contact the editor (see page 3). The descriptions included are those of the organisations. The editor accepts no responsibility for any statements made in this section.

Skills for Justice

Head Office Centre Court, Atlas Way, Sheffield S4 7QQ
0114 261 1499
Email: info@skillsforjustice.com
www.skillsforjustice.com

Northern Ireland Office 7th Floor, 14 Great Victoria Street, Belfast BT2 7BA
028 902 58028

Scotland Office 140 Causewayside, Edinburgh EH9 1PR
Tel: 0131 662 5234

Wales Office 1 Caspian Point, Pier Head Street, Cardiff Bay, Cardiff CF10 4DQ
Tel: 01656 750133

Skills for Justice is the Sector Skills Council covering employers, employees and volunteers working in the justice, community safety and legal services sectors. Its mission is to help employers and individuals become better skilled to deliver public benefits and to influence employers, policy makers and the skills system to take full account of workforce development needs.

Ad Esse Consulting Ltd

76 New Cavendish Street, London W1G 9TB
Tel: 0845 366 8528
Email: seriousfun@ad-esse.com
www.ad-esse.com
Twitter: @ad_esse

Ad Esse is a specialist management consultancy, delivering sustainable performance improvement. We are results-orientated, we measure and demonstrate what we do, providing a significant return on investment for our clients. We engage fully with the specific needs of our clients, and adapt for the particular challenges and objectives – this understanding and flexibility forms the basis of our unique approach to performance improvement.

Backstop Support Ltd – Recruitment, Consultation and Training

9 Disraeli Road, Putney, London SW15 2DR
Tel: 0844 499 3398 Fax: 020 8785 9904
Email: info@backstop.org.uk
www.backstop.org.uk

Recruitment and training agency specialising in providing high quality staff, and training and consultancy that provides criminal justice managers and practitioners with the skills needed to manage and work with offenders.

Being the Best You Can Be

17 Cottrell Road, Whitchurch, Cardiff CF14 1PZ
Tel: Paddy Doyle 07966 025446;
Melva Burton 07962 185691
Email:
paddydoyle@beingthebestyoucanbe.co.uk;
melvaburton@beingthebestyoucanbe.co.uk
www.beingthebestyoucanbe.co.uk

Provides coaching for agencies in the criminal justice and community safety sectors. Established by two experienced former probation managers and HMIP associate inspectors who have undertaken postgraduate coach training, BTBYCB offers bespoke packages of team and individual coaching to improve performance and enhance excellence. Coaching can be tailored to meet specialist performance issues such as chairing MAPPA meetings and operating with confidence in multi-agency settings.

BUSEC

Suite 5, Spain Buildings, 28 The Spain, Petersfield, Hants GU32 3LA
Tel: 01730 710055 Fax: 01730 710066
Email: admin@busec.co.uk
www.busec.co.uk

Provides professional assessment as a route to membership of the Chartered Institute of Personnel and Development (CIPD). This is specifically designed for personnel and training practitioners with at least five years middle/senior management experience and three years in HR. Candidates meet the CIPD professional standards by demonstrating practical application of competence through a variety of assessment methods. Professional assessment is an alternative to the academic, exam-based, route to membership.

Delivers ILM-endorsed programmes, recruitment and selection, employment law, performance management, and train the trainer. Also provides a range of NVQs and coaching. BUSEC has worked with a number of CJ agencies, including probation.

The Centre for Public Innovation

32/36 Loman Street, London SE1 0EH
020 7922 7820 Fax: 020 7922 7821
Email:
monica.fenwick@publicinnovation.org.uk
www.publicinnovation.org.uk

The Centre for Public Innovation (CPI) is a social enterprise working to develop innovation, better performance and outcomes in health, social care and criminal justice. Its aim is to improve service outcomes for end users, in particular, end users from disadvantaged communities. It specialises in innovation and outcome management delivered through training and consultancy services.

Cherry and Coburn CIC

Directors: Sally Cherry and Diane Coburn.
Email: sally@cherryandcoburn.co.uk
Tel: 07846 087647
Email: diane@cherryandcoburn.co.uk
Tel: 07979 577222
www.cherryandcoburn.co.uk
Management Development, Coaching and Action Learning Set facilitation training, for Criminal Justice organisations, accredited by the Chartered Management Institute. This social enterprise company has been established by the team who developed and ran the highly successful management development programme at Midlands Regional Probation Training Consortium (now closed). Training is contextualised for Criminal Justice and if learners undertake accreditation they gain a nationally recognised qualification. The Management Development programme is Skillsmark endorsed by Skills for Justice.

Child Bereavement UK

The Saunderton Estate, Wycombe Road
Saunderton, Bucks HP14 4BF
Tel: 01494 568900
Email: enquiries@childbereavementuk.org
www.childbereavementuk.org
Child Bereavement UK is the UK's leading national organisation that supports families

and provides training to professionals across the entire spectrum of child bereavement. We support families and educate professionals both when a baby or child of any age dies or is dying, or when a child is facing bereavement. Every year we deliver training across a breadth of issues to around 5000 professionals at the front line of bereavement support.
In the UK, when a baby or child dies, or a child is bereaved, many of those affected are unable to access good quality support which meets their individual needs. Child Bereavement UK believes all families should have the support they need to rebuild their lives when a child grieves or when a child dies. Our aim is to make sure they do.

Paul Cooper Consultants Ltd

19 Mossley Hill Road, Mossley Hill, Liverpool L18 4PT
Tel: 0151 724 4133 Mob: 07734 108 753
Email: guru1@talktalk.net

Specialises in the application of law to criminal justice practice and management (compliance, enforcement, breach, court skills, witness skills, indeterminate detention (IPPs) lifers, oral hearings, Human Rights Act, data protection and new legislation and case law) and to the work of the Youth Offending Service. Courses include Report Writing, Hate Crime, and Sentence Planning. Management development programmes for middle managers and customised courses for senior managers include performance management, change management, planning, leadership, recruitment and selection and discipline and capability. Customised management programmes may also be developed for charitable organisations. Accredited with the Open College Learning Network. E-learning and web-based programmes can be developed to meet client needs.

Delight Training Services Ltd

19 Chestergate, Macclesfield, Cheshire SK11 6BX
01625 421045 Fax: 01625 421064
Email: admin@delight.co.uk
www.delight.co.uk

Training providers specialising in teambuilding; leadership development; intervention skills; behavioural change; business people skills; structured programmes.

Equality Works

London office: Shepherdess Walk Buildings, 2 Underwood Row, London N1 7LQ
Tel: 020 7251 4939
Manchester office: 10th Floor, Bridgewater House, Whitworth Street, Manchester M1 6LT
Tel: 0161 200 8540
www.equalityworks.co.uk

A consultancy and training company specialising in integrating equalities into workplace learning and staff development. The approach is based on integrating a clear professional analysis of equalities and the way discrimination is embedded in organisations. Services include consultancy, research, facilitation and coaching.

Forensic Psychology Practice Ltd

The Willows Clinic, 98 Sheffield Road, Boldmere, Sutton Coldfield B73 5HW
Tel: 0121 377 6276 Fax: 0121 377 6027
Email: info@forensicpsychology.co.uk
www.forensicpsychology.co.uk

A private practice of forensic and clinical psychologists which provides psychology services to social, health and criminal justice agencies tasked with the assessment, management or treatment of individuals who present a risk to themselves or others.

Experienced in developing and running treatment programmes for sex offenders with learning disabilities in both health and criminal justice settings. Provides specialist training in working with sex offenders for practitioners in probation and NHS settings; acts as consultant to National Probation Service in managing high risk offenders in the community; and currently contracted to provide psychological life sentenced prisoner reports to HM Prison Service. Experienced in working with mentally disordered offenders and developing risk assessment protocols for private and criminal justice agencies.

GB Learning Consultancy

3 Basildon Close, Sutton, Surrey SM2 5QJ
Tel: 07906 613081 or 07914 397701

Email: info@gblearningconsultancy.co.uk
www.gblearningconsultancy.co.uk

Specialist management, leadership, and learning and development consultancy. Developers of the Living Leadership Toolkit with an excellent reputation for leadership and management development in the public sector, including both the NPS and NOMS. Specialists in the design of open and e-learning materials.

Grey Cell Training Ltd

Cherrybrook, 12 Lakeside, Irthlingborough, Northants NN9 5SW
Tel: 01933 653845 Fax: 01933 697888
Email: enquiries@greycelltraining.co.uk
www.greycelltraining.co.uk

Grey Cell provides strategy consultation and generic training programmes for national and local government. Offers over 90 courses which reflect the needs of the CJ and local government systems and each individual organisation.

Groupwork Consultation & Training Ltd

PO Box 363, Southsea, Hants PO4 0YP
Tel: 023 9275 0030 Fax: 023 9275 0109
Email: dave@groupct.co.uk or simon@groupct.co.uk
www.groupworktraining.co.uk

Groupwork Consultation & Training Ltd (GCT Ltd) is an accredited and established national groupwork training organisation founded in 1987. It specialises in providing theoretical and practical social group work training to group work practitioners primarily in the public sector: probation areas, social service departments, health authorities, drug projects, and voluntary organisations. Courses, including foundation, intermediate and certificate level groupwork courses, are held in London and at clients' premises. Two day courses in anger management and CBT are also run. GCT Ltd is a Member of the Institute for Learning and Development.

Grubb Institute

Cloudesley Street, London N1 0HU
Tel: 020 7278 8061 Fax: 020 7278 0728
Email: info@grubb.org.uk
www.grubb.myzen.co.uk

Works with leaders, managers and professionals on role and institutional transformation, using a systemic and group relations approach and applied Christian theology. Offers consultancy, development and learning opportunities in one-to-one role consultation, teams and groups, and whole systems. Works across the community in a range of organisations, and has a track record within the criminal justice field.

HealthCV Ltd

3 Beckside Gardens, Huddersfield, West Yorkshire HD5 8RS
Tel: 0845 460 1032 Fax: 01484 304614
Email: info@healthcv.com
www.healthcv.com

Health and lifestyle screening, health promotion activities, stress management courses (general and managers), and employee assistance programmes. Also specialises in lifestyle health workshops and courses, open drop-in events, employee wellbeing schemes, health profiles, risk assessment, and relaxation techniques. Validated Trainer with the International Stress Management Association ISMA(UK).

Ignition Creative Learning Ltd

Suite 155, R&R Consulting Centre, 41 St Isan Road, Cardiff CF14 4LW
Tel/fax: 0700 394 6217
Email: info@ignition-learn.com
www.ignition-learn.com

A national and international provider specialising in domestic violence and abuse work. Ignition is outside consultant to several probation areas running IDAP and delivers essential staff supervision and consultancy. The company also offers a range of one-day practical training courses for IDAP facilitators Aspects of Excellence, which focus on enhancing core practice, such as improved conduct of critical dialogue or structuring skills practise to develop non-abusive behaviours (in session three of IDAP modules) meaningful and effective. These courses are compliant with guidelines on programme integrity and treatment management. Ignition provides supervision for IDAP women's safety workers and training for case managers on effective work with men sentenced to IDAP or otherwise showing evidence of domestic violence or abuse issues.

JW & Associates Ltd

Managing Director – Joe Woods
Consultancy, Project Development and Training
8 Oak Tree Gardens, Tansley
Derbyshire DE4 5WA
Tel mobile: 077 177 66 123
email: joe@jwassoc.co.uk website: www.jwassoc.co.uk

JW & Associates provides a range of expertise to the Criminal Justice System in the UK and Europe and also to other fields in both Public and Private sectors. Specialising in management consultancy, project development and training, the Company offers extensive management experience of a range of work in both probation and prison settings. The range of Associates also cover other disciplines including Local Authority Management and Education. The company has a particular specialist knowledge of Offender Management. JW & Associates can provide help with business planning, long term strategic direction and implementation within the day to day realities of operational practice. In Project management the company uses Prince 2 methodology to provide a project development service which identifies and manages risks as well as ensuring that objectives and benefits are achieved within budget, on time and to the required quality. JW & Associates also provides a range of training events and will prepare and present half day, full day, or week long courses The company has wide ranging expertise in providing quality training and will provide bespoke courses and keynote speeches to meet your business and staff needs.

LAURUS OD Solutions

Sefton House 1, Molyneux Way
Liverpool, L10 2JA
Tel : 0151 526 1346
www.laurusodsolutions.co.uk
LAURUS is a joint venture agreed between the five North West Probation Trusts to deliver learning, development and assessment.
Our experienced and well-established staff have a proven track record in delivering effective training solutions and LAURUS is now a centre of excellence for the delivery of quality training, organisational development and qualification provision.

LAURUS provides core training for all grades of probation staff, as well as bespoke training packages for a range of employees in the justice sector. We are an accredited assessment centre for the Probation Qualification Framework and other qualifications including assessor and IQA awards, PTLLS, management and restorative practice.

We welcome enquiries about learning, development and qualification from providers of probation services in the public, private and voluntary sectors.

We are a recognised Skillsmark provider and hold the Matrix standard for Information, Advice and Guidance.

Linda Gast Training

54 Somers Road, Malvern, Worcs WR14 1JB
Tel/fax: 01684 564363
Email: training@lindagast.co.uk
www.lindagast.co.uk

Leader of established training network working across the criminal justice sector. A track record in all aspects of diversity, particularly from a management perspective, offering up to date workshops and courses for working with hate crime offenders. A continuing focus on 'people' skills; performance management, supervision and appraisal skills and sentence planning and objective setting events are all offered with detailed handbooks to support the training. Also PSO training on how to deliver effective supervision using a cognitive behavioural framework; ILM coaching and mentoring qualifications at levels 3, 5, and 7; ILM management qualifications at levels 3 and 5, along with training in a range of management issues. All events individually tailored to commissioners' requirements.

Link Training and Development

Oldacre House, Court Drive, Shenstone, Lichfield, Staffs WS14 0JG
Tel: 01543 481884
Email: info@linktraining.co.uk

Link Training is a network of three independent trainers. All have experience of working in the probation service, helping to develop best practice, and recognise the value to customers of linking their knowledge and skills to deliver quality training. The workshops are focused around the skills necessary for effective engagement with offenders, the courts, other services providers and meeting the challenges of NOMS. The practical application of models, research and ideas is encouraged and developed. The workshops are tailored to meet the varying skills development requirements of offender managers and supervisors, key workers and case administrators.

LMT Training and Consultancy

Ellastone House, Maenclochog, Pembrokeshire SA66 7LQ
Tel: 01437 532888 Mob: 07721 955216 Fax: 05601 146100
Email: info@lmt.uk.com
www.lmt.uk.com

Tailor-made training, mentoring and consultancy for practitioners and managers working in the crime and disorder arena. Practice areas covered include: risk assessment and management; offence behavioural and cognition analysis; pro-social modelling; motivational enhancement; groupwork; diversity; cognitive behavioural methods. Management provision includes staff, cultural and transition management and team building. The Pathway Plus programme is available for YOTs and other services working with young people.

Lucy Faithfull Foundation

Bordesley Hall, The Holloway, Alvechurch, Birmingham B48 7QA
Tel: 01527 591922 Fax: 01527 591924
Email: bordesley@lucyfaithfull.org
www.lucyfaithfull.org

A national charity providing specialist assessment and treatment for sexual abusers of children, their families and victims. Provides consultancies and training to social service departments, probation and YOTs. Takes referrals from agencies, courts and solicitors (not from clients directly).

Midlands Regional Probation Training Consortium

Suite 415, 4th Floor, Fort Dunlop, Fort Parkway, Birmingham, B24 9FD
Tel: 0121 730 3360, Fax: 0121 730 3361
Email:
firstname.surname@swm.probation.gsi.gov.uk
Sarah Winwin Sein (director)
Joanna Bell (eff pract trg mgr east)

John Richards (eff pract trg mgr east)
Michelle Walters (learning & devpt mgr qual trg)
Vacancy (learning & devpt mgr voc awards)
Alan Clark (learning & devpt mgr qual trg)
Sally Cherry (learning & devpt mgr man dev)
Dawn Bakewell (admin mgr)
Natalie Ryan (rgnl trg off eff pract)
Sheelah Carpenter (rgnl trg off)
Natalie Cole (pa/tng centre co-ordinator)
Jane Cook (finance & clerical off)
Lesley Rawlinson (admin asst)
Elaine Blewitt (admin off learning & devpt qual trg)
Sarah Walker (admin off, accs profs)
Chelsea Andrews (admin off learning & devpt man devpt)
Karen Robinson (admin off learning & devpt voc awards)
Vacancy (admin asst)

New Leaf Training and Counselling – Becky Wright

PO Box 4, Taunton, Somerset TA1 9FN
Tel/fax: 07590 684888
Email: info@new.leaf.uk.com
www.newleaf.uk.com

Provider of anger and stress management services. Held a contract with Avon & Somerset Probation Area for many years providing post-traumatic stress counselling. Now offers individual counselling and group work for those who have difficulty in managing anger and stress. Individuals can self refer to the service. MBACP (accredited) counsellor and UKRC registered independent counsellor. Has also delivered workshops within the prison system.

Noble Openshaw Ltd

4 Copthall House, Station Square, Coventry CV1 2FL
Tel: 01667 456031
Email: admin@noble-openshaw.co.uk
www.noble-openshaw.co.uk

Noble Openshaw provides business solutions and management services to public, private and voluntary sector organisations. Incorporated in 2003, the company now has more than 20 Associates available for deployment in support of an ever expanding portfolio of clients.
Services are focussed in 3 key areas:
· Cost Reduction through efficiency savings and business process improvement. We have developed our own ABC Functional Costing Tool specially designed for identifying improvements and savings in the provision of people services.
· Project Management Associates are Prince2 qualified or experienced.
· Independent investigation external assessment and audit. Associates include experienced HR specialists as well as former senior public sector managers.

PQF/VQ Regional Team—Yorkshire & Humberside Region

West Yorkshire Probation Area Head Office
Cliff Hill House, Sandy Walk
Wakefield WF1 2DJ
Tel: 01924 885300

Roger Geeson (Regional PQF/VQ Manager)
07887 744014
Email:
roger.geeson@west-yorkshire.probation.gsi.gov.uk

David Atkinson (Regional Eff Pract Training Mgr) 07887 744012
Email:
david.atkinson@west-yorkshire.probation.gsi.gov.uk

Sally Cherry Associates

Tel: 07846 087647
sally@sallycherryassociates.co.uk
www.sallycherryassociates.co.uk

Provider of coaching, training, facilitation and consultancy.
Sally Cherry Associates provides management and leadership coaching, facilitation of action learning sets, team days etc. Also training in pro – social modelling, motivational interviewing and other training for working with offenders and other 'difficult' service users, including short courses for staff of third sector organisations.
Sally Cherry is author of Transforming Behaviour: Pro-Social Modelling in Practice and also formerly ran the Management Development unit, the OAST (Offender and Accomodation Skills Training) and LiHMO (Living Here, Moving On – group work for Approved Premises) programmes at Midlands Regional Probation Training Consortium.
See website for more information.

Tavistock Centre for Couple Relationships

Central London office: 70 Warren Street, London W1T 5PB
City Centre office: 7 Artillery Lane, London E1 7LP
Tel: 020 7380 1975
Email: tccr@tccr.org.uk
www.tccr.org.uk

Offers training and consultation services in the field of relationships. As well as training directly involved with couples, the Tavistock consults to managers and supervisors who work in agencies involved with family relationships.

TQMI Ltd

The Heath Business & Technical Park, Runcorn, Cheshire WA7 4QX.
Tel: 01928 513171 Fax: 01928 513174
Email: info@tqmi.co.uk
www.tqmi.co.uk

Established in 1987 TQMI is a management consultancy which works with organisations determined to improve their performance in the light of challenges facing them from customer expectations, technology, government, competition and cost effectiveness.

Wardell Associates

21 Linkside, London N12 7LE
Tel: 020 8723 4357 Mob: 07825 177573
Email: info@wardellassociates.co.uk
www.wardellassociates.co.uk

Established in 2003, Wardell Associates specialise in risk management and safeguarding practice for multi-agency professionals. training and consultancy for criminal justice and MAPPA/safeguarding partnerships. The directors have over 25 years experience as practitioners and managers in probation, youth justice and social care and have contributed to national and London-wide developments. Delivers accessible high-quality training to criminal justice and safeguarding partnerships.

Charlie Watson Staff Development & Training

Mulberry Barn, Main Road, Stanton-in-Peak, Derbyshire DE4 2LW
Tel/fax: 01629 636986 Mob: 07739 468351

Email: charlie.watson@virgin.net
www.mentoringuk.org.uk

Learning and development programmes in the criminal justice, voluntary and higher education sectors concentrating on: interactional skills, involving engagement and motivation techniques; diversity; management development, including supervision and appraisal; presentation skills; groupwork; teambuilding; managing conflict; risk and public protection; academic delivery and placement supervision. NVQ assessor and verifier practice training. CJNTO endorsed.

ELECTRONIC MONITORING SERVICES

Ministry of Justice contractors are responsible for the management and enforcement of home detention curfew, curfew orders and other applications of electronic monitoring within the criminal justice system of England and Wales.

Serco Monitoring (England and Wales)

PO Box 45, Norwich NR3 1BF
Tel: 01603 428300 Fax: 01603 428311
Dave Weston (General Manager)
Andy Homer (Operations Support Manager, Agency/Customer Liaison)
Colin Flynn (Finance & Commercial Mgr)
Martin Elvin (Monitoring Centre Manager)
Tel: 08080 011 024
Email: taggingreturns@serco.com

Serco Home Affairs Monitoring Centre
PO Box 45, Norwich, Norfolk NR3 1BF

Monitoring Centre 24 hour helplines for all enquiries regarding electronic monitoring for HDC, court orders, bail, immigration monitoring, tracking, control orders.

Service delivery support (office hours): 0808 096 5124 Ext 395
Email: sdo@serco.com

Legal enquiries: 0808 096 5124 Ext 328
Email: breachdept@serco.com

London & Eastern
Tel: 080 8096 5124 Fax: 0870 070 0321

West Midlands & Wales
Tel: 080 8015 2369 Fax: 0870 070 0321

Secure email: neworders
amendments@serco.com.cjsm.net

Field Services London & Eastern
Areas Covered
Bedfordshire, Cambridgeshire, Essex,
Hertfordshire, London (Metropolitan),
Norfolk, Suffolk

East Anglia Field Base tel: 01638 750449
London Field Base tel: 020 8668 9429

Field Services West Midlands & Wales
Areas Covered
Dyfed-Powys, Gwent, North Wales, South
Wales, Staffordshire, Warwickshire, West
Mercia, West Midlands
West Midlands Field Base tel: 0121 212 0278
Wales Field Base tel: 0292 049 1131

Equipment Recovery
Tel: 01603 428337 or 0808 096 5124 (24-hour
answerphone)

G4S Care & Justice Services

PO Box 170, Manchester M41 7XZ
Tel: 0161 862 1000 Fax: 0161 749 9022/7620

Email: em.comms@uk.g4s.com
John Wheater (Managing Director)
Steve Rigby (Chief Operating Officer)
Peter Ashton (Chief Technical Officer)
Mark Preston (Commercial Director)
Diane Thomas (Marketing Manager)
Stuart Featherstone (Customer Relationship
Manager)

Compliance Information
Email: G4Scompliance@uk.g4s.com
If your query is urgent, call 0161 862 1753 (or
0161 862 1200 out of hours)

General Enquiries
Available 24 hours, 7 days a week
Email: ControlCentre@uk.g4s.com
Tel: 0161 862 1200

GLOSSARY OF COMMONLY USED ABBREVIATIONS AND SLANG

The following is a glossary of abbreviations and slang commonly used in the Probation and Prison Services. It is hoped that it will be of use to trainees and others struggling to understand contact records and referral forms. This glossary does not claim to be comprehensive. It has been compiled by the editor from his personal experience and with extra help from Terry Bond, Rod Pickin, Keith Norton and Angela Brown. Abbreviations particularly associated with NVQs, CRAMS or prisons are indicated, but there is obviously some cross over between categories. Any suggestions from colleagues will be gratefully received.

A1	Assessor Award (NVQ)
AA	Acceptable Absence, Alcoholics Anonymous
ABH	Actual Bodily Harm (or AOBH)
ACR	Automatic Conditional Release (prison)
ADAs	Additional Days Awarded (internal prison punishment)
AKA	Also Known As
AOBH	Assault Occasioning Actual Bodily Harm (or ABH)
APD	Approved Parole Date
APEL	Accreditation Of Prior Experience And Learning (NVQ)
ARD	Automatic Release Date (prison)
ART	Aggression Reduction Training
ASRO	Addressing Substance Related Offending (programme)
ASW	Approved Social Worker (mental health)
AU or UA	Unacceptable Absence
AUR	Automatic Unconditional Release (prison)
Bilking	making off without payment
BWNB	Bench Warrant No Bail
Br	Breach (of order/licence)
C&G	City & Guilds (NVQ)
CAR	Cumulative Assessment Record (NVQ)
CALM	Controlling Anger & Learning To Manage (programme)

CAR-ATS	Counselling, Assessment, Referral & Throughcare Services
CJ	community justice (NVQ)
CJNTO	community justice national training organisation (NVQ)
CM	Case Manager
CPS	Crown Prosecution Service
CPU	Child Protection Unit
CRAMS	Case Recording And Management System
CRD	Conditional Release Date
CRN	Client Reference Number
CRO	Community Rehabilitation Order (formerly Probation Order)
CSCP	Cognitive Self Change Programme
CS	Community Service (now unpaid work)
DCR	Discretionary Conditional Release (prison)
Deps	Depositions (witness statements)
D/H	Dwelling House
DIDs	Drink Impaired Drivers (programme)
Dip-ping	Pick Pocketing
DipSW	Diploma in Social Work
DLP	Discretionary Lifer Panel (prison)
DNA	Did Not Attend
DO	Duty Officer
DoB	Date of Birth
DRR	Drug Rehabilitation Requirement
DTTO	Drug Treatment & Testing Order (now DRR)
DV	Domestic Violence
DWD	Drive Whilst Disqualified
EDR	Earliest Date of Release (prison)
EEM	European Excellence Model
ETS	Enhanced Thinking Skills (programme)
ETE	Education, Training and Employment
EV	External Verifier (NVQ)
F2050	Code name for main prison file on prisoner
F2052SH	Section of F2050 relating to self harm (prison)
F75	Progress report on lifer (now obsolete) (prison)
FLED	Facility Licence Eligibility Date (in open prisons)

FTA	Fail to Attend	OCR	Oxford, Cambridge, Royal Society (NVQ)
FTS	Fail to Surrender (to bail)		
FWW	Formal/Final Written Warning	OGRS	Offender Group Reconviction Score
GBH	Grievous Bodily Harm	on the game	Prostitution
GOAD	Good Order and Discipline (prison)		
HDC	Home Detention Curfew (prison)		
HDCED	Home Detention Curfew Eligibility Date (prison)	on the rule	prisoner segregated under Rule 43 (prison)
HOC	Home Office Circular		
HV	Home Visit	OPL	Over The Prescribed Limit (drunk driving)
IEP	Integrated Employability Programme		
		OV	Office Visit
IG54/ 94	Prison service instruction relating to Schedule 1 offenders	Page 16	prison service version of contact sheet
IPP	Intensive Probation Programme	PDA	Practice Development Assessor
IV	Internal Verifier (NVQ)	PDH	Plea and Directions Hearing
kiting	issuing dud cheques	PED	Parole Eligibility Date (prison)
LDR	Latest Date of Release (prison)	Perp	Perpetrator of Sexual Offence
LED	Licence Expiry Date (prison)	PH	Preliminary Hearing (Crown Court)
LIDS	Local Inmate Database System (prison computer system)	POA	Public Order Act, Prison Officer's Association
LJA	Local Justice Area (formerly Petty Sessional Area)	PPU	Public Protection Unit
		PSD	Pre-sentence Disclosure
LSP	Life Sentence Plan (prison)	PSI	Prison Service Instruction
LSP3E	Progress Report On Lifer (formerly F75) (prison)	PSO	Probation Service Officer, Prison Service Order
MAPPP	Multi Agency Public Protection Panel	PSO 4400	Prison service instruction relating to child protection and harassment
MAPPPA	Multi Agency Public Protection Panel Arrangement	PSR	Pre-sentence Report
		RMIS	Resource Management Information System
MAL-RAP	Multi Agency Lifer Risk Assessment Panel (prison)	ROTL	Release on Temporary Licence (home leave) (prison)
MDT	Mandatory Drug Test		
MOWOP	Make Off Without Payment (bilking)	R & R	Reasoning and Rehabilitation (programme)
		RTO	Road Traffic Offence
MPSO	Money Payments Supervision Order	Rule 43	Prison rule enabling prisoner to request segregation for their own protection
NA	Next Appointment, Not Applicable		
NAI	Non Accidental Injury (to child)		
NBW	Bench Warrant No Bail (BWNB)	Sch 1	Offence listed in Schedule 1 1993 Children & Young Persons Act (a sexual or violent assault on a child)
NEO	No Evidence Offered		
NFA	No Fixed Abode		
No DL	No Driving Licence		
		SED	Sentence Expiry Date (prison)
No Ins	No Insurance	SEU	Sentence Enforcement Unit (Home Office)
Nonce	(Offensive) prison term for sex offender	SOTP	Sex Offender Treatment Programme
NPD	Non Parole Date (prison)	SPO	Senior Probation Officer
NS	Home Office National Standards	SSSO	Suspended Sentence Supervision Order
OASys	Offender Assessment System	SSR	Specific Sentence Report

TC	Telephone Call/Contact
TDA	Take (motor vehicle) and Drive Away
TICs	Offences Taken Into Consideration
TOPs	Targeted Offenders Project
TPO	Trainee Probation Officer
TWOC	Take (motor vehicle) Without Owners Consent
UAL	Unlawfully At Large (prison)
V1	Verifier Award (NVQ)
VDT	Voluntary Drug Test

VLO	Victim Liaison Officer
VOU	Victim Offender Unit
VP	Vulnerable Prisoner
Wt no bail	Warrant issued not backed for bail
YJ	Youth Justice
YOT	Youth Offending Team

Map of Probation Areas

1 TEESSIDE
2 MERSEYSIDE
3 GREATER MANCHESTER
4 NOTTINGHAMSHIRE
5 WEST MIDLANDS
6 WARWICKSHIRE
7 NORTHAMPTONSHIRE
8 BEDFORDSHIRE
9 HERTFORDSHIRE
10 GLOUCESTERSHIRE

AVON & SOMERSET PROBATION TRUST

Out of hours emergency contact point
Glogan House Tel: 01278 424165

Victim enquiries Tel: 03000 492 100 Fax: 0117 930 2525

Email:
firstname.lastname@avon-somerset.probation. gsi.gov.uk

Queensway House
The Hedges, St Georges
Weston-super-Mare
North Somerset BS22 7BB
Tel: 03000 49 2210 Fax: 03000 49 2251
Direct dial: 03000 49 + ext

Board
Kuipers, Joe (Chair) 2208
Berk, Elaine (Lead PA and PA to board) 2208
Roberts, Anne (Board Secretary) 2206

Chief Officer's Group
Lewis, Sally (CE) 2208
Berk, Elaine (PA to CE, Board & Annette Hill) 2208
Hill, Annette (ACO, HR) 2204
Neale, Danielle (Dir of Finance) 2202
McAdam, Diane (ACO BDU/IT/ETE) 2203
Dauncey, Debbie (PA to D McAdam & D Neale) 2207
Thomas, David (ACO, LDU Somerset & N.Somerset) (based at Taunton) 2668
Heaton, Maria (PA to D Thomas & A.King) 2209
King, Anne (ACO, Interventions) 2455
Harrison, Marilyn (ACO, LDU Bristol) (based at Central) 2458
Brandt, Peter (ACO, LDU Banes & S.Glouc) (based at Central) 2201
Doust, Michelle (PA to M.Harrison & P.Brandt) (based at Central) 2459
Bristow, Brenda (Area Business Mgrs) 2224
Heyworth, Elaine (Senior Project Mgr) 2605

Human Resources/Payroll
Scarbro, Anna (HR Business Partner) 2712
Mercer-Matthews, Gill (HR Business Partner) 2218
Willcocks, Sue (HR Business Partner) 2220

Banks, Sally (Asst HR Off) 2219
Downey, Nicola (Asst HR Off) 2217
Dyer, Carol (Asst HR Off) 2221
Silcox, Kenna (Asst HR Off) 2216

Communications
Geake, Rachael (Comms Off) 2211 – 07711 036534

Information Technology
Helpdesk: 03000 49 2255
Thompson, Bruce (Systems Mgr) 2234
Bennett, Lee 2239
Edwards, Ed (AT Coord) 2240
El Hack, Yasir 2244
Gleed, Nick 2235
Harrison, Peter 2238
Motlow, Ben (Network Mgr) 2237
Shepherd, Scott 2236
Thompson, Shirley (IT Training Coord) 2242
Locke, Joanne 2241
Weaver, Sara 2243

Finance
Estates, Procurement and Transport
Clark, Jane (Finance, Contracts & Estates Mgr) 2231
Pegler, Richard (Transport Coord) 2226

Financial
Ridley, Victoria (Finance Mgr) 2227
Summers, Brendon (Finance Mgr) 2225
Young, Alison (Snr Mgmt Accountant) 2228
Olley, Paula (Mgmt Accountant) 2229
Darby, Catherine (Mgmt Accountant) 2230
Woodey, Dawn (Finance Officer) 2233
Malkerson, Guy (Costing Accountant) 2232

Business Development Unit
Allen, Dave (Info & Quality Mgr) 2212
Hampson, Sandra (Info & Quality Officer) 2215
Sumner, Alexis (Info & Quality Officer) 2213
Kelly, Mel (Business Process Off) 2013

Staff Development
Wilson, Jim (Lead Training Off) 2223
Smith, Fleur (Training Off) 2222

General
Pearce, Jane (Office Support) 2210

North Somerset IMPACT Team
Tel: 03000 49 2259
Morelli, Massimo (Team Leader) 2714
Slack, Dave 2267

Edgell, Kerri (PSO) 2261
Mitchell, Tracy (Case Admin) 2266
Hooley, Rachel (PO) 2284
Fussell, Ashley (PSO) 2262
Greenway, Karen (PSO) 2263
Reeve, Jacqui (Case Admin) 2259
Jones, Paul (Police Off) 2265
O'Connor, Dan (ETE Team Leader) 2715
Hawley, Janice (ETE) 2264
MAPPA Admin Line: 01275 816949
Fax: 01275 816187
Mailbox E-mail:
publicprotectionteam@avonandsomerset.
pnn.police.uk
MAPPA Coordinator: Liz Spencer
07803008893
ViSOR Administrator: Amy Coppack
01275 816569
Public Protection Unit
Avon & Somerset Constabulary
Police HQ, PO Box 37, Valley Road
Portishead, Bristol BS20 8QJ

The Old Convent
35 Pulteney Road, **Bath** BA2 4JE
Tel: 03000 492 550 Fax: 03000 492 717
Direct dial 03000 49 + ext

Reed, Liz (Local Business Officer) 2557

**Offender Management Assessment
Team**
Day, Kevin (Middle Mgr) 2554
Brazier, Tony (Middle Mgr) 2402

POs
Jenkinson, Liam 2555
Lane, Sue 2449
Reade, Gemma
Smith, Kim 2087
Weldon, Clive 2118
Whittaker, Nina 2544

PSOs
Barling, Bridget 2536
Gill, Rebecca 2538
Heckbert, Murray 2372
Liddiard, Ben 2535
Quinn, Lorraine 2540
Silver, Deborah 2550
Wilson, Adam 2552
Cases Admin
Acres, Carole 2537
Fox, Dianne 2543
Clark, Jacqui 2550
McGill, Charlotte 2539
Morgan, Lisa (p) 2002

Programmes
Rakoczi, Jenny (Middle Mgr) 2346

BaNES IMPACT
(based at Bath Police Station, Manvers St,
Bath BA1 1JN)
O'Hagan, Rosie (Middle Mgr) 07920
878228

POs
Blacker, Sam 01225 842424
Denne, Emily 01225 842526
Leary, Michaela 01225 842526
Starbuck, Kim (PSO) 01225 842569
Matthews, Natalie (Case Admin) 01225
842410

Unpaid Work Unit
Coltman, Frank (Sess Supvr) 07595
004794

Consortium
Spurrell, Helen 2548

One The Bridewell
1–2 Bridewell Street, **Bristol,** BS1 2AA
Tel: 03000 49 2000 Fax: 03000 49
2078/2077
Direct dial: 03000 49 + ext
Team Leaders
Hunt, Allason 2498
Lane, Russell 2461
Rixon, Anna 2428
Summers, Clare 2542
Cragg, Rachael (on secondment 2012)
2383
Stewart-Gentle, Angela 2305
Tye, Sarah (Local Business Officer) 2392

POs
Bennett, Bridget 2501
Boow, Emma 2430
Brewitt, Helen 2341
Darts, Caroline 2317
Dawson, Andrew 2303
Davies, Jessica 2765
Dobbs, Nicky 2506
Fegredo, June 2083
Goedhart, Adriana 2464
Hector, Katherine 2281
Hutchinson, Stuart 2516
Lewis, Beverley 2443
Martin, Clive 2444
Merrett, Beth 2312
Pengelly, Janna 2432
Preston, Boyce 2536
Steele, Sarah 2508
Studley, Marina 2760
Ssali, Sula 2441

Thomson, Matthew 2370
Thompson, Steve 2397
White, Emma 2786
Woodroffe, Emma 2334
Wray, Nicky 2377

PSOs
Abbott-Hauxwell, Josie 2351
Adie, Janine 2752
Asadi Lucy 2325
Boulton, Gemma 2337
Brown, Hannah 2439
Bryant, Carla 2466
Clark, Sarah J 2435
Coombs, Holly 2447
Dadds, Stacey 2560
Damsell, Mark 2365
Excell, Natalie 2433
Griffin. Annie 2511
Groom, Hannah 2452
Handley, Ceris 2320
Harewood, Sheila 2393
Kerr, Anyha 2037
Mather, Laura 2778
O'Brien, Catherine 2318
Phillips, Beth 2464
Radford, Sara 2081
Rawlings, Francesca 2777
Rees, Robyn 2440
Royle, Fiona 2751
Sahota Imroze 2364
Taylor, Ali 2740
Williams, Deborah 2475
Case Admin
Allison, Nichola 2507
Barker, Jenny 2517
Budd, Paul 2451
Clark, Emily 2410
Cook, Rita 2515
Eddy, Emma 2504
Graham, Freddy 2436
Green, Paula 2442
James, Susan 2450
Jane, Atarah 2374
Jenner, Polly 2382
McLeod, Jamie 2439
Nicholls, Amy 2302
Oval, Ruth 2300
Watkins, Shirelle 2304

IMPACT
03000 49 2020
Team Leaders
Hook, Mike, 2719
Scott, Robin 2387

POs
Ealey, Emma 2331

Gupta, Gurmit 07919 697733
Fitzgerlad, Declan 2330
Light, Rachel 7252
Pace, Alex 2726
Parker, Sarah 2391
Pasco, Mark 2366
Romain, Maria 2363
Walsh, Jonathan 2349
Welsh, Clare 0777847 0384

PSOs
Bailey, Claire 2720
Bridal, Deb 2722
Champagine, Cynthia 2323
Day, Liz 2361
Drury, Dani 2085
Farah, Shamis 2021
Martin, Nicola 2124
Nutt, Lisa 2360
Potter, Brian 2315
Ralph-Brown, Katherine 2123
Richards, Jules 2296
Scott, Marvre 2367
Wildish, Katie 2353
Case Admin
Bradshaw, Thomas 2399
Dick, Becky 2311
Evans, Debbye 2357
Hill, Chloe 2404
Rich, Dan 2727
Snook, Richard 2728
Tout, Tricia (Area Bus. Co-ord.) 2729

IRIS
03000 49 2111
Birch, Fiona (Team Ldr) 2260
Burgess, Lucy (Dev. Mgr) 07500 999 067
Broad, Sally (OMU Off Supvr) 0117 373
263 (HMP Bristol)
Parsons, John (OMU Off Supvr) 0117 373
337 (HMP Bristol)
Robertson, David (OMU Off Supvr) 0117
373 384 (HMP Bristol)
Kehoe, Kevin (Det. Sergeant Police) 2025

POs
Fisher, Rachel 2737
Goodhind, Ben 2499
Guerreiro, Harriet 2373
Hanbidge, Matthew 2119
Hooper, Lois 2448
Richards, Matt 2505
Webb, Richard 2386
Wellman, Tom 2401
Meas, Kim (PSO) 2768
Wakefield, Dan (PSO) 2326
Dawson, Tom (Case Admin) 2400
Williams Aleysha (Case Admin) 2299

Police Field Intelligence Officers
Baker, Dan 07557 170982
Booth, Craig 07585 307111
Hatter, Gaby 07774 335961
Tyas, Andy 07827 979134

Central Office
Marlborough Street, **Bristol** BS1 3NU
Tel: 03000 49 2 519 Fax: 0117 930 2525
Direct dial: 03000 49 + ext
Harrison, Marilyn (ACO LDU Bristol)
2458
Brandt, Peter (ACO, LDU Banes &
S.Glous) 2201
Doust, Michelle (PA) 2459
Watson, Sybil (Dev Mgr) 2460
Beeson, Lesley (Local Business Off) 2456
Programmes
Van der Eerden, Barbara (Treatment
Mgr) 2309
Bradley, Steve (Treatment Mgr) 2396
Henry, Olivia (Treatment Mgr) 2379
Dunstan, Nicky (Middle Mgr) 2376
Rakozi, Jenny (Middle Mgr) 2346

POs
Burnett, Laurence 2358
Calderwood, Islay 2785
Clarke, Simon 2764
Essam, Odette 2378
Harley, David 2327
Banfield, Rose (PSO) 2388
Clark, Sarah L (PSO) 2389
Mountford, Guy (PSO) 2338
McGreevy, Lisa (PSO) 2359
Norton, Nick (PSO) 2375
Pretty, Kelly (PSO) 2354
Windle, Debra (PSO) 2329
Ramakrishnan, Bhuvana (Case Admin)
2313
Waller, Barbara, (Programme Admin),
2310

Courts Team
Whitefield, Nick (Team Leader) 2462
Bryant, Carla 2466
Brown, Diane 2471
Cook, Bev 2465
Comerford, Joanne 2469
Cornelius, Paul 2476
Danclar-Doody, Dawn 2467
Glanville, Amy 2301
Hill, Abigail 2463
Knill, Lisa 2474
Weston, Hannah 2114
Case Admin
Ashworth, Victoria 2477
Dinnis, Jane 2757

Eddy, Sarah 2012
Fox, Nicola 2475
Gifford, Stacey 2769
Miles, Karen 2470
Smith, Lauren 2756
McAllister, Gerry (Bail Info Off) 2472

South Glos Team
Ring, Lisa (LDU Team Ldr) 2761
Yates, Tony (LDU Team Ldr) 2479

POs
Davies, Neal 2490
Faulkner, Melissa 2489
Hutt, Andy 2481
Jackson, Audrey 2553
Middleton, Jayne 2485
Young, Carrie 2483

PSOs
Bishop, Ellen 2759
Hudson, Sarah 2493
Martin, Alison 2480
Sunderland, Rachel 2558
Swan, Jane 2758
Case Admin
Baker, Jonathan 2486
Dempster, Sarah 2494
Kelley, Joanna 2487
Regan, Leila 2488

Community Payback
Britton, Jeremy (Team Leader) 2347
Wellman, Stewart (Middle Mgr) 2395
Matthews, Christian (Team Mgr) 2321
Wainwright, Paul (Team Mgr) 2381

CP Supervisors
Bartlett, Keith 07711 089747
Briody, Jane 07714 399582
Dawes, Carlos 07525 408074
Mulholland, Simon 07768 241202
Nepean, James 07525 408075
Sabin, Sheila 07768 241206
Scott, Mike 07774 968672
Ward, Richard 07768 241811

PSOs
Clark, Colin 2322
Batten, Howard 2394
Billingsley, Jenny 2345
Campbell, Mary 2368
Willoughby, Claire 2335
Case Admin
Lane, Asha 2308
Sinclair, Ben 2763
Nowell, Hannah 2339
Hardwick, Josh 2350
Clarke, Lisa 2609

Szczelkun, Emma (Lead Admin
Interventions) 2332
Fullergreen, Jennifer 2342
Caseley, Joanna 2405
Cook, Lee 2343
Osbiston, Faye 2109

Victim Contact Team
VLOs
Ellis, Liz 2669
Harvey, Bridgette 2316
Stuart, Wendy 03000 47 2644
Summerhayes Alex 07899 964088
Whateley, Anna 2534
Women's Safety Officers
Bateman, Gurdarshan, 2385
George, Rebecca, 07595 007 550
Whitehead, Joanna, 2117
Admin
D'Arcy, Jason, 2344
Edwards, Sarah, 2390
Smith, Dawn, 2328

ETE Team
Thompson, Suzanne (Team Ldr) 2398
Bromham, Paul (LBM) 2380

ETE Officer
Cain, Paulette 2755
Griffiths, Michaela 2496
Hatwood, Jodie 2497
Ngozi, Kwesi 2356
Seward Lyn (New Futures Officer) 2791
White, Vicky 2403
Williams, Mike 2371
Case Admin
Saunders, Amanda 2080
Unstead, Tessa 2355
Woods, Eleanor 2336

Bristol Crown Court Liaison Office
Small Street, Bristol BS1 1DA
Tel: 0117 976 3071/2 Fax: 0117 976 3073

Admin
Taynton, Colin (CA) 0117 976 3071
Marshall, Sheralyn (CA) 0117 976 3071

Riverside House

West Quay
Bridgwater, Somerset TA6 3HW
Tel: 03000 49 2600 Fax: 03000 49 2617
Direct Dial 03000 49 + EXT

Pat Fensom (Local Business Off) 2598
Powell, Angela (LDU Team Leader) 2658
Harris, Tracey (Middle Manager) 2584

Offender Management (OM)
POs
Brooks, Marie 2590
Chin Mike 2687
Darbin, Steve 2591
Grover, Maggie 2612
Symons, Karen 2583
Walkley Julia 2268
Smith, Chantelle (Desistance Officer) 2577

PSOs
Kirby, Anna 2586
Sanchez, Paula 2613
Tuke, Mark 2575
Pike, Kate 582
Smith, Elaine (p) 2295
Case Admin
Bright, Leanne 2576
Chorley, Ruth 2574
Miller, Susan 2563
Montague, Emma 2579

Programmes
Hextall, Nigel (Middle Mgr) 2662
Denslow, Shelley (Local Business Mgr,
Interventions) 2593

Treatment Mgrs
Bradley, Steve 2396
Ellis, Liz 2669
Rexworthy, Frances 2675
Vale, Alan 2602
Harper, Sandra (PO) 2572

PSOs
Harris, Danielle 2608
Smith, Clare 2611
Packman, Heidi 2615
Tucker, Paul 2011
Coysh, Emma (Case Admin) 2564
Clarey, Sally (Case Admin) 2787

Community Payback
Harris, Tracey (Team Ldr) 2584
Day, Denise (Team Manager) 2674
Denslow, Shelley (Lead Admin,
Interventions) 2593

PSOs
Daniells, Sue 2603
Hale, Lynn 2606
Smith, Maxine 2578

Stretch, Sharon (UPW Admin) 2592
Emest, Peter (Supervisor Placement
Mgr) 07711 089779
Ball, Debbie (Case Admin) 2607
Shepherd, Jane (Case Admin) 2589

ETE
PSOs
Mobsby, Melayn 2682
West, Jackie 2594
Foreman, Christine (Case Admin) 2601

IMPACT Team
Knott, Christopher (PO) 2595
Carver, Aileen (PSO) 2610
Kingsbury, Marian (Specialist Admin)
2573

11 Canon Street
Taunton TA1 1SN
Tel: 03000 49 2666 Fax: 03000 49 2700
Direct dial: 03000 49 + ext
Minehead report centre tel: 07974 109850

Thomas, David (Local Delivery Unit Ldr,
ACO) 2668
Heaton, M (PA) based at HQ 2209
Local Business Officer – vacancy

Offender Management (Cluster A&B))
Team Leaders
Hamilton, Liz 2667 (p)
Hextall, Nigel 2662 (p)
Cluster A

POs
Murray, Graeme 2431
Waugh, Nicola 2685
Webster, Robin 2680
Barrie, Colette (PSO) 2693
Rawles, Colette (PSO) (p) 2683
Curtis, Mandy (Case Admin) 2655
Long, Sarah (Case Admin) (p) 2793
Rosewarne, Pauline (Case Admin) 2599
(p)
Cluster B

POs
Bawden, Kerrie 2789 (p)
Hammacott, Liz 2776
Roberts, Paul 2684

PSOs
Baker, Jane (p) 2696
Booth, Simon 2654
McKee, Rachel (p) 2698
Winterton, Olivia (p) 2686
Cottrell, Kara (Case Admin) 2664
Ross, Becky (Case Admin) (Courts) 2665
Alcohol Worker
Baker, Jane, PSO (p) 2696
Long, Sarah 2127

IMPACT
Kelly, Phil (Team Leader) 2645
Montag, Barbara (PO) 2692
Penelhum, Margaret (PO) 2691
Carver, Aileen (PSO)
Breakwell, Jim 2657
Stevenson, Matt 2660
Brown, Rosie, (Admin Officer), 2661
Price, Carol 2697 (Accommodation
Officer)
Ashton, Richard (Learning and
Development Officer) 2688

Taunton Crown Court
Shire Hall, Taunton TA1 1EU
Tel: 01823 338599 Fax: 01823 338946
Crown Court PSO/Administrator
Radford, Kathy (p, PSO) 01823 338599

North Somerset Magistrates'
Court Probation Office
North Somerset, Court House
The Hedges, St Georges

Weston-super-Mare
North Somerset BS22 7BB
Tel: 03000 49 2269 Fax: 03000 49 2298
(main)
Direct dial: 03000 49 + ext
Clarke, Annette (Local Business Off)
2273

Offender Management Assessment Team
Team Leaders
Harris, Andy 2280
Thatcher Sally 2289
Bessant, Matthew (PSO) 2271

POs
Hammacott, Liz 2776
Hooley, Rachel 2284
Lockwood, Daniel 2285
Maynard, Sally 2276
Somerville-Ashby, Helen 2270
Tiernan, Joe 2269
Woods, Doug 2291

PSOs
Brown, Hannah 2439
Coltham, Joy 2274
Coveney, Helen 2276
Lock, Clare 2293
Samotyi, Carly 2287
Stafford, Tracy 2288
Smith Elaine 2295 ((p) covering WSM &
B'Water)
Davies, Matt 2369
Case Admin
Cole, Peter 2275

Druce, Marion 2277
Gotsell, Susan 2278
Hector, Elizabeth 2282
Rosewarne, Pauline 2599

McFarlane, Mona (Receptionist) 2269
Pask, Lyndon (CP Supervisor) 077660
86515

Yeovil Office
Court Ash House, Court Ash
Yeovil BA20 1HG
Tel: 03000 49 2262 Fax 0300 039 2647
Frome Reporting Centre – 07912 668018
/ 07730 091081

LDU 3 Offender Management
Team Leaders
Evans, Claire 2630
Friend, Anne 2620

Taylor, Lesley (LBO) 2783
Reception 2622
Antrobus, Karen (Restore Trust) 2790

POs
Elliott, Jennifer 2628
Geraghty, Dominic 2631
Henderson, Richard 2434
Knell, Tim 2618
Miller, Bob 2642
Smerdon, Becca 2632

PSOs
Bushell, Karen 2636
Cox, Stephen 2624
Denman, Becky 2639
Ferrero, Marion 2638
Flower, Joan 2643
Hole, Kate, 2656
Smith, Kerren 2640
Stewart, Alison 2629
White, Deanne 2623
Hall, Linda (Case Admin) 2634
Hallett, Vicky (Case Admin) 2646
Staffe, Abby 2641

Programmes
Keith Lusty Treatment Manager – 2621
Paul Tucker, (PSO) 2011

Community Payback
Roberts, Joy, (Quality Assurance
Manager) – 2627
Daniels, Sue (PSO) 2603

ETE
Emily Janas (ETE Officer) 2631

Yeovil Impact Team
Yeovil Police Station, Horsey Lane
Yeovil BA20 1SN

Tel: 01935 402249
Fax: 01935 402282
Kelly, Phil, (Team Leader), 2645
Thorne, Sharon (PO)
Higginbotham, Coral (PSO) Case Admin
Ashford, Kay (Case Admin)
Jane Piggott / Joe Harper – 2784
Hale, Pauline (Case Admin)
Kensett, Amanda
PC Jim Breakwell

HMP Bristol Office
HMP Bristol, 19 Cambridge Road
Horfield, Bristol BS7 8PS
Tel: 0117 372 3383 Fax: 0117 372 3322
firstname.lastname@hmps.gsi.gov.uk

Withers, Peter (Snr Prison Off) 07796
337722
Deloni-Daure, Yvonne (Prison Off) 0117
372 3383
Headley, Richard (Prison Off) 0117 372
3023
Frater, Natasha (PSO) 0117 372 3023

Staple Hill Office
Staple Hill Police Station, Broad Street
Staple Hill, Bristol BS16 5LX
Fax: 01454 867256

O'Hagan, Rosie (Middle Mgr) 0117 945
4223
Mob: 07920 878228
Austin, Matt 0117 945 4257; 07919 697720
Sole, Stuart 0117 945 4126; 07789 753628
Brain, Lucy 0117 945 4257; 07919 697720
Smart, Charmaine (PSO) 0117 945 4257;
07919 017261
Morgan, Lisa Case Admin (p) 0117 945
4126

Taunton Office
Taunton Police Station
Upper High Street, Shuttern
Taunton TA1 3QA
Fax: 01823 363250

Montag, Barbara 01823 363020; 07917
883847
Carver, Aileen (PSO) 01823 363020;
07789 753626
Brown, Rosie (Admin Off) 01823 363020;
07919 697717

Youth Offending Teams
12 Charlotte Street
Bath BA1 2NF
Tel: 01225 396966 Fax: 01225 338063

Kenham House
Wilder Street, **Bristol** BS2 8PD
Tel: 0117 903 6480 Fax: 0117 903 6481

48–50 Elm Park
Filton, South Gloucestershire BS34 7PP
Tel: 01454 868553 Fax: 01454 868560

5–7 West End
Street BA16 0LG
Tel: 01458 440820 Fax: 01458 449100

59 Oxford Street
Weston-super-Mare
North Somerset BS23 1TR
Tel: 01275 888360 Fax: 01275 888361

Approved Premises

Ashley House Approved Premises
14 Somerset Street, Kingsdown
Bristol BS2 8NB
Tel: 0117 924 9697 Fax: 0117 944 4290
Pitman, John (Mgr)
Assistant Managers
Greenhill, Brendan
Hopkins, Clive
Hunt, Colin
Jefferies, Jessica
Stutt, Jean
Wilde, Sally
Williams, Matt
Marks, Hayley (Night Supervisor)
Morris, Eddie (Night Supervisor)
Burke, Terry (Hostel Admin)

Bridge House Approved Premises
78 Filton Road, Bristol BS7 0PD
Tel: 0117 969 3123 Fax: 0117 931 2167

Ashby, Richard AP Mgr

Miners, David Mgr

PSOs
Gilroy, Alistair
Hesketh, Christopher
Mockridge, Leigh
Richardson, Des
Hatfield, Catherine
Rosario, Octavian
Bragg, Jodie (NSA)
Oly, Marcia Johnson (NSA)
Tutton, Stephen (NSA)

Brigstocke Road Approved Premises
6 Brigstocke Road
Bristol BS2 8UB
Tel: 0117 942 5851 Fax: 0117 944 5945
Jacobs, Gillian (Admin)
David Miners (Middle Mgr)

Kerensa Holgate (PO)

PSOs
Robert Walker
Stephen Mudzamiri
Graham, Jon
Jefferies Julie
Lake, Catherine
Orchard, Patrick
Bakary Gibba
Bull, Adam
Vadher, Jig

Glogan House
59 Taunton Road, Bridgwater TA6 3LP
Tel: 01278 424165 Fax: 01278 446054
Cornelius, Simon (Interventions Mgr)
Rixon, Anna (Middle Mgr)

PSOs
Andrews, Wayne
Bourton, Bob
Day, Alison
Foxwell, Tony
McGill, Dave
Murkin, Robert
Reid, Steve
Jacky Burrows
Martin Stafford pt (NSA)
Shaun Concannon pt (NSA)
Bowie, Geoffrey (NSA)

Institutions

HMP Bristol
19 Cambridge Road, Bristol BS7 8PS
Tel: 0117 372 3100 Fax: 0117 372 3153
Direct dial: 0117 372 + ext

Pye, Denise (Middle Mgr) 3265
Broad, Sally (PSO ROTL, Offender
Supvr) 3337
Frater, Natasha (PSO Prolificis/IOMU)
3017
Jack, Ron (PSO Bail Info Off/Offender
Supvr) 3383
Stevenson, Frances (PSO, HDC) 3263

PSO Offender Supervisors
Dutson, Poppy 3337
Chaplain, Cassandra 3212
Champion, Esther 3290
Groves, Shaun 3337

HMP Leyhill
Wotton-under-Edge
Glos GL12 8BT
Tel: 01454 264000 Fax: 01454 264005
Direct dial: 01454 26 + ext
Mailbox: OMU.leyhill@hmps.gsi.gov.uk

Trundley, Katy (Middle Mgr) 4178
POs
Clare Daly 4030
Anna Hothersall 4036
Anne Weatherley 4118
Rachel Wedmore
Lesley Hall 4257
Claire Tonkinson 4032
Jayne Middleton
 Hannah Gregory
PSOs
Sue Hancock 4019
Angela Smith 4026
Emma Gray 4215
Kevin Edmonds OS 4137

HMP/YOI Eastwood Park
Falfield, Wotton-under-Edge
Glos GL12 8DB
Tel: 01454 382100 Fax: 01454 382101
OMU Fax: 01454 382092
Direct dial: 01454 382 + ext

Crallan, Katherine (p, Head of OMU)
01454 382046
Bovill, Carolyn (Accom Off) 01454 382335

PO/Offender Supervisors
Forbes, Angela 01454 382097
Hall, Lesley 01454 382 065
Hood, Colette 01454 382065
Maye, Rebecca 01454 382057
Watterson, Emma 01454 382057
Unit Admin 01454 382057

HMP/YOI Ashfield
Shortwood Road, Pucklechurch
Bristol BS16 0QJ
Tel: 0117 303 8000 Fax: 0117 303 8001

HMP Shepton Mallet
Cornhill, Shepton Mallet BA4 5LU
Tel: 01749 823300 Fax: 01749 823307
(probation)
Direct dial: 01749 82 + ext
Breckenridge, Allyson (PO) 3427
Hillier, Sara 3428(PO)
Farrell, Nicky (PSO) 3533

Local Justice Areas
Bath & Wansdyke
Bristol
North Avon
North Somerset
Sedgemoor
South Somerset & Mendip
Taunton Deane & West Somerset

Crown Courts
Bristol
Taunton

BEDFORDSHIRE PROBATION TRUST

Victim enquiries tel: 01234 358978

Email:
firstname.lastname@bedfordshire.probation.
gsi.gov.uk

Head Office
3 St Peter's Street Bedford MK40 2PN
Tel: 01234 213541 Fax: 01234 327497

Hennigan, Linda (CO)
Harding, Alison (ACO)
Osborne, Emma (ACO, based at Frank
Lord House, Luton)
Morgan, Katie (ACO)

Administration
Jones, Sara (PA to CO & Board)
Chapple, Belinda (PA to A Harding & S
Jennings)

Corporate Services & HR
Jennings, Sue (ACO)
McSweeney, Barbara (p, Comms Mgr)
Foinette, Nicole (HR Advisor)
Dempster, Claire (Training & HR
Advisor)

Performance and Information Unit
Brown, Andrew (Performance & Info
Mgr)
Mainwaring, Mick (IT Mgr)

Finance
Keith, Deborah (Head of Finance)

MAPPA/Victim Liaison Unit
Greyfriars Police Station
4th Floor
Greyfriars
Bedford MK40 1HR

Victim unit
Tel: To be advised Fax: To be advised

MAPPA unit
Tel: To be advised

De Souza, Chris (MAPPA Coord)
Ince, Josie (MAPPA Admin)

Bedford/Central Bedfordshire LDU

41 Harpur Street
Bedford MK40 1LY
Tel: 01234 350401 Fax: 01234 328658

LDU Management
Harding, Alison (ACO- based at Head Office)
Blows, Dawn (JS Admin & Information Mgr)
Brewer, Richard (JS, Admin & Information Mgr)

Offender Management
Gould, Dean (Acting Team Mgr)
Judge, Gabrielle (Team Mgr)
De St-Aubin, Doug (Partnerships Mgr)

Integrated Offender Management
Burnell, Karen (Team Mgr)

Unpaid Work Unit
Layne, Jacqui (Deputy Manager)
Di Salvo, Carina (Admin)

Training
Breakey, Paul (PDA)

Programmes
Nezis, Rebecca (Team Mgr)

Bedfordshire Youth Offending Service

Borough Hall Cauldwell Street
Bedford MK40 90P
Tel: 01234 363922

Corbett, Sue (Head of Integrated Youth Services and Youth Offending)
Seall, Clive (Service Manager)
Harper, Louise (InterimPA)

Bedfordshire Youth Offending Service

Bedfordshire Youth Offending Service
Enterprise House
36–40 Old Ford End Road
Bedford MK40 4PF
Tel: 01234 276400 Fax: 01234 276434
Secure email:
firstname.lastname@bedford.gov.uk.cjsm.net
Weatherall, Brian (Interim Team Mgr)
Campbell, Melissa (Interim Operations Manager)
Ruskin, Geoff (SNR Pract, Statutory Risk Countrywide)
McEvoy, Julie (SNR Pract, Intensive Superveillance & Support Countywide)
Easton, James (SNR Prac. Victim and Restorative Approaches Manager)

Boss, Donna (Information Manager)
Wilkinson, Paula (PO)

Luton LDU

Frank Lord House
72 Chapel Street Luton LU1 5DA
Tel: 01582 413172 Fax: 01582 418279

LDU Management
Harding, Alison (ACO, based at Head Office)
Osborne, Emma (ACO)
Morrison, Audrey (Admin & Info Mgr)

Administration
Duke, Andrea (PA to E Osborne)

Offender Management
Berg, Gill (Team Mgr)
Burrows, Matthew (Team Mgr)
Hooper, Steve (Team Mgr)

CT & Prevent
Beaumont, Sue (Mgr)

Unpaid Work Unit
Nezis, Rebecca (Team Mgr)
Anderson, Stephen (Dep Team Mgr)
Caveney, Marian (Snr Admin)

23–27 Napier Road

Luton LU1 1RF
Tel: 01582 735153 Fax: 01582 451536

Programmes
Nezis, Rebecca (Team Mgr, based at Frank Lord House)
Belony, Wendy (p, Snr Admin)

Integrated Offender Management
Delmar, Elaine (Team Mgr)

Luton Youth Offending Service

16 Rothesay Road Luton LU1 1QX
Tel: 01582 547900 Fax: 01582 547901
Non secure email: yos@luton.gov.uk
Secure email:
lutonyos-general@luton.gov.uk.cjsm.net

Briddon, Anita (Hd of YO Service)
King, Liz (Service Manager)
Collins, Dave (Ops Mgr)
Southwell, Verity (Ops Mgr)
Thompson, Jo (Ops Mgr)
Robinson, Steve (Bail Supvn Off)
Vacancy (Bail Supvn Off)
Swiecicki, Noreen (Admin & Finance Mgr)
Hutchinson, Troy (Info & Sys Mgr)

Court Services

Magistrates' Court Liaison Office
Shire Hall 3 St Pauls Square Bedford
MK40 1SQ
Tel: 01234 358402 Fax: 01234 358070

Pettengell, Louise (Court Support Admin)

Crown Court Liaison Office
Luton Crown Court
7–9 George Street Luton LU1 2AA
Tel: 01582 452079

Crown Court Switchboard
Tel: 01582 452846 Fax: 01582 485529

Haynes, Cheryl (Team Mgr, based at
Frank Lord House)

Magistrates' Court Liaison Office
The Court House
Stuart Street Luton LU1 5DL
Tel: 01582 482710 Fax: 01582 482995

Haynes, Cheryl (Team Mgr, based at
Frank Lord House)

Approved Premises (Hostels)

Accommodation Services Manager
Smith, Ali

36–40 Napier Road
Luton LU1 1RG
Tel: 01582 418200 Fax: 01582 737391

Andrews, Debra (Mgr)

80 Chaucer Road
Bedford MK40 2AP
Tel: 01234 340501 Fax: 01234 351715
Nichols, Magda (Mgr)

Institution

HMP Bedford
St Loyes Street Bedford MK40 1HG
Tel: 01234 373000 Fax: 01234 373568

Local Justice Areas

Bedford & Mid Bedfordshire
(*Bedford/Central Bedfordshire LDU*)
Luton & South Bedfordshire (*Luton
LDU*)

Crown Court

Luton

CAMBRIDGESHIRE AND PETERBOROUGH PROBATION TRUST

Out of hours emergency tel: Approved
Premises 01733 551678

Victim enquiries contact numbers:

Marilyn Ansell 03000 477400

Margaret Pool 03000 477400

Email:
firstname.lastname@cppt.probation.gsi.gov.uk

Head Office
Godwin House (2nd Floor), George Street
Huntingdon PE29 3BD
Tel: 03000 477000 Fax: 03000 477050
Direct dial: 03000+

Budd, John (CEO) ext 477001
Dyson, Mike (ACO) ext 477003
Hancock, Alison (ACO) ext 477004
Morrison, Roz (ACO) ext 477005
Ryder, Matthew (ACO)
Seaton, Paul (Treasurer) ext 477006
Salmon, Gaynor (Fin & Est Off) ext
477009

Gooch, Baden (Comm Eng Mgr) ext
477027
O'Sullivan, Jacqueline (Seconded to
NOMS)
Taylor, Jean (Change Mgr) ext 477025
Thompson, Kay (Staff Dev Admin) ext
477016
Faulkner, Keith (Team Mgr, Info) ext
477017
King, Bart (1st Line Supp) ext 477019
Clampin, Dawn (p, Intranet Pubs Officer)
ext 477023
Pereira, Chris (Perf Info Officer) ext
477020
Moore, Steve (IT Off) ext 477018
Donaldson, Sherron (Diversity Mgr) ext
477022
Sedzikowski, Sue (HR & Dev Mgr) ext
477011
Stackhouse, Joyce (HR Advisor) ext
477012
Gillies, Maureen (p, HR Admin) ext
477014
Jackson, Jackie (p, HR Admin) ext 477013
Panter, Shona (Bus Mgr) ext 477029
Sherwood, Karen (Bus Mgr) ext 477031

Huntingdon Office
Godwin House (Ground Floor), George Street
Huntingdon PE29 3BD
Tel: 03000 477400 Fax: 03000 477477
Humphrey, Emma (p, Team Mgr)
Turvill, Rachel (p, Progs Proj Op Mgr)
Beaumont, Lynn
Edmond, Diane (Treatment Mgr)
English, Doreen (p)
Holsgrove, Katie
Marsh, Linsey (p)
Mill, Danielle
Powney, Clare (p, PTA & QED Mgr)
Robinson, Paula (p)
Whitley, Helen
Wilson, Daniel

PSOs
Ansell, Marilyn (VLO)
Colomb, Stella (SO Facilitator)
Crate, Anne (p)
Ferrari, Sarah (Prog Tut)
Lowe, Jane
Pool, Margaret (VLO)
Stewart, Zoe (p)
Stimson, Kamila
Mansfield, Keith (p, CP Mgr)

Multi Agency Public Protection Panel
Cambridgeshire Police Authority
Copse Court, Thorpe Wood
Peterborough PE3 6SF
Tel: 01733 863116 Fax: 01733 868585

Jarvis, Andy (MAPPA Coord) 01733 863116

MAPPA Admin
Freeney, Pauline (p) 01733 863117/03000 477442
Jackson, Helen (p) 03000 477233
Jones, Sarah (p) 03000 400443
Pollard, Clare 03000 477360

Warkworth Lodge
Warkworth Street
Cambridge CB1 1EG
Tel: 03000 477200 Fax: 03000 477277

Seddon, Graeme (p, Team Mgr)

Swain, Mark (Team Mgr)

von Rabenau, Elisabeth (Reg Sex Offender Proj Mgr)
Waghorn, Hannah (Team Mgr)
Baker, Geraldine
Bardell, David
Bates, Gemma (Prog Tut)

Beale, Julie
Chalder-Mills, Julie (p, Prog Tut)
Gooch, Emily
Hawkes, Gary
Hudson, Becky
Jethva, Gita
Loosley, Suzanne
Lowes, Julie
Price, Morgan
Taylor, Amanda
Vickery, Anna
Vacancy (YOS)

PSOs
Bailey, Maxine (p)
Bromley, Amy
De Sousa, Jorge
Firman, Lewis
Flowerdew, Christopher
Lloyd, Linda (p)
Martin, Rachael
Payne, Barbara (p)
Sharman, Lyn
Stratfold, Deborah (p)
Templar, Ann

Programme Facilitators
Cameron, Katie
Curry, Suzanne
Norman, Viktorija
Patel, Rebecca
Tracey, Marcus

Comm Payback Managers
Bynoe, David (CP Proj Op Mgr)
Stimson, Darren (p)
Pease, Terri (p Temp PSO)

Cambridge Magistrates' Court
12 St Andrews Street
Cambridge

*(All mail to Warkworth Lodge Warkworth Street
Cambridge CB1 1EG)*

Castle Lodge
1 Museum Square
Wisbech PE13 1ES
Tel: 03000 477100 Fax: 03000 477150
Walker, Mick (Team Mgr)
Holloway, Stephen
Parker, Marsha
Talbot, Sophie
Thomas, Owy
Turner, Jayne
Wardell, Linda
Campbell, Anita (p, WSO)
Gibson, Joann (p, PSO)

Molloy, Val (PSO)
Moore, Alan (Comm Payback Mgr)

Magistrates' Court
Bridge Street
Peterborough PE1 1ED
Tel: 03000 477300 Fax: 03000 477310
Cochrane, Graham (Team Mgr)
Morphus, Becki (Team Mgr)
Anderson, Sue (p)
Block, Nigel
Brickley, Stephen
Crowley, Julie
Curphey, Joanne (PO & QED Mgr)
Davis, Matt
Douglas, Craig (YOS)
Drabble, Jacie
Goff, Christine (p, PTA)
Hoche, Anita (p)
Lace, Liz (p)
Lawrence, Victoria
Minns, Darren
Newington, Nicola (p)
Peacock, Kerrie
Stocks, Simone
Walker, Chris
Whaley, Claire
Whitwell, Natalie (p)
Willis, Mel (p)

PSOs
Beech, Garry
Garratt, Steve
Heighton, Tim
Latham, Lynda (p)
Munir, Mohammed
Sanders, Laura
Taylor, Clare (Temp PSO)
Walker Kelly-Anne (WSO)
Williams, Christine
Woods, Paul
Slyfield, Ann (Bus Mgr)

Crown Court
Tel: 01733 352763 Fax: 01733 565284

Gloucester House
23a London Road
Peterborough PE2 8AP
Tel: 03000 477350 Fax: 03000 477390

Wallis, Stuart (Interventions Mgr)

Prior, Marie (Team Mgr)

Edwards, Fiona
Fieldhouse, Nicola
Kerr, Sally
Morse, Mike (Prog Tut)

PSOs
Bester, Rachel
Clarke, Lucy (p)
Cummings, Lorna (p)
Hughes, Donna
Smith, Nick

Programme Facilitators
Barnacle, Sharon (IDAP)
Bibi, Khadeeja (p, WSO)
Corry, Kym
Venni, Ruth
Arnold, Jane, (CP Proj Op Mgr)
Hallam, Issy (p, Comm Payback Mgr)
Howes, Michael (Comm Payback Mgr)
Nutcher-Palmer, Barbara (p, Comm Payback Mgr)
Pollard, Clare (MAPPA Admin)

Approved Premises (Hostel)

5 Wesleyan Road
Peterborough PE1 3RW
Tel: 01733 551678 Fax: 01733 345161

Pease, Adrian (Team Mgr)

PSOs
Jenkins, Brian
Martin-James, Penny
Smith, Steve
Storey, Kevin (p)
Trower, Andreana

AP Supervisors
Friskey, Pamela
Mohammed, Kamran
Wilson, Tim
Wright, Richard (p)
Lane, Sandee (p, Admin)
Sidney, Jackie (p, Finance)

Institutions

HMP Littlehey
Perry Huntingdon Cambs PE18 0SR
Tel: 01480 335000 Fax: 01480 335070

Thomas, Francella (Team Mgr) 335546
King, Lesley 335507
Providence, Belinda 335508
Sandford, David 335510

PSOs
Fieldhouse, Adrian 335522
Garrett, Shaun 335496
Hazell, Susan
Jackson, Shane 335504
King, Janet
Murphy, Tracy 335535
Nolan, Gary 335532

Smith, Susan 335697
Turner, Donna (p, Admin)

HMP Whitemoor
Longhill Road, March PE15 0AF
Tel: 01354 602616 Fax: 01354 659861

OMU Fax 01354 602759
Legal visits tel: 01354 602654
Booking visits ext 2800
Fisher, Amanda ext 2526

PSOs
Calvert, Elizabeth ext 2832
Forte, Monica ext 2821
Humphrey, Dave ext 2469
Leigh, Maggie ext 2542

HMP Peterborough
Saville Road Westfield
Peterborough PE3 7PD
Tel: 01733 217500 Fax: 01733 217502

Szumlicki, Anna ext 5706
Browning, Cheryl (PSO) ext 3104
Jamison, Charlotte (PSO) ext 7144

Local Justice Areas
Cambridge (*Warkworth Lodge Cambridge*)
Huntingdonshire (*Huntingdon Office*)
Peterborough (*Magistrates' Court and Gloucester House Peterborough*)

Crown Courts
Cambridge
Peterborough

CHESHIRE PROBATION TRUST

Out of hours emergency contact numbers:
0151 357 3551or 01270 759181

E-mail:
firstname.lastname@cheshire.probation.gsi.gov.uk

Chief Executive Office
11 Hunters Walk, Off Canal Street
Chester, CH1 4EB
Tel: 01244 605850
Cossins, Angela (Chief Executive)
McCrorie, Ben (Projects Mgr)
Fredriksen, Tracey (Executive Assistant to CE)
Evans, Christine (ACE & Treasurer)
Vacant (Executive Assistant to Treasurer)
Bryan, David (Board Secretary)

Communications & Information Security
Gaughran, Liz (Communications & Info Security Off)

Finance
Tel: 01244 605854
Venables, Graham (Mgr)

Human Resources & Staff Development
Tel: 01244 605853
Collins, Michelle (Mgr)

Jupiter House
Jupiter House, Jupiter Drive
Chester West Employment Park
Chester, CH1 4QS
Tel: 01244 665100 Fax: 01244 665101

Information Services
Alexander, Iain
Ferguson, Christopher
Iremonger, Gordon (Infrastructure Manager)
Quirk, Lee

Health & Safety
Woods, Steve (Health & Safety Off)

Service Development Unit
Hulse, Steve (Contracts & Partnerships Off)
Meade, Donna (Service Development Mgr)
Thornden-Edwards, Kim (ACE)
Trueman, Karen (EA)
Theilade, Annemarie (Diversity Mgr)
Wallace, David (Info & Performance Mgr)

Cheshire West and Chester Local Delivery Unit
Jupiter House, Jupiter Drive
Chester West Employment Park
Chester, CH1 4QS
Tel: 01244 665100 Fax: 01244 665101

Orell, Marie (ACE)
Wilson, Cathy (EA)
Blackwell, Mandy (Business Admin)
Corbett, Catherine (SPO)
Jones, Brenda (Business Admin)
O'Mahony, Cathy (SPO)
Peters, Cherryl (SPO)
Bayles, Angela
Biddle, Malveen
Cox, Helen
Cunliffe, Sally (Courts)
Devine, Chris

Entwistle, Ben (Courts)
Gray, Nicky
Hadden, Kelly
Hudson, Steve (Programmes)
Humphries, Rachel
Jones, James
Jackson, Helen
Kernahan, Chris (Courts)
Mansutti, Helen
Nolan-Beattie, Cathy (Courts)
Orr, Rose
Parry, Enfys
Teese, David
Thorne, Tim
Warburton, Helen
Williams, Nick

PSOs
Ballard-East, Caroline
Bowman, Trudy (Courts)
Burrell, Clare
Davies, Lisa (Courts)
Graham, Kim (Courts)
Hammersley, Claire
Holleran, Steve (Programmes)
Howell, Karen
Jooste, Emma
Littler, Kelly
Powell, Claire (Courts)
Riccio, Marian (Programmes)
Roberts, Karen
Rose, Rachel
Rawlinson-Doyle, Janice (Courts)
Stewart, Chris (Victims)
Williams, Stella (Victims)
Hutt, Vicky (Crewe Victims)

Chester Community Payback
Skyner, David (SPO)
Cringle, Dave (Practice Mgr)
Crawford, Karen (PSO)
Green, Sam (PSO)
Millington, Grenville (Placement Mgr)

Marshall Memorial Hall
Woodford Lane
Winsford, CW7 2JS
Tel: 01606 551166 Fax: 01606 861267

Miklaszewicz, Janina (SPO)
Long, Belynda
Pritchard, Carol
Robson, Jackie
Shepherd, Cheryl

PSOs
Buckley, Gill
Dibbert, Diane
Simpson, Penny

Learner Practitioner
Halliwell, Krista

MAPPA
Smith, Ian (SPO)

Warrington Local Delivery Unit
Howard House, 10A Friars Gate
Warrington, WA1 2RW
Tel: 01925 650613 Fax: 01925 445109
Bendon, Kerri (SPO)
Lane, Rebecca (SPO)
Neary, Jackie (SPO)
Ashraf, Farah
Barnard, Karen
Birch, Jean
Hall, Steph
Jenkins, Lisa
Jones, Vikki
Lawlor, Jim
Mitchinson, Gail
Murphy, Jo
Norman, Philip
Sykes, Jan
Woodruff, John

PSOs
Gomme, Emma
Gibbons, Julie (Victims Warrington)
Hamlett, Andrea
Lea, Sarah
Lilly, Alan
Mapson, Frank (Courts)
Morris, Emma (Courts)
Pownall, Andrew
Phillips, Veronica (Courts)
Shaw, Julie (Courts)
Tickle, Tony
Whittle, Beth

Warrington Community Payback
Brown, Yasmine (PSO)
Johnston, James (PSO)
Leech, Sandra (Placement Mgr)
McGregor, Sheila (Practice Mgr)
Richards, Jeff (Placement Mgr)

Runcorn Local Delivery Unit
Norton House, Crown Gate
Runcorn, WA7 2UR
Tel: 01928 713555 Fax: 01928 701985

Davidson, John (ACE)
Gilmour, Elly (EA)
Crawford, Ann (SPO)
Jones, Sian (SPO)
McDonagh, Christine (SPO)
Taylor, Karen (SPO)
Willet, Jenny (Business Admin Runcorn
& Warrington)

Balchin, Susan
Bennette, Diane
Davies, Emma
Eagles, Jackie
Ferris, Shane (Programmes)
Foulkes, Richard
Kneale, Elaine
Madoc-Jones, Viv
McIntyre, Kevin
Nolan-Beattie, Cathy (Courts)
Plumb, Michelle (Programmes)
Pugh, Karen
Sawula, Sophie
Wyatt, Sue
PSOs
Anderson, Sue (Courts)
Beech, Catherine
Bradley, Elizabeth
Cavallaro, Eileen
Derrig-Vanzie, Cathryn (Courts)
Hallett, Michelle (Courts)
Harrison, Sophie (Programmes)
Lawlor, Chris (Victims)
Prior, Gemma (Programmes)
Seddon, Lisa (Programmes)
Simpson, Richard (Courts)
Shearer, Sandra (Community Payback)
Wilton, Dave
Learner Practitioners
Johnson, Sue
Stoneley, Kaye

Cheshire East Local Delivery Unit
Cedric Fullwood House
Gateway, Crewe, CW1 6YY
Tel: 01270 257781 Fax:01270 251181
Link, Sandra (ACE)
Waddington, Jo (EA)
Day, Julie (SPO)
O'Rourke, Jacqueline (SPO)
Wilde, Judith (Business Admin)
Collier, Rachel (Programmes)
Esegbona, Clem
Owen, Mark
Primmer, David
Rowntree, Rosie
Royle, Lynn
Spanswick, Emma
Varty, Jan
Whitwell, Danielle

PSOs
Ayers, Sue (Programmes)
Boliver, Mike (Courts)
Chaloner, Rae
Done, Joanne
Esegbona, Helen
Isherwood, Michael (Courts)

Jackson, Gail (Achieve)
Jenkins, Lee (Courts)
Kusiar, Pam
Lewis, Melissa (Programmes)
May, Rachel (Programmes)
McGuinness, Angela
Stacey, Colin (Programmes)
Whittaker, Thomas

Bradshaw House
45 Cumberland Street,
Macclesfield, SK10 1BY
Tel: 01625 423974 Fax: 01625 421345

King, Clare (SPO)
Yates, Donna (SPO)
Wilde, Judith (Business Admin)
Delaney, Sarah
Fagan, Erin
Horner, Ken
McKeith, Deborah
Scott, Christine
Sergeant, Dave
Whalley, Michael
Wilson, Sally

PSOs
Gregory, Janet
Perez, Sarah
Winney, Emma (Courts)
Learner Practitioner
Pearce, Tristram

Macclesfield Community Payback
Hamlett, Elaine (Practice Mgr)
Brown, Charlotte (PSO)
Tavourari-Green, Isobel (PSO)

Youth Offending Teams

Ellesmere Port
St Thomas House, Whitby Road,
Ellesmere Port, CH65 6TU
Tel:0151 337 6501

Keatley, Sarah

Macclesfield
Park View, Clarke Terrace,
Macclesfield, SK11 7QD
Tel: 01625 378160

Robertson, Kerry

Halton & Warrington
Unit 10 Turnstone Business Park,
Mulberry Ave,
Widnes, WA8 0WN
Tel:01514955840

Hial, Nadia

Approved Premises

Linden Bank
10 London Road,
Elworth, Sandbach, CW11 3BD
Tel: 01270 759181 Fax: 01270 759579

Rowe, Peter (Mgr)

PSOs
Buckley, Steve
Blevins, Richard
Coss, Jean
Foster, Julia
Jaroszek, Richard
O'Driscoll, Sally
Rozitis, Richard
Vesty, Annette

Bunbury House
Alnwick Drive, Stanney Grange
Ellesmere Port, CH65 9HE
Tel: 0151 357 3551 Fax: 0151 356 2102
O'Hea, Brendan (Mgr)

PSOs
Clarke, Graham
Connolly, Kay
Corley, Stephanie
Harvey, Ingrid
Joinson, Julie
Jones, Ian
Price, Jill
Roberts, Tracey

Institutions

HMP/YOI Styal
Wilmslow SK9 4HR
Tel: 01625 553000 Fax: 01625 553204
Maude, Manjit (SPO)
McGillivray, Andrea
Nicholson, Paul

PSOs
Ward, Catherine
West, Lindsey

HMP Risley
Warrington Road, Risley, Warrington WA3 6BP
Tel: 01925 733000 Fax: 01925 764103
Fax: 01925 766975 (Probation)
Burton, Rachel
Marquez, Ellen Marie
Moss, David
Ramsdale, Sue
Scott, Andrew

PSOs
Bywater, Mark
Lilly, Alan

HMYOI Thorn Cross
Arley Road, Appleton Thorn,
Warrington, WA4 4RL
Tel: 01925 605100 Fax: 01925 605101
Parkinson, Hillary

PSOs
Astall, Julie
McCaskill, Jane

ACHIEVE Project
Norton House, Crown Gate
Runcorn, WA7 2UR
Tel: 01928 713555 Fax: 01928 701985
Hill, Tracey (Runcorn) (Project Mgr)
Barker, Val (Thorn Cross YOI)
Hallwood, Catherine (Runcorn)
Jackson, Gail (Crewe)
Lloyd, Carol (Chester)
Lowe, Dianne (Warrington)
Johnson, Andrew (HMP Styal)
Mahar, Dennis (Chester)
Snow, Heather (Runcorn)

Belief in Change Programme
HRM Risley, Warrington Road, Risley,
Warrington, WA3 6BP
Tel: 01925 733000 Fax: 01925 764103
Edmondson, Lorna (BIC Reintegration Mgr) (temp)
McFadden, Sam (BIC Programme Facilitator)
Hawksworth, Alexandra (BIC Programme Facilitator) (temp)

Local Justice Areas
Chester, Ellesmere Port & Neston
(*Jupiter House Chester*)
Halton (*Norton House Runcorn*)
Macclesfield (*Bradshaw House Macclesfield*)
South Cheshire (*Cedric Fullwood House Crewe*)
Vale Royal (*Marshall Memorial Hall Winsford*)
Warrington (*Howard House Warrington*)

Crown Courts
Chester
Knutsford
Warrington

CUMBRIA
PROBATION TRUST

Out of hours emergency contact point
Bowling Green Approved Premises 01228
522360

Email:
firstname.lastname@cumbria.probation.gsi.
gov.uk

Probation Headquarters
Magistrates' Court, Rickergate
Carlisle CA3 8XP
Tel: 03000 473750 Fax: 03000 473751
Bruce, Russell (Chief Executive
(Interim))
Walker, Sara (P.A. to Chief Executive
(Interim) & Director of Operations)
Moore, Fiona (Director of Legal Services
/ Board Secretary)
Sait, Sargon (Director of Corporate
Services / Treasurer)
Ward, Sarah (Director of Operations)
Roebuck, Duncan (Business Development
Manager)
Penton, Joanne (Information,
Performance & Quality Manager)
Manson, Andrea (Health and Safety
Officer)
Kelleher, Anne (Information Systems
Officer)
Wilson, Stephen (Information Systems
Officer)
Patterson, Caroline (Information Support
Officer)
Graham, Andrew (Information Support
Officer)
Morgan, Ian (Finance Manager)
Bloomfield, Keith (Finance Officer
(Corporate Finance))
Greenop, Rebecca (Finance Officer)
Binnie, Claire (HR Manager)
Kirkwood, Christine (Human Resources
Officer)
Ruddick, Maureen (HR & Training
Adviser)

Carlisle Probation Office
Georgian House, Lowther Street
Carlisle CA3 8DR
Tel: 03000 473800 Fax: 03000 473840

Carlisle Magistrates' Court Tel: 03000
473858
Carlisle Crown Court Tel: 01228 882187
Craven, Mike (Head of LDU)
Marston, Pete (Team Manager (NW1))

POs
Fisher, Jen
Robinson, Sharon
Daines, Sue
Stephenson, Ben
Moloney, Bill
Darling, Richard

PSOs
Glaister, Caroline
Mennell, Josie
Glaister, Becki
McNeish, Jean (Probation Service Officer
)
Faith, Alan
Ward, Paul
Dawson, Robin (Team Manager (NW2))

POs
Stobart, Linda
Timperon, Jonathon
Gold, Rachel
Ritchie, Jane
Doggart, Clare

PSOs
McNeil, Charlotte
Murphy, Claire
Howat, Clint
Bright, Hannah (Team Manager (NW3))

POs
Paterson, Julie
Heath, Carrie
Hobbs, Kim
McQuillin, Alistair

PSOs
Harrison, Stuart
Annabel, Anderson
Keen, Nicola
Allison, Dawn
Wood, Gill
Robinson, Paul (Business Development &
Project Management Partner)

Programmes
Lear, Jon (Team Manager (ST4))
Loy, Helen (PO)
Buttery, Rob (PO (Barrow Office))
Thwaites, Ray (PSO)
Childs, David (PSO (Barrow Office))
Holliday, Marie (PSO)
Community Payback – N & W
Morley, John (Community Payback
Officer)

Achieve
Wackwitz, Gabriele -Marshall (ESF Case
Manager)

Penrith Probation Office (reduced opening hours)
Clint Mill, 1st Floor, Cornmarket
Penrith, Cumbria CA11 7HW
Tel: (01768) 864928 Fax: (01768) 861929
Hamilton, Stuart (Team Manager (NW4))
(Kendal Office)
Downie, Jack (Probation Officer)
Dalton, Janet (Probation Officer)

Public Protection Unit
Police Headquarters, Carlton Hall
Penrith, Cumbria CA10 2AU
Tel: (01768) 217453 Fax: (01768) 217611
Dawson, Robin Public (Protection Manager/ViSOR CPC)

West Cumbria Probation Office
Progress House, Regent Court

Guard Street, Workington

CA14 4EW
Tel: 03000 473900 Fax: 03000 473860

NW5
POs
Bowker, Pam
Kirkbride, Emily
Williams, Sian
Garrett, David

PSOs
Arrowsmith, Noreen
Blythe, Margaret
Chisnall, Lindsey
Sewell, Wisha
Moran, Laura

NW6
Jackson, Barbara (Team Manager)

POs
Hallam-Davies, Steve
Garrett, Lyndsay
Crane, Marie
Edwards, Diane
Scott, Helen
Bushell, Lindsay (IOM)

PSOs
Cartner, Lee
Asquith, Cara
O'Rourke, James

Archieve
Gartland, Antonia (ESF Case Manager (West))

Community Payback – N & W
Halder, Teresa (Placement Manager (PSO))

Corporate Services
Martin, Julie (Business Development & Project Management Partner)

Barrow Probation Office
77 – 79 Duke Street, Barrow in Furness

Cumbria LA14 1RP
Tel: 03000 473950 Fax: 03000 473960
Caroline Green Head of LDU
Hubbard, Stephen (Team Manager (ST1))

POs
Waterston, Darren
Waite, Rebecca
Jones, Sian

PSOs
Evans, Maureen
Wilson, Claire
Thomson, Dawn
Garnett, Gabriella

Scafell / IOM Project
POs
Sutton-Riley, Emma
Tricia Kelly (Team Manager (ST2))
King, Caroline
Hunt, Debra
Shinn, Josie
Gregory, Gemma
Davies, Patty

PSOs
Carruthers, Brian
Garside, Lyndsey
Thorpe, Gary

Community Payback – South
Halfpenny, Lynn (Community Payback Manager)
Birkby, Paul (Probation Service Officer)

Partnership Workers
Achieve North West
Annette Nixon, (Achieve Manager)
Yates, Jason (ESF Case Manager (South))

Kendal Probation Office
Busher Lodge, 149 Stricklandgate

Kendal LA9 4RF
Tel: 03000 473910 Fax: 03000 473930
Hamilton, Stuart (Team Manager (ST3))

POs
Wyatt, Lee
Worsley, Rob
Critchlow, Peggy

Dalton, Janet

PSOs
Evans, Erica
Baker, Stephen
Crook, David
Emmett, Victoria
Lowis, Rachel

Bowling Green Approved Premises
90 Lowther Street

Carlisle CA3 8DP
Tel: 03000 473850 Fax: 01228 590967
Miles, Clive (Team Manager)
Crack, Dick (PSO AP)
Schollick, Peter (PSO AP)
Mitchelhill, Paul (PSO AP)

HMP Haverigg
Probation Office, Haverigg

Millom LA18 4NA
Tel: 01229 713000 Fax: 01229 713027
Cooper, Gill (Senior PO)

POs
McCormick, Janet
Benn, Colin
Carroll, Sean
Casson, Joanne

PSOs
O'Brien, Diane
Wilson, Lorraine
Rafferty, Brett
Bell, Mike
Murray, Rachel
Ingram, George

Seconded Staff

YOS
5 Brunswick Road, Carlisle, CA1 1PB
Rachel, Gold (PO) 01228 227090
Bell de Zarza, Morag (PO) 01228 227090

YOS
67 Wood Street, Maryport, CA15 6LD
Sarah Fitzsimons (PO) 01900 706040

YOS
Newbridge Hse, Ewan Close
Barrow-in-Furness, LA13 9ED
Sargent, Julie (PO) 01229 407560
Gregory, Gemma (PO) 01229 407560

Laurus OD Solutions, Barrow Probation Office
Parkes, Ruth (PO) 03000 47 3936

DERBYSHIRE PROBATION TRUST

Out of hours emergency tel:
Burdett Lodge 01332 341324

Victim enquiries contact number: 01332 340047

Email:
firstname.lastname@derbyshire.probation.gsi.gov.uk

Head Office
18 Brunswood Road
Matlock Bath, Derbyshire DE4 3PA
Tel: 01629 55422 Fax: 01629 580838

Mead, Jo (Chief Exec)
Wilmot, Gillian (Chair of Board)
Finniear, Vicky (PA to Chief Exec & Chair)

Allsop, John (Dir of Business Services)
Bond, Corry (PA/Board Admin Sec)

Sandra Marjoram (Operations Manager – Public Protection)
Jennie Pugh (PA)
Booker, Philip (Comms Off)
Cartledge, Isobel (SPO Training)
Rush, Bernadette (HR Mgr)
Radford, Gary (Finance Mgr)
Angrave, Richard (Perf & Info Mgr)
Harton, Jon (IT Mgr
Potter, Anji (Information Governance Mgr)

MAPPA Public Protection Unit
Derbyshire Constabulary HQ
Butterley Hall Ripley Derbyshire DE5 3RS
Direct dial: 01773 + number
Fax: 01773 572976

Nuttall, Brian (MAPPA Coord Mgr) 573601
Taylor, Paul (Dep MAPPA Coord) 573602
Raybould, Verity (MAPPA Admin) 573634
Smith, Amy (MAPPA Admin) 573635
Winnington, Nicola (MAPPA Admin) 573635
Redfern, Joanne (ViSOR Admin) 573632

Derby Crown Court Team
Top Floor Derby Combined Court Centre
The Morledge Derby DE1 2XE
Tel: 01332 622549 Fax: 01332 622548

Crown Court Liaison Team
Mandair, Narinder (CCLO)

PSOs
Abbott, Danielle
Barnes, Sharon
Edwards, Shaaron

South Derbyshire Magistrates' Court
The Magistrates' Court Shire Hall
19 St Mary's Gate **Derby** DE1 3JR
Tel: 01332 293081 Fax: 01332 293082

South Derbyshire Magistrates' Court Team
Robinson-Stanley, Clifton (MCLO)

PSOs
Allan, Katie
Ardern, Cathy
Dallison, Jane
Doyle, Kirsty
Hutchinson, Karen
Low, Jo
Morgan, Mikki
Silo, Joanna
Winkley, Charlotte

2 Siddals Road
Derby DE1 2PB

Derby Central Reception
Tel: 01332 340047 Fax: 01332 340056

Sein, Sarah Winwin (Director of
Probation – City)
Whittaker, Rachel (PA)
Wild. Ben (Ops Mgr – OM &
Specifications)
Dunkley, Charlotte (Partnerships Mgr)
Anderson, Sara (Office Services Mgr)

Offender Management Units

Offender Management Unit 2 & SMU
Gardner, Martin (SPO)
Gell, Lois (SPO)
MacLachlan, Iain (SPO)
Barrett, Vickie
Bowden, David
Davey, Claire
Egginton, Matthew
James-Moore, Kathryn
Johnson, Claire
Kelly, Paula
Lawton, Adele
Lloyd, David
Nudd, Daniella
Roots, Susie
Schofield, Bob

Walkman, Emma
White, Lavina

PSOs
Biddick, Sharon
Deiedrick, Karlana
Harris, Karan
Kvintas, Julie
McArdle, Natalie
Sheldon, Sue
Giles, Ceri
Smith, Nic

Offender Management Unit 2
O'Neill, Sarah (SPO)
Johnson, Kat (SPO)
Ahmed, Sofena
Ayodeji, Andrew
Curry, Laura
Day, Vicky
Duncan, Samantha
Higgs-Ward, Jody
Khakh, Gurinder
Khalida, Tabasum
Mitchell, Jacqueline
Reid, Alia
Sandhu, Harjit
Wallis, Helen

PSOs
Gates, Daniel
Marshall, Mary
Nuttal, Corinne
Rai, Parmjit
Richardson, Lisa
Shearer, Francesca
Wilkinson, Paul

Diversity & Engagement
Malcolm, Robert (Diversity &
Engagement Mgr)

Employment, Training & Education
Burgess, Sheila (ETE Mgr)
Amy Bayne (Reach Worker)

PSOs
Beresford, Geraldine
Buckley, Wendy
Eames, Kerry
Hosty, Gemma
Whatton, Pam

Terrorism & Extremism
Smith, Catrin (SPO)

Victim Liaison
Page-Smith, Marion (SPO)
Pidgeon, Maxine (PSO)

Community Payback Unit
Tel: 01332 348936
Wagstaff, Neil (Div CP Mgr, South)

CPOs
Allbones, Jessica
Allen, Sandra
Braybrooke, Tanya
Collier, Lianne
Hilliard, Neil
Hough, Samantha
Martin, Majory
Sheldon, George
Woolley, Leona

CP Supervisors
Ilic, Peter (CP Placement Supvr)
Jordan, Denise
Meakin, Richard
Pierpoint, Heather
Sandhu, Diljit

Derby Probation Centre
Willow House 1a Willow Row
Derby DE1 3NZ
Tel: 01332 361200 Fax: 01332 294011

Lawrence, Neelum (Office Mgr)

Courts Team
Thandi, Sandeep (SPO)

Employment, Training & Education
Joyce, Sara (PSO)

IOM
Wild, Ben (SPO)
Fisher, Lyn
Gilchrist, Elizabeth
Jagpal, Nimrit
Raven, Mark

PSOs
Salmon, Robert
Sansom, Michelle
Tissington, Miranda

Practice Tutor Assessor
Sheree, Coleman

Programmes
Parker, Sue (SPO)
Heini, Claire (Treatment Mgr)
Smith, Nicola (Treatment Mgr)
Jennens, Julie (Act up Treatment Mgr
Tyler, Lucy (Act up Treatment Mgr)
Neville, Bill

PSOs
Ali, Lisa
Baker, Sherisse
Barnes, Amber

Cobb, Barbara
Groom, Julie
Lamzed, Judith
Millington, Lyndsey
Parveen, Zureena
Smith, Amy

RSOU
Bouse, Martin
Curtis, Helen
Blagden, Deborah (RSOU Facilitator)
Foster, Debbie (RSOU Facilitator)

3 Brimington Road
Chesterfield S41 7UG
Tel: 01246 276171 Fax: 01246 556505
Hickey, Janet (Director of Interventions)

Gibson, Kay (PA)

McMahon, Louise (Office Services Mgr)
Mortimer, Andrew (Info Off)

Offender Management Unit 1,
Chesterfield
Kenny, Danielle (SPO)
Blackburn, Rebecca
Evans, Becky
Milner, Sarah
Small, Nikki
Taylor, Sarah
Walker, Angie

PSOs
Ashton, Claire
Miller, Claire
Pepper, Sarah

Offender Management Unit 2 –
Bolsover & North East
Hume, Tracey (SPO)
Baker, Lawrence
Emslie, Ann
Hannant, Katy
Holmes, Philip
James, Marcus
Morley, Claire
Schreder, Mark

PSOs
Jackson, Sandy
Quigley, Hannah
Webster, Mark

Offender Management Unit 3
Alfreton North Division
Beardmore, Di (SPO)
Doxey, Gemma
Ingman, Rachel

PSOs
Campbell, Fiona
Hartley, Matthew
Wood, Rachel

Courts
Kenny, Danielle (SPO)
Miller, Rachel (breach)
Self, Louise (breach)

Employment, Training & Education
Woolliscroft, Daniel (Temp ETE Mgr)
Goodall, Deborah (North & West) (PSO)
Schofield, Paul (PSO)

Victim Liaison
Sampson, Adrienne (PSO)

Practice Tutor Assessor
Herward, Rebecca

Programmes
Trivett, Diane (Treatment Mgr)

PSOs
Dennis, Laura
Fitter, Simon
Lewis, Claire
Wilcockson, Mark
Weatherall, Lindsey

Community Payback Unit
Clay, Stephen (Divnl CP Mgr North &
West)

CPOs
Fury, Mike
Guy, Mark
Ludlam, Craig
Smith, Alfred

CP Supervisors
Lennon, Bevin (CP Placement Supvr)
Clayton, Melanie
Crich, Amanda
Gee, Jeff

Chesterfield Magistrates' Court
The Court House
Tapton Lane **Chesterfield** S41 7TW
Tel: 01246 278340 Fax: 01246 237582

Chesterfield Court Team
Randall, Laura (MCLO)
McAteer, Matt (MCLO)

PSOs
Gillott, Julia
Shannon, Katie
Starnes, Jeremy

Bayheath House
Rose Hill West
Chesterfield S40 1JF
Tel: 01246 279928 Fax: 01246 232678

Substance Misuse Unit
Kenny, Paul (SPO)
Cooper, Sarah
Dymond, Laura
Lawal, Christopher
Shelton, Laura
Turner, Phillip
Turner, Carly

PSOs
McMahon, Richard
Mather, Sara
Smith, James
Statham, Beverley

4 Lime Grove Walk
Matlock DE4 3FD
Tel: 01629 582148 Fax: 01629 57872

(*Wednesdays – Friday only*)

Offender Management Unit
Brown, Stephen
Taylor, Gemma
Ashwood, Rebecca (PSO)
Weston, Jackie (PSO)

Chesterfield House
24 Hardwick Street **Buxton** SK17 6DH
Tel: 01298 25558 Fax: 01298 79132
Watkins, Janice (Off Mgr)
Mortimer, Andrew (Info Off)

Offender Management Unit
Langley, Sarah (SPO)
Brown, Stephen
Chapman, Louise
Long, Jane
Rogers, Jane
Smith, Ellen
Whitlaw, Claire

PSOs
Ashwood, Rebecca
Elliott, Lisa
Glover, Tony
Weston, Jackie

Courts
Smith, Ellen

Employment, Training & Education
Goodall, Deborah (West & North) (PSO)

Substance Misuse
Whitlaw, Clare
McNicholas, Sally (PSO)

Community Payback Unit
Bates, Deborah (CPO)
Fox, Joy (CP Placement Supvr)
Crich, Amanda (CP Supvr)

34 South Street
Ilkeston DE7 5QJ
Tel: 0115 930 1123 Fax: 0115 944 2606

Macleod, Karen (Director of Probation
(County & Public Protection)

Swann, Samantha (PA)

Watkins, Janice (Off Mgr)
Masters, Sara (Info Off)

Offender Manager Uunit 1
Knowles, Kaye (SPO)
Baugh, Raelene
Don, Jennifer
Gooch, Dan
Howett, Mark
Kemp, Kathy
Southall, Francine
Wood, Graham
PSOs
Jackson, Ian
Roberts, Dunya
Smyth, Nicola

Offender Management Unit 2 –
Alfreton East
Beardmore, Diane (SPO)

Liegis, Eduards

Penman, Linda

Shankland,, Nicola
PSOs
Wood, Sally

Substance Misuse Unit
Vacant (SPO)
Briggs, Jo
Cammack, Jane
Purewal, Harjit
Wilkinson, Jennie
PSOs
Godfrey, James
Murphy, Gill
Roberts, Hannah

Employment, Training & Education
Beresford, Geraldine (PSO)
Martinson, Daryl (PSO)

Victim Liaison
Farry, Christine (PSO)

Health & Safety
Brown, Faye (H&S Mgr)

Youth Offending Teams

Derby Youth Offending Team
2nd Floor St Peter's House
Gower Street Derby DE1 9BR
Tel: 01332 256820 Fax: 01332 256830
Adler, Keren
Markham, Simon

Ilkeston Youth Offending Team
Kingfisher House Cotmanhay Road
Ilkeston DE7 8HU
Tel: 01629 531779 Fax: 0115 909 8184
Boyer, Sue

Chesterfield Youth Offending Team
56 Cobden Road, Chesterfield S40 4TD
Tel: 01629 537615 Fax: 01246 347651
Evans, Rebecca

Buxton Youth Offending Team
Area Education Office
Kents Bank Road, Buxton SK17 9HR
Tel: 01629 531085 Fax: 01298 308411
Gittins, Jane

Other Secondments

Derbyshire County Council
Community Safety Team
Mason, Glenn (SPO)

Derby City Council
Bacon, Mary (PSO)

Midlands Consortium
Ryan, Natalie

HMP Nottingham Prison
Webb, Jonathan

NOMS London
Britton, Penny
Maclennan, Rachel
Price, Kevin
Francis, Deanna (SPO)

NOMS Leicester
Revell, David

Approved Premises (Hostel)

Burdett Lodge
6 Bass Street Derby DE22 3BR
Tel: 01332 341324 Fax: 01332 202089

Dosanjh, Michael (AP Mgr)
Clay, Sharon (Bursar)

Hostel Officers
Bremmer, Carol
Carson, Lynn
Gilligan, Dominic
Hatto, Julie
Richardson, David
Wrighte, Shelley

Hostel Support Workers
Bano, Shamshad
Gordon, Fitzroy
Grocott, Rachel
Reed, Rosie
Stanley, Tracey
Thomas, Joyce
Turner, Jonathan
Webster, Rebecca

Institutions

HMP Sudbury
Sudbury, Ashbourne DE6 5HW
Tel: 01283 584000 Fax: 01283 584001
Direct dial: 01283 58 + ext number
Parker, Sue (SPO) ext 4073
Bingham, Carrie ext 4198
Dawkins, Jon ext 4075
Morgan, Jon ext 4228
Preston, Melanie ext 4076
Tugnait, Vandna ext 4232
Rowley, Lauren (PSO) ext 4233

HMP Foston Hall
Foston Derby DE65 5DN
Tel: 01283 584300 Fax: 01283 584314
Direct dial: 01283 58 + ext number
Fitch, Adrian ext 4495
Jones, Corinne ext 4464
Johnson, Sally ext 4409

PSOs
Leek, Rebecca ext 4437
Meyers, Helen ext 4494
Scoffham, Barbara ext 4437
Taylor, Clare ext 4491
Wardle, Amy ext 4482

Local Justice Areas
North East Derbyshire & Dales
(*Magistrates' Court, Brimington Road and Bayheath House Chesterfield, Lime Grove Walk Matlock*)
Southern Derbyshire (*South Derbyshire Magistrates' Court, Siddals Road and Willow Row Derby, South Street Ilkeston*)
High Peak (*Chesterfield House Buxton*)

Crown Court
Derby

DEVON & CORNWALL PROBATION TRUST

Out of hours emergency tel:
Lawson House 01752 568791

Victim enquiries tel:
Exeter 01392 421122 Plymouth 01752 827500

Torbay 01803 213535 N Devon 01271 321681

Email:
firstname.surname@devon-cornwall.probation.gsi.gov.uk

Corporate Services
Queen's House, Little Queen Street
Exeter EX4 3LJ
Tel: (01392) 474100 Fax: (01392) 413563
Menary, Rob (Chief Executive) 01392 474127
Clewlow, Ian (Deputy Chief Executive/Board Secretary) 01392 474116
Lamb, Carol (Treasurer/Finance ACO) 01392 474125
Tucker, John (Trust Business Development Manager) 01392 474133
Baines, Carol (P'Ship & Joint Commissioning Manager) 01726 223942 (Cornwall & Plymouth)
Perkins, Simon (P'Ship & Joint Commissioning Manager) 01392 455483 (Devon & Torbay)
Luffman, David (Finance Manager) 01392 474146
Kyme, Marie (HR Business Partner) 01392 473980
Legon-Taylor, Victoria (HR Business Partner) 01392 473981
Fowler, Sandra (Learning & Development Manager) 01392 474145
McCloy, Paula (Corporate Services Support Manager/PA Chief Executive) 01392 474127
Sussex, Trev (ICT Systems Manager) 01392 474121
Mandeville Norden, Rebecca (Research & Information Manager) 01392 474139
Felix-Mitchell, Jacquie (PR & Communications Officer) 01392 474104
Adam, Barry (Health & Safety Advisor) 01752 827554
Lim, Mona (Diversity and Equality Advisor) 01392 474119

Murphy, John (Business Manager –
Procurement) 01803 219333
Williams, Ros (Business Manager –
Interventions/Turnaround) 01752 827553

DEVON & TORBAY LDU

3/5 Barnfield Road
Exeter EX1 1RD
Tel: 01392 421122 Fax: 01392 434839
Coker, Charlotte (Assistant Chief Officer)
McGrail, Zilla (PA to ACO)

Business Support East
Hutchings, Dorothy (Divisional Business
Support Officer)
Paprocka, Ellie (PA and MAPPA
Coordinator)
Hampton, Nikki (PA to PJCM)

Courts (East)
Hamilton, Mike (Senior Probation
Officer)

POs
Annison, Keith
Emmen, Peter
Mannion, Christie
Murdock, Leah (Probation
Officer/Quality Development Manager)
Smith, Tina
Spiller, Paul
Turnbull, Adam

PSOs
Boniwell, Tracey
Munday, Susan
Taylor, Carol (Senior Legal Proceedings
Officer)
Case Admin
Duddridge, Kensie (Crown)
Hughes, Samantha
Selby, Annette

High Risk of Harm (East)
Bailey, Rachel (Victim Liaison Officer)

OM (East)
Senior POs
Bishop, Sasha
Hamilton, Mike
Keehner, Cindy

POs
Banham, Caron
Ford, Mark
Glide, Judith
Hadaway, Paul
Haydon, Carol
Holloway, Angela
Moore, Bernard

Western, Shaz
Savage, Viv
Stockley, Rachel
Wilson, Laura

PSOs
Lovell, Gemma
Sails, Jacqueline
Smith, Shirley
Welland, Sue
White, Christopher
Case Admin
Bingham, Sophie
Browne, Judi
English, Martin
Mitchell, Jan
Hurley, Kirsten
Smith, Kyle
Williams, Sarah
Wolske, Annette

Kingsley House
Castle Street
Barnstaple EX31 1DR
Tel: 01271 321681 Fax: 01271 329864

Business Support North
Gammons, Annabel (PA to SPO)
Burns, Jackie (Receptionist)
Edmonds-Hughes, Cass (IT Skills
Facilitator)

Courts (North)
POs
Palmer, Jo
Jones, Sara
Wright, Melanie
Thompson, Jo (Legal Proceedings
Officer)
Case Admin
Bottrill, Anthony
Tippett, Sharon

High Risk of Harm (North)
Palmer, Jo (Victim Liaison Officer)

OM (North)
Wells, Jenny (Senior Probation Officer)

POs
Bennett, Jane
Dawson, Lesley
Fairweather, Christine
Sylvester, Alison
Tilby, Gaynor

PSOs
Jones, Tessa
Slade, Wendy
Piper, Julie (Case Admin)

Thurlow House
Thurlow Road **Torquay** TQ1 3EQ
Tel: 01803 213535 Fax: 01803 290871

Business Support (Torbay)
Medd, Sarah (Business Manager)
Foulger, Angie (Divisional Business
Support Officer)
Dixon, Jackie (Personal Assistant/ICT
Skills Facilitator)
Hewett, Diane (Personal Assistant)
Receptionists
O'Toole, Tracy
Sydenham, Joanne
Wileman, Lorna

Courts (Torbay)
Bown, Gary (Senior Probation Officer)

POs
Harrison, Lyn
Herron, David
Winter, Debbie
Hughes, Chaylla (Probation Support
Officer)
Date, Sallie (Case Admin)
Whorton, Jennifer (Bail Information
Officer)

High Risk of Harm (Torbay)
Victim Liaison Officers
Britton, Colin
Randle, Heidi

OM
Drennan, Alex (Middle Manager)
Jones, Mandy (Senior Probation Officer/
Quality Development Manager)
Sanders, Hayley (Senior Probation
Officer)
POs
Alsop, Kathryn
Ferris, Christopher
Hamilton, Lois (Quality Development
Manager)
Kimble, Steve
Mitchell, Philippa
Moore, Polly
Norton, Jen
Whitney, David

PSOs
Aggett, Sarah
Caulfield, Michael
Webb, Heidi
Dark, Jacqui
Lord, Kelly
Lucas, Lisa
Scattergood, Shirley

Walker, Jan
Trump, Simon (Housing Link worker)
Case Admin
Crawford, Jill
Donohue, Siobhan
Edwards, Sharon
Jay, Justine

Shrublands House
8 Morgan Avenue Torquay TQ2 5RS
Tel: (01803) 293788 Fax: (01803) 294031

DRR & ATR (Torbay)
POs
Broaders, Gabriel
Tucker-Last, Jamie
Winser, Tulane (Probation Support
Officer)
Cowling, Chrystal (Case Admin)

Youth Offending Team
Ivybank, 45 St David's Hill
Exeter EX4 4DN
Tel: 01392 384933 Fax: 01392 384985

POs
Cook, Naomi
Watts, Sallyanne

Youth Offending Team
1st Floor Bridge House
Courtenay Street Newton Abbot TQ12
2QS
Tel: 01626 202700 Fax: 01626 202701
Rogers, Andrew (Probation Officer)

Torbay Youth Offending Team
Commerce House
97–101 Abbey Road Torquay TQ2 5PJ
Tel: 01803 201655 Fax: 01803 201721
Heather, Emily (Probation Officer)

Plymouth LDU

St Catherine's House
5 Notte Street **Plymouth** PL1 2TS
Tel: (01752) 827500 Fax: (01752) 267189
Benden, Mark (ACO)
Trelford, Siobhan (PA to ACO)
Hodgson, Sharon (PA to ACO)

Business Support
Jesson, Kathy (Business Manager –
Plymouth & Cornwall)
McConochie, Christine (Divisional
Business Support Officer)
Hodgson, Sharon (PA)
Lawrence, Jayne (PA)
Receptionists
Griffiths, Sharon
Land, Lynn

Mooney, Joanne
Blundell, Paul (Building Technician)
Monck, Daniel (Quality Development
Officer)

Courts
Clark, Brian (Senior Probation Officer)

POs
Casey, Charles
Garvey, Sarah
Ross, Bernie
Wooler, Tony

PSOs
Fry, Karen
Lee, David
Case Admin
Copleston, Lianna
Smith, Laurence
Wills, Nicola

DRR
PSOs
Corry, Vanessa
Trelford, Siobhan
Burns-Jones, Dianne (Case
Administrator)

High Risk of Harm
POs
Atkinson, Michael
Costello, Anne
Reeby, Lorraine
Measures, Debbie (Victim Liaison
Officer)
Titre, Marie (Case Admin)

OM – Team 1
Munn, Chris (Senior Probation Officer)

POs
Edgecombe, Helen
Narin, Jill
Pepperell, Kelly

PSOs
Amphlett, Kirsten
Rowe, Dawn
Lee, David
Case Admin
Perego, Solene
Toft, Barbara

OM – Team 2
Wellock, Neil (Senior Probation Officer)

POs
Carson, Tim
Downing, Vanessa
Lawrance, Nadine (Treatment Manager)

PSOs
Clarke, Sarah
Bennett, Paul
Case Admin
Dent, Karen
Eaton, Julian

OM – Team 3
Munn, Chris (Senior Probation Officer)

POs
Auty, Angela
Best, Kate
Cannan, Serena
Hollingsworth, Nicola

PSOs
Lester, Scott
Saunders, Janis
Case Admin
Beer, Patricia
Sabulis, Paul

OM – Team 4
Van-Waterschoot, Lucy (Senior Probation
Officer)

POs
Richards, Jane
Southern, Rob
White, Deborah

PSOs
Oxford, Lucy
Prior, Claire
Sherwin, Lisa
Case Admin
Chapman, Claire
Kinsley, Jing
Rawlings, Jennifer

Plymouth Youth Offending Team
Floor 3 Midland House
Notte Street **Plymouth** PL1 2EJ
Tel: 01752 306999
Aisbitt, Ian (PO)

CORNWALL LDU

Tremorvah Wood Lane
off Mitchell Hill **Truro** TR1 1HZ
Tel: 01872 326250 Fax: 01872 261311
Nason, Jon (ACO)
Logue, Mel (PA to ACO)

Business Support
Jesson, Kathy (Business Manager –
Cornwall & Plymouth)
Emmett, Lucy (Divisional Business
Support Officer)

Courts
Ciocci, Tony (Senior Probation Officer)

POs
Brown, Tony
Lewis, Mary
O'Hagan, Gail
Vincent, Amy (Case Admin)
Endean, Joni (Case Admin)

OM (Mid)
Coad, Lorna (Senior PO)
Brocklehurst, Jo (PO)
Payne, Sara (PO)
Berryman, Alison (PSO)
Bishop, Shelly (Case Admin)
Thomson, Lesley (Case Admin)

Endsleigh House
Roskear
Camborne TR14 8DN
Tel: 01209 612006 Fax: 01209 612551

High Risk of Harm
Butterworth, Stephen (PO)
Skewes, Nicola (PO)
Wells, Peter (Victim Liaison Officer)
Lanyon, Maria (Case Admin)

OM (West)
Parkinson, Ann (Senior Probation
Officer)

POs
Beddow, Jonathan
Bray, Brydie
Hazeldine, Michael
Rowe, Sarah
Stubbings, Pauline
Williams, Richard
Coad, Lorna (Quality Assurance Officer)
Rees, Michelle (Quality Assurance
Officer)
Gough, Brendan (PSO)
Spear, Ashley (PSO)
Case Admin
Harris, Carly
McKenzie, Anita
Skinner, Julie
Tregoning, Meg

3 Kings Avenue
St Austell PL25 4TT
Tel: 01726 223920 Fax: 01726 63553

Court Services
Ciocci, Anthony (PO)
Thomas, Hannah (PO)

OM (East)
Hearnshaw, Cate (Senior Probation
Officer)

POs
Cann, Joanna
Doble, Elizabeth
Frazer, Mark
Swan, Mark

PSOs
Hancock, Hayley
Heard, Elizabeth
McGougan, Kay
Case Admin
Rowley, Deborah
Shirley, Tracey
Wilson, Jacqueline

OM (West)
Rees, Michelle (Quality Assurance
Officer)

Lucknow Road
Restore, 3 Lucknow Road, **Bodmin** PL31
1EZ
Tel: 01208 78311 Fax: 01208 79006

OM (East)
Fitzsimmons, Christopher (Senior PO)

POs
Shirley, Ian
Wilson, Gail
Goodright, Emma

PSOs
Stacey, Sharon
Ryan, Rose
Martins, Denise (Case Admin)

High Risk of Harm
Brown, Heather (Victim Liaison Officer)

Cornwall Youth Offending Service
Chiltern House, Truro
Godfrey, Trudi (PO)

Interventions

3/5 Barnfield Road
Exeter EX1 1RD
Tel: 01392 421122 Fax: 01392 434839
Proctor, Anne (ACO)
Wilson, Deborah (PA to ACO)

CP (East)
Champion, Dawn (Unpaid Work
Supervisor)
English, Brent (PSO)
May, Alfred (Unpaid Work Supervisor)

ETE (Devon)
Greenhill, Laura (PSO)
Vosper, Dayna (Case Admin)

IDAP (East)
Boniwell, Tracey (Women's safety
worker)
Bennett, Neal (Programme Tutor)
Willett, Rachel (PO)

TSP (East)
Furness, Des (PSO)

TVSO (East)
Clark, Dee (PO)

Kingsley House
Castle Street
Barnstaple EX31 1DR
Tel: 01271 321681 Fax: 01271 329864

CP (East)
Ford, Geraldine (Community Payback
Manager)
Johns, Pauline (PSO)
Slade, Wendy (PSO)
Tomkinson, David (Unpaid Work
Supervisor)
Edmonds-Hughes, Cassandra (Case
Admin)
Wheatley, Janet (Case Admin)

Thurlow House
Thurlow Road **Torquay** TQ1 3EQ
Tel: 01803 213535 Fax: 01803 290871

CP (East)
PSOs
Britton, Colin
Steer, Cheryl
Unpaid Work Supervisors
Bammens, Russell
Cloherty, David
Pitt, Barry

ETE (Devon)
Palmer, Bev (PSO)
Taylor, Patricia (PSO)
Roberts, Louise (Case Administrator)

IDAP (East)
Lewis, Maddi (Programmes Interventions
Manager)
Offord, Jade (PA)

TSP (East)
Lewis, Maddi (Programmes Interventions
Manager)

PSOs
Austen, Nicci
Waine, Rosie

Randle, Steve (Programme Tutor)
Harley, June (Case Admin)

TVSOGP (East)
POs
Arube, Zarha
Fraser, James
Nunn, Melanie

St Catherine's House
5 Notte Street **Plymouth** PL1 2TS
Tel: (01752) 827500 Fax: (01752) 267189

CP (West)
Wakley, Richard (Community Payback
Manager)
Unpaid Work Case Managers
Haskell, Norman
Tricker, Paul
Unpaid Work Supervisors
Allen, Sam
Brownlow, John
Cowling, Edgar
Dean, Darren
Wilson, Cathy (PSO)
Pring, Cas (Case Admin)
Wood, Sam (Case Admin)

ETE (Devon)
Murray, Clare (PSO)
Mannion, Alyson (Case Admin)

IDAP (West)
POs
Bishop, Gary
Lamerton, Mark
Gunn, Hilary
Toms, Min

TSP (West)
Jolley, Olivia (Case Administrator)
Meara, Eleanor (Probation Support
Officer)

TVSOGP (West)
POs
Henderson, Alastair
Hart, Michelle

Tremorvah Wood Lane
off Mitchell Hill **Truro** TR1 1HZ
Tel: 01872 326250 Fax: 01872 261311
Nason, Jon (ACO)
Logue, Mel (PA)

ETE (West)
Endean, Joni (Case Administrator)

IDAP (West)
McConnel, Su (Programmes
Interventions Manager)

POs
Davies, Linda
Hopwood, Mags
Macdonald, Lorna
McDonald, Joe
Bose, Julian (Treatment Manager)

SARS
Islam, Sanjida (PSO)

TSP (West)
Bose, Julian (Programme Tutor)
Gay, Peran (PSO)

TVSOGP (West)
Gates, Liz (Treatment Manager)

Endsleigh House
Roskear
Camborne TR14 8DN
Tel: 01209 612006 Fax: 01209 612551

CP (West)
Tonkin, Robert (Unpaid Work Case
Manager)
Unpaid Work Supervisors
Adams, Bob
Cotton, Steve
Barbagallo, Sharon (Case Admin)

ETE (West)
Campbell, Samantha (PSO)

3 Kings Avenue
St Austell PL25 4TT
Tel: 01726 223920 Fax: 01726 63553

CP (West)
Unpaid Work Case Managers
Richards, Geoff
Rowe, Sandra
Mitchell, Ted (Unpaid Work Supervisor)
Wallis, Laura (Case Admin)

ETE (West)
Fildes, Timothy (PSO)
Williams, Jacqueline (Case Admin)

LIAP (West) & TSP (West)
Coley, Helen (PO/ Treatment Manager)

Lawson House
13/14 Paradise Place
Stoke **Plymouth** PL1 5QE
Tel: 01752 568791 Fax: 01752 606815
Webb, Georgia (Hostel Manager)

PSOs
Brown, Tessa
Buckley, Linda
Davies, Neil
Holgate, Max
Wetton, Steven

Nightcare Supervisors
Black, Paul
Chudley, Len
French, Neale
Kelly, Mark
Dicken, Sylvia (Resource Admin)

Meneghy House
East Hill Tuckingmill
Camborne TR14 8NQ
Tel: 01209 715050 Fax: 01209 612595
Cookson, Andrew (Hostel Manager)

PSOs
Aldridge, Kevin
Dronfield, Adrian
Harris, Vernon
Hill, Steve
Lucock, Anddrew
Parker, Karen
Nightcare Supervisors
Bond, Mark
Davey, Keith
Pascoe, Darren
Rundle, Matthew

Turnaround

3/5 Barnfield Road
Exeter EX1 1RD
Tel: 01392 421122 Fax: 01392 434839

Turnaround East
POs
Davis, Mandy
Heale, Rebecca
Quick, Louise
Hayford, Linda (Case Admin)
Soper, Vicki (Case Admin)

Kingsley House
Castle Street
Barnstaple EX31 1DR
Tel: 01271 321681 Fax: 01271 329864

Turnaround East
POs
Arscott, Louise
Milton, Mark
Thorne, Vanessa (Case Admin)

Thurlow House
Thurlow Road **Torquay** TQ1 3EQ
Tel: 01803 213535 Fax: 01803 290871
Ansell, Ian (ACO)
Hunt, Lisa (PA)

Turnaround East
Dubash, Nariman (Senior Probation
Officer)
Hunt, Lisa (PA)

POs
Cort, John
Gaywood, Anthony
Eames, Mary (PSO)
Bancroft, Jayne (Case Admin)

Tolvean
Coach House, **Tolvean**
West End, Redruth TR15 2SF

Turnaround West
POs
Element, Jane
Thorne, Kelly
Robson, Phil (Probation Support Officer)
Murray, Louise (Case Administration)

Hyde Park House
2nd Floor (Probation)
Mutley Plain, **Plymouth** PL4 6LF
Tel: (01752) 434567

Turnaround West
POs
Blake, Chloe
Davis, Simon
Hirons, Alicia
Vaudin, Michele (Case Admin)

St Austell
1st Floor, St Austell Police Station,
Palace Road, **St Austell** PL25 4AL
Tel: 01752 434567

Turnaround West
Nason, Kerri (Senior Probation Officer)

POs
Arrowsmith, Paul
Rees, Michelle
Davies, George (PSO)
Broad, Emma (Case Admin)

Institutions

HMP Channings Wood
Denbury Newton Abbot TQ12 6DW
Tel: 01803 814600 Fax: 01803 814601
Mcgregor, Jamie (Senior Probation
Officer)

POs
Gaubert, Ian
Johnson, Tig
Norton, Jen
Young, Judy

PSOs
Campbell, Kate
Gray, Chris
Programme Co-ordinators
Gue, Kevin

O'Toole, Patrick
Belief in Change Facilitator
Dan, Sam
Hannis, Fran
Holland, Darren
Jones, Laura
Wilson, Michelle

HMP Dartmoor
Princetown Yelverton PL20 6RR
Tel: 01822 322000 Fax: 01822 322001
Mcgregor, Jamie (Senior Probation
Officer)
Stewart, Val (Probation Officer)

PSOs
Chakrabarti, Santosh
Parnell, Mark
Walsh, Amanda
Willmott, Beverley
Butcher, Shirley (Senior Practitioner)

HMP/YOI Exeter
New North Road
Exeter EX4 4EX
Tel: 01392 415650 Fax: 01392 415651
Mcgregor, Jamie (Senior Probation
Officer)
Foster, Nikki (Probation Officer)

PSOs
Ballm, Carole
Burns, Melanie
Davies, Trina
Haslam, Carl
Wright, Alison
Stephens, Tanith (Senior Practitioner)

Remand in Custody
Tel: 01392 415836 Fax: 01392 415782

Local Justice Areas
Devon & Torbay
North Devon
Plymouth/South Devon
Cornwall

Crown Courts
Exeter
Barnstaple
Plymouth
Truro

DORSET
PROBATION TRUST

Out of hours emergency contact points:
Weston Approved Premises: Weymouth 01305
775742

The Pines Approved Premises: Bournemouth
01202 391757

Email:
firstname.lastname@dorset.probation.gsi.gov.
uk

Poole Office & Programmes Unit
63 Commercial Road Parkstone
Poole BH14 0JB
Tel: 01202 307200
Fax: 01202 307223 (Reception)
01202 307260 (OM) 307240 (centre)
Direct dial: 01202 307+ ext

Head Office
Wiseman, John (Chief Exec) 277
Ridge, Tina (Dir of Public Protection &
Offender Management) 247
Watkins, Liz (Dir of Business
Development & Offender Services) 248
Lane, Ben (Dir of Corporate Services &
Infrastructure) 249
Douglas, Matthew (Hd of Offender
Services) 201
Shepherd, Toni (Hd of Dorset County
LDU) 246
Howard, Gail (HR/L&D Mgr / Board
Secretary) 275
Humphreys, Liz (PA to CE, Trust Chair
and Trust Exec) 277
Cowling, Clare (PA to Trust Exec) 276

Offender Management – Poole
Norton, Denise (Unit Manager) 267
Brand, Jayne 258
Clark, Juliette 272
Morgan, Mark 264
Oliver, Richard 230
Smith, Paul 225
Hunter, Owen 262
Finch, Kay (PSO) 273
Reeves, Kelly (PSO) 271
Millington, Melissa (Snr Admin) 210

Programmes Unit
Russell, Kay (Unit Mgr) 251
King, Janet
Peterson, Martin 215
Rubie, Val 208
Watson, Claire 213
Watts, Claire 216
King, Janet (Treatment Manager) 207

PSOs
Fehr, Sonya 265
Fitzpatrick, Lee
Foot, Christine 224

Martin, Jane 204
McKay, Ian 205
Shutt, Paul 211
Strehl, Valerie
Lourens, Carolyn (Senior Administrator)
212

ETE Unit
Counterson, Rachel (ETE and
Accommodation Unit Manager) 226
Macpherson, Gordon (ETE Operations
Co-Ordinator) 242

ETE Officers/PSOs
Baker-Holmes, Lorna 202
Bascombe, Rima 299
Cannie, Claire 243
Chadwick, Jason-Lee 299
Fitzpatrick, Lee 203
Harrison, Marian 203
Huxtable, Rachel 299
Strehl, Valerie (Senior Attendance Centre
Officer/PSO)
Towers, Wendy (Snr Admin) 253
Curtis, Lisa (ETE Admin) 298
Watts, Michael (Chef/Trainer) 219

Accommodation
Sanderson, Nikki (PSO)
Saunders, Helen (PSO)

Business Development
Woolcock, Sarah (Business Development
Manager) 268/07919572578
Bascombe, Rima ((p) Partnership
Development Officer)
Topliss, Oliver ((p) Partnership
Development Officer)
Lowe, Martin

**Performance, Information &
Infrastructure**
Prowse, Matt (Performance, Information
& Infrastructure Manager) 254
Weller, John (IT Support Off) 257
Webber, Jan (Team Administrator) 256

Law Courts Westwey Road
Weymouth DT4 8SU
Tel: 01305 774921 Fax: 01305 780102
Direct dial: 01305 + ext

**Offender Management and Court &
Assessment**
Ireland, Duncan (Unit Manager) (OM &
Courts) 752606
Rogers, Ray (Performance & Information
Officer) 752609

Evans, Janet (p, OM and C&A Off)
752616
Moverley, Sarah (p) 752614
Phoenix, Laura (p) 774921
Pursglove, Melanie (p) 752612
Staddon, Linda (p) 752615
Townley-Walker, Sarah (p) 752613
Worth, Maggie (p) 752608
Fisher, Carol (PSO) 752617
McGown, Sandra (PSO) 752618
Emburey, Wendy (Snr Administrator)
752600

Accommodation
Chadwick, Jason (PSO) 752619/07717
766179

Human Resources
Southam, Vanessa (HR Officer)
752628/07919 572567
Watts, Carly ((p) Team Administrator)

Community Payback Unit
Unit 19 Sandford Lane
Wareham BH20 4JH
Tel: 01929 556513 Fax: 01929 553756
Direct dial: 01929 + ext
Crawford, Mel (Unit Manager) 557657
Jones, Julie Anne (Operations
Co-ordinator) 557644
Mason, Tony (Operations Co-ordinator)
557645
Richardson, Rosemary (Individual
Placement Officer) 557648

PSOs
Carey, Francis 557647
Hudson, Shellie 557655
Thomas, Diana 557654
Smyth, Deirdre 646
Brett, Steve (Site Admin/Task Coord)
557641
Hall, Karen (Performance & Information
Officer) 557651

Finance & Infrastructure
Hillman, Matthew (Finance Manager)
557659
Curtis, Glo (Finance Officer) 557661
Johnson, Paul (Finance Assistant) 557662
Watts, Carly ((p) Team Admin) 557660

South West / South East Training Team
Effective Practice Training Unit
Cooney, Barry (Effective Pract Training
Mgr) (mob: 07813 715 519)
Jones, Myra (Bus Admin for the EPTM)
557658

7 Madeira Road
Bournemouth BH1 1QL
Tel: 01202 200200 Fax: 01202 200280
Direct dial: 01202 200 + ext

Morgan, Elaine (Head of Bournemouth &
Poole LDU) 245

Court & Assessment
Fax: 01202 2002255
Macdonald, Jennifer (Unit Mgr) 221
Freelander, Viv (Senior Admin) 222
Chapman, Anna (p) 272
Denton, Kerry (p) 265
Marland, Penny (p)
Martin, Alison (p) 206
Newman, Rachael (p) 206

Breach Unit (CAT)
PSOs
Higgins, Sue 253
Stevens, Mel 244
Wheeler, Steve (Breach Off) 282

Offender Management –
Bournemouth
Fax: 01202 200247

Team 1
Garrod, Michaela (p) 259
Greaves, Kate (Unit Mgr) 223
Ennis, Joe (p) 258
McCormack, Kirstin (p) 230
Mitchell, Ann (p) 226
Marsh, Natalie (p) 216
Richley, Samantha
Solly, Chris
Topliss, Oliver (p) 232
Wilkins, Charlotte (p) 202
Langley, Sue (PSO) 249
McGeachy, Kerry-Louise (PSO) 263
Millington, Melissa (Snr Admin) 229

Team 2
Ward, Martin (Unit Mgr) 215
Dixon, James (p) 211
Hawker, Jocelyn (p)
Holmes, Debbie (p) 212
James, Denice (p) 214
Johnson, Tim (p) 260
Priest, Amy (p) 231
Mathias, Kate (p) 235
Pilgrim, Amanda (VLO) 234
Millington, Melissa (Snr Admin) 229

Accommodation
Glover, Kelly (PSO, SP Hubb)

Human Resources
Haywood, Marie (HR Officer & Training Coordinator) 269
Mackenzie, Ann (Team Administrator) 270

MAPPA
Middleton-Roberts, Kristy (MAPPA Coord) 239
Vaughan, Becky (MAPPA Sec) 207
Vieira, Paulo (Performance & Information Officer) 218

Victim Liaison
Pilgrim, Amanda (Victim Liaison Officerp) 234

Magistrates' Court Liaison Office
The Law Courts Stafford Road
Bournemouth BH1 1LE
Tel: 01202 291392 (Magistrates' Admin)
Tel: 01202 293341 (Magistrates' Office)
Fax: 01202 789468

Crown Court Liaison Office
The Courts of Justice
Deansleigh Road
Bournemouth BH7 7DS
Tel: 01202 430565 (Admin)
Fax: 01202 430522

Dorset Youth Offending Team
Monkton Park Winterborne Monkton
Dorchester DT2 9PS
Tel: 01305 221400

Goodchild, Mike (p)

Bournemouth & Poole Youth Offending Team
5 Hyde Road Kinson
Bournemouth BH10 5JJ
Tel: 01202 453939 Fax: 01202 453940

Harcombe, Samantha (p)
Hussey, Caroline (p)

Approved Premises

Weston Approved Premises
2 Westwey Road **Weymouth** DT4 8SU
Tel: 01305 775742 Fax: 01305 766510

Miller, Carol (Unit Mgr)
Beale, Cheryl (OSO)
Burgis, Debra (PSO)
Broomhead, Natasha (PSO)
APAs
Crane, Louise

Heslop, Delena
Jarman-Norris, Andrew
Logan, Alex (Sandy)
Darby, Tony
Fry, David
Loveless, Pauline
Read, Sandra
Shapland, Jess

The Pines Approved Premises
11 Cecil Road Boscombe
Bournemouth BH5 1DU
Tel: 01202 391757 Fax: 01202 391867

Baptiste, Toni (Unit Mgr)
Morrell, Paul (OSO)
Welch, Susan (PSO)

APAs
Bedford, Martin
Brown, Simon
Collinson, Peter
Cooke, Jacie
Moore, Anne
Penny, Carol
Bracher-Howard, Susan
McGrath, Andy
O'Leary, Sue

Institutions

HMP Dorchester
7 North Square Dorchester DT1 1JD
Tel: 01305 714500 Fax: 01305 714501
OMU Fax: 01305 714630
Direct dial: 01305 + 71 ext
Dryer, Lorraine (PSO) 4632
Mitchell, Tori (PSO) 4629

HMP The Verne
The Verne Portland DT5 1EQ
Tel: 01305 825000 Fax: 01305 825001
Fax: 01305 825028 (OMU/Probation)
Direct dial: 01305 82 + ext

Benson, Deborah (p) 50384
Hewson, Sharon (p) 5226

HMPYOI Portland
104 The Grove, Portland DT5 1DL
Tel: 01305 715600 Fax: 01305 715859
Direct dial: 01305 71 + ext

Dolder, John (p) 5867
Simpson, Jackie (p) 5911

PSOs
Cox, Vanessa 5767
Hamilton, Ian 5823
Monger, Michelle 5856

Payne, Keith 5863
Richards, Caroline 5852

HMP Guys Marsh
Shaftesbury SP7 0AH
Tel: 01747 856400 OMU Fax: 01747
856529
Direct dial: 01747 85 + ext

PSOs
Gaines, Fiona 6407
Harper, Susan 6550
Moger, Barry 6438
Moon, Donna 6438
Peate, Martin 6404

Local Justice Areas
East Dorset
West Dorset

Crown Courts
Bournemouth
Dorchester

DURHAM TEES VALLEY PROBATION TRUST

Out of hours emergency tel:
01642 826606/456811

Victim enquiries contact tel: 01642 247438

Email:
firstname.lastname@dtv.probation.gsi.gov.uk

Head Office
6th Floor Centre North East
73–75 Albert Road
Middlesbrough TS1 2RU
Tel: 01642 230533 Fax: 01642 220083

Bruce, Russell (Chief Exec)
Thomas, Brian (Dir of Bus Dev)
Carey, Carina (Dir of Offender Services)
Hine, Sue (Dir of Offender Services)
Norman, Keith (Dir of Offender Services)
Saiger-Burns, Lucia (Dir of Offender
Services)
Willoughby, Hazel (Dir of Offender
Services)
Holdhusen, Barbara (Dir of HR)
Rackstraw, David (Board Sec/Head of
Legal Services)
Craig, Philip (Dir of Finance)
Armstrong, Jill (Staff Dev Mgr)
Harrison, Denise (HR Mgr)
Petrie, Rod (H&S Mgr)
Vitty, Helen (IT & Info Mgr)
Miers, Alison (Finance Mgr)

Collins, Helen (Bus Dev Mgr)
Gleeson, Joanne (Bus Dev Mgr)
Gill, Barbara (Prob Mgr, Community
Supervision Services (CSS))
Graham, John (Prob Mgr, Preferred
Provider Network)
Thomas, Neil (Prob Mgr)
Mantle, Angela (PA to CE)
Burnip, Diane (PA to Directors) (based at
Chester-le-Street)
Camidge, Anya (PA to Directors)
Dobson, Sara (Buss Dev Off)
Wood, Laura (Buss Dev Off)
Gallant, Julie (Alliance &
Volunteer/Mentor Coord)
Dixon, Gill (T&D Officer – Pract Dev)

Seconded
Morton, Helen (Prob Mgr)
North, Saphron (Acting Prob Mgr)
Bentley, Michael
Burns, Darryl
Lane, Mike
Brown, John
Murphy, Anne
Stokeld, Keith
Teggert, Melanie

PSOs
Bryson, Jean
Cawson, Sheena
Horner, Pat
Kemp, Karen
Lawson, Alison
Lopez Real, Annie
Maddison, George
McKay, Debbie
Middleton, Debra
Pape, Yvonne
Patterson, Lisa
Pitt, Allison

160 Albert Road
Middlesbrough TS1 2PZ
Tel: 01642 247438 Fax: 01642 244651

Court Services
Roy, Rosana (Prob Mgr)
Turbitt, James (Dep Prob Mgr)
Blackett, Juliet
Jenkinson (nee Griffiths), Charlotte
Padgett, Chris (Admin Mgr)

PSOs
Felstead, Carol
Ferguson, Barbara
Gorbutt, Jane
Holmes, Jim
John, Jennifer

Mahmood, Mahmood
Menzies, Maria
Smith, Val

Public Protection Unit
Bagley, John (Prob Mgr)
Adair, Steven
Barber, Jem
Bennett, Maree
Carlton, Melanie
Cotterill, Sarah
Douglas, Lynn
Frostwick, Gemma
Gardner, Gill
Hird, Rebecca
Hopton, Julie
Knox, Amanda
Martin, Sam
Pawson, Julie
Whitehead, Tony

MAPPA
Bake, Andrew (Prob Mgr/MAPPA
Coord)
Currie, Carol (Admin Mgr)

**Prolific & Other Priority Offender
Scheme (PPO)
Middlesbrough**
Bateman, Jan (Prob Mgr)
Redgwell, Jeanette
Foster, Louise
Harburn, Andrea

PSOs
Bedford, Jane
Coates, Eddie
Downing, Faye

Forest House
Aykley Heads Business Centre
Durham City DH1 5TS
Tel: 0191 383 9083 Fax: 0191 383 7979

Public Protection Unit
Megan, Sarah (Prob Mgr)
Lumley, Mari
Wilson, Hayley
Reay, Gillian
Shek, Po-Ming
Simpson, Alison
Timoney, Pearl
Winn, Lesley

MAPPA
Storey, Hugh (Prob Mgr/MAPPA Coord)

**154/156 Borough Road
Middlesbrough** TS1 2EP
Tel: 01642 210717 Fax: 01642 230621

Offender Management Unit
Barnett, Sharon (Prob Mgr)
Bonas, Robin (Prob Mgr)
Westmoreland, Lynda (Admin Mgr)
Almond, Gail
Ashton, Stephen
Roberts, Fiona
Bullen, Carolyn
Fryett, Russell
Holmes, Claire
Iverson, Julie
Johnson, Gill
Johnson, Kelly
MacDonald, Andrea
Mahoney, Beth
Matthews, Barbara
Neasham, Laura
Rabjohns, Tracey
Ubaka, Anselm
Williams, Jennifer

PSOs
Byers, Karen
Collingwood, Deborah
Heywood, Kimberley
Holden, Jan
Lane, Jodie
Marson, Louise
Spaven, Tracey
Whitaker, Elaine

Community Supervision Service
Golden, Claire (PSO)

Unpaid Work
Smart, Olly (PSO – Compliance)
Smithyman, Sue (PSO – Compliance)

**Prolific & Other Priority Offender
Scheme (PPO) Middlesbrough**
Middlesbrough Police Headquarters
Bridge Street West
Middlesbrough TS1 2AB
Tel: 01642 303305/6/7/8 Fax: 01642
303159

O'Keeffe, Keri-Ann

Place, Shirley
Williams, Sue (PSO)
Finlay, David (Police Officer)

Teesside Crown Court
Russell Street Middlesbrough TS1 2AE
Tel: 01642 250469 Fax: 01642 230541

West, Doug (Prob Mgr)
Nolan, Mike

PSOs
Borg, Paul

Faye, Jeremy
Smith, Joan
Stott, Caroline

Mowlam House
1 Oxford Street
South Bank Middlesbrough TS6 6DF
Tel: 01642 452346 Fax: 01642 466021

*Note: South Bank & Redcar work as one
team across two sites*

Offender Management Unit
Sam-Drysdale, Sandra (Prob Mgr)
Hill, Susan (Admin Mgr)
Baines, Wendy
Boyd, Debbie
Edgar, Lisa
Devon, Alan
Spaldin, Louise
Waters, Nicola

PSOs
Chisanga, Vee
Cotter, Melissa
Mackin, Chris

Community Supervision Service
Foster, Alison (PSO)
Williams, Linda (PSO)

**Prolific & Other Priority
Offender Scheme (PPO) Redcar**
Douglas, Chris (PSO)
Garbutt, Claire (PSO)

38 Station Road
Redcar TS10 1AG
Tel: 01642 494395 Fax: 01642 489424

*Note: South Bank & Redcar work as one
team across two sites*

Offender Management Unit
Waddington, Mike (Prob Mgr)
Coombs, Laurence
Helmke, Sandra
Hernandez, Frieda
Hodge, Rachel
O'Brien, Sue
Urban, Lynne
Ward, Ellen
Ward, Kate

PSOs
Smith, Debbie
Young, Melissa
Wilkinson, Sarah

Unpaid Work
Vaughan, Brian (PSO – Compliance)

**Prolific & Other Priority Offender
Scheme (PPO) Redcar**
Langbaurgh District Police Headquarters
Troisdors Way
Kirkleatham Business Park
Redcar TS10 5AP
Tel: 01642 302085/302086

Parker, Richard (Prob Mgr)
Brown, John
Marshall, Jo
Nijjar, Candy
Rawson, Les (Police Officer)

Advance House
St Mark's Court
Teasdale, Thornaby
Stockton-on-Tees TS17 6QX
Tel: 01642 606111 Fax: 01642 607764

Offender Management Unit
Howard, Joe (Acting Prob Mgr)
Garbutt, Jenny (Admin Mgr)
Armstrong, Ian
Bell, Emma
Bligh, Carolyn
Brown, Matt
Day, Joanne
Ellison, Laura
Field, Gemma
Day, Kim
Grainger, Liz
Leishman, Martin
McFee, Michelle
O'Connor, Stella
Robson, Justine
Smart, Claire
Smart, Claire
Taylor, Peter
Vaux, Lizzie

PSOs
Eddon, Mark
Evison-McCabe, Alex
Hussain, Liaquet
Kelly, Emma
McConnell, Christine
Moppett, Stephanie
Moseley, Elisabeth
Raw, Stacey

Community Supervision Service
Paterson, Don (PSO)

Unpaid Work
Andrew, Paul (PSO – Compliance)
Johnson, Dave (PSO – Compliance)

**Prolific & Other Priority
Offender Scheme (PPO) Stockton**
Evans, Jeff (Mgr)
Askins, Liz
Barber, Louise
O'Neill, Jane
Sowerby, Andrea
Walton, Victroria (PSO)
Evans, Keith (Outreach Wkr)
Fleet, Jacqui (Police Officer)

Programmes
Dargue, Darren
Raynel, Cora
Starkie, Erika
Willett, Barbara (NSOG Technician)

Avenue Road
Hartlepool TS24 8BL
Tel: 01429 265101 Fax: 01429 231854

Offender Management
Keay, Julie (Prob Mgr)
Gaffney-Williams, Sarah
Hutchinson, Karen
Jewett, Natalie
McShane, Julie
Robertson, Ann
Shaw, Jan
Stoddart, Steve

PSOs
Sawdon (nee Caizley), Alison
Caizley, Alison
Currie, Bob
Johnson, Alan
Parkin, Pauline
Richmond, Kay
Turner, Jean

Court Services
I'Anson, Dougie (PSO)

Community Supervision Service
Gill, Audrey

Unpaid Work
Cameron, Mark (PSO – Compliance)

**Prolific & Other Priority
Offender Scheme (PPO), Hartlepool**
The Willows, Raby Road, Hartlepool,
TS24 8AF
Tel: 01429 868044 Fax: 01429 405588

Sparrow, Gemma (Prob Mgr)

Douglas, Stewart
Wilkinson, Julie
Davison, Nicola (PSO)
Forsyth, Hayley (Outreach Wkr)

Dunn, Brian (Police Officer)
Low, Sandra (PPO Coord)

Beechburn House
8 Kensington
Cockton Hill Road
Bishop Auckland DL14 6HX
Tel: 01388 602182 Fax: 01388 458403

Offender Management
Raine, Helen (Prob Mgr)
Hallimond, Claire
McEvoy, Siobhan
Priestman, Elizabeth
Richardson, Rachel (IOM)
Todd, Jayne
Watson, Jane

PSOs
Dale, Tracey
Davidson, Ingrid
Hardy, Janice
Hood, Jacqui
Moore, Kendra (IOM)

Community Supervision Service
Ashley, Mark (PSO)

Oakdale House
Oakdale Terrace
West Lane **Chester-le-Street** DH3 3DH
Tel: 0191 388 7951 Fax: 0191 388 1252

Offender Management
Passmore, Barbara (Prob Mgr)
Bruce, Karen (Admin Mgr)
Randles (nee Anderson), Kay (IOM)
Guy, Sarah
Hancox, Joanne
Thompson, Helen

PSOs
Buckingham, Jane
Gray, Eileen (IOM)
McHugh, Maureen
Robinson, James (Courier/Caretaker)

Unpaid Work
Hounam, Ken (Dep Prob Mgr)
Forster, Norman (PSO – Compliance)
Harker, Brian (PSO)

Court Services
Blackburn, Karen (Prob Lead Mgr)

84 Claypath
Durham DH1 1RG
Tel: 0191 386 1265 Fax: 0191 386 4668

Offender Management
Anderson, Diane (Prob Mgr)
Cadwallader, Steve
Francis, Hannah
Hunter, Beryl
Ridley, Karen

PSOs
Hunter, Fiona
Jobling, Lynsey

Programmes
Buckingham, Howard

PSOs
Cooper, Elaine
Hamilton, Diane
McKenzie, Aidan

Unpaid Work
Eggelstone, David (Prob Lead Mgr)
Hunt, Gill (Prob Mgr)
Best, Linda (PSO)

Durham Crown Court
Old Elvet Durham DH1 3HW
Tel: 0191 384 8130 Fax: 0191 386 2695

Liivand, Ann
Rodgers, Gary (PSO)

Highfield House
Parliament Street
Consett DH8 5DH
Tel: 01207 502821 Fax: 01207 583989

Offender Management
Cunningham, Martin (Prob Mgr)
Anderson, Paula
Brown, Diane
Eckert, Danielle
Newton, Louise
Reid, Colin

PSOs
Carney, Liz
Gibson, Tracey
Wardman, Alison

Community Supervision Service
Docherty, Val (PSO)

Court Services
Russell, Julie (PSO)
Smith, James (PSO)
Waterworth, Marion (PSO)

Unpaid Work
Thompson, Keith (PSO)

9 Corporation Road
Darlington DL3 6TH
Tel: 01325 486231 Fax: 01325 382760

Offender Management
Capstick, Anna (Prob Mgr) (IOM)
King, Peter (Prob Mgr)
Leighton, Rhonda (Prob Mgr, Restorative Justice)
Vacancy (Snr Psych)
Sedgewick, Leila (Admin Mgr Psych)
Mitchell, Suzanne (Admin Mgr)
Casswell, Glyn
Chapman, Erica
Clayton, Rob
Close, Suzanne
Hewitt, Gemma
Hill, Christine
James, Laurence
Longstaff, Laura
Longworth, Emma (IOM)
McAndrew, Kathryn
Strike, Claire

PSOs
Armstrong, Helen
Auld, Caroline
Briggs, Maria (IOM)
Edgar, Kevin
Ferry, Julie
Park, Philip

Community Supervision Service
Wilson, Pat

Victim Liaison
Edgar, Penny (VLO)

Court Services
Robertson, Brenda (PSO)
Sibert, Maureen (PSO)

Programmes
Shah-Storyan, Naheed
Hancock, Susan (PSO)

Unpaid Work
Crosby, Helen (Dep Prob Mgr)

PSOs
Hooper, Mark
Jones, Stephen
Muligan, Mike

Greenwell Road
Newton Aycliffe DL5 4DH
Tel: 01325 315444 Fax: 01325 329599

Offender Management
Lambert, Steve (Prob Mgr)
Brown, Donna

Davies, Andrea
Davies, Andrea
Johnson, Susan
Michna, Jan
Potts, Laura
Sygrove, Julie
Taylor, David

PSOs
Alderton, Julie
Banham, Stephen
Bell, John
Hopson, Alison (PSO)
Maddison, Dawn (MARAC Coord)

Community Supervision Service
Kelly, Michael (PSO)

Court Services
Parry, Kevin (Prob Mgr)
Stokeld, Keith
McGuire, Craig (PSO)
Payne, Hilary (PSO)

Durham House
60 Yoden Way
Peterlee SR8 1BS
Tel: 0191 586 2480 Fax: 0191 586 3442

Offender Management
Nicolson, Kay (Prob Mgr)
Ghosh, Marc (Prob Mgr)
Barry, Lin (Admin Mgr – Volunteers)
Berry, Steven (IOM)
Burnett, Karen
Cuthbertson, Haley
Davison, Ken
Farrow, Philippa
French, Nichola
Richards, Paul
Smith, Janette
Watkin (née Craggs), Anna
Zahra (nee Stewart), Louise

PSOs
Dinsdale, Brian
Green, Sandra
Harland, David
Haston, Gilly
Leigh, Fiona
Neale, Gay

Community Supervision Service
Trotter, Jeanne (Prob Mgr)
Harland, David (PSO)

Court Services
Hodgson, Melanie
Dougherty, Eileen (PSO)
Rogers, Sharon (PSO)

Unpaid Work
Playfor, Duncan (PSO)
Quinn, Stephen (PSO)
Vincent, Marie

Milbank House
1 Milbank Street
South Bank Middlesbrough TS6 6DD
Tel: 01642 515315/6 Fax: 01642 290677

Unpaid Work
Wooding, Gordon (Dep Prob Mgr)

PSOs
Henderson, Gary
Hey, Anthony
Lunn, Michael
McKenna, Mike
Merrick, Janet
Millar, David
Smallwood, Dave

Programmes
Beckett, Tina (Prob Lead Mgr)
Brittain, Tracey (Prob Mgr)
Anderson, Jenny (Admin Mgr)

PSOs
Ayton, Lisa
Bell, Simon
Foggin, Hilary
Hill, Katy
Strike, Nigel
Whitehead, Angela
Davies, Bill (Prog Support Wkr)
Fisher, Tracey (Prog Support Wkr)
Hunter, Derek (Prog Support Wkr)

Victim Liaison
Aldus, Beverley (VLO)

Youth Offending Service

Hartlepool
The Archive Building
Upper Church Street
Hartlepool TS24 7EQ
Tel: 01429 523986 Fax: 01429 523971

Cooper, Paula

South Tees
(Middlesbrough and Redcar)
51a Kings Road
North Ormesby
Middlesbrough TS3 6NH
Tel: 01642 501500 Fax: 01642 501800

Tunnacliffe, Katie

Stockton
Floor 3 Bayheath House,
Prince Regent Street
Stockton-on-Tees TS18 1DF
Tel: 01642 527597 Fax: 01642 527598
Clement, Sandra
Smart, Claire

Durham
Orwell House No 9 Mandale Business
Park
Belmont Industrial Estate
Durham DH1 1TH
Tel: 0191 372 8060

Coleman, Paul
Dixon, Jo

Newton Aycliffe
Unit 5 Parsons Court Welbury Way
Aycliffe Industrial Estate
Newton Aycliffe DL5 62E
Tel: 0191 372 8000

Coe, Emma

Johnson, Leanne

Darlington
Central House Gladstone Street
Darlington DL3 6JX
Tel: 01325 346831 Fax: 01325 346846
Joyce, Ian

Approved Premises (Hostels)

Probation Hostel
13 The Crescent
Linthorpe Middlesbrough TS5 6SG
Tel: 01642 826606 Fax: 01642 829782
White, Susan (Admin Mgr)
Osborne (nee Jackson), Becky (SRW)
Liebig-Denham, Annette (SRW)
Bielby, Aisha (RSW)
Bowers, Emma (RSW)
Dos Santos, Sarah (RSW)
Findlay, Pam (RSW)
Gavagham, Dave (RSW)
Menzies, Russell (RSW)
Merrit, Drew (RSW)
Steel, Val (RSW)
Barrow, Pip (NCW)
Matthews, Carol (NCW)

Nelson House Probation Hostel
Middlesbrough Road
South Bank Middlesbrough TS6 6LZ
Tel: 01642 456811 Fax: 01642 468671

Allan, Julie (Prob Lead Mgr)
Davis, Glen (Dep Prob Mgr)

Heaviside, Jennifer (SRW)
Watling, Steve (SRW)
Baker (nee Woodhead), Jackaleen (SRW)
Ayton, Chris (RSW)
Jackson-Clapham, Debra (RSW)
Moulsher, Philip (RSW)
Nichols (nee Welsh), Angela (RSW)
Sparrow, David
Stallard, Kay (RSW)
Thompson, Sid (RSW)
Warrior, Joan (RSW)
Daniel, Malcolm (NCW)
Lawton, Terry (NCW)

Institutions

HMP Kirklevington Grange
Yarm Cleveland TS15 9PA
Tel: 01642 781391 Fax: 01642 790530
Discipline ext 201
Special visits (via communications office)
ext 230

Kitching, Caroline (Prob Mgr)
Hewerdine, Lynne
Pritchard, Nick
Thomas, Jeff (PSO)

HMP Holme House
Stockton-on-Tees TS18 2QU
Tel: 01642 744000 Fax: 01642 744001
Direct dial: 01642 74 + ext
Probation Clerk ext 4327
Special visits ext 4280
Probation fax: 01642 744264

Cooke, Sally

Doswell, Paul
Ford, Allison
Rennie, Debbie
Hatchwell, Victoria (PSO Accom)
Manning, Karen (PSO)
Turver, Andy (PSO)

HMP Durham
Old Elvet Durham DH1 3HU
Tel: 0191 386 2621 Fax: 0191 386 2524

Thomas, Neil (Prob Mgr)
Bell, George
Harrison, Linda
Penzer, Anne

PSOs
Clift, Lynn
Cook, Susan
Cooper, Barry
Copeland, Ena
Evans, Harvey
Lewis, David

Lochore, Margaret
O'Neill, Fiona
Snowball, Sharon
Walton, Andy

HMP Frankland
Brasside Durham DH1 5YD
Tel: 0191 332 3000 Fax: 0191 332 3001

Hancock, Derek

Linsley, Kay

McKenzie, Lisa
O'Keeffe, Peter
O'Sullivan, Claire

HMYOI Low Newton
Brasside Durham DH1 5YA
Tel: 0191 376 4000 Fax: 0191 376 4001
Langthorne, Chris
Thompson, Sarah
Hind, Linda (PSO)
Herrington, Claire (PSO)

HMYOI Deerbolt
Bowes Road
Barnard Castle DL12 9BG
Tel: 01833 633200 Fax: 01833 633201

Auckland, Mary
Thomas, Jenny
Begg, Maureen (PSO)
Lowery, Mark (PSO)
Thresher, Kathryn (PSO)

Local Justice Areas
Hartlepool
Langbaurgh East
North Durham
South Durham
Teesside

Crown Court
Teesside
Durham

ESSEX PROBATION TRUST

Central Bail Referral tel: 01268 557550

Out of hours emergency contact point
Basildon Hostel: 01268 557550

Victim enquiries tel: 01268 412241

Email:
firstname.lastname@essex.probation.gsi.gov.
uk

Head Office
Cullen Mill 49 Braintree Road
Witham CM8 2DD
Tel: 01376 501626 Fax: 01376 501174

Archer, Mary (CE)
Bamber, Alex (Director)
Brennan, Robin (Director)
Kennerson, Shirley (Director)
Mangan, Pete (Director)
Messam, David (Director)
Mozzanica, Louise (Director)
Came, Debbie (Director Finance)
Farmer, Paul (Director, HR & Central
Services)

McCann, Helen (Training and Central
Services Mgr)
Rowlands, Gill (p, NVQ Assessor)
Mott, Sam (p, HR Mgr)
Butt, Andrew (H&S Mgr)
Gorrie, Paul (Finance Mgr)
McKay, Lynne (Comms Mgr)
Sadler, Steven (Business Development
Mgr)
Juniper, Laurel (Ptnshps Mgr)
Chapman, Liz (p, Mgr Operational
Investigations)
Mackman, Matthew (Perf Mgr)
Neill, Lorraine (Internal Verifier)
Turl, Gordon (DRR Mgr)
Pearce, Helen (Diversity Officer)
Cooke, John (Ptnships Mgr)
Lane, Laurence (Ptnshps Officer)
Dewitt, Jane (Bus Change Mgr)

South Essex Local Delivery Unit
Carraway House Durham Road
Laindon **Basildon** SS15 6PH
Tel: 01268 412241 Fax: 01268 544241

Castle, Katie, (p, SPO, Mgr OM)

Kay, Michael (SPO, Mgr OM)
Port, Sarah (SPO, Mgr-OM)
Harbon, Jacqui (Staff Devpt Off)
Allison, Sue (p)
Bigg, Melanie
Colnbrook, Lee
Curtin, Rich
Grant, Katherine (part time)
Linahan, Rosan
Walters, Neil

OMs
Jones, Julie (Staff Devpt Off)
Austin, Michelle
Bearman, Fiona
Bird, Lindsay

Farrier, Kirsty
Fisher, Marion (Courts)
Fisher, Natalie
Ford, Elaine
Gardiner, Claire
Karby, Leigh
Kreyling, Joseph
Moody, Natalie
Morris, Katy
Njeru, Stephanie
Price, Sue
Prosser, Tim
Smith, David
Turner, Diane
Waterfield, Kathleen
Webster, Maggie

Programmes
Routh, Jo (Mgr)
Norman, Stacey (p, Treatment Mgr)
Baker, Steve (Programme Tutor)
Sturch, Tony (Programme Tutor)
Taiani, Heidi (Programme Tutor)

Women's Safety Officers
Keevil, Claire (p)
Lester, Emma (p)
Pond, Catherine (p)
Stearn, Jo-ann (p)

Victim Unit
Davison, Natalie (p, Mgr)
Anderson, Debbie (Victim Liaison Officer)
Clark, Roland (Victim Liaison Officer)
Levy, Marion (Victim Liaison Officer)
Watson, Chris (Community Payback Co-ordinator)
Parratt, Margaret (Support Services Mgr)
Fallon, Carol (ETE Officer)
Brown, Paul (Housing Liaison Officer)

Basildon Crown Court
The Gore Basildon SS14 2EU
Tel: 01268 458118 Fax: 01268 458116

Cadzow, Anna (Court Officer)
Clark, Dawn (Court Officer)
Giles, Frances (Court Officer)
Turner, Janet (p, PSO)

Mid Essex Local Delivery Unit
4th Floor Ashby House Brook Street
Chelmsford CM1 1UH
Tel: 01245 287154 Fax: 01245 491321

Colby, Adam (SPO, Mgr OM)
Gherendi, Ioan (SPO, Mgr OM)
Macdiarmid, Susan (SPO, Mgr OM)

Hards, Joanne (Report Writer)
Griffiths, Henry (Staff Devpt Off OM)
Bell, Dominic
Campbell, John
Culliton, Robert
Evans, Anne Marie
Fairchild, Christine
Gibbons, Kirsty
Hyatt-Butt, Tariq

OMs
Sadler, Mark (Staff Devpt Off OM)
Anderson, Charlotte
Austin-Carroll, Sarah (p)
Chapple, Melanie
Clayton, David
Cuney, Letita
Dallas, Michelle
Davis, Gary
Dow, Maggie
Grace, Caroline
Hopwood, Amanda
Jaynes, Peter
Jones, Rhys
Murphy, Michelle (p)
Magee, Sean
Overland, Jamie
Pulham, Laura (p)
Robb, Christine
Slater, David

Programmes
Brown, Katherine (Mgr)
Boutel, Helen (Programme Tutor)
Chatten, Chris (Programme Tutor)
Griffin, Sarah (Treatment Mgr)
Meadows, Rachel (Treatment Mgr)
Harris, Kerry (Programme Tutor)
Fraser, Michelle (Programme Tutor)
Kennedy, Greg (Programme Tutor)
Lunn, Christopher (Programme Tutor)

Unpaid Work
Richardson, Jill (Community Payback Co-ordinator)
Powers, Martin (Support Services Mgr)
George, Kathryn (p, ETE Officer)
Rayner, Rachel (p, ETE Officer)
Felice, Paul (Housing Liaison Officer)

North East Essex Local Delivery Unit
Ryegate House 23 St Peter's Street
Colchester CO1 1HL
Tel: 01206 768342 Fax: 01206 768348

Aguste, Pauline (SPO, Mng Offender Management)

Colby, Adam (SPO, Mng Offender Management)

Rickman, Penny (SPO, Mng Offender Management)
Hogg, Jenni (Staff Devpt Off)
Bevis, Michelle
Chenoufi, Jennifer
Colby, Adam
Coward, Wendy
Doy, Natalie (p)
Duffett, Emma (p)
Gourlay, Robert
McPhillips, Anthony
Meadows, Max
Sacre, Jamie
Stow, Denise

OMs
Atkinson, Caroline (Courts)
Bond, Lucy
Campbell, Carol (p)
Cassi, Elisabeth
Clarke, Anne
Cock, James
Coker, Steven
Duffus, Alastair

EsPOsito, Kathleen (p)
Gibson, Jenny (Staff Devpt Off)
Haggerty, Sheila (p)
Leader, Lisa
Lee, Adrian (Courts)
Martin, Sharon
Mohtram, Krishun
Moore, Laura
Morris, Sian
Munson, Wayne
Paige, Catherine
Quance, Karen
Snowling, Elana (p)
Vasquez-Walters, Elisa
White, Paul
Wright, Sue

Courts
Double, Linda (Court Officer)

Programmes
James, Hayley (Manger, Interventions)
Ross, David (Programme Tutor)
Steele, Beau (p, Treatment Mgr)
McGregor, Tim (Treatment Mgr)

Programme Tutors
Bennett, Alan
Morris, Karen
Speed, Joanne
Copeland, Leanne

Unpaid Work
Minns, John (Community Payback Co-ordinator)
Woodhouse, Karen (Support Services Mgr)
Watts, Amanda (ETE Officer)
Perrot, Claire (Housing Liaison Officer)

Crown Court Liaison Office
Crown Court New Street
Chelmsford CM1 1EL
Tel: 01245 358833 Fax: 01245 258136

Alun Gower (SPO, Mgr Courts)
Clarke, Jeanette (Court Officer)
Diwell, Kevin (Court Officer)
Jarman, Gail (Court Officer)

Thurrock Local Delivery Unit
Five Wells West Street
Grays Thurrock RM17 6XR
Tel: 01375 382285 Fax: 01375 394715

Rossi, Bill (SPO, Mgr-OM)
Toper, Sue (SPO, Mgr-OM)
Redgwell, Tracey (Staff Devpt Off)
Fasulo, Selina
Hogben, Sarah (p)
Main, Darryl
Thompson, Sarah

OMs
Archer, Jacqueline
Beveridge, Caroline
Cain, Nicola
Callender, Claire (p)
Cuthbert, Julia (p)
Gale, Emma
Hubbard, Carol
Hussain, Imraan
Jones, Barbara
Palmer, Jane
Seeley, Keri (p)
Sibley, Joanne
Sturman, Thomas

Programmes
Rodway, Debbie (Mgr)
Halsey, Kyle (Treatment Mgr)
Bryant, Jack (Programme Tutor)
Cherifi, Sindy (Programme Tutor)
Coleman, Liz (Programme Tutor)
Mahnaz, Janet (Programme Tutor)
Watson, Chris (Community Payback Co-ordinator)
Ofeke, Anne (Support Services Mgr)
Gray, Trevor (ETE Officer)
Reynolds, James (Housing Liaison Officer)

West Essex Local Delivery Unit
Centenary House 4 Mitre Buildings
Kitson Way **Harlow** CM20 1DR
Tel: 01279 410692 Fax: 01279 454116

Bishop, Neeve (SPO, Mgr, Offender
Management)
Mason, Frances (SPO, Mgr Offender
Management)

McGeehan, Georgina (SPO, Mgr
Offender Management)
Prince, Melissa (Staff Devpt Off) (p)
Brunton, Jason
Hughes, Gerry
Martin, Nicola
Osborne, Kelly (p)
Sampson, Carol
Stubbs, Erin
Winch, Clair Louise

OMs
Akers, Valerie
Beveridge, Caroline
Clarke, Lorraine
D'Silva, John
Fisher, Jacqueline
Hart, Nick
Hawkins, John
Hawley, Drew
Matthews, David
Morgan, Martina (p)
Perry, Kathy
Phillips, Sheridon
Redman, Debbie
White, Rowena

Programmes
Saward, Adrian (Mgr)
Coombes, Paul (Treatment Mgr)
Parnham, Joanne (Programme Tutor)
Wilson, Tracy (Programme Tutor)
Pond, Beth (Programme Tutor)

Unpaid Work
Hill, Adele (Community Payback
Co-ordinator)
Brown, Roger (Support Services Mgr)
Simons, Jennet (ETE Officer)

**South East Essex and South End Local
Delivery Unit**
Blue Heights 45 Victoria Avenue
Southend-on-Sea SS2 6BA
Tel: 01702 337998 Fax: 01702 333630

*Crown Court enquiries to Crown Court
Liaison Office, Chelmsford*

Brenkley, Sam (p, SPO, Mgr-OM)
Butlin, Carolyn (SPO, Mgr-OM)
Griffiths, Clare (SPO, Mgr-OM)
Osler, Alex (p, SPO, Mgr-OM)
Frost, Michelle (Staff Devpt Off)
Atkins, Sarah
Connolly, Terry
Edosomwan, Jonathan
Ekpunobi, Kelly
Finnessey, Jane
Jess, Michael
Moore, Bruce (p)
Pocock, Rebecca (p)
Roberts, Dawn
Stack, Anne
Wright, Joanne

OMs
Jones, Tony (Staff Devpt Officer)
Aston, Mike
Atkins, Sarah
Beasley, Jacqui
Bolton, Christine
Browning, Louisa
Carbutt, Carol
Catling, Dione
Chamberlain, Lucy
Cook, Jacqui
Dawson, Anne
Eve, Rebecca
Farrey, Larissa
Gunn, Ted (p)
Harris, Karla
Hobart, Toni (p)
Kinder, Keith
Lee, Sue
O'Leary, Leigh (p)
Penton, Kelly
Penton, Sue
Pickford, Pauline
Savage, Joanne
Smith, Kevin
Smith, Tina (p)
Summerhayes, Lesley (p)
Williamson, Charlotte
Wyman, Sharon (p)

Programmes
Catto, Mark (Mgr, Interventions)
Childs, Ben (Treatment Mgr)
Merenda, Natalie (Treatment Mgr)
Burr, Stephen (p) (Programme Tutor)
Johnson, Susan (p) (Programme Tutor)

Programme Tutors
Cutts, Kirstie (p)
Garnett, Pippa
Halsey, Kyle

Speller, Lee
Owens, Jan (Community Payback Co-ordinator)
Sales, Debra (p, Support Services Mgr)
Olusina, Louis (ETE Officer)
Scott, Emma (p, Internal Verifier)

Youth Offending Services

Essex Youth Offending Service
Head Office
Suite 4 Empire House,
Victoria Road Chelmsford CM1 1PE
Tel: 01245 265151 Fax: 01245 346396

Mid Essex Youth Offending Team
Suite 2 Empire House
Victoria Road Chelmsford CM1 1PE
Tel: 01245 358092 Fax: 01245 358337

North Essex Youth Offending Team
Stanwell House Stanwell Street
Colchester CO2 7DL
Tel: 01206 573188 Fax: 01206 564660

West Essex Youth Offending Team
Suite 3–5 Level 10 Terminus House
The High Harlow CM20 1XA
Tel: 01279 427495 Fax: 01279 436494

South Essex Youth Offending Team
31 Battleswick
Basildon SS14 3LA
Tel: 01268 520612 Fax: 01268 270924
Budd, Louise

Thurrock Youth Offending Service
Five Wells West Street
Grays RM17 6SX
Tel: 01375 413900 Fax: 01375 413901
Bullock, Gemma

Southend Youth Offending Service
4th Floor Queensway House
Essex Street Southend-on-Sea SS1 2NY
Tel: 01702 534300 Fax: 01702 534301

Robertson, Karen

Approved Premises (Hostel)

Felmores Approved Premises
1 Felmores Basildon SS13 1RN
Tel: 01268 557550
Fax: 01268 558661

Moore, Sheetal (Mgr)
Pocock, Rebecca (p, Dep Hostel Mgr)

Hostel Officers
Amobi, Chris
Hargreaves, Kyle

Kreyling, Annette
Wood, Anne (p, Finance Asst)

Institutions

HMP/YOI Bullwood Hall
High Road Hockley SS5 4TE
Tel: 01702 562800 Fax: 01702 207464

Ward, Gill (Snr Pract)

HMP/YOI Chelmsford
200 Springfield Road
Chelmsford CM2 6LQ
Tel: 01245 272000 Fax: 01245 272001
01245 272074 (probation)
Winters, Terry (Mgr)
Grant, James (p)
Oviatt, Leigh (p)
Rockenbach, Chloe
Shreeve, Alison

OMs
Campbell, Carol (p)
Elliott, Laura
Ling, Kevin
Prior, Jacalyn
Vale, Luke
Virtcheva-Gana, Eleonora (p)
Williams, Jon

Local Justice Areas
Mid-North Essex (Mid Essex Local Delivery Unit)
Mid-South Essex (South Essex Local Delivery Unit)
North-East Essex (North East Essex Local Delivery Unit)
North-West Essex (West Essex Local Delivery Unit)
South-East Essex (South East Essex Local Delivery Unit)
South-West Essex (Thurrock Local Delivery Unit)

Crown Courts
Basildon
Chelmsford
Southend

GLOUCESTERSHIRE PROBATION TRUST

Out of hours emergency contact point
Ryecroft Approved Premises: (01452) 380268

Victim enquiries: (01242) 534546

Email:
firstname.lastname@gloucestershire.
probation.gsi.gov.uk

Head Office
Twyver House, Bruton Way
Gloucester GL1 IPB
Tel: (01452) 389200 Fax: (01452) 389230

Fitzsimons, Tony (Board Chair)

Bensted, John (Chief Executive)
Cryer, Naomi (Director of Business
Services) ext 214
Myatt, Maxine (Acting Director of
Operations) ext 211
Riches-Jones, Liz (PACE, Board) ext 232
Jones, Laura (PA to Director) ext 234
Training
Kerr-Rettie, Kathy (Staff Dev Mgr) ext
215
Hawkins, Julie (Staff Dev Ass) ext 262
IT
Fogarty, Tim (Business Sys & Info Mgr)
ext 209
Allen, Brian (IT Off) ext 205
Boggon, Campbell (Info & IT Supp Off)
ext 238
Patel, Raj (Info & IT Supp Off) ext 207
Perratt, Alan (Info Off) ext 206
Boseley, Sophie (IU Administrator) ext
208
HR
Hall, Vicki (HR Manager) ext 216
Richards, Jackie (HR Admin) ext 217
Finance
Newman, Louise (Treasurer) ext 213
Maloney, Debra (Finance Mgr) ext 224
Longbotham, Rachel (Finance Off) ext
203
Darlow, Sharon (Finance Off) ext 204
Health & Safety
Westhead, Chris (Facilities Mgr, H&S
Advisor) ext 222
Salcombe, Karen (H&S Administrator)
ext 200
Area Managers
McBride, Stephanie (CP / ETE) ext 219
Temple, Richard (OM) ext 220
Yates, Ted
(IOM/Programmes/HMP/Community
Initiatives) ext 233

Gloucester Offender Management Team
Hughes, Dan (Perf Man) ext 263
Powell, Valerie (Perf Man) ext 259

POs
Allen, David ext 274
Bennett, Catherine ext 273
Broderick, Tessa ext 274
Clee, Mark ext 276
Cooper, Andrew ext 285
Cooper, Lesley ext 281
Oatley, Diane ext 270
Rea, Mary ext 266
Shearman, Kerry ext 282
Sonnichsen, Kirsten ext 265
Wake, Robert ext 268
Pearson, Pauline
Waldron, Amanda ext 277
Walford, Verity ext 283

PSOs
Boughton, Angie ext 275
Cassidy, John ext 271
Grant-Jones, Pauline ext 264
Hall, Joanne ext 286
Rennebach, Rachel ext 287
Smith, Stephen
Tracey, Patrick 01452 427011
Support Staff
Moss, Elizabeth (SASO) ext 258
Andrews, Amy ext 272
Head, Zoe ext 284
Keith, Emma (Accom) ext 298
Lovell, Jane ext 260
Morgan, Deborah ext 267
Morris, Clare ext 278
Powick, Carolyn
Taylor, Sharon ext 279
Trigg, Tina ext 260
Community Initiatives
Dower, Kevin Community Initiatives
Co-Coordinator ext 226
Programmes
James, Shirley (Programmes Man) ext
261
Adlard, Stephen (PSO) ext 250
Mills, Christina (PO) ext 249
Fowler, Miranda (PSO) ext 296
Leishman, Angela (PO) ext 248
Jones, Karen (PSO) ext 251
Patterson, Chris (PSO) ext 294
Neil Hewitt (PSO) ext 299
Whitney, Vicky (PSO) ext 295
Support Staff
Symons, Nicola (SASO) ext 257
Daws, Monique ext 256
Keable, Sheena ext 200
Lethbridge, Tracy ext 253
Merry, Jan ext 254
Timur, Judith ext 255
Wilson Sarah ext 252

Barlow, Kerry ext 243
Teague, Michelle ext 245
Palmer, Mavis ext 247

ETE Team
Berry, Dave (ETE Mgr) ext 288
Ayling, Carol (ETE Wkr) ext 290
Hirst, Veronica ext 293
Jones, Gillian ext 293
Mashta, Hussain ext
Lewis, Joanne ext 292
Trigg, Lillian (ETE Wkr) ext 291
Ward, Susan ext 289
Weaving, Sally ext 289

Community Payback
Walker, Lisa (CP Project Off) ext 240

Butcher, Suzanne (PSO) ext 244
Taylor, Beverley (PSO) ext 246
CP Supervisors
Allan, Daryl ext 200
Dobbin, Matthew ext 200
Hanson, Steve ext 200
Hills, David ext 200

Cheltenham and Tewkesbury

County Offices
St George's Road
Cheltenham GL50 1QF
Tel: 01242 534500 Fax: 01242 534590

Offender Management
Dennison, Alex (Perf Mgr) ext 506
Bombera, Isoline (PO) ext 540
Donald, Nick (PSO) ext 524
Moxon, Vicky (CMO) ext 543
Belshaw, Lisa (PO) ext 527
Clayton, Sharon (PO) ext 553
Hall, Anita (PO) ext 529
Jones, Carolyn (PO) ext 541
Ustok, Lisa (PO) ext 532
Read, Matthew (PO) ext 525
Simson, Kate (PO) ext 533
Smith, Elaine (PO) ext 533
Cowmeadow, Hillary (PSO) ext 53444
Hayley, Lynda (PSO) ext 528
Pettipher, Leanne (PSO) ext 544
Cudmore, Jean (VLO) ext 546
Usman, Melanie (PO) ext 526

Support Staff
Gleed, Sian (SASO) ext 549
Bircher, Jane (IT Training Off) ext 551
Cook, Tina ext 531
Frazier, Lesley ext 527
Hughes, Kerry ext 537
Keeling, Angela (Data Quality and Dev Officer) ext 523

Middlecote, Lesley ext 536
Patel, Hansa ext 500
Stanley, Rosamund ext 534
Spashett Louise ext 542
Woodfield, Joanne ext 500
Jones, Gillian (ETE Wkr) ext 504
Jones, Sue ext 500
Garrington, Ann (Accom Off), ext 516

Stroud & Cotswolds

118 Cainscross Road
Stroud GL5 4HN
Tel: 01453 760100 Fax: 01453 760107

Offender Management
POs
Gibbs, Kate ext 122
Johnson, Leanne ext 110
Pritchard, Clive ext 129
Taylor, Sue ext 104
Williams, Jan ext 112
Phelps, Tanya (PSO) ext 113
Carter, Sarah (PSO) ext 280

Support Staff
Ellis, Lisa ext 127
Maquire Patricia ext 126
Powell, Susan ext 100
Ward, Sue ext 102
Hirst, Ronnie (ETE Off) ext 121

Forest Team
The Court House, Gloucester Road,
Coleford GL16 8BL
Tel: 01594 837090 Fax: 01594 837256

Offender Management
Coombs, Sue (PO)
Sims, Clare (PO)

Support Staff
Tooze, Gillian

Youth Offending Team
48 London Road **Gloucester** GL1 3NZ
Tel: 01452 547540 Fax: 014520 551114

Slack, Sue

Integrated Offender Management / Drug Intervention Programme
Holland House, 59 Landsdown Road,
Cheltenham GL51 6QH
(01242) 27 then extension

Knott, Jane (Perf Manager) ext 6675

Hall, Tracy (PSO) ext 6271
Fletcher, James (PSO) ext 6812
Jones, Paula (PSO) ext 6802

Donnelly, Laura (PO) ext 6828
Wilford, Huw (PO) ext 6803
Cousins, Terry (PO) ext 6818

Support Staff
Thomas, Rebecca
Skelham, Jacqueline ext 6827

MAPPA
Public Protection Bureau Wilton House
63 Lansdown Road **Cheltenham** GL51
6QD
Tel: 01242 247979 Fax: 01242 276879

Scully, Mark (MAPPA Mgr Coord) 01242
247974
Ridge, Kirsty (Admin) 01242 247980

Approved Premises

Ryecroft Approved Premises
78 Ryecroft Street, Tredworth
Gloucester GL1 4LY
Tel: 01452 380268 Fax: 01452 302969

Dennison, Mark (Prob Rehabilitation
Mgr)
Cottrell, Susan (Asst Mgr)
Wessex, Mark (Asst Mgr)

Supervisors
Bees, Harry
Bolton, Peter
Gilbert, Thomas
Piwowarski, Grzegorz
Pyrce, Claire
Morgan, Greg
Trotman, Lucy
Wooding, Clive

Support Staff
Baldwin, Julie (Admin)

Institution

HMP/YOI Gloucester
Barrack Square Gloucester GL1 1JN
Tel: 01452 453000 Fax: 01452 453001

Knight, Anthony (Perf Mgr)

Baker, Jacqui (PSO)
Gough, Petra (PSO)
Farr, Derek (PSO)

Local Justice Areas
Gloucestershire

Crown Court
Gloucester
Worrall, Sian (PSO) 01452 426719

HAMPSHIRE PROBATION TRUST

Out of hours contact point
The Grange Probation Hostel Tel: 023 9236
3474

Victim enquiries tel: 0300 047 2055

Email:
firstname.lastname@hampshire.probation.gsi.
gov.uk

Head Office
1st Floor, Cromwell House, Andover Road
Winchester SO23 7EZ
Tel: 0300 047 2000 Fax: 01962 865278
Crook, Barrie (CE)
Hatch, Belinda (PA to CE)
Bailey, Sharon (p, Dir Finance &
Resources)
Reavey, Diane (p, Prop Mgr)
Straw, Christine (Dir of HR)
Gray, Rachel (p, PA to Dir of HR)
Fry, Chris (p, Bus Change Mgr)
Young, Neill (p, Comms Mgr)
Heppenstall, Samara (Snr Inf & Perf
Analyst)
Clayton, Rosie (p, Info & Perf Analyst)
Bahaj, Julia (Diversity Advisor) Mob:
07974 971896
Goodchild, Nicky (Women and Equalities
Liaison Off)
Crowther, Teresa (HR Servs Mgr)
Charlton, Maggie (HR Servs Adv)
King, Emma (p, HR Servs Adv)
Howson, Monica (Payroll Mgr)
Okami, Julia (Personnel Asst)
Rooke, Ginette (Personnel Asst)
Quiggin, Sean (Mgr Shared IT Services)
Hacker, John (Info Systems Mgr)
Collins, Nicki (IT Tech & Support Mgr)
Clarke, Paul (p, IT Network Support Off)
Hammonds, Katie (IT Network Support
Off)
Hedley, Clare (p, IT Asst)
Jones, Rachael (p, Finance Mgr)
Scott, Barry (Asst Finance Mgr)
Dunn, James (Finance Off)
Stranks, Helen (p, Finance Off)
Maltby, Vicki (Finance Asst)
Wenman, Paula (p. Finance Asst)
Townsend-Brown, Angela (Bus Support
Mgr)
Reid, Bill (Reception)
Blake, Lisa (p, Admin Off)

IT Helpdesk Tel: 0300 047 2036

Hampshire LDU
Mitchell, Chris (Dir Offender Mgmt)
Roscoe, Martin (p, Ops Mgr Crt Martial)
Josling, Sarah (p, PA to Dir of OM and
Dir of Offender Services)

Offender Services
Swyer, Barbara (Dir Offender Services)
Davies, Jonathan (P&Q Mgr)
Barrett, Niki (p, Ops Mgr CP/AP)
Loveridge, Rachael (p, Ops Mgr Acc
Prog/ETE)
Vacancy (Bus Support Mgr)
Blackman, Jo (p, Admin Off)
Weston, Natalie (p, Admin Off)

ETE Team
Vicki Scarfield (Mgr)
Davies, Sarah (Admin)
Hall, Samantha (Admin)

Training Unit
Witt, Margaret (L&D Coord)
Sitaram, Shashi (IT Trainer)

Winchester Probation Team
1st Floor, Cromwell House, Andover Road
Winchester S023 7EZ
Tel: 0300 047 2050Fax: 01962 866228

Hampshire LDU
Pearce, Melanie (p, Ops Mgr) (Aldershot,
Fareham, Havant, HMP Winchester, IOM
North and East)
Holmes, Sue (Ops Mgr) (Basingstoke,
Eastleigh, New Forest, Test Valley,
Winchester, IOM West)
Moore, Sarah (Bus Support Mgr)
Vacancy (Commissioning Mgr)
Orman, Lin (Performance & Quality
Manager)
Cavanagh, Siobhan SPO (Winchester,
WCC)
Shone, Lynne (p, Admin Off)
Abbott, Heidi (p)
Keevash, Dave (IOM – West Hampshire)
Spiers, Daniel
Sherwood, Heather
Scott, Jo
Smith, Amy

PSOs
Riley, Amanda
Morrison, Allison
Vigar-Taylor, Su (p, IOM Engagement
Officer)
Admin
Nayyar, Sarah
Field, Sara

Rothery, Dianne
Risden, Karen (Receptionist)

Victim Contact Unit
Tel: 0845 6040 150 Fax: 01962 844983
Black, Tracey (SPO)
Ball, Liz
Turner, Kirsty
Rooney, Debi
Smith, Victoria (p, Admin)

Winchester Combined Court Centre
The Law Courts Winchester SO23 9EL
Tel: 01962 849256 Fax: 01962 870405

Hampshire LDU
Cavanagh Siobhan (SPO)
Nayyar, Sarah (Admin)
Stainton, Kate (Court PO)
Williams, Tina
Stroud, Sarah (p, Court PO)

Youth Offending Teams

Wessex Youth Offending Team
Hampshire County Council, Elizabeth
Court II (East), The Castle,
Winchester, Hampshire SO23 8UG
Tel: 01962 845501 Fax: 01962 846078

Interventions
Smailes, Alison (Head of Service)

Aldershot Probation Team

Imperial House
2 Grosvenor Road
Aldershot GU11 1DP
Tel: 0300 047 2200 Fax: 01252 329515

Hampshire LDU
Baker, Sheila (SPO)
Edom, Matthew (SPO)
Despicht, Kathy (p)
Dobson, Rachel (p)
Etherington, Kate (IOM)
Gallichan, Gail
Lowe, Rachel
Regan, Cliff
Pullen, James

PSOs
Buckle, Gill
Hutton, Suzanne
Nicholls, Lara
Hocking, Angela (ETE Off)
OM Admin
Burrell, Elaine (p)
Evans, Gemma
Freeland, Julie

Jones, Phil (Receptionist)

Southern Support HQ
Hamble Lane, Hamble, Southampton
Tel number unknown at present
Rowlands, Jacqueline (MAPPA
Co-ordinator)
Watt, Julia (Deputy MAPPA Co-ordinator)

Andover Probation Team

The Court House
West Street **Andover** SP10 1QP
Tel: 0300 047 2400 Fax: 01264 335457

Hampshire LDU
Caroline Gray (p, SPO)

POs
Brown, Joanne
Rees-Jones, Stephen
Thomas, Jeremy
Bainbridge, Adam
James, Michele (PSO)(p)
OM Admin
Gray, Liz
Priestley-Cooper, Jenny
White, Celia (p)

Basingstoke Probation Team

Level Two St Clement House
1–3 Alençon Link
Basingstoke RG21 7SB
Tel: 0300 047 2100 Fax: 01256 812374

Hampshire LDU
Cluff, Jeff (SPO)
Appleby, Allan (SPO)
Markie, Jacqui (p, IOM, SPO)
Alderton, Judith
Burley, Emma (p)
Davis, Melanie
Durnell, Caroline (p, Court)
Griffiths, Ceri (p)
O'Donovan, Emma
Shearing, Hazel
Stace, Andrea (IOM)
Stacey, Kevin
Steed, Julie (p)
Tickner, Christy

PSOs
Date, Alice
Finch, Jane (Court)
Haxby, Jo
Souter, Lynda
Saunders, Cara (BPO)
Smith, Ben (BPO)
Haddon, Alison (ETE Off)

Hocking, Angela (ETE Off)
OM Admin
Berrecloth, Jane (p)
Doublet, Sue (Breach)
Ellis, Jill
Hughes, Jane
Hunt, Alison (p)
Oliver, Leigh
Sadler, Nicola (p)
Steadman, Debbie (p, Admin Officer)
Nagle, Janet (reception)
White, Janet (p) (evening reception)

Level 1 St Clement House
1–3 Alençon Link
Basingstoke RG21 7SB
Tel: 0300 047 2100 Fax: 01256 357292
(Progs only)

Programmes
Hall, Louise (p, Prog Mgr)
Browning, Tom (p, Prog Mgr)
Cleal, Davina (Treatment Mgr IDAP)
George, Amy (Treatment Mgr)
Gorman, Laura (Facilitator)
Vince-Reece, Hannah (SOGP Facilitator)
Hayes, Emma (Prog Off)
Parker, Phil (Facilitator)
Niknejad, Leila (Facilitator)
Small, Rebecca (Facilitator)
Smith, Julia (Facilitator)
Standing, Paula (Facilitator)
Kelley, Emma (Psych Off)
Vacancy
Rabika, Adria (Women's Safety Wkr)
Prog Admin
Grimston, Alison (p)
Larcome, Sharon (p)
Tambascia, Katie (p)

Community Payback (North)
Skinner, Alan ((N) CP Mgr)
Robertson, Paula (Placement Mgr)
Mills, Stephen (Placement Mgr)
Pickford, Julie (PSO)
Wyatt, Leona (p) (PSO)
Evans, Gemma (p) (PSO)

Fareham Probation Team

20 High Street
Fareham P016 7AF
Tel: 0300 047 2350 Fax: 01329 825023

Hampshire LDU
Morgan, Catherine (SPO)
Skinner, Corinne (SPO)
Caswell, Paul
Crooks, Avril

Davies, Susan (p)
Haynes, Claire (p)
Herbert, Lorraine (p)
Paradise, Erika (IOM)
Pencavel, Katie (p)
Talbot, Polly (Court)
Gilroy, Vicky
Winkworth, Jane (p)
Bone, Rebecca

PSOs
Burns, Jill
Chuter, Sam (IOM)
Smith, Penny
Phillip, Roy (EO IOM)
Shaw, Kristina
Pickering, Debbie (p, ETE Off)
Admin
Clarke, Christine (p)
Collingwood, Julie (p, OM)
Ginn, Nikki
Orridge, Helen
Penny, Sharon
Rushton, Nikki
Emery, Kay (p, Reception)

Fareham Magistrates' Court
c/o 20 High Street Fareham
Hampshire PO16 7AF
Tel: 01329 220846 Fax: 01329 220846

Manuel, Rachel (p, PO)
Talbot, Polly (PO)
Starr, Brian (PSO))

Elmleigh Road
Havant P09 2AS
Tel: 0300 047 2300 Fax: 023 9249 8275

Allen, Rob (Health & Safety Adv)

Havant Probation Team

Hampshire LDU
Marsh, Rob (SPO)
Sealey, Judi (SPO)
Coffey, Mick
Jenkins, Carolyn
Keys, Carly (p)
Meads, Genevieve (p)
Prew, Georgina
Taylor, Susannah
Gifford, Jo
Temperley-Chapman, Sharon (p)
Smith, Sam (IOM)
Davenport, Amy

PSOs
Edwards, Paul
Logan, Sue

Spencer, Patrick
Wallis, Karyn
Eade, Rebecca (IOM Engagement
Officer)
Henderson, Yvonne (ETE Off)
Hobbs, Rosemary (p, OMA)
Blake, Lisa (Admin Off)
Collins, Debbie (OMA)
Power, Beth (p) (OMA)
Webb, Rebecca (OMA)
Maslen, Lisa (p)
Cafferky, Janet (p) (Reception)

West Shore House
West Street **Hythe** SO45 6AA
Tel: 023 8084 3684 Fax: 023 8084 2354

Hythe Probation Team

Hampshire LDU
Veck, Nicola (SPO)
Pontin, Amanda
Kavanagh, Lewis
Bridgeman, Joanne (p)
Goodeve, Jayne (PSO)
Pearce, Elaine (PSO – IOM West
Hampshire)
Buston, Natalie (p, admin)
Fovargues, Jax (p, admin)
Marshall, Elaine (p, admin)

8 Sea Street
Newport
Isle of Wight P030 5BN
Tel: 0300 047 2700 Fax: 01983 528994

Portsmouth and Isle of Wight LDU
Hyslop, Alex (SPO)
Lightburn, Marilyn (SPO)

POs
French, Daniella
Stead, David
Janvrin, Jane
Mitchell, Kirsty
McCulloch, Amy
Puckett, Nicola
Sanders, Donna
Shardlow, Rob
Charlesworth, Ian

PSOs
Bacon, Justine
Kennedy, Jo
Greenhalgh Barry
Reid, Linda
Woodhouse Matt
Yates, Rebecca
Gulliver, Pauline

Offender Services Community Payback
Swan, Jane (Placement Mgr)

Island House
Priestlands Place
Lymington S041 9GA
Tel: 0300 047 2450 Fax: 01590 671521

Hampshire LDU
Hatton, Dean (SPO) Lymington and IOM
West Hampshire SPO
Shergold, Aggie (PSO)
Smith, Brian (PSO)
Lee, Emma
Garland, Sandra (IOM West Hampshire)
Lewis, Zara (Court Martial Reports
Service (p))
Pagett, David
OM Admin
Charton, Kathy
Martin, Holly
Sparks, Debbie
Taylor, Kerry

Portsmouth Probation Team
PO Box 703 **Portsmouth** POI 2WZ
Tel: 0300 047 2500 Fax: 023 9285 1618

Portsmouth and Isle of Wight LDU
Beattie, Sarah (Dir of Offender Mgmt)
Gwyther, Natasha (PA to Dir of OM)
Shave, Nikki (Op Mgr)
Turtle, Steve (P&Q Mgr)
Wells, Andy (L&D Mgr)
Coombes, Clayton (Commissioning Mgr)
Judd Estelle (SPO OM1)
Fitch, Sarah (SPO OM2)
Welch, Yasmin (SPO MAPPA)
Vacancy (SPO, IOM Team)
Richards, Teresa (Bus Sup Mgr)
Shawl, Richard (Legal Services Mgr)
Vacancy (Admin Off)

MAPPA
Watt, Sue
Gaites, Tim
Bowes, Tom
Frampton, Pat
Harvey, Matt
Arnold, Denise (PSO)
Bradshaw, Mike

Offender Management Team 1 (OM1)
POs
Connolly, Ellie
McKeown, Cora
Eames Laura

Cherry, Sam
Sims, Crystal

PSOs
Gough Kelly
Punton, Bridge
Sedgeley, Clare

Offender Management Team 2 (OM2)
Clemson, Kim
Rushforth, Rachel
Wyeth, Leslie

POstin, Laura
Gamer, Kayley

PSOs
Wade, Pete
Barnard, Dennis

IOM Team
POs
Goman, Rebecca
Peckham, Jennifer

PSOs
Babbington, John
Judd, Pete
Savege, Vicky (PPOC)
Whitelock, Kate (EO)

Training Unit
Evans, Trish (p, Org Dev Mgr)
Keysell, Ben (Training Officer)
Sherwood-Plant, Siobhan (VQ Centre
Co-ordinator)

Community Payback Unit (SE Region)
PO Box 703 Portsmouth PO1 2WZ
Tel: 0300 047 2500 Fax: 023 9287 1183

Chambers, Steph ((SE) CP Mgr)
Harris, Jeff (Placement Mgr)
Pervin, Eddie (Placement Mgr)
Bastable, Jane (PSO)
Francis, Steve (PSO)

Administration Team
McInnes, Helen (Admin team leader)
Taylor, Suzie (p)
Whittaker, Elizabeth
Geraish, Emma
Wright, Alison
Rees-Truman, Hannah
Prosser, Wendi
Clough, Kim
Clark, Tracy
Woods, Karen

Programmes South East Unit
6th floor Enterprise House
Isambard Brunel Road
Portsmouth PO1 2RX
Tel: 0300 047 2500 Fax: 023 9282 7841

Programmes
Simpson, Sandra (p) (Prog Mgr)
Whitefield, Sarah (p, Treatment Mgr)
Programme Officers
Burr, Carianne (p)
Vacancy
Vacancy
Minton, Jenna
Warburton, Jane (Prog Off)
Programme Admin
Adkins, Anna (p)
Correa, Helen (p)
Terracciano, Sarah

SOGP Team
Facilitators
Kelly, Bernadette
Tilford, Richard
Toovey, Adele
Wright, Hayley

IDAP team
Tripp, Russell (Treatment Mgr, Prog Off)
Bennett, Alison (Women's Safety Wkr)
Todd, Sandra (Women's Safety Wkr)
Dyke, Matthew (Prog Off)
Palombo, Ashleigh (Prog Off)
DeVine, Ishret (Prog Off – half time EH
and half time Women Safety Worker TQ)

Portsmouth Reporting Office
52 Isambard Brunel Road, **Portsmouth**
PO1 2BD
Tel: 0300 047 2600 Fax: 023 9273 5192

Court Unit
Tel: 0300 047 2600 Fax: 023 9275 5663
Burgess, Heather (SPO)

POs
Bizley, Jane
Piper, Ceri
Devereux, Jan
Eden, Julie
Hahn, Colin
Joslin, Susie
Joyce, Jackie
Osbourne, Estelle
Vosper, Jo
Doran, Anna
Smith, Chas
Hepner, Nina

PSOs
Ball, Jackie
Webb, Hayley
West, Lyn
Thompson Sam
Borg, Mark

Breach Unit
Tel: 0300 047 2600 Fax: 023 9273 5192
Richards, Ian (PSO, BPO)
Stubbs, Lisa (PSO, BPO)

ETE
Tel: 0300 047 2600 Fax: 023 9287 1801

Wishart, Corinne (ETE Off)

7 Town Quay House
Town Quay
Southampton SO14 2ET
Tel: 0300 047 2800 Fax: 0300 047 2873

Southampton LDU
Galovics, Maria (Director of Offender
Management)
Welsh, Christina (P/A to Director of
Offender Management)
Svendsen, Jo Inge (Operations Manager)
Willcocks, Alison (Business Support
Manager)
James, Nigel (P & Q Manager)
Henderson, Gavin (Commissioning
Manager)
Hardy, Susan (L & D Manager)
O'Connor, Lou (ETE / PSO)
Tuck, Trudi (ETE Officer)
Joanne Cooper ETE Officer)
Thorne, Lin (Reception)
O/Neill, Val (Reception)

MAPPA Team 1
SPO
Black, Tracey

POs
May, Simon
Townsend, Lucinda
Winter, Emma Jane
Bell, Amanda
Murray, Andrea
PSO
Sherwood, Alex (PQF)

MAPPA Team 2
SPO
Alford, Alison

POs
Phillips, Heather
Gunn, Mark
Power, Claire

Ducommun, Yvonne
Major, Rosie
Barton, Verity

POs
Pilkington, Michelle (PQF)
CAs
Bulpitt, Carol
Powell, Jacqueline
Mitchener, Lisa
Donovan, Leanne

Young Adult Offender Team
SPO
Walker, Karen

POs
Boulton, Neil
Pettit, Hayley
Viney, Lauren

PSOs
Keites, Hayley
Palmer, Donna
Garrett, Kerry (PQF)
CAs
Kitson, Nicola

OMT 1
SPO
Barrett, Sally

POs
Cato, Len
Hearn, Jenny
Goldspink, Claire (Women's Programme)
Maidment, Hayley
Collins, Yvonne (Women's Programme)

PSOs
Butt, Laura (Women's Programme)
Evans, Heather (Women's Programme)
Leigh, Brian
Kennelly, Gerry
Taylor, Kirsty (PQF)
CAs
Risk, Delia
Butcher, Jodi

OMT 2
SPO
Morris, Pete

POs
Brown, Neil (DRR)
Baxter, Kevin (DRR)
Flint, Janet (DRR)
Barclay, Michelle
Baynham, Myra
Brider, Heather

PSOs
Hopper, Sarah
Steinicke, Claire
Gladdis, Jayne
Cleeve, Kate (DRR)
CAs
Hussain, Shanaz
Lovell, Sandra

Programmes Unit – Town Quay, Southampton
Rowlands, Jonathan (SPO / Programme Manager)
Connell, Soozin (GOBP Treatment Manager)
Morariu, Romona (Psych. Off.)
Cleal, Davina (Programme Off., Town Quay) + (IDAP Treatment Mngr, Basingstoke)
Gover, Tanya (IDAP, Programme Off.)
Selvage, Michele (Programme Tutor)
Waddington, Sue (IDAP, Treatment Mgr.)
De Vine, Ishret (Women's Safety Worker)
Miles, Nikki (Women's Safety Worker)
Gatt, Jan (Programme Admin.)
Knight, Rachel (Programme Admin.)
Storey, Alison (Programme Tutor)
Shashi Dhar (Programme Tutor (p))
Beament, Casey (Programme Tutor)

TV-CSOP Team – Town Quay, Southampton
Savage, Corinna (SPO/ Programme Manager)
Metcalfe, Suzie (SOGP Treatment Mgr.)
Hendricks, Caroline (SOGP Facilitator)
Saunders, Clare (SOGP Facilitator, PO)
Downer, Alex (Sex Offender Facilitator)

Southampton Central Police Station
Southern Road, **Southampton** SO15 1AN
IOM Team
Tel: 023 8053 3318 or 023 8053 319
SPO
Walker, Karen
PO
Horrocks, Allison

PSOs
Palmer, Vicky
Skinner, Joanne
CA
Barnes, Clare

Southampton Magistrates' Court
100 The Avenue Southampton SO17 0EY
Tel: 023 8033 6113 Fax: 023 8033 6122

Southampton LDU
Barrett, Sally (SPO Courts)
Glew, David (PO)
Paul, Debbie (PO)

PSOs
Bennett, Keith (PSO)
Williams, Eve (PSO)
Thomas, Colette (PSO)
Ryder. Zoe ((p) PO)
Nicholas. Wendy (f/t PSO)

Old Bank House
66–68 London Road
Southampton S015 2AJ
Tel: 0300 047 2950 Fax: 023 8023 5778
SPO
Robbie Turkington

POs
Bridger, Jane
Sharratt, Matthew
Lidstone, Fiona
Whitehead, Kira
Thomas, Liz
Broughton, Steve
Ryder, Zoe
CAs
West, Tracey (Court Admin)
Nelson, Rosemary (Court Admin)

SW Breach Team – Southampton
Hall, Leo (BPO)
Hill, Jo (BPO)
Darlington, Joanne (Breach Admin)
Farthing, Debbie (Breach Admin)

**SW Region Offender Services
Community Payback**
Taggart, Kelly ((SW) Op Mgr Int/CP)
Annell, Sharon (Placement Mgr)
Simpson, Matt (Placement Mgr)
Pocock, Nicola (PSO)
Crouch, Liz (PSO)

Southampton Crown Court
The Courts of Justice
London Road Southampton S015 2AA
Tel: 023 8023 2642 Fax: 023 8023 5929

PSOs (working at both Courts)
Thomas, Colette
Williams, Eve
Bennett, Keith
Cupid, Kenny
Wiltshire, Elaine

Bail Officer
Jones, Kirsty

Wessex YOT (NE & NW)
180 Culver Road **Basingstoke** RG21 3NL
Tel: 01256 464034 Fax: 01256 327210

Offender Services
Humphrey, Jean (Area Mgr)
Smailes, Alison (TM Mgr)
Lambert, Penny
Tomkins, Peter
Williams, Nina

Portsmouth YOT
Floor 4 Core 6, Civic Offices, Guildhall
Square,
Portsmouth PO1 2EA
Tel; 023 92688450 Fax: 023 92834677
Gardner, Jon (Service Mgr)
Purser, Kathy
Read, Mary

Offender Services
Ballard, Jeff (Area Mgr)
Barham, Lynn (Team Manager –
Community Payback)
Briggs, Paul (Team Manager – South
East Hampshire)
Rees, Mary
Swift, Georgia
Williams, Lin

SW Hampshire YOT
Hampshire House
4th Floor, 84–98 Southampton Road,
Eastleigh, Hampshire, SO50 5PA
Tel.: 023 8049 8000 Fax: 023 8038 3355

Southampton YOT
28 – 29 St Mary's Street, Southampton,
Hampshire, SO14 1AT
Tel.: 023 8083 4900
Morse, Sue, YOT Manager

Wessex YOT (Isle of Wight)
62 Crocker Street Newport
Isle of Wight PO30 5DA
Tel: 01983 522799 Fax: 01983 523175

Offender Services
Morgan, Lisa (Team Mgr)

**Wessex YOT (Intensive Supervision &
Surveillance)**
2nd Floor Ashville House 260–262
Havant Road Drayton **Portsmouth** PO6
1PA
Tel: 023 9228 3900 Fax: 023 9238 1318

Offender Services
Earles, Richard (Team Mgr)

Approved Premises (Hostels)

Dickson House Approved Premises
77 Trinity Street Fareham PO16 7SL
Tel: 01329 234531 Fax: 01329 284523

Newman, Mark (SPO)

Moloney, Mike (Support Services Off)

Residential Services Officers
Binfield, Iris
Dobson, Gemma
Kitching, Peter
Trueman, Sarah
Wheeler, Philip
Knott, Patricia (Res Adm Support Off)
Boulter, Jamie (Night Wk Supvr)
Rogers, Mary (Night Wk Supvr)

The Grange Approved Premises
145 Stakes Road Purbrook PO7 5PL
Tel: 023 9236 3474 Fax: 023 9236 3481
Christie, Steve (SPO)
Residential Services Officers
Clark, Michelle
Floyd, Keith
Leeds, Kelly-Ann
Swain, Georgia
Bone, Darren (Night Wk Supvr)
Kerley, David (Night Wk Supvr)
Bloor Katherine (Res Admin Support Off)
Starkie, Erin (Res Off)

Landguard Road Approved Premises
32 Landguard Road Shirley
Southampton SO15 5DJ
Tel: 023 8033 6287 Fax: 023 8033 6290
McKie Jenny (SPO)
Davidson, Donna (Support Serv Off)
Residential Services Officers
Austin, Ruby
Collins, Paul
Pickering, Darren
Payne, Kayleigh
Grayling, James (Night Wk Supvr)
Fisher, Barbara (Night Wk Supvr)
Reilly, Lynn (Res Admin Support)
Morgan-Jones, Debbi (Res Asst)

Institutions
HMP Isle of Wight
Direct dial: 01983 55 + ext
O'Driscoll, Paul (SPO for Prison Cluster
and Public Protection) ext 4119

POs
Snell, Patricia
Crawford, Colin
Courtney, Ben

Owen, Bryony
Ellis, Michelle
Murray, Karen
Pennell, Stephen
Croset, Paula
Tate, Angela

PSOs:
Pond, Dawn (Accomodation Officer,
Camp Hill)
Jenkins, Su (Public Protection, Albany)

Parkhurst Site
Newport Isle of Wight PO30 5NX
Tel: 01983 554000 Fax: 01983 554001

Albany Site
Newport Isle of Wight PO30 5RS
Tel: 01983 556300 Fax: 01983 556362

Camp Hill
Newport Isle of Wight PO30 5PB
Tel: 01983 554600 Fax: 01983 554799

HMP Kingston
122 Milton Road **Portsmouth** PO3 6AS
Tel: 023 9295 3100 Fax: 023 9295 3186

Direct dial: 023 9295 + ext

Offender Management Unit
Donnelly, Sarah (Supvr) 3236

HMP Winchester
Romsey Road Winchester SO22 5DF
Tel: 01962 723000 Fax: 01962 723001;
01962 723008 (probation)

Direct dial: 01962 723 + ext
Neary, Paul (SPO) ext 161
Desjardins, Tracey
Evans, Lisa (p)
Rynne, Martin 160
Walden, Amy ext 180
Beatson, Jennifer (PSO Bail Info) ext 036
Carter, Judith (PSO Bail Info) ext 036
Howell, Steve (PSO) ext 157
Smith, Ann (PSO) ext 035
Vigar Taylor, Su (IOM Engagement
Officer) ext 247
Eade, Rebecca (IOM Engagement
Officer) ext 247
Smith, Victoria (IOM Case Administrator)
ext281

Local Justice Areas
Isle of Wight
New Forest (Totton Team)
North East Hampshire (Aldershot)

North West Hampshire (Andover,
Basingstoke)
South East Hampshire (Havant,
Portsmouth)
South Hampshire (Fareham)
Southampton (Southampton)

Crown Courts
Newport
Portsmouth
Southampton
Winchester

HERTFORDSHIRE
PROBATION TRUST
Email:
firstname.lastname@hertfordshire.probation.
gsi.gov.uk

Head Office
Argyle House, Argyle Way
Stevenage, Herts, SG1 2AD
Tel: 01438 747074 Fax: 01438 316207

Webb, Tessa (Chief Executive)
Hughes, John (Director Interventions)
Johnson-Proctor, Steve (Director
Operations)
Riccardi, Lisa (Director Corp Services)
Forth, Adrian (Director Finance &
Business Dev)
Holmes, Alex (Interventions Mgr)
McSweeney, Barbara (p, Comms Officer)
Collett, Jo (HR & Staff Development
Mgr)
Blaney, Mark (Finance Mgr)
Rea, Emma (p, SDO/LDO)
Watson, Sam (Acting Centre Mgr)
Spencer, Lucy (Perf Improvement Mgr)
Hook, Doug (Partnership Commissioning
Mgr)

Eastern LDU, Cheshunt
Bishop College, Churchgate,
Cheshunt, EN8 9XL
Fax: 01992 785160 Fax: 01992 785175

Hylton, Gary (Acting SPO)

Johnson, Di (UPW Project Manager)

Pearse, Faye (Acting Dep Centre Mgr)

POs
Bruno, Tina
Gordon, Shanti (p)
Kinsey, Ian (p)
Kusevra, Ozcn
Ling, Darren

Reynolds, Zoe
Breed, Sarah (p)
Choudhury, Keron
St Luce, Cheryl (Court)

PSOs
Bouma, Esther (Gen)
Ferguson, Sarah (Gen)
Curtis, Chris (Gen)
Winters, Hazel (Gen)
Roskilly Caitrin (Gen)
Clay, Natalie (Gen)
Williams, Di (Gpwk)
Carter, Richard (PSO Unpaid Work)
Williams, Di (Gpwk)
Barnes, Amanda (Court)
Hill, Shirley (UPW)

Eastern LDU, Stevenage
Argyle House, Argyle Way
Stevenage SG1 2AD
Tel: 01438 747074 Fax: 01438 765206

Martindale, Clare (SPO)
Cowen, Jon (SPO)
Brooks, Dawn (ETE/Treatment Mgr)
Watson, Sam (Acting Centre Mgr)
Johnson, Di (UPW Project Mgr)
Downes, Tom (p, SDO)
Phipps, Tom (Job Deal Mgr)

POs
Bibi, Majabin
Bolton, May
Doole, Katherine
Downes, Tom (p)
Jones, Kelly
Moss, Nik
Oliver-Blais, Merle
Rayner, Kate
Tooley, Neil
Duncan, Jacky (Court)

PSOs
Pearson, Tony (Court)
Pratt, John (Court)
Winter, Louise (Court)
Cotton, Janette (Gen)
Ebeling-Jones, Cheryl (Gen)
Ganatra, Anjana (Gen)
Frankland, Alison (Gen)
Johnston, Anne (p, Gen)
Parker, Heather (Gen)
Stewart, Cindy (Gen)
Insaf, Ayse (Gen)
Cooper, Lee (Gpwk)
Graham, Rose (Gpwk)
Suchley, Clare (Gpwk)
White, Catherine (Gpwk)

Smith, Alexandra (Job Deal)
Turner, Chantel (Job Deal)

Sex Offender Specialists
Von Rabenau, Elisabeth (SPO)
Gurr, Lydia
Roderick, Liz (p)
Shirley, Matthew
Dale, Rebecca
Francis, Annabel (Circles)

Central LDU
62–72 Victoria Street
St Albans AL1 3XH
Tel: 01727 847787 Fax: 01727 792700

List, Terry (SPO)
Leng, Sally (SPO)
Harvey, Kate (ETE/Court SPO)
Toofail, Jackie (Treatment Mgr)
Mayles, Shelley (Centre Mgr)
Harding, Karen (UPW Project Mgr)
Kinsey, Ian (p, SDO)

POs
Adams, Katie (p)
Ewington, Mark
Farrance, Denese
Ferguson, Dave
Golding, Victoria (p)
Goodall, Anika
Kielthy, Anne
Kozlowska, Beata
Turner, Sarah
Willis, David
Dowling, Jackie
Wojdyla-St James, Barbara (Court)

PSOs
O'Neill, Desmond (Gen)
Hillhouse, Lynne (Gen)
Ivey, Linda (p, Gen)
McGovern, Maureen (Gen)
McKenna, Natalie (Gen)
Terywall, Naznean (Gen)
Chambers, Teresa (Gen)
Szyman, Michelle (Gen)
Brooks, Michaela (Court)
Che, Simon (Court)
Gilbride, Aiden (Court)
Harrison, Nicola (Court)
Runham, Jennifer (Court)
Marino, Colette (Gpwk)
Woolfe, Ashlea (p, Gpwk)
Williams, Rodney (Gpwk)
Wright, Lex (Gpwk)
Berardi, Patrizia (UPW)
Mullings, Sonia (ETE)

Victim Unit
Tel: 01727 792709 Fax: 01727 792706

Pleasants, Sue (Victim Dvpt Mgr)
Radcliffe, Frank (VLO)
Isaacs, Susan (VLO)
Davies, Lynda (WSO)
Ford, Donna (WSO)

South & West Herts Probation Centre
16–22 King Street Watford WD1 8BP
Tel: 01923 240144 Fax: 01923 699195
Bond, Nicola (SPO)
Mentern, Hannah (SPO)
Holmes, Mignon (ETE/Treatment Mgr)
Spencer, Jeffery (UPW Project Manager)
De Castro, Eunice (Centre Mgr)
Stark, Laura (SDO)

POs
Boorman, Laura
Carroll, Joanne
Cox, Sarah (p)
Goodall, Anika
Hopkins, Alison
Mikk, Jaanus
Pinder, Julie
Ross, Sarah-Jane
Smallman, Gary
Urwin, Sue
Whyman, Robert
Munna, Jubeda
Street, April
McFarlane, Julia (p, Court)

PSOs
Adams, Samantha (Gen)
Kane, Lauren (PSO)
Almond, Dawn (p, Gen)
Flaherty, Mary (Gen)
Foley, Louise (Gen)
Graham, Sara (p, Gen)
Hughes, James (Gen)
Isherwood, David (Gen)
Kropidlowska, Emilia (Gen)
O'Donnell, Carole (Gen)
Butcher, Clare (p, Gen)
Taylor, Hollie (Gen)
Bruce, Sara (Gpwk)
Woolmer-Thomas, Paul (Gpwk)
Osho, Jenyo (Gpwk)
Moreton, Tom (Gpwk)
Napier, Rebecca (Court)
Foley, Louise (UPW)
Buckley, Lauren (UPW)

Crown Court Probation Office
Bricket Road St Albans AL1 3JW
Tel: 01727 753290 Fax: 01727 868276
IOM Team
Hatfield Police Station, Comet Way
Hatfield, AL10 9SJ
Spencer, Maureen (SPO)

POs
Smith, Nicola (p)
Marco, Francesca
Hughes, Sarah
Jervis, Andrea
Keyte, Bernie

PSOs
Johnson, Monique
Morris, Emma
Maurice, Jane

MAPPA
Police HQ, Stanborough Road
Welwyn Garden City, AL8 6XF
Johnson, Morris (SPO)

Youth Offending Team

S&W, Watford
Tel: 01923 229012
Baker, Jill

N Herts, Stevenage
Tel: 01438 219420
Jeffery, Peter

S&W, Hemel Hempstead
Tel: 01442 388755
Tiernan, Janet

Institution

HMP The Mount
Molyneaux Avenue, Bovingdon
Hemel Hempstead, HP3 0NZ
Tel: 01442 836300 Fax: 01442 836301

PSOs
Watkins, Craig
Borg, Michelle
Joseph, Kelly
Warren, Jenny
Cowen, Hayley
Heck, Sally
Shults, Peter
Robson, Clare

Local Justice Areas
Central Hertfordshire (*Mid Herts Probation Centre*)
East Hertfordshire (*Head Office*)

North Hertfordshire (*North Herts Probation Centre*)
West Hertfordshire (*South & West Herts Probation Centre*)

HUMBERSIDE PROBATION TRUST

Email:
firstname.lastname@humberside.probation.gsi.gov.uk

Head Office
Liberty House Liberty Lane
Kingston-upon-Hull HU1 1RS
Tel: 01482 480000 Fax: 01482 480007

Wright, Peter (CE)
Birt, Janet (PA to CE)
Munsn, Kate (Director of Probation, Hull & East Riding, MAPPA – Safeguarding)
Ware, Ian (Director of Probation, N & NE Lincs) (See Scunthorpe/Grimsby)
Gore, Martin (Director, Corporate Services)
Fridlington, Kevan (Asst Director of Probation, Public Protection)
Green Jackie (Asst Director of Probation, N & NE Lincs) (See Scunthorpe/Grimsby)
Gilbert, Amy (Asst Director of Probation, Hull)
Redfern, Kate (Asst Director of Probation, Interventions, Prisons & East Riding)
Rhodes, Sharon (Head of Human Resources)
Stathers, Kerrie (Head of Information Services)
Wright, Jean (Head of Learning and Organisational Development)
Shipley, Barrie (Finance Mgr)
Tallant, Chris (PQF Manager)
Archer, Kevin (H&S Advisor)

Hull Office
Liberty House Liberty Lane
Kingston-upon-Hull HU1 1RS
Tel: 01482 480000 Fax: 01482 480003

Hull Offender Management Unit
Adegbembo, Sally (p, SPO)
Bate, Liz (SPO)
Campbell-Williams, Tara (p, SPO)
Harvatt, Diane (SPO)
Scargill, Vicki (SPO)

Forton, Alison (Business Mgr, Hull &
East Riding)
Franks, Terry/Watkins, Wendy (Bus
Mgr, Hull & East Riding)
Arnett, Elaine (Bus Mgr Interventions,
Humberside)
Allison, Vicky (p)
Bassett, Laura
Birkett, Lynne
Boyne, Linda
Brown, Kathryn
Cormack, Shona (p)
Cripps, Rosie
Dee, Rebecca
Dent, Jane
Duncan, Hannah (p)
Elkomi, Gamal
Hall, Sally (p)
Hamson, Louise (p)
Hancock, Jane
Hardy, Rebecca (p)
Harrison, Catherine
Harrison, Sonja
Henderson, Peter
Hill, Katrina
Hockney, Gary
Holmes, Heidi
Johnstone, Selina (p)
Kelly, Paul
Langdon, Jonathon
Leighton, Katie (p)
MacKenzie, Michelle
Ormerod, Sarah
Oyston, Sam
Parrott, Andrea (p)
Peck, Julie
Porteous, Mandy-Lee (p)
Sage, Clare
Stride, Gemma (p)
Sutton, Emma
Watts, Sally
Wells Gareth
Westmoreland, Chris
Williams, Mark
Wilson, Lee

PSOs
Bahn, Steve
Billam, Lesley
Clark, Mike
Kimenia, Macharia
Mansson, Magnus
McAllister, Carmel (p)
Matthews, Claire
Njord, Chris
Proctor, Tracey
Robson, Rebecca

Tennison, Leanne (p)
Trowell, Paula
Waddy, Rachel (p)

CAs
Adams, Judith (p)
Adamson, Sue (p)
Beadle, Caron
Drummond, Sarah
Fussey, Diane
Haldenby, Angie (p)
Marshall, Jenna
Sargerson, Karen
Weavers, Gemma

IOM
Baker, Sue (SPO)
Sefton, Wendy (SPO)
Clark, Rebecca
Frank, Joy
Kiney, Brighid
Mitchell, Nick
Walkington, James
Wilkinson, Andrea

PSOs
Lupkin, Cynthia
Green, Sharon
Kirkpatrick, Joe (p)
Brooks, Carol (CA)
Watkins, Wendy (CA)

TWP
Beaulah, Sue
Whittle, Julie
Taylor, Zoe PSO

Court Services
Watson, Alexa (SPO)
Armstrong, Rob
Sambrook, Mark
Sugden, Matthew
Sleight, Maxine (Prosecutions Officer)
Wadforth, Neil (Prosecutions Officer)

PSOs
Billam, Lynne
Burton, Helen (p)
Dee, Kathryn
Dhamrait, Neelam
Edmonson, Paula
Jarvis, Tina
Longhorn, Mandy (CA)

Victims Team
Dent, Pamela (Victim Mgr)
Cross, Jackie (WSW/VLO)
Gowland, Paul (VLO)
Jones, Ellen (WSW/VLO)
Rookyard, Tracey (WSW/VLO)

Interventions Team
Sellors, Rupert (SPO)
Taylor, Donna (SPO)
Barnes, Alison
Garrett, Tony
Graham, Glynis
Hurst, Phil
Swales, Liza

PSOs
Adamson, Liz
Allen, Elaine
Clark, Jamie
Cunningham, Mo
Kerr, Laura
Mounce, Pauline
Pickering, Lisa (p)
Rymer, Jane (p)
Wong, Jimmy

Community Payback Unit
POstill, Bill (Unit Mgr)
Williams, Gwendoline (PSO)

Practice Tutor Assessors
Birkett, Lynne (p)
Henderson, Peter
Watts, Sally (p)

Hull MAPPA Team
Humberside Police
Queens Gardens, Dock Street
Hull HU1 3DJ
Tel: 01482 480000/0845 606062

Crown Court Office
Hull Combined Courts Centre
Lowgate Hull HU1 2EZ
Tel: 01482 308635

East Riding PPO & East Riding OM Unit
8 Lord Roberts Road
Beverley
E Yorks
HU17 9BE
01482 282930
Galloway, Brenda (SPO)
Bates, Elizabeth
Fraser, Robert
Gaunt, Christine
Morrell, David
Priestley, Ray
Prout, Lisa
Street, Catherine
Walmsley, David

PSOs
Boxhall, Lesley
Duncan, Maggie

Jarvis, Louise
Throssel, Sara
Case Admin
Cawley, Rose (p)
Heath, Sue

St Johns Avenue
Bridlington E Yorks YO16 4NG
Tel: 01262 672512 Fax: 01262 400336
Atkin, Sarah (p, SPO)
Hall, Rachel (p)
Lee, Stephen
Wilson, Jennifer

PSOs
Stephenson, Lesley
Wild, Jonathon
Franks, Terry (Case Admin)

Queen Street
Grimsby NE Lincs DN31 1QG
Tel: 01472 357454 Fax: 01472 355572

Ware, Ian (Director of Probation N & NE Lincs)
Green, Jackie (Asst Director of Probation N & NE Lincs)
Barker, Sam (Bus Mgr N & NE Lincs)

Grimsby Offender Management Unit
Bolton, Wendy (SPO)
Coleman, Sarah (SPO)
Adams, Michelle
Drury, Jenny
Ford, Jo
Gillender, Clare
Lowery, Kirsten
Lynn, Kerry-Jo
Lynn, Phil
McGrath, Anne-Marie (p)
Martin, Julia (p)
Martland, Arthur
Parnell, Diane
Phillips, Kerry (p)
Ratcliffe-Cooper, Enid (p)
Sanghera, Paramjit
Sprakes, Marie
Talbot, Becky (p)
Thomas, Lorraine
Woods, Gemma
Woods, Heather

PSOs
Curtis, Nichola
Duffield, Paul
Frith, Linda (p)
Huxford, Karen
Iggo, Amanda
Jackson, Linda

Peart, Rachel

CaseAdmin
Humphries, Helen
Nesbitt, Caroline
Seward, Katie

IOM/DRR/DIP/PPO
Leake, Sonia (SPO)
Lewis, Helen
Smith, Sophie
Woods, Heather

PSOs
Cassidy, Joanne
Drinkall, Gemma
Hazzard, Laura
Hoyle, Sarah
Kirby, Jihan
Suiter, John
Whittingham, Lisa (p)
Stratford, Emma (CA)

Court Services Team
Hamilton-Rudd, Nick (SPO)
Binns, Alison (p)
Jackson, Robert
Marshall, Graham

PSOs
Austwick, Rachel
Fairbank, Martin
Hookham, Di

Victims Team
Glendenning, Dawn (PSO, WSW, VLO)

Practice Tutor Assessor
Martland, Arthur (p)

Interventions
PSO
Capes, Debbie
Doherty, Carole
Duffield, Kate
Kong, Alison

Community Payback Unit
POstill, Bill (Unit Mgr)
Blythin, Lynette (PSO)

Grimsby Crown Court
Tel: 01472 357454

Park Square
Scunthorpe N Lincs DN15 6JH
Tel: 01724 861222 Fax: 01724 289343

Ware, Ian (Director of Probation N & NE Lincs)
Green, Jackie (Asst Director of Probation N & NE Lincs)

Holland, Claire (PA)
Barker, Sam (Bus Mgr N & NE Lincs)

Scunthorpe Offender Management
Corkhill, Kirsty (SPO)
Gould, Angi (SPO)
Brown, Matthew
Christian-Cooper, Nicola
Devine, Jessica (p)
Dixon, Natalie
Dunderdale, Lucie
Harding, Keith
Hartley, Denise
Harvey, Ruth
Jones, Peter (p)
Kirby, Laura
Pitts, Alison
Taylor, Rachael (p)
Thrower, Keith
Walker, Amanda
Wright, Lizzie (p)

PSOs
Chadi, Allel
Exton, Zoe (p)
Gunn, Helen
Henry, Su (p)
Jacomb, Donna
Lings, Diane
Wilson, Ann
Case Admin
Cochrane, Hayley
Mitcheson, Claire
Westfield, Helen
Wood, Jackie

IOM
DRR/PPO
Evans, Adrian SPO
Anderson, Shaun
Emerson, Julie
Firth, Rebecca

DIP
Whitehand, Donna (PSO)

Court Services Team
Hamilton-Rudd, Nick (SPO)
Ross, Di (p)
Austwick, Rachel (PSO)
Ellse, Linda (PSO)

Interventions
Sellors Rupert (SPO)
Taylor, Donna (SPO)
Jones, Peter (p)

PSOs
Atherton, Gary
Franklin, Lyndsay

Howe, Miranda (p)
Permaine, Erica
Perry, Emma

Community Payback Unit
POstill, Bill (Unit Mgr)
Adams, Liz (PSO)

Victims' Team
Bearne, Ann (WSW)

Practice Tutor Assessor
Ratcliffe-Cooper, Enid (p)

Youth Offending Teams

Hull Youth Offending Team
Dock Office Chambers
New Cross Street Hull HU1 3DU
Tel: 01482 609991

Hookem, Michelle
Young, Pete (PSO)

East Yorkshire Youth Offending Team
Council Offices, Main Road
Skirlaugh Nr Hull HU11 5HN
Tel: 01482 396623

Peck, Julie (PO)

North Lincolnshire Youth Offending Team
22–24 Cole Street
Scunthorpe DN15 6QS
Tel: 01724 298549

NE Lincolnshire Youth Offending Team
44 Heneage Road
Grimsby DN23 9ES
Tel: 01472 325252

Chung, Emma

Approved Premises (Hostels)

41 Queens Road
Kingston-upon-Hull HU5 2QW
Tel: 01482 446284 Fax: 01482 470704

Catterson, Neil (SPO)

Assistant Wardens
Baker, Paul
Higginbottom, Chris
Jatau, Ezekiel
Robinson, Andy
Rollinson, Sonja
Scarah, Dawn
Tongrack, Joanne
Wells, Carol (AO)

Victoria House 31 Normanby Road
Scunthorpe DN15 6AS
Tel: 01724 289124 Fax: 01724 289126

Robotham, Delyse (SPO)

Assistant Wardens
Adams, John
Clarke, Peter
Evans, Tony
Hayes, David
Ives, Dean
Shepherd Chris
Spindley, Roy
Clayborough, Dawn (AO)

Institutions

HMP Hull
Hedon Road
Kingston-upon-Hull
E Yorks HU9 5LS
Tel: 01482 282200 Fax: 01482 282400

Cook, Darran (SPO)
Boyd, Christine
Heald, Fliss
Fishwick, Rachel (p)

PSOs
Allison, Maria
Birt, Chris
Burnett, Sarah
Gibson, Claire
Riby, Sam
Stainforth, Wendy
Swales, Amy

HMP Full Sutton
Moor Lane Full Sutton York YO41 1PS
Tel: 01759 475100 Fax: 01759 371206
Jackson, Caroline (SPO)
Collins, Susan
Kiddle, Jo (p)

HMP Everthorpe
Brough East Yorkshire HU15 1RB
Tel: 01430 426500 Fax: 01430 426501

Elmugadem, Mohamed (SPO)

Hastings, Joanne (p)
Haynes, David
McCartney, Sarah (p)
Newton, Becky
Winters, Chris (p)

PSOs
Foster, Helen
Rowe, Debbie
Wilkinson, Sue
Wilson, Sally

HMP Wolds
Everthorpe Brough
East Yorkshire HU15 2JZ
Tel: 01430 428000 Fax: 01430 428001

Elmugadem, Mohamed (SPO)
Smith, Pat
Futter, Suzanne (p, PSO)

Local Justice Areas
Bridlington
Beverley & The Wolds
Goole & Howdenshire
Grimsby & Cleethorpes
Hull & Holderness
North Lincolnshire

Crown Courts
Great Grimsby
Kingston-upon-Hull

KENT
PROBATION TRUST

Out of hours emergency contact tel:
Fleming House 03000 473110

Victim enquiries tel:
Maidstone 01622 202120

Email:
firstname.lastname@kent.probation.gsi.gov.uk

Area Office
Chaucer House 25 Knightrider Street
Maidstone ME15 6ND
Tel: 03000 473040 Fax: 01622 751638
Direct Dials 03000+ ext below

Billiald, Sarah (Chief Executive) 473015
Baillieu, Adrian (Dir of Corporate
Services) 473001
Hazell, Sandy (p, PA Board Sec) 473028
Preston, Helen (Dir of Organisational
Effectiveness) 473014
Jarvis, Collette (head of bus improvement
& people dev) 473150

Communications
Boulden, Michelle (Comms Officer)
473011
Mattison, David (Communications
Developer) 473010

Diversity
Dowarris, Colin (p, Diversity Mgr)
473009

Estates & Area Office Admin
McCarthy, Anne (Area Bus Mgr) 473003
Vacancy (Bus Mgr) 473019

Finance
Collins, Pauline (Finance Mgr) 473025
Jacques, Julia (Payroll Mgr) 473039

H&S Officer
Wilson, David (H&S Officer) Tel: 01795
662651, Fax: 01795 429622

Human Resources
Davis, Caroline (Head of HR) 473007
Brace, Dawn (HR Officer) 473023
Jones, Laura (p, HR Officer) 473018
Judd, Stephanie (HR Officer) 473013
Bradford, Emma (p, HR Asst) 473627
Fuller, Tracey (p, HR Asst) 473627
Harley, Elaine (p, HR Admin) 473012
Hayler, Paul (HR Asst) 473032

Professional Development Managers
Coley, David (based Maidstone)
Peall, Jeanne (p, based Gravesend)
Puce, Eriks (based at Canterbury)

Learning & Development Department
Ralphs Centre, 24 Maynard Road
Wincheap Estate
Canterbury CT1 3RH
Tel: 03000 473154 Fax: 03000 473210
Tel: 03000 473185 Fax: 03000 473210
Peall, Jeanne (p, SPO, PDM based at
Gravesend) 03000 473163
Port, Jane (Training Delivery Mgr) 03000
473558
Wilding, Rebecca (Learning & Devpt
Admin) 03000 473182
Markelyte, Inga (Traing & Development
Administrator) 03000 473163

Finance, Performance & Standards

Performance & Standards
Preston, Helen (Dir Organisational
Effectiveness)
(based at Chaucer House) 03000 473014
Prudhomme, Barbara (PA/Support
SPOC) 03000 473005
Coldwell, Jacq (SFO SPOC/co-or) 03000
473016

Quality/Lean Team
(based at Chaucer House)
Vacancy (Quality Mgr) 03000 473038
Mason, Denise (Lean Off) (based at
Tunbridge Wells)

Performance & Standards Unit (PSU)
58 College Road Maidstone ME15 6SJ
Tel: 03000 473216 Fax: 01622 697101
Email: is.unit@kent.probation.gsi.gov.uk

Webb, Peter (IT Infrastructure Mgr) 03000 473330
Wickens, Julie (PSU Mgr) 03000 473318
Wright, Julie (PSU Mgr) 03000 473314
Craker, Vicky (Term-time ICT Training Off) 03000 473348
Bamblett, Peter (Tech Support Off) 03000 473331
Sanders, Steven (Tech Support Off) (Canterbury) 03000 473186

Performance & Standards
(based at Chaucer House) 03000 473040
Jacques, Rob (Business Intelligence Mgr) 03000 473026
Kennedy, Mark (Perf Analyst) 03000 473021
Baker, Ricky (Performance Analyst Support Officer)

Interventions Commissioning & Partnerships

Business Development
Chaucer House, 25 Knightrider Street Maidstone ME15 6ND
Tel: 03000473040 Fax: 01622 751638
Email: business.development@kent.probation.gsi.gov.uk

Clark, Robert (Dir Bus Development)
Cohn, Howard (Commissioning Mgr)
Gardner, David (Comm Mgr Health & Subs Misuse)
Franks, Michelle (Business Analyst & Support Off)

Community Payback

Management Office
27–35 New Road Chatham ME4 4QQ
Tel: 03000 473100 Fax: 03000 473470

Binning, Suki (Dir of Interventions) based at Gravesend (03000 473599)
Lee, Carol (Resource Mgr) based at Canterbury (03000 473412)
Watson, Sara (PA) based at Gravesend (03000 473525)

CP Resource Team
Tel: 03000 473100 Fax: 03000 473470

Bravo, Chrissie (Resource Admin) (03000 473632)
Gage, Natalie (Resource Admin) (03000 473441)
Wells, Louise (Resource Admin) (03000 473437)
Ellis-Shrubsole, Julie (Resource Admin) (03000 473495)
Bennett, Justin (Education & Training Coord) (03000 473431)

East Kent District
Cullen, Stuart (CP Mgr)
Tel: 03000 473457

(covering Ashford, Folkestone, Canterbury, Thanet & Dover)

Folkestone
Tel: 03000 473219
Gooding, Michelle (PSO-CP) 03000 473257
Sas-Bilinska, Joanna (Placement Officer-CP) (03000 473602)
Wilkinson, Jane (PSO-CP) 03000 473602

Canterbury
Tel: 03000 473154
Gregory, Hazel (Placement Officer-CP) (03000 473206)
Stapleford, Kerry (PSO-CP) (03000 473604)

Thanet
Tel: 03000 473218

Craig, Ian (Placement Officer CP) 03000 473385
Foster, Gary (PSO-CP) 03000 473247

Central & West Kent District
Majuqwana, Alison (CP Mgr) (03000 473294)

(covering Maidstone, Swale & Tunbridge Wells)
Brown, Gemma (Placement Officer – CP) (03000 473651)
Foster, Gary J (Placement Officer-CP) (03000 473385)
Harvey, Emily (PSO-CP) (03000 473604)

Jenkinson, Linda (PSO-CP) (03000 473325)
Turner, Kathleen (PSO-CP) (03000 473321)
Morris, Christopher (PO/QDO) (03000 473611)

North Kent District
Simpson, Liz (CP Mgr) (03000 473 019)

(covering Gravesend & Medway)

Gravesend
Legg, Pat (PSO-CP) (03000 473060)
Pluck, Steve (Placement Officer-CP)
(03000 473063)

Medway
Crealock, Nick (PSO-CP) (03000 473443)
Kirby, Kevin (PSO-CP) (03000 473433)
VACANCY (PSO-CP)
Woolley, Allan (Placement Officer-CP)
(03000 473548)

ETE Team
58 College Road
Maidstone ME15 6SJ
Tel: 01622 687521 Fax: 01622 697101
Email: unit mail box: ETE Team

Leigh, Donna (ETE Commissioning Mgr)
ext 134
Hammond, Jodie (ETE County Admin)
01622 697117
Heywood, Tara (ETE Business Admin)
01622 687521

ETE Officers
Austen, Louise (Folkestone & Dover)
03000 473122
Burls, Glynis (Thanet & Canterbury)
01843 227479; 01227 769345
Macey, Gemma (Sittingbourne &
Sheerness) 01795 423321
Read, Emma (Gravesend & Medway)
03000 473487
Treharne, Janet (Maidstone & Tunbridge
Wells) 01622 687521

ETE Groupwork Tutors
Attack, Claire (p) (Maidstone) 01622
687521

Job Deal
Mepham, Pamela (Project Mgr)
Haddon, Sally (p, Caseworker) 03000
473335

Sex Offender Resource Team (SORT)
58 College Road
Maidstone ME15 6SJ
Tel: 01622 687521 Fax: 01622 697101
ADMIN FOR SORT NOW 27–35 NEW
ROAD, CHATHAM, KENT ME4 4QQ
Tel: 03000 473217 Fax: 01634 400522
Ratledge, Paula (Operations Mgr –
Canterbury) 03000 473162)

Maurice, Carol (Medway (Admin) 03000
473413

Programme Facilitators
Wallace, Tracey (Medway)
Campbell, Henry (PO) (Gravesend)
03000 473047
Fyles, Susan (PO) (Canterbury) 03000
473184
Goulbourne, Theresa (p, PO) (Thanet)
03000 473532
Hammond, Claire (PO) (Canterbury)
03000 473149
Hay, Jenny (PO, Treatment Mgr)
(Maidstone) 01622 697120
Smith, Laura (PO SOGP) 473055

General Offender Behaviour Programmes
27–35 New Road
Chatham ME4 4QQ
Tel: 03000 473217 Fax: 01634 400522

Maurice, Carol (Groupwork Coord,
Medway) 03000 473413

Ratledge, Paula (Op Mgr – Accredited
Prog. Canterbury) 03000 473162

Programme Facilitators
Clark, Hayley (PSO, Canterbury) 03000
473159
Henderson, Nichola (PSO, Canterbury)
03000 473176
Hughes, Cath (PSO, Medway) 03000
473414
Jagger, Maria (PSO, Medway) 03000
473439

Treatment Managers
Crealock, Carol (Canterbury) 03000
473146
Doherty, Fiona (Canterbury) 03000
473157
Wheal, Sarah (Medway) 03000 473453

Mentor Unit
Vacancy (Comm Serv Unit Resource
Mgr) (based Medway) (03000 473517)

Private Drink Drive
Gibson, Catherine (p, Admin) (based
Medway) 03000 473414

Offender Management

Court Services Team
Probation Office Maidstone Crown Court
The Law Courts Barker Road
Maidstone ME16 8EQ
Tel: 01622 202121 Fax: 01622 677312

King, Barney

PSOs
Smedley, Georgia
Stevens, Julie
Strydom, Angela
Wilson, Susan

Canterbury Crown Court
Liaison Probation Office The Law Courts
Chaucer Road Canterbury CT1 1ZA
Tel: 01227 819299/819301 Fax: 01227
764961
Williams, Susan-Anne
Jeacock, Linda (SPO)
Sookun, Prakash (PSO)

Magistrates' Court Staff

Canterbury
Tel/fax: 01227 766254
Gillon, Anne (03000 473144)
Gurr, Michaela

Thanet
Tel/fax: 01843 223297
Lawrence, Carmen (473509)
Lovell, Christine (473510)

Folkestone & Ashford
Neve, Susan (PSO) 01303 852134
Rickwood, Helen (PSO) 01303 852134
Williams, David (PSO) 01233 650637

Dartford
Tel: 01474 569546

Louch, Deborah
Watson, Stewart

Maidstone
Tel: 01622 661897

Vacancy

Sevenoaks
Tel: 01732 460353
Hooper, Laura (PO)

Tunbridge Wells
Tel: 01892 559350

Medway
Tel: 01634 849284
Russell, Ishbell
Harvey, Nick
Webb, Laura
Grenhalgh, Julie

Swale
Tel: 01795 475782

East Kent
Allen, Cynthia (Director of East Kent)
03000 473151
Redman, Julia (Dist Bus Mgr) 03000
473167
Lowry, Caroline (PA/Sec to Dis Mgr)
(based at Canterbury) 03000 473148
Fax: 01227 785143

(*covers Canterbury, Dover, Folkestone,
Ashford and Thanet*)

Canterbury Unit
Ralphs Centre 24 Maynard Road
Wincheap Estate Canterbury CT1 3RH
Tel: 03000 473154 Fax: 01227 85992

Callingham, Debbie (SPO) 03000 473180
Sahagian, Karen (Bus Mgr) 03000 473169
Bassett, Linda (03000 473170)
Corkhill, Rebecca (Progs)
Fyles, Susan (Sort) 03000 473184
Gillon, Anne (03000 473144)
Goldspring, Joanne (p)
Gurr, Michaela
Hammond, Claire (Sort) 03000 473149
Harris, Rachel (03000 473178) (PO &
Quality Dev Officer)
Hollins, Sue (p, Treatment Mgr, IDAP)
03000 473189
Moore, William (03000 473196)
Ruck, Abbie (PPO & IOM Coord) (02000
473141)
Thompson, Jan (Manager Mentor Unit)
03000 473164
Walczak, Rebecca (03000 473181)
Williams, Sue (03000 473190)
Puce, Eriks (PDM) 03000 473156
Crealock, Carol (Treatment Mgr) 03000
473146
Doherty, Fiona (Treatment Mgr) 03000
473157
Holloway, Suzanne (Women's Safety Wkr)
03000 473193

PSOs
Clark, Hayley (Prog Facilitator) 03000
473159
Curteis, Michael (03000 473175)
Harrison, Caroline (p) (03000 473147)
Hawksworth, Jeremy (Prog, IDAP) 03000
473165
Henderson, Nichola (Prog Facilitator)
03000 473176
Hughes, Cath (PSO Accredited
Programmes) 03000 473414
Mason, Alison (03000 473142)
Medlock, Pam (PSO) 03000 473445

Reeves, Tania (p) 03000 473194
Talbot, Lizzie IOM Support Off

Folkestone & Ashford Unit
The Law Courts Castle Hill Avenue
Folkestone CT20 2DH
Tel: 03000 473219 Fax: 03000
473280/473279

Barry, John (SPO) 473254
Kenny, Jo (SPO) 473253
Ling, Sarah (Bus Mgr) 473286
Boarder, Ellie
Boddington, Anita (PO & Quality Dev
Off) 473237
Bywater, Elizabeth (p, Sort)
Callister, Andy (p) 473236
Cox, Martin
Hadden, Richard (473261)
Heskett, Craig (473242)
Ivory, Tessa (p) 473267
Mowbray, David (473243)
Raeburn, Stephen (p) 473231
Soloman, Laura (p) 473255
Squire, Stephen (473233)
Stockle, Anthony (473269)
Wills, Tina
Wright, Stanley (473230)

PSOs
Evenden, Colin (473223)
Gough, Carly (p) 473239
Grace, Hedley (p) 473250
Hayward, Anna 473238
Hyden, Heather 473250
Jones, Romi (p) 473262
Lavelle, Jeanette (p) 473579
Morris, Wendy (p) 473270
O'Reilly, Jess
Rasmussen, Nichola (p) 473260
Stabler, Jim (473226)

Thanet Unit
38/40 Grosvenor Place
Margate CT9 1UW
Tel: 03000 473218 Fax: 01843 292958
Director Dial (03000+ no below)

Johnston, Mark (SPO) 473522
Scarr, Claire (p, SPO & p. Investigations
Off) 473417
Sahagian, Karen (Bus Mgr) 473169
Cesbron, Ben 473507
Cox, Deborah 473511
Davies, David 473224
Goulbourne, Theresa (p, Sort) 473532
Lawrence, Carmen (473509)
Lister, Jane (473514)

Lovell, Christine (473510)
Reader, Sally (p)
Ryder, Anne (473514)
Stevens, Candice (473508)
Wildman, Jennifer (p) 473516
Clarke, Terri (VLO) 473531

PSOs
Brackley, Amanda (Women's Safety Wkr)
473505
Cossell, Susan (473529)
Ford, Malcolm (p) 473172
Jones, Sarah 473526
Lewis, Janette 473515
Nicolaou, Sophie (473528)
Ruck, Wendy 473533
Smith, Julie (p) 473519

Central & West Kent
Kadir, Tracey (Director of Central & West
Kent)
Robinson, Danny (Dist Bus Mgr)
McGhie, Yvonne (PA Sec)
(based at Maidstone) 01622 687521

(*covering Maidstone, Swale & Tunbridge
Wells*)

Maidstone Unit
56–58 College Road
Maidstone ME15 6SJ
Tel: 01622 687521 Fax: 01622 697101

Hook, Heather (SPO & Investigation Off)
Coley, David (PDM)
Thomson, Kelly (SPO)
Doyle, Nick (PO)
Tancred, Tania (Snr Psychologist)
Smith, Jan (Bus Mgr)
Balsamo, Delaine
Bratton, Jane
Callar, Brian (Courts PO & Quality Dev
Off)
Goulbourne, Teresa (p)
Hay, Jenny (Sort, Treatment Mgr)
Plaiche, Aline
Sandy, Corinne (OM/Courts PO)
Smith, Tracy
Udale, Lisa
Wood, Richard

PSOs
Greenaway, Rose
Ludlow, Jacqueline
Marriott, Andrew
Marsh, Yvonne
Moat, Tina
Robinson, Carol (p)
Smith, Robin

Spekes, Melissa
Vardy, Ashley
Willock, Louise
Roberts, Sarah (Perf & Data Support Off)

Swale Unit
*Sittingbourne & Sheerness have been
amalgamated.
All phone calls and faxes to Sittingbourne.*

Thames House Roman Square
Sittingbourne ME10 4BJ
Tel: 01795 423321 Fax: 01795 474251
46 High Street
Sheerness ME12 1NL
Fax: 01795 663240
Houghton, Lynda (SPO)
Gardner, David (SPO)
Godmon, Karen
Kirk, Johanna (p)
Port, Jane (PO & Quality Dev Off)
Sampson, Jackie
Tindall, Pam
Varker, Annette
Williams, Debra
Willis, Sue (p)
Wood, Andrew (p)
Berry, Karen (p, VLO)
Macey, Gemma (ETE Off)

PSOs
Baldock, Jayne
Bunn, Sandra
Davis, Kevin
Dummott, Karen (p)
Foreman, Josie
Goodwin, Jayne
Ince, Donna
Marchant, Clive
Matthews, Daphne (p, Progs)
Shaw, Liz (p)

Tunbridge Wells Unit
17 Garden Road
Tunbridge Wells TN1 2XP
Tel: 03000 473130 Fax: 03000 473139
Direct Dials 03000+ ext below

Wickens, Joanne (SPO, also covering
courts)

Hall, Julie (SPO)
Collison, Mark 473131
Crocker, Alan
Gosling, Becki
Griffiths, Paul 473134
Henderson, Kathryn (p) 473127
Hooper, Laura 473129
Kimber, Kevin 473128

Lane, Jane 473135
Nightingale, Nadine 473133
O'Sullivan, Chloe (PO & Quality Dev Off)
473119
Strong, Thomas 473137
Tomlinson, Rachel (p)

PSOs
Boon, Stephen
Baker, Alison (p) 473116
Dicks, Jacqueline
Lindeman, Anna
McCulloch, Susan
McVeigh, Vanessa 473138
Paterson, Tami 473136

North Kent
O'Reilly, Maurice (Director of North
Kent) 03000 473440
Wickens, Tina (Dist Bus Mgr) 03000
473459
Roberts, Diane (PA/Sec to Dist Mgr)
03000 473423
(based at Medway)

(*covering Gravesend & Medway/Chatham*)

Dartford & Gravesham
Joynes House New Road
Gravesend DA11 0AT
Tel: 03000 473058 Fax: 03000 473070
Moyse, Susan (SPO) 473054
Peel, Steve (SPO)
Mason, Toni (Bus Mgr) 473461
Berry, Chas 473046
Burr, Fran 473643
Campbell, Henry (Sort) 473047
Choudhury, Rejaur 473058
Dorrell, Karen (p) 473052
Harris, James 473048
Logan, Sue 473065
Morris, James 473049
Peall, Jeanne (p, Professional Devp Mgr)
473050
Tupper, Kelly 473647
Watson, Stewart 473064
Whitwell, Jenny (p) 473051

PSOs
Burns, Kim 473053
Dodd, Steve 473061
Sandhu, Kininjit 473634
Lucas, Toneka 473067
Flood, Trish (p) 473068
Roe, Julie 473058
Sharp, Carole 473045
Taft Morris, Lesley (p) 473056
Davey, Una 473095

Burgess, Marcus (Perf & Data Support Off) 473057

Medway Unit
27–35 New Road Chatham ME4 4QQ
Tel: 03000 473217 Fax: 03000 473467
Direct Dials 03000+ ext below
Faturoti, Laura (SPO) 473054
Whittall, Andrea (SPO) 473524
Harris, Sonia (p, SPO SFOs, SPO Victim Liaison) 473455
Mason, Toni (Bus Mgr) 473461
Leggatt, Cheri (BA) 473416
Akers, Joanne (p) 473438
Ashley, David 473217
Campbell, Valerie 473650
Graham, Trudie 473463
Greenhalgh, Julie 473633
Harvey, Nick 473444
Hughes, Pauline (p) 473448
Leek, Katherine (p) 473490
Linton, Donna (473096)
Munn, Davina 473418
Plank, Sally 473450
Rawlings, Kelly (p, PO) 473491
Samuda, Evonne 473424
Smith, Laura 473055 (PO SOGP)
Webb, Laura 473434
Thompson, Allison (PO & Quality Dev Off) 473409
Jagger, Maria (Accred Prog Coord) 473439
Maurice, Carol (Accred Prog Coord) 473413
Conelly, Tracey (VLO) 473462

PSOs
Alderson-Rice, Nick 473442
Andreou, Theo 473458
Baker, Katie (p) 473494
Cooney, Bernard 473607
Dix, Dannielle (PO & VQ Assessor) 473592
Eva, Diane 473422
Gooderham, Katie 473101
Hastings, Clare 473608
Hayes, Simon 473454
Keable, Angela 473410
Laverie, Deborah 473421
Ravate, Dawn (PSO)
Sanders, Jodie 473429
Silvey, Sonja (p) 473465
Tremain, Julie 473430
Wheal, Sarah (Treatment Mgr) 473453
Bennett, Justin (ETE Coord) 473431
Baker, Alison (CA) 473408
Attack, Carol (CA) 473411

Glykys, Karen (CA) 473432
White, Lorraine (CA) 473436
Edwards, Kayleigh (CA) 473630
Windley, Wendy (CA) 473465
Greenwood, Sarah (CA) 473452

Public Protection
Approved Premises (Hostel)

Fleming House
32 Tonbridge Road
Maidstone ME16 8SH
Tel: 03000 473110 Fax: 01622 685249
Direct Dials 03000+ ext below
Email: unit mail box: Fleming House
Hughes, Tina (SPO Mgr) 473112
Vecchiolla, Emma (Temp Dep Mgr) 473110
PSO/Office Supervisors
Curtis, Joanne (p) 473110
McDermott, Sally
McGrath, Richard
Sandhu, Kirinjit
Turner, Lewis
Lawrence, Sharon (CA) 473110
May, Theresa (Finance Admin) 473111
Waking Night Supervisors
Bourne, Nicholas
Boyd, Andy
Suleyman, Muzahir
Twining, John (Night Support Worker)

MAPPA Joint Coordination Team

Kent Police HQ
Sutton Road Maidstone ME15 9BZ
Tel: 01622 650459 Fax: 01622 654679
Gibson, Isobel (Det Chief Inspector)
Horton, Vicki (Police MAPPA Admin)
Brooks, Fiona (MAPPA Admin)
DeFroand, Sara (MAPPA Admin)
Bennewitz, Tristen (Visor Admin)
Jezusek, Teresa (p, Visitor Admin)

Medway Police Station
Eastbridge Purser Way Gillingham ME7 1NE
Tel: 01634 792444 Direct dial: 04 2444
Fax: 01634 792249
Mob: 07807 340205

Brown, Deborah (PPO Coord – Medway) 03000 473420

Victim Liaison Service
27–35 New Road
Chatham ME4 4QQ
Tel: 03000 473217 Fax: 03000 473467

Harris, Sonia (p, SPO, Victim Liaison)
03000 473455

Scanlan, Paula (VL Admin) 03000 473447

Goodwin, Jo (PSO)
Berry, Karen (p, VLO) (Sheerness)
Clarke, Terri (VLO) (Thanet)
Conelly, Tracey (VLO) (Medway)
Barber, Sharon (p, VLO) (Maidstone)
King, Joanna (Admin IDAP (Canterbury)
03000 473166
Brackley, Amanda (p, Women's Safety
Wkr based Thanet)
Holloway, Suzanne (Women's Safety Wkr
based Canterbury)

Criminal Justice Partners
Youth Offending Teams

East Kent
Apollo House Chapel Place
Ramsgate CT11 9SA
Tel: 01843 587976 Fax: 01843 590009

Townsend, Sian

Avenue of Remembrance
Sittingbourne ME10 4DD
Tel: 01795 473333 Fax: 01795 420016

Central & West Kent
Bishops Terrace Bishops Way
Maidstone ME14 1LA
Tel: 01622 772149 Fax: 01622 772104

Burr, Fran
Bennett, Peter

Queen's House Guildhall Street
Folkestone CT20 1DX
Tel: 01303 224287 Fax: 01303 224329

Corkill, Rebbeca

West Kent
Joynes House New Road
Gravesend DA11 0AT
Tel: 01474 544366 Fax: 01474 544569

Vacancy

Social Services Department
Croft House East Street
Tonbridge TN9 1HP
Tel: 01732 362442 Fax: 01732 352733

Burr, Fran

Medway Area
The Family and Adolescent Centre
67 Balfour Road Chatham ME4 6QU
Tel: 01634 336223 Fax: 01634 336260

Kramer, Julie (p)
Laws, Jackie (PSO)

Institutions

HMYOI Rochester
1 Fort Road Rochester ME1 3QS
Tel: 01634 803100 Fax: 01634 803101
Direct dial: 80 + ext

Parole Clerk tel: 01634 803032
Discipline tel: 01634 803211
Special visits tel: 01634 803350

Kempster, Leanne (Resettlement Mgr &
Public Protection) ext 3213
Greenhalgh, Julie (Resettlement Mgr &
Offender Supvr) ext 3030
Moss, Cheryl (PSO Offender Supvr) ext
3177
Willoughby, Emma (PSO, Offender
Supvr) ext 3024

Sheppey Prison Cluster Probation Team

HMP Standford Hill
Church Road Eastchurch
Sheerness ME12 4AA
Tel: 01795 884500 Fax: 01795 880041
Direct dial: 01795 88 + ext
OMU ext 4777

Pellatt, Kate (SPO) Head of Public
Protection based at Swaleside
Sennett, Paul ext 4780
Brown, Janet (PSO) ext 4780

HMP Swaleside
Brabazon Road Eastchurch
Sheerness ME12 4AX
Tel: 01795 804100 Fax: 01795 804200;
01795 804128 (probation)
Direct dial: 01795 80 + ext
Tel: 01795 804102 (SPO Office)
Tel: 01795 804137 (Probation Officer)
Fax: 01795 804128
OMU ext 4025
Lifer Clerks ext 4166
Special visits ext 4177/4187
Email:
visitsbookingswaleside@hmps.gsi.gov.uk

Pellatt, Kate (SPO, Head of Public
Protection based at Swaleside)
Campbell, Valerie ext 4128
Dold, Gavin ext 4137
Gurr, Michaela ext 4103
Allison, Marie (p, PSO) ext 4103

HMP Elmley
Church Road Eastchurch
Isle of Sheppey ME12 4AY
Tel: 01795 882000 Fax: 01795 882001
Direct dial: 01795 88 + ext
OMU (Sheppey Cluster Public Protection Coord)
Knott, Louise ext 2154
Martin, Sarah ext 2230
Legal visits tel: 01795 882327

Pellatt, Kate (SPO, Head of Public Protection based at Swaleside)
Nicolaides, Michael (DSPO, Dep Head of Public Protection) ext 2074
Coleman, Deborah ext 2065
Green, Joseph ext 2065
Vacancy ext 2065
Young, Pam ext 2053
Bail info tel: 01795 882288
Fax: 01795 880140

HMP Maidstone
36 County Road Maidstone ME14 1UZ
Tel: 01622 775332 Fax: 01622 775487
Probation Clerk tel: 5380

Williams, Jessica (SPO)

Peel, Steve (SPO Head of Public Protection) ext 5332
Email: steve.peel@hmps.gsi.gov.uk
Alexander, Sara ext 5498
Emes, Jenny ext 5382
Gooderham, Katie ext 5356
Hambly, Gemma ext 5481
Thomson, Helen ext 5477
Vacancy ext 5356

HMP/YOI East Sutton Park
Sutton Valence Maidstone ME17 3DF
Tel: 01622 785000 Fax: 01622 785019
Direct dial: 01622 785 + ext
Probation Clerk tel: ext 5060/5061/5066

Vacancy (p, SPO based HMYOI Rochester)
Nettleton, Terry ext 5036
Wall, Delia (p, PSO) ext 5079

HMP Canterbury
46 Longport Canterbury CT1 1PJ
Tel: 01227 862800 Fax: 01227 862801

(*There are no probation staff in HMP Canterbury as the population are foreign nationals.*)

HMP Blantyre House
Goudhurst Cranbrook TN17 2NH
Tel: 01580 213200 Fax: 01580 211060

King, Patricia

Local Justice Areas
Central Kent (*Thanet, Maidstone and Swale Units*)
East Kent (Court Services Team Maidstone, Probation Office Canterbury Crown Court, Magistrates' Court staff)
North Kent (Canterbury and Thanet Units)

Crown Courts
Canterbury
Maidstone

LANCASHIRE PROBATION TRUST

Out of hours emergency tel: 01254 395997

Central Bail Referral no: 01254 832299

Email:
firstname.lastname@lancashire.probation.gsi.gov.uk

Head Office
99–101 Garstang Road
Preston PR1 1LD
Tel: 01772 201209 Fax: 01772 884399
Robinson, Kevin (Chief Executive)
Barker, Penny (Director of Operations)
McKevitt, Kerry (Director of HR)
Mattinson, Louise (Director of Finance)
Thompson, Geraldine Byrne (Assistant Chief Executive Business & Commercial Development)
Mayo, Anne (Secretary to Board)

Communications
Preston, Roger (SPO)
Rees, Lucy (Communications Mgr)
Williamson, James (Communications Officer)

Finance
Gwen Knowles (Payroll Officer)
Doyle, Sam (Admin Officer)
Douglas, Rachel (Assistant Management Accountant)
Milroy, Stephen (Financial Accountant)
Simons, Gaynor (Management Accountant)
McGuirk, Lydia (Finance & IT Assistant)

HR Team & Staff Development Unit
Woods, Richard (HR Mgr)
Hall, Susan (OD Mgr)
Ogdon, Karen (HR Officer)
Turner, Clare (HR Officer)
Chati, Imran (HR Officer)
Ahmed, Bilal (HRD Support Officer)
Kirkby, Maureen (HRD Support Officer)
McNeela, Harriet (HRD Support Officer)
Ward, Ann Marie (Org Dev Officer)
Bradley, Stephanie (HR Assistant)

Health and Safety
Hamer, Natalie (H&S Advisor)
Executive Support
Crossland, Bev (Secretary)
Blackburn, Dawn (Secretary)
Hartley, Rachael (Secretary)
Staton, Jill (Secretary)
Holmes, Sandra (Secretary)
Flatley, Daniel (Executive Support
Assistant)
Admin
Halsall, Janice (Receptionist/Typist)
Mcloughlin, Sandra (Receptionist/Typist)

Information Unit
Pourmahak, Mahmood (ICT Systems
Administrator)
Johnson, Kim (Info & Statistics Officer)
Allsop, Mark (Info Service Mgr)
St John-Foti, Diane (Info Systems Officer)
Hussian, Saquib (Service Desk Officer)
Brooks, Paul (Applications Developer)

Business and Commercial Development Team
Dyer, Rachel (Business and Commercial
Development Mgr)
Tune, Linda (Business and Commercial
Development Officer – Projects)
Bowler, Jonathon (Business and
Commercial Development Officer –
Contracts)
Mohammed, Sajid (Administrator)

Business Process Team
Clarke, Dr. Charlotte (Mgr)
Birkett, Lee (Co-ordinator)
Conley, Elizabeth (Co-ordinator)

Corporate Services Team
Smith, Debbie (Mgr)
Higson, Sheila (Procurement
Co-ordinator)
Smith, Darren (Estates Co-ordinator)
Atherton, David (Admin)

Unit 1 Block B

Albert Edward House
The Pavilions **Preston** PR2 2YB
Tel: 01772 256630 Fax: 01772 208540
Booth, Lynda (Project Mgr)
Beddow, David (Team Mgr)
Foster, Jane (PO/Union Rep)

Performance Quality Standards Unit
Seed, Elaine (PQSU Acting PO)
Lawson, Amanda (PQSU Accrington)
Kett, Alison (PQSU Burnley)
Johnson, Lisa (PQSU Blackpool)
Wilson, Joy (PQSU Lancaster)

Peripatetic Team
Roger, Peel
Finnesey, Jane
Lauraus
Ferguson, Diane (Learning and
Assessment Officer) (AEH)
Giddings, Melanie (Learning &
Assessment Officer) (AEH)
Whittaker, Pamela (Quality Assurance
Mgr) (Old Roan Liverpool)
Fairclough, Emma (Practice Development
Assessor) (Lancaster)

Eastern
84 Burnley Road **Accrington** BB5 1AF
Tel: 01254 232516 Fax: 01254 396160

Offender Management
McCloy, Kirsten (SPO)
Shinks, Elaine (SPO)

POs
Cookson, Gayle
Dornan, Liz
Edmondson, Alison
Hall, Elizabeth
Hamid, Sobia
Haynes, Michelle
Hopewell, Keith
Kay, Jonathan
Kimberly, Gayle
Musker, Heidi
Parkinson, Christopher
Przybysz, Linda
Rodgers, Susan
Standing, Deborah
Torczuk, Raymond
Learner Practitioner POFs
Ahmed, Tahir
Port, Steven

PSOs
Bromley, Shirley
Drabble, Jackie

Molloy, Dan
Shouib, Kanwal
Smith, Fiona
Treitl, Linda
Walker, Stephen

Community Payback
Holt, John (Project Supervisor)

Achieve
Chati, Zubeir (Case Manager)

Sumner Building
40b Preston New Road
Blackburn BB2 6AH
Tel: 01254 265221 Fax: 01254 685385
Thomas, Janet (Assistant Chief
Executive)
Bange, Joanne (DM Secretary)
Admin
Etherington, Beverley (Office Mgr)

13/15 Wellington Street
St Johns **Blackburn** BB1 8AF
Tel: 01254 265221 Fax: 01254 697852

Offender Management
Daud, Mohammed (District Information
Systems Officer)
Cass, Andrew (IOM Manager)

SPOs
Moses, Richard
Kenny, Mick
Sunderland, Marcus

POs
Banks, Bernadette
Beardsworth, Jenna
Bent, Sarah
Bridgeman, Paul
Chadderton, Sheila
Cooper, Steven
Commisioning, Michael
Davies, Mary
Dryden-Bircher, Danielle
Elwell, Irene
Emmot, Pauline
Endicott, Coleen
Jordan, Joanne
Lambert, Jeremy
Mack, Liam
Moorhouse, Beverley
Singleton, Janette
Small, Helena
Spokes, Craig
Stone, Sharon
Wilson, John
Learner Practitioner POFs

Cardwell, Emma
Hurst, Kevin
Law, Ben

PSOs
Caddy, Sara
Crook, Christine
Desai, Rukshana
Foster, Jaqueline
Gough, Kay
Maden, Helen
Moor, Wendy
Nolan, Lynne
O'Hanlon, Sharon
Pollard, Wendy
Ramsden, Joanne
Solkar, Akeela
Sharples, Jeremy

Programmes
Harrison, Phillippa
Walmsley, Jason

Community Payback
Luke, David (Project Supervisor)

Victims
Socratous, Kirsty (PSO)

Achieve
Chati, Fahim (Case Mgr)

Probation Centre
55 Preston New Road
Blackburn BB2 6AY
Tel: 01254 261764 Fax: 01254 53603

Programmes
Smith, Louise (Treatment Manager)
Walker, Hayley (PSO)

**Probation Department Burnley
Combined Court**
PO Box 30 Hammerton Street Burnley
BB11 1XD
Tel: 01282 855344 Fax: 01282 455211

Powel, Nicholas (PSO)

Birkett, Kate (PSO)

1st Floor Stephen House
Bethesda Street **Burnley** BB11 1QW
Tel: 01282 425854 Fax: 01282 838947
Lock, Linda (Assistant Chief Executive)

Offender Management
Strachan, Ian (SPO)
Watson, Pauline (SPO)
Willetts, Rachel (SPO)

Pollard, Michelle (Public Protection Manager)

POs
Campbell, Colin
Cridford, Stephen
Entwistle, Stephen
Green, Lesley
Hartwell, Susan
Johnson, Christine
Johnson, Wendy
Leeming, Jackie
Mattison, James
Rudkin, Elise
Smith, Ray
Uttley, Catherine
Waterworth, John
Bedford, Ruth (Learner Practitioner PQF)

PSOs
Brierley, Christine
Caddy, Sara
Dawson, Anna
Greenwood, Nicola
Johnson, Cathy
Parker, Elaine
Peel, Victoria
Pollard, Barbara
Slater, Peter
Sharples, Jeremy
Todd, Zoe
Tomlinson, Lindsey
Williams, Victoria

Programmes
PSOs
Green, Zoe
Harrison, Philipa
Johnson, David

Community Payback
Slater, Lorraine (Practice Mgr)

Project Supervisors
Fort, Barry
Stanworth, Peter
Zia, Majid

Victims
Warbrick, Louise

Admin
Brittain, Anna (Admin Officer)
Richardson, Pauline (Office Mgr)

25 Manchester Road
Nelson BB9 9YB
Tel: 01282 615155 Fax: 01282 619693

Offender Management
Munro, Anne (SPO)

POs
Fryer, Kate
Matson, David
O'Connor, Alan
Pearson, Emma
Roberts, Alyson
Roberts, Marie
Ross, Roderick
Taylor, Michael
Learner Practitioner POF
Gildea, Peter
Winter, Diane

PSOs
Cox, John
Eatough, Geoffrey
Khan, Imrana

Community Payback
Project Supervisors
Blezard, Paul
Sargeant, Michael

Achieve
Sullivan, Barry (Case Mgr)

Central/Southern

The Crown Court
The Law Courts
Ring Way **Preston** PR1 2LL
Tel: 01772 844799 Fax: 01772 844788
Flynn, Jeanette (SPO)

POs
Collum, Seamus
Green, Julie
Imisson, Jo

PSOs
Calvert, Barbara
Evans, Justine

50 Avenham Street
Preston PR1 3BN
Tel: 01772 552700 Fax: 01772 552701

Offender Management
O'Donnell, Philip (Assistant Chief Executive)
Javed, Anna (SPO)
Harker, Jane (SPO)
Whitehouse, Martin (SPO)
Michelbach, Hayley (DM Secretary)
Boydell-Cupitt, Susan (SPO)
Harker, Jane (SPO)
Beddow, David (OMI Project Team Leader)

POs
Ainsworth, Claire
Barker, Alexandra
Barrass, sherry
Booth, Sophie
Brooks, Patricia
Caine, Carol
Carr, Susan
Chester, Eve
Craven, Rachel
Deasha, Greg
Gilmore, Rachel
Hesketh, Phiona
Howard, Lawrence
Johnrose, Peter
Loxley, Sarah
McBride, Kieran
Mayren, Scott
Micallef, Linda
Mounsey, Claire
Peel, Roger
Pilkington, Arlene
Rea, Alison
Sherdley, Victoria
Stringfellow, Gemma
Learner Practitioner POFs
Flanagan, Pamela
Hassan, Adam
Heath, Nicola

PSOs
Bradley, Janet
Bryan, Paul
Blackwell, Maria
Buchanan, Wendy
Carlton, Phil
Da Costa, Louise
Griffiths, Alincia
Hewitt, Lynne
Hyett, Hannah
Maudsley, Tom
Richardson, Zoe
Rocks, Helen
Unsworth, Rob
Van De Sande, Lynda
Westcott, Viv

Community Payback
Ward, Christopher (SPO)
Baxter, Stephanie (Practice Mgr)

Project Supervisors
Tamimi Al, Tamim
Bradley, Richard
Singh, Lakwinder

Programmes
Treatment Managers
Ashley, Sammy

Gawthorpe, Jane

POs
Arkwright, Kate
Godfrey, Michael
Halliwell, Carly
Loughlin, Colm
Parkinson, Lucy
Suleman, Rehana
Wilkinson, Emma

Victims
Nelson, Michelle (PSO)

Prosecution Officers
Cairns, Ralph
Lythgoe, Michelle

Achieve
Jones, Catherine (Case Mgr)

Information Unit
Truswell, Debbie (District Information
Systems Officer)
Admin
Mahmood, Anila (Secretary/Typist)

Leigh Street
  Chorley PR7 3DJ
  Tel: 01257 260493 Fax: 01257 233177

NOMS (ETE)
Fiddler, Susan (Public Protection)

Achieve
Heffernan, Shaun (Case Manager)

Offender Management
Turner, Chris (SPO)
Ashraf, Farzana (SPO)

POs
Finch, Janet
Brooker, Martin
Burns, Vikki
Carroll, Stephen
Cook, Catherine
Howson, Natalie
Leach, Marilyn
Lloyd, Tracy
McGarry, Samantha
Mackley, Alison
Rees, Sharon
Warbrick, Kevin
Learner Practitioner PQFs
Gillespie, Emma
Leonard, Clare

PSOs
Kirkham, Liz
Melling, Ruth

Ralley, Stuart
Shouib, Humayun

Community Payback
Williams, Gary

Admin
Ramsbotham, Maureen (Office Mgr)

Information Systems
Massam, Daniel

Probation Office
High Street
Skelmersdale WN8 8AP
Tel: 01695 720248 Fax: 01695 556579

Offender Management
Shields, Dorothy (SPO)

POs
Choraffa, Lynne (PO)
Edwards, Jacqueline
McGrath, Fran
McGuire, Annette
Kerrigan, Emmy
Sansbury, Joanne

PSOs
Albers, Michelle
Holden, Elizabeth
McGrath, Fran
Morris, Adam
Willis, Robert

Community Payback
Blakemore, Stephen (Project Supervisor)

Achieve
Case Managers
Brooks, Angela

West District

384 Talbot Road
Blackpool FY3 7AT
Tel: 01253 394031 Fax: 01253 305039

Offender Management
Fisher, Louise (Acting Assistant Chief
Executive)
Waine, Margaret (DM Secretary)
MacKenzie, Eileen (Secretary)
Ali, Rifat (Office Manager)
Harrison, Dave (SPO)
Lloyd, Tracey (SPO)
Taylor, Michele (SPO)
Whittaker, Lisa (SPO)

Achieve
Owens, Ellen (Case Manager)

Offender Management
POs
Aitken, Nicoll
Aspin, Julie
Barrer, Lynn
Boyle, Wendy
Brown, Janine
Calvert, Sarah
Cordwell, Eleanor
Dean, John
Etherington, Darren
Gerard, Patricia
Griffiths, Yvonne
Heslop, Robert
Hill, Chris
Ivett, Nicola
Jones, Simon
Kassam, Shiraz
Keighley, Lydia
Lambert, Dawn
Ledgard, Joy
Mulcahy-Webster, Bernie
Naden, Emma
Rahim, Mohammed
Sorksy, Lucinda
Tomlinson, Nicola
Weatherington, Janine
Weatherington, Brian
Walsh, Jane Anne
Whittaker, Lesley
Learner Practitioner PQFs
Bowden, Nicola
Crawley, Donna
Flintoff, Kirsty
Gradwell, Rachel

PSOs
Andrews, Tracey
Booth, Katie
Bullough, Louisa
Brookes, Neal (Unison Rep)
Ementon, Helen
Jones, Carol
Duckworth, Beverley
Moran, Peter
Moulds, Charmaine
Myers, Joey
Normanton, Roxanne
Southworth, Helen
Todd, Zoe
Wallbank, Rachelle

Community Payback
Project Supervisors
Harold, Alan
Maun, Adam

Victims
Brownwood, John
Johnson, Elizabeth

Admin
MacMahon, Katherine (Case Management)

2 Avroe Crescent
Blackpool Business Park
Blackpool FY4 2DP
Tel: 01253 685050 Fax: 01253 349759

Offender Management
Westrop, Wendy (SPO)
Cairns, Pamela (PSO)
Simpson, Gail (PSO)

Programmes
Fisher, Louise (Assistant Chief Executive)
Johal, Gurjit (SPO)
Nagy, Sheila (Practice Manager)
Sargent, Adam (Programmes Facilitator)

PO/Programme Tutors
Bidder, Patsy (Scheduler)
Bartley, Michael
Koowaroo, Natasha
McCarthy, Jessica
McHugh, James
Maister, Jane
Poulter, Fiona
Whitehouse, Paul

PSOs
Coleman, Lee
Disley, Alan
Eynon, Glynn
Haworth, Melanie

Wolstenholme, Caroline
Women's Safety Workers
Mortimer, Sarah

Wilkinson, Niomi

Community Payback
Barlow, Julie (Practice Manager)
Halstead, Shaun (Project Supervisor)

Eccles, Paul (Project Supervisor)

Victims
Westrop, Wendy (SPO)

Garnett, Elizabeth (Victim Contact Team Admin)

9 The Esplanade
Fleetwood FY7 6UW
Tel: 01253 879500 Fax: 01253 776581
Direct dial: 01253 879 + ext

Offender Management
Rigg, Judy (SPO)

POs
Brooks, Karen
Christian, Diana
Crabtree, Joanne
Foster, Jane
James, Caroline
Joynes, Nicola
Lawson, Joanne
McClements, Julia
Tierney, Emma (Learner Practitioner PQF)

PSOs
Connelly, Sharon
Howard, Lesley
Joynson, Gail
Webster, David

41 West Road
Lancaster LA1 5NU
Tel: 01524 63537 Fax: 01524 848519

Offender Management
Dann, Joanne (Assistant Chief Executive)
Staniforth, Gillian (SPO)

POs
Blyth, Janene
Bruno, Maggie
Byrne, Michelle
Carr, Vicky
Frankland, Roger
Graydon, Lindsey
Hall, Becky
Johnson, Helen
McGuaran, Andra
Ralston, Cathy
Seath, Stephanie
Shields, Stephen
Smith, Doug
Thompson, Donna
Wilson, Joy
Learner Practitioner PQF
Dunn, Lauren
Halstead, Hilary
Housley-Smith, Elizabeth
Livesey, Danielle

Admin
Larn, Carol (Secretary)

Community Payback
Green, Barry (Project Supervisor)
Scanlon, Roger (Project Supervisor)
Larn, Carol (Secretary)
Watson, Jane (Office Mgr)

Achieve
Hartin, Kerry (Case Mgr)

Youth Offending Teams
Blake Street **Accrington** BB5 1RE
Tel: 01254 389456 Fax: 01254 872614

(inc Hyndburn, Rossendale, Clitheroe, Ribble Valley)

Exchange Building
Ainsworth St
Blackburn BB1 8AF
Tel: 01254 666995 Fax: 01254 666652

Orwin, Alex

Stanley Buildings
1–3 Caunce Street
Blackpool FY1 3DN
Tel: 01253 478686 Fax: 01253 478687

Wilson-Gil, Nicola (PO)

Burnley and Pendle
Easden Clough, Morse Street
Burnley BB10 4PB
Tel: 01282 470750

Murray, Martin (PO)
Johnson, Emma (PO)

Halliwell House
15/17 Halliwell Street
Chorley PR7 2AL
Tel: 01257 516051 Fax: 01257 516053

Cook, Catherine

Team Wyre and Fylde Office
Marsh Mill, Fleetwood Road North
Thornton, Cleveldeys FY5 4JZ
Tel: 01253 869576

Marton House
Aalborg Place
Lancaster LA1 1BJ
Tel: 01524 384780 Fax: 01524 842467

Rollitt, Steve

Preston YOT
143–161 Corporation Street
Preston PR1 2UG
Tel: 01772 532047 Fax: 01772 532130
Bretherton, Gaynor
Da Costa, Louise

Approved Premises (Hostels)

Edith Rigby House
6 East Cliff, Preston,
Lancashire, PR1 3JE
Drummond, Shona (AP Mgr)

Storer, Georgina (AP Deputy Mgr)
AP Assistant Managers
Gee, Wendy
Sweeney, Sharon
Whittle, Tracey
AP Supervisors
Duckworth, Kim
McGrath, Michelle
Steele, Gina
Ashurst, Charlotte (AP Case Administrator)
Storer, Georgina (AP Duty Manager)

Highfield House
Lydia Street Wood Nook
Accrington BB5 0PX
Tel: 01254 395997 Fax: 01254 398536
Drummond, Shona (Mgr)
Eccleston, Victoria (Deputy Mgr)
Luca, Victoria (Supervisor)
Chiappi, Daniela (PO)

Assistant Managers
Edmondson, Gabrielle
Mayers, Jane
Pattisnson, Mark
Hostel Supervisors
Dennett, Gareth
Foster, Margaret
Marsh, Jeremy
McCormack, Ptraick
Parkinson, Joanne
Mason, Angela (Case Administrator)

Haworth House
St Peters Street
Blackburn BB2 2HL
Tel: 01254 59060 Fax: 01254 672062

Javed, Anna (Mgr)
Lawson, Amanda (Dep Mgr)
Eccleston, Victoria (Deputy Mgr)
Krasowski, Carol (AP Assistant Manager)
Yates, Louise (PO)

Assistant Managers
Bird, Ashley
Cookson, Bill
Roberts, Paul
Shingleton, Iain

Hostel Supervisors
Almond, Yvette
Lysons, Sheila (Case Administrator)

Institutions

Northern
HMP Garth
Ulnes Walton Lane
Leyland Preston PR26 8NE
Tel: 01772 443300 Fax: 01772 443301

Probation General Office ext 3383

Threlfall, Paul (Acting SPO)

POs
Bewley, Caroline
Dickson, Katrina
Little, Stephanie
Morton, Sharn

HMP Kirkham
Preston PR4 2RN
Tel: 01772 675400 Fax: 01772 675401

Probation Clerk/special visits ext 5614
ROTL Clerk ext 5612
HDC Clerk ext 5613
Prison Admin/temp release enquiries ext 5472
Truesdale, Gemma (SPO)

Johnson, Wendy (SPO)

PSOs
Hulse, Jacqui
Orwin, Gayle
Williams, Jo
Wilson, Carlene

PSOs
Brown, Iain
Nicholls, Caroline
Ritchie, Victoria
Walmsley, Hayley

HMYOI Lancaster Farms
Stone Row Head Off Quernmore Road
Lancaster LA1 3QZ
Tel: 01524 563450 Fax: 01524 563451
Bail info 01524 563820
Bail info/HDC Fax: 01524 563833
Special visits 563542
Threlfall, Paul (Acting SPO)
Boothman, Barbara (PO)
Smith, Anthony (PO)
Edwards, Julie (PSO)

HMP Preston
2 Ribbleton Lane, Preston PR1 5AB
Tel: 01772 444550 Fax: 01772 444551

Special visits 01772 444715
Bail info 01772 444587
Bail info fax: 01772444553
Reception fax: 01772 444563

Healthcare fax: 01772 444554

Probation Clerk tel: 01772 444899

Hall, Lynn (SPO)
Boothman, Phil
Dowbakin, Bernadette
Thompson, Becky
Weigh, Stephen

PSOs
Byrne, Gerard
Dixon, Joanna
Duxbury, Sarah
Horsfall, Jane
McLoughlin, Leanne
Nisbet-Gorman, Alison Ralley, Stuart
Sheikh, Asad
Taylor, Charlene

Achieve
Buckley, Shaun (Case Mgr)

HMP Wymott
Ulnes Walton Lane
Leyland PR26 8LW
Tel: 01772 4424000 Fax: 01772 444001
Threlfall, Paul (Acting SPO)_
McLean, Janice
Ralph, Clare
Webb, Clare
Phillips, Owen (Treatment Mgr)

Local Justice Areas
Blackburn, Darwen & Ribble Valley (Sumner House Preston, Wellington Street and Preston New Road Blackburn) Burnley, Pendle & Rossendale Stephen House Burnley, Nelson) Chorley (Leigh Street Chorley) Fylde Coast (Talbot Road and Avroe Crescent Blackpool, The Esplanade Fleetwood, Morecambe) Hyndburn (Burnley Road Accrington) Lancaster (West Road, Lancaster) Ormskirk (Skelmersdale) Preston (Avenham Street Preston) South Ribble

LEICESTERSHIRE & RUTLAND PROBATION TRUST

Out of hours tel: Kirk Lodge 0116 270 8327; Howard House 0116 254 9059

Victim enquiries tel: 0116 257 3803

Central hostels referral tel: 0116 244 8028
Fax: 0116 244 8696

Email:
firstname.lastname@leicestershire.probation.
gsi.gov.uk

Head Office
2 St John Street Leicester LE1 3WL
Tel: 0116 251 6008 Fax: 0116 242 3250
Email:
firstname.lastname@leicestershire.
probation.gsi.gov.uk

West, Helen (Chief Exec)
Worsfold, Trevor (Director)
Kennedy, Paul (Director)
Peters, Carrie (Director)
Pinfold, Colin (p, Director)
Pollard, Karen (Director)
Wilson, Jane (Board Chair)
Brookes, Sarah (Board Secretary)
Trivedi, Chetan (HR and Staff
Development)
Irwin, Gaynor (IT)
Stretton, Caroline (Finance)
Say-Ludlow, Jim (Health and Safety)
Thomas, Mandy (Premises)
Davies, David (REACH Project)
Wisniewska, Dreda (SPO Risk)

Offender Management Teams

2 Cobden Street
Leicester LE1 2LB
Tel: 0116 262 0400 Fax: 0116 248 0561

Leicester 1 Offender Management
Team
E-Mail:
Leicester1Mail@leicestershire.probation.
gsi.gov.uk
Hulait, Jaspal (SPO)
Singh – Here, Dalminder (PDM)
Haque, Dot
Hodgins, Ellen (p)
Howes, Julie (p)
Ingamells, Beverley
Mann, Rachael (p)
Neale, Rachel
Parry, Jasmine
Reynolds, Cherilee
Singh Hayre, Jasdeep

PSOs
Jones, Kim
Sullivan, Liam
Tobin, Patricia
Wagstaff, Stephen

MAPPOM
(Multi Agency Prolific & Priority
Offender Management)
Mansfield House, 74 Belgrave Gate,
Leicester, LE1 3GG
Tel: 0116 222 8476 Fax: 0116 248 4688
Mailbox:
mappommail@leicestershire.probation.
gsi.gov.uk

Strong, Grace (SPO)

Holland, Richard (PDM)
Cassie, Louise
Frazer, Rachael
Langridge, Tony
Mason, Claire
Stevens, Richard
Wilkinson, Ruth
Wright, Nicola (p)

PSOs
Broad, Kim (p)
Griffin, Chris
Hallam, Claire
Wright, Esther

Resettlement Team (Under 12
Months)
Bailey, Becky (p)
Baumber, Becky (p)
Foreman, James
Noble, Laura (p)
Prideaux, Katrina

Psychology Team
Castledine, Sue (Psychologist)

Probation Centre
2 Cobden Street Leicester LE1 2LB
Tel: 0116 262 0400 Fax: 0116 253 0819

Leicester 2 Offender Management
Team
E-mail:
Leicester2Mail@Leicestershire.probation.
gsi.gov.uk
Bearne, Bob (SPO)
Wickenkamp, Danielle (PDM)
Alabi, Stella
Cameron, Natalie
Cawston, Martin
Cousins, Nicola
Griffiths, Richard
Henry, Jenny
Keysell, Elspeth
Pearce, Jo
Rawle, Paul
Trevor, Ruth
Watson, Emma

PSOs
Baker, Laura
Cooke, Emily
Lad, Anjna
Okan, Olive
Parmar, Nalini
Reece, Neil
Schilling, Tim

Leicester 3 Offender Management Team
Maclean, Carolyn (SPO)
Duckham, Selena (PDM)
Tilley, Hannah
Hadley, Jennie
Hubbard, Joanne
Illston, Suzanne
Shah, Beena
Price, Amy
Allard, Natalie
Hulbert, Emily
Renshaw, Eleanor
Woolverton, Andy

PSOs
Bhavsar, Anjuna
Spencer, Shona
Jones, Sarah
Newbrooks, Clare
Dickson, Joanne
Pattni, Sheetal
Wilton, Katie

Health Team
E-Mail:
healthtrainerteam@leicestershire.
probation.gsi.gov.uk
Pearce, Jan (SPO)
Health Trainers:
Aherne Tim
Archer, Paula
Gatward, Leroy
Haywood, Steve
Wright-Robinson, Jackie
Clarke, Sarah (Administrator)

27 London Road
Coalville LE67 3JB
Tel: 01530 836688 Fax: 01530 834136
E-mail:
CoalvilleMail@Leicestershire.probation.
gsi.gov.uk

Lake, Nicola (SPO)
Pearce, Alison (p, PDM)
Flint, Brendon
Howe, Phillip
Kirby, Arlene
Waite, Anthony

PSOs
Barney, Christopher
Bonser, Paul (p)
Kitching, Suzanne (p)
Newton, Neil

35 Station Road
Hinckley LE10 1AP
Tel: 01455 615645 Fax: 01455 891147

Marriage, Ghislaine (p, SPO)
Gregory, Mark (p, PDM)
Costello, Maxine
Gill, Jasvir
Goodwin, Keeley
Hinson, Kristina

PSO
Howarth, Diane
Newton, Neil

12 Southfield Road
Loughborough LE11 2UZ
Tel: 01509 212904 Fax: 01509 218954
E-mail:
LoughboroughMail@Leicestershire.
probation.gsi.gov.uk

Lake, Nicola (SPO)
Pearce, Alison (p, PDM)
Brown, Jenny (p)
Cusack, Steve (p)
Morfett, Richard
Mouland, Janet (p)
Thompson, Michelle (p)
Warmington, Christine (p)
Williams, Sarah (p)

PSOs
Luik, Naomi (p)
Neale-Badcock, Stephen
Williams, Dawn

Parkside, Station Approach, Burton Street
Melton Mowbray LE13 1GH
Tel: 01664 410410 Fax: 01664 412771
Middleton, Glynis (p, SPO)
Beaumont, Glenn (PDM)
Clay, Madeleine
Coles, Nicola
Roskell, Sharon
Appleton, Jane
Vega, Jane

28 Station Road
Wigston Leicester LE18 2DH
Tel: 0116 257 3800 Fax: 0116 257 0240

Marriage, Ghislaine (SPO)
Gregory, Mark (PDM)

Bowers, Sonia
Coleman, Deborah
Gravestock, Lisa (p)
Jones, Martin
Kotecha, Rahul
Wiltshire, Jeanette

PSOs
Brighty, Stacey
Browne, Marc
Hewitt, Julie

Victim Liaison Team
Tel: 0116 257 3803
Email:
victim.liaison@leicestershire.probation.
gsi.gov.uk
Pearce, Jan (SPO)
Lapidge, Theresa
Sword, Alexandra (Administrator)

PSOs
Chiavolini, Alessandra
Turnock, Paula

Interventions

Probation Centre
2 Cobden Street **Leicester** LE1 2LB
Tel: 0116 262 0400 Fax: 0116 253 0819

Programme Provision
Wynter, Colin (SPO)
Sex Offender Team
Gardner, Mark
Lawler, Linda
Marshall, Peter
Modi, Panna
Smillie, Phil
Yorke, Tina

PSOs
Baggott, Tanya
Bhogaita, Aarti
Collins, Judith (p)
Cuke, Charlene (p)
Devshi, Sajan
Evill, Anthony
Gosling, Paul
Heath, Linda (Women's Support Worker)
Jones, Catherine
Mistry, Vanisha
Mitchell, Paul
Parks, Emma (p)
Ross, Natalee
Seniuk, Stefan

LEAF Team (Learning Employment Accommodation Finance)
E-Mail:
Leaf@leicestershire.probation.gsi.gov.uk
Fax: 0116 242 8447
Brotherton, Chris (SPO)
Hobbs, John (Accommodation Manager)
Smith, Kathy (Skills Dev Coord)

PSOs
Bullock, Emma (p)
Dorrington, Sam (p)
Hallisey, Michael
Hobster, Mark
Jones, Tracey (p)
Straw, Trisha
Thomas, Suzanne (p)

REACH Project
Brotherton, Christine (p, SPO)

PSOs
Hunt, Suzanne (Mentor-Coordinator)
Badat, Ismail
Bourne, Elizabeth
Bugby, Adam
Dorrington, Sam (p)
Jones, Tracey (p)
Whiteley, Hannah

Volunteers
Wain, Stuart (COSA & Volunteer
Co-ordinator)

Community Payback Team
Tel: 0116 262 2245 Fax: 0116 248 0563
Barber, Pam (SPO)
Johnston, Lee (PDM – Deputy Manager)
Bradley, Chloe (PO – Deputy Manager)

PSOs (Community Payback Officers)
Flannagan, Lucy
Godfrey, Graham
Hodson, Karen
Ingram, Maxine
Mason, Anthony
Sahota, Baljit
Samana, Ketna
Sharp, Suzanne
Staszak, Irek
Mann, Elayne
Parsons, Lisa
Pilkington, Alex
Turnock, Paula
Wright, Denise
Yusufzai, Amana

2 Cobden Street
Leicester LE1 2LB

Offender Management Drugs Team

Leicester LE1 2LB
Tel: 0116 262 0400 Fax: 0116 242 4502
E-Mail:
OMDMail@Leicestershire.Probation.gsi.
gov.uk
Chivers, Andrew (SPO)
Beaumont, Glenn (PDM)
Boddington, Katy
Bonner, Joanne
Castanha, Jessica
Crocker, Alison
Dixon, Danielle
Goodliffe, Andrew
Ludlam, Melanie
McGrath, Frances
Wheeler, Helen

PSOs
Ardley, Karen

Courts Team

Members of the Courts Team work from
both courts

Leicester Crown Court

90 Wellington Street, Leicester LE1 6HG
Tel: 0116 204 4990 Fax: 0116 254 1437
E-mail:
ltscrowncourt@leicestershire.probation.
gsi.gov.uk

Leicester Magistrates' Court

Pocklington Walk Leicester LE1 9BE
Tel: 0116 255 3799; 0116 254 2693
Fax: 0116 255 3805
E-mail:
ltsmagscourt@leicestershire.probation.
gsi.gov.uk

Jones, Megan (SPO)
Charlton, David
Cotterill, Amelia
Houghton, Paul
Jones, Sian
Piper, David
Pugh, John
Vega, Jane
Yates, Paul

PSOs
Acton, Susan
Bonser, Paul
Edan, Peter
Garvey, Amanda
Hawkins, Darren
Majid, Furhan
Patel, Jaimy
Reed, Janet

Saujani, Radhika
Smith, Anita

Integrated Offender Management Team (IOM)

Mansfield House Police Station
74 Belgrave Gate Leicester LE1 3GG
Tel. No: 0116 248 4678

Scotson, Tim (SPO)

City IOM

Sayer, Beverley

County IOM

Megennis, Helen

MAPPA Coordination Unit

Mansfield House Police Station
74 Belgrave Gate Leicester LE1 3GG
Admin office tel: 0116 248 6606 Fax: 0116
248 6608
Gullick, Andy (SPO)

Youth Offending Teams

Leicester City Youth Offending Service

Eagle House, 11 Friar Lane
Leicester LE1 5RB
Tel: 0116 299 5830 Fax: 0116 233 6003

Dhokia, Anita
Meakin, Tarnya

PSOs
Berridge, Jane
Bulsara, Hina

Leicestershire Youth Offending Service

County Hall – 3rd Floor
Glenfield, Leices LE3 8RA
Tel: 0116 305 0030 Fax: 0116 305 7220

James, Linda
Turner, Carly

PSO
Muskwe, Chester

Criminal Justice Drugs Team

Quality of Life

7a Cumberland Street
Leicester LE1 4QS
Tel. No. 0116 2389977
Hancock-Smith, Sarah (SPO)

PSOs
Barron, Angie (Project Worker)
Benvenuto, Celine
Harrison, Emma

McGann, Jenna
Roberts, Jon (Service User Engagement
Coordinator)
Roberts, Ros (Project Worker)

CJ Pathway
Castle House 6–8 Nelson Street
Leicester LE1 7BA
Tel: 0116 257 5700 Fax: 0116 257 5749
Duty desk tel: 0800 7311 118

Talbott, Charlotte (SPO)
Chadwick, Liz (SPO)
Radford, Jan
Thoor, Inderjit (Clinical Treatment Mgr)

PSOs
Baxter, Sue
Bingham, Nicola
Brockie, Sarah
Cave, Joanne
Chapman, Brian
Chapman, Nicola
Chavda, Raj
Duncan, Jude
Francis, Dulcie
Gamble, David (Service User
Engagement Coordinator)
Good, Justine
Hughes, Amy
Hyare, Rita
Jackson, Selena
Jagger, Drew
Jeanes, Eleanor
John, Elizabeth
Johnson, Nicholas
Johnson, Vikki
Jones, Mo
Jordan, Jennifer
Kaur, Manjit
Lewis, Andy
Millington, Rhian
Mistry, Roshni
Moore, Trish
Neal, Viv
Niland, Grania
O'Callaghan, Joe
Purewal, Sukhvinder
Randon, Melvyn (Data Mgr)
Reece, Charlotte
Steele, Joanne
Ruprai, Mandeep
Takhar, Jaskaren
Thomas, Amy
Thompson, Gerald
Walker, Martin
Wan, Siu
Ward, Louisa

Weaver, Sarah
Wilson, Karen
Wren, Alison

Approved Premises

Howard House Approved Premises
71 Regent Road Leicester LE1 6YF
Tel: 0116 254 9059 Fax: 0116 254 0303

Kirk Lodge Approved Premises
322 London Road Leicester LE2 2PJ
Tel: 0116 270 8327 Fax: 0116 244 8696

Central Referral Point
Hostel Team members work from either
hostel

Smith, Jeanne (SPO Mgr)
Hopkinson, Michael (PO Deputy)
Kotey, Amon (PO Deputy)

PSOs
Aouni, Karen
Berry, Donna
Bone, Sudeep
Churchill, Marcella
Crawford, Helena
Dublin, Andrew
Frearson, Hannah
Gundry, Kelly
Higham, Andy
Jeggo, Steve
Kedie, Oliver
Leech, Phil
Paige, Oliver
Patel, Dipika
Mason, Kerry
Randhawa, Manjit
Roberts, Paul
Wood, Debbie
Institutions

HMP Gartree
Gallowfield Road
Market Harborough LE16 7RP
Tel: 01858 436600 Fax: 01858 436601

Cripps, Ian (SPO)
Statham, Sarah-Jane
Mann, Rachael
Fowler, Joanne

HMP Leicester
117 Welford Road, Leicester LE2 7AJ
Tel: 0116 228 3000 Fax: 0116 228 3001
Direct dial: 0116 228 + ext
Probation fax: 0116 228 3112

Cripps, Ian (SPO)
Evens, Sally

PSOs
Briers, Zoe
Lail, Andeep

HMYOI Glen Parva
Saffron Road Wigston LE18 4TN
Tel: 0116 228 4100 Fax: 0116 228 4262
Direct dial: 0116 228 + ext
Cripps, Ian (SPO)
Clayton, Rebecca
Patel, Kusum
Weaver, Lestroy

PSOs
Clarke, Anthony
Gargan, Gill
Kilpatrick, Andy
Matthews, Annette
Saunt, Shelley

HMP Stocken
Stocken Hall Road Stretton
Nr Oakham LE15 7RD
Tel: 01780 795100 Fax: 01780 795091
Evans, Graham
Fish, Mike
Walworth, John

PSOs
Cassidy, Jane
Clegg, Ann

Local Justice Areas
Leicester (2 Cobden Street Leicester)
Ashby-de-la-Zouch (Coalville)
Market Bosworth (Hinckley)
Loughborough (Loughborough)
Melton, Belvoir & Rutland (Melton
Mowbray) ˙
Market Harborough & Lutterworth
(Wigston)

Crown Court
Leicester

LINCOLNSHIRE PROBATION TRUST

Out of hours emergency contact point
Wordsworth House tel: 01522 528520

Victim enquiries tel:
Lincoln 01522 510011; Skegness 01754
763906; Grantham 01476 583131

Email:
firstname.lastname@lincolnshire.probation.
gsi.gov.uk

8 Corporation Street
Lincoln LN2 1HN
Tel: 01522 510011 Fax: 01522 514369
Davies, Martin (CEO)
Adey-Johnson, Pete (Director LDU West)
Gregory, Melanie (Director Corporate
Services)
Rushby, Pete (Head of Finance/Board
Sec/Treasurer)
Bateman, Andrew (Finance Project
Manager)
Burke, Tony (Information Systems Mgr)
Callery, Bev (Business Development
Mgr)
Hough, Quin (H&S Off)
Martel, Rachel (Communications Mgr)
McMahon, Paul (Mgr OM)
Millar, Dusty (HR and Training Mgr)

Morris, Andy (OM Project Manager)
O'Meara, Tricia (Business Mgr LDU
West)
Reed, Sarah (Mgr OM)
Smith, Nigel (Performance and
Excellence Mgr)
Collett, Becky (p)
Croft, Nicole
Garnett, Hilary
Loffhagen, Jane
Miller, Leanne
Nisbet, Steve
Plant, Kim (p)
Reddish, Michael
Taylor, Katy (p)
Vaughan, Tammy
Waller, Stacey (p)
Welsh, Sara (p)

PSO/CSOs
Banks, Janice
Birks, Rachel (p)
Dean, Jackie
Flewers, Leanne
Gostelow, Elaine
King, Nigel (p)
Maddocks, Darren
Simpson, Nicci (p)
Smith, Laura
Strowger, Amy
Wild, Layla (p)
Williams, Sarah
Young, Sally (p)
Murphy, Lindsay (VCO)

IOM Team
Crook, Dave (IOM Project Manager)
Morrissey, Matthew (IOM Team Leader
East)

Newborn, Clare (p, IOM Team Leader West) (p)

POs
Bennett, Tracey (IOM West & South Kesteven Cases)
Peacock, Jean (IOM East)

PSOs
Broxholme, Leanne (IOM South Kesteven)
Ross, Stephanie (IOM West)
Sturton, Paul (IOM West)
Williams, Marie (IOM East) (p)

Health Support Service
Connell, Tony (Health Support Mgr)
Miechowski, Helen (PSO/CSO)

Community Payback
Temperton, Kristy (Community Payback Mgr)
Byrne, Mick (Unit Mgr)

PSOs
Holmes, Wendy
Kilgallon-Porter, Cecily
Merrix, Joanne (p)

Programmes
Temperton, Kristy (Programmes Mgr)
Baker, Graham
de Vries, Aggie
Gray, Holly (CSOG/IDAP PO)

PSO Tutors
Cochrane, Nicolette
Edwards, Fiona
McBride, Claire
Smith, Karen

Lincoln Magistrates' Court Office
The Courthouse High Street
Lincoln LN5 7QA
Tel: 01522 533352/560063 Fax: 01522 546332

PSO/CSOs
French, Jolyon
Raby, Amanda

Lincoln Crown Court
The Castle
Castle Hill
Lincoln LN1 3AA
Tel: 01522 526767 Fax: 01522 528779

Dunkling, Marilynne

Police Station
Morton Road
Gainsborough DN21 2SY
Tel: 01427 612260 Fax: 01427 612975

Reed, Sarah (Mgr OM)
Page, Dan
Wood, Janine (p)
Nolan, Linda (PSO/CSO)

The Town Hall
North Parade
Skegness PE25 1DA
Tel: 01754 763906 Fax: 01754 760202

Lynch, Andy (Mgr OM)
Davies, Mark
Sarin, Raish (p)

PSO/CSOs
Clarke, Alan
Hartley, B (p)
Hoy, Caroline (p)
Jennings, Nicola
Murray, Wayne
Swift, Vicky
Nicholls, Alan (VCO) (p)

Police Station
Eastfield Road
Louth LN11 7AN
Tel: 01507 604427 Fax: 01507 608642

Lynch, Andy (Mgr OM)
Bradley, Louise
Kosoko, Shahara
Turner, Sarah (PSO/CSO)

Probation Centre, The Annexe
The County Hall
Boston PE21 6DY
Tel: 01205 316300 Fax: 01205 316301

Oliver, Joanne (Director LDU East)
Pollard, Simon (Business Mgr LDU East)
Gilbert, Mike (Mgr OM)
Jones, Angela (p)
Jones-Lobley, Bobbi
Lawson, Amy (p)
Read, Camilla
Roberts, Angie
Wilson, Angela

PSO/CSOs
Blackman, Paul
Lee, Kathy (p)
Lyon, Michelle
Moss, Esther
Weston, Sara
Wilkinson, Michelle

Interventions
The Old School Carlton Road
Boston PE21 8LN
Tel: 01205 316350 Fax: 01205 316351

Programmes
Temperton, Kristy (Programmes Mgr)
Briggs, Mel (p)
Butterfield, Karen (p)
Hancock, Paul (PSO Tutor) (p)
Hodgson, John (PSO Tutor)
McDonald, Callum (PSO Tutor)
Walukiewicz, Eleanor (PSO Tutor)

Community Payback
Temperton, Kristy (CP Mgr)
Rate, Rebecca (Unit Mgr)
Wright, Richard (Acting Unit Mgr) (p)

PSOs
Harris, Nigel
Hopkinson, Jenny (p)
Windle, Sadie

Broadgate House
Westlode Street
Spalding PE11 2AD
Tel: 01775 722078
Fax: 01775 713936

Gilbert, Mike (Mgr OM)
Hutchinson, Sandie
Hopkins, Cheri (p, PSO/CSO)
Day, Jenny (PSO/CSO)

Grange House
46 Union Street
Grantham NG31 6NZ
Tel: 01476 583131 Fax: 01476 583130

Campbell, Rebecca (Mgr OM)
Leachman, Beccy
Long Fiona (p)
Michelson, Sally
Walters, Zoe
Drury, Verity

PSO/CSOs
Conlin, Emma (p)
Dearden, Francesca
Hamblett, Chris
Jutsum, Sue
Leivers, Bev (p)
Patel, Kiran
Payne, Chris (p)
Saunderson, Debbie (p)
Baker, Georgina

Programmes
Temperton, Kristy (Programmes Mgr)
Smith, Annette (Women's Safety Wkr)

Multi Agency Public Protection Panel
Lincolnshire Police HQ
PO Box 999 **Lincoln** LN5 7PH
Tel: 01522 558255 Fax: 01522 558299

Hilton, Nicole (MAPPA Mgr)

Youth Offending Service (East)
The Old Courthouse North Street
Horncastle LN9 5EA
Tel: 01507 528250 Fax: 01507 528251
Jackson, Angela

Youth Offending Service (South)
The Old Barracks Sandon Road
Grantham NG31 9AS
Tel: 01476 591522 Fax: 01476 569166

Evans, Tracey

Youth Offending Service (West)
8 The Avenue Lincoln LN1 1PB
Tel: 01522 554550 Fax: 01522 553563

Smith, Paul

Approved Premises (Hostel)

Wordsworth House
205 Yarborough Road
Lincoln LN1 3NQ
Tel: 01522 528520 Fax: 01522 526077

Laughton, Keith (Mgr)
Bhatti, Cherie (PSO)

Support Workers
Clipsham, Margaret
Cottingham, Matthew
Greasley, Allan

Supervisors
Paynter, Malcolm
Pell, David
Roberts, Chris
Smith, Rebecca
Taylor, Roly

Institutions

HMP Lincoln
Greetwell Road Lincoln LN2 4BD
Tel: 01522 663000 Fax: 01522 663001

Probation Fax: 01522 663001
Legal Visits ext 31554
Discipline/Offender Admin ext 3075

Aylward, Ali (Mgr OM)
Byrne, Clare
Sackfield, Helen

PSOs
Armstrong, Phil
Broughton, Lesley
O'Rourke, Diane

HMP North Sea Camp
Frieston Boston PE22 0QX
Tel: 01205 769300 Fax: 01205 769301
Probation Fax: 01205 769383

Gilbert, Mike (Mgr OM)
Edmondson, Sarah

Wilks, Helena
Norman, Donna (PSO)

Local Justice Areas
East Lincolnshire – Skegness, Louth
South Lincolnshire – Grantham, Spalding,
Elloes, Bourne, Stamford
West Lincolnshire – Gainsborough,
Lincoln, Sleaford

Crown Court
Lincoln

LONDON
PROBATION TRUST

1 Hammersmith
2 Kensington & Chelsea
3 Westminster
4 Islington
5 City
6 Southwark
7 Lambeth

London Probation Trust has offices in every
London borough and is organised on a
borough and functional basis.

London Postcodes by Borough
 Barking & Dagenham
IG11, RM6, RM7 (part), RM8, RM9,
RM10

Barnet
N2, N3, N10, N11 (part), N12, N14 (part), N20, N22, NW2, NW4, NW7, NW9, NW11, EN5

Bexley (with Beckenham)
SE2 (part), SE9 (part), SE28 (part), DA1 (part), DA5, DA6, DA7, DA8 (part), DA14, DA15, DA16, DA17 (part), DA18 (part)

Brent
NW6 (part), NW10, HA0, HA9

Bromley
SE20, SE26 (part), BR1 (part), BR2, BR3, BR4 (part), BR5, BR6, BR7, TN16 (part)

Camden
N7, N19, NW1 (part), NW2 (part), NW3, NW5, NW6 (part), NW8, WC1, WC2 (part)

Croydon
SE19, SE25, SW16, CR0, CR2, CR3, CR5, CR6, CR7, CR8

Ealing
W3, W4, W5, W7, W13, UB1, UB2, UB4 (part), UB5, UB6

Enfield
N9, N11 (part), N13, N14 (part), N18, N21, EN1, EN2, EN3, EN4

Greenwich
SE3, SE7, SE8, SE10, SE18

Hackney and City of London
EC1, EC2, EC3, EC4, E2, E5, E8, E9, N1 (part), N4, N16

Hammersmith & Fulham
SW6, W6, W12, Part of W11, Part of W14

Haringey
N2 (part) N4 (part), N6, N8, N11 (part), N15, N17, N22

Harrow
HA1, HA2, HA3, HA4 (part), HA5, HA7, HA8

Havering
RM1, RM2, RM3, RM4, RM7 (part), RM11, RM12, RM13, RM14

Hillingdon
HA4 (part), HA6, UB3, UB4 (part), UB7, UB8, UB9, UB10

Hounslow
TW3, TW4, TW5, TW6, TW7, TW13, TW14, UB2 (part), W4

Islington
WC1 (part), N1 (part), N4 (part), N5 (part), N7 (part), N16 (part), N19

Kensington & Chelsea
SW10, W11, W8, SW5 & part of W10

Kingston-upon-Thames
SW19, SW20 (part), KT1, KT2, KT3, KT4 (part), KT5, KT6 (part), KT9

Lambeth
SE5, SE11, SE21, SE24, SE27, SW2, SW4, SW8, SW9, SW12

Lewisham
SE3 (part), SE4, SE6, SE8, SE9 (part), SE10 (part), SE12, SE13, SE14, SE23, SE26 (part), BR1 (part)

Merton
SW17 (part), SW19, SW20, SM4, CR4, CR0 (part)

Newham
E6, E7, E12, E13, **E15**, E16, **E20**

Redbridge & Waltham Forest
E4, E10, E11, E15, E17, E18, IG2, IG3, IG4, IG5, IG6, IG7, IG8, IG10 and parts of E15, E7, IG11, IG10, RM6 and RM8

Richmond-upon-Thames
SW13, SW14, TW1, TW2, TW9, TW10, TW11, TW12

Southwark
SE1, SE5, SE11, SE15, SE16, SE17, SE21 (part), SE22, SE23 (part), SE24 (part), SE26 (part)

Sutton
SM1, SM2, SM3, SM5, SM6, CR4 (part)

Tower Hamlets
E1, E3, E14

Wandsworth
SW4 (part), SW8 (part), SW11, SW12 (part), SW15, SW16 (part), SW17 (part), SW18, SW19 (part)

Westminster
SW1, W1, W2, W9, NW1, NW8 & part of W10

Email:
firstname.lastname@london.probation.gsi.gov.uk

Head Office
151 Buckingham Palace Road
London SW1W 9SZ

Tel: 0300 048 0000 (switchboard)
Fax: 0300 048 0297 (reception)

Napo Greater London Branch
151 Buckingham Palace Road
London SW1W 9SZ
Tel: 0300 048 0099 Fax: 0300 048 0295
Email:
nps.LondonNAPO@London.probation.gsi.
gov.uk

Chair: Pat Waterman

Vice Chair: Patricia Johnson

Vice Chair: David Masterson

Health & Safety Convenor: Paul Fairbrass

Anti-Racism/Equal Rights Officer:
Charron Culnane

Senior Union Administrator: Beverley
Cole

LONDON LOCAL DELIVERY UNITS
Barking Dagenham and Havering LDU

Olympic House
4th Floor 28/42 Clements Road
Ilford, Essex IG1 1BA
Tel: 020 8514 5353 Fax: 020 8478 4450

Havering Probation Office
1 Regarth Avenue
Romford, Essex RM1 1TJ
Tel: 01708 742 453 Fax: 01708 753 353

Havering Court Team
NE London Magistrates Court (sitting at Havering)
Havering Magistrates' Court
Probation Suite, The Courthouse
Main Road, Romford RM1 3BH
Tel: 01708 502 501 Fax: 01708 736 533

Barking & Dagenham
29/33 Victoria Road
Romford RM1 2JT
Tel: 01708 753 555 Fax: 01708 752 096

Barnet and Enfield LDU

Hendon
Suite B, Denmark House
West Hendon Broadway
West Hendon, London NW9 7BW
Tel: 020 8457 6820 Fax: 020 8457 6822

The Old Court House
Windmill Hill, Enfield
Middlesex EN2 6SA
Tel: 020 8366 6376 Fax: 020 8367 1624

Enfield Substance Misuse Unit
The Centre, 12a Centre Way
Claverings Industrial Estate
Montagu Road, Edmonton
London N9 OAH
Tel: 020 8379 6972 Fax: 020 8379 6965

Barnet Substance Misuse Unit
Suite B, Denmark House
West Hendon, Broadway
West Hendon, London NW9 7BW
Tel: 020 8457 6820 Fax: 020 8457 6822

Barnet Youth Offending Team
3rd Floor, Barnet House
1255 High Road, Whetstone
London N20 0EJ

Tel: 020 8359 5535 Fax: 020 8359 5530

Brent LDU

Brent Probation Office
440 High Road, Willesden
London NW10 2DW
Tel: 020 8451 6212 Fax: 020 8451 3467

Brent Youth Offending Team
5th Floor, Chesterfield House,
9 Park Lane, Wembley
Middlesex HA9 7RH
Tel: 020 8937 3810 Fax: 020 8937 3811 or
020 8937 4789

Bexley and Bromley LDU

Bexley Probation
Norwich Place
Bexleyheath, Kent DA6 7ND
Tel: 020 8304 5521 Fax: 020 8301 5737

Bexley Magistrates' Court
Norwich Place
Bexleyheath, Kent, DA6 7ND
Tel: 020 8304 5521 Fax: 020 8301 5737

Bexley Youth Offending Team
Howbury Centre, Slade Green Road
Erith, Kent DA8 2HX
Tel: 020 3045 5073
Fax: 01322 356 380

Bromley Probation
6 Church Hill Orpington
Kent BR6 0HE
Tel: 01689 831616 Fax: 01689 875253

Bromley Magistrates' Court
1 London Road, Bromley
Kent BR1 1RA
Tel: 020 8466 7391 Fax: 020 8466 6217

Bromley Youth Offending Team
8 Masons Hill, Bromley
Kent BR2 9EY
Tel: 020 8466 3080 Fax: 020 8466 3099

Crosby House
9–13 Elmfield Road
Bromley, Kent BR1 1LT
Tel: 020 8464 3430 Fax: 020 8466 1571

Camden and Islington LDU

53 Holloway Road
London N7 8JD
Tel: 020 7609 0913 Fax: 020 7700
2553/6936

401 St John Street
London EC1V 4RW
Tel: 020 7014 9800 Fax: 020 7014 9801

Camden Youth Offending Service
218–220 Eversholt Street
London NW1 1BD
Tel: 020 7974 6181 Fax: 020 7974 4163

Islington Youth Offending Service
27 Dingley Place, London EC1V 8BR
Tel: 020 7527 7050 Fax: 020 7527 7066

Croydon LDU

Church House
1A Old Palace Road
Croydon, Surrey CR0 1AX
Tel: 020 8686 6551 Fax: 020 8688 4190

Croydon Magistrates' Court
2 Barclay Road, Croydon
Surrey CR9 3NE
Tel: 020 8688 0739 Fax: 020 8681 7325
Tel: 020 8688 0611 (breach)

Substance Misuse & PPO Unit (IOM)
51 Wandle Road
Croydon, Surrey CR0 1DF
Tel: 020 8686 4441 Fax: 020 8680 7951

Ealing LDU

Ealing Probation Office
Leeland House, Leeland Road,
West Ealing, London W13 9HH
Tel: 020 8840 6464 Fax: 020 8579 8165

Acton Probation Office
4 Birkbeck Road
Acton, London W3 6BG
Tel: 020 8992 5863 Fax: 020 8993 5942

Ealing Youth Offending Team
2 Cheltenham Place, Acton
London W3 8JS
Tel: 020 8993 9555 Fax: 020 8993 6292

Ealing Magistrates' Court
The Court House, Green Lane
Ealing, London W13 0SD
Tel: 0208 566 3882
Fax: 020 8566 2045

Greenwich LDU

39 Greenwich High Road
London SE10 8JL
Tel: 020 8465 6000 Fax: 0208 465 6009

Greenwich Probation Office
Riverside House, Beresford Street
Woolwich, London SE18 6DH
Tel: 020 8855 5691 Fax: 020 8309
8693/8694

Greenwich Youth Offending Service
The Woolwich Centre,
35 Wellington Street,
London, SE18 6HQ

Tel: 020 8921 8700

Hackney and City of London LDU

34 Englefield Road
Hackney, London N1 4EZ
Tel: 020 7241 9900 Fax: 020 7241 9901

Reed House
2–4 Rectory Road
Stoke Newington, London N16 7QS
Tel: 020 7923 4656 Fax: 020 7923 4084

Hackney Youth Offending Team
Hackney Service Centre
1 Hillman Street
Hackney, London E8 1DY
Tel: 020 8356 7404 Fax: 020 8356 4708

City of London Magistrates' Court
Probation Liaison Department
c/o Central Criminal Court
Old Bailey, London EC4M 7EM
Tel: 020 7332 1139 Fax: 020 7332 1139

Hammersmith and Fulham LDU

191A Askew Road
London W12 9AX
Tel: 020 8811 2000 Fax: 020 8811 2001

Hammersmith Magistrates' Court
181 Talgarth Road
Hammersmith, London W6 8DN
Tel: 020 8846 3250 Fax: 020 8700 9494

Women's Community Project Team
Based at Minerva Project
Unit 6 The Lanchesters
162–164 Fulham Palace Road
Hammersmith, London W6 9ER
Tel: 020 8237 5593/0208 237 5594
Fax. 020 8748 0077

Hammersmith & Fulham Youth Offending Team
Cobbs Hall, 266–284 Fulham Palace Road
Fulham, London SW6 6LL
Tel: 020 8753 6200/6201 Fax: 020 8753 6242

Haringey LDU

Telfer House
Church Road, Highgate, London N6 4QJ
Tel: 020 8341 9060 Fax: 020 8341 4260

Wood Green Crown Court Team
Woodall House, Lordship Lane
Wood Green, London N22 5LF
Tel: 020 8826 4100 Fax: 020 8881 2665

71 Lordship Lane
Tottenham, London N17 6RS
Tel: 020 8808 4522 Fax: 020 8885 5946

Haringey Youth Offending Team
476 High Road, Tottenham N17 9JF
Tel: 020 8489 1508/1523 Fax: 020 8489 1588

Harrow and Hillingdon LDU

The Court House
Harefield Road
Uxbridge UB8 1PQ
Tel: 01895 231 972 Fax: 01895 257 972

Rosslyn Crescent
Harrow, Middlesex HA1 2SU
Tel: 020 8427 7246 Fax: 020 8424 2101

Harrow YOT
Harrow Civic Centre
2nd Floor, North Wing
Station Road, Harrow
HA1 2XY
Tel: 020 8736 6755
Fax: 020 8736 6766

Hillingdon YOT
Link 1A
Hillingdon Civic Centre

High Street Uxbridge
Hillingdon UB8 1UW
Tel: 01895 277 957
Fax: 01895 277 946

Hounslow LDU

Banklabs House
41a Cross Lances Road
Hounslow TW3 2AD
Tel: 020 8570 0626 Fax: 020 8814 1238
IOM Team Fax: 020 8570 1190

Feltham Magistrates' Court
Hanworth Road
Feltham, Middlesex TW13 5AF
Tel: 020 8890 8747 Fax: 020 8893 2368

Hounslow Youth Offending Team
Redlees Centre, Worton Road
Isleworth TW7 6DW
Tel: 020 8583 6363 Fax: 020 8847 9418

Isleworth Crown Court
36 Ridgeway Road
Isleworth Middlesex TW7 5LP
Tel: 020 8380 4500 Fax: 020 8758 9650

Kensington Chelsea and Westminster LDU

Westminster Probation Office
1–5 Dorset Close
Marylebone, London NW1 5AN
Tel: 020 7563 3600 Fax: 020 7563 3601

Central London Court Team
Westminster Magistrates Court
179 Marylebone Road
London NW1 5BR
Tel: 0300 048 0350 Fax: 0300 048 0396

Kensington & Chelsea Youth Offending Team
36 Oxford Gardens
London W10 5UQ
Tel: 020 7598 4700 Fax: 020 7598 4715

Westminster Youth Offending Team
6a Crompton Street
London W2 1ND
Tel: 020 7641 5307 Fax: 020 7641 5311

Kingston and Richmond LDU

45 High Street
Kingston-upon-Thames
Surrey KT1 1LQ
Tel: 020 8939 4130 Fax: 020 8549 7626

Kingston Youth Offending Team
Eagle Chambers, 18 Eden Street
Kingston-upon-Thames
Surrey KT1 1BB
Tel: 020 8547 6920 Fax: 020 8547 6959

Richmond Youth Offending Team
2nd Floor, 42 York Street,
Twickenham TW1 3BW
Tel: 020 8891 7050 Fax: 020 8891 7473

Lambeth LDU

117 Stockwell Road
London SW9 9TN
Tel: 020 7326 7700 Fax: 020 7326 7701

Harpenden House
248–250 Norwood Road
London, SE27 9AW
Tel: 020 8766 5700 Fax: 020 8766 5746

Lewisham LDU

208 Lewisham High Street
Lewisham, London SE13 6JP
Tel: 020 8297 7300 Fax: 020 8297 7301

Lewisham Youth Offending Team
23 Mercia Grove, Lewisham
London SE13 6BJ
Tel: 020 8314 7474 Fax: 020 8314 3505

Merton and Sutton LDU

Probation Resource Centre
Martin Harknett House
27 High Path, Wimbledon
London SW19 2JL
Tel: 020 8545 8500 Fax: 020 8543 1178

103 Westmead Road
Sutton, Surrey SM1 4JD
Tel: 020 8652 9670 Fax: 020 8770 3592

Newham LDU

Olympic House
4th Floor, 28/42 Clements Road
Ilford, Essex IG1 1BA
Tel: 020 8514 5353 Fax: 020 8478 4450

20 Romford Road
Stratford, London E15 4BZ
Tel: 020 8534 5656 Fax: 020 8534 8285 (1st
Floor)
Fax: 0208 534 1470 (2nd Floor)
Fax: 0208 281 5253 (3rd Floor)

Stratford Magistrates' Court
389–397 High Street
Stratford, London E15 4SB
Tel: 020 8437 6060 Fax: 020 8534 7356

Newham Youth Offending Team
192 Cumberland Road
Plaistow, London E13 8LT
Tel: 020 8430 2361 Fax: 020 8430 2299

Plaistow Police Station
444 Barking Road, London E13 8HJ
OMT4 Tel: 0208 217 3919
IOM/PPO Tel: 0208 217 5875
JIGSAW Tel: 0208 217 5723

Redbridge & Waltham Forest LDU

Ilford Probation Centre
Redbridge/Waltham Forest OMT1,
OMT2, OMT3
277–289 High Road
Ilford, Essex IG1 1QQ
Tel: 020 8478 8500 Fax: 020 8553 1972

Waltham Forest Probation Office
Redbridge/Waltham Forest OMT4,
OMT5, OMT6
1b Farnan Avenue
Walthamstow, London E17 4TT
Tel: 020 8531 3311 Fax: 0208 523 1733

**Barking Magistrates' Court (formerly
Redbridge Magistrates' Court**
Redbridge/Waltham Forest CRT2
850 Cranbrook Road
Barkingside, Essex IG6 1HW
Tel: 0208 551 9724
Fax: 0208 262 4210

**Snaresbrook Crown Court
Probation Liaison Unit**
Redbridge/Waltham Forest CRT 1
Hollybush Hill, London E11 1QW
Tel: 020 8530 7561
Fax: 020 8530 1399

Southwark LDU

**ViSOR Team, Central Extrenism Unit,
Restorative Justice**
21 Harper Road
London SE1 6AW
(ViSOR) Tel: 020 7940 6183 (CEU) Tel:
020 7407 7333

**2 Great Dover Street (OMT1, OMT2,
OMT3, IOM1 and Programmes)**
London SE1 4XW
Tel: 020 7740 8400 Fax: 020 7740 8449

Camberwell Green Magistrates' Court
15 D'Eynsford Road
London SE5 7UP
Tel: 020 7703 0822 Fax: 020 7703 8319

Tower Bridge Magistrates' Court
211 Tooley Street
London SE1 2JY
Probation enquiries regarding Tower
Bridge Magistrates' Court should contact
Camberwell Green Magistrates' Court

Inner London Crown Court
21 Harper Road
London SE1 6AW
Tel: 020 7407 7333 Fax: 020 7403 8637

Southwark Crown Court
1 English Grounds, Battle Bridge Lane
London SE1 2HU
Tel: 020 7403 1045 Fax: 020 7403 8602

Blackfriars Crown Court
1–15 Pocock Street
London SE1 0BT
Tel: 020 7021 0769 Fax: 020 7401 9138

Tower Hamlets LDU

Olympic House
4th Floor, 28/42 Clements Road
Ilford, Essex IG1 1BA
Tel: 020 8514 5353 Fax: 020 8478 4450

50 Mornington Grove
Bow, London E3 4NS
Tel: 020 8980 1818 Fax: 020 8983 0020

377 Cambridge Heath Road
Bethnal Green, London E2 9RD
Tel: 020 7739 7931 Fax: 020 7729 8600

Tower Hamlets Youth Offending Team
54th Floor, Mulberry Place
5 Clove Crescent
London E14 2BG
Tel: 020 7364 1144 Fax 020 7364 0362

Wandsworth LDU

79 East Hill
London SW18 2QE
Tel: 020 8704 0200 Fax: 020 8704 0201

Lavender Hill Magistrates' Court
176a Lavender Hill
London SW11 1JU
Tel: 020 7228 9047 Fax: 020 7924 4775

Wandsworth Youth Offending Team
177 Blackshaw Road
Tooting, London SW17 0DJ
Tel: 020 8871 6222 Fax: 020 8682 4255

PUBLIC PROTECTION
Approved Premises
General enquiries contact Head Office
151 Buckingham Palace Road
London SW1W 9SZ
Tel: 0300 048 0000 (switchboard)
Fax: 0300 048 0297 (reception)

Central Referral Scheme
151 Buckingham Palace Road
London SW1W 9SZ
Tel: 020 7407 7293 Fax: 020 7357 7140

Seafield Lodge Approved Premises
71/73 Shoot Up Hill
London NW2 3PS
Tel: 020 8452 4209 Fax: 020 8450 2037
Manager: Andrew Wisdom

Camden House Approved Premises
199 Arlington Road
London NW1 7HA
Tel: 020 7482 4288 Fax: 020 7284 3391
Manager: Rob Hutt

Westbourne House Approved Premises
199 Romford Road
Forest Gate, London E7 9HL
Tel: 020 8534 0673 Fax: 020 8534 8286
Manager: Barbara Thomas

Beckenham Approved Premises
4 Beckenham Road
Beckenham, Kent BR3 4LR
Tel: 020 8658 3515 Fax: 020 8663 6244
Manager: Diane Orlebar

Tulse Hill Approved Premises
147 Tulse Hill
London SW2 2QD
Tel: 020 8671 4086 Fax: 020 8671 8546
Manager: Grace Harris

Canadian Avenue Approved Premises
7 Canadian Avenue
London SE6 3AU
Tel: 020 8690 3234 Fax: 020 8314 0650
Manager: Janet Irish

Ellison House Approved Premises
370 Albany Road
London SE5 0AJ
Tel: 020 7703 3332 Fax: 020 7252 6327
Manager: Angela Clarke

Ealing Approved Premises
2 Corfton Road
London W5 2HS
Tel: 020 8997 7127 Fax: 020 8810 6213
Manager: Alan Holland

Kew Approved Premises
96 North Road
Richmond-upon-Thames
Surrey TW9 4HQ
Tel: 020 8876 6303 Fax: 020 8876 7402
Manager: Hans Weijman

Voluntary Approved Premises

Katherine Price Hughes Hostel
28 Highbury Grove
London N5 2EA
Tel: 020 7226 2190 Fax: 020 7354 3221
Manager: Ted Owen

Hestia Streatham
298 Leigham Court Road
London SW16 2QP
Tel: 020 8769 8096 Fax: 020 8664 7392
Manager: Teresa Goede

Hestia Battersea
9 Cologne Road
London SW11 2AH
Tel: 020 7223 3006 Fax: 020 7924 2156
Manager: Teresa Goede
Prisons

London (Prisons)
General enquiries contact Head Office
151 Buckingham Palace Road
London SW1W 9SZ
Tel: 0300 048 0000 (switchboard)

Fax: 0300 048 0297 (reception

HMP Brixton
Jebb Avenue, London SW2 5XF
Tel: 020 8588 6336 Fax: 020 8588 6342

HMP Belmarsh
Western Way, Thamesmead
London SE28 0EB
Tel: 020 8331 4400 Fax: 020 8317 8719

HMP Holloway
1 Parkhurst Road, London N7 0NU
Tel: 020 7979 4400 Fax: 020 7979 4763

HMP Pentonville
Caledonian Road, London N7 8TT
Tel: 020 7023 7180 Fax: 020 7023 7250

HMP Wandsworth
Heathfield Road
London SW18 3HS
Tel: 020 8588 4229 Fax: 020 8588 4011

HMP Wormwood Scrubs
Du Cane Road, London W12 0AE
Tel: 020 8588 3238 Fax: 020 8588 3549

Resettlement
Resettlement Coordinator
151 Buckingham Palace Road
London SW1W 9SZ
Tel: 0300 048 0000 (switchboard)
Fax: 0300 048 0297 (reception)

Home Detention Curfew (HDC) SpoC tel:
0300 048 0111

Serious Further Offences
151 Buckingham Palace Road
London SW1W 9SZ
Tel: 0300 048 0000 (switchboard)
Fax: 0300 048 0297 (reception)
Manager: Yvette Howson
SFO SPoC tel: 0300 048 0018

REHABILITATION SERVICES
Offending Behaviour Programmes
General enquiries contact Head Office
151 Buckingham Palace Road
London SW1W 9SZ
Tel: 0300 048 0000 (switchboard)
Fax: 0300 048 0297 (reception)

191A Askew Road
London W12 9AX
Tel: 020 8811 2000 Fax: 020 8811 2001

Crosby House
9–13 Elmfield Road
Bromley, Kent BR1 1LT
Tel: 020 8464 3433 Fax: 020 8460 9990

Camden House (including Camden Women's Centre)
199 Arlington Road
London NW1 7HA
Tel: 020 7428 8430 Fax: 020 7428 8494

2nd Floor King's House
The Green, Southall
Middlesex UB2 4QQ
Tel: 020 8574 9954 Fax: 020 8813 9124

Ilford Probation Centre
277 High Road
Ilford, Essex IG1 1QQ
Tel: 020 8478 8500 Fax: 020 8478 8518

Marylebone Road Probation Office
179 Marylebone Road
London NW1 5BR
Tel: 0300 048 0350 Fax: 0300 048 0396

Hendon Probation Office
Suite B, Denmark House
West London Broadway, London NW9 7BR
Tel: 020 8457 6923 Fax: 020 8457 6823

Probation Resource Centre
Martin Harknett House
27 High Path
Wimbledon SW19 2JL
Tel: 020 8545 8500 Fax: 020 8543 1178

Norwich Place Bexleyheath
Kent DA6 7ND
Tel: 020 8304 5521 Fax: 020 8301 5737

Reed House
1–4 Rectory Road
Stoke Newington, London N16 7QS
Tel: 020 7923 4656 Fax: 020 7923 4084

2 Great Dover Street
London SE1 4XW
Tel: 020 7740 8420 Fax: 020 7740 8449

208 Lewisham High Street
Lewisham, London SE13 6JP
Tel: 020 8297 7300 Fax: 020 8297 7301

90 Lansdowne Road
London N17 9XX
Tel: 03000 480300 Fax: 03000 480339

117 Stockwell Road
Stockwell, London SW9 9TN
Tel: 020 7236 7700 Fax: 020 7326 7701

Community Payback London
Control Centre
Tel: 020 7740 8222

Employment and Skills
General enquiries contact Head Office
151 Buckingham Palace Road
London SW1W 9SZ
Tel: 0300 048 0034

Victim Liaison Units
All London cases should be referred to
Central Administration at Acton

Ilford Victim Liaison Unit
4th Floor, Olympic House
28–42 Clements Road
Ilford IG1 1BA
Tel: 020 8514 5353 Fax: 020 8478 4450

Acton Victim Liaison Unit
4 Birkbeck Road
Acton, London W3 6BE
Tel: 020 8993 0934 Fax: 020 8993 0497

Bromley Victim Liaison Unit
Crosby House
9/13 Elmfield Road
Bromley, Kent BR1 1LT
Tel: 020 8290 2158 Fax: 020 8313 1621

Kingston Victim Liaison Unit
45 High Street
Kingston-upon-Thames KT1 1LQ
Tel: 020 8939 4119/4127/4135 Fax: 020 8549 7626

Crown Court Teams

Crown Courts in the London Area	Borough in which situated
Blackfriars Crown Court	Southwark
Central Criminal Court	City of London
Croydon Crown Court	Croydon
Harrow Crown Court	Harrow
Inner London Crown Court	Southwark
Isleworth Crown Court	Hounslow
Kingston Crown Court	Kingston-upon-Thames
Royal Courts of Justice (Criminal Division, Court of Appeal)	Westminster
Snaresbrook Crown Court	Waltham Forest
Southwark Crown Court	Southwark
Wood Green Crown Court	Haringey
Woolwich Crown Court	Greenwich

Blackfriars Crown Court
1–15 Pocock Street, London SE1 0BT
Tel: 020 7021 0769 Fax: 020 7401 9138

Central Criminal Court
Old Bailey, London EC4M 7EM

Tel: 020 7192 2224/2228 Fax: 020 7236 6692

Croydon Crown Court
The Law Courts
Altyre Road, Croydon CR9 5AB
Tel: 020 8681 5039 Fax: 020 8681 6604

Harrow Crown Court
Hailsham Drive
Harrow, Middlesex HA1 4TU
Tel: 020 8424 2294 Fax: 020 8424 9346

Inner London Crown Court
21 Harper Road, London SE1 6AW
Tel: 020 7940 6173 Fax: 020 7403 8637

Isleworth Crown Court
36 Ridgeway Road
Isleworth Middlesex TW7 5LP
Tel: 020 8380 4500 Fax: 020 8758 9650

Kingston Crown Court
6/8 Penrhyn Road
Kingston-upon-Thames KT1 2BB
Tel: 020 8240 2551 Fax: 020 8240 2555

Court of Appeal
Room E303, Royal Courts of Justice
London WC2A 2LL
Tel: 020 7947 6092 Fax: 020 7947 6704

Snaresbrook Crown Court
Crown Court, Hollybush Hill
Snaresbrook, London E11 1QW
Tel: 020 8530 7561 Fax: 020 8530 1399

Southwark Crown Court
1 English Grounds, Battle Bridge Lane
London SE1 2HU
Tel: 020 7940 8149 Fax: 020 7403 8602

Wood Green Crown Court Team
Woodall House, Lordship Lane
Wood Green, London N22 5LF
Tel: 020 8826 4100 Fax: 020 8881 2665

Woolwich Crown Court
2 Belmarsh Road
London SE28 0EY
Tel: 020 8312 7000 Fax: 020 8317 1605

Local Justice Areas
Courts without phone numbers are often not staffed. Please phone another team in the LJA.

Central London LJA
City of London Magistrates' Court, Tel: 020 3126 3382
Westminster Magistrates' Court, Tel: 020 3126 3050

Hammersmith Magistrates' Court, Tel: 020 8846 3250

North East LJA
Barkingside Magistrates' Court, Tel: 020 8551 9724
Havering Magistrates' Court

East LJA
Thames Magistrates' Court
Stratford Magistrate' Court
Waltham Forest Magistrates' Court

North West LJA
Hendon Magistrates' Court, Tel: 020 8511 1312
Brent Magistrates' Court

North LJA
Highbury Corner Magistrates' Court, Tel: 020 7609 0913
Tottenham Magistrates' Court

West LJA
Uxbridge Magistrates' Court, Tel: 01895 455 130
Ealing Magistrates' Court, Tel: 020 8566 3882
Feltham Magistrates' Court, Tel: 020 8890 8747

South East LJA
Bexley Magistrates' Court, Tel: 020 8304 5521
Bromley Magistrates' Court, Tel: 020 8466 7391
Greenwich Magistrates' Court

South LJA
Camberwell Green Magistrates' Court, Tel: 020 7703 0822
Croydon Magistrates' Court, Tel: 020 8688 0739

South West LJA
Wimbledon Magistrates' Court

GREATER MANCHESTER PROBATION TRUST

Out of hours emergency contact point
Tel: 0161 226 1179

Email:
firstname.lastname@manchester.probation.gsi.gov.uk

Head Office
5th Floor Oakland House
Talbot Road Manchester M16 0PQ
Tel: 0161 872 4802 Fax: 0161 872 3483
Hamilton, Roz (Chief Exec)
Noah, Chris (Dir, Ops & Local
Partnerships)
Greenhalgh, Judith (Dir, Corp Services)
Geddes, Lyndy (Dir, Commercial)
Groves, Nigel (ACE, Performance and
Policy)
Carman, Andrea (ACE, Business &
Commissioning Mgr)
Tumelty, Joe (ACE, Interventions)
Thornley, Lucy (ACE, People and
Development)
Parmar, Sangita (HR Manager)
Hayton, Elaine (IT & Bus Systems Mgr)
Vacant (Marketing & Comms Mgr)
Patel, Bhimji (Finance Mgr)
Wilson, Matthew (Business and
Development Manager)
O'Neill, Steven (Community Payback
Area Manager)
Hickey, Simon (Systems & Tech Support
Mgr)
Ventris, Michael (Project Mgr Achieve
North West)
Clarke, Rebecca (Head of Research and
Policy)
Woods, Jane (Bus &Exec Support Mgr)
Lowe, Deborah (PA to the Chief Exec)
Kay, Debbey (PA to the Deputy Chief
Executives)

Manchester Crown Court
Crown Court Buildings Crown Square
Manchester M3 3FL
Tel: 0161 954 1750/3 Fax: 0161 839 3856
Smith, Celia (Prob Ops Mgr)

Minshull Street Crown Court
Courts of Justice Minshull Street
Manchester M1 3FS
Tel: 0161 954 7654/7661/7662 Fax: 0161
954 7664

Smith, Celia (Prob Ops Mgr)

Bolton Crown Court
Liaison Office, Black Horse Street
Bolton BL1 1SU
Tel: 01204 372119 Fax: 01204 380963
Smith, Celia (Prob Ops Mgr)

Magistrates' Court Building
Manchester and Salford Magistrates
Court

Crown Square, Manchester M3 3FL
Tel: 0161 830 2250 Fax: 0161 834 3064
Martin, Chris (Prob Ops Mgr)

Offender Management
Bolton

St Helena Mill
St Helena Road Bolton BL1 2JS
Tel: 01204 387699 Fax: 01204 382372
Brimley, John (ACE)
Berry, Susan (Prob Ops Mgr)
Hickey, Joanne (Prob Ops Mgr)
Long, Joe (Prob Ops Mgr)
Roberts, Andrew (Prob Ops Mgr)
Williams, Heather (Bus & Perf Mgr)

Bolton Community Payback Unit
St Helena Mill
St Helena Road Bolton BL1 2JS
Tel: 01204 387699 Fax: 01204 382372

Bolton Magistrates Court
PO Box 24 The Courts Civic Centre
Bolton, BL1 1QX
Tel: 01204 558200 Fax: 01204 364373

Bury

Argyle House
Castlecroft Court
Castlecroft Road Bury BL9 0LN
Tel: 03000477900 Fax: 03000477999
Elliott, Nigel (ACE -Bury and Rochdale
LDU)
Elliott, Nigel (Acting ACE –Bury and
Rochdale LDU)
Parkes, Glenn (Prob Ops Mgr)
Trudi Brown (Prob Ops Mgr)
Janice France (Acting Prob Ops Mgr)
Olajide, Tunde (Bus & Perf Mgr)

**Bury and Rochdale Community
Payback**
Middleton Office
St Michael's House
Oldham Road Middleton M24 2LH
Tel: 0300 047 7770
Fax: 0300 047 7769
Harrison, Kevin (Community Ops Mgr)

Bury Magistrates Court
The Courthouse, Tenters Street, Bury
BL1 1QX
Tel: 0161 447 8600 Fax: 0161 447 8630

Manchester and Trafford

Longsight
Victoria Park Laindon Road
Longsight Manchester M14 5YJ
Tel: 0161 224 0231 Fax: 0161 248 6953
Edwards, Chris (ACE)
Kyle, Tim (ACE)
Lowe, Dawn (Bus & Perf Mgr)
Connolly, Andrew (Prob Ops Mgr)
Nicolls, Steve (Prob Ops Mgr)

Cheetham Hill
20 Humphrey Street
Cheetham Hill Manchester M8 7JR
Tel: 0161 795 1777 Fax: 0161 720 6707
Parmar, Sushma (Prob Ops Mgr)
Johnston, Graham (Prob Ops Mgr)
Wild, Andrea (Bus & Perf Mgr)

Moss Side
87 Moss Lane West
Moss Side Manchester M15 5PE
Tel: 0161 226 3515 Fax: 0161 232 0649
Orr, Cranmer (Prob Ops Mgr)
Martin, Patricia (Prob Ops Mgr)
Lowe, Dawn (Bus & Perf Mgr)

Miles Platting
Varley Street
Miles Platting Manchester M10 8EE
Tel: 0161 205 7444 Fax: 0161 205 7563
Coyle, Rob (Prob Ops Mgr)
Wild, Andrea (Bus & Perf Mgr)

Wythenshawe
258 Brownley Road
Wythenshawe
Manchester M22 5EB
Tel: 0161 436 1919 Fax: 0161 498 8304
Burton-Francis, Sheron (Prob Ops Mgr)
Scanlon, David, (Prob Ops Mgr – IOM South)
Shepherd, Andrea (Bus & Perf Mgr)

Manchester Community Payback Unit
Victoria Park Laindon Road
Longsight Manchester M14 5YJ
Tel: 0161 224 0231 Fax: 0161 248 5378
Badachha, Simi (Community Ops Mgr)

Manchester and Salford Magistrates Court
Manchester Crown Court
Crown Square
Manchester M3 3FL
Tel: 0161 9541791 Fax: 0161 9541761
Martin, Chris (Prob Ops Mgr)
Jones, Steph (Bus & Perf Mgr)

Intensive Alternative to Custody
Vektor House
6–10 Hanover Square
Manchester M4 4AH
Tel: 0161 832 3200 Fax: 0161 832 3200
Pandolfo, Paul (Bus Mgr)
Davis, Paul (Prob Ops Mgr)
Wild, Andrea (Bus & Perf Mgr)

Trafford
Newton Street Stretford
Manchester M32 8LG
Tel: 03000 478350 Fax: 03000 478097
Cavanagh, Paul (Prob Ops Mgr)
Bulman, Kevin (Prob Ops Mgr)
Jones, Stephanie (Bus & Perf Mgr)

Trafford Community Payback Unit
Newton Street Stretford
Manchester M32 8LG
Tel: 03000 478350 Fax: 03000 478097

Trafford Magistrates Court
PO Box 13 Ashton Lane Sale Cheshire
M33 7NR
Tel: 0161 976 3333 Fax: 0161 975 4673

Oldham

128 Rochdale Road
Oldham OL1 2JG
Tel: 0300 047 8545 Fax: 0300 047 8568
Jarvis, Sarah (ACE)
Araya, Christina (Bus & Perf Mgr)
Dale, Kelly (Prob Ops Mgr)

64 Bridge Street
Oldham OL1 1ED
Tel: 0300 047 8500 Fax: 0300 047 8541
Janet Armstrong-Burns (Prob Ops Mgr)
Derek Rhoden ((Prob Ops Mgr)
Claudia Ricketts (Prob Ops Mgr)

Oldham Community Payback Unit
64 Bridge Street
Oldham OL1 1ED
Tel: 0300 047 8500 Fax: 0300 047 8541
Kevin Harrison (Community Payback Locality Mannager)

Oldham Magistrates court
St. Domingo Place West St, Oldham
OL1 1QE
Phone: 0161 785 8819 or 0161 652 5885
Fax: 0161 633 0602

Rochdale

193/195 Drake Street
Rochdale OL11 1EF
Tel: 0300 047 7700 Fax: 0300 047 7707
Elliott, Nigel (ACE)
McGartland, John (Bus & Perf Mgr)
Brown, Trudi (Prob Ops Mgr)
Murphy, Alison (Prob Ops Mgr)
Albuquerque-Neale, Maria (Prob Ops Mgr)

Middleton Office
St Michael's House
Oldham Road Middleton M24 2LH
Tel: 0300 047 7770 Fax: 0300 047 7769
Perry, Hellen (Prob Ops Mgr)

Salford

2 Redwood Street
Pendleton Salford M6 6PF
Tel: 0161 736 6441 Fax: 0161 736 6620
Seale, Manjit (ACE)
Jones, Debra (Bus & Perf Mgr)
McDonagh, Mary (Prob Ops Mgr)
Phillips, Annette (Prob Ops Mgr)
Rothwell, Alison (Prob Ops Mgr)
Fuller, Clare (Prob Ops Mgr)
Thornton, Lisa ((p) Prob Ops Mgr)

Salford Community Payback Unit
2 Redwood Street Pendleton
Salford M6 6PF
Tel: 0161 736 6441 Fax: 0161 736 6620
Cope, Stephen (Community Payback Locality Mgr)

Stockport

19/37 High Street
Stockport SK1 1EG
Tel: 03000 477 500 Fax: 03000 477 599

Farooq, Mohammed (ACE)
Hilton, Jenny (Bus & Support Mgr)
Berry, Eloise (Prob Ops Mgr)
Phillips, Mandy (Prob Ops Mgr)
Saunders, Phil (Prob Ops Mgr)

Stockport Community Payback Unit
19/37 High Street
Stockport SK1 1EG
Tel: 03000 477 508 Fax: 03000 477 599
Humphriss, Andy (Community Ops Mgr)

Stockport Magistrates Court
The Court House
PO Box 155
Edward Street, Stockport SK1 3NF

Tel 03000 477 518 or 03000 477 560
Fax: 0161 429 7928

Tameside

Francis Thompson Drive
Off Water Street
Ashton-under-Lyne OL6 7AJ
Tel: 03000 47 7600 Fax: 0161 343 7475
Barnes, Richard (ACE)
Ross, Enda (District Manager – Acting)
Johnson, Julie (Bus & Perf Mgr)
Allen, Fuschia (Prob Ops Mgr)
Gartside, Lisa (Prob Ops Mgr)
Lowe, Louise (Prob Ops Mgr)
Dale, Kelly (Prob Ops Mgr (p))

Priority & Prolific Offenders & DRR Team
Tameside DIP Good Hope Mill
98 Bentinck Street
Ashton-under-Lyne OL5 7SS
Tel: 0161 343 5622 Fax: 0161 343 4754

Schofield, Ceri (Prob Ops Mgr)

Tameside Community Payback Unit
Francis Thompson Drive
off Water Street
Ashton-under-Lyne OL6 7AJ
Tel: 03000 47 7600 Fax: 0161 343 7475
Humphriss, Andrew (Community Ops Mgr)

Wigan

81 Gloucester Street
Atherton M46 0JS
Tel: 01942 876889 Fax: 01942 886109
Buckley, Angie (ACE)
Lattimer, Debbie/Tracy Smith (Bus & Perf Mgr)
Buckley, Danielle (Prob Ops Mgr)
Leslie, Nicola (Prob Ops Mgr)
Thomson, Neil (Prob Ops Mgr)

Wigan Community Payback Unit
81 Gloucester Street
Atherton M46 0JS
Tel: 01942 876889 Fax: 01942 886109

Cooney, Martin (Community Ops Mgr)

Wigan Magistrates Court
Darlington Street Wigan
Phone: 01942 496410

Units

MAPPA Support Unit
c/o SOMU
MAPPA Support Unit
3rd Floor
Nexus House
Alexandria Drive
Ashton-under-Lyne
OL7 0QP
Tel: 0161 856 3636 Fax: 0161 855 2487
Cope, Angela (Prob Ops Mgr)
Campbell, Zoe (MAPPA/Visor Admin Mgr)

Intensive Alternative to Custody
Vektor House
6–10 Hanover Square
Manchester M4 4AH
Tel: 0161 832 3200 Fax: 0161 832 3200

Pandolfo, Paul (Bus Mgr)
Davis, Paul (Prob Ops Mgr)

Interventions

12 Minshull Street
Manchester M1 3FR
Tel: 0161 237 5173 Fax: 0161 228 6745

Probation Programmes & Development Unit
Tumelty, Joe (ACE)
Dransfield, Linda (Prob Ops Mgr)
Grundy, Peter (Bus & Perf Mgr)
Forsyth, Jane (Prog Mgr)
Nixon, Dave (Prog Mgr)
Willis, Julie (Prog Mgr)

Probation Programmes & Development Unit – SORT
2 Redwood Street
Pendleton Salford M6 6PF
Tel: 0161 736 3515
McGinn, Des, (Prog Mgr)

Youth Offending Services

Bolton Youth Offending Service
Le Mans Crescent
Bolton BL1 1SA
Tel: 01204 331263 Fax: 01204 331258

Bury Youth Offending Service
Seedfield Resource Centre
Parkinson Street Bury BL9 6NY
Tel: 0161 253 6862

Manchester Youth Offending Service
c/o Crime & Disorder Group (room 9030)

Town Hall Extension
Manchester M60 2LA
Tel: 0161 234 4564 Fax: 0161 234 4914

Manchester North Youth Offending Service
Abraham Moss Centre Crescent Road
Crumpsall Manchester M8 5UF
Tel: 0161 908 8368 Fax: 0161 908 1835

Manchester Central Youth Offending Service
Daisy Mill 345 Stockport Road
Longsight Manchester M13 0LF
Tel: 0161 227 3430 Fax: 0161 227 3460

Manchester South Youth Offending Service
Greenbow Road Newall Green
Manchester M23 2RE
Tel: 0161 219 2680 Fax: 0161 437 3856

Oldham Youth Offending Service
Medtia Place 80 Union Street
Oldham OL1 1DT
Tel: 0161 621 9500

Rochdale Youth Offending Service
Townhead Offices John Street
Rochdale OL16 1LB
Tel: 01706 925353

Salford Youth Offending Service
Encombe House
10/12 Encombe Place Salford M3 6FJ
Tel: 0161 607 1900 Fax: 0161 832 4306

Stockport Youth Offending Service
1st Floor Owl House
59/61 Great Underbank
Stockport SK1 1NE
Tel: 0161 476 2876 Fax: 0161 476 2858

Tameside Youth Offending Service
31 Clarence Arcade Stanford Street
Ashton-under-Lyne OL6 7PT
Tel: 0161 342 7680 Fax: 0161 330 3149

Trafford Youth Offending Service
Ground Floor,
Stretford Public Hall
Chester Roaddx, Stretford
M32 0LG
Tel: 0161 911 8201 Fax: 0161 911 8202

Wigan Youth Offending Service
93 Victoria Road
Platt Bride Wigan WN2 5DN
Tel: 01942 776886 Fax: 01942 776856

Approved Premises (Hostels)

Hostels Management Unit & Central Admissions Unit
64 Manley Road Whalley Range
Manchester M16 8ND
Tel: 0161 227 1849 Fax: 0161 227 9052

Central Referrals
Tel: 0161 226 8465 Fax: 0161 227 9052
Tumelty, Joe (ACE)
Archer, Carol (Bus & Perf Mgr)

Bradshaw House Approved Premises
147/151 Walmersley Road
Bury BL9 5DE
Tel: 0161 761 6419 Fax: 0161 763 4353
Wood, Nick (Prob Ops Mgr)

St Joseph's Approved Premises
Miller Street Patricroft
Eccles Manchester M30 8PF
Tel: 0161 789 5337 Fax: 0161 707 9085
Murphy, Lindsey (Prob Ops Mgr)

Withington Road Approved Premises
172/174 Withington Road
Whalley Range Manchester M16 8JN
Tel: 0161 226 1179 Fax: 0161 227 8041
Croall, David (Prob Ops Mgr)

Chorlton Approved Premises
10/12 Oswald Road
Chorlton-cum-Hardy
Manchester M21 1LH
Tel: 0161 862 9881 Fax: 0161 862 9554
Hunt, Sean (Prob Ops Mgr)

Wilton Place Approved Premises
10/12 Edward Street
Werneth Oldham OL9 7QW
Tel: 0161 624 3005 Fax: 0161 628 6936
Lees, Wendy (Prob Ops Mgr)

Ascot House Approved Premises
195 Wellington Road North
Heaton Norris Stockport SK4 2PB
Tel: 0161 443 3400 Fax: 0161 432 9739
Williams, Robbie (Prob Ops Mgr)

Hostels for Men
Ascot House Stockport
Bradshaw House Bury
Chorlton House Manchester
St Joseph's Salford (specialist MDO hostel)
Wilton Place Oldham
Withington Road Manchester

Prisons

HMP Manchester
Southall Street Strangeways
Manchester M60 9AH
Tel: 0161 817 5600 Fax: 0161 817 5601
Direct dial: 0161 817 + ext
Visits tel: 0161 817 5656
Probation fax: 0161 817 5970
HDC admin tel: 0161 817 5653
Johnston, Graham (Hd of Off Mgt) ext 6087

HMP Buckley Hall
Buckley Road
Rochdale OL12 9DP
Tel: 01706 514300 Fax: 01706 711797
Parole Clerk ext 290
Special visits ext 312

HMP/YOI Forest Bank
Agecroft Road Pendlebury
Salford M27 8FB
Tel: 0161 925 7000 Fax: 0161 925 7001
Direct dial: 0161 925 + ext
Probation Office: ext 2153
Bail Info Off 0161 925 7000 ext 2018
Bail Info fax: 0161 925 7019
Booking visits ext 7029/7030
Healthcare Centre ext 7065
Healthcare Centre fax: 0161 925 7055

Local Justice Areas
Bolton
Bury
Manchester City
Oldham
Rochdale, Middleton & Heywood
Stockport
Tameside
Trafford
Wigan & Leigh

Crown Courts
Manchester
Bolton

MERSEYSIDE PROBATION TRUST

Out of hours emergency tel: 0151 257 6090

Email:
firstname.lastname@merseyside.probation.gsi.gov.uk

Head Office
Burlington House Crosby Road North
Waterloo Liverpool L22 0PJ
Tel: 0151 257 6090 Fax: 0151 257 6154

Hennessey, Annette (CEO)
Pakula, Anne (Head of Operations)
Gotts, Paul (Treasurer)

Assistant Chief Officers
Chadwick, Jayne (HR & Staff Dev)
Murray, Peter (Info Performance &
Planning)
Turner Sonia (Interventions)

Divisional Managers
Marlow, Jan (Approved Premises & Acc
Unit)
Legal Services
Aspinall-Brew, Nadine (Solicitor
Communications
Felton-Aksoy, Kathy (Comm Off)
Finance
McDonald, Colin (Principal Accountancy
Assistant
Stamper, Kevin (Payroll/Payments
Manager)
Clarkson, Libby (Purchasing Officer)
Christian, Dave (Commissioning
Manager)
Human Resources
Beigan, Carla (HR Mgr)
Thurston, David (H&S Advisor)
Crowley, Ann-Marie (PQF Coordinator)
Information Services
Steele, Box (Project & ICT Mgr)
Steele, Rachael (Research & Performance
Info Unit Mgr)
Goodwin, Rosemary (Performance &
Quality Mgmt Unit Mgr)
Phillips, Jenny (Quality Assurance OM)
Pickstock, Katie (Quality Assurance OM)
Achieve Northwest
Bennett, Chris (Project Dir)
Bratherton, Robert (Finance Mgr)

Liverpool Crown Court
PO Box 69 Queen Elizabeth II
Law Courts Derby Square
Liverpool L69 2NE
Tel: 0151 236 5302 Fax: 0151 255 0682

Hamilton, Richard (Team Mgr)

Caton, Barry
Leonard, Jacci

PSOs
Cummins, Susan
Harrison, Christine

Marston, Paul
Poole, Amy
Reil, Sue
Williams, Jan

Achieve Northwest Team

Wirral Probation Centre
40 Europa Boulevard Birkenhead
Wirral, Merseyside CH41 4PE
Tel: 0151 666 0400 Fax: 0151 666 0402

Jones, Anne-Marie (Regional Quality
Assurance Manager)

PSOs
Adamson, Helen
Baglow, Kenny (based HMP Liverpool)
Fearon, Ronnie
Jones, Chris
Keefe, Catherine

North Liverpool Probation Centre
Cheadle Avenue Old Swan
Liverpool L13 3AE
Tel: 0151 254 7000 Fax: 0151 254 7204

Taylor, Jeannette (Project Mgr)

PSOs
Fletcher, Barry
Underwood, Mike (based 4 Trinity Road
Bootle)
Watson, Louise (based St Helens
Probation Centre)

MAPPA Coordinator
25 Crosby Road North,
Waterloo Liverpool L22 1RG
Tel: 0151 920 4444 Fax: 0151 928 9143

Phillips, Jayne (Team Mgr)

Knowsley LDU

Knowsley Probation Centre
Poplar House, Poplar Bank, Huyton,
Liverpool LS36 9US
Tel: 0151 480 5020 Fax: 0151 481 5095/6
Metherell, David (ACO)

Kayani, Nick (Partnership & Interagency
Mgr)

Offender Management
Hughes, Peter (Team Mgr)
Branford-Ellis, Patsy
Gilbert, Nicky
McGee, Carol
Markland, Kate
Williams, Sarah
Williams, Ian

PSOs
Bell, Emma
Huhwaite, David
Griffiths, Alex (Team Mgr)
Foster, Ian
Loyden, Frank
Lynch, Katie
McCully, Simon
Patterson, Pat
Wardle, Rebecca
PSOs
O'Connor, Claire
Thulbourn, Kayleigh
Morris, Judith (Team Mgr)
Corcoran, Angela
Heston, Debbie
Kelly, Michelle
Morley, Fiona
Nelson, Sam
Rainford, Jane
PSOs
Fletcher, John
Nijs, Rebecca
Rimmer, Hayley

DRR
Bradley, Claire
Owens, Steve
Kildare, Irene (PSO)

PPO
Grady, Claire
Graham, Nora (PSO)

Victim Liaison
Nash, Emma (PSO)

Youth Offending Service Knowsley
Youth Justice Section Fairclough Centre
193 Liverpool Road Huyton
Merseyside L36 3RD
Tel: 0151 443 3079 Fax: 0151 443 3086

Lopez, Donna

Liverpool

Liverpool Magistrates' Court
111 Dale Street Liverpool L2 2JQ
Tel: 0151 236 0603 Fax: 0151 236 5417

Hamilton, Richard (Team Mgr)
Loughran, Pete
Pennington, Nicola

PSOs
Aston, Barbara
Brownrigg, Catherine
Carroll, Liz
Cherry, Anne
Hughes, Alex

McManniman, Diane
O'Neill, Jan
Patterson, George
Pilkington, Barbara
Smith,Jenny
Thompson, Jennie

Bail Information
Charnock, Jacqui (PSO)
O'Grady, Stuart (PSO)

North Liverpool Community Justice Centre
5 Boundary Street Liverpool L5 2QD
Tel: 0151 298 3636 Fax: 0151 298 3601

McIlveen, John (Team Mgr)
Lawrence, Pauline
Tubb, Eileen (PSO)

PPO Liverpool
Eaton Road Police Station Eaton Road
Liverpool L12 3HF
Tel: 0151 777 4431 Fax: 0151 777 4445

Dickinson, Ann (Team Mgr)
Ashes, Ken
Hypolite, Diana
Massey, Joanne
Taylor, Kate

PSOs
Hypolite, Addissa
Lewis, Alan
Melia, Chris

Youth Offending Service Liverpool
Customer Focus Centre
80–82 Wavertree Road Liverpool L7 1PH
Tel: 0151 255 8213 Fax: 0151 255 8607

Pope, Alan
Pritchard, George
Proudlove, Sarah

North Liverpool LDU

North Liverpool Probation Centre
Cheadle Avenue Old Swan
Liverpool L13 3AE
Tel: 0151 254 7102 Fax: 0151 254 7204

Quick, John (ACO)

Sofia, Nikki (Partnership & Interagency Mgr)

Offender Management
Williams, Clare (Team Mgr)
Alexander, Kathryn
Barnes, Roger
Harvey, Mike
Kenwright, Kathleen

Lyon, Alison
Macaulay, Robert
Phillips, Tony
Ralph, Renée
Riley, James
Thompson, Kerry

PSOs
Bradshaw, James
McGenity, Lisa
Rotherham, Karen
McIlveen, David (Team Mgr)
Dykes, Ste
Grunnill, Paul
Jones, Ann
Lightfoot, Julie
Lynch, Valerie
McGrath, Alison
Perkins, Tony
Turner, Emma
Wilson, Wayne
Wynn, Paul

PSOs
Given, Mike
Lloyd, Neil
McBurney, Gill

Women's POD
Daley, Jeanette
Gore, Amanda
Hamilton, Amanda
Williams, Lucy
PSOs
Eccleston, Yasmin
McKeown, Jenny
Riley, Sandra

Intensive Alternative to Custody
Churchill, Gail (Team Mgr)
McClelland, Fiona
Kent, Linda
Smith, Mark
Powell, Audrey (PSO, Mentor)
Hughes, Gareth (PSO)
Sheldrake, Hayley (PSO)

DRR
Monteith, Tracey (Team Mgr)
Daelman, Louise
Gowan, Steve
Jameson, Keith
May, Patsy
Underwood, Shanel (PSO)

Victim Liaison
Byrne, Diane (PSO)

142/148 Stanley Road Kirkdale
Kirkdale, Liverpool L5 7QQ
Tel: 0151 286 6159 Fax: 0151 284 7847

Offender Management
Dauphin, Colin (Team Mgr)
Beuschlein, Barbara
Chambers, Clare
Dinwoodie, Claire
Keating, Lisa
Nuttall, Leslie
Richmond, Stephanie
Smith, Jan
Stanton, Rachel
Thomas, Andrea

PSOs
Gillies, Ros
O'Doherty, Barry
Teese, Paul
Wells, Emma

South Liverpool LDU

South Liverpool Probation Centre
180 Falkner Street Liverpool L8 7SX
Tel: 0151 706 6644 Fax: 0151 708 5044
Chambers, Steve (ACO)

Dean, Michelle (Partnership & Interagency Mgr)

Offender Management
Manley, Nanci (Team Mgr)
Craig, Michael
Griffiths, Christine
Hanson, Caroline
Hutchinson, Danielle
Lowe, Helen
Rolfe, Katin
Stevenson, Kerry
Wiltshire, Sasha
Fisher, John (PSO)
Wood, David (Team Mgr)
Adamson, Jo
Bozkurt, Claire
Kennedy, Irene
Mohamed, Ibrahim
Nenna, Paul
Pickstock, Marie
Tracey, Anna
Buoey, Carol (PSO)
Li, Amanda (PSO)
Morris, Judith (Team Mgr)
Arnold, Maxine
Anderson, Nicola
Baker, Fiona
Gill, Helen
Houghton, Nick

Jones, Candice
Jones, Gavin
McAnallen, Donna
McGovern, Jamie
Oldham, Paul
Williams, Debbie
Adekanmbi, Mji (PSO)
Bradshaw, Bernie (PSO)
Fullalove, Linda (PSO)

Black Mentor Scheme
Diskaya, Mayling (PSO)
Rogers, Darren (PSO)

Victim Liaison
Parkinson, Julie (PSO)

Sefton LDU
Holt, Paul (ACO) based at Waterloo)

4 Trinity Road
Bootle, Merseyside L20 7BE
Tel: 0151 286 5667 Fax: 0151 286 6900

Offender Management (South Sefton)
Milnes, Mike (Team Mgr)
De Gale, Hamilton
Hayes, Malcolm
Moorhead, Justin
Roach, Lynsey
Feehan, Sue (PSO)
Keenan, Joy (Team Mgr, PPO and DRR)
Bailey, Janine
Chadwick, Pat
Clarke, Ruth
Conroy, Martin
Dillon, Jayne
Phillips, Hilton
Platt, Jonathan
Kite, Clare (PSO)
McDonnell, Rebecca (PSO)
McLean, Ian (PSO)
Pendleton, Chris (PSO)

Victim Liaison
Chambers, Martin (PSO)
25 Crosby Road, South Waterloo,
Liverpool L22 1RG
Tel: 0151 920 4444 Fax: 0151 928 9143

Offender Management (North Sefton)
Stamper, Lena (Team Mgr)
Brotherstone, Cathie
Eisner, Julien
Gallivan, Michelle
Hall, Rachel
Jones, Pam
Seel, David
Johnson, Angela (PSO)
Taylor, Lynn (PSO)

South Sefton Magistrates' Court
The Court Building
29 Merton Road, Bootle L20 3BJ
Tel: 0151 285 6236 Fax: 0151 933 8602
Khazi, Sharon

PSOs
Dawber, Jacqueline
Hilton, Bernie
O'Brien, Pam
Reilly, Moira

PPO Sefton
Marsh Lane Police Station
Marsh Lane Liverpool L20 5HJ
Tel: 0151 777 3077

Farrell, Debbie
Munro, Lee

Youth Offending Service Sefton
Supervision Assessment/Court Services
Sefton Youth Offending Team
Police Station Marsh Lane
Liverpool L20 5HJ
Tel: 0151 285 5127 Fax: 0151 934 2779

Doherty, Eddie
Murphy, Jennifer

St Helens LDU

St Helens Probation Centre
St Mary's House 50 Church Street
St Helens Merseyside WA10 1AP
Tel: 01744 630229 Fax: 01744 606224

Metherell, David (ACO based at Knowley
Probation Centre)
Aubrey, Cath (Partnership & Interagency
Mgr)

Offender Management
Kuyateh, Jeanette (Team Mgr)
Davidson, Sally
Dryhurst, Jim
Kelly, Lisa
Nowell, Clayton
Plews, Paula

PSOs
Ingram, Louise
Sweeney, Carol
Wood, Jean

Rooney, Karen (Team Mgr)
Bellamy, Mary
Curzon, Anna
Harris, Helen
Jones, Jo
Malone, Zara
Platt, Sarah

Sweeney, Michelle
Haworth, Roz (PSO)
Shaw, Chris (PSO)

Court Services
Carroll, June

PSOs
Bennett, Claire
Ingram, Elizabeth

DRR St Helens
O'Neale, Steve
Moran, Kelly (PSO)

Victim Liaison
Myler Sharon (PSO)

PPO St Helens
St Helens Police Station
College Street, St Helens
WA10 1TG
Tel 0151 777 6826/7/8 Fax 0151 777 6888

Briggs, Danuta
Cleworth, Geoff
Whitby, Nicola (PSO)

Youth Offending Service St Helens
Youth Offending Team
2 Tickle Avenue Parr
St Helens WA9 1RZ
Tel: 01744 677990 Fax: 01744 675577

Martine, Karen

Wirral LDU

Wirral Probation Centre
40 Europa Boulevard Birkenhead
Wirral Merseyside CH41 4PE
Tel: 0151 666 0400 Fax: 0151 666 0400

Brown, Sue (ACO)
Baird, Allen (Partnership & Interagency
Mgr)

Offender Management
Kelly, Mary (Team Mgr)
Bygrave, Hazel
Fishwick, Donna
Gibbons, Laura
McNiffe, Peter
Nickeas, Jason
Osborne, Stephen
Kennedy, Paul (PSO)
Wilkins, Ian (PSO)
Roberts, Kelly (Team Mgr)
Bestwick, Helen
Foster, Rob
Freeman, Sue
Jones, Carla

Marmion, Christopher
Minnis, Nicola
O'Donnell, Shaun
O'Grady, Anne
Byron, Paul (PSO)
Cummins, Pauline (PSO)
Morrison, Stephanie (PSO)
Pat Kimmance (Team Mgr)
Beggs, John
Foster, Rob
Marshall, Andrea
O'Neill Con
Robinson, Kate
Chandler, Collette (PSO)
Cowell, Steph (PSO)
Dennis Rona (PSO)

Court Services
Smeda, Mike
Taylor-Watson, Susan
Totty, Stella
Charnock, Sam (PSO)
McKenzie, Lisa (PSO)
Surridge, Andrew (PSO)

Victim Liaison
Haselden, Patricia (PSO)

DRR Wirral
Arches Initiative 23 Conway Street
Birkenhead Wirral CH41 6PT
Tel: 0151 666 6867 Fax: 0151 666 6802

Forshaw, Karen
Toole, John
Kinsey, Rebecca (PSO)
Lucas, Ian (PSO)

PPO Wirral
Old Court Building Manor Road
Wallasey Merseyside CH44 1BU
Tel: 0151 606 5760

Hamill, Una
Wright, Noel

Youth Offending Service Wirral
Hamilton Building Conway Street
Birkenhead Wirral CH41 4FD
Tel: 0151 666 4536 Fax: 0151 666 5651
McAllister, Christine

Interventions
Turner, Sonia (ACO, based at
Headquarters)
Armstrong, Paul (Div Mgr –
Programmes, based at MDU)
Marlow, Jan, (Div Mgr – Approved
Premises (based at Headquarters)

Accommodation Unit

Southwood Approved Premises
24 Southwood Road, Liverpool, L17 7QB
Tel: 0151 280 1833 Fax: 0151 280 3027

Reddy, Sharon (Accom Mgr)

PSOs
Arno, Sandi
Edwards, John
Mathison, David

Approved Premises

Stafford House

10 Croxteth Road, Toxteth, Liverpool L8 3SA
Tel: 0151 726 8286 Fax: 0151 727 2059

Kelly, Becky (Team Mgr)
Dunleavy, John (Prob Residential Off)
Rose, Francis (Project Co-ordinator/Assessor)
Lyon, Ruth (Prob Residential Off)

Hostel Supervisors
Bell, Clare
Diboe, Margo
Gillings, Paul
Molloy, Brian
Santangeli, Jenny

Merseybank

26 Great Howard Street Liverpool L3 7HS
Tel: 0151 255 1183 Fax: 0151 236 4464

Gay, Martin (Team Mgr)
Hurst, Sheila (Prob Residential Off)
Warren, Garry (Prob Residential Off)

Hostel Supervisors
Birchall, Lorraine
Freeman, John
Gillings, Paul
Harvey, Raoul
Morris, Stephen

Southwood

24 Southwood Road Liverpool L17 7BQ
Tel: 0151 280 1833 Fax: 0151 280 3027

Walker, Paul (Team Mgr)
Gee, Anthony (Prob Residential Off)
Rhodes, Paul (Prob Residential Off)

Hostel Supervisors
Bilbao, Tina
Cassells, Clark
Edwards, John
Glen, Jim
Kelly, Collette
Kormoss, Tony

Adelaide House

115 Edge Lane Liverpool L7 2PF
Tel: 0151 263 1290 Fax: 0151 260 4205

(independently managed female approved premises)

Thomas, Pat (CEO)
Kelly, Julie (Deputy Manager)

Programmes (GOBPs)

South Liverpool Probation Centre
180 Falkner Street Liverpool L8 7SX
Tel: 0151 706 6611 Fax: 0151 708 9687
Dykes, Jill (Progs Team Mgr)
Mannix, Nancy (Progs Team Mgr)
Watkins, Douglas (Treatment Mgr)

Programme Tutors
Bibby, Richard
Burns, James
Burton, Kayleigh
Butler, Sue
Campbell, Tom
Coulton, Kelly
Fisher, Jo
Halpin, Dawn
James, Alison
Khandamirian, Patrick
Lennard, Jane
Maher, Damien
Malone, Pat
McCarthy, Jacki
MacDougall, Paula
Wakelam, Dominica

Programmes (SO, DV and Hate Crime)

Merseyside Development Unit
6/8 Temple Court Liverpool L2 6PY
Tel: 0151 229 2000 Fax: 0151 236 4265

Green, Cindy (Progs Team Mgr)

Thomson, Angela (Progs Team Mgr)
Anderson, Carole (Treatment Mgr)

Programme Facilitators
Bakhtiary-Nejad, Patricia
Cook, Roy
East, Caroline
Gallagher, Julie
Hutchinson, Ian
Johnson, Emma
Johnson, Norris
Porter, Elizabeth
Ross, Bernadette
Shaw, Steph
Waller, Tracey
Walsh, Jenny

Walsh, Leanne
Woods, Kath

Unpaid Work

Knowsley & St Helens
South Knowsley Probation Centre
597 Princess Drive Liverpool L14 9NE
Tel: 0151 480 4544 Fax: 0151 480 3618

Kavanagh, Jennifer (Snr Ops Mgr)

Houghton, Janet, (Stakeholder
Engagement Officer)
Waine, Susan (Ops Mgr)
Dunn, Karen, (CSO)
Francis, Lorraine (CSO)

North Liverpool
North Liverpool Probation Centre
Cheadle Avenue Old Swan
Liverpool L13 3AE
Tel: 0151 254 7102 Fax: 0151 254 7204

Donoghue, Patrick (Ops Mgr)

South Liverpool
South Liverpool Probation Centre
180 Falkner Street Liverpool L8 7SX
Tel: 0151 706 6688 Fax: 0151 708 5044

Ashby, Maurice (Ops Mgr)

CSOs
Barrett, Kate
Clark, Louise
Cliff, Anita
Ginley, Vicky
Henry, Emma
Parkinson, Joe

Sefton
25 Crosby Road North Waterloo
Liverpool L22 1RG
Tel: 0151 920 4444 Fax: 0151 928 9143

Lavin, John (Ops Mgr)
Cowley, Brian (CSO)

Kelly, Lisa (CSO) Wirral
Wirral Probation Centre
40 Europa Boulevard Birkenhead
Wirral, Merseyside CH41 4PE
Tel: 0151 666 0400 Fax: 0151 666 0402

Humphreys, Barry (Team Mgr – all
CSOs)
Bromley, Rod (Ops Mgr)
Loughran, Julie (CSO)
O'Donnell, Gillian (CSO)

Institutions
Holt, Paul (ACO) based at Waterloo

HMP Altcourse
Higher Lane Fazakerley
Liverpool L9 7LH
Tel: 0151 522 2000 Fax: 0151 522 2121

Burns, Julie
Curtis, Naomi
Lawrenson, Phillip

HMP Kennet
Parkbourn Maghull
Merseyside L31 1HX
Tel: 0151 213 3000 Fax: 0151 213 3103

Hamilton, Elaine (p, Team Mgr)
Holleran, John
Maguire, Jan
Morrison, Andy

HMP Liverpool
Hornby Road Liverpool L9 3DF
Tel: 0151 530 4000 Fax: 0151 530 4001
Probation fax: 0151 524 1941

Vellacott, Sheila (Head of Offender
Management Unit)

Bowers, Kate
Brundell, Paul
Horrocks, Christine
Lock, Peter
Rogerson, James

PSOs
Ayres, Lesley
Basley, Jana
Cunningham Alison
Dooley, David
Draper, Rebecca
Hampson, Susan
Lumsden, Ken
Morris, Diane

Local Justice Areas
Knowsley (Knowsley LDU, Unpaid Work
Knowsley & St Helens)
Liverpool (North & South Liverpool LDU,
N Liverpool Community Justice Centre,
Unpaid Work N & S Liverpool)
North Sefton (Sefton LDU, Unpaid Work
Sefton)
St Helens (St Helens LDU, Unpaid Work
Knowsley & St Helens)
South Sefton (Sefton LDU, Unpaid Work
Sefton)
Wirral (Wirral LDU, Unpaid Work
Wirral)

Crown Court
Liverpool

NORFOLK AND SUFFOLK PROBATION TRUST

Out of hours emergency contact point (Norfolk)
John Boag House 01603 429488

Out of hours emergency contact point (Suffolk)
The Cottage (01473) 408266

Email:
firstname.lastname@nspt.probation.gsi.gov.uk

Centenary House
19 Palace Street
Norwich NR3 1RT
Tel: 01603 724000 Fax: 01603 664019
Direct dial: 01603 30 + ext

Graham, Martin (CEO) ext 2232
Gillian Lewis (Board Chair)
Blackman, Judith (Director Norwich & Kings Lynn LDU) ext 2233
Macdonald, Stuart (Director Business Devpt) ext 2237
Parker, Kelley (Director Ipswich & Bury LDU) 01473 282315
Pestell, Steve (Director Corporate Services) 01473 282317
Sharp, Julia (Director Interventions) ext 2244
Wardley, Sarah (Director Public Protection & Waveney LDU) ext 2239
Aspin, Steven (Director Finance) ext 2231
Wade, Belinda (Finance Mgr) ext 2230
Watchorn, Kemi (HR Mgr) ext 2238
Lewis, Gill (HR Mgr) 01473 282297
Herbert, Rachel (Asst HR Mgr) ext 2235
Sendall, Robbie (Health & Safety Mgr) ext 2241
Symonds, Robin (IT Mgr) ext 2200
Fullman, David (Diversity Mgr) 2248

Training
Foy, Rosemary (Training Mgr) ext 2236
Racher, Bev (PTA) 01533 669000
Pooley, Gill (PTA) 01603 724000
Smith, Kirstie (PTA) 01603 724000
Whitehead, Annette (PTA) ext 2246
Dobell, Stacey (PTA) 01473 408130
Stevens, Amber (PTA) 01473 282238
Brame, Rachel (PTA) 01473 282326
Curtis, Sally (PTA) ext 2116

Business Development Unit
Baker, Stephen (Procurement & Contracts Mgr) ext 2072

Leborgne, Claire (Offender Pathways Devpt Mgr) ext 2071
Jay, Nicky (Offender Pathways, Devpt Mgr)
Palmer, Rob (Offender Pathways, Devpt Mgr) 01473 282211
Wright, Andrew (Business Improvement Manager) ext 2247
Bergdahl, Jo (Performance Information Unit Mgr) 01473 282237
Boast, Leanne (Communications Officer) ext 2242
Rose, Jo (Restorative Justice Development Officer) ext
Stone, Katie (Restorative Justice Development Officer) 01473 408130

MAPPA
Monk, Donna (MAPPA Mgr)

Interventions – Programmes Unit
Ramshaw, Charles (Prog Mgr IDAP, SOTP) ext 2067
Shaw, John (Operational Support MGR) ext 2006
Wooltorton, Jo (Treatment Mgr DIDP, OTO, WESWAR (Spoc)) ext 2041
Feeney, Michael (Treatment Mgr IDAP) ext 2045
Richards, Matt (Treatment Mgr OSAP) ext 2054
Gale, Marie ext 2080
Medhurst, Ian (Programme Facilitator) ext 2127
Ryan, Liz (Treatment Mgr TVP) ext 2066
Weedon, Michelle ext
Young, Amanda 2152

PSOs
Bruce, Scott
Colbourn, Lynne ext 2079
Cullum, Stuart 2064
Clement, Jane (IDAP)
Feeney, William ext 2049
Fenn, Sharon 2057
Hampson, Nichola ext 2046
Harper, Louise ext
Hewitt, Steve ext 2059
Page, Viv ext 2060

Integrated Offender Management (Norfolk)
East, Paul (SPO) ext 2073
Cocker, Nicki ext 2181
Shuter, Wayne ext 2178
Gooding, Kevin (PSO) ext 2088
Pritchard, Hayley (PSO) 01493 333336
Steward, Kathy (PSO) 01553 669000

Victim Liaison
Burbidge, Kathy (VLO) ext 2011
Blanchard, Victoria (WSO) ext 2013
Bliss, Kim (WSO) ext 2014

Norwich Offender Management
Belham, Charlotte (SPO) ext 2069
DeVaux, Paula (SPO) ext 2114
East, Paul (SPO) ext 2184
McLoughlin, Leon (SPO) ext 2162
Tennant, James (Acting SPO) ext
Plunkett, Carly (Acting SPO) ext
Anderson, June (OSM) ext 2144
Whyte, Juliet (OSM) ext 2141
Probation Officers
Atkins, Tina ext
Black, Thomas ext 2120
Cleaver, Anne ext 2123
Coman, Matthew ext 2165
Connor, Elizabeth ext 2150
Cooper, Michael ext 2113
Day, Alyson ext 2130
Devaux, Dan ext 2163
Dyde, Sally ext 2171
Foulger, Sarah ext 2118
Gall, Jason ext 2110
Garnham, Jo ext 2159
Good, Philippa ext 2152
Hutchings, Joanne ext
Jackson, Gareth ext 2157
Kennedy, Helen ext 2108
Loome, Alex ext 2177
Louise, Pippa ext 2169
Lynch, Rosanna ext 2133
Marsden, Gill ext 2106
Reeve, Caroline ext 2100
Robinson, Samantha ext 2117
Shuter, Wayne ext
Smith, Chris ext 2137
Weedon, Michelle ext
Young, Amanda ext 2152

PSOs
Baker, Aaron ext 2145
Cullum, Stuart
Forrest, Paula ext 2115
Hanton, Matthew (TPO) ext 2086
Hill, Abi ext 2008
Macdonald, Stacey ext 2173
Menezes, Liz ext
Myhill, Tracey ext 2179
Nixon, Lisa (TPO) ext 2105
Noakes, Amy ext
Noble, Phil ext 2183
Pyzer, Stephen ext 2029
Racher, Karen ext 2122
Riches, Jason ext 2078
Riley, Nicole (TPO) ext

Smith, Michael (TPO) ext
Stebbing, Luke ext
Wood, Karen (TPO) ext
Wood, Tracey ext 2124
Woodhouse, Tracey ext 2124
Young, Hannah ext 2107

Crown Court Office
Tel: 01603 728268
Orson, Emily

Magistrates' Court
Tel: 01603 724056/7

PSOs
Cockrill, Alan
Cooper, Katie
Malone, Robert
Rutherford, John
Whitaker, James

Community Payback Unit
Tel: 01603 30 + ext Fax: 01603 302297
Hunter, Richard (CPU Scheme Mgr) ext 2074
Houseago, Sally (Locality Mgr) ext 2035

PSOs
Young, Mark ext 2025

Ipswich Office
Peninsular House
11–13 Lower Brook Street
Ipswich IP4 1AQ
Tel: (01473) 408130 Fax: (01473) 408136
Direct dial: 01473 28 + ext

Gillian Lewis (Board Chair)
Parker, Kelley (Director Ipswich & Bury St Edmunds LDU) ext 2315
Pestell, Steve (Director Corporate Services) ext 2317
Fullman, David (Diversity Mgr) ext 2309
Foy, Rosemary (SPO, Training Mgr) ext 2312
Morgan, Elizabeth (SPO, VQ Centre Mgr) ext
Palmer, Rob (SPO, Pathways Devpt) ext 2211
Sykes, Tim (MAPPA Mgr) ext 2308
Bergdahl Jo (SPO, Performance Unit Mgr) ext 2237
Green Mandy (SPO, Women's Offender Project) ext 2268
Lewis, Gill (HR Mgr) ext 2297
Coopoosamy, Ruby (Supt Services Mgr) ext 2283
Carey Godfrey (p, Project Co-ordinator)

Integrated Offender Management
Woods, Victoria (SPO) ext 2212
Rohlfing, Kate (PO) ext 2289
Roberts, Jennie (PSO) ext 2293

Ipswich Offender Management
Abbott, Pat (SPO) ext 2231
Mark McLelland-Brown (SPO) ext 2346
Brame, Rachel (Acting SPO) ext 2284
Stevens, Amber, (Acting SPO) ext 2284
Collings, Mark (OSM) ext 2322
Baldwin, Claire ext 2281
Black, Sharon ext 2331
Cossey, Alison (p) ext 2249
Dance, Alison (p) ext 2330
Dunn, Nikki ext 2265
Dickson, Sarah
Hawkins, Vicky ext 2332
Joiner, Elise ext 2226
Larter Tracey (p) ext
Lockhart, Sue ext 2282
MacDonald, Carolyn ext 2329
Mendham, Dene (p) ext 2267
Needham, Marcus ext
Petch, Emma ext 2270
Pratt, Melvin ext 2266
Scuffins, Carol ext 2223
Sharpe, Don ext 2272
Smith, Rachael ext 2334
Staines, Leslie ext 2256
Stock, Corrina ext 2229
Amy Tuffin ext 2205

PSOs
Black, Jeanette ext 2234
Chitty Sharon (TPO) ext 2314
Crawford, Nicky ext 2274
Lee, Sarah ext 2272
Parcell, Jayne ext 2273
Shaw Sara (p,) ext 2343
Wallis, Karen ext 2313
Westren, James ext 2276

Crown Court Office
Tel: 01473 228526/228527

Magistrates' Court
Tel: 01473 408270

PSOs
De'ath, Ashleigh
John, Shelley
Lane, Val
Stone, Liz

Interventions – Programmes
Clarke, Richard (p, SPO) ext 2236
Low, Gordon (SPO) ext 2344
Maudsley, Richard (Treatment
Mgr/Facilitator) ext 2310

Lister, Simone (Treatment
Mgr/Facilitator) ext 2232
Lockhart, Sue ext 2282
Meadows, Karen (p TVP) ext 2215
Reid, Heather (p, TVP Treatment Mgr)
ext 2213
Rickatson, Carmel (p, TVP) ext 2221
Tozer, Neil (p) ext 2221
White, Colin (p, TVP) ext 2221

PSOs
King, Michelle (p) ext 2219
Morse, Allwyn (p) ext 2220

Victim Liaison
Sage, Lorri (WSO/VLO) ext 2348
Wilkins, Sarah (VLO) ext 2254

Community Pay Back
Morrison, Kevin (Locality Mgr) ext 2264
John Wesley (Placement Mgr) ext 2263

Purfleet Quay
  King's Lynn PE30 1HP
  Tel: 01553 669000 Fax: 01553 776544
  Direct dial: 01553 6690 + ext

Offender Management
Parke-Chatten, Pauline (SPO) ext 14
Vacancy (p SPO)
Bliss, Lesley (OSM)
Probation Officers
Barnes, Amanda ext 07
Bertram, Angela ext 12
Coleman, Guy ext 05
Cooper, Sharon ext 04/39
Farelly, Joanne
Nash, David ext 09
Wallis, Sarah

PSOs
Arnold, Tracy (TPO) ext 02
Barker, Andrew ext 10
Bolger, Jenna ext 31
Driver, Len ext 44
Garner, Roy ext 03
Jobsz, Tracy
Mahoney, Philippa (TPO) ext 08
Taylor, Victoria ext 30
Thompson, Rebecca ext 45
Vassie, Lisa (PPO) ext

IOM
Steward, Kathryn (PSO)

Interventions
Cooper, Sharon (Treatment Mgr ART)
ext 04/39
Allen, Rita (PSO IDAP) ext 46
Harpley, Jenny (PSO) ext 36

Victim Liaison
Bliss, Kim (WSO/VLO) ext
Bolger, Jenna (WSO) ext 31
Taylor, Victoria (VLO) ext 30

Community Payback Unit
Houseago, Sally (Locality Mgr) ext 58
Goldsmith, Terence (PSO, Placement
Supervisor) ext 56
Murphy, Fred (PSO, Placement
Supervisor)

Waveney & Yare Officer
203 Whapload Road
Lowestoft NR32 1UL
Tel: (01502) 501800 Fax: (01502) 525779

Offender Management
Cuell, David (SPO) 01502 527313
Woodley, Michaela (SPO) 01502 525769
Payne, Paul (OSM) 01502 527306
Probation Officers
Bransby, Alison 01502 527320
Brogan, Rachel 01502 527325
Ford, Helen 01502 527771
Hannant, Andrew 01502 527311
Herring, Jo 01502 527316
Kansal, Kate (p temp)
Massey, Kate (p) 01502 525751
Maudsley, Lindsay 01502 527319
Moonoosamy, Krishna 01502 527318
Tandy, Anne (p) 01502 525754
Wilkinson, Emma 01502 527305
Payne, Paul (OSM)
Williamson, Jodi 01502 525776
Zagdan, Charlene 01502 525757

PSOs
Ayres, Sylvia (TPO) 01502 525765
Baldry, Maureen 01502 527321
Berry, Christina (TPO) 01502 527326
Burley, Peter (p) 01502 525762
Craske, Sue 01502 527327
Fisher, Sarah (p) 01502 527323
Gore, Hannah 01502 527329
Hewitt, Kathryn 01502 527327
Jackson, Barry 01502 525772
King, Lucy 01502 525758
Martin, Jon 01502 525764
McMormack, Julie 01502 525759
McKinnell, Duncan 01502 525761
Smith, Steve 01502 527360
Taylor, Stuart 01502 527328
Integrated Offender Management
Interventions – Programmes
Hipperson, Sarah (Treatment
Mgr/Facilitator) 01502 525763
Alden, Graham 01502 527314

Davis, Shayne (p)
Chapman-Wright, Ian (p, PSO Treatment
Mgr)
King, Sarah (p, PSO) 01502 525766

Victim Liaison
Vicky Blanchard (WSO/VLO) 01502
527308
Doherty, Patricia (WSO) 01502 525774

Community Payback
Murphy, Tracey (Locality Mgr) 01502
527324
Leer, Colin (p, Placement Mgr) 01502
527317
Scully, Eamonn (PSO, Placement
Supervsior) 01502 525767

West Suffolk Probation Centre
Dettingen Way
Bury St. Edmunds IP33 3TU
Tel: (01284) 716600 Fax: (01284) 716606
Direct dial: 01284 716 + ext

Offender Management
Foden, Jackie (SPO) ext 634
Greenhalgh, Karen (SPO) ext 629
McNamara, Adele (SPO)
Layzell, Karen (OSM) ext 627
Probation Officers
Gallagher, Ann ext 640
Ofverberg, Julian ext 624
Puscasu, Ioana ext 643
Smeeth, Sarah ext 615
Steel, David (p) ext 620
Tozer, Neil ext 633
Wood, Janet ext 644

PSOs
Barber, Ann (p) ext 645
Beckett, Anna ext 608
Bluett, Marie (p) ext 647
Lewis, Fran (CRT) 638
Melvin, Peter (p) ext 614
Reader, Shelley ext 655
Salmons, Marie (p) ext 611
Snodgrass, Andrew (p) ext 621
Stoodley, Carl ext 664
Tooley, Craig ext 607
Wogan, Chris ext 649

Integrated Offender Management
Tattersall, Beth ext 637
Bouyer Herb (PSO) ext 636

Interventions – Programmes
Low, Gordon (p, SPO) ext 632
Bowman, Anna (p, Treatment Mgr)
Clarke, Richard (SPO, IDAP)
Tozer, Neil (p) ext 633

Chapman-Wright, Ian (p, PSO, Treatment Mgr) ext 631
Beckett, Anna ext 608
Griffiths, Kaye
Key, Martyn ext 641
Wogan, Chris ext 649

Victim Liaison
Bluett, Marie (WSO) ext 647
Barber, Ann (VLO) ext 645

Community Payback
Morrison, Kevin (Locality manager)
Foster, Bryan (p, Placement manager)

Youth Offending Teams

Norwich
Tel: 01603 877500

Kemsley, Hannah

Great Yarmouth
Tel: 01493 847400

Vacancy

Kings Lynn
Tel: 01553 819400
Johnson, Richard

Youth Offending Service

Bury St Edmunds
Tel: 01284 352378
Cuthbert, Ann

Ipswich
Tel: 01473 583570
Nikki Dunn (p)
Vacancy (p)

Lowestoft
01502 405375
Vicki Grice (p)

Approved Premises (Hostels)

John Boag House
1 Drayton Road, Norwich NR3 2DF
Tel: 01603 429488 Fax: 01603 485903

Leaberry, David (Mgr)

Winchester, Claire (Deputy Mgr)

PSOs
Anderton. Andy (p)
Eliot, Stef (p)
Caron-Mattison, Joe
Davison, Cathy (p)
Foster, Frank (p)
Young, Janet (p Finance & Admin Officer)

Lightfoot House
37 Fuchsia Lane, Ipswich IP4 5AA
Tel: (01473) 408280 Fax: (01473) 408282

Leaberry, David (SPO Mgr)
Dickson, Sarah (Dep Mgr)

PSOs
Murray, Jim (p)
Portfleet, Theresa
Royal, Chris
Smith, Jason
Chaplin, Lynne (Finance & Admin Officer)

The Cottage
795 Old Norwich Road
Ipswich IP1 6LH
Tel: (01473) 408266 Fax: (01473) 408268
Leaberry, David (SPO Mgr)
Carr, Taryn (Dep Mgr)

PSOs
Ball, Reg
Butler, Maria (p)
Ramshaw, Steph
Smith, Jason
Williams, Richard (p)
Chaplin, Lynne (Finance & Admin Officer)

Institutions

HMP/YOI Norwich
Knox Road **Norwich** NR1 4LU
Tel: 01603 708600 Fax: 01603 708601
Probation Fax: 01603 708619
Discipline ext 8791

Probation Clerks
Carpenter, Brian (HDC) ext 8753

Moore, Andy (Public Protection) ext 8804
Nichols, Sue (Public Protection) ext 8804
Roper, Dan (SPO) ext 8802

POs
Coleman, Sam
Mulford, Gill

PSOs
Colk, Miranda
Fulcher, Jon
Gregory, Tonia
Hurn, Emma
Millbank, Lindsey
Montague, Michael

HMP Wayland
Griston, Thetford IP25 6RL
Tel: 01953 804100 Fax: 01953 804220
Direct dial: 01953 858 + ext

Probation Clerk (visits, gen enquiries) ext 073
Probation Typist (sch 1, temp release) ext 071
Bateman, Peter (SPO) ext 072

POs
Baker, Elizabeth
Dawson, Annetta
Huggins, Wendy
Mead, Nikki
Wright, Julie
Cox, Martin
Payne, David

HMP Bure
Coltishall, Norfolk NR10 5AJ
Tel: 01603 266800

Roper, Dan (SPO)
Cummins, John
Pett, Bev
Perrett, Andrew
McIntyre, Philip (PSO)

Interventions – Programmes Unit
Vacancy SPO

Programme Facilitators
Attfield, Dan
Bentley, Jayne
Carter, Joanne
Golden, Deborah
Hogarth, Rosa
Mason, Chris
Monk, Ian
Wilson, Kate

HMP Blundeston
Lowestoft NR32 5BG
Tel: (01502) 734500 Fax: (01502) 734503
direct dial (01502) 73 + ext
probn clerk ext 4769

Hacon, Linda (p SPO) ext 4568

POs
Moreno, Rene ext 4771
Peacock, Mark
Steel, David (p) ext 4580

PSOs
Bennett, Lisa
Grimble, Anna
Hathway, Taff ext 4759
Suso, Hayley ext 4769

HMP Highpoint South
Stradishall, Newmarket CB8 9YG
Tel: (01440) 743100 Fax: (01440) 743049
Direct dial (01440) 74 + ext
Admin clerk ext 3022

Hopwood, Andrew (SPO) ext 3314
Grant, Donna (Practice Manager) ext 3008

POs
Gladden, Angela (p) ext 3022
Meiklejohn, Jamie (p) ext 3215
Pearson, Nicky ext 3128
Stainton, Jayne ext 3022
Turnbull, Christine ext 3081
White, Colin (p) ext 3128

PSOs
Culver, Jennifer ext 3216
Kingfisher, Wendy ext 3216
O'Neill, Terry ext 3078
Smith, Emily ext 3132

HMP Highpoint North
Stradishall, Newmarket CB8 9YN
Tel: (01440) 743500 Fax: (01440) 743568
Direct dial (01440) 74 + ext
Admin clerk ext 3566
Hopwood, Andrew (SPO) ext 3571
Probation Officers
Gladden, Angela (p) ext 3559

PSOs
Case, Adrian ext 3558
Griffiths, Kaye ext 3556
Johns, Carla ext 3556
Orton, Kate ext 3528
Vann, Claire ext 3555

HMP/YOI Hollesley Bay
Hollesley, Woodbridge IP12 3JW
Tel: (01394) 412400 Fax: (01394) 412769
Direct dial (01394) 41 + ext
Parole clerk ext 2500
Dyde, Clare ext 2487

Crown Courts
Ipswich
Norwich

Local Justice Areas
Norwich
Great Yarmouth
SE Suffolk
North Norfolk
NE Suffolk
Central Norfolk
West Norfolk
W Suffolk
South Norfolk

NORTHAMPTONSHIRE PROBATION TRUST

Central bail referral number
Bridgewood Hostel tel: 01604 648704

Out of hours emergency contact point
Bridgewood Hostel tel: 01604 648704

Victims enquiries contact number
Tel: 01604 658060 or 01536 526821

Email:
firstname.lastname@northamptonshire.
probation.gsi.gov.uk

Head Office
Walter Tull House 43–47 Bridge Street
Northampton NN1 1NS
Tel: 01604 658000 Fax: 01604 658004

Senior Management Team
Budd, John (Chief Executive)
Geaney, Mary (Director of Interventions,
Partnerships & Community)
King, Helen (Director of Corp Services)
Meylan, Denise (Director of Offender
Management)
Harper, Tansi (Trust Chair)
Bedford, Roland (Board Sec)

EMT Support Unit
Pardoe, April (PA to CEO & Trust Chair)
Sanders, Katie (PA to Director of
Interventions, Partnerships &
Community)
Wakelin, Sarah (PA to Director of
Offender Management)
Sampson, Jackie (PA to Director of Corp
Services, Admin Asst to Board Secretary)

**Business Development &
Communications**
Robinson, Becky (Bus Dev & Comms
Asst)

Finance & Estates
Brown, Linda (Accountant)
Hickman, Helen (Finance Off)
Humphries, Angela (Finance Asst)
Medley, John (H&S and Estates Officer)

Human Resources Unit
Brady, Walter (HR Business Partner)
Bradley, Julie (HR Advisor Equalities)
Aworth, Caroline (HR Admin)
Smith, Emma (HR Admin)
Bushby, Amy (HR Advisor)

Information Services Unit
IT helpdesk tel: 01604 657090

Cornhill, Alan (Unit Manager)
Tebbutt, Bernice (Info Systems Trainer)

Performance Unit
Garcha, Permjit (Unit Mgr)
Harris, Len (Data Analyst)
Jones, Mandie (Data Analyst)

Northampton
Contact information as for Head Office,
above

Community Payback
Chester, Matt (Unit Mgr)
Daft, Joh (Dep Mgr)
Peyando, Barry (Induction Placement
Off)
Robinson, Lindsey (Induction Placement
Off)
Wieczorek, Matthew (Induction
Placement Off)
Samat, Ranjit (Placement Dev Off)
Wright, Malcolm (Placement Dev Off)
Christie, Jim (Placement Dev Off)
Killeen, Patrick (Placement Dev Off)
Dudman, Glenn (Placement Dev Off)
Kapoor, Ashok (PSO)
Jennings, Margot (Admin)
Kinsella, Lorraine (Admin)

County Office
Bharadia, Bhavina (Admin)
Ashley, Jane (Clerical Off)
Lewis, Debbie (Clerical Off)

Court Team
Donoghue, Lesley
Griffiths, Paul

PSOs
Burton, Tracy
Clements, Stella
Leduc, Angela
Lishman, Stevie
Knight, Stephanie
Parker, Karen (Admin)
Newman, Barbara (Admin)
Edwards, Sarah (Admin)

DaRT
Whitaker, Sue (Unit Manager)
Hicks, Gina
Smart, Karen (Admin)

Offender Management Unit
Buckingham, Jess (Unit Mgr)
Whelan, Beth (Unit Mgr)
Woodward, Jenny (Unit Mgr)

Burns, Gary (Unit Manager)
Aitken, Karen
Bampton, Lindsey
Cartwright, Rebecca
Grant, Richard
Hancock, Rob
Hare, Nicola
Jones, Hannah
Kennedy, Jo
Kiernan, Sandra
Kingsbury, Prudence
Lad, Divya
Mallard, Liz
Martin, Lesley
Maguire, Siobhan
Richardson, Mikaela
Salmon, Ginny
Silcott, Chantel
Steele, Karen
Thompson, Gary
Wallace, Noreen
Woodward, Teresa
Kintu, Sarah
Reast, Carrie

PSOs
Bicka, Marta
Burgazzi, Elaine
George, Jen
Hewett, Shirley
Holmes, Bekke
James, Paul
Newbold, Andy
Pratt, Marie
Prendiville, Johnny
Roquecave, Debbie
Grice, Deborah (VLO)
Smith, Claire

Admin
Battersby, Jackie
Geary, Tricia
McGee, Anna
Primus-Wilson, Claudette
Taylor, Inge
Shakespeare, Shamel

Partnerships
Kellock, Jim (Unit Mgr)
Clark, Barbara (ETE Advisor – REACH)
Hurling, Jo (ETE Advisor)
Bazeley, Kirsty (Admin)

Practice Development
Barrett, Sarah (PDA)

Programme Delivery Unit
Kellock, Jim (Unit Mgr)
Bullock, Sally (Treatment Manager)

Blackshaw, Charlotte (Treatment Mgr)
Ettinger, Simone (IDAP Facilitator)
Randall, Natalie (Programme Facilitator)
Sanders, Cheryl (CSOG Facilitator)
Wigley, Glenn (Programmes Facilitator)
Wrighton, Sarah (Programmes Facilitator)

Regional Sex Offender Unit
Programmes Facilitators
Handscombe, Naomi
Long, Rachel
Thornhill, Kimberley
Wilson, Helen

Integrated Offender Management Unit (Countrywide)
Presbury, Debs (Unit Manager)
Fielding, Lorna
Roberts, Beccy
Walker, Ruth
Nichols, Emma
Paintin, Gary
Driver, Tracy (PSO)
Fontana, Caterina (PSO)
Newman, Gemma (Admin)

20 Oxford Street
Wellingborough NN8 4HY
Tel: 01933 303680 Fax: 01933 303699

County Office
Rice, Candice (Admin)

Unpaid Work
Edwards, Gary (Induction Placement Off)
Griffin, John (PSO)
Robinson, Elaine (Placement Dev Off)

Court Team
Bartley, Delia (PSO)
Gardner, Christopher (PSO)
Ziaja, Laura (Admin)

DaRT
Cox, Debbie (PSO)
Williams, Christine (PSO)
Arnold, Gary (Admin)

Offender Management Unit
Enfield, Claire (Unit Mgr)
Bayliss, Rosie
Earl, Louise
Essam, Helen
Gabriel, Gail
Jones, Mari
Jones, Matthew
Lewis, Lawrence
Tew, Helen
Pratt, Joe

PSOs
Hartung, Dorothy
Holmes, Carly
Pearce, Emma
Pratt, Liz
Robinson, Andy
Smith, Kerry
Bishop, Deb (Admin)
Patel, Shila (Admin)

Programme Delivery Unit
Gibbons, Paulette
Westley, Linda

Unit 5 Baron Avenue
Telford Way Industrial Estate
Kettering NN16 8UW
Tel: 01536 521740 Fax: 01536 524282

County Office
Brown, Amanda (Admin)
King, Helen (Admin)
Headland, Yvonne (Clerical)

Community Payback
Abela, Frank (Dep Mgr)
Cookson, Laurie (Induction Placement Off)
Docherty, Kathryn (Induction Placement Off)
Allen, Simon (Placement Dev Off)
Corbett, Alan (Workshop Supvr)
Chandler, Jenine (Placement Dev Off)

Offender Management Unit
Roberts, Pam (Unit Mgr)
Hammond, Alison
Hegarty, Eamon
O'Shea, Mel
Rowley, Lorna
Donoghue, Dominic
Flunder, Jennifer
Guy, Jodie
Johnson, Brian
Tomlinson, Leanne

PSOs
Clark, Julie
Ellis, Caroline
Everest, Karen
Sludden, Patrick
Gardner, Chris
Preskey, Tony (BASS Officer)
Carson, Lindsay
Pettit, Jane
Pollock, Jade
King, Marilyn (Admin)
Ingham, Debbie (Admin)

Partnerships
Grimmit, Nigel (ETE Advisor – REACH)
Stapleton, Lynn (ETE Advisor)

Programmes Delivery Unit
Harcourt, Diane (PSO)
Geraghty, Amanda (Treatment Manager)
Johnson, Karen (Admin)
O'Brien, Leanne (Admin)

Crown Court
85/87 Lady's Lane
Northampton NN1 3HQ
Tel: 01604 637751 Fax: 01604 603164

Donoghue, Lesley

Youth Offending Teams

Youth Offending Team South
52–53 Billing Road
Northampton NN1 5DB
Tel: 01604 602400 Fax: 01604 639231

Osbourne, Liz

Bryson, Caroline

Youth Offending Team North
73 London Road
Kettering NN15 7PQ
Tel: 01536 533800 Fax: 01536 312240
Woolley, Julie
Seabrook, Clare

MAPPA Team
Northamptonshire Police Headquarters
Wotton Hall Northampton NN4 OJQ
Tel: 03000 111 222 ext 5265

Chantler, Mike (Unit Mgr)

Todd, Jackie (MARAC Coordinator)

Admin
Kent, Jacqui
Addis, Karen

Approved Premises (Hostel)

Bridgewood House
45–48 Lower Meadow Court
Northampton NN3 8AX
Tel: 01604 648704 Fax: 01604 645722

Coleman, Lisa (Unit Mgr)

Probation Hostel Officers
Armitt, Kim
Busby, Cheryl
Lloyd-Williams, Debby
Mason, Michelle
Savage, Michael

Waking Night Supervisors
Downer, Kim
Knight, Bridget
Paul, Robert
Thornton, Emma
Waring, Dean
Cooke, Linda (Admin)

Institutions

HMP Onley
Willoughby Rugby
Warwickshire CV23 8AP
Tel: 01788 523400 Fax: 01788 523401

Doran, Paul (Unit Mgr)
Stephens, Chris (PO)

PSOs
Aslett, Peter
Baker, Daniel
Farnan, Michael
Gallant, Tio

HMP Wellingborough (Closing 31.12.2012)
Millers Park Doddington Road
Wellingborough Northants NN8 2NH
Tel: 01933 232700 Fax: 01933 232847

Mackenzie, Rachel (Unit Mgr) ext 2853
Biddle, Graeme
Lansberry, Denise
Tuft, Sophie

PSOs
Abraham, Natalie
Bailey, Yvonne
Davis, Sharon
Doyle, Pippa
Green, Lissa
Judge, Stephen
Ryan, Nicola

HMP Rye Hill
Willoughby Nr Rugby, Warwickshire
CV23 8SZ
Tel: 01788 523300 Fax: 01788 523311
Mackenzie, Rachel (Unit Mgr)
Baggott, Martin
Dade, Emma
Gary, Jane
McCarthy, Sinead
Addison, Lesley

PSOs
Knights, Jackie
Healy, Anna

Local Justice Areas
Corby (Corby)
Daventry (Northampton)
Kettering (Kettering)
Northampton (Northampton)
Towcester (Northampton)
Wellingborough (Wellingborough)

NORTHUMBRIA PROBATION TRUST

Out of hours emergency tel:
0191 477 5600

Victim enquiries tel:
0191 261 2541

Email:
firstname.lastname@northumbria.probation.
gsi.gov.uk

Head Office
Lifton House Eslington Road
Jesmond Newcastle-upon-Tyne NE2 4SP
Tel: 0191 281 5721 Fax: 0191 281 3548
Direct dial: 0191 240 + number

Hall, Nick (Chief Exec) 7332
Gardiner, David (Director of Ops) 7303
Bilcliff, Jackie (Dir of Finance & Business
Services/Treasurer) 7352
Israni, Roshan (Dir of People Mgmt &
Org Dev) 7333
Mackie, Chris (Dir of Legal
Services/Trust Secretary) 7351
Taylor, Barry (Dir of Performance, ICT &
Best Value) 7366
Bone, David (ICT Mgr) 7345
Mann, Louise (Service Dev Mgr) 7349
Menzies, Sue (Comms Mgr) 7330
Nesbit, Don (Perf Mgr) 7362
White Sam (Finance Mgr) 7326
Dixon, Anita (p, HR Business Partner)
7306
Emmerson, Claire (Accountancy Mgr)
7325
Fullard, Lynn (Business Support
Manager Operations) * based at Dene
House
McDine, Julie (p, HR Business Partner)
7379
Rigby, Matt (Perf & Info Mgr) 7343
Tate, Lynsay (p, Accountancy Mgr) 7323
Taylor, Julie (Properties & Procurement
Mgr) 7339
Wilson, Gillian (Business Risk Mgr) 7304
Clennell, John (H&S) 7331

Secondments
Elliott, Megan (p, NAPO)
Foreman, Siobhan
Middlemass, Lee (Union PSO)
Clarkson, Laura (St Nicholas Hosp)
Kelly, Janet (Newcastle City Council)
Armour, Kristy (NOMS)

Training Centre
Dene House Durham Road
Low Fell Gateshead
Tyne & Wear NE9 5AE
Tel: 0191 491 1693 Fax: 0191 491 3726

Murphy, Steve (Org Dev Mgr)

Smith, Mary (Unit Mgr, North East
Learning & Assessment Unit)
Walker, Sally (p, Org Dev Adviser)
Doggett, Steven (Org Dev Adviser –
Service Delivery)
Edison, Elaine (PO Org Dev)
Stephenson, Sharon (p, Org Dev Adviser)
Wilks, Elizabeth (NVQ Assessor)
Stafford, Phil (Learning & Dev Off, OM
& IT)

Newcastle Local Delivery Unit

Newcastle Management Unit
Lifton House, Eslington Road
Jesmond Newcastle-upon-Tyne
NE2 4SP
Tel: 0191 240 7376

Mackintosh, Jane (Dir of Offender
Mgmt) 7350
Hardington, Gary (Partnership Mgr)
7369

5 Lansdowne Terrace
Gosforth, Newcastle-upon-Tyne NE3
1HW
Tel: 0191 213 1888 Fax: 0191 213 1393

North Team
Cornick, Judith (Team Mgr)
Baker, Mike
Clark, Malcolm
Dale, Paul (p)
Humphries, James
Manson, Allison (p)
Masendeke, Sally

PSOs
Adams, Maggie
Pearson, Kim
Wilcox, Chris
Williamson, Georgina

Reducing Re-Offending Team
Gilbert, Steve (Team Mgr)
Gartland, Elaine
Harrington, Kathryn
Lennox, Mark
Reed, Paula (DRR)
Rothwell, Diane (DRR)

PSOs
Brickland, David (IOM)
Burrell, Anthony (IOM)
Dinning, Sean (IOM)
Hudson, Sharon (IOM)
Johnson, Heather (IOM)
Connor, Rachel (DRR)
Ellison, Gladys (DRR)
O'Reilly, Michael (DRR)

70–78 St James Boulevard
Newcastle-upon-Tyne NE1 4BN
Tel: 0191 261 9091 Fax: 0191 233 0758

City Team
Hughes, Karen (Team Mgr)
Anderson, Claire (p)
Anderson, Shirley
Collins, Nicola
Lowes, Elaine
Martin, Deborah
Shenton, Nicola
Smyth, Sue
Wood, Lorraine (p)

PSOs
Bickley, Kate (p)
Kelly, Sheliagh
MacQueen, Gay
Sullivan, Lucy

717 West Road
Newcastle-upon-Tyne NE15 7PS
Tel: 0191 274 1153 Fax: 0191 275 0963

West Team
McKenna, Maureen (Team Mgr)
Binley, Karen
Burrows, Gerry (p)
Garrity, Val
Grierson-Smith, Marie (p)
Key, Helen
McKale, Jonathan
Pyle, Colin

PSOs
Burrell, Anthony (p)
Colloby, Cheryl (p)
Fearon, Lee
Lawson, Rachel
Mullen, Angela

4 Glendale Terrace
Byker, Newcastle-upon-Tyne NE6 1PB
Tel: 0191 276 6666 Fax: 0191 224 2878

East Team
Wallace, Joanne (Team Mgr)
Capper, Elaine (p)
Coombe, Jennifer
Coxon, Adrian
Gwilym, Matthew
Higgins, Rob (p)
Mynott, Cynthia
O'Kane, Kathy
Robinson, Jennifer
Sharpe, Ian (p)
Stafford, Sandra
Thorpe, Simon

PSOs
Attley, Paul
Cardiff, Teresa
Cowen, Kate
Hall, Heather
Patterson, Victoria
Taylor, Paul

Northumberland Local Delivery Unit

Former Employment Exchange
South View Ashington
Northumberland NE63 0RY
Tel: 01670 840880 Fax: 01670 814858

Kelly, Liz (Dir of Offender Mgmt)

Tel: 01670 813053 Fax: 01670 814858

County Team
Familton, Bev (Team Mgr)
Dungait, Lynn
Hogg, Ben
Kirk, Carole
Roberts, Joanne
Singer, Stephen
Storey, Fiona

PSOs
Coxon, Debbie
Davidson, Stacey
Warburton, Julie

27 Bondgate Without
Alnwick Northumberland NE66 1PR
Tel: 01665 602242 Fax: 01665 605184

Jaimin, David
McCarthy-Smith, Lesley (PSO)

23 Castlegate
Berwick-upon-Tweed TD15 1LF
Tel: 01289 306165 Fax: 01289 332693

(*All post to 27 Bondgate Without*)
Willcock, Sarah (p)

32/34 Richard Stannard House
Bridge Street Blyth
Northumberland NE24 2AG
Tel: 01670 352441 Fax: 01670 352921

Ryland, Mark (Team Mgr)

Armstrong, Andrea (p)
Brannon, Tom
Currie, Ivan
Elliott, Katherine
Foster, Chris (p)
Moor, Leigh (p)
Pugh, Jan
Wylie, Sarah (Prac Dev)

PSOs
Cox, John (PSO)
Hadland, Simone (PSO)
Knox, Clare (p)
Mills, Rachel (DRR)

Blyth Police Station
Tel: 01661 861913

Connor, Gary (Reducing Re-offending Mgr)
Elliott, Neil (IOM)
Peacock, Graham (IOM)
Hamilton, Ann (PSO)
Harrison, Tracey (PSO)

4 Wentworth Place
Hexham, Northumberland NE46 1XB
Tel: 01434 602499 Fax: 01434 606195

Ackerman, Sarah (OM)

North Tyneside Local Delivery Unit

North Tyneside Management Unit
Lovaine House, 9 Lovaine Terrace
North Shields, Tyne & Wear NE29 0HJ
Tel: 0191 293 0515 Fax: 0191 257 6170

Turner, Margaret (Dir of Offender Mgmt)
Cox, Jackie (Mental Health & Learning Disabilities Coordinator)

Public Protection Management Unit
Lifton House Eslington Road
Jesmond Newcastle-upon-Tyne NE2 4SP
Tel: 0191 281 721 Fax: 0191 281 3548
Direct dial: 0191 240 + number

McLean, Wynne (Safeguarding Communities Mgr) 7348

Stephenson, Maggie (Reviewing Mgr) 7373

MAPPA Unit
Northumbria Police, Middle Engine Lane Wallsend NE28 9NT
Tel: 0191 295 7495 Fax: 0191 295 7497
McCartney, Jeff (p, MAPPA Dev Mgr)

Love, Amanda (MAPPA Coord)

Lovaine House
9 Lovaine Terrace
North Shields Tyne & Wear NE29 0HJ
Tel: 0191 296 2335 Fax: 0191 257 6170

Caush, Natalie (Team Mgr)
Armstrong, Angela

Brent, Claire (p)
Coleman, Sarah (p)
Fellows, Debra
Jones, Hannah (p)
Rudram, Anna
Wade, Martin
Wallwork, Charlie
Weatherly, Chantal (p)

PSOs
McPeake, Ciaran
Minhas, Virinder
Richardson, Clare
Tinkler, Ashleigh

13 Warwick Road
Wallsend, Tyne & Wear NE28 6SE
Tel: 0191 262 9211 Fax: 0191 295 4824

Seddon, Amanda (Team Mgr)
Brennan, Louise
Falcus, Lindsay
Jones, Stephanie (Practice Dev)
Penfold, Keith
Southern, Elizabeth
Ward, Clare (p)

PSOs
Allison, Pam
Bowler, Howard
Murray, Hannah (p)
Sherriff, Amanda
Williamson, George

North Tyneside Reducing Re-offending Team
19 Station Road Wallsend
Tyne & Wear NE28 6HD

Tel: 0191 240 8126 Fax: 0191 240 8127

Booth, Richard (Reducing Re-offending Mgr)
Heron, Bill (DRR)
Vacancy (PPO)

PSOs
Barrett, Michelle (PSO DRR)
McBeth, Pam (PSO PPO)

South Tyneside Local Delivery Unit including Area Court Services

South Tyneside Management Unit
Secretan Way
Millbank South Shields NE33 1RG
Tel: 0191 4969748 Fax: 0191 496 9784

O'Neill, Karin (Dir of Offender Mgmt)

South Tyneside IOM Unit
5–7 Cornwallis Street South Shields
Tyne & Wear NE33 1RG
Tel: 0191 497 4600 Fax: 0191 496 7911

Coulthard, Gail (Reducing Re-offending Mgr)
Dixon, Ian
Hawes, Scott (PPO)
Jones, Vikki (PPO)
Ruddick, Angela (DRR)

PSOs
Carter, Alan (PSO IOM)
Cliff, Andrea (PSO IOM)

Secretan Way Millbank
South Shields Tyne & Wear NE33 1RG
Tel: 0191 4552294 Fax: 0191 427 6919

Harrison, Kenneth (Team Mgr)

Lamb, Mark (Team Mgr)

Atkinson, Jonelle
Carson, Mandy
Hayes, Mary
Hill, Linda
Hills, Carla
Jamieson, John
Key, Gareth
Main, Allison
Malins, Petra
O'Connor, Alita
Pagan-Jones, Nerys
Robinson, Kerry (p)
Rose, Simon

PSOs
Anderson, Kaye
Fascia, Julie

Johnston, Carole
O'Neill, Maria
Scott, Gemma
Spedding, Helen

Court Services

North of Tyne Court Services
Ford, Lucy (Team Mgr) * based at Lifton
House – Tel: 0191 240 7391

Court Services Unit
Market Street
Newcastle-upon-Tyne NE99 1TB
Tel: 0191 296 2335 Fax: 0191 257 6170
Connor, Stephen
Lloyd, Philip

PSOs
Foster, Neil
Maxwell, Sandra
Mullen, Angela

North Tyneside Magistrates' Court
Tel: 0191 296 4263
Connor, Stephen
Douthwaite, Lynda
Lathbury, Simon (PSO)

SE Northumberland Magistrates' Court
Tel: 01670 843805 Fax: 01670 826180

Bridgeman, Nicola (p)
Flynn, Tony
Lee, Vanessa (p)
Bonham, Cheryl (p, PSO)

South of Tyne Court Services
Murphy, Kirsty (p, Team Mgr) * based at
John Street Tel: 0191 510 2030
Wilsdon, Maureen (p, Team Mgr) *
based at Lifton House Tel: 0191 240 7390

Sunderland Magistrates' Court
Tel: 0191 514 8949
Cavanagh, Ian
Stube, Lori
Scott, Sara

PSOs
Brown, Malcolm
Brown, Victoria
Cutting, Alan
Grace, Paul
Richardson, Ian

Gateshead
Tel: 0191 477 5821 ext no 246 Fax: 0191
429 3903

Hunter, Colin

PSOs
Dickinson, Kevin
Hodgson, Louise (p)
Heaton, Catherine

South Shields
Tel: 0191 427 4482

Dent, Sharon
Davison, Susan (PSO)
Gibson, Kim (p, PSO)
Hanson, Amy

Victim Liaison/Restorative Justice Unit
Dene House, Durham Road
Low Fell, Gateshead
Tyne & Wear NE9 5AE
Tel: 0191 491 7933 Fax: 0191 491 3726
Thompson, Mark (Team Mgr)

Clinton, Roy

Houghton, Madeleine

PSOs
Graham, Lisa
Hodgson, Kath (p)
Riley, Gillian
Smith, Dawn
Tempest, Kerry (p)

The Law Courts Quayside
Newcastle-upon-Tyne NE1 2LA
Tel: 0191 230 1737 Fax: 0191 233 0759

Badham, Savina (p)

Bell, Andrea
O'Farrell, Paul

PSOs
Brough, Anjali (p)
Thornton, Christina
Wilkinson, Peter

Durham Prison
Tel: 0191 332 3400 Fax: 0191 386 2524
Cliff, Marian (PSR writer)
Codling, Neil (PSR writer)

Gateshead Local Delivery Unit

Gateshead Management Unit
Warwick Street Gateshead
Tyne & Wear NE8 1PZ
Tel: 0191 478 9978 Fax: 0191 478 9979

Strike, Martyn (Dir of Offender Mgmt)

Wesley Court
Blaydon, Tyne & Wear NE21 5BT
Tel: 0191 414 5626 Fax: 0191 414 7809

Bunney, Crawford (Team Mgr)
Armstrong, Anne (p)
Bowers, Tracey
Cockburn, Ben
Crowther, Lynn
Loughrey, Terry (p)
Marsh, Charlotte (p)
Smith, Clair
Turner, Melanie
Ul-Haq, Ehtesham

PSOs
Bleanch, Graham
Clark, Paula
Morren, Alex
Smiles, Simon

Warwick Street
Gateshead, Tyne & Wear NE8 1PZ
Tel: 0191 478 2451 Fax: 0191 478 1197

McElderry, Jim (Team Mgr)
Vacancy (Reducing Re-Offending Mgr)
Edwards, Ian
Finnigan, John
Halpin, Aidan
Hope, Katherine (p)
Hutchinson, Jenny (PPO)
Lawrence, Bob
Lee, Stephen
Maughan, Jennifer
Norton, Michael (DRR)
Robinson, Sharon (IOM)
Robson, Colin
Simpson, Kerry
Vipond, Richard

PSOs
Baker, Dawn
Boyne, Steph (IOM)
Cole, Liz (DRR)
Elliot, Bev
Hannen, Heidi (p)
Middlemass, Lee
O'Donnell, Sheree
Vickers, David

Community Payback
70–78 St James' Boulevard
Newcastle-upon-Tyne NE1 4BN
Tel: 0191 261 9091 Fax: 0191 233 0758
Hinder, Mick (OM Co-ordinator North)
Redford, Paul (CP Placement Supvr)
Offender Managers:
Aitchison, George
Dingwall, Ed
Harrington, Jim
Harrison, Reg

Lowther, Jimmy
Offender Supervisors:
Bass, Karen
Coates, George
Tait, David
Taylor, Ian (p)

Wallsend
13 Warwick Road
Wallsend Tyne & Wear NE28 6SE
Tel: 0191 262 9211 Fax: 0191 295 4824
Archer, Mark (OS Co-ordinator North)
Offender Supervisors:
Lamb, Kevin
Scott, Richard (p)

Former Employment Exchange
South View Ashington
Tel: 01670 813053 Fax: 01670 814858
Offender Supervisors:
Holgate, Steve
Paterson, Bill
Rice, Vincent

John Street
45 John Street Sunderland
Tyne & Wear SR1 1QU
Tel: 0191 510 2030 Fax: 0191 565 7746
Simpson, Dawn (CP Manager South)
O'Neill, Mick (OM Co-ordinator South)
Offender Managers:
O'Neill, Richie
Penty, Barbara
Sanderson, David
Withers, Viv
Offender Supervisors
Fay, Kevin
Griffiths, Edwin (p)
Mason, Phil

Warwick Street Gateshead
Tyne & Wear NE8 1PZ
Tel: 0191 478 2451 Fax: 0191 478 1197
Forster, Maureen (CP Manager North)
Baker, Maureen (CP Placement
Supervisor)
Offender Supervisors:
Kirton, Ian

Secretan Way Millbank
South Shields Tyne & Wear NE33 1HG
Tel: 0191 455 2294 Fax: 0191 427 6919
Offender Supervisors:
Gibson, Mark

Sunderland Local Delivery Unit

Sunderland Management Unit
45 John Street Sunderland
Tyne & Wear SR1 1QU
Tel: 0191 515 5190 Fax: 0191 515 5191

Gavin, Mauren (Dir of Offender Mgmt)

Hylton Road
Pennywell
Sunderland SR4 8DS
Tel: 0191 534 5545 Fax: 0191 534 2380

Oxley, Ann (Team Mgr)
Airey, Tony
Barnes, Helen
Bell, Joanne
Cutter, Anne-Marie
Davison, Olwen
Jones, Vickki
Main, Alex
Middleton, Linda
Murray, Hannah
Myers, Louise
Rafiq, Mohammed (p)
Smith, Lindsay
Stobbart, Susan
Tomlinson, Amy

PSOs
Glendinning, Alan
Mardghum, Alan
Walker, Joan

Mainsforth Terrace West
Hendon Sunderland SR2 8JX
Tel: 0191 514 3093 Fax: 0191 565 1625

Stafford, Keith (Team Mgr)
Bright, Kelly
Devlin, Linda
Haran, Margaret
Jennings, Dawn
McQuillan, Steve
Nairne, Finlay (p)
Smith, Susan

PSOs
Bosher, Shaun
Fascia, Paul
Ferries, Amy

Citi Team
Kings Road Southwick
Sunderland SR5 2LS
Tel: 0191 548 8844 Fax: 0191 548 6834
Visram, Ann (Partnership Mgr)

PSOs
Bower, Peter
Coxon, John
Giles, Julie (p)
Manley, Lynn (p)
Price, Carol
Quinn, Michael (p)

1st Floor Empire House
Newbottle Street Houghton-le-Spring
Tyne & Wear DH4 4AF
Tel: 0191 584 3109 Fax: 0191 584 4919

Scott, Mark (Team Mgr)
Baker, Pam (p)
Blaylock, Johanne
Brown, Jo
Haberfield, Lee
Jones, Victoria (p)
Lowerson, Angela
Nolan, Michael
Oyolu-Barker, Chin Chin

PSOs
Amor, Helen
McElvie, Tom
Robertson, Tracey
Walker, Jeanette

Sunderland IOM

Unit 4 Bridge House
Bridge Street Sunderland SR1 1TE
Tel: 0191 564 1325 Fax: 0191 567 4764

Stratford, Mary (IOM Mgr)

Dowson, Catherine
Gettings, Sarah
Murray, Alison (PO, PPO)

PSOs
Beton, Carol (IOM)
Hutchinson, Claire (DRR)
Houghton, Karen (p, DRR)
Thompson, Keith (DRR)

Programmes & ETE

70–78 St James' Boulevard
Newcastle-upon-Tyne NE1 4BN
Tel: 0191 241 8115 Fax: 0191 261 1548

Francis, Anne (Interventions Manager)

NSOG Programme Team
Walton, Peter (Team Mgr NSOG/CDVP)
Flynn, Alan (Treatment Mgr)
Barnes, Matthew
Dymore, Claire (CDVP)
Gow, Sue

Ions, Kenneth
Loxley, Felicity (p)
Strachan, Ian
Wallace, Stacey (p)

Sexual Behaviour Unit
Tel: 0191 260 2540 Fax: 0191 261 1548
Devine, Eileen
Kennington, Roger

CDVP Team

Warwick Street
Gateshead NE8 1PZ
Tel: 0191 243 8106 Fax: 0191
Carr, Richard (Treatment Mgr)
Bosanko, Kay (Treatment Mgr)
Deary, Kath (p)
Gunn, Ann (p)
Jones, Mike
Turner, Daphne

PSOs
Hirst, Eunice
Tobin, Neville
Towns, Alan

70–78 St James' Boulevard
Tel: 0191 261 9091 Fax: 0191 233 0758

Talbot, John (Prog Mgr)

Aikman, Debbie (p, Treatment Mgr)

PSOs
Miller, Claire
Patterson, Liz
Reay, Rebecca (p)
Smith, Anthony
Southern, Samantha
Stevenson, Malcolm

45 John Street
Sunderland, Tyne & Wear SR1 1QU
Tel: 0191 510 2030 Fax: 0191 565 7746

Brunger, Sheila (p, Quality Mgr)
Patterson, Kerrie (p, Treatment Mgr)

PSOs
Starforth, Anna (Treatment Mgr)
Brown, Allyson
Craig, Tonya
Cullerton-Jones, Jane
Gerrard, Jason
Jackson, Suzanne
Lowerson, Catherine (p)
McGough, Carol
Miles, Paul
Price, Kevin

ETE Referral Unit & Specific Interventions
Dene House – Annex
Durham Road Gateshead NE9 5AE
Tel: 0191 491 7938 Fax: 0191 49137269

Taylor, Richard (Specific Interventions Co-ordinator)

Charlton, Eve (ETE Off)

Former Employment Exchange
South View, Ashington

Northumberland, NE63 0RY

Tel: 01670 840880 Fax: 01670 814858

Randall, Barbara (Interventions Project Lead)

Approved Premises (Hostels)

Cuthbert House Bail Hostel
Derwentwater Road Bensham
Gateshead NE8 2SH
Tel: 0191 478 5355 Fax: 0191 490 0674

Pooley, Geoff (Mgr)

PSOs Approved Premises
Beall, Fiona
Clark, Paula
Douglas, Jason
Swanston, Dean

Pennywell House Bail Hostel
Hylton Road Pennywell
Sunderland SR4 8DS
Tel: 0191 534 1544 Fax: 0191 534 1049

Saddington, Debbie (Mgr)

PSOs Approved Premises
Gregg, Michael
Greaves, Aly
McManus, Paula
Whillians, Christine

Ozanam House Probation Hostel
79 Dunholme Road
Newcastle-upon-Tyne NE4 6XD
Tel: 0191 273 5738 Fax: 0191 272 2729

Gelder, Chris (Mgr)
Bell, Geoff (Deputy)

Central Referral Service
Tel: 0191 272 2626 Fax: 0191 272 1126

Nugent, Peter (Central Referring Officer)

St Christopher's House Bail Hostel
222 Westmorland Road Cruddas Park
Newcastle-upon-Tyne NE4 6QX

Tel: 0191 273 2381 Fax: 0191 272 4241

Faill, Peter (Mgr)
Yoxall, Gail (Dep Mgr)

Youth Offending Teams

Northumberland Youth Offending Team
The Riverside Centre
North Seaton Industrial Estate
Ashington Northumberland NE63 0YB
Tel: 01670 852225 Fax: 01670 854193

Graham, Helen

North Tyneside Youth Offending Team
153 Tynemouth Road
North Shields Tyne & Wear NE30 1ED
Tel: 0191 643 8605 Fax: 0191 643 8606

McNiven, Helen

Newcastle Youth Offending Team
Block D 4th Floor Jesmond Quadrant
3 Archbold Terrace Sandyford
Newcastle-upon-Tyne NE2 1BZ
Tel: 0191 277 7377 Fax: 0191 277 7368

Davison, Rebecca

Gateshead Youth Offending Team
Former Felling Police Station
Sunderland Road Felling
Gateshead Tyne & Wear NE10 0NJ
Tel: 0191 440 0500 Fax: 0191 440 0501

Vacancy

South Tyneside Youth Offending Team
30 Commercial Road
South Shields Tyne & Wear NE33 1RW
Tel: 0191 427 2850 Fax: 0191 427 2851

Vacancy

Wearside Youth Offending Team
Lambton House 145 High Street West
Sunderland Tyne & Wear SR1 1UW
Tel: 0191 566 3000 Fax: 0191 566 3002

Lawther, Susan

Institutions

HMP Northumberland
Morpeth Northumberland NE65 9XF
Tel: 01670 762300 Fax: 01670 762301
Probation fax: 01602 762307

Direct dial 01670 762 + ext

Probation Clerk 453/446
Risk Mgmt Coord 638
SOTP Treatment Mgr 458
Sentence Mgmt Clerk 450
Sentence Mgmt Officers 636/447
Downing, Dorothy (Team Mgr) 452
Airey, Tony
Alexander, Paul

Dent, Sharon

McDermott, Angela
Nicholson-Fawcett, Tracy
Wylie,Karen
Stasik, Mark (PSO)

HMP Frankland
Finchale Avenue Brasside
Durham DH1 5YD
0191 332 3000 Fax: 0191 332 3001

Local Justice Areas
Alnwick
Berwick-upon-Tweed
Gateshead District
Houghton-le-Spring
Newcastle-upon-Tyne
North Tyneside
South East Northumberland
South Tyneside
Sunderland
Tynedale

Crown Courts
Newcastle-upon-Tyne

NOTTINGHAMSHIRE PROBATION TRUST

Out of hours emergency contact point
Trent House Tel: 0115 841 5630

Email:
firstname.lastname@nottinghamshire.
probation.gsi.gov.uk

Head Office
Marina Road, Castle Marina
Nottingham NG7 1TP
Tel: 0115 840 6500 Fax: 0115 840 6502
Direct dial: 0115 840 + ext

Chief Officer Group
Fax: 0115 840 6453
Geraghty, Jane (Chief Executive) 0115
840 6463
Goldstraw, Christine (Board Chair) 0115
993 6455

Moore, Rob (Dir of Finance & Resources) 0115 993 6519
Goode, Alan (LDU Dir Projects) 0115 840 6506
Hill, Nigel (LDU City) 0115 840 6389
Taylor, Mark (LDU County) 0115 840 6537
Wright, Sheila (LDU Dir Interventions) 0115 840 6461
Tingle, Ralph (Treasurer & Financial Advisor) 0115 840 6468
Francis, Gill (Asst Dir Ext Relations) 0115 840 6490
Balmer, Claire (Area Manager Interventions)
Baumber, Luke (Area Manager City)
Smith, Sue (Area Manager County)

Central Administration
General enquiries 6500

Finance & Payroll
Enquiries 6464
Kooner, Jagjeet (Mgr) 0115 993 6515

Human Resources
Enquiries 0115 993 6528
Best, Elizabeth (Mgr) 6485

Learning & Development
Enquiries 6475
Tomlinson, Karen (Mgr) 6510

Management Information & Services & Facilities & Support
Enquiries 6472
Laurenti, Louise (Mgr) 6495

Health & Safety
Brown, Faye (Mgr) 8502

Accommodation & Advice Unit
Buckley, Michael (Mgr) 6524

Access (ETE) Team
Cooke, Steve (Mgr) 6459

Nottingham City

206 Derby Road
Nottingham NG7 1NQ
Tel: 0115 845 5100 Fax: 0115 845 5101

South Nottinghamshire
Khan, A (SPO)
Urquhart, J (SPO)

POs
Bashir, S
Bellingham, D A
Columbinc, T
Douglas, J M

Faulkner, D S
Fryer, J F
Green, J
Kennedy, W L
Mulligan, A E
Murphy, P J
Peake, C N W
Rouse, N
Sharma, R

OMPSOs
Anderson, M
Dinnall A
Evans C
Mycock, S A
Cooke, C
Kurcewicz, A L
Lavelle, L A
Morton, C
Page, J C
Slater, S J
Spray, E C
Taylor A
Willis, Z X

Unpaid Work Team
Mack, C (SPO)

POs
Clare, J C
Mitchell, R
Stephens, V C

OMPSOs
Anderson, J V
Dawson, G A
Heppenstall, S
Jefferson, T
Lewis, S L
Mawani, R
Reilly, S L
White, J
Whittaker, A L

Domestic Violence and High Risk
Tel: 9082970 Fax: 0115 845 5213
Julie Burton (SPO)
PO
Paul Marriott

PSOs
O'Dare, Helen
Preston, Julie
Ryan, Marie
Taylor, Alice

Diversity
Green, P
Annison L

OMPSO
Clarke, D

Community Payback
Jeacock, C (Senior CSO)
Goulder, J A
Byfield, M
Guthrie, M A
Wilson, J
Nesbitt, A P
Russo, R R
Weston, D

City Enforcement Team – Derby Road
Tel: 0115 845 5113
Hewitt, J (PSO)

Nottingham City

Castle Quay
9 Castle Boulevard, Nottingham NG7 1FW
Tel: 0115 908 2900 Fax: 0115 908 2915

City North
Caesar, B (SPO)
Ahluwalia, N
Benjamin, E
Brown, D J
Cross, H
Dyson, G
Fahy, N
Flewitt, W J
Fothergill, T F
Garner, K E
Giordmaina, C L
Haque, R
Hunt, A J
Leech, M
Malyan, H
Ramsey, S E
OM

PSOs
Beeby, M
Henman, N
Kouser, S
Melhado, D L
Roe, J S
Skervin, C
Unwin, M
Wilson, L
Yates, T

City South
Jones, Sarah (SPO)
Abdullah, M
Adas, R J
Bernard, J B
Burnett, S E

Conway, B S
Jordan, W
Lowe, E M K
Mansaram, C
Muller, M W
Parker, G
Raymond, L
Robinson, D
Sawyers, M E
Stafford, L M
Standing, O W

OM PSOs
Boothe, C
Buxton, E
Gosden, R
Howle, A R
Kimberley, M
Veira, M H
Amey, S L

Programmes
Martin, S (SPO)
Goulder, J
Haq, N
House, D C
Jabeen, S
Muyunda, S Y
Rayment, L P
Tribe, S E
Turner, D A
Weaver, P

OMPSOs
Berrisford, L M
De'ath, J A
Humphrey, M
Jacobson, S P
Jarratt, K
Keijzer, A
Morris, L
Mugglestone, A C
Tuke, N E
Whitsed, N

Castle Gate House
24–30 Castle Gate, Nottingham NG1 7AT
Tel: 0115 915 1414 Fax: 0115 915 1412

Adult Offending Team (AOT)
Walker, Angela (SPO)
Green, H J
Hester, V
Martin, W J
Rowe, E M
Woolley, R G
Zieba, H M

OMPSOs
Barnes, W K
Barrett, M A
Brady, M M
Firth, V L
Gregory, S
Hibbert, R
Iftikhar, R
Russell, C E
Taylor, A
Wilkins, Z
Wilson, J (Treatment Mgr)
Blair, K (Team Leader)
Shaw, R (Team Leader)
Boynton, T J (Team Leader)
Drug Workers
Bibi, Y
Chambers, T
Logan, L M
McDonald, M
Semmelroth, J L
Green, J
Hubbard, C J
Kerry, H L
Mann, J
O'Love, R J
Sawula, S
Banks, D
Crossley-Morris, M
Haflidadottir, G
Remm, K
Sabat, S
Yassin, N
Substance Misuse Practitioner
Baker, C
Baxter, M
Berry, P
Skinner, K E
Smith, R D

Fit For Work
Hampton, S (Health Training Coord)
Lee, R (PSO)

Magistrates' Court Liaison Team
Carrington Street, Nottingham NG1 2EE
Tel: 0115 908 2312 Fax: 0115 908 2319
E-mail:
magistrates.courtsadmin@
nottinghamshire.probation.gsi.gov.uk
Marley, T (SPO)
OM

PSOs
Dyer, M D
Marshall, E J
Short, D M
Stoddart, L B

Crown Court Liaison Team
Canal Street, Nottingham NG1 7EL
Tel: 0115 910 3540 Fax: 0115 958 6135
E-mail:
crown.courtsadmin@nottinghamshire.
probation.gsi.gov.uk
Canal Street, Nottingham NG1 7EL
Tel: 0115 910 3540 Fax: 0115 958 6135
E-mail:
crown.courtsadmin@nottinghamshire.
probation.gsi.gov.uk
Marley, T (SPO)
Davies, J L
Goode, L J
Smillie, R L
Wass, H S

PSOs
Baird, M E
Brown, A
Dominy, M A
Kinkaid, G
Mahal, J
Mallows, J S

Arrival Square
Mansfield NG18 1LP
Tel: 01623 460800 Fax: 01623 460801

Ashfield Team
West, S (SPO)
Butler, A
Hardy, J
Roulstone, J E
Saddington, M
Walsh, H P
Belshaw, K J
Calvert, J
Deakin-Cooper, M S
Downey, A
Hickinbottom, A
Maurer, F J

OMPSOs
Jeal, E
Maycock, K A
Romanko, H L

Mansfield Team
Bannister, J (SPO)
Allcock, E
Castick, G
Harris, C H
Muyunda, S Y
Perrell, C A
Rudkin, C L
Scott, A L
Toft, A
Young, L K

OMPSOs
Bano, R
Boardman, D
Evers, H
Harper, J M
Smeeton, E

Substance Misuse Team (County)
Perkins, D (SPO)
Barling, L M
Gardner, E V
Hand, S
Hilton, D V

OMPSOs
Dean, B
Deane, M C
Ealden, D R
Moore, D L
Richardson, N
Lever, D J
May, K (Senior Substance Misuse
Practitioner)

Substance Misuse Practitioner
Bush, S
Freeston, S
Guy, A
Rowlands, H

Courts Team
Bannister, J (SPO)
Hand, J
Nisbet, C (OM PSO)
Harrison, L (OM PSO)

Unpaid Work Team
Nesbitt, A (CSO)
Russo, B (CSO)
Dangerfield, M (PSO)

11 Appleton Gate
Newark NG24 1JR
Tel: 01636 652650 Fax: 01636 652651
Williams, A (SPO)
Codrington-Hopkins, R
Denham, S J
Johnson, S P
Payne, H E

OMPSOs
Goodwin, E
Gravestock, D
Orton, A L
Shereston, N

Access (ETE)
Phillips, D (Employment Off)

11 Newcastle Street
Worksop S80 2AS
Tel: 01909 473424 Fax: 01909 530082
Snell, N (SPO)
Burton, M
Ellis, C E
Mortimer, S C
Phillips, S
Ruston, V
Street, K S
Wass, R

OMPSOs
Drew, M
Eaton, E
Mallows, J S
Percival, G
Witts, P

Community Service Team
Weston, D (CSO)

Adult Offender Team (County)
Perkins D (SPO)
Austin, S L
Gatland, S
Szulc, C J

MAPPA
Public Protection Unit, CID HQ, Holmes
House
Ratcliffe Gate, Mansfield NG18 2JW
Tel: 01623 483052 Fax: 01623 483053
email:
mappa@nottinghamshire.pnn.police.uk

Hilton, J (SPO, MAPPA Mgr & Coord)
Williams, I (ActDI, Policy & Strategy
Offi)

Youth Offending Teams

City
2 Isabella Street, **Nottingham** NG1 6AT
Tel: 0115 915 9400 Fax: 0115 915 9401
Green, S S
Shaw, J J
Ramsey, K (OMPSO)

County North
Dale Close
100 Chesterfield Road South
Mansfield NG19 7AQ
Tel: 01623 433433 Fax: 01623 452145

Parr, AS

Ground Floor, Block B
65 Northgate, **Newark** NG24 1HD
Tel: 01636 479929 Fax: 01636 613972
Simpson-White, F

Approved Premises (Hostels)

106 Raleigh Street
Nottingham NG7 4DJ
Tel: 0115 910 5450 Fax: 0115 910 5451
Feather, B (Operational Manager)
Foster, S M
Harris, K
Headley, B
Jones, M M E
Storer, B L

5 Astral Grove
Hucknall, Nottingham NG15 6FY
Tel: 0115 840 5720 Fax: 0115 840 5721
Snowden A (AP Manager)
Amos, S E
Bennett, M
MacKenzie, C
Morris, J

Trent House
392 Woodborough Road
Nottingham NG3 4JF
Tel: 0115 841 5630 Fax: 0115 841 5631
Rodgers, T (Operational Manager)

Institutions

HMP Nottingham
Perry Road, Sherwood, Nottingham NG5 3AG
Tel: 0115 872 3000 Fax: 0115 872 3005
Singh, G (SPO)
Cina, E M R
Maidens, K M
Smith, S J
OM

PSOs
Middleton, K
Melbourne, M F L
Miller, M
Morgan, R

HMP Ranby
Retford, Nottinghamshire DN22 8EU
Tel: 01777 862000 Fax: 01777 862001
Ryer, N (SPO)
Henry, T
White, R L
OM

PSOs
Bal, S
Hammond, E
Haynes, S
Parmley, C
Thomas, K

HMP Whatton
New Lane, Whatton, Nottingham NG13 9FQ
Tel: 01949 803200 Fax: 01949 803201
Ryer, N (SPO)
Clegg, J P
Dyjasek, M
Griffiths, M A
Hodgson, H R E
Middleton, P M
Roworth, K R
Tocher, M
Wright, P N

OMPSOs
Lawrence, C
Reilly, L L

STAFFORDSHIRE & WEST MIDLANDS PROBATION TRUST
Victim enquiries tel: 0121 248 6100; 01785 231728, 02476 838308, 01902 875750

Email: firstname.lastname@swm.probation.gsi.gov.uk

Trust Executive Office

1 Victoria Square
Birmingham B1 1BD

Tel: 0300 200 2300 Fax: 0121 634 1411

Maiden, Mike (CE)
Bates, Ged (Dir of Operations)
Holland, Catherine (Dir of Exec Services)
Barr, Alistair (Dir of Finance)
Appleby, Sue (Payroll Mgr)
Armstrong, Kim (Exec Admin Mgr)
Bannister, David (Training Officer-Business Support)
Bell, Ali (Hd of PR & Comms)
Chahal, Palvinder (Exec Programme Mgr)
Cutayar, Mark (Property & Estates Mgr)
Daly, William (Hd of Property & Estates)
Flaxman, James (Performance & Systems Info Mgr)
Gill, Stephen (Hd of Business Transformation)
Grafton, Phil (Trust Solicitor and Head of Governance)
Kerslake, Mike (Quality Improvement Mgr)

Financial Service Manager – Vacant POst
Knott, David (Hd of HR, Learning & Development)

Madders, Michael (Hd of IT Services)
Maydew, Chris (Exec Support Mgr)
Mitchell, Rita (Risk Mgr)
Noble, Jackie (HR Mgr)
Osborne, Tony (Org Dev Mgr)
Sawbridge, Judith (Knowledge Mgr)
Singh, Harjinder (Ext Partnerships
Comm Mgr)
Whelan, Paula (Hd of Diversity)

(Accountancy Services Mgr) Vacancy
POst
Yates, Christopher (ITSD Support Mgr)

University Court
Staffordshire Technology Park
Beaconside Stafford ST18 0GE
Tel: 01785 223416

Trust Executive Staff
Bowden, Sandra (HR Mgr)
Clewlow, Linda (Financial) Planning
Manager
Hewitt, Ian (Dep Hd of Property &
Estates)
Parekh, Mohamed (Senior IT
Engineer/Information Security Officer)
Scott, Peter (Partnering & Competition
Mgr)
Thompson, Jacqui (Data Protection/FOI
Off)

Substance Misuse Strategy
Hay, Catherine (SPO/Mgr)
Tel: 01785 223416 Fax: 01785 223108

King Edward House
5th Floor King Edward House
135A New Street Birmingham B2 4QJ
Tel: 0121 329 7900 Fax: 0121 329 7992

Byford, Nigel (Hd of Public Protection)
Elphick, Bronwen (Hd Interventions)
Royal, Pat (Hd Probation Birmingham)

Effective Practice
Shaw, Judith (SPO) (University Court)

**Bail & Support Services Project
(BASS) West Midlands Area**
Jones, Stuart (SPO) Based at Sheriffs
Court

Volunteers Mentoring Co-ordinator
*at Birmingham King Edward House 0121
329 7929*
Jellett, Victoria (Mentor Co-ordinator)

Business Interventions Unit
Cole, Diane (Admin Mgr)

Timms, Sharon (Partnerships
Monitoring/DRR Commissioning Off)
Ellis, Philip J (Progs Implementation
Mgr)

Employment Training & Education Unit
At Horninglow Street, Burton DE14 1PH
Tel: 01283 564988 Fax: 01283 567978
Self, Mark (ACO ETE)
Centenary House, Mackadown Lane
Kitts Green, **Birmingham** B33 0LQ
Tel: 0121 248 3660 Fax: 0121 248 3661

Carr, Caroline (Ptrship & Commissioning
Mgr for Skills for Life & ETE)
at Centenary House 0121 248 3660
Gaughan, John (ETE PSO)
at Coventry 024 7663 0555
Kane, Lorraine (ETE PSO)
at Dudley 01384 440682
Pearce, Gavin (ETE PSO)
at Stourbridge 01384 429 366
Mohammed, Sohail (ETE PSO)
at Selly Oak St 0121 248 6680
Henry, Jackie (ETE PSO)
at Perry Barr 0121 248 6348
Rupende, Yvonne (ETE PSO)
at Unity House, 0121 533 4500
Vacancy (ETE PSO)
at Unity House 0121 258 9358
Smart, Charles (ETE PSO)
at Walsall 01922 721341
Iftikhar, Ali (ETE PSO)
at Wolverhampton 01902 576000
Rees, Jennie (ETE PSO)
at Hamstead Rd 0121 248 6500
Anderson, Patricia (ETE PSO)
At Cannock Office
Stevens, Christine (ETE PSO)
Collings, Chelsea (ETE PSO)
Based at Melbourne House
Lockely, Sophie (ETE PSO)

Dudley Probation

District Management Unit
McNulty, Adrian (Hd of Probation
Dudley) based 44 New road, Stourbridge
Brown, Steve (Admin Mgr) based Atlantic
House
Bailey, Sally (SPO) based 44 New Road,
Stourbridge

**44 New Road
Stourbridge DY8 1PA**
Tel: 01384 429366 Fax: 01384 441354
Fergus, Michael (SPO)
Jhali, Sharnjit

Bishop, Claire
Jerrison, Jayne
Fountain, Joanne
Garratt, Liz
Taylor, Barbara
Ali, Asif (PSO)
Graham, Sonia (PSO)
Dee, Brian (PSO)
Simmons, Rachel (PSO)
Walker-Smith, Jenny (PSO)

Atlantic House
Dudley Road, Lye, **Stourbridge** DY9 8EL
Tel: 01384 429529 Fax: 01384 422934
Mayers, Julie (SPO)
Storer, Jim
Brecknell, Davina
Harper, Keeley
Rushton, Claire
Young, Jodie
Dee, Elaine (PSO)
Farrar, Susan (PSO)
Stephens, Fay (PSO)

The Court House
The Inhedge
Dudley DY1 1RR
Tel: 01384 862424 Fax: 01384 862425
Brookes, Angie (SPO)
Goldie, Joanne (SPO)
Hampton, Jane
Higgitt, Gary
Reid, Karen
Thornton, Amy
Turner, Stuart
Vaughan-Phillips, Louise
Whittam, Jayne
Wilkinson, Sara

PSOs
Leather, Debbie
Nash, Paul
Brown, Shirley
Partridge, Susan
Round, Deborah
Tyler, Ami

Courts & Allocation
Goldie, Joanne (SPO)

Dudley Magistrates' Court Office
Tel: 01384 862424 Fax: 01384 862437
Kaur-Thandi, Palbinder
Mills, Phil
Hawley, Anne (PSO)
Jordan, Oliver (PSO)
Spiteri, Paula (PSO)

Dudley Youth Offending Team
Brindley House Hall Street
Dudley DY2 7DT
Tel: 01384 813060 Fax: 01384 813270
Platt, Andy
Grizzle, Subira (PSO)

Sandwell Probation

Unity House
14–16 New Street
West Bromwich B70 7PQ
Tel: 0121 358 9358 Fax: 0121 358 9480
Connelly, Jane (Hd of Probation Sandwell)
Brown, Steve (Admin Mgr) based Atlantic Hse (Dudley Probation)

OM Team 1
Johnson, Eric (SPO)
Brown, Damian
Cookson, Diane
Crawford-Brown, Junior
Glean, Janice
Jennings, Karen
Samira, Daljit
Trainor, Timothy
Williams, Morene
Price, John

PSOs
Summers, Susan
Facer, Rebecca
Hubbold, Melissa
Riley, Paul

OM Team 3
Hird, Maria (SPO)
Greensill, Carole
McGhee, James
Cooner, Sarnjit Singh
Robinson-Wright, Lorraine
Taylor, Owen
Tracey, Danny
Vasia, Archana

PSOs
Buchanan, Sonia
Fearon, David
Wheeler, Monica

OM Team 4
Kuffa, Tony (SPO)
Brown, Adele
Francis, Vanessa
Griffiths, Sian
Jester, Katie
Morgan, Claradell
Queely, Claudine
Walker, Teresa

PSOs
Bevin, Fay
Sendur, Leila
Heer, Kulji
Radford, Edwina
Ryan, John

Substance Misuse
Gould, Ian (SPO)
Forrest, Sean
Vacancy (PSO)
Smith, Karen (PSO)

PPO Team & Projects
Bibi, Shaida (SPO)
Rai, Harmail [IOM co-ordinator]
Browne, Philippa (PSO) [Time4change]
Edwards, Claudette (PSO) [DIP/Housing Wkr]
*based: West Bromwich Police Station
Tel: 0345 113 5000 Fax: 0121 626 9130
Kernarne, Emma
Stewart, Cynthia (PSO)
Reeve, Adam (PSO)

Courts & Allocation
Gould, Ian (SPO)

Sandwell Magistrates' Court Office
Tel: 0121 358 9463 Fax: 0121 544 8105
Kooner, Juskaren
Fergus, Paul

PSOs
Balu, Amarjit
Mervyn, Jackie
Oakley, Stacey
Oldham-Smith, Trevor

Sandwell Youth Offending Team
6–8 Unity Walk, Owen Street,
Tipton DY4 8QL
Tel: 0845 352 7701 Fax: 0845 352 7731

Murphy, Brian (PO)
Bloice, Lawrence (PSO)

Coventry Probation

Sheriff's Court
12 Greyfriars Road
Coventry CV1 3RY
Tel: 02476 838300 Fax: 02476 838332

District Management Unit
Chand, Sarah (Hd of Probation Coventry)
McCarthy, Terry (Effective Practice SPO)

OM Team 1
Holten, Noelle (SPO)
Taylor, Caroline
Whittem, Gavin
Wibberley, Steve
Williams, Paul
Dent, Lucy
Davies, Sandra
Humphrey, Jo

PSOs
Briffa, Colin
Khan, Imtiaz
Ferron, Lynne
Patton, Brian

OM Team 2
Heath, Alison (SPO)
Jaspal, Sunny
Lynch, Leeanna
Butler, Anika
Peynado, Fenton
Almquist, Debbie
Gill, Duljit
Robertson, Helen
Smith, Clare

PSOs
Goolding, Melanie
Oakley, Jon
Chana, Kiran

OM Team 3
Mole, James (SPO)
Fleming, Sandra
Ford, David
Golby, Chris
Newbold, Denise
Rose, Samantha
Farmer, Emma
Taylor, Sarah
Thorpe, Elaine
Nutting, Marie (PSO)
Lusby, Nichola (PSO)

OM Team 4
Makin, Nick (SPO)
Chambers, Kalvin
Hoo, Marcus
Laidler, Karen
Norton, Deborah
Parsonage, Kirstin
Purdy, Lynn
Osidpie, Emily
Gheent, Harvi

PSOs
Miller, Cath
Rudd, Charlotte
Griffin, Leigh

Team Substance Misuse, DRRs & PPOs
O'Donoghue, Deirdre (SPO)
Atwal, Ranjit
Browett, Guy
Fisher, Matthew

PSOs
Groves, Rose (PSO)
Springer, Enmore (PSO)
McEwan, Aaron (SPO)
Butler, Heather (Accommodation Officer)

Coventry & Warwickshire Programmes
Ditchburn, Margaret (SPO)
Darby, Hannah (PSO)

PSOs
Bains-Rousseau, Rupinder
Griffin, Leigh
Kenny, Julia
McKenzie, Dan
Cadman, Nicola
Owen, Jo (Treatment Mgr)
Porter, Kevin (PSO)
Price, Simon (Treatment Mgr)
Sweatman, Matthew (PSO)
Pre-Qualifying Assessors
Hayward, Mark

70 Little Park Street
Coventry CV1 2UR
Tel: 02476 838300 Fax: 024 7655 3393

Coventry Courts & Allocation Team
Winston, Muhammad (SPO)
O'Neil, Jim

PSOs
Barrett, Ann Marie
Bilverstone, Stuart
Cowley, Steve
Hall, Michael
Rollason, Karen

Coventry Youth Offending Team
Ground Floor Christchurch House
Greyfriars, Lane Coventry CV1 2GY
Tel: 024 7683 1414 Fax: 024 7683 1400
Sadler, Caron
Gordon, Lindsay
David, Sabrina

Solihull LDU

Centenary House
Mackadown Lane Kitts Green
Birmingham B33 0LQ
Tel: 0121 248 3660 Fax: 0121 248 3661

District Management Unit
Levy, Paul (Hd Probation Solihull)

OM Team 1
Francis, Ireca (SPO)

POs
Brennan, Helen
Dodd, Claire
Whitehurst, John
Connelly, Bill (PSO)
Fitzsomons, Elaine (PSO)
Bailey, Nadia

Substance Misuse
O'Connell, Michael (SPO)
Chapman, Sarah (PSO)
Chatwin, Patricia (PO)
Dickenson, Nicole (PO)
Oluwole, Lawal (PSO)

Solihull Magistrates' Court Team
O'Connell, Michael (SPO)
McCauley, Chris

Solihull Magistrates' Court
Homer Road Solihull B91 3RD
Tel: 0121 711 7331 Fax: 0121 711 7050

PSOs
Fitzsimons, Elaine
Hipkiss, Andy
Reeve, Max
Williams, Claudette

ETE
Gaughan, John (PSO)

Rear of Solihull Magistrates' Court
Homer Road Solihull B91 3RD
Tel: 0121 248 6849 Fax: 0121 248 6848

OM Team 3
Green, Beverley (SPO)
Buckley, Jane
Purba, Sandeep (PSO)
Gissey, Sharon
Stephen Mills (PO)
Murland, Ceri-Lisa
Williams, Claudette (PSO)
Walker, Yvonne (PSO)

Solihull Youth Offending Team
Keeper's Lodge Chelmsley Road
Chelmsley Wood Birmingham B37 7RS
Tel: 0121 779 1750 Fax: 0121 779 1755
Lennon, Anna (PSO)

Stafford Probation

University Court
Staffordshire Technology Park
Beaconside Stafford ST18 0GE
Tel: 01785 223416 Fax: 01785 223108

Lomas, Simon (Hd of Prob Stafford)
Brown, Len (Deputy Hd of Prob Stafford)
McConnell, Kate (Dep Hd of Prob Stafford)

Horninglow Street
Burton-upon-Trent DE14 1PH
Tel: 01283 564988 Fax: 01283 567978

Lawrence, Diane (SPO)
Bi, Safina
Burroughs, Tammie
Coates, Julie
King, Elizabeth
Lindsay, Rachel (p)
Lowrence, Nicola
Montgomery, Adele
Reynolds, Paula
Stretton, Daniel

PSOs
Brake, Vicky
Brotherhood, Rhiannon
Crouch, Zoe (p)
Palin, Rachel
Redfern, Sarah
Davies, Helen (p)

200a Wolverhampton Road
Cannock WS11 1AT
Tel: 01543 506112 Fax: 01543 501029

Coplestone, Kathryn (SPO)
Freeman, Hayley (p) (SPO)
Ammi, Angela
Cantrill, Suzanne
Fiero, Roma
Kaur, Baljeet
Mayer, Julie
Neville, Dean

PSOs
Ball, Sarah
Burgess, Val
Edwards, Anita
Daughton, Katy (p)
Tromans, Charmine
Tyler, Rachel

Cross Street
Leek ST13 6BL
Tel: 01538 399355 Fax: 01538 399245

Hodgkinson, Ian (p, SPO)
Bentley, Stephanie
Flowers, Stephanie
Pointon, Tim
Szymichowski, Claire
Beardmore, Paul (p, PSO)
Heath, Pam (PSO)

South Walls
Stafford ST16 3BL
Tel: 01785 223415 Fax: 01785 224159

Perry, Steve (SPO)
Pilling, Steve
Brookes, Kelly
Wright, Joanne
Elliot, Lynne
Mills, Mike
Stourbutts, Robert
Charlton, Julie

PSOs
Caddick, Janice (p)
Chatterley, Julie
Edwards, Anita (p)
Edwards, Sarah
Watkins, Sarah

Moor Street
Tamworth B79 7QZ
Tel: 01827 302600 Fax: 01827 302649

Brown, Laura (SPO)
Burke, Richard
Gilbert, Sylvia
Hope, Victoria
Jakeman, Darren
Simon, Emma
Styles, Kim

PSOs
Collins, Diane
Dunne, Kathryn
Garrow, June (p)
Wiggan, Tammy

Newcastle Team
Melbourne House Etruria Office Village
Forge Lane Festival Park
Stoke-on-Trent ST1 5RQ
Tel: 01782 202800 Fax: 01782 202804

Burnham, Dolores (SPO)
Groombridge, Andrew
Hough, Stephanie
Toohey, Michael
Atkins, Peter
Bettany, Kevin
Ryan, Bob

Lambert, Edward
Sadler, Amy
Smith, Suzi
Watts, Alison
Beardmore, Paul (p, PSO)
Dean, Emily (PSO)
Lowndes, Denise (PSO)
Dixon, Emily (PSO)

Youth Offending Team

Seabridge Youth & Community Centre
Newcastle-under-Lyme ST5 3PJ
Tel: 01782 297615 Fax: 01782 297616

Vacancy

Anson House
Lammascote Road
Stafford ST16 3TA
Tel: 01785 277022 Fax: 01785 277032

Atkins, Peter

Leaning, Victoria

Brotherhood, Rhiannon

The Old House
Eastern Avenue Lichfield WS13 7SQ
Tel: 01543 512103 Fax: 01543 512100

Tatton, Tracy

South Staffordshire Mentally Disordered Offenders Team
Marston House St George's Hospital
Corporation Street Stafford ST16 3AG
Tel: 01785 221306 Fax: 01785 221371

Molloy, Saul

Housing Unit – South
(based at University Court)
Tel: 01785 231738 Fax: 01785 243028

Yarwood, Ellen (SPO)
Griffiths, Linsey (Accom Officer)

Chase Court
200a Wolverhampton Road
Cannock WS11 1AT
Tel: 01543 506112 Fax: 01543 501029

Coplestone, Kate (SPO) (p)
Freeman, Hayley (SPO) (p)
Smith, Jenny (p)
Robinson, Helen
Davies, Martin (PSO)
Hira, Herminder (PSO)

The Chase Prolific Offender Project
Stafford Police Station
Eastgate Street Stafford ST16 2DQ
Tel: 01785 234024 Fax: 01785 234028

Parkes, Jonathan (SPO)
Grice, Kelly
Hibbert, Sharon
Preston, Andrew
Pilling, Steve
Treble, Lesley
Hewston, Tarnia (PSO)

Newcastle & Moorlands Prolific Offender Project
IOM, Longton Police Station
Sutherland Road, Longton
Tel: 01785 233222
Leake, Jason

Trent Valley Prolific Offender Project
(based at Tamworth Police Station)
Spinning School Lane Tamworth B79 7AP
Tel: 01782 234600 Fax: 01782 234605.

Parkes, Jonathan
Gilbert, Sylvia
Woolhouse, John
Gooch, Amy (PSO)

Stoke-on-Trent Probation

Melbourne House
Etruria Office Village
Forge Lane Festival Park
Stoke-on-Trent ST1 5RQ
Tel: 01782 202800 Fax: 01782 202804

Staplehurst, Angela (Hd of Probation Stoke-on-Trent)

Stoke North
Gough, Mick SPO
Almond, Bob
Bromley, Phil
Matthews, Ruth
Proctor, Wendy
Skelton, Ken
Brookes, Jacqui (PSO)
Salter, James (PSO)
Hare, Karen
Heap, Caroline (p)
Nixon, Sue
Parsons, Jennifer (p)
Skelton, Julie (p, PSO)
Evans, Mavis (PSO)
Malam, Janine (PO)
Grindey, Kerry (PO)

Francis, Lisa (PO)
Breen, Helen (PO)

Stoke Central
Hulme, Heather (SPO)
Brereton, Simon
Dunne, Steve
Pitt, Joanna
Shaw, Kerry
Knox, Jennifer (PSO)
Dean, Tracy
Spong, Emma
Rutter, Barbara (PSO)
Stevenson, Laura
Tomczak, Karen
Williams, Andrew
Sutton, Nicholas (PSO)

Stoke South
Hudson, Sue (SPO)
Garland, Sharon
Barnett, Leanne
Brough, Gordon
Newton, Angela
Swann, Victoria
Hinds, Colin
Smith, Racheal
Steele, Hayley
Towner, Claire (p)
Turner, Debra
Gordon, John (PSO)
Litherland, Sylvia (p, PSO)
Watkin, Michelle (p, PSO)
Dancer, Amy (PSO)
Flannagan, Kate (PO)

Youth Offending Team
Ringway House Bryan Street
Hanley Stoke-on-Trent ST1 5AJ
Tel: 01782 235858 Fax: 01782 235860

Moss, Kelly

Criminal Justice Mental Health Team
Now at: The Hope Centre, Huntbach
Street, Hanley, Stoke on Trent, ST1 2BL
Tel 01782 275195

Lindsey, Terry (CJMH Team)
IOM North Team
Northern IOM Team
Based at Longton Police Station
Sutherland Road, Longton, Stoke on
Trent, Staffs

Tel: 01785 233222

Williamson, Jeanette (SPO)
Burdon, Julie
Williams, Debbie

Stoddart, Neal (PSO)
Holford, Joe (PSO)
Barber, Rachael
Dehal, Rupinder
Garner, Maureen
Rhodes, Shelley (PO)
Nixon, Anne-Marie (PSO)

Housing Unit – North
(based at Hanley)
Tel: 01782 212608 Fax: 01782 208589

Yarwood, Ellen (SPO)
Walton, Bernard (Accom Officer)

Courts

**North Staffordshire Magistrates'
Court**
Baker Street, Fenton, Stoke on Trent,
Staffs
Tel: 01782 415219

Mountford, John (SPO)
Platt, Linda
Steer, Jean

PSOs
Vernon, Louise
Archer, Suzanne
Da Silva, Karel
James-Harford, Tina
Rogers, Emma
Brookes, Anne (p PSO)

Crown & County Court
Bethesda Street Hanley
Stoke-on-Trent ST1 3BP
Tel: 01782 286831 Fax: 01782 287994

Mountford, John (SPO)
McLoone, Chris (PO)
Vernon, Darren (PSO)

Crown & County Court
Victoria Square Stafford ST16 2QQ
Tel: 01785 223 433 Fax: 01785 224156

Mountford, John (SPO)
Whitmore, Andrew (p)
Cairns, Esther (PSO)

Wolverhampton Probation

Prue Earle House
Union Street Horseley Fields
Wolverhampton WV1 3JS
Tel: 01902 576000 Fax: 01902 576097

District Management Unit
Appleby, Neil (LDU Head)
Vann, Barbara (Admin Mgr)
Tel: 01902 576009 Fax: 01902 576095

PPO/IDOM Coordinator
Brigue, Parveen (SPO)

SPOs
Altaf, Azhar
Briscoe , John
Gaddu , Diamond
Walker, Stephen

POs
Anand, Vijay
Aston, Jenny
Birdi, Sharon
Chamberlain, Sarah
Chumber, Amir
Cooper, Heather
Cornwell, Rachel
Easthope, Norma
Evans, Jo
Grant, Sheena
Lloyd, Fran
Mail, Stephanie
Mangot, Harbinder
Meredith, Nina
Mills, Louise
Moore-Graham, Merna
Patel, Shanta
Pschenyskyj, Denise
Rowley, Emily
Sharman, Dave
Taylor, Tarnia
Teale, Ian
Uppal, Pinder
Wallace , Clare
Wilson, Jean

PSOs
Daley, Carol
Garcha, Daive
Davies, Katie
Dee , Jill
Grant, Carol
Hyatt, Basil
Mpofu, Edith
Ramzan, Mohammed
Randle Katy
Sinckler , Sharon
Teale , Tracey
Thompson , Gemma
Timmins , Chuchie

Forensic Mental Health
Patel, Lalita (SPO)
Thackwray, Michelle

Court & Allocation Unit
Tel: 01902 576034 Fax: 01902 576010
Patel, Lalita (SPO)

Wolverhampton Magistrates' Court
Law Courts North Street
Wolverhampton WV1 1RA
Tel: 01902 711449 Fax: 01902 772361

Patel, Lalita (SPO)
Pearson, John (PO)

PSOs
Kneller, Jo
McManus, Sally
Ross, Peter
Russon, Janet
Williams, Odette

Wolverhampton Crown Court
Pipers Row Wolverhampton WV1 3LQ
Tel: 01902 481108/9 Fax: 01902 713355

Patel, Lalita (SPO)
Wilkins, Ian (PO)

PSOs
Jones, Jackie
Nash, Kate
Vogan, Jayne

Wolverhampton Youth Offending Team
c/o Social Services Department
Beckminster House Birches Barn Road
Wolverhampton WV3 7BJ
Tel: 01902 553722 Fax: 01902 553733

Link SPO

Walker, Stephen

POs
Denny, Nicola
Kaur, Rajinder
Mitchell, Carol
Osbourne, Annette

PSOs
Winstone, Diane

Walsall Probation

Walsall Probation Complex
Midland Road Walsall WS1 3QE
Tel: 01922 721341 Fax: 01922 618676

District Management Unit
Hall, Kobina (LDU Head Walsall)
Vann, Barbara (Admin Mgr)
Tel: 01922 618501 Fax: 01922 618644

SPOs
Clark, Joseph
Jackson , Judith
Jordan, Carla
Smith, Paul

POS's
Allison , Una
Arrowsmith , Ben
Astley , Debbie
Ball, Pamela
Brown, Vassel
Corbett, Victoria
Cunningham , Julian
Dhillon, Surrinder
Geal Elizabeth
Hamkalo, Michelle
Head, Nigel
Kelsey, Hayley
Littlehales, Sue
Oakley, Tricia
Osmond , Andy
Robinson , Angela
Sagar , Vid
Thompson , Sally

PSOs
Beere, Yvonne
Goode, Debbie
Heath, Lisa
Kaur, Bilwinder
Panesar, Pam
Paul , Anthony
Preedy , Karen
Richards , Marjorie
Titley , Janine
Wallbank , Jenny
Wells , Angela
Wood, Stephen

Walsall Magistrates' Court
Stafford Street Walsall WS2 8HA
Tel: 01922 721471 Fax: 01922 621488

SPO

Clark, Mandy
Hamkalo, Michelle (PO)
PSOs
Bull, Martin
Carolan, Bernie
Dhani, Hasmukh
Ford, Lesley
Tarajia, Zaynab

Youth Offending Team
Blakenall Village Centre Thames Road
Blakenall Walsall WS3 1LZ
Tel: 01922 714966 Fax: 01922 492462

Link SPO
Smith, Paul

POs
Mills, Pamela
PSOs
Gainer, Martin

Birmingham Probation

5th Floor King Edward House
135A New Street Birmingham B2 4QJ
Tel: 0121 329 7900 Fax: 0121 329 7992

Royal, Pat (Birmingham Hd of Probation)
Edwards, Jamie-Ann (Dep Hd Probation Birmingham)
Walton, Neil (Admin Mgr)

Victoria Law Courts
Corporation Street
Birmingham B4 6QU
Tel: 0121 248 6080
Fax: 0121 248 6081 (court info)
Fax: 0121 248 6096 (court liaison)

Aziz, Naheed (SPO)
Campbell, Emily (SPO)
Phillips, Dave
Coombs, Caroline

PSOs
Altaf, Samina
Bansal, Amarjit
Brown, Vanessa
Crawford, Jean
Grimes, Sarah
Hardy, Neil
Kaur, Ranjit
McIntear, John
Palmer, Maureen
Raphael, Melissa
Samuels, Lorraine
Waldo, Valena
Young, Mary
Brissett, Maxine
De Souza, Susie

Drug Intervention Programme
Tel: 0121 248 1283 Fax: 0121 248 1276
Finucane, Gabe (SPO)
Smith, Liz (PM)

PSOs
Nevin, Louise
Kaur, Narinder
Rollins, Gina
Blewitt, Juliette
Edwards, Dot
Johnson, Julia

Queen Elizabeth II Law Courts
1 Newton Street Birmingham B4 7NA
Tel: 0121 248 0099 Fax: 0121 248 0045

Crown Court Team
Durbin, Ray
Fellowes, Richard
Spence, Audrey
Jones, Martin

PSOs
Grundy, Victoria
Jordan, Althea
Andrews, Faye

11–15 Lower Essex Street
Birmingham B5 6SN
Tel: 0121 248 6460 Fax: 0121 248 6461

Homeless Offenders Resettlement Unit
Baker, Kirsty (SPO)
Ashford, Lynne
Carmen, Stephen
Grewal Amarjit
Lidell, Catherine
McLeish, Gillian
Minto, Sharon
O'Shea, Rebecca
Phillips, Rebecca
Braithwaite, Kevin (PSO)

12 High Street
Saltley, Birmingham B8 1JR
Tel: 0121 248 6150 Fax: 0121 248 6151

Team 1
Karra, Geeta (SPO)
Smith, Richard (SPO Temp)

POs
Ahmed, Shaheen (PO)
Barnett, Mabel
Burch, Jeff
Johnson, Debby
King, Maxine
Morris, David
Ormsby, Janet
Simms, Arlene
Spillane, Kerry

PSOs
Allport, Amy
Edwards, Maureen
Johns, Sue
Kalia, Reena (PSO)
Williams, Martin

Team 2
Key, Megan (SPO)
Ayee, Jackie (SPO Temp)

POs
Ashley, Wendy
Blackman, Gywllym
Farmer, Louise
Martin, Lisa
Matthews, Kim
Maye, Owen
Smith, Keith
Woods, Pat

PSOs
Ashraf, Omara
France, Charlene
Spencer, Christopher (PSO)
Talbot, Viv

Team 3
Murphy, Majella (SPO)

POs
Cain, Claudia
Leach, Margaret
McGrainor, Katie
Roberts, Janine
Smythe, Karen
Twist, John

PSOs
Eason, George
Panton, Shirley
Kelley, Steven
Gordon, Sammi
Robins, Toby

Greencoat House
259 Stratford Road
Sparkbrook Birmingham B11 1QS
Tel: 0121 248 5611 Fax: 0121 248 5613

Garton, Kashmir (Dep Hd of Probation, Birmingham East)

Team 1
Fitzer, Zelda (SPO)

POs
Brown, Carolyn
Campbell, Jennifer
Collinge-Lowe, Alina
Edwards, Cheryl Ann
Edwards-Jones, Debbie
PSOs
Rollason, Juliette (PSO)
Sharman Paul (PSO)
Wookey, Stephen (PSO)

Team 2
Stokes, Elaine (SPO)

POs
Britton, Matthew
Lee, Alison
Dale, Rebecca
James, Maria
Mohammed, Weddad
Rhoden, Sonia
Thomas, Katherine

PSOs
Burgess, David
Perkins, Eve
Pratty, Claire
Rowley, Glenda
Thomas, Ian
Ware, Jim

Team 4
Manning, Paul (SPO)
Abrams, Pat
Barnett, Pat
Madeley, Helen
Moss, Alison (SPRAC)
Parchment, Lorna
Pritchard, Andy
Rehman, Rafia
Richards-Myles, Monesha
Thurman, Bernadette

PSOs
Allen, Julie
Bearsmore, Rennie
Mathieson, Rebecca
More, Mandip
Moulton, Patricia

326 Bristol Road
Selly Oak, Birmingham B29 6NA
Tel: 0121 248 6680 Fax: 0121 248 6681

Stevenson, Jackie (Dep Hd of Probation,
Birmingham South)

Team 1
Kennedy, Jennifer (SPO)

POs
Anderson, Dawn
Bassi, Hardeep
Blake, Sara
Dickman, Susan
Hobday, Lisa
Knowles, Ann
Seadon, Sally
Sumner, Gary
Steer, Nicolas

PSOs
Abanikanda, Tunde
Gooden, Michelle
Grant, Stacey
Mukadam, Aishah
Rich, Brian
Robinson, Keith
Sheard, Mary
Walker, Jackie

Team 2
Yeap, Christine (SPO)

POs
Botham, Joanne
Cansfield, Karen
Flynn, Val
Francis, Aaron
Frati, Catherine
Hanley, Richard
Mullings, Janet
Sewell, Jean
Stevenson, Fiona
Watkins, Laurence
Williamson, Zoe
Young, Terese

PSOs
Adams, Karl (PSO)
Bott, Catherine
Graham, Elaine (PSO)
Hadley, Paula (PSO)
Swingler, Claire

Team 3
Dunbar, Janet (SPO)
James, Donna (PSO)

Birmingham South Sector
Tel: 0345 113 5000

Central Team
Pasha, Naveed (SPO)

Sutton Coldfield Police Station
Lichfield Road Sutton B74 2NR
Tel: 0345 113 5000

North OMU
Davy-Sharpe, Mel
Hunk, Emma
Longthorn, Debra
Stannard, Andrew

Bournville Lane Police Station
341 Bournville Lane Bournville
Birmingham B30 1QX
Tel: 0345 113 5000 EXT 7822 6610

South OMU
Branson, Jennifer
Gordon, Michael
Tudor, Pam
Blewitt, Juliette (PSO)

Thornhill Road Police Station
Handsworth Birmingham B30 9BT
Tel: 0345 113 5000 ext 7862 6788

West OMU
Bailey, Rema
Green, Ben
Guinan, John
Hazeley-Jones, Chris

Stetchford Police Station
Stechford Birmingham B33 8RR
Tel: 0345 113 5000 ext 7844 6821

East OMU
Ballard, Claire
Beardmore, Rennie
Caesar, Yvette
Hedderick, Bev
Pratty, Claire

MAGU
Richards, Sandra (SPO)
Felton, Stuart
Lam, Angela
Salter, Helen

18–28 Lower Essex Street
Birmingham B5 6SN
Tel: 0121 248 6400 Fax: 0121 248 6401

Rai, Ravinder (SPO)
Benjamin, Audrey
Burt, Tania
Canicle, Jakki
Edwards, Althea
Jan, Araf
Lindo, Elizabeth
McGuinness, Matthew
Neal, Suzanne
Rogers, Jennifer

PSOs
Bailey, Eileen
Bennington, Claire
Gray, Diane
Johns, Val
Shinji, Rajinder

76 Walsall Road Perry Barr
Perry Barr Birmingham B42 1SF
Tel: 0121 248 6340 Fax: 0121 248 6341

Team 1
Thawait, Pratima (SPO)

POs
Bevan, Catherine
Hope, Kathryn
Philippides, Toni
Scott, Valerie
Rogers, Tom
Stewart, Mervin
Thompson, Jennifer
Ward, Rosie
Worley, Nick

PSOs
Bassan, Ravinder
Boylan, Lindsay
Clarke, Cynthia
Creighton, Denise
Gessey, Vanessa
Finch, Andre
Lerenzo, Sebastian
Powell, Wayne
Scott, Dominique
McGowan, Yvonne (ELO)

Team 2
Cookson, David (SPO)

POs
Akram, Safraz
Begum, Farzana
Joseph, Drayton
Eggleton, Joanne
Hancel, Kerry
Mair, Patsy
Vernon, Maureen
Sohal, Kulvinder
Yorke, Julia

PSOs
Estridge, Shelley
Larman, Karon
Malone, Angela
Ochi, Emmanuel
Riley, Laura
Smith, Anne
Williams, Joel

Team 3
Ainslie, Sam (SPO)

326/328 Hamstead Road
Handsworth Birmingham B20 2RA
Tel: 0121 248 6500 Fax: 0121 248 6501

Brown-Richards, Pat (Dep Hd of
Probation, Birmingham)

Poland, Michael (SPO)

SWEET & MAXWELL
FREEPOST
PO BOX 1000
ANDOVER
SP10 9AH
UNITED KINGDOM

Thank you for purchasing The Probation Directory 2013.

☑ Don't miss important updates

So that you have all the latest information, The Probation Directory is published annually. Sign up today for a Standing Order to ensure you receive the updating copies as soon as they publish. Setting up a Standing Order with Sweet & Maxwell is hassle-free, simply tick, complete and return this FREEPOST card and we'll do the rest.

You may cancel your Standing Order at any time by writing to us at Sweet & Maxwell, PO Box 1000, Andover, SP10 9AH stating the Standing Order you wish to cancel.

Alternatively, if you have purchased your copy of The Probation Directory from a bookshop or other trade supplier, please ask your supplier to ensure that you are registered to receive the new editions.

All goods are subject to our 30 day Satisfaction Guarantee (applicable to EU customers only)

Yes, please send me new editions of The Probation Directory to be invoiced on publication, until I cancel the standing order in writing.

☐ All new editions

Title   Name

Organisation

Job title

Address

Postcode

Telephone

Email

S&M account number (if known)

PO number

All orders are accepted subject to the terms of this order form and our Terms of Trading (see www.sweetandmaxwell.co.uk). By submitting this order form I confirm that I accept these terms and I am authorised to sign on behalf of the customer.

Signed   Job Title

Print Name   Date

UK VAT Number: GB 900 5487 43. Irish VAT Number: IE 9513874E. For customers in an EU member state (except UK & Ireland) please supply your VAT Number. VAT No

(BC003) V9 (09.2012) LC / JK

Delivery charges are not made for titles supplied to mainland UK. Non-mainland UK please add £4/€5 per delivery. Europe – please add £10/€13 for first item, £2.50/€3 for each additional item. Rest of World – please add £30/€38 for first item, £15/€19 for each additional item..

Goods will normally be dispatched within 3-5 working days of availability. The price charged to customers, irrespective of any prices quoted, will be the price specified in our price list current at the time of dispatch of the goods, as published on our website, unless the order is subject to a specific offer or discount in which case special terms may apply.

UK VAT is charged on all applicable sales at the prevailing rate except in the case of sales to Ireland where Irish VAT will be charged at the prevailing rate. Customers outside the EU will not be charged UK VAT.

Thomson Reuters (Professional) UK Limited – Legal Business (Company No. 1679046). 100 Avenue Road, Swiss Cottage, London NW3 3PF. Registered in England and Wales. Registered office: Aldgate House, 33 Aldgate High Street, London EC3N 1DL. Trades using various trading names, a list of which is posted on its website at sweetandmaxwell.co.uk

"Thomson Reuters" and the Thomson Reuters logo are trademarks of Thomson Reuters and its affiliated companies.

SWEET & MAXWELL

 THOMSON REUTERS

POs
Farmer, Liz
Green, Janet
Hewitt, Christine
Kataria, Meena
Kewley, Robert
Mukwamba, Michael
Mulowoza, Christine

PSOs
Bhopal, Varinder (PSO)
Bryan, Alan (PSO)
Byrne, Sarah
Caines, Michelle
Hamilton, Adele
Mills, Olive
Ram-Jakhu, Sodhi
Uppal, Dalvinder

Birmingham Youth Offending Service
Youth Offending Service Head Office
18 Gravelly Hill North
Erdington Birmingham B23 6BQ
Tel: 0121 464 0600 Fax: 0121 464 0609

Youth Offending Service (North)
Pype Hayes Hall Pype Hayes Park
Pype Hayes Birmingham B24 0HG
Tel: 0121 303 0252 Fax: 0121 464 0921
Evers, Genene
Crisp, Ruth

Youth Offending Service (South)
Halescroft Square, Off Shenley Hill
Birmingham B31 1HD
Tel: 0121 476 5111 Fax: 0121 411 2198
Brown, Keren
James, Clare

Youth Offending Service (East)
15 Commons Lane Washwood Heath
Birmingham B3 2US
Tel: 0121 464 7719 Fax: 0121 464 6261

Coleman, Angela

Youth Offending Service (West)
115 All Saints Street
Hockley Birmingham B18 7RJ
Tel: 0121 464 8484 Fax: 0121 464 7575

Myerscough, Karen
Baker, Joanne

Youth Offending Service
Highgate Centre
157–159 St Lukes Road Highgate
Birmingham B5 7DA

Tel: 0121 464 1570 Fax: 0121 464 1596
King, Maria
Milinkovic, Victor

Youth Offending Service

(Birmingham Youth Court)
c/o 52 Newton Street
Birmingham B4 6NF
Tel: 0121 233 3600 Fax: 0121 236 0828

Jenoure, Jean (PSO)

Accredited Programmes
5th Floor King Edward House
135A New Street Birmingham B2 4QJ
Tel: 0121 329 7900 Fax: 0121 329 7992

Elphick, Bronwen (Head of Interventions
– Effective Practice)
Ellis, Philip (Programmes Implementation
Mgr)
Black Country Programmes Unit

Unity House
14–16 New Street
West Bromwich B70 7PQ
Tel: 0121 358 9358 Fax: 0121 358 9487
Mudoch, Mike (SPO)

PSOs
Bennett, Francesca
Byron, Mark
Hothi, Sak
James, Jane
Murphy, Jaci
Nash, Karen
Saddler, Stephen
Sarai, Kulvinder
Whitehouse, Sally
Burton, Carol (Treatment Mgr)
Pope, Kerrie-Anne (Treatment Mgr)
White, Elaine (Treatment Mgr)

Women Safety Workers
Walsall Probation Complex
Midland Road Walsall WS1 3QE
Tel: 01922 721341 Fax: 01922 725616
Green, Becky (Women's Safety Wkr

Birmingham & Solihull Programmes Unit
18–28 Lower Essex Street
Birmingham B5 6SN
Tel: 0121 248 6460 Fax: 0121 248 6461

D'Ippolito, Angela (SPO)
Afzal, Kaiser (Treatment Mgr)
Bolton, John (Treatment Mgr)

Ferber, Rozanne (Women's Safety Wkr)
Campion, Sally (Treatment Mgr)

PSOs
Byng, Jodie
Froome, Robert
Ghag, Navnéet
Gibbs, Charlotte
Halsey, William
Harris, Chris
Minott, Marsha
Richards, Laurie
Tandy, Rachael

Melbourne House
Etruria Village
Forge Lane Festival Park
Hanley Stoke-on-Trent ST1 5RQ
Tel: 01782 202800 Fax: 01782 202858

Cooper, Sally (Acting Deputy Head)
(based at Dorrington Drive & Melbourne
House)
Parsons, Jen (PO)
Willis, Emma (Treatment Mgr/Tutor)
Wood, Tony (Acting SPO)
MacKinnon, Nicola (IDAP TM)

PSOs
Paterson, Rebecca
Richards, Lisa (p)
Riley, Michael
Pope, Richard
Woolridge, Laura-Jane

Horninglow Street
Burton-on-Trent DE14 1PH
Tel: 01283 565951 Fax: 01283 567978

Cooper, Sally (SPO, Progs Mgr) (based at
Dorrington Drive)
Bibi, Sophina (PSO)

Dorrington Drive
Dorrington Industrial Park
Stafford ST16 3BF
Tel: 01785 279951 Fax: 01785 279959

Cooper, Sally (SPO, Progs Mgr)
Cooper, Andrew (Treatment Mgr)
Taylor, Ross (PSO)
Welch, Karen (PSO)

Moor Street
Tamworth B79 7QZ
Tel: 01827 302616 Fax: 01827 302649

Cooper, Sally (SPO, Progs Mgr) (based at
Dorrington Drive)
Harper, Ian (PSO)

Community Payback Division

5th Floor King Edward House
135a New Street **Birmingham** B2 4QJ
Tel: 0121 329 7900 Fax: 0121 329 7995
Mason, John (Head of Community
Payback)
Tolley, Pat (Admin Mgr)
Huckerby, Keith (H&S Off)

Unity House
14 – 16 New Street
West Bromwich B70 7PQ
Tel: 0121 358 9358 Fax: 0121 358 9480

Walton, Martin (Unit Mgr) also covers
Walsall
Williams Charles (PSO)
Hawkins, Craig (Dep Unit Mgr) also
covers Walsall
Williams, Nicola (PSO)
Balfour, Richard (PSO)
Whale, Paul (PSO)

162 Halesowen Road
Netherton **Dudley** DY2 9PS
Tel: 01384 456482 Fax: 01384 457441

Mills, John (Unit Mgr) also covers
Wolverhampton
Coley, Trevor (Dep Unit Mgr) also covers
Wolverhampton
Ralph Andy (PSO)
Smith, Michael (PSO)
Warmer, Barry (PSO)
Pankhania, Manjula (PSO)

Sheriffs Court
12 Greyfriars Road, Coventry CV1 3RY
Tel: 02476 838300 Fax: 02476 838332

Smith, Penny (Unit Mgr)
McKinnell, Chris (Dep Unit Mgr)
Hughes Charlotte (PSO)
Lee, Mark (PSO)
Lowndes, Jacqui (PSO)
Massey Stephen (PSO)
Patrick, Ray (PSO)

Prue Earle House
Union Street, Horseley Fields,
Wolverhampton WV1 3JS
Tel: 01902 576000 Fax: 01902 576097
Hyatt, Marinda (PSO)
Hill, Karen (PSO)
Green, Matthew (PSO)
Colburn, Gemma (PSO)
Lockley, Shelia (PSO)

Walsall Probation Complex
Midland Road Walsall WS1 3QE
Tel: 01922 721341 Fax: 01922 723080
Cross, David (PSO)
Irving, Marshall (PSO)
Leslie, Tracey (PSO)
Thompson, Maria (PSO)

United Friendly House
76 Walsall Road
Perry Barr Birmingham B42 1SF
Tel: 0121 248 6348 Fax: 0121 248 6324

Choudhury, Sheku (Unit Mgr)
Barlow, Lynne (Dep Unit Mgr)
Badesha, Jas (PSO)
Byron – Scott, Shalene (PSO
Oram, Andrew (PSO)
Stokes, Tony (PSO)
Uppal, Balvinder (PSO)

11–15 Lower Essex Street
Birmingham B5 6SN
Tel: 0121 248 6334 Fax: 0121 248 7136
*Areas covered are: Sparkbrook, Saltley,
Selly Oak Chelmsley Wood*

Community Payback Unit
Kennedy, Yvonne (Unit Mgr)
Loft, Lesley (Dep Unit Mgr)

PSOs
Al-Moghraby, Mazen
Dennis, Beverley
Hamilton, Nyasha
McLarnon ,Nonnie
Meacham, Robert
Millard, Angie
Mohammed, Khalik
Reid, Kenneth
Sterling, Conrad
Walker, Lionel

Dorrington Drive

Dorrington Industrial Park
Common Road, Stafford ST16 3BF
Tel: 01785 228608 Fax: 01785 228708
Roberts, Peter (Deputy Unit Mgr)
Grice, Julie (PSO)

Melbourne House
Etruria Office Village, Forge Lane
Festival Park, Etruria**, Stoke-on-Trent**
ST1 5RQ
Tel: 01782 202951 Fax: 01782 202858
Keeling, Neil (Deputy Unit Mgr)
Hughes, Kim (Placement Mgr)
Lowndes, Chris (Placement Mgr)

PSOs
Birt, Kathleen
Bromfield, Peter
Scarrat, Wendy
Lowndes, Tony

**Unit 1 Crossfields Industrial Estate
Lichfield** WS13 6RJ
Tel: 01543 263299 Fax: 01543 419360
Walker, Steve (Unit Manager)
Pearson, Ian (Deputy Unit Mgr)
Bradley, Shirley (Placement Mgr)
Harries, Marc (Placement Mgr)
Ryan, Tori (PSO)
Thompson, Cliff (PSO)

**Executive Business Unit – Learning &
Development**
826 Bristol Road Selly Oak
Birmingham B29 6NA
Tel: 0121 248 6720 Fax: 0121 248 6721

Armstrong, Kim (Exec Admin Mgr)
(based at Trust Executive Office Victoria
Square), Birmingham B1 1BD

Knott, David (Head of HR, Learning &
Development) 0121 634 1340 (based at
Trust Executive Office, Victoria Square,
as above)

Business Support Training
Harman, Lucy (Bus Support Training
Mgr) (based at Fort Dunlop, Fort
Parkway, Birmingham B24 9FD)
Brown, Eve (Business Support Trainer)

Effective Practice Training
Gill, Andy (Training Mgr) (based at Trust
Executive Office, as above)

Pre-Qualifying Training
Dunkley, Rose (PQF Manager) (based at
Fort Dunlop, as above)
Aston, Jeff (Deputy Manager, PQF)
Glennie, Karin (Practice Tutor)
Richmond, Rita (Practice Tutor)

Training Admin Unit
Thompson, Eleshia (Course
Administrator)
Beard, Julie (PQT Administrator)
Leighton, Joseph (Training Support Asst)
Robinson, Karen (PQT Administrator)

Training Assessors
Billingham, Ruth
Chaudhry, Geet
Bushell-Edwards, Alyson
Hayward, Mark

Linton, Hazelle
Male, Anita
Rackley, Lisa
Rattigan, Sylvia
Richardson, Sue
Vacancy (Training Assessor)

Regional Sex Offender Unit

5th Floor King Edward House
135A New Street Birmingham B2 4QJ
Tel: 0121 329 7900 Fax: 0121 329 7992

Farmer, Mark (Regional Mgr)
Cole, Diane (Admin Mgr)

RSOU – Selly Oak
826 Bristol Road Selly Oak
Birmingham B29 6NA
Tel: 0121 248 6760 Fax: 0121 248 6761

Clarke, Dave (SPO/Prog Mgr)
Gibbs, Caroline (Treatment Mgr)
Millington, Sonia (Treatment Mgr)
PO Facilitators
Bough, Diane
Bond, Jonathan
Day, Stuart
Gibbs, Amy
Jones, Sezal
Marsh, David
Mordecai, Jo
Ring, Lindsey
Twist, Lorraine
Willett, Andrea

RSOU – Staffordshire
Stafford Programmes Unit
Dorrington Drive
Dorrington Industrial Park
Common Road Stafford ST16 3DG
Tel: 01785 279951 Fax: 01785 279959

Jones, Roderick (SPO)
Baverstock, Laura (Treatment Mgr)
Dalgarno, Claire (PO/Facilitator)
Joslyn, Jean (PO/Facilitator)
Patterson, Rob (PO/Facilitator)
Ward, Jenny (PO/Facilitator)

West Mercia Sex Offender Unit
Courtside House Telford Square
Malinsgate **Telford** TF3 4EQ
Tel: 01952 299366 Fax: 01952 200896

RSOU – West Mercia
135 Abbey Foregate
Shrewsbury SY2 6AS
Tel: 01743 231525 Fax: 01743 244914

Daly, Maggie (Treatment Mgr)
Barrington, Karyn (PO/Facilitator) Based at Telford
Willetts, Diane (PO/Facilitator)

RSOU – West Mercia
3–4 Shaw Street
Worcester WR1 3QQ
Tel: 01905 723591 Fax: 01905 724833

Jones, Roderick (SPO)
Edgar, Karen (PO/Facilitator)

Public Protection

Public Protection Business Unit
King Edward House
135a New Street
Birmingham B2 4QJ
Tel: 0121 329 7900 Fax: 0121 329 7994
Byford, Nigel (Hd of Public Protection)
Tel: 0121 329 7904
Townsend, Viv (Head of Approved Premises) Tel: 021 329 7932
Beckford, Audrey (Dep Hd Public Protection – Prisons) Tel: 021 329 7932
Kaur, Christine (Admin Mgr) Tel: 0121 329 7933
Green, Emma (Central Referral Officer) 0121 329 7937

Approved Premises (Hostels)

Bilston
23 Wellington Road
Bilston Wolverhampton WV14 6AH
Tel: 01902 497688 Fax: 01902 498150

Blake, Sonia (SPO Mgr)
Walker, Glenford (PO Dep)
Butler, Janet (PSO)
Madders, Lynn (PSO)
Willis, Davis (PSO)

Carpenter House
33 Portland Road Edgbaston
Birmingham B16 9HS
Tel: 0121 248 3680 Fax: 0121 248 3690
Mullis, Dave (SPO Mgr)
Collier, Catherine (PO Dep)
Shaw, Bharti (PSO)
Hodson, Christine (PSO)
Ollerenshaw, Richard (PSO)

Crowley House
(for women)
31 Weoley Park Road Selly Oak
Birmingham B29 6QY
Tel: 0121 472 7111 Fax: 0121 415 4072

Clarke, Tracy (SPO Mgr)
Davenport, Jen (PO Dep)
Bishop, Leah (PSO)
Cox, Ira (PSO)
Clarke, Natalie (PSO)
Tustin, Kerry (PSO)

Elliott House
(for mentally disordered offenders only)
96 Edgbaston Road, Moseley
Birmingham B12 9QA
Tel: 0121 440 2657 Fax: 0121 446 6818

Fleming, Natasha (SPO Mgr)
Field, Richard (PO Dep)
Booth, Samantha (PSO)
Kelly, Brian (PSO)
Campbell, Chantelle (PSO)

Welford House
31 Trinity Road Aston
Birmingham B6 6AJ
Tel: 0121 523 4401 Fax: 0121 515 1355

Mullis, Dave (SPO Mgr)
Harvey, Victoria (PO Dep)
Coleman, Lloyd (PSO)
Kane, Kenneth (PSO)
Robinson, Elaine (PSO)

Stonnall Road
85 Stonnall Road
Aldridge Walsall WS9 8JZ
Tel: 01922 459574 Fax: 01922 455373

Blake, Sonia (SPO Mgr)
Canning, Michael (PO Dep)
Hawley, Karen (PSO)
Page, Roy (PSO)
Vacancy (PSO)

Sycamore Lodge
Clay Lane Langley
Oldbury B69 4TH
Tel: 0121 552 9930 Fax: 0121 544 6994

Dee, John (SPO Mgr)
Branwood, Dave (PO Dep)
Belal, Ahmed (PSO)
Bagharian, Kuldip (PSO)
Wood, Sharon (PSO)

Wenger House Probation & Bail Hostel
21a Albert Street
Newcastle-under-Lyme ST5 1HJ
Tel: 01782 717423 Fax: 01782 714332
Admin: 01782 622683

Downing, Sue (SPO Mgr)
Adams, Carl (PO Deputy)
Azarpour, Reza (PSO)

Forrester, June (PSO)
Weaver, Peter (PSO)

Staitheford House Probation & Bail Hostel
14 Lichfield Road Stafford ST17 4JX
Tel: 01785 223417 Fax: 01785 224153

Williams, Ruth (SPO Mgr)
Breeze, Stuart (PO Dep)
Butler, David (PSO)
Mottram, Ann (PSO)
Steele, Heather (PSO)

Wharflane House Bail Hostel
34 Rectory Road Shelton
Stoke-on-Trent ST1 4PW
Tel: 01782 205554 Fax: 01782 205552

Downing, Sue (SPO Mgr)
Holsey, John (PO Dep)
Graham, Patrick (PSO)
Scarratt, Ian (PSO)
Walters, Sandra (PSO)

Prisons

HMP Birmingham G4S
Winson Green Road
Birmingham B18 4AS
Tel: 0121 598 8000 Fax: 0121 345 2501
Special visits ext 8263 Fax: 0121 345 2469
General Probation Enquiries:
0121 598 8249/8181

Thompson, Jacky (SPO) ext 8119
Collins, Yvonne ext 8181
Jordan, Pat ext 8294
Lau, Natalie ext 8294

HMP/YOI Brinsford
New Road Featherstone
Wolverhampton WV10 7PY
Tel: 01902 532450 Fax: 01902 532451
Special visits tel: 01902 533605
Probation enquiries: 01902 533544

Davidson, Paulette (SPO) ext 3517
Vacancy
Burns, Louise ext 3532
Sidaway, Yvonne ext 3637
Shotton, Julie ext 3476
Pratley, Jacqueline (PSO) ext 3641
Tabberer, Phil (PSO, Bail Info) ext 3571
Thomas, Mark (PSO) ext 3633

HMP Hewell
Hewell Lane Redditch B97 6QS
Tel: 01527 785000 Fax: 01527 400501

Moran, Paula (SPO) 01527 794080
Kyle, Suzanna 01527 785230

HMP Stafford
54 Gaol Road Stafford ST16 3AW
Tel: 01785 773000 Fax: 01785 773314
Cavanagh, Ian
Stockall, Steve

HMP Dovegate (Serco)
Moreton Lane Uttoxeter ST14 8XR
Tel: 01283 829400 Fax: 01283 829469
Butler, Sally
Chown, Nicola
Kidd, Sharon
Matile, Miles (PO)
Davies, Paul (PO)

HMP Drake Hall
Eccleshall Nr Stafford ST21 6LQ
Tel: 01785 774100 Fax: 01785 774010 s/b
Fax: 01785 858010

Large, Malcolm (SPO)
Boult, Chris
Watts, Alison

HMYOI Swinfen Hall
18 The Drive Swinfen Nr Lichfield WS14 9QS
Tel: 01543 484000 Fax: 01543 484001

Large, Malcolm (SPO)
Reynolds, Paula (PO)
Robertson, Les (PO)
Windridge, Kelly

HMP Featherstone
New Road Wolverhampton WV10 7PU
Tel: 01902 703000 Fax: 01902 703001 s/b
Tel: 01902 703095

Large, Malcolm (SPO)
Dwight, Ellie (PO)
Gilbride, Sue
Lawton, Stephen
Oram, Rachel (PSO)

HMP Oakwood (G4S)
New Road, Wolverhampton WV10 7PU
Tel: 01902 7997000
Probation Office Tel: 01902 7999923
Thompson, Jacky (SPO)
Hughes, Anna (PO)
Jones, Adrian (PO)
Wallace, Lucinda (PO)

MAPPA Team (West Midlands)

West Midlands Police
Room 710A
Lloyd House, Colmore Circus,
Queensway,
Birmingham B4 6NQ

Tel: 0121 609 6954 Fax: 0121 609 6950
Batham, Angie (Mappa Co-ordinator SPO)
Rogers, Tom Deputy Mappa Co-ordinator
Paten, Sarah Snr Mappa Administrator

MAPPA TEAM (Staffordshire)
MAPPA Unit
PO Box 3167
Stafford ST16 9JZ
Fax: 01785 235172
White, Mark (Mappa Co-ordinator SPO)
Tel: 01785 235249
Charlesworth, Margaret (PO) Tel: 01785 235224
Barlow, Claire (PO) Tel: 01785 235010
Terry-Short, Pam (MAPPA Administrator) Tel: 01785 235170
Groom, Andrea (MAPPA Administrator) Tel: 01785 235123
Brown, Ann (VISOR Administrator) Tel: 01785 235008

Victim Liaison Unit

52 Newton Street
Birmingham B4 6NF
Tel: 0121 248 6100 Fax: 0121 248 6101
Darby, Paul (SPO)
Gallagher, Nicola (PO)
Bebbington, Christine (PSO)
Fitzmaurice, Tracy (PSO)
Montague, Lucy (PSO)
Nembhardt, Osbourne (PSO)
McBean, Angela (PSO)
Birch, Kelly (PSO)

5th Floor King Edward House
135A New Street **Birmingham** B2 4QJ
Tel: 0121 329 7900 Fax: 0121 329 7994
Tudor, Barbara (Victim/Offender Development Officer)

Sheriff's Court
12 Greyfriars Road
Coventry CV1 3RY
Tel: 02476 838308/9/10 Fax: 02476 838434
Vacancy

Prue Earle House
Union Street, Horseley Fields,
Wolverhampton WV1 3JS
Tel: 01902 875750 Fax: 01902 875754
Durbin, Jackie (PSO)

University Court
Staffordshire Technology Park
Beaconside Stafford ST18 0GE
Tel: 01785 231728 Fax: 01785 674519

Darby, Paul (SPO)
Vacancy
Parker, Rachel (PSO)

Local Justice Areas
Birmingham
Central & South West Staffordshire
Coventry
Dudley & Halesowen
North Staffordshire
Sandwell
Solihull
South East Staffordshire
Sutton Coldfield
Walsall & Aldridge
Wolverhampton

Crown Courts
Birmingham
Coventry
Stafford
Stoke-on-Trent
Wolverhampton

SURREY & SUSSEX PROBATION TRUST

Out of hours emergency tel: 01483 571635; 01273 622300

Victim enquiries tel: 01483 568561 (Surrey) 01273 810411 (Sussex)

Email:
firstname.lastname@sspt.probation.gsi.gov.uk

Trust Head Office
SSPT Headquarters operates over three sites. The main HQ is Brighton; staff located in Guildford are indicated by the symbol (G), Hillside by the symbol (H)
4th Floor, Invicta House, Trafalgar Place, Brighton
East Sussex BN1 4FR
Tel: 01273 627800 Fax: 01273 625207

Guildford Office
College House, Woodbridge Road, Guildford
Surrey, GU1 4RS
Tel: 01483 534701 Fax: 01483 453701

Hillside Cottage
Ferry Lane, Portsmouth Road, Guildford, Surrey, GU2 4EE
Tel: Direct Dials Only

Board
Steele, John (Trust Board Chair)
Wells, Steve (Solicitor & Trust Secretary)

Trust Executive Team
Smart, Nick (Chief Executive)
Berrill, Judith (Dir of HR) 01273 627847
Browne, Jane (Dir, Service Design) 01273 627843
Whitworth, Anne (Dir of Finance and IT) 01273 627844
D'Arcy, Mary (Dir of Interventions) 01273 627842
Hayde, Elspeth (Dir of HR) 01273 627847
Pedrick, Lin (Dir, Surrey LDU) (G) 01483 863538
Radley, Amanda (Dir, West Sussex LDU) 01273 627839
Rogers, Leighe (Dir, Brighton & Hove and East Sussex LDU) 01273 627841
Saunders, Andrea (Dir of Public Protection) 01273 627840
Watkin, Valerie (Dir of Quality and Corporate Services)
Alcock, Jennie (PA to Chief Executive and Board) 01273 627833
Cubey, Diane (PA to Directors) 01273 627831
Lewis, Louise (PA to Directors) 01273 627832
Pollard, Trish (PA to Directors) (G) 01483 863510

Communications
Hustwayte, Rob (Mgr)
Nicholls, Rob

Commissioning
Eley, Hannah (Commissioning Mgr) (G)
Cossutta, Jane (Contract Mgr)
Gieler, Stefan (Bench Marking Mgr)

Corporate Services
Lane, Brenda (Corp Estate Mgr) (G)
Simpson, Jan (Support Services & Recall Mgr)
Patching, Rachel
Rolf, Jason

Finance
Robinson, Jenny (Financial Controller)
Chauhan, Sangita
Goldberg, Mauricia
Howe, Harriet
Kuo, Claudia
May, Roderick
Shaddick, Angela
Warland, Chris

Health & Safety
Ilesley, Christine (H&S Off) (H) (01483 269182)
Hood, Bisi (H&S Off)

Human Resources
Adams, Kylie (G)
Attree, Sara
Barrett, Belinda (G)
Brigham-Wilmot, Justine
Filby, Lynsey (G)
Hussain, Imran (G)
King, Kay (G)
Lucas, Tracy
Muir, Julia
Parker, Jo (G)
Rowley, Julie (G)
Thompson Carole (G)

ICT
Kellet, James (Mgr)
Edwards, Phil (H) (01483 269180)
Ehsan, Azeem
Lansana, Emmanuel (H) (01483 269180)
Newman, Lesley
Piper, Walter

Information Assurance and Security
Graham, Jay

Learning & Development
Marsh, Christine (Prof & Org Dev Mgr)
Hilling, Peter (Core Training Mgr) (H) (01483 269189)
Dawson, Angela (G)
Jones, Phil (Brighton)
Layzell, Judith (H) (01483 269183)
Pollard, Trish (H)
Whitehead, Alison (Worthing)

MAPPA
Bamford, Mark (Mgr)
Burns, Brenda (H)
Henry, Louise (H)
Gray, Kim (H) (01483 269192)
Johnson, Marguerite
Maddocks, Tristan
Meyer, Victoria

Projects, Performance & Excellence
Bowler, Rebecca
Finella, Giorgio
Hooper, Rhian (G)
Murray, Laura
Snashall, Peter
Thrussell, Jackie

Brighton LDU

Lancaster House
47 Grand Parade, Brighton BN2 9QA
Tel: 01273 810300 Fax: 01273 810399

Offender Management Team
Piggott, Debbie (SPO)
Andrews, Emily
Barnes, Simon
Burgess, Giovanna
Conduct, Emma
Coney, Yve
Cooper, Kate
Dawes, Lisa
Duncan, Angie (Women's Safety Worker)
Griffiths, Anthony
Hanmer, Poppy
Hewland, Teresa
Ivors, Cameron
Ley, Suzanne
Lovell, Sarah
Mahoney, Catherine
Oko, Steve
Paul, Katy
Potter, Jodie
Ring, Maya
Roughly, Lucy
Smith, Naomi
Spiers, Angela
Wilson, Stella
Woodbridge, Kelly

Integrated Offender Management Team
Edwards, Martin (SPO)
Davis, Helen (QDO)
Melrose, Rea (QDO)
Bletchley,Amber
Burgess,Giovanna
Catling,Sarah
Dawes,Lisa
Eason, Cathryn
Enzor, Suzanne
Fowler, Jennifer
Gerrard, Jake
Hanmer,Poppy
Herring, Sharon
Hewland, Teresa
Knight, Debbie
Mayhew,Ben
Paul,Katy
Radcliffe,Stephen
Williams, Louise

Public Protection Team
Burden, Mark (SPO)
Bridger, Rick
Carter, Liz

Garland, Marie (High Risk Floating
Support Worker)
Gerrard, Wendy
Gregory, Eleanor
Hardy, Alison
Kelly, Linda
Lloyd-Pay, Anthony
Manning, Sue
Peacock, Phillipa
Williams, Beth

Programmes Team
Porter, Louise (Mgr)
Bell, Matilda
Burt, Tim
Coleman, Sharon
Mowinski, Joanna
Nicholson, Sarah
Powley, Dean
Rudd, Wendy
Saunders, Hannah
Stevens, Teresa
Strong, Lynne
Swift, Amy
Tilbury, Guy

Court Team
Peters, Kerrin (SPO)
Hollington, Abigail
Kirov, Charmelle
Lambert, Anna
McLean, Janis
Rich, Trudy
Roe, Stepha
Soopraya, Gerard
Thomas, Anne

Community Payback Team
Brown, Lara (Ops Mgr)
Berry, Stephen
Bligh, Sean
Bradshaw, Zorina
Clements, Peter
Coulson, Charlie
Dale, Joanna
Day, Sarah
Fox, Alex
Garcka, Gillian
Green, Shane
Houlton, Diane
Lennie, Gary
Mearns, Loraine
Rachad, Fatima
Spencer, Sian
Streeter, Mark

Victims' Liaison Team
Colishaw, Stacey
Herring, Sharon
Lunderstedt, Max

Accommodation Services Team
Bond, Kat
Deighton, Sacha

Corporate Services
Porcas, Sarah (Support Services Mgr)
Agyei, Sarah
Crawley, Corinne
Matthews, Nathaniel
Watts, Ann
Wheeler, Wendy

Offender Employment and Skills
Franks, Debbie

Learning & Development
Davis, Helen
Jones, Paul
Whitehead, Alison

East Sussex LDU

1 St Leonards Road
Eastbourne, East Sussex BN21 3UH
Tel: 01323 749555 Fax: 01323 738484

Programmes Team
Furlong, Michaela
Marshall, Vanessa
Ncube, Emmanuel
Warner-Swann, Johanna

Community Payback Team
Downs, Nick
Lanigan, Joseph
Lennie, Gary

35 Old Orchard Road
Eastbourne, East Sussex BN21 1DD
Tel: 01323 746200 Fax: 01323 439755

Offender Management Team
Young, Keith (SPO)
Bennett, Sarah
Brennan, Sarah
Connaboy,Chris
Crockett,Peter
Gregory,Hannah
Lacey, Karen
Lang, Joanna (QDO)
Mould, Hannah
Neal, Holly
Webb, Helen
Westbrook, Paul
White, Marc

Whitmore, Lee (QDO)
Winthe, Serge

Integrated Offender Manager Team
Freeborn,Lance (SPO)
Collier,Jodie
Hunt,Jenny
Little, Joanne
Lynch, Lynda
Taylor,Abigail
Taylor, Jason

Public Protection Team
Callum, Gordon (SPO)
Bettridge, Jennifer
Danetesh-Pour, Siameck
Dove, Joe
Flay, Helen
Mould, Hannah
Radcliffe, Claire

Court Team
Broom, Brenda
Cooper, Peter
Harris, James
McWall, Karen
Murphy, Cheryl
Needham, Christine

Housing Coordinator
Kinsey, Sharon

Corporate Services
Reed, Pat (Support Services Mgr)
Boyes, Jessica
Mould, Hannah

Offender, Employment and Skills
Ramakrishnan, Kim

Community Payback
Westbrook, Paul

(Hastings) Crozier House
1A Shepherd Street, St Leonards-on-Sea,
East Sussex TN38 0ET
Tel: 01424 448600 Fax: 01424 448601/2

Offender Management Team
Richardson, Martin (SPO)
Everson, Martha
George, Marian
Glover, Sarah
Goddard, Nicky
Jones, Liam
Lawrence, Diana
Ockenden, Elly
Sullivan, Andrew
Tipper, Tracey

Integrated Offender Management Team
Maxwell, Nicola (SPO)
Everst, Chris
Ferguson, Chris
Hamblin,Phil
Jinks,Dean
Morris,Susan
Skipworth, Helen (QDO)
Willis,Joanne
Willis, Joanne

Public Protection Team
Callum, Gordon (SPO)
Blackburn, Michael
Mould, Hannah
Osborne, Laura
Satchell, David
Tanner, Tanya

Programmes Team
Coleman, Sharon
Delaney, Mick
Durham, Yvonne

Community Payback Team
Bond, Peter
Browning, Lee
Wardroper, Tom
Webb, Mick

Court Team
Batchelor, Kimberly
Corby, Roshenda

Victim Liaison Team
Bayliss, Caroline

Accommodation Services Team
Scott, Louise

Corporate Services
Reed, Pat (Support Services Mgr)
Hitchman, Paula
Murphy, Kirstie

Learning & Development
Warrick, Judith

Surrey LDU

College House
Woodbridge Road, **Guildford** GU1 4RS
Tel: 01483 534701 Fax: 01483 453702

Offender Management Team
Jefferies, Victoria (SPO)
Allen, Graham
Campbell, Rebecca
Chivers, David
Grayson, Anna
Green, Andy

Holt, Anna
Johnson, Nicola
Moore, Margaret
Mortimer, Canan
Pain, Leigh
Percy, Lily
Rosati, Jo
Silvester, Jo
Stone, Alan

Public Protection Team
Moffitt, David (SPO)
Fuller, Anne
Lee, Alistair
Oakley, Lauren
Potter, Gemma
Trenchard, Susan

Programmes Team
Porter, Louise (Mgr)
Reynolds, Emma (Treatment Mgr)
Carter, Heidi
Clay, Maribel
Coggan, Carol
Henderson, Clive
Kerr, Liam
Winstone, Lisa

Community Payback Team
Martin, Rosie (Mgr)
Coles, Garry
Curtis, Victoria
Harding, Lisa
Houghton, Angela
Nani, Kler
Palmer, Michael
Ponsford, Chris
Puttick, Terry
Reynolds, Helen
Westwood, Emma

Substance Misuse Team
Homyer, Ros (Mgr)
Hall, Carl (Dpt Mgr)
Allen, Angela
Bateman, Lee
Crowsley, Louisa
Heathcote, Jacquie
Paszkiewicz, Ewa
Shonk, Tina
Singleton, Debbie
Tartari, Seren

Court Team
English, Alison
Lunnon, Sally
Morrison, Rosina
Mulligan, Ali
Robinson, Lucy

Sale, Heather
Wilmott, Lewis

Corporate Services Team
Gibson, Christine (Support Services Mgr)
Edwards, Kate
Leach, Bernice
Shonk, Tina

Offender, Employment and Skills
McLaren, Sue

Guildford Police Station
Margaret Road, Guildford, Surrey GU1
4PZ

*(Correspondence to Guildford Probation
Centre
College House Woodbridge Road Guildford
GU1 4RS)*
Tel: 01483 534701 Fax: 01483 453702
(Guildford Probation)
Tel: 01483 500923

**Integrated Offender Management
Team**
Jefferies, Victoria (SPO)
Cannon, Sarah
Evans, Hannah
Hussain,Becci
O'Keefe,Alex
Pearce,Corrine
Raynor, Mandy
White, Lucy

Allonby House
Hatchlands Road, **Redhill** RH1 6BN
Tel: 01737 763241 Fax: 01737 765688

Offender Management Team
Maxwell, Nicola (SPO)
Bergin, Kim
Berry, Michelle
Bradley, Jan
Bruton, Olive
Glenn, Nicola
Godly, Gemma
Groves, Jo
Mott, Helen
Saunders, Katy
Shaw, Lindsay
Steele, Nataile
Thomas, Nicola
Waghorn, Maggie
Westwood, Jane
Wilson, Pete

Public Protection Team
Moffitt, David (SPO)
Baldwin, John

Clarkson, Jacqui
Derbyshire, Gordon
Fellows, Sam
Jones, Sally

Community Payback Team
Martin, Rosie (Community Payback Mgr)
Ditzel, Nick (Operations Mgr)
Allsop, Kayleigh
Botha, Kate
Dean, Paul
Dear, Emma
Evans, Les
Hilliard, Brian
Holder, Lucy
Pool, Tony

Substance Misuse Team
Bheenick, Melissa
Greenwood, Leah

Court Team
Clare, Lyn
Freeman, David
Heley, Helen
Regan, John
White, Jo

Corporate Services
Hambleton, Emma (Support Services Mgr)
Frost, Shelley
Greenfield, Katherine
Jeffree, Susan

Integrated Offender Management Team
Edwards, Charles (SPO)

Amor, Charlotte

Ayers, Carol
Cissokho, Kirsty
Coombes, Jessica
Neubert, Catherine
Rozmanowski, Nicole
Spruce, Nicola
Weller, Vicky

Swan House
Knowle Green, **Staines-upon-Thames,**
Middlesex TW18 1XS
Tel: 01784 459341 Fax: 01784 449932

Offender Management Team
Burchmore, Lucy (SPO)
Arnold, Sally
Baker, Nicola
Clake, Matt
Cooper, Jonathan
Daly, Es

Erb, Melody
Fern, Scott
Levett, Richard
Lewin, Joanna
O'Connell, Louise
Todd, Claire
Unwin, Carly
Williams, Zoe
Wolfe, Jacci

Public Protection Team
Moffitt, David (SPO)
Calvert, Anne Marie
Hillsdon, Freya
Parsons, Jennifer (QDO)
Williams, Zoe
Wilson, Lisa

Substance Misuse Team
Bheenick, Mellisa
Murray, Lynn
Irving, Morine

Court Team
Dev, Meena
Cameron, Vivienne
Mason-Thompson, Maria
McGuigan, Steve
Smart, James

Corporate Services
Meek, Charlotte (Support Services Mgr)
Backen, Katharina
Rowesell, Justine

Integrated Offender Management Team
Fletcher, Tamsin (SPO)
Arthur, Kim
Badiel, Kirpal
Cox, Caroline
Pilatowicz, Lisa
Rogers, Kirsty
Stocker, Cathy

West Sussex LDU
8 Market Avenue
Chichester, West Sussex PO19 1YF
Tel: 01243 787651 Fax: 01243 781151

Offender Management Team
Rolls, Kathryn (SPO)
Ajaegbu, Christiana
Bowles, Louise
Brown, Victoria
Clement, Dee
Elphick, Elyse
Fellows, Kimberley
Taylor, Christie
Thorne, Michael

Treharne, Owain
Walsh, Caroline

Integrated Offender Management Team
Jones, Paul (SPO)
Bolton, Sophie
Carter, Kay
Churchill, Richard
Earney, Craig
McGuire, Kathy
Ryan, Sally
Smith, Adam

Court Team
Shaw, Chris (SPO)
Bristow, Candida
Brown, Victoria
Cotton, Carla
Guy, Sarah
Taylor, Steve

Programmes Team
Lockwood, Richard
Macfarlane, Sylvia

Community Payback Team
Sanderson, Sam (Mgr)
Goody, Jackie
Gowler, Jackie
Palin, Shelley
Springett, Sally
Turner, Andrea
Turner, Kate

Corporate Services
Broad, Trudy (Support Services Manager)
Rumke, Judith
Vincent, Soctt

Goffs Park House
Old Horsham Road
Crawley, West Sussex RH11 8PB
Tel: 01293 525216 Fax: 01293 525215

Offender Management Team
Pope, Joe (SPO)
Blair, Lisa
Budden, Claire
Dolby, Sonia
Honeycombe, Victoria
Mancey, Christine
Parsons, Dawn
Smith-Byrne, Teresa
Sweeney, Vicky
Triggs, Nicola
Wells, Michelle
Wilson, Susan

Integrated Offender Management Team
Barnett, Sylvia
Bradley, Jan
Delaney, Mick
Dowse, Phillipa
Hounslow, David
Langley, Janice
Paterson, Rose
Sweeney, Vicky
Thurley, Graham
Triggs, Nicola
Wood, Jo

Programmes Team
Drummond, Yvonne
Barker, Graham
Goodchild, Heather
Murray, Ian

Community Payback Team
Ditzel, Nick (Mgr)
Ali, Ehsan
Benson, Paul
Cox, John
Palin, Shelley
Pool, Anthony
Streeter, Stephen
Tomlinson, Rachel

Court Team
Adams, Trish
Bray, Jason
Clarke, Lesley
Di Lauro, Guisj
Dowse, Philippa
Henderson, Kerry
Lane, Chris
Nicholas, Harvinder
Thurley, Dorren

Victims Liaison Team
Jarvis, Fiona (Mgr)
Price, Natalie
Thorpe, Jennie

Accommodation Services Team
Hudson, Lisa
Maddock, Ana

Corporate Services
O'Shea, Fiona (Support Services Mgr)
Holmes, Janet
Lockett, Louise
Sherwood, Elsa

Offender, Employment and Skills
Whatley, Graham

Learning & Development
Bruton, Shane

Public Protection Team
Now based at Crawley Police Station,
Northgate Avenue,Crawley,RH10 8BF
Marcus, Bailey (SPO)
Bannister, Claire
Barton, Jo
Carter, Yvonne
Greenfield, Alex
Oakes, Victoria

Meadowfield House
East Street, **Littlehampton**, West Sussex
BN17 6AU
Tel: 01903 711500 Fax: 01903 711555

Public Protection Team
Bailey, Marcus (SPO)
Allnutt, Claire
Banner, Charlotte
Carey, Louise
Greene, Shelly
Feeney, Claire
Knapman, Bev
Tattersall, Lisa
Wilson, Jane

Community Payback Team
Gear, Beverley (Mgr)
Cairns, Rob
Unsted, Lesley

Accommodation Service Team
Grainger, Jill

Mental Health Team
Eliades, Nicola

Corporate Services
Buss, Catherine (Support Services Mgr)
SSA/PPT Vacancy
Hand, Tyler

4 Farncombe Road
Worthing West Sussex BN11 2BE
Tel: 01903 216321 Fax: 01903 204287

Offender Management Team
Butler, Michelle (SPO)
Howell, Angela
Knight, Kate (QDO)
Krause, Hollie
Laine, Sarah
Leach, Sarah
Lovely, Linda
Lexus, Helen
Miles, Peter
Saunders, Melanie
Skinner, Amy
Thompson, Rachel
Williams, Emily

Integrated Offender Management Team
Baird, Cheryl (QDO)
Berrman, Ian
Burns, Raymond
Carr, Catherine
Davis-Monk, Vivien
Denyer, Zoe
Hill, Karen
Khamlichi, Lamyaa
Scott, Louise
Thompson, Andrea

Court Team
Shaw, Chris (SPO West Sussex)
Adams, Judith
McGowan, Laura
Scarletson, Gemma
Sharples, Henry
Ward, Lisa
Youngs, Martyn

Corporate Services
Buss, Catherine (Support Services Mgr)
SSA (Vacancy)
SSA (Vacancy)

Offender, Employment and Skills
Purcell, Suzanne (Mgr)
Clark, Karen
Yates, Nik

Interventions Managers
(*Staff are located at offices throughout the Trust*)

Community Payback
Martin, Rosemary (CP Mgr Operations Redhill)
Sanderson, Sam

Programmes
Porter, Louise (SPO Mgr Surrey and Sussex) (Guildford and Brighton)

Substance Misuse
Homyer, Ros (Mgr) (Guildford)

Victim Liaison
Jarvis, Fiona (SPO Mgr) (Crawley)

Courts

Brighton Crown Court
Edward Street, Brighton, East Sussex
BN2 0LG
Tel/fax: 01273 695941

Evident, Gray

Brighton Magistrates Court
Edward Street, Brighton, East Sussex
BN2 0LG
Tel: 01273 669500 Fax: 01273 669519

Archer, Deborah

Bower-Feck, Veronica
Rich, Trudy

Hove Court Centre
The Court House, Lansdowne Road
Hove, East Sussex BN3 3BN
Tel: 01273 778843 Fax: 01273 720532

Blyghton, Anne

Harbane, Jean

Guildford Crown Court
Bedford Road, Guildford GU1 4ST
Tel: 01483 568561 Fax: 01483 306724

Jones, Simon (Mgr, Surrey Court Team)
Lane, Lynda
Lawlor, Karen
McClure, Tracey
Price, Natalie
Thorpe, Jennie
Wilson, Joanna

Victim Liaison Team
Considine, Mary

Lewes Combined Court Centre
The Law Courts
High Street, Lewes, East Sussex BN7
1YB
Tel: 01273 487608 Fax: 01273 487610

Booth, Sally
Cromarty, Liz
Evident, Gary,
Harbane, Jean
Hurworth, Clare
Murray, Stewart
Rhodes, Lawry

Youth Offending Team

West Green Youth Centre
West Green Drive, **Crawley,** West Sussex
RH11 7EL
Tel: 01293 643450 Fax: 01293 643472

Malone, Eluned

East Sussex Youth Offending Team
Ground Floor Offices, Queens
Apartments, Robertson Terrace,
Hastings TN34 1JN
Tel: 01424 726520

Preston, Peter
Saunders, Rita

Centenary House
POst 1.34, Durrington Lane, Worthing,
West Sussex BN13 2QB
Tel: 01903 839920 Fax: 01903 839965

Alcorn, Chris

Quadrant Court
35 Guildford Road, **Woking** GU22 7QQ
Tel: 01372 363655 Fax: 01372 363675

Wells, Toby (Cty Mgr)

The Mansion
Church Street, **Leatherhead** KT22 8DP
Tel: 01372 363655 Fax: 01372 363675

Patchet, Mark (Mgr East)
Defai, Paula
Miles, Paul

Approved Premises

162 Marine Parade
Brighton BN2 1EJ
Tel: 01273 622300 Fax: 01273 623486

Rayfield, Michael (SPO)
Smithson, Paul (Deputy Mgr)
Bickerstaff, Kate
Bridges, Melanie
Collins, Frank
Croskell, Ian
Dury, Min
Glover, Natasha
Hare, Wendy
Howard, Mark
O'Riordan, Nessa
Ndluvu, Ndaba

St Catherine's Priory
Ferry Lane, Portsmouth Road
Guildford GU2 4EE
Tel: 01483 571635 Fax: 01483 454130

Jones, Allan (SPO)

Brown, Jude (Deputy Mgr)

Chard, Gillian
Doe, Robert
Gwarisa, Bob
Lake, Angela
Lee, Adrian
Oakes, Nick
Olejnik, Sam
Stewart, Nicole
Warner, Catherine

Institutions

HMP Bronzefield
Woodthorpe Road, Ashford, Middlesex
TW15 3JZ
Tel: 01784 425690 Fax: 01784 425691

Davis, Hayley

Larkins, Georgina (Mgr)
Bheenick, Melissa
Clark, Matthew
Geller, Eli
Taylor, Josephine
Vermessen, Emmanuelle

HMP Coldingley
Shaftesbury Road, Bisley, Woking GU24
9EX
Tel: 01483 344300 Fax: 01483 476149

Skeet, Lorraine
Thomas, Adam
Wardell, Amie

HMP Downview
Sutton Lane Sutton Surrey SM2 5PD
Tel: 020 8196 6300 Fax: 020 8196 6301

Turner, Lesley (Mgr)
Davis, Hayley
Redfern, Holly
Woghiren, Sharon

HMP Ford
Arundel, West Sussex BN18 0BX
Tel: 01903 663000 Fax: 01903 663001
Probation tel: 01903 663195/663186 Fax:
01903 663197

Leeming, Su (Mgr)
Brownsey-Joyce, Carole
Mckenzie, Mia
Parker, Ashley

HMP High Down
Sutton Lane, Sutton, Surrey SM2 5PJ
Tel: 020 7147 6300 Fax: 020 7147 6301

McLean, Marion (Mgr)

Allen, Steph
Ballantine, Jim
Beck, Marianne
Bedborough, Carole
Brown, Jude
Butler, Jo
Clark,Richard
Hart,Maria
Jacobson,Tim
Swift, Sarah

HMP/YOI Lewes
1 Brighton Road, Lewes, East Sussex
BN7 1EA
Tel: 01273 785100 Fax: 01273 785101

Fordham, Colin (Mgr)
Bescoby, Steve
Earnshaw, Claire
Jones, Kevin
Littlejohn, Emily
Patterson, Kate
Taylor, Malolm

HMP Send
Ripley Road, Send, Woking GU23 7LJ
Tel: 01483 471000 Fax: 01483 471001

Turner, Lesley (Mgr)
Briam, Ginny
Coulson, Louise
Coutts, Natash
Russell, Jan

Local Justice Areas
North Surrey
North West Surrey
South East Surrey
South West Surrey
Sussex (Central)
Sussex (Eastern)
Sussex (Northern)
Sussex (Western)

Crown Courts
Chichester
Lewes
Guildford

THAMES VALLEY PROBATION TRUST

Email:
firstname.lastname@thames-valley.probation.
gsi.gov.uk

Head Office
Kingsclere Road, Bicester
Oxon OX26 2QD
Tel: 01869 255300 Fax: 01869 255344

Gillbard, Paul (CEO)
Fearn, Malcolm (p, Board Chair)
Lawrence-Wilson, Richard (p, Sec to
Board)
Marsh, Nicki (PA to CO/Chair)
Hudson, Lesley (p, Dir of HR)
Mackenzie, Gaynor (p, Dir of HR)
Wilson, James (Dir of Finance)

Kempster, Helene (PA to Dir Oper)
Mitchell, Sarah (PA to Dir HR & Dir Finance)
Ransom, Joanna (p, Recep/Admin)
Dally, Joe (p, Recep/Admin)
Medhurst, Elizabeth (Bus Proc Imp Mgr)
McIntyre, Shauna (p Diversity SPO)

Communications
Tarrant, Fiona (Comms Mgr)

Human Resources
Francis, Jones, Adele (HR Adviser, Mgmt Info & Rec)
Heron, Diane (HR Adviser)
Khanum, Naheed (p, HR Adviser)
Brooks, Anne (HR Officer)
Game, Elly (p, HR Officer)
Syred, Anne (p, HR Admin Ass)
Eaves, Eddie (H&S Adviser)

Learning & Development
Jones, Karen (Train & Org Dev Mgr)
Claxton, Naomi (p, Offender Mgr – Learning & Dev)
Beckley, David (Training Admin)
Coleman, Lynda (p, Training Admin)
Fell, Sue (p, Training Admin)
Sweetland, Judith (Training Admin)
Mafham, Val (Trainer)

Finance & Facilities
English Bridget (Financial Accountant)
Harvey, Susie (p, Financial Accountant)
Chapple, Wendy (Finance Off)
Roberts, Sonia (Finance Off)
Fearn, Vicky (p, Payroll Mgr)
Dean, Vanessa (p, Payroll Off)
Durrant, Julia (p, Senior Facilities & Est Off)
Smith, Esther (p, Asst Facilities & Est Off)

Performance Information Unit
Gower, Alan (Info Mgr)
Grimes, Julie (Snr Info Analyst)
Harrison, Yvette (Snr Info Analyst)
Searle, Mark (Info Analyst)
Chan, Alice (Compli Off)
Spayne, Chris (p, Compli Off)

2a Wynne-Jones Centre
Walton Road, **Aylesbury,** Bucks HP21 7RL
Tel: 01296 483174 Fax: 01296 415212

Cook, Sue (Asst Dir)

Court, Mary (PA)

Offender Management Unit
Brigue-Parker, Rekha (SPO)
Gallagher, Gillian (SPO)
Fisher, Stella
Jenner, Jeannie (p)
North, Kate
Pask, Jessica
Adams-Rimmer, Jane (p, Offender Mgr, Learning & Dev)
McConnell, Elena (p LDU Interventions Co-ordinator)

PSOs
Cowley, Pauline
Davis, Douglas
Hagen, Michael
Karachiwala, Sahera
Malone, Cindy
Rogers, Adrienne (p)

Substance Misuse Offender Management Unit IOM
Richards, Lyn (SPO)
Chapman, Rosemary (p)
Evans, Catherine
Macpherson, Anne
Richardson, Jo (p)
Christie, Dod (PSO)
Foy, Selina (PSO)
Mobeen, Shamah (PSO)
Simmons, Allister (B2E Keyworker)
Johnson, Linda (p Job Deal Adviser)

Administration
Deeks, Avril (Div Admin Mgr)
Brown, Carole (Asst Div Admin Mgr)

IT Unit
Tel: 01296 393925 Fax: 01296 398490

Baker, Ralph (Snr IT Support Off)
Briscoe, Neil (IT Support Off)
Shergill, Jas (IT Support Off)
Proctor, Christine (IT Admin)

Bucks Unpaid Work Unit
Swift, Erica (UPW Scheme Mgr)
PCMs
Evans, Julie
Hall, Jan
Hopping, Eleanor
Wright, Paul

Aylesbury Crown Court
38 Market Square, Aylesbury, Bucks HP20 1XD
Tel: 01296 339770 Fax: 01296 435665

15 Canada Close
Marley Way, **Banbury**
Oxon OX16 2RT
Tel: 01295 268436/7 Fax: 01295 268120

Czajewski, Stephen (Asst Dir)

Offender Management Unit
Burrell, Anne (p SPO)
Meech, Liz (SPO)
Ferron, Denise (p)
Gowney-Hedges, Hannah
Hoggins, Michelle
Netten, Kate (p)
Robinson, Zoe
Ruff, Simon
Wilson, Pat
Yard, Gregory

PSOs
Barrett, Laura
Bryan, Rachel
Burden, Lauren (p)
Doolan, Mike
Ivory, Catrina
Loveridge, Louise (p)
Morrison, Donald (p)
Ormerod, Mandy

Administration
Maines, Joy (Div Admin Mgr)
Robson, Angela (Asst Div Admin Mgr)

Units 9 & 10, Talisman Business Centre
Talisman Road, **Bicester**
Oxon OX26 6HR
Tel: 01869 328500 Fax: 01869 328528;

Enforcement
Rich, Valerie (p, SPO)
Hafeez, Mohammed (Legal Proceedings Mgr)
Porter, Ian (Legal Proceedings Mgr)
Barwick, Mikaela (Admin)

B2E Team
Mayson, Sarah (p, B2E Mgr)
Lant, Tracy (p, B2E Co-ordinator)

Oxfordshire Unpaid Work Team
Swift, Erica (UPW Scheme Mgr)
Clayton, Julie (County UPW Admin)

PCMs
Major, Diane
Rawding, Kirsty
Spargo, Julia (p)

Public Protection Unit
Johnson, Debbie (SPO)
Ricks, Linda (SPO)

Davis, Clive (Treatment
Manager/Facilitator)
Stewart, Lucy (p, Treatment
Manager/Facilitator)

Facilitators
Amar, Urfan
Cox, Sarah
Davis, Clive (p)
Davies, Kim
Kleinman, Susan (p)
Loveday, Marian (p)
Lovelock, Jo
McMahon, Claire (p)
Mullaney, Louise
Sexton, Lesley
Small, Damian
Stewart, Lucy (p)
Subenko, Pauline (p)
Vince-Reece, Russell
Crane, Rosalie (Women's Safety Wkr)
Wook, Sue (p, Women's Safety Wkr)

Central Interventions Unit
Cockbill, Leona (p, CIU Mgr)
Myatt, Emma (p, CIU Mgr)
Smith, Lyn (Facilitator)
Tingey, Lisa (Facilitator)

MAPPA Unit
Thames Valley Police
Fountain Court, Kidlington OX5 1NZ
Tel: 01865 293101 Fax: 01865 293292

Honeysett, Clare (p SPO Prevent)
Stirling, Bob (MAPPA Mgr)
Bates, Andrew (Principal Forensic Psych)
Mob: 07796 948297
Haigh, Alex (p, PO)

Thames Valley Restorative Justice Service
Units 9 & 10, Talisman Business Centre
Talisman Road, Bicester
Oxon OX26 6HR
Tel: 01869 328562

Emerson, Geoff (p, RJ Mgr)
Stevens, Caroline (New Leaf Project
Worker)

James Glaisher House
Grenville Place, **Bracknell** RG12 1BP
Tel: 01344 420446 Fax: 01344 301274

McCartney, Graham (Asst Dir)

Offender Management Unit
Mellish, Louise (SPO)
Avarne, Grace (p)
Billington, Kerri-Ann

Gash, Nicola
Henstridge, Jennie
Johnston, Lucy (p)
Morris, Helen (p, Offender Mgmt –
Learning & Dev)

PSOs
Evans, Alessandra
Mattu, Nikku
Otieno, Carol (p)
Perry, Richard
Russell, Christopher
Swindells, Catherine (p)

**Substance Misuse Offender
Management Unit IOM**
Blakesley, Clive
Powers, Julia
Crawford, Mary (p, B2E Keyworker)

Administration
Coston, Jacqueline (Div Admin Mgr)
Lagarde, Michelle (Asst Div Admin Mgr)

Easton Court
23a Easton Street
High Wycombe, Bucks HP11 1NT
Tel: 01494 436421 Fax: 01494 450132

Cooke, Sue (Asst Dir)

Offender Management Unit
Walls, Charlie (SPO)
Morris, Sally (p, SPO)
Blowfield, Anna (p)
Brown, Alma
Davies, Clare
Glynn, Beth
Halliwell, Jenni
Lang, Karen
Lowe, Liz
Malone, Siobhan
Nair, Renuka (p)
O'Kelly, Catherine (p)
Weston, Timothy

PSOs
Barker, Emily
Bowell, Lynda
Brown, Karen
Capon, Emma
Dow, Elizabeth
Morris, Delia
North, Laura (p)
Patis, Emma
Scott, Cazz

**Substance Misuse Offender
Management Unit IOM**
Richards, Lyn (SPO)
Urbanska, Jana
Clifford, Emily (PSO)

Administration
Deeks, Avril (Div Admin Mgr)
Brown, Carole (p, Asst Div Admin Mgr)

**301 Silbury Boulevard, Witan Gate East
Milton Keynes** MK9 2YH
Tel: 01908 679734 Fax: 01908 230050

Vigurs, Kilvinder (Asst Dir)

Ellis, Liza (p PA)
Hazell, Paulette (p, PA)

Offender Management Unit
Hayat, Zareen (PSO)
Mansell, Lorraine (SPO)
McConnell, Elena (p, SPO)
Pickering, Linda (SPO)
Bairstow, David
Elmore, Claire
Gianneto, Kate
Harris, Ann (p)
Litchfield, Theresa
Longley, Luke
Nickels, Kate
Potter, Mandy
Rogers, Carol
Rothery, Rachel
Spencer, Johnson
Cockbill, Leona (p LDU Interventions
Co-ordinator)

PSOs
Allen, Katie
Anstey, Susan
Beale, Katie (p)
Carty, Angela (p)
Deards, Amy
Hancock, Jessica
Martin, Viv
Murphy, Brynmor
Oldfield, Amanda
Patidar, Prity (p)
Quelch, Ria
Snell, Martin
Stafford, Ruth (p)
Vickery, Sally (p)
Lant, Tracy (p, B2E key Worker)
Harbage, Lorraine (p Job Deal Adviser)

**Substance Misuse Offender
Management Unit IOM**
Butt, Denise (SPO)
St Amour (p SPO)

Glenn, Ashleigh
Hunter, Katie
Jones, Allan (p)
Oke, Manny
Outram, Natalie
Shrimpton, Becky (p)

PSOs
Bircham, Anne (p)
Duke, Vincent
Harbage, Lorraine (p)
Hughes, Bryony
Kiely, Stephen
Stubbs, Christine (p)
Vippond, Keith

Administration
Maddison, Michelle (p, Div Admin Mgr)
Ellis, Liza (p Asst Div Admin Mgr)

Mill Lane
Newbury RG14 5QS
Tel: 01635 43535 Fax: 01635 42103

Amahwe, Gabriel (Asst Dir)

Offender Management Unit
Kueberuwa, Norma (SPO)
Aldridge, Richard
Lewis, Rowena (p)
Randle, Gill (p)
Reeves, Catriona (p)
Tyson, Peter (p)
MacDonald, Christina (PSO)
Moore, Niki (p, PSO)
Willmott, Vickie (PSO)

Administration
Bull, Helen (Div Admin Mgr)
Andrews, Helen (Asst Div Admin Mgr)

Macmillan House Unit
Unit 1 St Aldates, Courtyard, 38 St
Aldates, **Oxford** OX1 1BN
Tel: 01865 240750 Fax: 01865 240780

Czajewski, Stephen (Asst Dir)
Netting, Kathy (p, PA)

Offender Management Unit
Webb, Nicola (Quality Improvement Mgr)
Harvey, Vicki (SPO)
Hume, Duncan (SPO)
Rogers, Katharine (SPO)
Banks, David
Duffy, Andrea (p)
Harvey, Julian
Hewitt, Joy
Hudson, Natalie
Jefford, Michelle (p)

Johnson, Corina (PO and LDU
Interventions Co-ordinator)
Lampton, Victoria (p)
Lane, Vivien
MacGowan, Caroline
Newman, Sarah
Roe-French, Chris
Watt, Rachel
Webb, Oxana
West, Sarah (p)
Wickham, Tania (p)

PSOs
Aitkins, Russell
Ashton, Ian (p)
Baldauf-Clark, Beatrix (p)
Bishop, Laura
Brailey-Maskery, Juliet (p)
Colton, Lee
Gannon, Sophia
Grillo, Andrew
Mackay, Joanne
Nelms, Lisa
Perry, Alex
Phillips, Caroline
Smith, Julie
Walter, Dudley
Williams, Caroline (p)
Halime, Aziz (B2E Keyworker)
Khalid, Asif (B2E Keyworker)

Administration
Maines, Joy (Div Admin Mgr)
Robson, Angela (Asst Div Admin Mgr)

Old Music Hall
106–108 Cowley Road, **Oxford** OX4 1JE
Tel: 01865 403225 Fax: 01865 403258

**Substance Misuse Offender
Management Unit**
Bennett, Lynn (p, SPO)
Everatt, Lou (SPO)
Honeysett Clare (p, SPO)
Medley, Stephanie (p)
Morris, Bernard
Powell, Sabrina
Bennett, Lynne (p, Substance Misuse
Wkr)
Parveselli, Caroline (p, Substance Misuse
Wkr)
Savage, Jan (Substance Misuse Wkr)
Lesnik, Andrew (PSO)
Winstone-Partridge, Elizabeth (p, PSO)
Barnes, Louise (p, Job Deal Adviser)

Administration
Maines, Joy (Div Admin Mgr)
Robson, Angela (Asst Div Admin Mgr)

Oxford Magistrates' Court Office
Tel: 01865 202039 Fax: 01865 200078

The Old Shire Hall
The Forbury, **Reading** RG1 3EH
Tel: 0118 967 4430 Fax: 0118 967 4431

Reading Crown Court Team

Greyfriars House
30 Greyfriars Road, **Reading** RG1 1PE
Tel: 0118 956 0466 Fax: 0118 955 1300

Amahwe, Gabriel (Asst Dir)
Browne, Carol (p, PA)

Offender Management Unit
Holland, Sarah (p, Partnerships)
Clairmonte, Claire (SPO)
Fisher, Claire (SPO)
Powell, Hannah (SPO)
Williams, Kevin (SPO)
Anglin, Vicci
Boden, James
Constant, Aimee
Graham, Debbie
Harding, Hannah (p)
Howe, Dawn
Jara-Duncan, Laura (p)
Jennings, Lucy
Knight, James
Newton, Nicole (p)
Ohsan-Ellis, Berenice
Rees, Maryanne
Rooke, Simon
Smith, Mark
Bull, Richard (Offender Mgr, Learning & Dev)
Marshall, David (Offender Mgr, Learning & Dev)
Raven, Bex (Offender Mgr, Learning & Dev)
Young, Beckie (Offender Mgr, Learning & Dev)
Hunt, Martin (p, LDU Interventions Co-ordinator)

PSOs
Boatfield, John
Burns, Linda
Choloniewska, Honorata
Chrisp, Lin
Cole, Jeannette (p)
Eggleton, Rebecca
Godfrey, Joanna
Gibson, David
Hunt, Martin (p)
Jackson, Tom
Jan, Jenkinson

McDonald, Linda
O'Boyle, Julie
Phasey, Rosalind
Taylor, Eileen (p)
Thomas-Williams, Sandra
Wilson, Maxine (p)
Mills, Selina (p, B2E Keyworker)

Substance Misuse Offender Management Unit IOM
Badhen, Asha (SPO)
Cannell, Sabrina (p)
Farrall-Hyder, Ruth
Latawiec, Tomek
Tagoe, Gina

PSOs
Collins, Sarah
Hartley, Ben
Hendrick, Maria
Owen, James
Watts, Daniel

Administration
Bull, Helen (Div Admin Mgr)
Andrews, Helen (Asst Div Admin Mgr)

Reading Magistrates' Court Team
Tel: 0118 956 0466 Fax: 0118 955 1305

Victim Liaison Unit
Tel: 0118 955 1255 Fax: 0118 955 1304

Boyd, Gillian (p, SPO)

Hogg, Joanna (p)
Oakes, Helen (p)
Sutherland, Sarah (p)
Troup, Ian (p)
Bolton, Karen (PSO)
Dowling, Frances (p, PSO)
Ogilvie, Claire (PO)
Brent, Linda (p, Coord)
Morgan, Helen (p, Coord)

Berks Unpaid Work Unit
Mondaye, Andrew (UPW Scheme Mgr)
Fletcher, Jackie (Admin Serv Mgr)

PCMs
Aitken, Becca
Brazier, Carly (p)
Harris, Laura (p)
Hawker, Emily (p)
Katuscakova, Julia
Ladlow, Christina
Lambert, Michelle
Senyah, Chris
Vernon, Caroline
Wells, Liz

Public Protection Unit
Gange, Callie (p, Facilitator)
Naidoo, Sharon (Womens Safety Wkr)

Central Interventions Unit
Arnold, Susan (Treatment Manager)
Brown, Tim (Facilitator)
Havercan, Rhian (p, Facilitator)
Sutherland, Nandi (p, Facilitator)

Revelstoke House
Chalvey Park, **Slough** SL1 2HF
Tel: 01753 537516 Fax: 01753 552169

Graham, McCartney (Asst Dir)
Clarke, Jackie (p, PA)

Offender Management Unit
Walls, David (Partnerships)
Ennis, John (SPO)
Rich, Valerie (p SPO)
White, Debbie (SPO)
Bourget, Robbie
Clarke, Victoria
Connell, Catherine
Cudby, Teri
Cunnington, Sarah
Goodall, Phil
Jordan, Hazel
Nagib-Ali, Abdallah
Oztemel, Deniz (p)
Stokes, Lauren
Ward, Maggi (p)
Whitelam, Sandra
Cawdell, Mark (Offender Mgr, Learning
& Dev)
Hewstone, Peter (Offender Mgr,
Learning & Dev)

PSOs
Bhatti, Jas
Cann, Frances
De Silva, Mauren (p)
Gumbs, Veronica
Ladha, Farzana
Norman, Gemma
Mahmood, Saima
Rakkar, Pazz
Sahota, Jatinder
Smith, Matthew
Southall, Claire
Stafford, Linda
Whelan, Siobhan
Yasmin, Saiqa
Rehal, Amrita (Job Deal Adviser)
Stevens, Melanie (B2E Keyworker)

**Substance Misuse Offender
Management Unit IOM**
Azad, Usha (SPO)
Candlish-Stuart, Patrick
Thornton, Hayley (p)
Wood, Marie (p)
Clarke, Frank (Substance Misuse Wkr)

PSOs
Fidler, Anna
Gray, Lesley
Soper, Laura
Wright, Cara (p)

Administration
Coston, Jacqueline (Div Admin Mgr)
Lagarde, Michelle (Asst Admin Mgr)

Approved Premises (Hostels)

AP Central Referral Unit
8 Straight Road
Old Windsor SL4 2RL
Tel: 01753 850586 Fax: 01753 852861

Simpson, Simon (AP Area Mgr)
Bradley, Felicity (p, CRU Co-ordinator)

112 Abingdon Road
Oxford OX1 4PY
Tel: 01865 248842 Fax: 01865 794680
Mob: 07836 235707

Perry, Sheila (AP Area Mgr)
Maidment-Vint (Oper Mgr)

Clark's House
Clark's Row, Oxford OX1 1RE
Tel: 01865 248841 Fax: 01865 790756
Mob: 07836 637934

Perry, Sheila (AP Area Mgr)
Maidment-Vint, Vicky (Oper Mgr)

Manor Lodge
8 Straight Road, Old Windsor SL4 2RL
Tel: 01753 868807 Fax: 01753 620466

Simpson, Simon (AP Area Mgr)
Sandum, Shelley (Oper Mgr)

1 Haddon Great Holm
Milton Keynes MK8 9AL
Tel: 01908 569511 Fax: 01908 265949

Simpson, Simon (AP Area Mgr)
Mathew, Bijoy (Oper Mgr)

St Leonard's
2 Southcote Road, Reading RG30 2AA
Tel: 0118 957 3171 Fax: 0118 956 0677

Perry, Sheila (AP Area Mgr)
Richardson, Kay (Oper Mgr)

Voluntary Hostel

Elizabeth Fry
6 Coley Avenue, Reading RG1 6LQ
Tel: 0118 957 2385 Fax: 0118 951 0340

Titcomb, Fiona (Mgr)
Oke, Caroline (p, Dep Mgr)
Yapp, Anita (Dep Mgr)

Institutions

HMYOI Aylesbury
Bierton Road, Aylesbury HP20 1EH
Tel: 01296 444000 Fax: 01296 444001

Sparshott, Felicity (SPO)
Nelson, Sarah
Phillips, Dave (p)
Thorpe, Rodney
Waters, Martyn
Stennings, Patrick (SPO)
Taylor, Zo (PSO)

HMP Bullingdon
PO Box 50, Bicester X25 1WD
Tel: 01869 353100 Fax: 01869 353101

Drake, Paul (SPO)
Eastwood, John
Grant, Joy
Lebeanya, Uche
Tartakover, Julie (p)
Wheatley, Dorothy (p)

PSOs
Chapman, Amanda
Hawkins, Tracy
Howard, Dawn
Lewis, Christine
Taylor, Melanie
Whareham, Lisa (p)
Woodruff, Jennifer (p)

Bail Information Unit
Fax: 01869 353171

HMP Grendon
Grendon Underwood
Aylesbury HP18 0TL
Tel: 01296 443000 Fax: 01296 443001

Foster, Karen (SPO)

Benson, Claire
Sims, Rebecca
Sugarman, Donna

HMP/YOI Reading
Forbury Road, Reading RG1 3HY
Tel: 0118 908 5000 Fax: 0118 908 5004

Ager, Jackie (SPO)
Evans, Sarah
Bentley, Alice (PSO)
Grace, Jennifer (PSO)
Pawlow, Keely (PSO)

HMP Spring Hill
Grendon Underwood
Aylesbury HP18 0TL
Tel: 01296 443000 Fax: 01296 443002

Foster, Karen (SPO)
Charles, David
Cooper, Bridget (p)
Stokes, Paul
Whymark, Gay (p)
Blackman, Elaine (PSO)
Sharpe, Abigail (PSO)

HMP Woodhill
Tattenhoe Street
Milton Keynes MK4 4DA
Tel: 01908 722000 Fax: 01908 867063
Butt, Denise (p SPO)
Lynch, James (SPO)
Ali, Jay
Fox, Mandy
Smith, Clare (p)

PSOs
Easthope Claire
McCarthy, Dee (p)
Shippen, Jane
Staff-Lonie, Sue
Tomkin, Joanna

HMP Huntercombe
Huntercombe Place, Nuffield
Henley-on-Thames RG9 5SB
Tel: 01491 643100 Fax: 01491 643101
Drake, Paul (SPO)
Clark, Susan
Hutchins, Lucy (p)

Local Justice Areas
Central Buckinghamshire (*Wynne-Jones Centre Aylesbury*)
East Berkshire (*James Glaisher House Bracknell, Greyfriars House Reading, Revelstoke House Slough*)
Milton Keynes (*Silbury Boulevard Milton Keynes*)
Northern Oxfordshire (*Banbury, Bicester*)
Oxford (*Oxford*)
Reading (*Reading*)
West Berkshire (*Newbury*)
Wycombe & Beaconsfield (*High Wycombe*)

Crown Courts
Aylesbury
Oxford
Reading

WARWICKSHIRE PROBATION TRUST

Out of hours emergency contact
Augustus House Approved Premises 01926
339331

Victim enquiries Tel: 0845 120 2325 Fax:
0845 120 2326

Warwick Crown Court enquiries Tel:
01926 682274/01926 682277 Fax: 01926
682287

Email:
firstname.lastname@warwickshire.probation.
gsi.gov.uk

Warwickshire Justice Centre
Newbold Terrace Leamington Spa CV32
4EL
Tel: 01926 682217 Fax: 01926 682290

Area Executive Team
Stafford, Liz (CE) 01926 682285
l'Anson, Cathy (Admin Off) 682281
Wade, Andy (ACO Offender Mgmt)
682282
McGovern, Donald (ACO Interventions)
682284
Morrison, Christie (Admin Off) 682279
Miles, Emma (Temp Admin) 682279

Business Support Unit
Goodyear, Kevin (Temp Mgr, Business
Support) 682307
Newbold, Sue (Admin Off, Training
Admin) 682305

Finance Unit
Chappell, Sue (Finance Admin) 682299
Tew, Annette (Finance Admin) 682301

Human Resources Unit
Caswell, Heather (Mgr) 682308
Jewsbury, Tricia (Deputy Mgr) 682311
Chambers, Rosey (Learning &
Development Advisor/Practice Tutor
Assessor) 682309
Elmhirst, Nicola (Advisor) 682312
Jolly, Anne (Advisor) 682311

Information Unit
Wood, Paul (Temp Mgr) 682298
Vacant (Off)

Winstanley, Lorna (Systems Admin)
682296
Mistry, Vanita (Admin) 682297

Offender Management
Tel: 01926 682217 Fax: 01926 682290

Team 1 South
Sahota, Kiran (SPO) 682234
Cory, Nick 682212
Ghafoor, Meena 682265
Kent, Stephen 682215
Mannion, Danny 682211
Ramswell, Amy 682213
Sullivan Karen 682264
Jones, Abigail 682266

PSOs
Leighton, Kelly (PSO) 682259
Townsend, Nikki (PSO) 682254

Team 2 South
Lawson, Neil (SPO) 682233
Bains, Kiran 682202
Chapman, Helen 682225
Hewitt, Lucy 682201
Treveil, Richard 682203
Trevor, Victoria 682263
Turner, Polly 682204

PSOs
Godfrey, Leroy 682223
Hobbins, Angela 682222
O'Sullivan, William 682210
Smith, Amy 682226
Dimmick, Jane (AOA) 682232

Quality & Performance
Baxendale, Nadine (Perform & Pract Dev
Mgr) 682260
Dalton, Gemma (Quality Development
Coach) 682254

Community Payback
Adams, Dave (Deputy Manager, CP)
682231
Dalman, Martyn (CPO) 682253
Griffin, Velma (CPO) 682250

Crown Court Unit
Fax: 01926 682287
Burt, Christine (PSO) 682274
Bosanko, Lynn (admin) 682277

Victim Contact Unit
Chilton, Earl (Mgr)
Roberts, Carys (VLO) 684082
Lund, Darren (VLO) 684084

Partnerships Unit
Henshaw, Ian (Partnership Proj Mgr)
682259

Hardy, Len (Ontrak Transition Mgr) 682244
Sandhu, Manny (Ontrak PSO) 682219
Halford, Helen (Accom Off) 682245
Roberts, Janette (Ontrak Admin) 682243

Domestic Abuse Unit
Kalm, Indi (PSO) 682248
Course, Michelle (admin) 682251

Integrated Offender Management Scheme (IOM)
Morgan Cathy (IOM Co-ordinator

Bulmer, Holly (PSO)

Warwickshire Youth Justice Service
Warwickshire Justice Centre
Newbold Terrace **Leamington Spa** CV32 4EL
Tel: 01926 682650

Tregear, Lesley (Hd of Youth Justice Service)
Jones, Natalie (Pract, Northern Justice Centre)
Parmar, Sarah (Pract, Northern Justice Centre)
Weatherall, Brian (Pract, Southern Justice Centre)

The Courthouse
Newbold Road, **Rugby** CV21 2LH
Tel: 01788 534900 Fax: 01788 547576

Chapman, Thomasina (SPO)
Ghaiwal, Kanwal (Peripatetic)
Brown, Katie
Cooper, Jolie
Furnival, Monika
Jones, Andrew
Kelly, Hazel
Smith, Darren

PSOs
Sambhi, Pam
Marsella, Linda
Winton, Sarah
Hallam, Caroline (Temp to Jan-13)
Clarke, Sally (AOA)

Community Payback
Eaves, Craig (CPO)

Warwickshire Justice Centre
Vicarage Street **Nuneaton** CV11 4JU
Tel: 02476 483140 Fax: 02476 482864

Team 1 North
Evans, Bev (SPO) 482819
Burnett, Chris 482848

Burns, Roy 482845
Chapman, Sarah 482868
Crunkhorn, Sue 482856
Farndon, Suzanne 482847
Hill, Natalie
Kockelbergh, Marion 482857
Moore, Tara
Parmar, Deena 482846
Tolley, Liz
Wood, Kelly 482850

PSOs
Brammer, Holly
Dewis, Hayley 482834
Hewitt, Joanne 482830
Howe, Faye 482999

Team 2 North
Mitchell, Kathleen (SPO) 482821
Ademefun, Ade 482840
Dimbleby, Natalie 483005
Doughty-Lee, Niki 482855
Gilbert, Beverley 482832
Guru, Sam 482820
van der Molen, Jenny 482853

PSOs
Davies, Loukia
Devine, Catherine 482836
Cook, Val 482833
Hallam, Caroline
Cadman, Nicola (PSO Progs) 482818
Lewis, Linda (AOA) 482839

Community Payback
Baxter, Sue (CPO) 482825
Smith, Les (CPO) 482823

Joint Programmes Unit

Coventry
Staffordshire and West Midlands Programmes Unit
Sheriffs Court 12 Greyfriars Road
Coventry CV1 3RY

Ditchburn, Margaret (Progs Mgr)
Price, Simon (Treatment Mgr)
Kenny, Julia (PSO)
Darby, Hannah (PSO)
McKenzie, Dan (PSO Seconded to NOMS Training)
Hamid, Hana (Prog Admin)

Approved Premises (Hostels)

Augustus House
33 Kenilworth Road
Leamington Spa CV32 6JG
Tel: 01926 339331 Fax: 01926 312518

Bains, Peter (Mgr)
Gravenor, Frank (Dep Mgr)

Residential PSOs
Chamberlain, Chris
Frost, Melanie
Kavanagh, Maxine
Kettyle, Heather
Wallis, Steve
Simons, Sharon (Admin)

McIntyre House
125 Edward Street Nuneaton CV11 5RD
Tel: 024 7664 1423 Fax: 024 7635 3982

Bains, Peter (Mgr)

Bevan, Shelley (Dep Mgr)

Residential PSOs
Allen, Angela
Barlow, James
Moorie, Linda
Wallis, Julia
Simons, Sharon (Admin)

Local Justice Area
Warwickshire

Crown Court
Warwick (Sitting at the Warwickshire
Justice Centre, Leamington Spa)

WEST MERCIA PROBATION TRUST HEREFORDSHIRE, SHROPSHIRE, WORCESTERSHIRE, TELFORD & WREKIN

Out of hours emergency contact point
Braley House 01905 723975

Email:
firstname.lastname@west-mercia.probation.
gsi.gov.uk

Head Office
Stourbank House, 90 Mill Street
Kidderminster, Worcs DY11 6XA
Tel: 01562 748375 Fax: 01562 748407

Email:
head.office@west-mercia.probation.gsi.
gov.uk
www.westmerciaprobation.org.uk

Kelly, James (Board Chair)
Chantler, David (CEO)
Mallinson, Graham (Dir of Finance &
Business Services/Board Treasurer)

Brewerton, Anthony (Dir of Operations)
Barham, Keith (West Mercia YOT
Manager)
Ritson, Catherine (p, Area Mgr Perf)
Simmonds, Karen (Head Office Bus Mgr)
Bell, Jackie (PR & Comms Off)
Champken, Tina (Finance Mgr)
Smith, Linda (ICT Mgr)
Lewis, Darren (Systems Mgr)
Jones, Jeff (Info Mgr)
Cullen, Kerry (Personnel Mgr)
Bramford, Kate (Learning and Dev Mgr)
Hulston, Deborah (Learning and Dev
Off)
Instan, Joanna (Training Admin)
Blake, Barbara (IT Trainer)
Reeves, Catherine (p, H&S Off)
Ashmore, Tina (Bus Dev Unit Mgr)
Mistry, Chandry (Bus Dev Off)

Telford Local Delivery Unit

Telford Square
Malinsgate, Telford TF3 4HX
Tel: 01952 214100 Fax: 01952 214111

Branch, George (Hd of Service, Telford)
Hatfield, Michele (AIM Project Mgr)
Davies, Glyn (SPO and CP Offender
Management Shropshire and Telford
Wrekin)
Gandon, Michelle (SPO)
Cotton, Louise (SPO)
De Vos, Les (Treatment Mgr)
Gittins, Amanda (p, Resource Off)
Burd, Bev (UPO)
Muffit, Lynne (VLO)
Aldridge, Tina
Armstrong, Guy
Beeston, Nicola (p)
Briscoe, Kate
Cadmore, David
Cannon, Leila (p)
Challenger, Paul
Danesi, Rosa (p)
Emanuel, Jennifer
Hinde, Christopher
Pugh, Karli
Russell, Michelle
Smith, Susan
Stephens, William
Varnham, Maxine
Watts, Jim
Wheeler, Clare
Willetts, Di (RSOU)
Wilson, Fiona
Wright, Karen

PSOs
Bond, Kelly (p)
Hughes, Chris
Newcombe, Gillian (p)
Nicholls, Dorothy
Kaleta, Philip
CP
Ball, Alan (p)
Brown, Godfrey
Konkel, David (p)
Metcalfe, Donald (p)
Murray, Phil (p)
Richardson, Wendy
Wild, Paul (p)

Telford Magistrates' Court
Tel/fax: 01952 210074

Shropshire Local Delivery Unit
Shrewsbury, Ludlow, Market Drayton
Oswestry, Whitchurch

135 Abbey Foregate
Shrewsbury SY2 6AS
Tel: 01743 231525 Fax: 01743 244914

Currie, Tom (Hd of Service, Shrewsbury
and Lead Senior Mgr for CP, Lifers, Sex
Offenders, Mental Health and Domestic
Abuse)
Holland, Glyn (p, SPO)
Smith, Ruth (p, SPO)
Southwell, Debra (SPO)
Titley, Jenna (SPO and Programmes
Telford and Wrekin and Shropshire)
Briscoe, Mark (Treatment Mgr)
Daly, Maggie (RSOU Treatment Mgr)
Konkel, Carolyn (Resource Off)
White, Neil (UPO)
Cox, Lesley (VLO)
Heywood, Sue (PDA)
Buckley, Carol
Cannon, Helen (Shropshire IOM Unit)
Chilton, Lis
Collin, Chris
Harvey, Carrie (p)
Jeffries, Sandra (p) (Shropshire IOM
Unit)
Law, Margaret (p)
Obertelli, Joanne (p)
Owen, Lynne
Pennal, Jesse
Proctor, Anne
Ruffell, Clare (p)
Slawson, Robert

PSOs
Castle, Lindsay
Clarke, Janet

Joyce, Rose
Johnson, Colin
Norfolk, Gael (p)
Pearce, Anna
Price, Iain
Telford, Dawne
Worthington, Rachel (Shropshire IOM
Unit)
Young, Carl
CP
Barkley, Bev (p)
Coleman, Annita
Grant, Desmond
Heskey, Richard
Lockley, Tina (p)
McIntyre, Don
Whitby, Martyn (p)
Birch, Roberta (p, Interventions Resource
Mgr)

Crown Court Probation Office
The Law Courts, Shirehall
Abbey Foregate, Shrewsbury SY2 6LU
Tel: 01743 252934
Tel: 01743 252936

Herefordshire Local Delivery Unit
Gaol Street, **Hereford** HR1 2HU
Tel: 01432 272521 Fax: 01432 350408

Smith, Liz (Hd of Service, Hereford)
Ashworth, Julie (SPO and Programmes)
Smith, Ursula (SPO /VLU Mgr)
Powell, John (SPO and CP Offender
Management Herefordshire)
Lewis, Jane (Resource Off)
Angell, Sue (UPO)
Petts, Susanna (VLO)
Arndt, Jenna
Clarke, Lloyd
Denning, Andrew
Greig, Dennis
Jones, Daniel
Matthews-Jones, Nigel
Mills, Sue
Rees, Sharon
Rosoman, Richard

PSOs
Chilton, Barbara
Dovey, Amanda
Guy, Ginny
Morris, Sarah (p)
Swan, Jane (p)
Wainwright, Urszula
CP
Clother, Maurice (p)
George, Catherine (p)

Parsons, Nicola

Hereford Crown Court
The Shirehall, St Peter's Square
Hereford HR1 2HY
Tel: 01432 276118
Fax: 01432 274350

Worcestershire Local Delivery Unit

1–4 Windsor Court
Clive Road, Redditch
Worcestershire B97 4BT
Tel: 01527 585152 Fax: 01527 596459

Purewal, Manjinder (Deputy Director of
Operations / Hd Service Worcestershire)
Bentley, Mike (Deputy Hd of Service,
Worcs and Accredited Programmes)
Davis, Hyacinth (SPO)
Baynton, Glen (SPO)
Breen, Jan (CP Mgr Worcs)
Williams, Ruth (Resource Asst)
Allen, Karen
Chaudhry, Aftab
Chung, Dawn
Fowler, Claire (p)
Hammes, Anthony
Harris, Emma (p)
Middleton, Penny (p)
Morgan, Gail (p)
Morgan, Jane
Rees, Sarah (p)
Shelley, Emma (p)

PSOs
Bennett, Jeannie
Clarke, Alex
Firman, Katy
Griffiths, Samantha (p)
Heighway, Lee
Romanus, Lis (p)
CP
Harrison, Ian (p)
Pitt, Andrew
Sikanartey, Ninam (p)
Southwell, Keith

Stourbank House
90 Mill Street
Kidderminster, Worcestershire DY11 6XE
Tel: 01562 820071 Fax: 01562 862425

Purewal, Manjinder (Deputy Director of
Operations / Hd Service Worcestershire)
Bentley, Mike (Deputy Hd of Service,
Worcs and Accredited Programmes) –
based at Worcester
Kane, Nina (SPO)
Sinclair, Margaret (SPO)

Breen, Jan (CP Mgr Worcs)
Bradley, Denise (Resource Asst)
Andrews, Louise (UPO)
Mowbray, Nicola (VLO)
Akhtar, Azeem
Concannon, Iggy
Darlow, Teresa (p)
Johnson, Adam
Mellor, Ruth
Oliver, Sarah (p)
Slater, Neil (p)
Thomas, Jason
Thorp, Elizabeth (p)
Tolley, Steve
Wall, Tania Maria
Webster, Trevor
Wroblewska-Fairless, Dorota

PSOs
Betts, Lynn
Smith Jason
Stevens, Kate (p)
Thompson, Kirsty
CP
Purewal, Sanjeev (p)
Reeves, Stanford
Sikanartey, Ninam (p)

3–4 Shaw Street
Worcester WR1 3QQ
Tel: 01905 723591 Fax: 01905
20516/29057

Purewal, Manjinder (Deputy Director of
Operations / Hd Service Worcestershire)
King, Les (Deputy Hd of Service, Worcs)
Chiverton, Steve (SPO)
Lee, Martin (SPO)
Beard, Richard (SPO and Accredited
Programmes)
Stennett, Susannah (p, SPO)
Breen, Jan (CP Mgr Worcs)
Stewart, Jayne (Treatment Mgr)
Fairclough, Amanda (UPO)
Greaves, Lesley (UPO)
Martin, Carol (VLO)
Akhtar, Zafran
Bassett, Tania
Baynton, Glen
Britton, Christine
Da Silva, Claira
Dawkins, Helen
Foster, Andy
Greenman, Hilary
Gualano, Marco
Guest, Kerry (p)
Hudson, Thomas
Hutchinson, Chris

Murphy, Carol (p)
Perkins, Joanne
Purewal, Davs (p)
Rimoncelli, Polly (p)
Secrett, Rebecca
Sheath, Jan (p)
Taylor, Lee

PSOs
Ball, Kathryn
Charles, Kim
Dufty, Katy (p)
Evans, Susan
Hewitt, Stephen
Leeuwangh, Jonathan
McDonald, Dee (p)
McLeod, Steve (p)
Schwab, Richard
Sirman, Catherine
Smith, Kirsty
Teale, Gemma

CPOs
Bovington, Sarah (p)
Gibbons, Jenny (p)
Hall, Will
Hampton, Ian
Jones, Peter (p)
Morgan, Louise (p)
Penney, Craig
Porter, John (p)
Taylor, Louise (p)
Willis, Peter
Nash, Jenny (Progs Team Admin)

Worcester Crown Court
Tel: 01905 730800

Youth Offending Services

2nd Floor, Euston House
Euston Way, **Telford** TF3 4LY
Tel: 01952 385953

Kwarteng, Michelle

Tolladine Road
Worcester WR4 9NB
Tel: 01905 732200

Fields, Alistair

Approved Premises (Hostels)

Braley House Approved Premises
89 Ombersley Road
Worcester WR3 7BT
Tel: 01905 723975 Fax: 01905 617687

Bentlley, Mike (Deputy Hd of Service,
Worcs and Accredited Programmes)
Baynton, Jenny (AP Mgr)
Searle, Janis (AP Admin)

Assistant Wardens
Coleman, Neil
Jones, Pamela
Khan, Nadim
Newton, Tony
Weston, Mike
AP Supervisors
Marilyn Gibson (p)
Hewitt, Greg
Singh Kler, Kalbinder (p)
Wilson, Andrew

Institutions

HMYOI Stoke Heath
Market Drayton TF9 2JL
Tel: 01630 636000 Fax: 01630 636001
Probation fax: 01630 636164

Gaffney, Jane (p, SPO)
Davies, Felicity (p)
Vaughan, Lucy
Johnson, Adrienne (PSO)
White, Ashleigh (PSO)

HMP Shrewsbury
Shrewsbury SY1 2HR
Tel: 01743 273000 Fax: 01743 273001
Probation tel: 01743 273054
Probation fax: 01743 273003

Gaffney, Jane (p, SPO)
Adams, Sheila
Obertelli, Joanne (p)
Wilson, Jessica

HMP Hewell
Hewell Lane, Redditch B97 6QS
Tel: 01527 785000 Fax: 01527 785001
Legal visits 01527 785087
Legal visits fax: 01527 785010
Moran, Paula (SPO)
Koser, Razwana
McLean, Paula

HMP Long Lartin
South Littleton, Evesham WR11 3TZ
Tel: 01386 295100 Fax: 01386 295101

Chambers, Lucy
Drever, Marita

West Mercia Constabulary HQ
CID, Hindlip Hall, PO Box 55, Hindlip,
Worcester, WR3 8SP
Tel: 01905 332305

Clark, Peter (p, MAPPA Co-ordinator)
Slater, Neil (p, MAPPA Co-ordinator)
Vaughan, Esther (p, MAPPA Co-ordinator)

Local Justice Areas
Bromsgrove & Redditch
Herefordshire
Kidderminster
Shrewsbury & North Shropshire
South Worcestershire
Telford & South Shropshire

Crown Courts
Hereford
Shrewsbury
Worcester

WILTSHIRE PROBATION TRUST

Victim enquiries tel: 01793 509709
Email:
firstname.lastname@wiltshire.probation.gsi.
gov.uk
34 Marshfield Road, Chippenham SN15 1JT
Trowbridge BA14 8JQ
Tel: 01249 461577 Fax: 01249 445497
Rijnenerg, Liz (CE)
Aviss, Paul (Chair)
Patience, John (Secretary)
Nash, Philip (Treasurer)
Powell, Diane (ACE HR)
Taylor, Riana (ACE Interv)
Wootton, Lynne (ACE Off Mgmt)
Jeffery, Simon (Comm Dev Mgr)
Shaftoe, Claire (HR Mgr)
Quinney, Gemma (HR Asst)
Topping, Nicola (L&D Off)
Hussey, Simon (Finance Mgr)
Sullivan, Sandra (Finance Off)
Fairgrieve, Simon (Perf & Info Mgr)
Wheeler, Wayne (Sen LDU Perf & Info Off)
Elkins, Adrian (IT Off)
Reid, Simon (LDU Perf & Info Off)
Richardson, James (AIO)
Green, Hilary (PA to ACE)
Rumming, Janice (PA to ACE)
Tawn, Jan (PA to CE)
Phillips, Jan (LDU Mgr)
POs
Race, Heather
Parker, Charlotte
Owen, Karen
PSOs
Bull, Vicky
Jackson, Terry
Watson, Sandi

Wilshire, Tanya
Barnes, Karen
Jones, Debby (Health Trainer)
Easden, Vivien (Team Coord)
Newman, Tracy (Case Admin)
Scoble, Karen (Case Admin)
Cole, Alison (Gen Admin)
Programmes Team
Bennett, Mark (Treatment Mgr)
Parmenter, James
Gage, Emma (Prog Tutor)
Community Payback Office
Cope, Simon (CP Team Mgr)
Ashman, Anne (Admin Off)
Pimpernell, Linda (CP Off)
Young, Lynn (CP Off)
CP Supervisors
Mack, Doug
Rainbow, Malcolm
Pathways Development Unit
Potter, Lisa (Pathway Off)
Jackson, Sue (ETE Coord)
Woodman, Katherine (ETE Off)
Ranger, Lesley (Admin Off)
Lancashire, Cheryl (Admin Off)
Whittaker, Vicki (Admin Off)

2 Prospect Place
Trowbridge BA14 8QA
Tel: 01225 763041 Fax: 01225 775667
Hickey, Liz (LDU Mgr)

PSOs
Clifford, Maggie
Mercieca, Emma
Murray, Andrew
Rhodes, Emma
Treasure, Sharon

PSOs
Coombs, Laura
Lauder, Carolyn
Rygor, Hannah
Case Administrators
Heydon, Carolyn
Millican, Kelly
Reeve, Sara

The Boulter Centre
Avon Approach **Salisbury** SP1 3SL
Tel: 01722 327716 Fax: 01722 339557
Flynn, Lisa (LDU Mgr)
Fairgrieve, Laura (LDU Mgr)

PSOs
Jay, Tina
Lumber, Ruth
Steele, Kerry

Mason, Jessica
Taylor, Michael
Whittle, David
O'Shaugnessy, Debbie

PSOs
Baldwin, Joanna
Bird, Dale
Roscow, Susan
Wells, Laura
Regan, Sarah (Team Coord)
Brown, Joanna (Case Admin)
Neville, Michelle (Case Admin)
Thomson, Olivia (Case Admin)
Holden, Jess (Gen Admin)
Gostelow, Garry (Health Trainer)
Ryan, Tony (Health, Safety & Facilities Advisor)

Community Payback Office
Tel: 01722 320897

Uphill, Amanda (CP Off)
Aldridge, Peter (CP Supvr)

Centenary House
150 Victoria Road
Old Town **Swindon** SN1 3UZ
Tel: 01793 534259/536612
General fax: 01793 509707
Office Manager fax: 01793 509701
Interventions fax: 01793 509702

Wiltshire Victim Liaison Unit
Tel: 01793 509709 (direct line)
Fax: 01793 509702
Email:
nps.victims@wiltshire.probation.gsi.gov.uk

Offender Management
Murray, Amanda (Eff Pract Mgr)
Beddis, Anna (LDU Mgr)

PSOs
Bamford, James
Davies, Albertine
Derbyshire, Wayne
Hall, Louise
Hellier, Emma
Kipling, Laura
Jackson, Rob
Melvin, Joanna
Seddon, Andrew
Scarle, Jane
Watson, Zoe (IOM)

PSOs
Soane, Melanie
Bell, Sarah

Helmer-Pedley, Jessica
Webb, Victoria (IOM)
Frankham, Rachel
James, Michelle
Lansdowne, Lesley
O'Hara, John
Sheeran, Joanna
Matsushima, Carol (VLO)
Saunders, Dawn (VLO)
Fardon, Howard (LDU Perf & Info Off)
Bird, Kelly (Team Coord)
Truman, Claire (Team Coord)
Tuck, Craig (Health Trainer)
Case Administrators
Attree, Lisa
Austen, Mary
Butler, Alison
Greenslade, Julie
McNeill, Sharon
Probets, Joe
Hyde, Claire
Sadler, Caroline

General Administrators
Geddes, Christine
Teal, Alicia

Programmes Team
Glasscoo, Stephanie (Progs Team Mgr)
Fuller, James (Treatment Mgr)
Bath, Felicity
Attree, Nick
Mack, Leanne (Prog Tutor)
Blacklock, Sue (Women's Safety Wkr)
Affleck, Annette (Admin)
Graham, Karen (Interventions Coord)
McMullan, Carol (Team Co-ord)

Community Payback Office
Swindon 01793 534259/496622
Sargeant, Maryann (CP Off)
Geiran, Tracy (CP Coord)

CP Supervisors
Benfield, Roy
Howlett, David
Wood, Rachel (Int Admin)

Pathways Development Unit
Lane, Sarah (ETE Off)
Fenton, Kirsten (Pathway Off)
Frith, Russell (Case Mgr)

Youth Offending Team
The Limes 21 Green Road
Upper Stratton **Swindon** SN2 6JA
Tel: 01793 823153 Fax: 01793 820578

Norton, Melissa
Dudman, Jen

Wiltshire Council, Monkton Park
Chippenham SN15 1ER
Tel: 01249 709400 Fax: 01249 707901

Drew, Sharon

Wiltshire Council, Council House,
Bourne Hill, **Salisbury**, SP1 3UZ
Tel: 01722 432435 Fax: 01722 438062

Kelly, Tom

MAPPA Coordination
Room 54 Devizes Police Station
New Park Street **Devizes** SN10 1DZ
Tel: 0845 408 7000 Fax: 01380 733260

Hemming, Alan (MAPPA Coord) ext
7372398
Email:
alan.hemming@wiltshire.pnn.police.uk
Woolley, Denise (MAPPA Admin) ext
737580
Email:
denise.woolley@wiltshire.pnn.police.uk

SWITHC (IOM)
Melksham Police Station
SN12 6QQ
Tel: 01380 734001
Kennedy, Angela (SWITCH Mgr) ext
728222
Knight, Georgina (PO)
Hulm, Charlotte (PSO)

Institution

HMP Erlestoke
Devizes SN10 5TU
Tel: 01380 814250 Fax: 01380 818663

Minch, Alison (Head of OMU)
Larcombe, Laura
O'Pray, Andy
O'Shaughnessy, Debbie

PSOs
Patrick, Gina
Pearson, Andy
Piper, Stephen
Frost, Simon
Fuller, Lester

Local Justice Areas
NW Wiltshire (*Trowbridge*)
SE Wiltshire (*Chippenham, Salisbury*)
Swindon (*Swindon*)

Crown Courts
Salisbury
Swindon

YORK & NORTH YORKSHIRE PROBATION TRUST

Out of hours emergency contact point
Southview Approved Premises Tel: 01904
780358

Email:
firstname.surname@north-yorkshireprobation.
gsi.gov.uk

Head Office
Essex Lodge, 16 South Parade
Northallerton DL7 8SG
Tel: 01609 772271 Fax: 01609 772931

Brown, Pete (Chief Executive) (based at
P2K, York 01904 698920)

Bellamy CBE, Ken (Board Chair)

Widmer, Jaqui (PA to Chief Executive
and Board Chair)
Burns, Walter (Dir Corporate
Service/Trust Secretary)
Ryan, Mike (Dir York Local Delivery
Unit) (based at York Probation Office
01904 526000)
Seed, Kevin (Org Development Mgr)
Sheard, Jon (Dep Dir Finance) (based in
West Yorkshire 03000 487053)
Taylor, Justine (Dep Dir HR) (based in
West Yorkshire) 0300 487127

5/7 Haywra Crescent
Harrogate HG1 5BG
Tel: 01423 566764 Fax: 01423 565790

Interventions

The Court House
Bunkers Hill, **Skipton** BD23 1HU
Tel: 01756 794797 Fax: 01756 798614

Scarborough
3rd Floor, Pavilion House, Pavilion
Square
Scarborough YO11 2JN
Tel: 01723 366341 Fax: 01723 501932

108 Lowther Street
York YO31 7WD
Tel: 01904 526000 Fax: 01904 526001

Pavilion 2000 (P2K)
Amy Johnson Way
Clifton Moor, **York** YO3 4XT
Tel: 01904 698920 Fax: 01904 698929

Offender Management
Atkin, Joanne (Area Mgr Public Protection)

Interventions
Chatters, Sandra (Area Mgr)

York Crown Court
The Castle, York YO1 9WZ
Tel: 01904 651021 Fax: 01904 652397

Union Lane, Selby YO8 4AU
Tel: 01757 707241 Fax: 01757 213911

CRI (Crime Reduction Initiatives)
6 Peckitt Street, York YO1 9SF
Tel: 01904 675040 Fax: 01904 521108

Public Protection
North Yorkshire Police Headquarters
Newby Wiske DL7 9HA
Tel: 01609 789299 Fax: 01609 789214

Youth Offending Teams

North Yorkshire Youth Offending Team
Delta House, 12B North Park Road
Harrogate HG1 5PG
Tel: 0845 0349478 Fax: 01423 522949

North Yorkshire Youth Offending Team
2nd Floor, Pavilion House
Pavilion Square
Scarborough YO11 2JN
Tel: 0845 0349497 Fax: 01723 361368

City of York Council
1st Floor, George Hudson Street
York YO1 6ZE
Tel: 01904 554565 Fax: 01904 554566

Approved Premises (Hostel)

Southview Approved Premises
Southview, 18 Boroughbridge Road
York YO26 5RU
Tel: 01905 780358 Fax: 01904 780475
Weatherstone, Paul (Manager)

Institutions

HMYOI Northallerton
15A East Road
Northallerton DL6 1NW
Tel: 01609 785100 Probation fax: 01609 785102

HMP/YOI Askham Grange
Askham Richard, York YO23 3FT
Tel: 01904 772000 Fax: 01904 772001
Probation fax: 01904 772003

Local Justice Areas
Harrogate
Northallerton & Richmond
Scarborough
Selby
Skipton
York

Crown Court
York

SOUTH YORKSHIRE PROBATION TRUST

Out of hours emergency contact point
Norfolk Park Hostel, Tel: 0300 0470900

Email:
firstname.lastname@south-yorkshire. probation.gsi.gov.uk

Head Office
45 Division Street
Sheffield S1 4GE
Reception: Jeanne Bartles/Janet Wragg
Tel: 0300 047 0800
Fax: 0300 047 0899

Brown, Roz (CE)
Cutting, David (Solicitor and Secretary to the Board)
Cullen, Amanda (Dir of Corporate Services)
Marginson, Lynda (Deputy Chief Exec)
Jones, Graham (ACO Head of IBDU)
Razzell, Ian (Head of Information, Performance and Quality)
Moore, Robert (Commissioning Mgr)

PAs
Barber, Claire
Brown, Kaniz
Clarke, Kirsty
Hunt, Laura

Bell, Caroline (Head of Finance)
Cook, Susan (Accountant)
Andrew, Antonia (Accountant)
Judd, Carole (Head of HR)

HR Business Managers
Hollingsworth, Peter
Slater, Carrie
Barker, Sarah

Tinker, Angela (Support Mgr)

Anderson, Kathy (Hd of Diversity & Inclusion & L&D)

Cocken, Clare (PR & Comms Officer)
Abbott, Penny (H&S Business Partner)
Jenkins, Matt (Learning & Devt Officer)
Emmerson, Laura (Learning & Devt Officer)
Jenkinson, Paul (Learning & Devt Officer)
Green, Katherine (Learning & Dev Coord)
Doyle, Tina (Hd of Info Services Unit)
Myers, Gail (Snr Computer Off)

Vacant POst (Snr Computer Off)
Lawrenson, Hilary (Info Security Analyst)
Maughan, Ann (Process Dev Off)
Richardson, Neil (UNISON Rep)
Woodhouse, Joan (NAPO Rep)

MAPPA Unit
South Yorkshire Police Headquarters
Snig Hill, **Sheffield** S3 8LY
Tel: 0114 252 3319 Fax: 0114 252 3885
Clarke, Dean (MAPPA SMB Co-ord)
Odusanya, Julie (MAPPA Co-ord)
Saxby, Karen (Psychologist)
Betts, Melissa (Circles Co-ord)

3 West Bar
Sheffield S3 8PJ
Tel: 0300 047 0600 Fax: 0300 047 0716

Local Delivery Unit Support Unit
Jan Hannant (Hd of Probation)
Smith, Jenny (Support Mgr)
Gerrard, Gill (PA)

Offender Management Unit 1
Welch, Simon (Team Mgr)
Gayle, Hyacinth
Harley, Bryan
Johnson, Susan
McCuish, Linda
Manifold, Garry
Wainwright, Joy
Ward, Adele

PSOs
Hewitt, Keith
Armitage, Cath (Snr Case Admin)

Offender Management Unit 2
Vacant (Team Mgr)
Afzal, Taira
Beckford-Pcart, Marjorie
Bufton, Sally

Fenwick, Jessica
Machin, Helen
Teather, Laura
Woodhouse, Joan

PSOs
MacPherson, Niki
Wall, Michelle
Holdsworth, Gillian (Snr Case Admin)

Offender Management Unit 3
Gregory, Ian (Team Mgr)
Daughtry, Emma
Foster, Jayne
Jones, Karen
Lawrence, Aimee
Mellor, Sonya
Reeves, Sheila
Sullivan, Jeremy

PSOs
Macdonald, Gwendoline
Unsworth, David

Offender Management Unit 4
Cotterell, Rob (Team Mgr)
Moss, Susan
Newsum-Brown, Anthony
Penney, Sallyann
Price, Sharon
Storey, Ruth
Wake, Sarah
Williams, Elizabeth

PSOs
Clayton, Francine
Hutchinson, Geraldine
Perrelli, Ruth
Smyth Emma (Snr Case Admin)

Offender Management Unit 5
Connelly, John (Team Mgr)
Kenny, Helen
Kerr, Laura
McHale, Anne
Perch, Michael
Scott, Samantha
Shann, Christine
Taylor, Nicholas
Walker, Rebecca

PSOs
Galton, Jill
Herron, Janine
Horbury, John
Roe, Margaret

Offender Management Unit 8 (West Bar)
Jen Porter (Team Mgr)
Newton, Andrea

Jones, Karen
Perch, Michael
Kenny, Helen
Wood, Josie (Snr Case Admin)

Magistrates' Court
c/o 3 West Bar
Sheffield S3 8PJ
Tel: 0300 047 0777 Fax: 0300 047 0789

Offender Management Unit 8
PSOs
Akpaka, Berthrand
Barber, Sheila
Foster, Julie
Howard, Sadie
Hurst, David
Revill, Debbie

Crown Court
50 West Bar, **Sheffield**
Tel: 0300 047 0799 Fax: 0300 047 0798

(all mail to 3 West Bar, Sheffield S3 8PJ)

Offender Management Unit 8
PSOs
Askew, Sarah
Bunting, Kathryn
Gill, Linda

Sheffield IMPACT Team
42 Sidney St, **Sheffield** S1 4RH
Tel: 0300 0470750 Fax: 0300 0470774

Offender Management Unit 7
Kime, Sheena (Team Mgr)
McNerney, Phil (Team Mgr)
Beet, Hannah
Brown, Thomas
Edwards, Angela
Gregory, Sharon
Jones, Carol
Jackson, Melvin
Moreland, Gregory
Stephenson, Christine
Tully, Marianne

PSOs
Edmunds, Katy
Hodgkinson, Michael
Kerslake, Stephen
Neville, Helen
O'Neil, Isobel
Walton, Christine
Winter, Jane (Snr Case Admin)

Youth Justice Service
Star House, 43 Division St, **Sheffield S1 4GE**
Tel: 0114 228 8555 Fax: 0114 228 8500

Youth Offending Team
Forrest, Janet
Drabble, Philip
Holmes, Hannah
Taylor, Sam
Oates, Daniel (PSO)

Barnsley Local Delivery Unit
Acorn House, Mount Osbourne, Industrial Park
Barnsley S71 1HP
Tel: 0300 047 0000 Fax: 0300 047 0090

Local Delivery Unit Support Unit
Lanfranchi, Max (Hd of Probation)
Richmond, Gilly (Support Mgr)
Landon, Tracey (PA)

Offender Management Unit 2
Ludlam, Sue (Team Mgr)
Allsopp, Sarah
Barton, Esther
Bougnot, Anna
Edwards, Lynda
Jones, Samantha
Kennedy, Louise
Lindley, Kat
Middleton, Emma

PSOs
Dyson, Jane
Morrisroe, Simon
Waller, Lynda (Snr Case Admin)

Offender Management Unit 3
Westley-Morris, Ray (Team Mgr)
Dunnill, John
Firth, Emma
Havenhand, Kate
Horridge, Peter
Jones, Andrew
Scott, Marie
Taylor, Helen
Sam, Rose

PSOs
Padgett, Rosemary
Steele, Betty
Whyke, Larry
Rushton, Diane (Snr Case Admin)

Offender Management Unit 4
Niven, Chris (Team Mgr)
Couldwell, Amber
Green, Andrew

Kenny, Elanor
Philips, Darren
Shepherd, Luke

PSOs
Booth, Louise
Coniston, Diane
Crookes, Joan
Garrett, Sharon
Ormrod, Heather
Harrison, Alison (Snr Case Admin)

Court House
Churchfields, **Barnsley** S70 2HW
Tel: 01226 243331 Fax: 01226 294908

Offender Management Unit 5
Ford, Liz (Team Mgr)
Harper, Clare (Team Mgr)
Dyson, Rita

PSOs
Andrews, Stella
Crossland, Amy
Mcdermid, Charles
Rock, Julie

Youth Offending Team
Crookes Street
Barnsley S70 6BX
Tel: 01226 774986 Fax: 01226 774968

Marziano, Cristina
Shaw, Josephine

The Law Courts
College Road, **Doncaster** DN1 3HU
Tel: 0300 04070333 Fax: 0300 0470349

Court Team and Quality Assurance Team
Page, Paulette (Team Mgr)
Howkins, Sallyanne

PSOs
Bourne, Rod
Lambert, Aaron
Varney, Christine
Wilkinson, Melanie
Hamill, Kerry (Snr Case Admin)
Ottewell, Erica (Snr Case Admin)

Bennetthorpe
34 Bennetthorpe, Doncaster DN2 6AD
Tel: 0300 470200 Fax: 0300 0470299

Local Delivery Unit Support Unit
Maryke, Turvey (Hd of Probation)
Bowie, Chris (Support Mgr)
Steen, June (PA)

Offender Management Unit 2
Vacant (Team Mgr)
Beadle, Sally
Emmerson, Laura
Hubber, Tacita
Potter, Helen
Spence, Judith
Spivey, Kathreine
Sykes, Karen
Thomas, Vikki
Walker, Lorraine
Wilson, Kerry

PSOs
Torn, Shelley
Castleton, Tracey
Bishop, Rowena (Snr Case Admin)

Offender Management Unit 3
Turgoose, Josie (Team Mgr)
Bertie, Susan
Brown, Peter
Chesters, Joanne
Hosfield, Christopher
Morgan, Gaynor
Tapudzai, Menford

PSOs
Honey, Graeme)
Rachwalski, Gemma
Thomas, Patricia
Jane, Cheryl (Snr Case Admin)

Offender Management Unit 4
Maille, Doug (Team Mgr)
Barrow, Louise
Denovan, Melissa
Eagle, Sally
Glover, Andrew
Pass, Clare
Peat, Sarah
Popple, Teresa
Richards, Donna
Wormley, Zoe

PSOs
Lambert, Aaron
Wilson, Sharon
Bishop, Rowena (Snr Admin Off)

Offender Management Unit 5
Jackson, Ian (Team Mgr)
Broadbent, Anthony
Ellis, Paul
Jones, Helen
Maud, Rebecca
Mombeshora, Davie
Shaw, Lorna
Sherriff-Jones, Jo

PSOs
Lambert, Jayne
Gordon, Sophia
Houghton, Michelle
Porritt, Patricia
Weerdmeester, Maia
Jane, Cheryl (Snr Case Admin)

Youth Offending Team
Rosemead Centre, May Avenue
Balby, Doncaster DN4 9AE
Tel: 01302 736100 Fax: 01302 736103

Dallas, William
Tyson, Carla

Ashley Business Court
Unit 2/3 Rawmarsh Road, **Rotherham**
S60 1RU
Tel: 0300 047 0400 Fax: 0300 047 0486

Local Delivery Unit Support Unit
Mainwaring, Sarah (Hd of Probation)
Corby, Tracy (Support Mgr)
Plumb, Anne (PA)

Offender Management Unit 1
Lubienski, May (Team Mgr)
Wells, Emma (Team Mgr)
Booth, Rebecca
Carrington, Diane
Davitt, Rachel
Holland, Lindsey
Jones, Rachael
Lloyd-Jones, Gwen
Ogden, David
Peacock, Jane
Titus, Karen
Turner, Emma
Weston, Lisa
Younger, Stephen

PSOs
Bates, Karen
Cottam, Helen
Lane, Sarah
Patterson, Claire
Walker, Victoria
Hadfield, Susan (Snr Case Admin)
Saxton, Kathleen (Snr Case Admin)

Offender Management Unit 2
Mansaram, Ray (Team Mgr)
Deen, Shaheen
Cureton, Debbie
Gibbons, Nadine
Hoole, Paul
Saville, Jane
Tweddle, Claire

Ullah, Ali
Walker, Katy

PSOs
Heeds, Charlotte
Hirst, Richard
Maw, Claire
Tindall, Elizabeth
Oakley, Tracey (Snr Case Admin)

Offender Management Unit 3
Handy, Jill (Team Mgr)
Ogden, Dave
Brennan, Lenday
Ducker, Andrew
Hogan, Katy

PSOs
Lester, Kevan
Rimmer, Julia
Smith, Melanie (Snr Case Admin)

Youth Offending Team
4/6 Moorgate Road
Rotherham S60 2EN
Tel: 01709 516999 Fax: 01709 836584

Morris, Lisa
Sharman, Anne
Hoole, Michelle (PSO)

Rotherham Magistrates' Court
The Statutes, PO Box 15
Rotherham S60 1YW
Tel: 01709 361321 Fax: 01709 370172

Offender Management Unit 4
Andersson, Pam (Team Mgr)
Land, Judith (PSO)
Wainwright, Jeanett (PSO)

Group Programmes Unit
Masborough Street
Rotherham S60 1HW
Tel: 0300 047 0500 Fax: 0300 047 0530

Forbes-Williams Paulette (Interventions
& Business (Div Mgr)
Beard, Sarah (Support Mgr)
William, Barbara (Team Manager)
Wilson, Kelly (Prob Team Mgr)
Reading, Neil (Prob Team Mgr)
Cosgrove, Caroline
Edge, Philip
Ellis, Rhys
Glover, Lynda
Ibbotson, Bryan
Jones, Paula
Simpson, Rachel
Turner, Kate

Walton, Frank

PSOs
Cook, Katherine
Cowan, Libby
Grocott, Wayne
Hadfield, Joanne
McEvoy, Declan
Parker, Tracey
Parry, Stephen
Rose, Ellie
Ulman, Stephen
Wales, Steven
Welch-Jasnoch, Nicky
Wilkinson, Emma

Akers, Berrnard (GP Prog Support Wkr)

Laksevics, Abby (GP Prog Support Wkr)

Victim Unit
PSOs
Barlow, Sue
Brook, Anne
Denton, Margaret
Murphy, Lynda

Community Payback
269 Pitsmoor Road
Sheffield S3 9AS
Tel: 0300 0470727 Fax: 0300 0470744

Montgomery, Avril (Div Mgr)

Walker Steve (South Team Mgr)
Morton, Ann (North Team Mgr)
Dixon, Phil (North Deputy Team Mgr)
Project Officers
Blake, Bev
Fleet, Judith
Hatton, Rachel
Headen, Mark
Hunter, Kevin
Meades, Louise
Mills, Nichola
Slack, Phil

Supervisors
Badger, Brian
Cadet, David
Grubb, David
Illingworth, Peter
Longmuir, John
Robbins, David
Tomlinson, Ian
Turton, David
Whitworth, Stephen

Community Payback Unit
Unit 2/3 Rawmarsh Road, **Rotherham**
S60 1RU

Tel: 0300 047 0400 Fax: 0300 047 0486

Shaw, Steve (South Deputy Team Mgr)

Project Officers
Bargh, Alan
Bower, Kerry
Miller, Fiona
Sigfusson, Tony

Supervisors
Barks, Terry
Fallowfield, Ron
Hancock, Stuart
Hayes, James
Moule, Graham

Acorn House
Mount Osbourne Industrial Park
Barnsley S71 1HP
Tel: 0300 047 0000 Fax: 0300 047 0090

Morton, Ann (Team Mgr)
Dixon, Phil (Dep Team Mgr)

Project Officers
Chambers, Tracy
Dixon, Harry
Staves, Glyn
Swallow, Ian

Supervisors
Barrowclough, Susan
Biggin, Glen
Hodgson, Stanley
Lockie, Trish
Smith, Russell

Yarborough Terrace
Bentley, **Doncaster** DN5 9TH
Tel: 0300 047 0300 Fax: 0300 047 0324
Cran, Mel (Team Mgr)

Project Officers
Dale, Michael
Doyle, Brenda
McMaster, Val
Murdoch, Scott
Tottie, John

Supervisors
Dutchak, Peter
Gant, Chris
Wilson, Paul
Lynas, Julia (Support Mgr)
Crossland, Gillian (Snr Admin Off)

Approved Premises (Hostels)
Central bail referral number
Tel: 0300 0470900 Fax: 0300 0470919
Hostel administrative support

Tel: 0300 0470900 Fax: 0300 0470919

Parkin, Gillian (Support Mgr)

Norfolk Park Hostel
100–108 Norfolk Park Road
Sheffield S2 2RU
Tel: 0300 047 0900 Fax: 0300 047 0919

Pidwell, David (Div Mgr)

Rajaie, Kaveh (Team Mgr)
Greaves, Rita (Prob Hostel Wkr)
Hodgkinson, Faye (Prob Hostel Wkr)
Ellams, Stephen (Night Care Wkr)
Peters, Sandra (Night Care Wkr)
Sampson, Ann (Night Care Wkr)
Senior, Lowgan (Waking Night Wkr)
Skubala, June (Waking Night Wkr)
Flintham, Jacqueline (Hostel Support Wkr)
Wood, Charlotte (Hostel Support Wkr)
Anderson, Steph (Snr Admin Off)

Rookwood Hostel
Doncaster Road
Rotherham S65 1NN
Tel: 0300 047 0940 Fax: 0300 047 0949

Platt-Hopkin, Gill (Team Manager)
Andrews, Diane (Prob Hostel Wkr)
Bennett, Delroy (Prob Hostel Wkr)
FoxBerry, Tracy (Prob Hostel Wkr)
Evans, Jodi (Hostel Support Wkr)
Wadsworth, Ian (Hostel Support Wkr)
Bintcliffe, Kenneth (Night Care Wkr)
Fretwell, Darren (Night Care Wkr)
Marsh, Donna (Night Care Wkr)
Millington, Gill (Waking Night Wkr)
Wilks, John (Waking Night Wkr)
Croxton, Lisa (Snr Admin Off)
Hackleton, Donna (Snr Admin Off)

Town Moor Bail Hostel
38/40 Christchurch Road
Doncaster DN1 2QL
Tel: 0300 0470920 Fax: 0300 0470934

Aspden, Paul (Team Manager)

Carroll, Steven (Prob Hostel Wkr)
Hunt, Jenny (Prob Hostel Wkr)
Phipps, Serena (Prob Hostel Wkr)
Chehata, Paula (Hostel Support Wkr)
Isle, Val (Hostel Support Wkr)
Faulkner, Kim (Night Care Wkr)
Fox, Michelle (Night Care Wkr)
Slater, Stephen (Night Care Wkr)
Brown, Duncan (Waking Night Wkr)
Foster, Paul (Waking Night Wkr)

Hall, John (Waking Night Wkr)
Gauden, Susan (Snr Admin Off)

Institutions

HMP/YOI Doncaster
Marsh Gate, Doncaster DN5 8UX
Tel: 01302 760870 Fax: 01302 760851

Discipline (EDR Enquiries) ext 308
Discipline (Discharge) ext 265
Special visits 01302 342413

Probation direct dial: 01302 763 + ext
Probation Clerk ext 203
Houseblock 1 probation ext 287
Houseblock 2 probation ext 290
Houseblock 3 probation ext 291
Bail info ext 293
Bail info fax: 01302 368034
Gilmour, Claire (Team Mgr)
Fells, Helen
Marsh, Martin
Mockford, Mark
Petersen, Lynn
Wheatcroft, Deborah

HMP Lindholme
Bawtry Road, Hatfield Woodhouse
Doncaster DN7 6EE
Tel: 01302 524700 Fax: 01302 524750
Vernon, Glyn (Team Mgr)
Mackenzie, Philip
Musgrave, Rita

PSOs
Allison, Tracy
Hookway, Beverly
Selman, Clair
Winstanley, Jacqueline

HMP/YOI Moorland (Closed)
Bawtry Road, Hatfield Woodhouse
Doncaster DN7 6BW
Tel: 01302 523000 Fax: 01302 523001

Probation Clerk ext 3108

Vernon, Glyn (Probation Team Mgr)
Harrison, Janet
Skelding, Steve
Toole, Alison
Dix, Cathryn

HMP/YOI Moorland (Open)
Thorne Road, **Hatfield**
Doncaster DN7 6EL
Tel: 01405 746500 Fax: 01405 746501

Skelding, Stephen

Interventions Staff (Various Locations)
PSOs
Clarke, Lesley (*Acorn House, Barnsley*)
Holden, Rachel *Bennetthorpe, Doncaster*)
Hughes, Denise (*3 West Bar, Sheffield*)
Keye, Christy (*12 Main Street, Rotherham*)
Knowles, Alexandra (*3 West Bar, Sheffield*)
Askew, Sarah (3 West Bar, Sheffield)

Local Justice Areas
Sheffield (*3 West Bar, 42 Sidney St, 43 Division St,*)
Barnsley (*Barnsley Local Delivery Unit, Churchfields, County Way*)
Doncaster (*College Road, Bennetthorpe, Balby, Ashley Business Court, Rotherham*)
Rotherham (*Moorgate Road, Masborough Street, 269 Pitsmoor Road Sheffield*)

Crown Courts
Doncaster
Rotherham
Sheffield

WEST YORKSHIRE PROBATION TRUST

Out of hours emergency contact point
Elm Bank Hostel 01274 851551

Email:
firstname.lastname@west-yorkshire.probation.gsi.gov.uk

Head Office
Cliff Hill House
Sandy Walk, Wakefield WF1 2DJ
Tel: 03000 487000 Fax: 03000 487152

Executive Group
Hall, Sue (CE)
King, Jayne (Dir Finance & IT)
Mullen, Bernadette (Dir HR)
Siddall, Mark (Dir Operations)
Bryan, David (Dir of Legal Services & Secretary to the Trust)
Cavanagh, Christine (Dir of Business Development)

Interventions
Chandler, Andrew (Hd of Interventions)
Townend, Karen (Ops Mgr Community Payback)
Haddrick, David (Ops Mgr App Premises)
Burns, Janine (Ops Mgr Activities)

Policy & Practice
Mills, Elizabeth (Policy & Practice Unit Mgr)

Human Resources
Taylor, Justine (Dep Dir HR)
Mason, Barbara (HR Mgr)

Finance and IT
Sheard, Jon (Dep Dir Finance & IT)
Ingle, Phil (Head of ICT)

Business Development
Ridley, Diane (Head of Analysis, Research and Communication)

Bradford LDU

Fraternal House
45 Cheapside, Bradford BD1 4HP
Tel: 03000 487040 Fax: 03000 487381

Smallridge, Maggie (Hd of Probation)
Macpherson, Stuart (Ops Mgr)

Bradford City Courts
Probation Centre City Courts
The Tyrls, Bradford BD1 1LB
Tel: 03000 487040 Fax: 03000 487294

Merchant's House
1–7 Leeds Road, Shipley
Bradford BD18 1BP
Tel: 01274 809801 Fax: 01274 809884

Crown Court Bradford
Drake Street, Bradford BD1 1JA
Tel: 01274 840584 Fax: 01274 840588

Keighley Probation Office
11/19 Cavendish Street
Keighley BD21 3RB
Tel: 01535 662771/2 Fax: 01535 611346

Together Women Project
East Wing, 1st Floor
Broadacre House, Bradford BD1 5AA
Tel: 01274 301470

Youth Offending Team
Bank House, 41 Bank Street
Bradford BD1 1RD
Tel: 01274 436060 Fax: 01274 436061

HMP Wealstun
Thorp Arch, Boston Spa
Wetherby LS23 7AZ
Tel: 01937 444400 Fax: 01937 444401

Leeds LDU

Waterloo House
58 Wellington Street, Leeds LS1 2EE
Tel: 0113 243 0601 Fax: 0113 399 5374
Fax: 0113 234 41951

Moloney, Neil (Hd of Probation, Leeds)
Parker, Lisa (Operations Mgr)

379 York Road
Leeds LS9 6TA
Tel: 0113 285 0300 Fax: 0113 285 0301

Ball, Kevin (Operations Mgr)

Leeds Combined Court (Crown and Magistrates')
28 Westgate, Leeds LS1 3AP
Tel: 0113 399 5440 Fax: 0113 245 0967

Crown Court
1 Oxford Row, Leeds LS1 3GE
Tel: 0113 3995497 Fax: 0113 234 1952

Mill 2 4th Floor Mabgate Mills (POO and ICO Teams)
Mabgate, Leeds LS9 7DT
Tel: 0113 394 5421

Mill 1 3rd Floor Mabgate Mills (Substance Misuse Team)
Mabgate, Leeds LS9 7DT
Tel: 0113 397 1900 Fax: 0113 397 1901

HMP Leeds
Gloucester Terrace, Armley, Leeds LS12 2TJ
Tel: 0113 203 2600 Fax: 0113 203 2601

Bail information ext 2648/2640
Bail info fax: 0113 203 2869

Youth Offending Team Leeds East North East
Tech North, 9 Harrogate Road
Chapel Allerton, Leeds LS7 3NB
Tel: 0113 247 5710

Youth Offending Team Leeds West North West
Hough Lane Centre, Hough Lane
Bramley, Leeds LS13 3RD
Tel: 0113 395 0101 Fax: 0113 395 0102

Youth Offending Team Leeds South South East
47 Marshall Street, Holbeck
Leeds LS11 9RZ
Tel: 0113 214 5300 Fax: 0113 214 1517

Calderdale LDU

Probation Centre
173a Spring Hall Lane
Halifax HX1 4JG
Tel: 01422 340211 Fax: 01422 320998

Whitehead, Gini (Hd of Probation)

Youth Offending Team
Hoover Building, 21 West Parade
Halifax HX1 2TE
Tel: 01422 368279 Fax: 01422 368483

Kirklees LDU

Broadway House, Crackenedge Lane
Dewsbury WF13 1PU
Tel: 01924 464171/3 Fax: 01924 453279

Loney, Kathy (Hd of Probation)

21 St John's Road
Huddersfield HD1 5BW
Tel: 01484 826100 Fax: 01484 422218

Youth Offending Team
1st Floor, Somerset Buildings
Church Street, Huddersfield HD1 1DD
Tel: 01484 226263 Fax: 01484 226919

Wakefield LDU

20/30 Lawefield Lane
Wakefield WF2 8SP
Tel: 01924 361156 Fax: 01924 291178

Sinclair, Andrew (Ops Manager)

Grosvenor House
8–20 Union Street
Wakefield WF1 3AE
Tel: 01924 334300 Fax: 01924 780858

HMP/YOI New Hall
Dial Wood, Flockton
Wakefield WF4 4AX
Tel: 01924 803000 Fax: 01924 803001
Probation fax: 01924 844248

HMP Wakefield
5 Love Lane, Wakefield WF2 9AG
Tel: 01924 246000 Fax: 01924 2462799

Youth Offending Team
5 West Parade
Wakefield WF1 1LT
Tel: 01924 304155 Fax: 01924 304156

Interventions
Activities

Bradford/Calder Activities
Fraternal House
45 Cheapside, Bradford BD1 4HP
Tel: 0300 0487040 Fax: 0300 487381

Probation Centre
173a Spring Hall Lane
Halifax HX1 4JG
Tel: 01422 340211 Fax: 01422 320998

Kirklees/Wakefield Activities
5 Albion Street
Dewsbury WF13 2AJ
Tel: 01924 457744 Fax: 01924 458564

20/30 Lawefield Lane
Wakefield WF2 8SP
Tel: 01924 361156 Fax: 01924 291178

Leeds Activities
Waterloo House
58 Wellington Street, Leeds LS1 2EE
Tel: 0113 243 0601 Fax: 0113 399 5374

Victim Services

Bradford Calder Victim Services
Probation Office, Fraternal House
45 Cheapside, Bradford BD1 4HP
Tel: 0300 0487040 Fax: 0300 487383

173a Spring Hall Lane
Halifax HX1 4JG
Tel: 01422 340211

Leeds Victim Services
379 York Road, Leeds LS9 6TA
Tel: 0113 285 0300 Fax: 0113 285 0301

Wakefield Victim Services
20/30 Lawefield Lane
Wakefield WF2 8SP
Tel: 01924 361156

Skills for Work

Bradford
Fraternal House
45 Cheapside, Bradford BD1 4HP
Tel: 0300 0487040 Fax: 0300 0487383

City Courts
The Tyrls, Bradford BD1 1LB
Tel: 01274 704500

11/19 Cavendish Street
Keighley BD21 3RB
Tel: 01535 662771/2

Calderdale

Probation Centre
173a Spring Hall Lane
Halifax HX1 4JG
Tel: 01422 340211 Fax: 01422 320998

Leeds

Waterloo House
58 Wellington Street, Leeds LS1 2EE
Tel: 0113 243 0601 Fax: 0113 399 5374

379 York Road
Leeds LS9 6TA
Tel: 0113 285 0300

Dewsbury Probation Centre
5 Albion Street
Dewsbury WF13 2AJ
Tel: 01924 457744

Community Payback East
379 York Road
Leeds LS9 6TA
Tel: 0113 285 0300 Fax: 0113 285 0301

20/30 Lawefield Lane
Wakefield WF2 8SP
Tel: 01924 361156 Fax: 01924 29117

Community Payback West
21 St John's Road
Huddersfield HD1 5BW
Tel: 01484 826100 Fax: 01484 422218

Probation Centre,
173a Spring Hall Lane
Halifax HX1 4JG
Tel: 01422 340211 Fax: 01422 320998

Fraternal House
45 Cheapside, Bradford BD1 4HP
Tel: 01274 703700 Fax: 01274 703701

Approved Premises

Holbeck House Approved Premises
Springwell View, Springwell Road
Leeds LS12 1BS
Tel: 0113 245 4220 Fax: 0113 245 4910

Elm Bank Approved Premises
59 Bradford Road
Cleckheaton BD19 3LW
Tel: 01274 851551 Fax: 01274 851079

Albion Street Approved Premises
30 Albion Street
Dewsbury WF13 2AJ
Tel: 01924 452020 Fax: 01924 455670

Westgate Project
188–198 Westgate
Wakefield WF2 9RF
Tel: 01924 203730 Fax: 01924 203731

Voluntary Managed Approved Premises

Cardigan House Approved Premises
84 Cardigan Road
Leeds LS6 3BJ
Tel: 0113 275 2860 Fax: 0113 274 5175

St John's Approved Premises
259/263 Hyde Park Road
Leeds LS6 1AG
Tel: 0113 275 5702 Fax: 0113 230 5230

Ripon House Approved Premises
(Women-only hostel)
63 Clarendon Road
Leeds LS2 9NZ
Tel: 0113 245 5488 Fax: 0113 242 3675

Institutions

HMP Leeds
Gloucester Terrace, Armley, Leeds LS12 2TJ
Tel: 0113 203 2600 Fax: 0113 203 2601
Bail information ext 2648/2640
Bail info fax: 0113 203 2869

HMP/YOI New Hall
Dial Wood, Flockton
Wakefield WF4 4AX
Tel: 01924 803000 Fax: 01924 803001
Probation fax: 01924 844248

HMP Wakefield
5 Love Lane, Wakefield WF2 9AG
Tel: 01924 246000 Fax: 01924 2462799

HMP Wealstun
Thorp Arch, Boston Spa
Wetherby LS23 7AZ
Tel: 01937 444400 Fax: 01937 444401

Local Justice Areas
Batley & Dewsbury (Broadway House Dewsbury)
Bradford (Fraternal House Bradford, Bradford City Courts, Merchant's House Shipley)
Calderdale (Probation Centre Halifax)
Huddersfield (St John's Road Huddersfield)
Keighley (Keighley Probation Office)
Leeds District (Waterloo House & 379 York Road Leeds)

Pontefract (Harropwell Lane Pontefract)
Wakefield (Lawefield Lane Wakefield)

Crown Courts
Bradford
Leeds

WALES PROBATION TRUST YMDDIRIEDOLAETH PRAWF CYMRU

Email
Firstname.Surname@wales.probation.gsi.gov.uk

1. Office of Chief Executive
33 Westgate Street, Cardiff CF10 1JE
Tel: 029 2023 2999 Fax: 029 2023 0384
Direct dial: 02920 78 + ext

Fox, Sue (Chair, Based at Office 28)
Payne, Sarah (Chief Executive)
Barrow, Ian (Dir of Operations)
Savage, William (Dir of Commercial Affairs)
Vacancy (Dir of Corporate Resources & Organisational Development)
Seculer, Anthony (Trust Secretary)
Rabaiotti, Ella (Staff Officer to Chief Executive) ext 5015
Semmens, Leeanne (Interim Staff Officer to Dir of Operations) ext 5098
Harley, Christine (Ace, Business Development)
O'Leary, Susan (Ace, Business Planning)
Attwell, Julia (Ace, Business Monitoring and Review)
Donovan, Martin (Treasurer and Ace, Finance)
Hughes, Jonothan (Ace, Infrastructure)
Roach, Clare (Ace, HR and OD)
Kirk, Tony (Business Planning Mgr)
Morgan, Peter (Communications Mgr)
Williams, Katherine (PR Mgr)
Moyce, Natalie (E-Communications Mgr, Based at Office 39)
Clancy, Sarah (Business Support) ext 5085
Curtis, Simon (Performance & Information Mgr) ext 5101
Smith, Jayne (Pa to Trust Chair, Based at Office 28)
Viant, Gwenllian (Pa to Chief Executive) ext 5015
Williams, Clare (Pa to Dir) ext 5098
Hunter, Sally (Pa to Dir) ext 5036
Caple, Michelle (Pa to Dir) ext 5048

Davies, Davina (Pa to Ace) ext 5079
Meredith, Sian (Pa to Ace) ext 5059
Dilworth, Susan (Pa to Ace, Based at office 37)
Jones, Ceri J (Pa to Ace)

2. Cardiff & The Vale Local Delivery Unit
33 Westgate Street
Cardiff CF10 1JE
Tel: 029–2023 2999 Fax: 029–2023 0384
Direct dial 02920 78 + ext
Greenhill, Peter (ace) ext 5070
Reed, Gail (dace) 5042
Allsopp, Elizabeth (p, PA) ext 5003
Meakin, Tracy (p, PA) ext 5003
Coxon, Caroline (bus Manager) ext 5057

Offender Management
Griffiths, Carolyn (Team Manager) ext 5104

POs
Shaw, Linda ext 5080
Hamed , Janine 5044
Halsey, Jim ext 5147
Taylor, Phil 5008

PSOs
Pearson, Maria ext 5116
Jenkins, Leah ext 5064
Fitzgerald, Kate ext 5108
Grant, Christopher 5149
Warner, Helen (Team Manager) ext 5050

POs
Strong, Rebecca 5077
Morgan, Paul ext 5004
Dacey, Ian ext 5130
Richmond, Ruth ext 5148
Williams, Julie M 5127
Sheppard, Anita 5106
Bicknell, Helen 5142

PSOs
Cribb, Christine ext 5132
Jenkins, Angharad ext 5114
Holt, Heidi ext 5062
Sagoo, Sharon (PQF) ext 5091
Pallister, Sheila (Team Manager) ext 5006

POs
Gibbons, Kathy ext 5096
Morris, Graham ext 5066
Mulligan, Zelda ext 5063

PSOs
Sullivan, Steve ext 4997
Fisher Sharpe, Tracey ext 5105
Kingdom, Anna 5061
Bellamy, Nicola ext 5123

Irwin, Claire (Team Manager) ext 5122

POs
Anderson, Laura 5001
Chevis, Kat ext 5073
Reddington, Terry ext 5030
Hygate, Zoe ext 5141
Powell, Claire ext 5049
Rees, Sian ext 5088
Enos, Estella
Floyd, Nicola (PQF) ext 5088
Thomas, Mike (PSO) ext 5141
Jones, Bethan (PSO) ext 5099
Bamford, Aimee (PQF) 5117
Watkins Cath (Team Manager) ext 5021

POs
Morris, Lucy ext 5115
Hales, Natalie ext 5056
Blackhurst, Lisa ext 5020
Chandler, Rachael ext 5076
Pearce, Sarah ext 5013
Morley, Rebecca ext 5100
Edwards, Sally ext 5033
LeSauter, Alice

PSOs
Moore, Kirsty ext 5075
Bynon, Julie ext 5133
Sims, Karen ext 5125
Wareham, Karen 5087
Foulner, Jane (Team Manager) ext 5128

POs
Bailey, Ken ext 5071
Eynon, John ext 5109
Moore, Alastair ext 5043
Allsop, Lianne ext 5107
Atkins, Miriam ext 5032
Smith, Heather ext 5093

PSOs
Adams, Darren ext 5113
Barrett, Nicola 5016
Parkinson, Nadine ext 5029
Walsh, Lucy ext 5102
Scott, Jodie ext
Tingle Beth ext

Programmes
Law, Alex (Team Manager) ext 5136
Vowles, Gus (PSO/Treatment Monitor) ext 5097
Williams, Sarah (PSO/Treatment Monitor) ext 5124

PSOs
Rees, Nikki ext 5055
Baker, Byron ext 5140
Goldsworthy, Jason ext 5140

McTair, Grace ext 5119
Evans, Sara ext 5055
Watts, Amanda (VO) ext 5017
Williams, Amanda (VO) 5018
Swift, Samara (VO) 5018
McSwinney, Jo (VO) 5018

3. Vale District
Wales Probation Trust
Barry Police Station
Gladstone Road
Barry CF63 1TD
Phone 01446 450500 Fax 01446 450510
Shellens, Peter (Team Manager) 01446 450506

POs
Stockley, Pru 01446 450500
Smith, Jeremy 01446 450503
Brown, Lynsey 01446 450505
Humphrey, Laura 01446 731690
Horsell, Katie 01446 450500
Williams, Tara 01656 674741
Powell, Sally 01446 450500

PSOs
Arthur, Steve 01446 450501
Holmes, Louise 01446 450500
Jones, Kate 01446 450505
Moyle, Gaynor 01446 450505

4. 2a Lewis Street, Canton
Cardiff CF10 8JX
Tel: 029 20660 611 Fax: 029 2066 7870
Direct dial: 029 20660 + ext
Martin, Philip (Team Manager) ext 615

PSOs
Taylor, Yvonne ext 617
Franklin, Anna ext 622
Alecock, Trish ext 624

5. Cardiff Crown Court
Cathays Park, Cardiff CF10 3NL
Tel: 029 2034 8890 Fax: 029 2034 5705
Direct dial 029–2034 + ext
Plechowicz, Leanne (Team Manager) ext 8896
Nicholas, Colin (PO) ext 8896

6. Cardiff Magistrates' Court
Fitzalan Place, Cardiff CF24 1RZ
Tel: 029 2035 8460 Fax: 029 2049 8587
Direct dial 029–2035 + ext
Plechowicz Leanne (Team Manager) ext 8460

POs
Dunne, Michael 8460
Rees-Jones, Julian 8460

Newton, Robert 8460
Williams, Joan ext 8460

7. Cardiff Youth Offending Team
The Rise, Penhill, Cardiff CF11 9PR
Tel: 029 2056 0839 Fax 029 2057 8746
Heaton Jones, Saul (seconded PO)
Lucking, Bethan (seconded PO)
Manley, Sarah (seconded PSO)

8. Vale Youth Offending Team
91 Salisbury Road, Barry
Vale of Glamorgan CF62 6PD
Tel: (01446) 745820 Fax:(01446) 739549
Bicknell, Helen (seconded PO)

9. Gwent Local Delivery Unit
Newport Office,
Usk House,
Lower Dock Street,
Newport, NP20 2GD
Tel: (01633) 247300. Direct dial is (01633) 24 followed by 4 digit extension number
Fax: (01633) 247499
Davies, Nic (ace) ext 7402
Bush, Andrew (dlduh)
Ryan, Mary (p, PA) ext 7403
Kendall, Sally (p,PA) ext 7403
Holder, Rachael (Bus Mgr) ext 7413

Newport Team 1
Vernon, Claire (Team Mgr) ext 7401
Asher, Kate (PSO) ext 7367
Beck, Ruth (PSO) ext 7364
Collins, Kath (PO) ext 5038
Gibbon, Louise (PSO) ext 7365
Gilder, Gayle (PO) ext 7371
Harrison, Laura (PSO) ext 7366
Llewellyn, Janet (PO) ext 7368
Nicholas, Zara (PO) ext 7334
Sarwar, Zaheen (PO) ext 7369 (on secondment)
Wesley, Michelle (PO) ext 7341
Whittington, Fiona (PSO) ext 7335

Newport Team 2 – Court Team
Atkins, Debbie (Team Mgr) ext 7484
Bailey, Helen (PO) (based office 17)
Brown, Jo (PSO) ext 7381
Clarke, Anthony (PSO) ext 7340
Jenkins, Rebecca (PO) (based office 16)
McCormack, Caroline (PO) ext 7388
Mukhtar, Kauser (PO) ext 7338 (on secondment)
Phillips, Emma (PO)
Powell, Kate (PO) ext 7336
Smith, Rebecca (PSO) (based ncc)
Walters-Moore, Andrew (PSO) ext 7333
Welch, Janice (PSO) (based office 16)

Newport Team 3
Binding, Diana (Team Mgr) ext 7485
Clemson, Trish (PO) ext 7390
Edwards, Sarah (PO) ext 7394
James, Eleanor (PSO) ext 7395
Johns, Kirsty (PO) ext 7382
Lewis, Fran (PSO) ext 7393
Moore, Kate (PSO) ext 7383
Peckham, Tracey (PO) ext 7386
Porter, Rick (PO) ext 7380

Education, Training and Employment
Mitchell, Valerie (basic skills co-ord) ext 7420
Creswell, Sarah (PSO) ext 7416

Programmes Team
Davies, Alan (Team Mgr) ext 7486
Curtis, Sherrie (Programme Mgr) ext 7480
Feeney, Brian (PSO) ext 7474
Halligan, Jean (Treat Mgr) ext 7481
Ivens, Luke (PSO) ext 7471
Law, Kim (PSO) ext 7470
Price, Tasha (PSO) ext 7473
Tew, Stephanie (PSO) ext 7472
Thomas, Fiona (Treat Mgr) ext 7483
Richardson, Ann-Marie (Admin) ext 7475

Unpaid Work Team
Daniel, Darren (Team Mgr) ext 7431
Axenderrie, Paul (CPO) ext 7423
Bartlett, Claire (CPO) ext 7427
Bidgood, David (Snr CPO) ext 7421
Davies, Andrew (PSO) ext 7430
Mogford, Mike (CPO) ext 7422
Morgan, Glyn (CPO) ext 7425
Price, Marilyn (PSO) ext 7429
Russell, Graham (Upw Sup) ext 7424

Integrated Offender Management
Spacey, Nigel (Team Mgr) ext 7488
Bullock, Donna (PSO) ext 7444
Downes, Emma (PO) ext 7456
Forman, Louise (PO) ext 7454
Gittoes, Catherine (PO) ext 7448
Haskins, Lee (PO) ext 7457

Nicholls, Robert (PPOS) ext 7459
Pudge, Lindsey (Secondment)
Strange, Jeff (PO)
Walsh, Johanna (PSO) ext 7455
Wilding, Laura (PO) ext 7446

10. East Gwent Office
Torfaen House,
Station Road,
Sebastopol,
Pontypool NP4 5ES

Tel: (01495) 755221 Direct dial (01495) 74
followed by 4 digit extension number
Fax: (01495) 763233
Turner, Karen (Team Mgr) ext 5030
Boulter, Paul (PO) ext 5028
Ellis-Hall Karen (PO) ext 5035
Goodall, Lianne (PSO) ext 5036
Handy, Kailey (PSO) ext 5015
Jenkins, Jason (PSO) ext 5045
Jenkins, Rebecca (PO) ext 5022
Jones, Leigh (PO) ext 5018
Lavelle, Kate (PO) ext 5039
Strange, Jeff (PO) ext 5009
Webb, Ellen (PO) ext 5012
Welch, Janice (PSO) ext 5024
Williams, Sarah A (PSO) ext 5021
Wright, Hannah (PO) ext 5034
Young, Mark (PSO) ext 5017

Central Payroll
Finance Officers
Hamilton, Jo ext 5004
Howells, Helen ext 5003
Hencher, Della ext 5042

MAPPA Unit
Hale, Gareth (MAPPA Co-ordinator) ext 5031
Trotman, Rhonwen (Mappa Registrar) ext 5050

11. Caerphilly Office
Centenary House,
Unit 1 De Clare Court
5 Alfred Owen Way,
Pontygwindy Industrial Estate
Caerphilly, CF83 3HU
Tel: (02920) 885861, Direct dial (02920) 76 followed by 4 digit extension number
Fax: (02920) 760123
Davies, Nic (ACE) ext 0092
Bush, Andrew (DLDUH) ext 0083
Holland, Susie (PA to ACE) ext 0082
Rose, Zoe (Bus. Mgr) ext 0001

Rhymney Valley Team 1
Walters, Sharon (Team Mgr) ext 0081
Alexander, Sharon (PSO) ext 0050
Connolly, Lisa (PO) ext 0046
Howse, Sarah (PO) ext 0033
Johnson, Emma (PO)
Pizey, Sarah (PO) ext 0053
Taylor, Rachel (PSO) ext 0044

Rhymney Valley Team 2
Morgan, Leah (Team Mgr) ext 0090
Allen, Barbara (PO) ext 0065
Bailey, Helen (PO) ext 0020
Jones, Kristina (PO) ext 0027

Nash, Katie (PO) ext 0015
O'Connell, Siobhan (PO) ext 0037
Ravenhill, Sandra (PSO) ext 0014
Taylor, Janice (PO) ext 0013
Wood, Nadine (PSO) ext 0012

Other Staff
Hughes, Suzanne (VLO) ext 0016
Vallely, Gillian (PO – Progs) ext 0024
Palmer, Rosa (GMC) ext 0115

12. Ebbw Vale Office
50 Bethcar Street
Ebbw Vale, NP23 6HG
Tel: (01495) 309799, direct dial (01495) 35
followed by 4 digit number
Fax: (01495) 306997
Thomas, Sian L (Team Mgr) ext 6463
Brown, Deborah (Newday Case Mgr) ext
6477
Holloway, Dave (PO) ext 6474
Lewis, Sinead (PO) ext 0029
Rees-Jones, Julian (PO) ext 6471
Thomas, Iwan (PSO) ext 6468
Timothy, Sarah (PSO) ext 6482
Williams, Timothy (PSO) ext 6488

13. Blackwood Office
Chambers House,
49 Blackwood Road
Blackwood, NP12 6BW
Tel: (01495) 233405 (no DD)
Fax: (01495) 233407

Drug Rehabilitation Team 1
Nicholls, Heather (Team Mgr)
Birchmore, Alan (PO)
Davies, Frank (PSO)
Jill Packham (Team Mgr) Secondment
Phillips, Kelly (PO)
Tetley, Nicholas (PO)
Thomas Wan, Lisa (PO)

14. Crown Court
The Law Courts, Faulkner Rd, Newport,
Gwent NP20 4PD
Tel: 01633 266211
Fax: 01633 266891
Smith, Rebecca (PSO)

15. Caerphilly Magistrates Court
The Court House, Mountain Road,
Caerphilly, Glamorgan CF83 1HG
Tel: 02920 880174
Fax: 02920 880175

**16. Gwynedd, Ynys Mon, Conwy &
Denbighshire Local Delivery Unit**
25 Conway Road,
Colwyn Bay, Conwy LL29 7AA

Tel: (01492) 530600 Fax:(01492) 532283
direct dial 01492 52 (followed by
extension number)
Jones, Andy (ace) ext 4081
Jones, Sandra (pa) ext 4016
Partington, Catherine (bus mgr) ext 4019
Taylor, Joanne (Team Mgr –
Denbighshire) ext 4079
Honan, Carol (Team Mgr – Conwy) ext
4078
Goodwin, Phil (Team Mgr – Progs) ext
4027
Hughes, Sue (Admin – Progs) ext 4061

POs
Dhaliwal, Jaspal ext 4053
Donnelly, Paul ext 4042
Hughes, Paula ext 4047
Jones, Gillian ext 4032
Jones, Tim ext 4050
Kidd, Gareth ext 4032
Markwick, Nerys ext 4052
Murt, Carly ext 4038
Owen, Samantha ext 4072
Puw, Rhodri ext 4046
Schofield, Eleri ext 4040
Sowinska-Pritchard, Bernadetta ext 4037
Swinden, Elizabeth ext 4056
Williams, Paul ext 4041

PSOs
Kelly, Louise ext 4039
Mead, Damon ext 4045
Owen, Marina ext 4055
Parry, Eirian ext 4071
Thomas, Rachel ext 4077
New, Tony (Progs) ext 4066
Pritchard, Vivien (Progs) ext 4063
Roberts, Janet (Progs) ext 4062
Kitchen, Linda (CSO) ext 4065
Parry, Paul (CSO) ext 4064

Victim Liaison Unit
Kerr, Cassie (VLO) ext 4010
McKeaveney, Siobhan (VLO) ext 4012
Owen-Rees, Nia (VLO) ext 4011
McCabe, Julieanne (Admin) ext 4013

17. Llys Garth, Garth Road
Bangor Gwynedd LL57 2RT
Tel: (01248) 370217 Fax: (01248) 372422
Direct dial: 01248 374420 (then last two
digits of extension number)
Adlam, Doris (LDU Dev Mgr) ext 2023
Griffith, Hannah (Team Mgr) ext 2032
Thomas, Graham (Team Mgr – UPW) ext
2012

POs
Davies, Emma ext 2014
Evans, Ruth ext 2020
Jones, Delyth ext 2007
Jervis, Allison ext 2020
Owen, Lowri ext 2015
Griffith, Gerallt ext 2036
Rees, Awen ext 2014
Williams, Ffion ext 2018

PSOs
Healy, Diane ext 2027
Phillips, Liz ext 2021
Roberts, Sian ext 2022
Whatling, Michael ext 2019
Hughes, Catherine (Progs) ext 2030
Hughes, Karen (Progs) ext 2028
Owen, Cathy (Progs) ext 2031
Tyrer-Thomas, Catherine (Progs) ext 2041
Millichamp, Vicky (CSO) ext 2024
Reed, Paul (CSO) ext 2034

18. 14 Market Street
Caernarfon Gwynedd LL55 1RT
Tel: (01286) 674346 Fax: (01286) 672668
Williams, Sharon W (Team Mgr) ext 1810

POs
Dawson, Linda ext 1806
Jones, Rhys ext 1801
Middleton, Sue
Peters, Llyr ext 1818
Thomas, Catrin ext 1811
Williams, Lynne ext 1805
Williams, Eira ext 1807/4203

PSOs
Pugh, Richard ext 1813
Roberts-Price, Lynne ext 1813/4205
Williams, Caryl ext 1807/4203
Williams, Sian (Progs) ext 1812

19. Lombard Street, Dolgellau
Dolgellau Gwynedd LL40 1HA
Tel: (01341) 422476 Fax: (01341) 422703
Harrison, Marian (Progs) ext 4202

20. Gwynedd/Ynys Mon Youth Justice Service
Swyddfa Menai, Glan y Mor,
Y Felinheli, Gwynedd, LL56 4RQ
Tel: (01248) 679183 Fax: (01248) 679180

21. Conwy/Denbighshire Youth Justice Service
68 Conway Road
Colwyn Bay LL29 7LD
Tel: (01492) 523500 Fax: (01492) 523555

22. Rhondda Cynon Taff, Merthyr Tydfil & South Powys Local Delivery Unit
4–7 The Broadway
Pontypridd CF37 1BA
Tel: (01443) 494200 Fax: (01443) 494284
Direct dial (01443) 49 + ext
Stone, Neil (ACE) ext 4338
Richards, Emma (DLDUH) ext 4272
Sartin, Joanna (PA) ext 4245
Bradbury, Sue (PA) ext 4235
Smith, Earl (TM) ext 4233
Bevan, Natalie ext 4229
Boswell, Sarah ext 4204
Cain, Dominic ext 4273
Davies, Charlotte ext 4219
Evans, Deborah ext 4232
Griffiths, Helen ext 4264
Hughes, Mike J ext 4242
James, Heulwen ext 4266
Jones, Karen ext 4210
Li, Xue Bin ext 4237
Jones, Rhian ext 4220
Morgan, Catherine ext 4204
Owen, Emma ext 4238
Roberts, Stephen ext 4244
Thorne, Stephen ext 4215
Williams, Simone ext 4207

PSOs
Andrews, Angela ext 4202
Barnes, Amy (Bail Inf Officer) ext 4341
Cox, Joanne ext 4240
Elston, Diane ext 4262
Harris, Sarah ext
Howells, Cliff ext 4208
Hughes, Robin John ext 4223
Jones, Ceri ext 4227
Llewellyn, Anne ext 4211
Price, Alison ext 4203
Williams, Judith ext 4217
Williams, Andrea ext 4225
Pring, Abbi ext 4230
Lewis, Amanda ext 4250
Luke, Anthony ext 4234
Williams, Cindy ext 4216
Brown, Deborah ext 4228
Bell, Doreen ext 4271
Jones, Eirwen ext 4224
Price, Irene ext 4249
Williams, Janet ext 4214
Rutter, Karen ext 4268
Handy, Kailey ext 4241
Phillips, Leah ext 4206
Bickham, Libby ext 4259
Parsons, Linda ext 4213
Edwards, Martin ext 4340

Richards, Natalie ext 4270
Harris, Sarah ext 4221
Woodruff, Sheree ext 4207
Hughes, Sian ext 4239
Weightman, Ceri (SOVA) ext 4216
Gurman, Sue ext 4222
Gerlach, Suzanne ext 4261
Thomas, Val ext 4260

Victim Liaison
Thomas, Denise (women's safety wrkr)
ext 4231

Programmes
Hegarty, Trish (PO Treatment Monitor)
ext 4257
Evans, Simon (PSO Treatment Monitor)
ext 4258
Gerrard, David (PSO) ext 4256
Wilce, Andrew (PSO) ext 4254
Davies, Maxine (admin) ext 4263

Court Services
Towell, Ann (PSO) ext 4252

Unpaid Work
Evans, Lyn (Team Mgr, based at office
23)

Human Resources
Pring, Maxine (HR Manager) ext 4335
Bridgeway, Bev ext 4333
Fearn, Sam ext 4336
Light, Sheena ext 4337

Learning & Development
Chapman, Cara ext 4339
Price, Huw ext 4243
West, Kairen ext 4334

23. Oldway House, Castle Street
Merthyr Tydfil CF47 8UX
Tel: (01685) 728900 Fax: (01685) 728921
Direct dial (01685) 72 + ext
Bedwell, Marcus (Team mgr) ext 8912
POs
Beaumont, Patricia ext 8922
Davies, Melissa ext 8923
Haslehurst, Laura ext 8916
Jones, Emma ext 8914
Rance, Nichola ext 8918
Scott-Cowan, Pippa ext 8907
PSOs
Davies, Natalie ext 8920
Evans, Paula ext 8917
Hale, Phillip ext 8936
James, Claire ext 8903
Shemwell, Karen ext 8943
Programmes
Gibbins, Chantal (Team Mgr) ext 8929

PSOs
Haines, Beth ext 8905
Norgrove, Ross ext 8902
Boden, Emma ext 8909
Coleman, Phillip ext 8935
Fox, Lyn ext 8909
Unpaid Work
Evans, Lyn (Team Mgr) ext 8929
Victim Liaison
Kirby, Alison (PSO) ext 8925

24. Ground Floor, Plas y Fynnon
Cambrian Way
Brecon LD3 7HP
Tel: (01874) 614150 Fax: (01874) 610602
Fields, Dave (p, tm mgr)
Craig, Graham (PO)
Goulding, Dave (PO)
Davies, Donna (PSO)

25. Merthyr Tydfil Youth Offending Team
Merthyr CBC Youth Justice
47–48 Pontmorlais Centre
Merthyr Tydfil CF47 8UN
Tel: (01685) 389304 Fax: (01685) 359726

Webber, Stephanie (Seconded PO)

26. Rhondda Youth Offending Team
Unit 2, Fairway Court, Tonteg Road
Treforst Industrial Estate, Pontypridd
CF37 5UA
Tel: (01443) 827300 Fax:(01443) 827301

Owen, Robert (Seconded PO)
Smith, Rachel (Seconded PO)
Phillips, Leah (Seconded PSO)
27. Swansea, Neath, Port Talbot &
Bridgend Local Delivery Unit
Tremains House
Tremains Road, Bridgend CF31 1TZ
Tel: (01656) 674700 Fax: (01656) 674702
Direct dial (01656) 67 + ext
Blower, Dawn (ACE) ext 4748
Burridge, Marc (PA) ext 4766
Evans, Shelley (PA) ext 4775
Kenny, Joscelin (p) (based at 28)
Percival, Bev (Bus Mgr) ext 4728

Offender Management
Girton, Tracey (Team Manager) ext 4757
Mason, Deanne (Team Manager) ext
4771

POs
Hood, Maree ext 4722
Jury, Caren ext 4724
Williams, Emma ext 4805
Witts, Adrian ext 4777

Williams, Lynne ext 4727
Wybron, Steph ext 4791
Williams, Tara ext 4739
King, Laura ext 4837
Walton, Helen ext 4734

PSOs
Phillips, Rebecca ext 4706
Drinkwater, Sian ext 4716
Nye, Kelly ext 4788
Powell, Val ext 4707
Gwilliam, Pen ext 4740
Roche, Ann ext 4730
Yeates, Lauren ext 4838
Yip, Debra ext 4708
Lloyd, Sue ext 4736
Burridge, Lynne (PO) 679591

Programmes
Edwards, Meinir (TM) 02920 785035
(based at office 2)
Perriam, Helen (Treatment Monitor) ext
4712
James, Karen (Programmes
Administrator) ext 4721

PSOs
Clarke, Rob ext 4703
Llewellyn, Lisa ext 4720
Wybron, Nicola ext 4704

POs
James, Paul ext 4795
Thomas, Donna ext 4819
Wanklyn, Delyth ext 4710

PSOs
Lee, Peter ext 4704
Budge, Steve ext 4721
Lewis, Hannah ext 4720

Unpaid Work
Goodman, Gail (Team Manager) ext 4725
Francis, Sean (PSO) ext 4825
Galvin, Sue (PSO) ext 4705
Woolcock, Mark (Placement Officer) ext
4816

28. West Glamorgan House
12 Orchard Street **Swansea** SA1 5AD
Tel: (01792) 645505 Fax: (01792) 478132
direct dial (01792) 478 / 479 + ext

Richards, Tony (ACE) ext 159
Kenny, Joscelin (PA) ext 318
Thomas, Kate (Bus Mgr) ext 335
Dyer, Charlotte (Business Dev Mgr) ext
183
Offender Management
Team Managers
Roberts, Colette ext 323

Stephens, Jo ext 392
Lewis, Catrin ext 324
Turner, Monica ext 398

POs
Malik, Iqbal ext 175
Williams, Peter 344
Young, Joanna ext 167
Collins, Nicola ext 319
Rees, Julie ext 303
Evans, Heather 130
Banner, Helen ext 116
Evans, Heather ext 115
Reynolds, Andrew ext 393
Roberts, Shida ext 169
Metcalf, Angharad ext 102
Edwards, Suzanne (PSO) ext 105
Miles, Nicholas ext 394
Tyler, Susan (p) ext 327
Morgans, Leon ext 328
Humphreys, Sian (p) ext 320
Hurren, Jackie ext 125
Allen, Mike ext 182
Lewis, Audra ext 189
Nantel, Caroline ext 157
Protheroe, Tammy ext 345
Walsh, Jed ext 101
Edwards, Jeanne ext 196
Lewis, Rebecca ext 181
Carley, Michael ext 331
Macdonald-Mohan, Melissa ext 304
Trinder, Joel ext 164
Matthews, Jonathan ext 183

PSOs
Mobbs, Susan (p) ext 326
Jones, Jayne (p) ext 317
Meadowcroft, Sarah ext 309
Fox, Melanie ext 198
Thomas, Nicola ext 160
Jones, Ian ext 358
Jones, Teresa ext 156
Sparks, Ian ext 170
Reece, Karan ext 174
Scullion, Rachel ext 315
Reece, Karan ext 174
Programmes
Driscoll, Wayne (Team Mgr) ext 348
Lewis, Hannah (PSO / Treatment
Monitor) ext 354
Progs Tutors
Lee, Peter ext 356
Budge, Stephen ext 350
Davies, Dorian ext 357
Hazzard, Karl ext 333
Frame, Susan ext 359
Owen, Neil, ext 312
Victim Liaison

Lewis, Helen (VLO) ext 334
Lloyd, Susan (VLO) ext no ext
Court Services
Purchase, Sue (Team Mgr) ext 302

PSOs
Matthews, Fred ext
Steadman, Joanne ext
Flowers, Greg ext
Williams, Kerry ext
Richards, Susan ext
Richards, Claire ext
Michelle Porter (PO) ext 115
Unpaid Work
Goodman, Gail (Team Mgr) ext 171
Morse-Jones, Simon (Placement Officer) ext 112
Davies, Ian ext 107
Howells, Simon ext 127
Thomas, Jane ext 222
Grimes, Sarah ext 103
Neath/Port Talbot District
Nicholls, Rob (Team Mgr) ext 324

POs
Stringer, Susan ext 130
Hoyles, Lee ext 313
Rowlands, Emma-Jane ext 110
Davies, Wynne ext 179
Stringer, Susan ext 109

PSOs
Kovacs, Tina ext 343
Llewelyn, Einir ext 308

29. Bridgend Magistrates Court
Sunnyside Bridgend CF31 4AJ
Tel: 01656 673800
Jones, Anna (Court pso) 01656 640940
Thomas, Lindsey (Court pso) 01656 640940
30. Neath/Port Talbot Court
(01639) 765951 (Neath) (Mon/Wed/Fri)
(01639) 894064 (Port Talbot)
(Tues-Thurs)
31. Swansea Crown Court
St Helens Road, Swansea SA1 4PF
Tel: (01792) 461381 Fax: (01792) 457783

32. Bridgend Youth Offending Team
Tremains House, Tremains Road
Bridgend CF31 1TZ
Tel: (01656) 657243 Fax:(01656) 648218
Dyer, Caroline (Manager)
Morgan, Daniel (Operational Manager)
Thomas, Sianelen (PO)
33. Neath Port Talbot Youth Offending Team
Cramic Way, Port Talbot SA13 1RU

Tel: (01639) 885050 Fax: (01639) 882809
34. Swansea Youth Offending Team
Llwyncelyn Campus
Cockett Road, Cockett
Swansea SA2 0SJ
Tel: (01792) 522800 Fax: (01792) 522805
James, Barbara (seconded PO)
Kerr, Bridget (seconded PO)

35. South Wales Area MAPPA Unit
Public Protection Bureau
Police HQ, Cowbridge Road
Bridgend CF31 3SU
Tel: (01656) 306043/48 Fax:(01656) 303464
Rees, Nigel (MAPPA Mgr Co-ord)
Higgins, Bernard (dep MAPPA Mgr Co-ord)
Admin
Francis, Kate
Metcalfe, Chris
O'Brien, Carole
Richards, Lynda

Approved Premises (Hostels)
Lundbech, Dave (AP Services Officer)

36.West Wales Local Delivery Unit
Lloyd Street
Llanelli SA15 2UP
Tel: (01554) 773736 Fax: (01554) 758491
Evans, Eirian (ACE)
Osowicz, Deborah (Dep ACE)
Thomas, Deborah (EA)
Lovell, Rhian (Team Manager)
Hyett, Wendy (Team Manager)
James, Catrin (Business Manager)

POs
Davies, Catherine
Brennan, Jackie
Brenton, Liz (Secondment)
Jenkins, Georgina
Creed, Martyn
Jones, Dave
Thomas, Lowri Angharad
Worth, Tracey
Williams, Hannah

PSOs
Harries, Christine
Jenkins, Tim
McDowell, Kirsty
Lester, Michelle L
Cuthell, Keith
Belton, Mike (Programmes)
Bouleghlimat, Janet (Programmes)
Rees-Thomas, Michelle (Programmes)
Freshwater, Ian (Programmes)

Waters, Sian (Programmes)

37.7a-7b Water Street
Carmarthen SA31 1PY
Tel: (01267) 222299 Fax: (01267) 222164
Matthews, Jon (Team Mgr)

POs
Jones, Jayne
Morgan, Debbie
Hiscocks, Karen (p)
Kettle, Emily Jayne
Parker, Claire (p)

PSOs
Burd, Judith
John, Gaye (p)
King, Rosemary (PSO, Programmes)
Phillips, Clare (p, PSO, Victims Officer)
Glasson, Steven (CWO)

38. High Street, Haverfordwest
Haverfordwest SA61 2DA
Tel: (01437) 762013 Fax: (01437) 765423
Linck, Jacquie (UPW Team Manager)
Wakelam, Ruth (Team Manager)
Osuji, Iain (Team Manager)
Caveille, Loraine (Programmes Manager)
Summers, Keri (Business Manager)

POs
Brown, Nicola (p)
Chappill, Frank (p)
Jones, Gary
Horner, James
James, Kerri Diane (p)
Jarvis, Tara

PSOs
Bowen, Elizabeth
Hier, Emma
Turner, Vicky
Norman, Julie
Maguire, Allan (p, PSO, Programmes)
Giacci, Blanche (PSO, Programmes)
Inglesant, Bob (PSO, Programmes)
Jenkins, Jean Myfanwy (CWO)

39. 23 Grays Inn Road, Aberystwyth
Aberystwyth SY23 1DE
Tel: (01970) 636460 Fax: (01970) 624713
Alman, Mark (Team Manager)
Frisby, Daniel (PO, p, YOS)

POs
Spencer, Lesley
Rennie, Gemma
Simpson, Laura (p)

PSOs
Davies, Julian

Price, Jane
Davies, Ruth (PSO Victims Officer)

40. Carmarthenshire Youth Offending Team
West End, Llanelli, Carmarthenshire SA15 3DN
Tel: (01554) 740120 Fax: (01554) 740122
Owen, Robert (Seconded PO)

41 Pembrokeshire Youth Offending Team
County Hall, North Wing, Freemans Way
Haverfordwest, Pembrokeshire
SA61 1TP Tel: 01437 776038/776040
Brosnan, Mark (Seconded PO)

42. Ceredigion Youth Offending Service
Ceredigion County Council
Canolfan Rheidol, Rhodfa Padarn,
Nr Llanbadarn Fawr Aberystwyth SY23 3UE
Telephone: 01970 633730
Frisby, Daniel (p, Seconded PO)
Brosnan, Mark (p, Seconded PO)

43. MAPPA Unit
Dyfed-Powys Police Headquarters
Llangunnor Road, Carmarthen SA31 2PF
Tel:(01267) 226154 Fax: (01267) 226054
mappa@dyfed-powys.pnn.police.uk
Edwards, Andrew (MAPPA co-ord)

44. Wrexham, Flintshire & North Powys Local Delivery Unit
Ellice Way, Wrexham Technology Park
Wrexham LL13 7YX
Tel: (01978) 346200 Fax: (01978) 346206
Williams, Judith (ACE)
Owen, Tracey (Deputy LDU Head)
Jones, Toni (PA)
Garvey, Margaret (Bus Mgr)
Haggett, Carol (Trainee Forensic Psychologist)
Hughes, Sharon (Team Mgr)
Ryan, Jane (Team Mgr)

POs
Clarke, Jonathan
Croft, Katherine
Maggs, Christopher
McKenzie, Kirsten
Moon, Kelly
Mooney, Claire
Partington, Michelle
Pawulska, Jacqui
Preece, Llinos (p)
Shepherd, Julie
Smith,Kate

Webster, Frances
Woolford, Elen

PSOs
Davies, Patrick
Farrington, Rebecca
Hodgson, Nicky
Jones, Tracey
Owen, Elain
Woolford-Tab, Ffion
Davies, Teresa (PSO Progs)
Griffiths, Myfanwy (PSO Progs)
Joubert, Penny (PSO Progs)
Nicholls, Sian (PSO Progs)
Stach, Halina (PSO Progs)

Court Team East
Conway, Angela (Team Mgr)
Evans, Edwyn (p, PO)

PSOs
Arrowsmith, Stuart
Connah, Andrew
Mitchell, Emma (p)
Roberts,Pamela

Unpaid Work Community Payback
Purton, Richard (Team Mgr)
CSOs
Davies, Chris (p)
Harry, Brian
Hayes, Gillian
Lloyd, David
Hickman, Tracey
Richards, Sharon

45. Unit 6, Acorn Business Centre
Flint Flintshire CH6 5YN
Tel: 01352 792140 Fax: (01352 792141)
Brett, Emma (Team Mgr)

POs
Evans, Tracey (p)
Hooley, Emily
Humphries, Kat (p)
Lord, Christine
Ceri Maggs (p)
Murphy, Mike
Potts, Darren (p)
Roberts, Lynsey (p)
Thompson, Rachael

PSOs
Jones, Ceri (p)
Salazar, Annie
Wyn, Mair

46. Straight Lines House
New Road Newtown SY16 1BD
Tel: (01686) 611900 Fax: (01686) 611901
Arrowsmith, Stevie (Tm Mgr)

POs
Crewe, Trish
Jarman, Nicola
Jones, Hannah
Taylor, Helena
Brown, Anna-Marie (PSO)
Sandford, Tracy (PSO, Programmes)
Hickman, Tracey (CSO)

47. Crown Courts
Mold Crown Court
Law Courts, Civic Centre
Mold CH7 1AE
Tel & Fax: (01352) 751649

48. Flintshire Youth Offending Team
6th Floor, County Hall
Mold Flintshire CW7 5BD
Tel: (01352) 702603 Fax: (01352) 750601
Laing, Angharad (Seconded PO)

49. Wrexham Youth Offending Team
Unit 21, Whitegate Industrial Estate
Caia Park Wrexham LL13 8UG
Tel: (01978) 268140 Fax: (01978) 268169
Duckett, Sarah (seconded PO)

50. DIP Regional Commissioning Team
24 Wynnstay Road, Colwyn Bay, Conwy, LL29 8NE
Ffon/Tel: 01492 539780
Ffacs/Fax: 01492 535069
Playle, Katy Regional DIP Manager 07799697510
McKenna, Lisa – DIP Data Manager 07717766169
Edwards, Audrey – DIP Business Administrator 07904293533

51. Drug Interventions Programme (DIP)
"Hafod", 21 Grosvenor Road
Wrexham LL11 1BT
Tel: (01978) 366941 Fax: (01978) 366945

52. 10–12 Salisbury Street
Shotton, Flintshire CH5 1DR
Tel: (01244) 845920 Fax: (01244) 836483

53. Porthmadog Multi Agency Building
Uned A7 / Unit A7
Parc Busnes Penamser / Penamser Business Park
Porthmadog, Gwynedd LL49 9GB
Ffon/Tel: 01766 510280
Ffacs/Fax: 01766 512937

54. Caernarfon Criminal Justice Centre
Llanberis Street
Caernarfon, Gwynedd
LL55 2DF
Tel: (01286) 669700 Fax: (01286) 669797

55. MAPPA Unit
Crimes Services Division
North Wales Police
Ffordd William Morgan
St Asaph LL17 0HQ
Tel: 01745 588649 Fax: 01745 588648
Clark, Carolyn (Team Mgr – MAPPA/VLU)
Ellis, Paula (Admin)

Approved Premises (Hostels)

56. Plas y Wern Approved Premises
Ruabon, Llangollen Road. Nr Wrexham
LL14 6RN
Tel: (01978) 814949 Fax:(01978) 810435

Hughes, Sharon (Team Mgr)
Evans, Helen (Bus Admin)
Forster, Ceri (RSO)
Higgins, Gareth (RSO)
Hughes, Donna (PSO)
Scott-Melville, Ricky (RSO)
Thomas, Paula (RSO)
Barnes Bridgette (RSO)
Hughes, Joanna

57. Ty Newydd Approved Premises
Llandygai Road
Bangor, Gwynedd LL57 4HP
Tel: (01248) 370529 Fax: (01248) 371204
Marston, Joanna (Team Mgr)
Cox, Karen (Admin)
Jones, Tina (PSO)
Phillips, Len (PSO)
RSOs
Jones, Emma
Jones, Hefina
Sawicz, Phillip
Williams, Emyr
Williams, Gwenno

58. Mandeville House Hostel
9 Lewis Street, Canton
Cardiff CF11 6JY
Tel: 029 2039 4592 & 029 2023 2999 ext 4530
Fax:029–2023 3857
Higgins, Bernard (Team Mgr)
Taylor, Phil (PO)
AP Services Officers
Barrett, Nicola

Davies, Siobhan
Driscoll, Janice
Griffiths, Stuart
Lundbech, Dave

59. Quay House Probation Hostel
The Strand, Swansea SA1 2AW
Tel: (01792) 641259 Fax: (01792) 641268
Higgins, Bernard (Team Mgr)
Long, Peter (PO)
AP Services Officers
Frudd, Andrew
Oakley, Angela
Newcombe, Jeff
Powell, Andrew
Williams, Nigel

Institutions

60. HM Prison
Knox Road, Cardiff CF24 1UG
Tel: 029 2092 3100 Fax 029 2092 3318
Winston, Emma (Team Mgr)

POs
Davies, Gavin
Enos, Estella
Griffiths, Angharad
Rees, Sian
Wareham, Robert
Bailey, Jon (PSO)
Evans, Margaret (PSO)

61. HM Prison Parc
Heol Hopcyn John, Bridgend CF35 6AR
Tel: (01656) 300200 Fax: (01656) 300201
McAllister, Wil (Team Mgr)
Lewis, Amanda (PO)
Preece, Gail (PO)
Clinton, Lisa (PSO)

62. HM Prison
Oystermouth Road **Swansea** SA1 3SR
Tel: (01792) 485300 Fax: (01792) 632979
Gannon, Charisse (PO)
Barker, Jenny (PSO)
Thomas, Sharon (PSO)

63. H M Prison, 47 Maryport Street
Usk NP15 1XP
Tel: (01291) 671600 Direct dial (01291) 67 + ext
Fax: (01291) 671752
Hopkins, Michelle (PO) ext 3694
Sheppard, David (PO) ext 3693

64. H M Prison
Prescoed, Coed-y-Paen
Nr Pontypool NP4 0TB

Tel: (01291) 675000 Direct dial (01291) 67
+ ext
Fax: (01291) 675158
Daniel, Peter (PSO) ext 5118

Local Justice Areas
Cardiff
Cynon Valley
Merthyr Tydfil
Miskin
Newcastle & Ogmore
Neath Port Talbot
Swansea County
Vale of Glamorgan
Carmarthen
Ceredigion
De Brycheiniog
De Maldwyn
Dinefwr
Llanelli
North Pembrokeshire
Radnorshire & N Brecknock
South Pembrokeshire
Welshpool
NW Gwent
SE Gwent
Anglesey/Ynys Mon
Conwy
Denbighshire
Flintshire
Gwynedd
Wrexham Maelor

Crown Courts
Cardiff
Merthyr Tydfil
Swansea
Carmarthen
Haverfordwest
Caernarfon
Mold

PROBATION BOARD FOR NORTHERN IRELAND

Emergency out of hours contact point
02890565795

Headquarters
80/90 North Street, Belfast BT1 1LD
Tel: 028 9026 2400 Fax:

McCaughey, Brian (Dir)
van der Merwe, David (Deputy Dir)
Canavan, Maura (Asst Dir Finance)
Doran, Paul (Deputy Dir)
Robinson, Gillian (Head of HR)
Hamill, Hugh (Asst Dir)

Lamont, Cheryl (Deputy Dir)
McGreevy, Gail (Asst Dir, Comms)
Muldoon, Roisin (Asst Dir)
Moss, Peter (Sec to the Board)
McCutcheon, Brian (IT Mgr)
Cooper, Louise (Asst Dir)
McIlroy, Eithne (Asst Dir)

Assessment Unit
Tel: 028 9026 2400

McCusker, Paul (Area Mgr)
Carville, Carol (Acting Area Mgr)

POs
Farrelly, Ciaran
Greer, Bill
Taylor, Siobhan
McKee, Chris
Vaughan, Fiona
Sheppard, Paul
Winnington, Michael
Cavan, Mary
Stirling, Miss Mairi (p)
Cassidy, Joanne
White, Jennifer
Finn, Maighread (Fixed Term)
McKibbon, Fiona (Fixed Term)

PSOs
McIlveen, Paul
Gilliland, Claire (p)
McGarvey, Alistair

Psychology Department
Tel: 028 9026 2408

O'Hare, Geraldine (Principal Psych)
Houston, Aileen (Trainee Forensic
Psych)
Jordan, Robin (Trainee Forensic Psych)
McCann, Louisa (Trainee Forensic
Psych)
Twigg, Samantha (Trainee Forensic
Psych-Fixed Term)
Crawford, Nichola (Trainee Forensic
Psych-Fixed Term)
Fleming, Cassie (Psych Assistant)
Reid, Rebecca (Psych Assistant)

330 Ormeau Road
Belfast BT7 2GE
Tel: 028 9064 7156

Hunter, Christine (Area Mgr)
Maguire, Catherine (Area Mgr)
Graham, Joan (Area Mgr)
Grant, Deirdre (Area Mgr) (Community
Lifer Management)

POs
Woods, Geraldine
McClinton, Ms Janet
McKenna, Lorraine
Quail, Moira
Shaw, Stephen
Mawhinney, Nicola (FixedTerm)
McDermott, Alana (Fixed Term)
Moore, Laura (Fixed Term)
Pitman, Val (Awards Officer – Duke of Ed)

Unit 4 Wallace Studios
27 Wallace Avenue
Lisburn BT27 4AE
Tel: 028 9267 4211

POs
Robinson-McDonald, Rosaleen
Wylie, Margaret
Watters, Eilis (PSO)
Mills, Stephanie
Best, Paul (CSS-Fixed Term)
Semple, Claire (Fixed Term)

306 Antrim Road
Belfast BT15 5AB
Tel: 028 9075 7631

Nicholson, Mark (Area Mgr)

POs
Mulholland, Catherine
Bell, Sarah-Jane
Harvey, Laura
Reynolds, Aisling (p)
Smith, Mark
Quiery, Niamh (Fixed Term)
Cahill, Maria (PSO)
Wray, Steven (CSS)
Bowers, Colin (CSS-Fixed Term)
Milburn, Rhonda (PSO)
Lennon, Anthony
Potts, Gordon (PSO)
Gregg, Catherine (PO-Fixed Term)
McCartney, Nikki (PSO-Fixed Term)
McCusker, Sarah (PO)
Maitland, Jennifer (PO-Fixed Term)
Henry, Alan (PO-Fixed Term)
Kerr, Edel (PO-Fixed Term)
O'Boyle, Keelin (PO-Fixed Term)
McCann, Fergal (CSS)

Unit 5 Antrim Technology Park
Belfast Road Antrim BT41 1QS
Tel: 028 9448 0140

Learning & Development Centre
McAllister, Lesley (L&D Manager)

POs
O'Neill, Noreen
Pegg, Jackie
McMillan, Pauline

Glenshane House

202a Andersonstown Road
Belfast BT11 9EB
Tel: 028 9060 2988

Connolly, Mike (Area Mgr)
McKenna, Gloria (PO)
Kelly, Dessie (PO)
McGeough, Patrick (CSS)
Breen, Siobhan (PO)
McCarthy, Vincent (PO)
Maitland, Michael (PSO)
Moore, Geraldine (PO)
Power, Michelle (PO)
Scullion, Deirdre (PO-Fixed Term)
Gray, John (CSS)

297 Newtownards Road
Belfast BT4 1AG
Tel: 028 9073 9445

Lappin, Jane (Area Mgr)
Bailie, Kathryn (PO)
Simpson, Leanne (PO) (p)
Wainwright, Nicola (PO) (p)
Cooke, Norman (CSS) (p)
Cummings, Kyle (PO)
Ferguson, Michael (PO-Fixed Term)
Cochrane, Tom (CSS)
Nicholl, Irene (PSO)
Morrow, Kate (PSO) (p)
McCartney, Catherine (PSO-Fixed Term)
Finlay, Gemma (PO-Fixed Term)
Marner, Tom (CSS)

15 Castle Street
Newtownards BT23 3PA
Tel: 028 9181 7778
Cahir, Seamus (PO)
McCreery, David (PSO)
Burrows, John (CSS)
Doran, Marie (PO-Fixed Term)

2 Church Street
Downpatrick BT30 6EJ
Tel: 028 4461 4061

Reporting centre only

POs
Donnelly, Lynn

MacNeill, Eoin
Cooper, Amanda (Fixed Term)

12 Lodge Road
Coleraine BT52 1NB
Tel: 028 7035 3141
Dorsett, Ms Caroline
Nelis, Liam (PSO) (split loc)
Quigley, Mrs Marlyn (PSO)
Penn, Chris (CSS)
Quigg, Martina (PO)
Stewart, Denise (PO)
Archibald, Selina (PO) (p)

3 Wellington Court
Ballymena BT43 6EQ
Tel: 028 2565 2549
Doherty, Terry (Assist Dir)
Rodgers, Brigie (Proj Mgr)
Nelis, Liam (PSO) (Split loc)
Lees, Raymond (PO)
Adams, Bridgeen (PO)Tweed, Stephen (CSS)
Gray, John (CSS) Split loc
McMullan, Joanne (PSO)
McCartney, Nikki (PSO-Fixed Term)
Wilkinson, Stephen (PSO)
McWilliams, Jacqueline (Project Worker)
Dempsey, Colin (PO)
McKee, Mary (PO) (p)

8 Crawford Square
Londonderry BT48 7HR
Tel: 028 7126 4774
Barr, Nicola (AM)

POs
Clifford, Briege
O'Hagan, John
Millar, Maria
McDaid, Gabrielle
Curran Lisa
Quigley, Michael

7 Limavady Road
Londonderry BT47 1JU
Tel: 028 7134 6701
O'Kane, John (AM)
Dunlop, Raymond (PO)
Weir, Adam (PO) (ISU)
Higgins, Michael (PO) (ISU)
Ferguson, Liam (PSO)
Duffy, John (CSS)
Doherty, John (CSS)
Reid, Louise (PSO)
Hawes, Shauna (PO-Fixed Term)
Cunningham, Bernie (PO)

38 Fountain Street
Antrim BT41 4BB
Tel: 028 9442 8475
Reporting Centre

Seapark, 151 Belfast Road
Carrickfergus BT38 8PL
Tel: 028 9025 9576

Public Protection Team
Thompson, Paul (Area Mgr)

POs
McGlade, Ian
Carswell, Lyn
McKee, Mary

1d Monaghan Street
Newry BT35 6BB
Tel: 028 3026 3955
Leckey, Roisin (AM) (p)
Doran, Mrs Mary (PO)
McEvoy, Niall (PO)
Duffy, Damien (PO)
Bedard, Beverly (PSO)
Gray, James (CSS) (p)
Mageean, Fianait (PO Fixed Term)

12 Church Street
Portadown BT62 3LQ
Tel: 028 3833 3301
Hamilton, Stephen (AM)

POs
Atkinson, Emma
Cunningham, Victoria (p)
Cousins, Mrs Joanne
Doyle, Fergal
McAnallen, Annie
Woods, Lorraine (PSO)
Lyle, Stephen (CSS)
Grant, Jill (PO)
Powell, Gary (PSO)
Draffin, Julie (PO Fixed Term)
Chambers, Iris (PO Fixed Term)
Tracey, Claire (PO Fixed Term)

11a High Street
Omagh BT78 1BA
Tel: 028 8224 6051

McKeever, Patricia (Area Mgr)
Brady, Julie (PO) (p)
McKelvey, Ruth (PO) (p)
Nash, Paul (PO)
McGurk, Oonagh (PO)
Devlin, Peter (CSS)
McCausland, Neil (CSS)

14 Dublin Road Cathcart Square
  Enniskillen BT74 6HH
  Tel: 028 6632 4383 Carty, Selina (PO)
  Lattimore, Collette (PO) (p)
  Nealon, Bernadette (PO)
  Young, David (PO)
  Stevenson, Will (CSS)

Kirk Avenue
  Magherafelt BT45 6BT
  Tel: 028 7963 3341
  Montgomery, Miss Gillian (AM)

  POs
  Feeney, Ms Geraldine
  McLaughlin, Terry
  Grant, Michelle
  Campbell, Moire
  Wylie, Lorraine
  McMullan, Mrs Joanne (PSO)
  Wilkinson, Stephen (PSO)
  Loughran, Eddie (CSS)

30 Northland Row
  Dungannon BT71 6AP
  Tel: 028 8772 2866
  Flynn, Susan (PO)
  Devlin, Fiona (PSO)
  McCoy, Kristina (PO Fixed Term)

25 College Street
  Armagh BT61 9BT
  Tel: 028 3752 5243
  Devlin, Paul (Area Mgr ISU)
  Brecknell, Patricia (PO)
  Bailie Gael (PO) (ISU Rural)
  Teague, Grainne (PO) (ISU Rural)
  Rural Programmes Team
  Donaldson, Victor (PSO)
  Abernethy, Ms Jayne (PSO)
  Fitzpatrick, Anthony (PSO)
  Morrow, Kate (p, PSO)

40–44 Great Patrick Street
  Belfast BT1 2LT
  Tel: 028 9033 3332

  Programme Delivery Unit
  Moore, Jimmy (Area Mgr)
  O'Laughlin, Kathryn (Acting Area Mgr)
  (ISU)
  Bailie, Rosemary (AM – ISU)
  Arthur, Liz (AM) (ISU)

  POs
  Bell, Lesley (p)
  Kane, Deborah
  Lenzi, Shauneen

Barry, Mrs Patricia (ISU)
Loughran, Emer (ISU)
Duffy, Colum (ISU)
Graham, Brian (ISU)
Hall, Julie (PO-Fixed Term) (ISU)
Johnston, Emma
Belshaw, Stephen (ISU)
McMahon, Fergal (ISU)
Watson, Gary (PSO)
Campbell, Pamela (ISU)
Taylor, Claire
Crawley, Declan (ISU)
McConnell, Rachael (ISU)
Osborne, Clare (ISU)

  PSOs
  Kelly, Mrs Donna
  Rainey, Stuart
  Nelson, Claire
  McGeoghegan, Fiona
  Maher, Kitty
  Cahill, Philip (p)
  Wright, Anne (p)
  Scroggie, Shauna

Alderwood House
(Integrated Supervision Unit)
  Hydebank Wood Purdysburn Road
  Belfast BT8 7SL
  Tel: 028 9064 4953
  McGibbon, Gareth (Programmes
  Manager)
  Malone, Ms Kerry (Programmes
  Manager)

  POs
  McSherry, Mrs Tina
  Mullan, Ms Brigeen
  Armstrong, Nicola
  Watson, Ms Sarah
  Tracey, Damien
  McElnea, Miss Siobhan (ISU)
  Sands, Caroline
  McVeigh, Josie (PCO)

Victims Unit
  Office 40 Imperial Buildings
  72 High Street Belfast BT1 2BE
  Tel: 028 9032 1972

  POs
  Lamb, Linda
  Smith, Helen (p)
  Weir, Stephanie

Youth Justice Team
  North Street 028 90262483
  Ormeau Road 028 90647156

Andersonstown Road 028 90602988
North Street
McKenna, Jane (AM)
Paterson, Carolyn (Acting Area Manager)
McClenaghan, Joe (PCO)
Forsythe, Claire (PSO)
Ormeau Road
Clarke, Niamh (PO) (p)
Andersonstown Road
Richmond Emma (PO)

Institutions

HMP Magilligan
Co Londonderry BT49 0LR
Tel: 028 7775 0434/5
Smyth, Miss Julie (Area Mgr)

POs
Holmes, Paula
Quigley, Michael
Devlin, Ms Anne
Clarke, Jenni
McClay, Alison (p)
Monaghan, Siobhan
Turner, Seanagh
McNicholl, Sally
McLaughlin, Kevin
Dempsey, Kirsteen
Wiseman, Paul

HMP/YOI Hydebank Wood
Hospital Road Belfast BT8 8NA
Tel: 028 9049 1015
Davies, Chris (Area Mgr)

POs
Calvin, Marilyn
Sinnamon, Karen
McKee, Ms Briege
Coogan, Nicola
McKelvey, Claire (p)
Spence, Melissa

HMP Maghaberry
17 Old Road Upper Ballinderry
Lisburn BT28 2PT
Tel: 028 9261 2665
Simpson, Simone (AM)

POs
Brannigan, Oonagh
Conlon, John
Noade, Deirdre (p)
O'Neill, Oonagh
Quigley John
Willighan, Stephen
Connolly, Gary
Smyth, Stephanie
Sloan, Allison

Haslett, Andrea
Rooke, Genni
White, Philippa
McAuley, Nicola
Mills, Rory
Quinn, Nuala
McCann, Dermot (p)
Hopkins, Shirley

Inspire Project
72 North Street Belfast BT1 1LD
Tel: 028 9026 2515
O'Neill, Jean (AM)

POs
Richardson, Eileen
Mullan, Nuala
Murphy, Christine
Nicholson, Jacqueline
Doran, Andrea

On secondment
Lennox, Julie (PO)
McRoberts, Claire (Area Mgr)

On career break
POs
Bartlett, Patricia
Christie, Trisha
Mooney, Ms Angela
Shearer, Jill
Ramsey, Angela
Cunningham, Julie
Rutledge, Ali
Hobson, Bronwyn
Hill, Kieran
McGurnaghan, Gayle (AD)

REPUBLIC OF IRELAND
THE PROBATION SERVICE
AN TSEIRBHÍS PHROMHAIDH

All queries from outside the jurisdiction email internationaldesk@probation.ie

Abbreviations

APPO	Assistant Principal Probation Officer
SPO	Senior Probation Officer
APO	Assistant Principal Officer
HEO	Higher Executive Officer
EO	Executive Officer
YPP	Young Persons' Probation

Where no letters appear after a name, that person is a Probation Officer.

Dialing from UK 00 (international code) 353 (country code) and omit the first 0 of the local code (so, for example, Haymarket, Smithfield Officer 00 353 1 8173600.

Headquarters
Haymarket
Smithfield
Dublin 7
Tel: 01 817 3600 Fax: 01 872 2737

Geiran, Vivian (Dir)
Vacancy (Dir of Operations)
Vella, Suzanne (Dir of Corp Affairs/HR)
Dack, Brian (Asst Dir of Operations)
Gerry McNally (Asst Dir of Operations & Adult Community Supervision
Cooney, Paula (APPO, Risk Settlement & Prisoners)

Information & Statistics Unit
Brennan, Natasha (EO, Info IT)
Gormley. Aidan (Statistician)
Sweeney, Bill (EO, Info Mgr)
Burke, Eibhlis (Admin)

Haymarket
Smithfield Dublin 7
Tel: 01 817 3600 Fax: 01 872 2737

International Desk
Hanna, Emer (SPO)
Kennedy, Geraldine (Admin, Ops)
Email: internationaldesk@probation.ie

Community Funded Projects & Community Service Directorate
Dack, Brian (Asst Dir Community Service & Funded Projects)
Connolly, Anna (APPO Community Service)
Mc Donnell Paul (APO Community Programme Unit)

Funded Projects Team
Cornish, Simon (EO)
Kenny, Maurice (Admin)
Mansfield, Andrew (Admin)

Community Service Unit – Haymarket
Brennan, Claire (SPO)
McGuire, Leah
Kelly, Conor
O'Connor, Joan
Croghan, Paul
McCarthy, Justin

Zagibova, Danica
Higgins, Lilibeth (HEO)
Cummings, Yvonne (Admin)
McGovern, Linda (Admin)

Corporate Services & HR Directorate
Corporate Services
Hanney, Christine (APO)
Lally, Paul (HEO & Estate Mgmt)
Treacy, Patricia (EO)
Mooney, Graham (EO)
Thompson, Sean (Admin)
King, Eileen (EO)
Lynagh, Suzanne (Admin)
Gavagan, Mags (Admin)
Martin, Monica (Admin)

HR
Burke, Ita (APPO HR)
Wade, Linda (HEO)
Cawley, Leona (Admin)

Finance Unit
Callanan, Valerie (Accountant)
Geoghegan, Brian (EO)
Grimes, Carmel (Admin)
Reid, Pauline (Admin)

IT
O'Keeffe, Karen (HEO)
Hensey, Leah (EO)

Operations Unit
Finglas, Keith (Admin)
Kelly, Sarah (Admin to Dir)

Court Reports
Irwin, Paula (Admin Registry)
McPartlan, Lisa (Admin Registry)

Research/Training and Development
Santry, Brian (APPO)

Staff Training & Development Unit
Reade, Ann (SPO)
Christie, Irene
Boland, Maria (Admin)

Dublin South & Wicklow Region
390–396 Clonard Road
Crumlin Dublin 12
Tel: 01 492 5625 Fax: 01 492 5631

Moore, Mary (APPO)

Callery, Dot (Admin)

Haymarket
Smithfield Dublin 7
Tel: 01 817 3600 Fax: 01 872 2737

Dublin Court Liaison Team
Hanna, Emer (SPO)
McCabe, Janice
Donnelly, Declan
O'Halloran, Caoimhe
Anderson, Lisa
Connor, Siobhan

Dublin South Assessment Team
Ansbro, Anne (SPO)
Gates, Paul
Commins, Susan
McCarroll, Jane
Cole, Jennifer
Cotter, Laura
Duffy, Sarah
Broomfield, Darren
Hunt, Sinead

Homeless Offenders Team
O'Donoghue, Elizabeth (SPO)
Kane, Tara
Pickles, Rob
O'Reilly, Dorothy
Keane, Marie Anne
Kelly, Paula

The Cualann Centre
Main Street
Bray Co Wicklow
Tel: 01 204 2662 Fax: 01 204 2663

Wicklow Team
O Brien McNamara, Joan (SPO)
Alvey, Jan
O'Doherty, Anne
Johnston, Elizabeth (Admin)

Over Extra Vision
Wexford Road
Arklow Co Wexford
Tel: 0402 91 066 Fax: 0402 91 114

Wicklow Team
O Brien McNamara, Joan (SPO)
Doyle, Catherine
Murphy, Andrew
Cullen, Anne Marie (Admin)

Le Fanu Road
Ballyfermot Dublin 10
Tel: 01 623 3666 Fax: 01 623 3737

Dublin South Central Team
Macken, Nuala (SPO)
Meenaghan, Fiona
O'Higgins, Muireann
Connaughton, Linda (Admin)

Mark's Lane
Neilstown Road
Clondalkin Dublin 22
Tel: 01 623 6235 Fax: 01 623 6236

Dublin South Central Team
Macken, Nuala (SPO)
Groome, Tommy
Lowde, Sean
Aughney, Brenda (Admin)
Gibson, Marguerite (Admin)

Carmens Hall
Garden Lane (off Catherine Street)
Dublin 8
Tel: 01 709 3530 Fax: 01 709 3539

Dublin South Inner City Team
Foley, Tony (SPO)
McQuaid, Emily
Kavanagh, Siobhan
Clarke, Susan
Clarke, Nicholas
Dardis, Sandra
Krivtsova, Oksana
Murphy, Elaine
O'Neill, Yvonne (Admin)

Westpark Tallaght
Dublin 24
Tel: 01 462 3033 Fax: 01 462 3767

Dublin South West Team
O'Connor, Ciara (SPO)
Algottson, Gallagher, Anna
Cahill, Sharon
Charles, Anita
Kelly, Lorraine
Ward, Liz (Admin)

Foundation House
Northumberland Avenue
Dun Laoghaire Co Dublin
Tel: 01 230 1860 Fax: 01 230 1870

Dublin South East Team
Kelly, Anthony
O'Neill, Martina
Ryan, Mary
Lynch, Gaye (Admin)

Dublin North & North East Region

Haymarket
Smithfield Dublin 7
Tel: 01 817 3600 Fax: 01 872 2737
Wilson, Mark (APPO)

Dublin North Assessment Team
Lillis, Rachel (SPO)
Mulpeter, Maria
Nichol, Derek
Phibbs, Tracey
Dennan, Catriona
Kavanagh, Elaine
McGuigan, Sarah
Finnegan, Sarah

**Intensive Probation Supervision
(Bridge Project) Team**
Williamson, David (SPO)
McGarrigle, Sarah
Stapleton Doyle, Una
Trant, Aidan
Geiran, Elaine (Programme Development
Unit)

Second Floor Office Block
Donaghmede Shopping Centre
Grange Road **Donaghmede**
Dublin 13
Tel: 01 816 6800 Fax: 01 816 6801

Dublin North East Team
Kelly, James (SPO)
Corrigan, John
Dooley, Niamh
Ferguson, Darren
Smith, Eimear
Murphy, Claire
Moore, Karen (Admin)

Block 3 Grove Court
Grove Road **Blanchardstown** Dublin 15
Tel: 01 8662700

Dublin West Team
O'Sullivan, Cathal (SPO)
Purcell, Denise
Murphy, Dave
Odimuke, Victor
Power, Linda
Commins, Pat (Admin)

Haymarket
Smithfield Dublin 7
Tel: 01 817 3600 Fax: 01 872 2737

Dublin North Inner City Team
Williamson, David (SPO)
McArdle, Rita
Loughrey, Sile
Hynes, John

Poppintree Mall
Finglas Dublin 11
Tel: 01 864 4011 Fax: 01 864 3416

Dublin North Central Team
O'Sullivan, Cathal (SPO)
Adesida, Ademilola
Doyle, Barbara
O'Connell, Valerie
Fogarty, Fiona
Glynn, David
Lawlor, Breda (EO)
O'Grady, James (Admin)

St Laurence's Street
Drogheda Co Louth
Tel: 041 980 1580 Fax: 041 980 1583

Government Offices
Millennium Centre
Alphonsus Road **Dundalk**
Co Louth
Tel: 042 933 2163 Fax: 042 933 2501

Louth Team
McDonald, Mary (SPO)
Farry, Neasan
Faulkner, Monica
McAloon, Eadaoin
Norton, Sheena
Codd, Avril (YPP)
O'Malley, Rachel (YPP)
Jordan, Ita (Admin)
Ryan, Joy (Admin)
McKeever, Sinead (Admin)

Government Offices Kilcairn
Navan Co Meath
Tel: 046 909 0941 Fax: 046 909 0142

Meath Team
Quinn, Kerry (SPO)
Brennan, Mary
Kearney, Ian
Wason, Laura
McHugh, Martina (Admin)

Risk, Resettlement & Prisoners' Region

Government Offices
Shannon Lodge
Carrick-on-Shannon Co Leitrim
Tel: 071 9620966 Fax: 071 9621230
Cooney, Paula (APPO)

**Sex Offender & High Risk
Management Team**
Kenny, David (SPO)
Broderick, Geraldine
O'Brien, Tim
Gallahue, Liz

Arbour Hill Prison
Arbour Hill Dublin 7
Tel: 01 671 9519 Fax: 01 671 9565

Arbour Hill Prison & Shelton Abbey Team
Kenny, David (SPO)
Duffy, Paul
Richardson, Michelle
Darragh, Sandra

Shelton Abbey
Arklow Co Wicklow
Tel: 0402 32912 Fax: 0402 39924

Glennon, Ailish (SPO)

Morahan, Marion

Wheatfield Place of Detention
Cloverhill Dublin 22
Tel: 01 620 9437 Fax: 01 620 9457

Wheatfield/Cloverhill Team
Downey, Pauline (SPO)
Kilgannon, David
McNamara, Suzanne
McLaughlin, Ruth
Curtis, Victoria
Molloy, James
O'Neill, Jenny (Admin)

Cloverhill Remand Centre
Cloverhill Road
Clondalkin Dublin 22
Tel: 01 630 4942 Fax: 01 630 4939

Wheatfield/Cloverhill Team
Downey, Pauline (SPO)
Campbell, Fiona
Joyce, Phyllis (Admin)

Mountjoy Prison (Male)
North Circular Road Dublin 7
Tel: 01 806 2834 Fax: 01 830 2712

Mountjoy Male & Training Unit Team
Leetch, Judith (SPO)
Burke, Brigetta
Geary, Anne Marie
Nagle, Susan
Rock, Mark
O'Reilly, Rachel (Admin)

Training Unit Glengarriff Parade
North Circular Road, Dublin 7

Leetch, Judith (SPO)

Bentley, Philip
Taylor, Scarlet

Mountjoy Female Prison
Dochas Centre North Circular Road
Dublin 7
Tel: 01 806 2834 Fax: 01 830 2712

Glennon, Ailish (SPO)

Kinsella, Anne
Morris, Aine
Butler, Lucy
Purcell, Patricia
Gunn, Emma

Midlands Prison
Dublin Road
Portlaoise Co Laois
Tel: 0502 72210 Fax: 0502 72209

Midlands/Portlaoise Prison Team
Matthews, Deirdre (SPO)
Costigan, Marita
Kelly, Marie
Kavanagh, Jane Sarah
Martin, Catriona
Fahey,Caroline
Delahunt, Claire (Admin)

Castlerea Prison
Harristown Castlerea
Co Mayo
Tel/fax: 094 962 5277

Castlerea/Loughan Prison Team
Brett, Maeve (SPO)
Boyle, Olivia
Cahill, John (Admin)

Loughan House
Blacklion Co Cavan
Tel/fax: 072 53026
Cahill, John (Admin)

Castlerea/Loughan Prison Team
Brett, Maeve (SPO)
Lowe, Helen

Cork Prison
Rathmore Road Cork
Tel: 021 4503829 Fax: 021 450 1702

Cork/Limerick Prison Team
Coughlan, Tony (SPO)
O'Farrell, Tim
Murphy, Siobhan (Admin)

Limerick Prison
Mulgrave Street Limerick
Tel: 061 294718 Fax: 061 419812

Cork/Limerick Prison Team
Coughlan, Tony (SPO)
Griffin, Gerry

Young Persons' Probation Region

Haymarket
Smithfield Dublin 7
Tel: 01 817 3600 Fax: 01 872 2737

Regional Manager's Office
Doyle, Una (APPO)

YPP Dublin Court Liaison
Timoney, Lena (SPO)
Trainor, Mary
Hickey, Majella
McFadden, Neil
Gillespie, Eloise

390–396 Clonard Road
Crumlin Dublin 12
Tel: 01 492 5625 Fax: 01 492 5631

YPP Dublin South Team
Kelly, Janice (SPO)
Egan, Amanda
Byrne, Ambrose
Mdingi, Unathi
O'Dwyer, Geraldine
Jones, Anne Marie

Main Street
Ballymun Dublin 9
Tel: 01 842 1810

YPP Dublin North Team
McGagh, Mary (SPO)
Hickey, Bernadette
McCarthy, Elizabeth
Hughes, Alan
O'Toole, Ann-Marie
Brady, Margaret (Admin)

St Laurence's Street
Drogheda Co Louth
Tel: 041 980 1580 Fax: 041 980 1583

St Patrick's Institution
North Circular Road Dublin 7
Tel: 01 806 2941 Fax: 01 830 1261

YPP St Pats
Cronin, Rosemary (SPO)
Milne, Sarah
O'Brien, Maria
Connell, Brian
O'Reilly, Elaine
Ruane, Mary
Smith, Brenda (Admin)

Government Buildings
Cranmore Road **Sligo**
Tel: 071 914 5203 Fax: 071 914 4840

YPP North West
Mannion, John (SPO)
Meehan, Eileen (Admin)

Abbey Arch
8 Upper Abbeygate Street
Galway
Tel: 091 565375 Fax: 091 567286

YPP North West
Mannion, John (SPO)
Brady, Brid
Myles, Bridget

48–50 Lower Main Street
Letterkenny Co Donegal
Tel: 074 912 5264 Fax: 074 912 6008
Connery, Ian (Admin)

Grace Park Road
Athlone Co Westmeath
Tel: 090 648 3500 Fax: 090 647 5843

YPP North West
Mannion, John (SPO)
Meehan, Eileen (Admin)

Theatre Court
15 Lower Mallow Street
Limerick
Tel: 061 206 320 Fax: 061 206 339

YPP Limerick
Brosnahan, John (SPO)
Connolly, Blanaid
Kirwisa, Linda
Murphy, Sean
Moore, Michelle

17 Audley Place
Westview House
St Patricks Hill Cork
Tel: 0214681017

YPP Cork
Fox, Rosemary (SPO)
Buckley, Hilary
Henley, Karen
McCarthy, Ken

YPP Cork Court Liaison Team
O'Connell, Sinead (SPO)
Ahern, Maria
Walsh, Mary

West/North West & Westmeath Region

Grace Park Road
Athlone Co Westmeath
Tel: 090 648 3500 Fax: 090 648 3580
Fernee, Ursula (APPO)
Hannon, Clare (EO)

Westmeath/Longford/Roscommon Team
Gavin, Alma (SPO)
Byrne Fallon, Collette
Ryder, Tom
Leonard, Sinead
Keogh,Valerie
Connolly, Kieran
Ward, Enda (Admin)

Abbey Arch
8 Upper Abbeygate Street
Galway
Tel: 091 565 375 Fax: 091 567 286

Prendergast, Margaret (SPO)
Claffey, Thomas
Brosnan, Catriona
Claffey, Helen
Devine, Corina
Mitchell, Patrick
Flanagan, Marian (Admin)
O'Grady, Marion (Admin)

Government Buildings
Cranmore Road, **Sligo**
Tel: 071 914 5203 Fax: 071 914 4840

Sligo/Mayo Team
Morrin, Helena (SPO)
Kelly, Tracey
Leahy, Denise
Quinlan, Judy

Unit 10 F N 5 Business Retail Park
Moneen **Castlebar** Co Mayo
Tel: 094 902 8404/5 Fax: 094 9044218

Sligo/Mayo Team
Morrin, Helena (SPO)
Tallon, Miriam
Caldwell, Katie
Halligan, Colin
Byrne, Laura (Admin)

48–50 Lower Main Street
Letterkenny Co Donegal
Tel: 074 912 5264 Fax: 074 912 6008

Donegal Team
Mannion, John (SPO)
Coughlan, Tim

Duke, Anne
Lennox, Yvonne
McShane, Michelle
Connery, Ian (Admin)

Unit 15 Churchview
Cavan
Tel: 049 432 7474 Fax: 049 4327461

Cavan/Monaghan/Leitrim Team
Donnelly, Carmel (SPO)
Gervin, Alice
Stone, Clive
Murray, Aine
Reilly, Sinead
Fallon, Oliver
Noone, Catherine (Admin)

Midlands & South East Region

Government Buildings
Abbeyleix Road
Portlaoise Co Laois
Tel: 057 862 2644 Fax: 057 866 0218

Laois/Offaly Team
Brennan, Maura (SPO)
Heffernan-Price, Majella
Cummins, Mary
Doyle, Alan
Walsh, Ann
Hanlon, Joy (YPP)
Mannion, Carmel (Admin)

3 Catherine Street
Waterford
Tel: 051 872 548 Fax: 051 878 238

Waterford Team
Goode, Mary (SPO)
Bourke, Andrea
Kennedy, Sharon
Fisher, Geraldine
Murphy, Mary T
Fisher, Sean (YPP)
Mansfield, Patricia (Admin)
Tobin, Margaret (Admin)

Government Buildings
Anne Street **Wexford**
Tel: 053 914 2076 Fax: 053 912 3565

Wexford Team
Weir, Michelle (SPO)
Corcoran, Anna Mai
Gurrin, Catherine
Halpenny, Seamus
Brookes, Veronica(YPP)
Long, Carol (Admin)

Harbour House
   The Quay
   Clonmel Co Tipperary
   Tel: 052 23880 Fax: 052 25874

   Tipperary Team
   Devereux, Della (SPO)
   Aylward, Mary
   Cooney, John
   Hughes, Ina
   O'Brien, Tom
   McLoughney, Caroline
   O'Dwyer, Niamh
   Lyons, Mandy (EO)
   Stapleton, Kathleen (Admin)

Quinn House
   Mill Lane **Carlow**
   Tel: 059 913 5186 Fax: 059 913 5194

   Carlow/Kilkenny Team
   Kavanagh, Billy (SPO)
   Brown, Carolyn
   Carolan, Patricia
   McGagh, Aisling (Admin)

Government Offices
   Hebron Road Kilkenny
   Tel: 056 776 5201 Fax: 056 776 4156

   Regional Manager's Office
   Vacant

   Carlow/ Kilkenny Team
   Kavanagh, Billy (SPO)
   Lacey, Joan
   Macken, Lorna
   Walsh, Geraldine
   Young, Dolores
   O'Sullivan, Moyra (Admin)

Government Buildings
   Abbeyleix Road Portlaoise
   Co Laois (Temporary Base)
   Tel: 057 8622644

   Kildare Team
   Redmond, Helen (SPO)
   Canty, Lena
   Cowzer, Elaine
   Balfe, John
   Lavin, Dermot
   Alright, Kim (Admin)

South West Region

   St Nicholas Church
   Cove Street **Cork**
   Tel: 021 483 6700 Fax: 021 484 5146

Regional Manager's Office
   Boyle, Terry (APPO)
   O'Riordan, Jennifer (EO)
   Desmond, Maria (Admin)
   Barry, Kenneth (Admin)
   McCarthy, Mairead (Admin)

Assessment Team
   Coakley, Deirdre (SPO)
   McAuley, Robert
   Campbell-Ryan, Susan
   Lynch, Dympna
   O'Connor, Tracy

Cork Community Service
   Gill, Catherine (SPO)
   Busteed, Eleanor
   Casey, Sue
   O'Connell, Roseanne
   O'Leary, Paula
   Dunne, Richard
   Walsh, Bernadette
   Moylan, Breda

Cork Community Supervision
   Corcoran, John (SPO)
   O'Brien, Joe
   Carmody, Mairead
   Barry, Eleanor
   Coveney, Eugene
   O'Shea, Olivia

Ashe Street
   Tralee Co Kerry
   Tel: 066 712 2666 Fax: 066 712 1764

   Kerry
   Keane, Norma (SPO)
   Brassil, Nora
   O'Connor, Hannah (Admin)

Theatre Court
   15 Lower Mallow Street
   Limerick
   Tel: 061 206 320 Fax: 061 206 339

   Limerick City / County Supervision
   Coughlan, Hedvig (SPO)
   Cahill, Frank
   Ryan, Cathy
   Tierney, Catherine
   O'Donnell, Helena
   Coffey, Sarah

   Limerick Assessment & Clare Team
   Ryan, Eoin (SPO)
   Mohan, Sadie
   McNamara, Paula
   Minogue, Anne (Admin)

Quane, Mary (Admin)
Quigley, Ger (Admin)

Intensive Probation & Offending Behaviour (Adult)
Griffin, Margaret (SPO)
Roberts, Terence
McDermott, Niamh

CHANNEL ISLANDS, ISLE OF MAN, AND THE COURTS MARTIAL REPORT SERVICE

GUERNSEY PROBATION SERVICE
The Market Building Fountain Street
St Peter Port Guernsey GY1 1BX
Tel: 01481 724337 Fax: 01481 710545
Email: probation@gov.gg

Guilbert, Anna (CPO)
Crisp, Stuart (Snr Pract)
Clark, Kate (Snr Prac)
Tardif, Kerry (Snr Prac – Prison)
Le Poidevin, Bryn
Guilbert, Sarah (p)
Greening, Gemma
Murphy, Cathy
Richmond, Issy
Speers, David
Sullivan, Mark (Prison)
Le Cheminant, Louise
Pearce, Emma
Ray, Fiona (Trainee)
Langlois, Amy (Trainee)
Ogier, Gill (CJ Drug Wkr)
Knight, John (CJ Alcohol Wkr)
Chambers, Paul (RJ Wkr)
Lowe, Vanessa (Admin Mgr)

Victim enquiries contact Kate Clark

Community Service
Hill-Tout, Laurence (Mgr)
Stagg, Emma (Officer)
Browning, Roger (Supvr)

ISLE OF MAN PRISON AND PROBATION SERVICE
2nd/3rd Floors Prospect House
27–29 Prospect Hill
Douglas Isle of Man IM1 1ET
Tel: 01624 687323/24 Fax: 01624 687319
www.gov.im/dha/probation
Email: first name.surname@gov.im
Gomme, Alison (Head of Prison and Probation Service)
Ingram, Patricia (Director of Community Operations)

Callow, Andrea (Service Administrator)
Mylchreest, Gemma (Administrator)
Christian, Louise (Sec)
Wagstaff, Karen (Sec)
Morphet, Kirstie – Senior Practitioner

Probation Officers
Erani, Hilary
Ledger, Ian
Stott, Elaine
Watts, Lynda

Prison Probation Officers
Bass, John (Prison) 01624 891008
Cubbon, Dawn (Prison) 01624 891005

Youth Justice
Robertson, John (Youth Justice) 01624 687572

Community Service
Forrest, Karen (PSO)
Vacant post (PSO)

Family Court Welfare
Gilbert, Marilyn (Family Court Welfare)
Strickland, Briana (Family Court Welfare)

JERSEY PROBATION AND AFTER-CARE SERVICE
1 Lemprière Street
St Helier JE4 8YT
Tel: 01534 441900 Fax: 01534 441944
Email: initial.lastname@gov.je
www.probation.je and www.gov.je

Heath, Brian (CPO)
Cutland, Michael (ACPO)
Pallot, Karen (Mgr Support Services)
Trott, David (Team Ldr)
Austin, Natalie (JS)
Barrowcliffe, Sarah
Brown, Susan (JS)
Christmas, Jane (JS)
Baudains, Sarah (JS)
Langford, Chris
Lister, Lisa (JS)
Lynch, James
Luce, Emma
Ormesher, Adelaide
Pike, Chay
Saralis, Mark (Ct Liaison/Subst Misuse)
Taylor, Robert
Urquhart, Janette

Machon, Barbara (p, PSA) (Trainee PO)
Rose, Chantelle (p, PSA Restorative Justice)

Veloso, Maurilia (Trainee PO)
Dowinton, Melanie (Case Mgmt Asst)
Gosselin, Gillian (p, Case Mgmt Asst)
Bisson, Donna (Case Mgmt Asst)
Soares, Rui (p, Case Mgmt Asst)

Allix, Nicky (p, Asst CSM & Court Officer)
Le Marrec, Andy (Asst CSM)
De Abreu, Rui (p, CS Supvr)
Hague, Philip (p, CS Supvr)
Renouf, Trevor (p, CS Supvr)
Lennane, John (p, CS Supvr)
McHendry, Chic (p, CS Supvr)
Bisson, Peter (p, CS Supvr)
Vacancy x 3 (p CS Supvr)

Jersey Family Court Welfare Service
PO Box 656 1 Lempriere Street as above
Tel: 01534 440640 Fax: 01534 440645

Ferguson, Jane (Team Manager)
Vacancy (Senior Practitioner)
Fernandes, Elsa (Senior Practitioner)
Green, Eleanor (Senior Practitioner)
Rosier, Nicki (Administrator)

THE COURTS-MARTIAL REPORT SERVICE
Courts-Martial Report Service (CMRS)
Building 398 Trenchard Lines Upavon
Pewsey Wilts SN9 6BE
Tel: 01980 618050/618101/618065
Fax: 01980 618048
Foster, Kerry (Office Mgr)
Hogan, Sarah (Admin Officer)

CMRS Germany Office
Military Court Centre
Normandy Barracks
Sennelager BFPO 16

Numbers shown below are direct dial from the UK
Saunders, Rachel (PO) 0049 5254 982 4366

Fax: 0049 5254 982 4358
In Germany CMRS has responsibility for the following:

• representing NPS in the British Forces Germany community
• preparing PSRs on service personnel appearing in courts martial

•supervision of court orders imPOsed at a service civilian court on the army's civilian employees and their dependants

•assisting UK-based probation Officers to liaise with army units based in Germany

where soldiers may be subject to community orders imPOsed by UK civilian courts.

SCOTLAND

DIRECTORATE FOR CRIMINAL JUSTICE
Community Justice Services Division
Floor GRW, St Andrew's House, Regent Road, Edinburgh EH1 3DG
Tel: 0131 244 4236 Fax: 0131 244 3548
Email:
firstname.lastname@scotland.gsi.gov.uk

Director Criminal Justice: Bridget Campbell

COMMUNITY JUSTICE AUTHORITIES
The Management of Offenders etc (Scotland) Act 2005 established eight local Community Justice Authorities (CJAs) in Scotland to provide a coordinated approach to planning and monitoring the delivery of offender services by planning, managing performance and reporting on the performance of offender management services. The aim of these partnership arrangements is to target services to reduce re-offending and to ensure close cooperation between community based services, the Scottish Prison Service, and the voluntary sector.
Each CJA consists of elected members of local authorities. The CJA is supported by a chief Officer and a small team of staff. CJAs have been fully operational since April 2007.

1. Fife & Forth Valley CJA
Kilncraigs Business Centre
Greenside Street, Alloa FK10 1EB
Tel: 01259 727434
www.ffvcja.co.uk

2. Glasgow CJA
4th Floor, 11 Hope Street
Glasgow G2 6AB
Tel: 0141 287 0196
www.glasgow.cja.org.uk

3. Lanarkshire CJA
Floor 2
Beckford Street
Hamilton ML3 0AA
Tel: 01698 454234
www.lanarkshirecja.org.uk

4. Lothian & Borders CJA
Rosetta Road
Peebles EH45 8HL
Tel: 01721 726314
www.cjalb.co.uk

5. North Strathclyde CJA
Unit 905
Mile End Mill
12 Seedhill Road
Paisley PA1 1JS
Tel: 0141 887 6133
www.nscja.co.uk

6. Northern CJA
The Annexe
Westburn Road
Aberdeen AB16 5GB
Tel: 01224 665780
www.northerncja.org.uk

7. South West Scotland CJA
Suite 6, Sovereign House
Academy Road
Irvine KA12 8RL
Tel: 01294 277968
www.swscja.org.uk

8. Tayside CJA
Floor 7, City House
Overgate
Dundee DD1 1UH
Tel: 01382 435394
www.taysidecja.org.uk

PAROLE BOARD FOR SCOTLAND
Saughton House, Broomhouse Drive
Edinburgh EH11 3XD
General enquiries tel: 0131 244 8373
Fax: 0131 244 6974
www.scottishparoleboard.gov.uk

Chairman: Prof Sandy Cameron
Vice-Chairman: Sheriff Fiona L Reith QC

ABERDEEN CITY COUNCIL

Emergency out of hours tel: 01224 693936

Email: oohs@socialwork.aberdeen.net.uk

Social Care & Wellbeing
McBride, Fred (Dir of Social Care &
Wellbeing)
Business Hub 12, 2nd Floor West,
Marischal College,
Broad Street, Aberdeen, AB10 1AB.
Tel: 01224 523797 Fax: 01224 346012
Email: frmcbride@aberdeencity.gov.uk
Cowan, Thomas (Hd of Adult Services

Social Care & Wellbeing)
Business Hub 8, 1st Floor North,
Marischal College,
Broad Street, Aberdeen, AB10 1AB.
Tel: 01224 523162 Fax: 01224 523195
Email: tcowan@aberdeencity.gov.uk

Social Care and Wellbeing

Criminal Justice Social Work
Exchequer House 3 Exchequer Row
Aberdeen AB11 5BW
Tel: 01224 765000 Fax: 01224 576109

Simpson, Lesley (Service Mgr)
Email: lsimpson@aberdeencity.gov.uk
Balme, Jane (Research/Info Analyst)
Email: jbalme@aberdeencity.gov.uk

Specialist Criminal Justice Teams

Caledonian System
Edgar, Jackie (System Mgr)
Burrows, Sheena (Women's Wkr)
Milne, Julia (Women's Wkr)
Reid, Susan (Women's Wkr)
Edwards, Stacy (Children's Wkr)

**CJ Drug & Alcohol Team NOT Drug
Treatment & Testing Orders**
Murray, Lorna (SSW)
Halford, Vina (SW)
McLachlan, Louise (SW)
Sherriffs, Ronnie (SW) (p)
Greenaway, Jackie (Subst Misuse Wkr)
Watt, Gillian (Subst Misuse Wkr)
Vacancy (Subst Misue Wkr)
Brown, Sheena (Arrest Referral Wkr)
Donaldson, Michelle (Arrest Referral
Wkr)
Morrison, Karl (Arrest Referral Wkr)

SUPPORT WORK TEAM
Campbell, Karen (Senior Support Wkr)
Aspe, Elena (Community Support Wkr)
Bain, Victoria (Community Support Wkr)
Fraser, Caroline (Community Support
Wkr)
Gaunt, Paul (Community Support Wkr)
Mearns, Kathleen (Women's Support
Wkr)
Onder, Carol (Community Support Wkr)
Schiavone, Louise (Community Support
Wkr)

**Community Payback Order Teams
Team 1**
Wilson, Claire (p) (Acting SSW)
SWs
Cruickshank, Sarah

Magill, Sach
Mazzoleni, Marino
Roach, Phil

Team 2
Buchanan, Neil (SSW)
SWs
Allan, Sam
Brady, Ruth
Fogg, Noreen
Fyffe, Karaina (p)
Klimek, Dagmara
Michel-Stephen, Tina
Plumbridge, Brenda

Team 3
Trew, Carrie (SSW)
SWs
Campbell, Sheona
Goodman, Kerry
McAllister, Annie
McCubbin, Lyn
Noble, Lyndsey
Russell, Cara
Hendry, Christine (Support Wkr)

Team 4
Connon, John (SSW)
SWs
Adam, Kelly
Chan, Maria
Lorimer, Leanne (p)
Sandison, Steve
Scott, Mark
Taylor, Jenny
Urquhart, Amanda

Throughcare Team
Douglas, Julie (Acting, SSW)
SWs
Aitken, Adelle
Arnold, Kirsty
Forbes, Lora
Gillan, Gillian
Hogg, Nicola
MacPherson, Zara
Willox, Cheryl
Vacancy

Community Service

11 Willowdale Place
Aberdeen AB24 3AQ
Tel: 01224 624317 Fax: 01224 626544

Community Service Resource Team
Russell, Kevin (Team Ldr)
Paterson, Neil (Projects Off)
Order Supervising Officers
Donaldson, Sheila

Finnie, Pamela
Freeman, Derek
McWilliam, Shona
Murdoch, Colin
Reid, Nicola (p)
Riches, Carson
Rait, Gordon (Unpaid Work Case
Manager)

Penal Establishment

Social Work Unit
HMP Aberdeen
Craiginches 4 Grampian Place
Aberdeen AB11 8FN
Tel: 01224 238315 Fax: 01224 238343

Wilson, Claire p (Acting SSW)
Bruce, Lauren p (SW)
Sherriffs, Ronnie p (SW)
Fraser, Louise (SW)

Health Services

Social Work Department
Royal Cornhill Hospital
Cornhill Road Aberdeen AB9 2ZH
Tel: 01224 557734/557781 Fax: 01224
557730

Independent Sector

APEX Scotland
1st Floor 48a Union Street
Aberdeen AB10 1BB
Tel: 01224 611875 Fax: 01224 611890

*(supervised attendance orders,
employment)*
Tripp, Helen (Unit Mgr)

Victim Support (Scotland)
32 Upperkirkgate
Aberdeen AB10 1BA
Tel: 01224 622478 Fax: 01224 625439

SACRO
110 Crown Street Aberdeen AB11 6HJ
Tel: 01224 560550 Fax: 01224 560551

Mackie, Tracy (Snr Mgr Ops North)
Pirrie, Alex (Service Mgr for CJ)

Courts
Aberdeen High Court
Aberdeen Sheriff Court and Justice of the
Peace Court
Castle Street Aberdeen AB10 1WP
Tel: 01224 657200 Fax: 01224 657241

ABERDEENSHIRE COUNCIL

Director of Housing & Social Work
Woodhill House, Westburn Road
Aberdeen AB16 5GB
Tel: 01224 665490 Fax: 01224 664888
Johnson, Ritchie

Head of Adult & Criminal Justice Services
Woodhill House, Westburn Road
Aberdeen AB16 5GB
Tel: 01224 664940 Fax: 01224 664992
Philip English

Woodhill House
Westburn Road
Tel: 01224 664940 Fax: 01224 664957
Simpson, Mark (SW Mgr for CJ)

53 Windmill Street
Peterhead AB42 1UE
Tel: 01779 477333 Fax: 01779 474961

Joint Sex Offender Project
Millar, Corinne (Team Mgr)

Unpaid Work
Carlton House
Arduthie Road
Stonehaven AB39 2DL
Tel: 01569 768338 Fax: 01569 767906

Westland, Fiona (Team Mgr)

14 Saltoun Square
Fraserburgh AB43 9DA
Tel: 01346 513281 Fax: 01346 516885

Voluntary Throughcare
53 Windmill Street
Peterhead AB42 1UE
Tel: 01779 477333 Fax: 01779 474961

Aberdeenshire North Team
53 Windmill Street
Peterhead AB42 1UE
Tel: 01779 477333 Fax: 01779 474961

Leslie, Dawn (Team Mgr)

Winston House
39 Castle Street
Banff AB45 1FQ
Tel: 01261 812001 Fax: 01261 813474

14 Saltoun Square
Fraserburgh AB43 9DA
Tel: 01346 513281 Fax: 01346 516885

Aberdeenshire South Team

PO Box 42, Carlton House
Arduthie Road
Stonehaven AB39 2DL
Tel: 01569 768338 Fax: 01569 767906

Westland, Fiona (Team Mgr)

25 Station Road
Ellon AB41 9AE
Tel: 01358 720033 Fax: 01358 723639

93 High Street
Inverurie AB51 3AB
Tel: 01467 625555 Fax: 01467 625010

25 Gordon Street
Huntly AB54 8AL
Tel: 01466 794488 Fax: 01466 794624

Penal Establishment

Social Work Unit
HMP Peterhead
Peterhead AB42 2YY
Tel: 01779 485066

Gibson, Eileen (Team Mgr)

Courts
Banff Sheriff Court and Justice of the Peace Court
Banff AB45 1AU
Tel: 01261 812140 Fax: 01261 818394

Peterhead Sheriff Court and Justice of the Peace Court
Queen Street, Peterhead AB42 1TP
Tel: 01779 476676 Fax: 01779 472435

Stonehaven Sheriff Court
County Buildings, Dunnottar Avenue
Stonehaven AB39 2JH
Tel: 01569 762758 Fax: 01569 762132

ANGUS COUNCIL

Emergency out of hours tel: 01382 307964 / 01382 307940

Email: surname and initial@angus.gov.uk

Social Work and Health
St Margaret's House Orchard Loan
Orchardbank Business Park
Forfar Angus DD8 1WS
Tel: 01307 461460 Fax: 01307 474899

Peat, Robert (Director of Social Work and Health)

Social Work and Health
Ravenswood New Road
Forfar Angus DD8 2AF
Tel: 01307 462405 Fax: 01307 461261

Tim Armstrong (Snr Mgr, Children and
Families & Criminal Justice Services)

Criminal Justice Services
9 Fergus Square **Arbroath** DD11 3DG
Tel: 01241 871161 Fax: 01241 431898

Bowie, George (Service Mgr)
Fyfe, John (Team Mgr)
Winter, Vicki (Team Mgr)
Dickson, Fiona (Admin Officer)
Cavill, Steve (Research & Info Officer)
SWs
Beierlein, Jackie
Boyd, Gordon
Hendry, Alison
Jenkins, Wendy
Mackay, Donna
Pert, Angie
Power, Kendal
Richardson, Aileen
Ross, Ian
CJAs
Bancroft, Paul
Bell, Drew
Catherall, Phil (CSO)
Daly, Mark
Millar, Avril
Ness, Maureen
Richards, Lynn
Smith, Lynn

115 High Street
Arbroath DD11 1DP
Tel: 01241 433260 Fax: 01241 433271

Hope, Alan (Team Mgr)

SWs
DeVries, Linzi
McIntyre, Becky
Ritchie, Jillian
Smith, Colin
CJA
Coutts, Bruce

Courts
Arbroath Sheriff Court and Justice of the
Peace Court
Arbroath DD11 1HL
Tel: 01241 876600 Fax: 01241 874413

Forfar Sheriff Court and Justice of the
Peace Court
Market Street Forfar DD8 3LA
Tel: 01307 462186 Fax: 01307 462268

ARGYLL & BUTE COUNCIL

Part of Argyll, Bute & Dunbartonshire's
Criminal Justice Social Work Partnership

Email:
firstname.lastname@argyll-bute.gsx.gov.uk

Criminal Justice Services Headquarters
Argyll & Bute Council
Dalriada House Lochnell Street
Lochgilphead PA31 8ST
Tel: 01546 604580 Fax: 01546 604588
Direct dial: 01546 + number

Belton, Jon (CJ Services Mgr) 604567
Green, Kirsteen (Business Support
Manager) 604583

**Criminal Justice Services (Mid-Argyll
Area)**
Stead, John (Team Ldr, Kintyre,
Mid-Argyll, Lorn) 604571
Anderson, Jillian (SW) 604556
Livingstone, Iona (Community Payback
Officer – Kintyre, Mid Argyll) 604569
Green, Richard (Unpaid Work Officer –
Kintyre, Mid-Argyll, Lorn) 60455 or
07717540504

Criminal Justice Services (Cowal Area)
16 Church Street
Dunoon PA23 8BG
Tel: 01369 707829 Fax: 01369 703641
Direct dial: 01369 + number

Emmett, Beckie (Team Ldr, Cowal &
Bute) 707344
Cameron, Liz (SW) 707132
Donnachie, Paul (SW) 707345
MacNiven, Kathrine (Community
Payback Officer) 707128
Reynolds, George (Unpaid Work Officer –
Cowal & Bute) 707347

Criminal Justice Services (Isle of Bute)
35 Union Street
Rothesay Isle of Bute PA20 0HD
Tel: 01700 501300 Fax: 01700 505408

Corcoran, Kate (SW) 501325
Denholm, Georgette (Community
Payback Officer) 501343

Criminal Justice Services (Lorn Area, Isles of Mull, Colonsay, Coll & Tiree)
Soroba Road Oban PA34 4JA
Tel: 01631 572955/563068 Fax: 01631 566724
Direct dial: 01631 + number

MacLeod, Susan (SW) 572954
Anderton, Ann (Community Payback Officer) 572937

Criminal Justice Services (Kintyre, Isles of Gigha, Islay & Jura)
Old Quay Head Campbeltown PA28 6ED
Tel: 01586 559068 Fax: 01586 554912
Direct dial: 01586 + number
Gray, Ruth (SW) 559066
Livingstone, Iona (Community Payback Officer – Kintyre, Mid Argyll) 604569

Criminal Justice Services (Helensburgh & Lomond)
West Dumbarton Council
Municipal Buildings Station Road
Dumbarton G82 1QA
Tel: 01389 738484 Fax: 01389 738480
Direct dial: 01389 + number

Stevens, Craig (SSW) 738471
Dady, Phil (SSW) 738482
Pryce, Ruth (Unpaid Work Mgr) 738385

Courts
Campbeltown Sheriff Court & Justice of the Peace Court
Castlehill Campbeltown PA28 6AN
Tel: 01586 552503 Fax: 01586 554967

Dunoon Sheriff Court & Justice of the Peace Court (inc. Lochgilphead annex)
George Street Dunoon PA23 8BQ
Tel: 0300 790 0049 Fax: 01369 702191

Oban Sheriff Court & Justice of the Peace Court
Albany Street Oban PA34 4AL
Tel: 01631 562414 Fax: 01631 562037

Rothesay Sheriff Court
Eaglesham House, Mountpleasant Road
Rothesay Isle of Bute PA20 9HQ
Tel: 01700 502982 Fax: 01700 504112

CLACKMANNANSHIRE COUNCIL

Criminal Justice Service
Glebe Hall, Burgh Mews
Alloa FK10 1HS
Tel: 01259 452200/721069

Fax: 01259 723998

Landels, Stuart (Service Mgr, CJ Services)
Email: slandels@clacks.gov.uk

Criminal Justice Team
Buchanan, June (Team Mgr)
Email: jbuchanan2@clacks.gov.uk Secure email: jbuchanangsx@clacks.gsx.gov.uk
Donnelly, Mark (Research & Planning Officer)
Email: mdonnelly@clacks.gov.uk

Elflain, Lynne (SSW)
Miller, Anne (SSW)
SWs
Craig, Alison
Gordon, Lisa
Halton, Derek (p)
McCourt, Michele (p)
McGibbon, Mandy
Millar, Stewart
Morrison, Susan
Paterson, Caroline
Stewart, Zoe
Weld, Christina (p)
SW Assistants
Evans, Isobel
Rennie, Tom

Community Service Team
CS Officers
Binnie, Chris
Weir, Gary

Work Supervisors
Brown, James
Carruthers, Tam
McGrellis, Andy

Admin
Hutcheon, Louise
Lambert, Jeni
McDougall, Marilyn
McMurray, Tricia

HMP/YOI Glenochil
King O'Muirs Road
Tullibody FK10 3AD
Tel/fax: 01259 767315

Banyard, Libby (Team Mgr)
Email: libby.banyard@sps.gov.uk
Hughes, Caroline (SSW)
SWs
Ferguson, Linda
Gray, Dawn
Richley, Tim
Wilson, Jimmy

Dickson, Hazel
Kalwat, Teresa
SW Assistant
Atchison, Keri
Administrators
Hepburn, Susan
Bell, Susan

Courts
Alloa Sheriff Court and Justice of the
Peace Court
47 Drydale Street, Alloa FK10 1JA
Tel: 01259 722734/212981 Fax: 01259
219470

COMHAIRLE NAN EILEAN SIAR
WESTERN ISLES COUNCIL

Out of hours tel: 01851 701702

Email: imacaulay@cne-siar.gov.uk

michael.stewart@cne-siar.gov.uk

Criminal Justice Service
Social and Community Services Dept
Council Offices
Sandwick Road, Stornoway
Isle of Lewis HS1 2BW
Tel: 01851 822710

Macaulay, Iain (Dir Social & Community
Services)
Stewart, Michael (CJ Services Mgr)
Ross, Alison (CJ SW)
MacDonald, Maggie (CJ SW)
Murray, Donald (CJ SW)
MacKenzie, Angus (Community Services
Off)

Courts
Lochmaddy Sheriff Court
Lochmaddy HS6 5AE
Tel: 01478 612191 Fax: 0844 561 3015

Stornoway Sheriff Court and Justice of
the Peace Court
9 Lewis Street, Stornoway HS1 2JF
Tel: 01851 702231 Fax: 01851 704296

DUMFRIES & GALLOWAY
COUNCIL

Out of hours tel: 030 3333 3000

Email: allan.monteforte@dumgal.gov.uk

Education and Social Work Services
Woodbank, Edinburgh Road
Dumfries DG1 1NW
Tel: 01387 260417 Fax: 01387 260453

Alexander, J (Service Dir Social Work
Services)

Criminal Justice Social Work Services
39 Lewis Street
Stranraer DG9 7AD
Tel: 01776 706167 Fax: 01776 706884

Monteforte, A (Snr Social Work Mgr
Wigtown)

**Criminal Justice Social Work Services –
East**
122–124 Irish Street
Dumfries DG1 2AW
Tel: 01387 262409 Fax: 01387 267106

Lockerbie, N (Business Information Off)
Kerr, A (Admin Mgr)

Admin – East
Vacancy (Admin Assistant)
Brown, J (Snr Clerical Asst)
Vacancy (Snr Clerical Asst)
Sturgeon, L (Snr Clerical Asst)
Crawford, L (Snr clerical Asst)

Criminal Justice East
Glynn, J (Team Mgr)
Stokes-King, E (Snr SW)
Smith, N (Snr SW)
Jamieson, K (SW)
McCarron, A (SW)
McMeikan, E (SW)
McNaught, A (SW)
Henderson, A (SW)
Craik, S (SW)
Wilson, I (SW)
Gibson, J (SW)
O'Sullivan, A (SW)
Dudgeon, W (SW_
Macdonald, C (SW)
Charters, A (SW)
Ducker, S (SW)
Wilby, B (SW) (temp)
Fortune, P (SW Asst)
Dean, R (SW Asst) (Throughcare
Addiction Services)

Criminal Justice East
Town Hall
Annan DG12 6AA
Tel: 01461 203311 Fax: 01461 207026
Race, H (SW)
Wearn, D (SW)

Programme Delivery
52a Buccleuch Street
Dumfries DG1 2AP
Tel: 01387 262409 Fax: 01387 267106

McCallum, A (Team Mgr) (based at 39
Lewis St Stranraer)
Knipe, C (Snr SW)
Shannan, C (Snr Clerical Asst)
Thinsmith, G (SW)
Turnbull, S (SW)
Wells, D (SWA)
Bell A (Women's Service Worker)
Skae, D (Children's Service Worker)

39 Lewis Street
Stranraer DG9 7AD
Tel: 01776 706167 Fax: 01776 706884
Carnochan, C (SWA)
McDevitt, P (SWA
Stapleton, C (Women's Service Worker)

Unpaid Work
8 King Street
Dumfries DG2 9AN
Tel: 01387 262409 Fax: 01387 267106
Miller M, (Snr SW) (*based at Irish St,*
Dumfries)
Smeaton, E (CSO)
Mulholland, R (CSO)
Moffat, G (CSO)
Monteforte, W (CSO) (*based at 39 Lewis*
St Stranraer)
Lewis, R (CSO) (*based at 39 Lewis St*
Stranraer/Daar Rd Kirkcudbright)

**Criminal Justice Social Work Services
West**
39 Lewis Street
Stranraer DG9 7AD
Tel: 01776 706167 Fax: 01776 706884
McCallum, A (Team Mngr)
Guest, G (Snr SW)

Admin – West
Milligan, A (Snr Clerical Asst)
Loudon Hughes, M (Snr Clerical Asst)
King A (Snr Clerical Asst)
Hastie, A (Snr Clerical Asst)

Criminal Justice West
Blackwell, L (SW) (based at
Kirkcudbright)
Hollis, K (SW)
Whelan, N (SW)
Lewis, K (SW)
Loughrey, N (SW)
Walsh, P (SW)
Vacancy (SW)

Beagrie, S (SWA)
Westbrook, D (SWA) (Throughcare
Addiction Services)

MAPPA
Police Headquarters
Cornwall Mount
Dumfries DG1 1PZ
Slimmon, N (MAPPA Coord)
McDowell, C (Admin Asst)

Penal Establishment

HMP Dumfries
Terregles Street, Dumfries DG2 9AX
Tel: 01387 261218 Fax: 01387 264144
Hall, J (Snr SW)
McCall, S (SW Asst/Snr Clerical Asst)
Hodgson, A (SW)
Austin, K (SW)

Courts
Dumfries Sheriff Court and Justice of the
Peace Court
Dumfries DG1 2AN
Tel: 01387 262334 Fax: 01387 262357

Kirkcudbright Sheriff Court and Justice
of the Peace Court
Kirkcudbright DG6 4JW
Tel: 01557 330574 Fax: 01557 331764

Stranraer Sheriff Court and Justice of the
Peace Court
Stranraer DG9 7AA
Tel: 01776 702138/706135 Fax: 01776
706792

DUNDEE CITY COUNCIL

Out of hours contact tel: 01382 307964

Fax: 01382 432264

Friarfield House
Barrack Street
Dundee DD1 1PQ
Tel: 01382 435001 Fax: 01382 435073 or
435032
Direct dial: 01382 43 + ext

Martin, Jane (Head of Children's and
Criminal Justice Services) ext 6001
Lloyd, Glyn (Service Mgr) ext 5017
Hendry, Mike (Snr Officer) ext 5084
Naeem, Shahida (Planning Officer) ext
5084
McIlravey, Margaret (Admin Assistant)
ext 5052

Community Payback Order Team 1

Paterson, Grant (Team Manager) ext 5015

Social Workers
Dennis, Mhairi ext5012
Petrie, Lesley ext 5089
Robertson, Nicole ext 5081
Whitehead, Jim ext 5065

Support Workers
Baird, Joanna ext 5042
Brown, Colin ext 5098
Garrigan, Helena ext 2188
Massam, Elizabeth ext 5047
Reid, Wendy ext 5025 (Keep Well Nurse)

Community Payback Order Team 2

Beverley Hart – (Team Manager) ext 5004

Social Workers
Barrow, Trisha ext 5029
Breen, Ann ext 5513
Delaney, Fiona ext 5515
Duncan, Susan ext 5005
Reid, Mark ext 5026

Support Workers
McIver, Karen ext 5050
Mortimer, Scott ext 5035
Nelson, Dean ext 5033

Community Payback Order Team 3

Barrie, Jacqui (Team Manager) ext 5076
Social Workers
Dow, Ashley ext 5506
Duff, Iain ext 5056
Elder, Jill ext 5031
Hamilton, Lizzie ext 5038
Wallace-King, Gwen ext 5060
Support Workers
Brewster, Lesley (Snr Support Wkr) 5077
Allardice, Billy ext 5055
Barr, Heather ext 5007

Community Payback Order Team 4 (Women)

Barrie, Jacqui (Team Manager) ext 5076
Social Workers
Dow, Ashley ext 5506
Duff, Iain ext 5056
Elder, Jill ext 5031
Hamilton, Lizzie ext 5038
Wallace-King, Gwen ext 5060
Support Workers
Brewster, Lesley (Snr Support Wkr) 5077
Allardice, Billy ext 5055
Barr, Heather ext 5007

APEX Employability

Fax: 01382 435032

Cummings, Emma (Unit Manager) ext 5068
Alavuk, Tanya (PDM) ext 5068
Black, Cherry (PDM) ext 5020
Close, Ashley (PDM) ext 5002
Fowler, Vicky (PDM) ext 5068
Gordon, Duncan (PDM) ext 5020
McLean, Lara (PDM) ext 5068
Murray, Kathleen (PDM) ext 5090
Ritchie, Alison (PDM) ext 5008
Young, Julie (PDM) ext 5085
Yule, Liam (PDM) ext 5008
Watson, Shiona (Admin PDM) ext 5085

Tay Project

Coleman, Lucy (Team Manager) ext 5075

Social Workers
Doyle, Kelly ext 5091
Melrose, Jo ext 5091
Paton, Lisa ext 5003
Smith, Ron ext 5018

Support Worker
Kelegher, Joyce ext 5019

DTTO

Nurses
Campbell, Douglas ext 5028
Campbell, Sonya ext 5072
Henderson, Chris ext 5078
Keay, Morag ext 5030
Murray, Angela (Support) ext 5030

Public Protection Team

Lindsay, Stephen (Team Manager) ext 5046

Social Workers
Carnegie, Maureen ext 5074
Howitt, Elizabeth ext 5057
Laing, Ann ext 5516
Lewis, Anne ext 5024
Marshall, Sandra ext 5093
Milne, Janice ext 5043
McDonald, Teresa ext 5514
Reading, Heidi ext 5516
Walker, Debbie ext 5024
Support Workers
Cosgrove , Lara ext 5513
Lyttle, Claire ext 5054
Rollo, Pauline ext 5054

East Port House

65 King Street Dundee DD4 1JY
Tel: 01382 431450 Fax: 01382 431449

Courts

Dundee Sheriff Court and Justice of the Peace Court

Dundee DD1 9AD
Tel: 01382 229961 Fax: 01382 318222

EAST AYRSHIRE COUNCIL

East Ayrshire Council Headquarters
London Road
Kilmarnock KA3 7BU
Tel: 01563 576597
Fax: 01563 576210

Taylor, Susan (Head of Service: Children & Families and Criminal Justice)

Social Work Headquarters
15 Strand Street
Kilmarnock KA1 1HU
Tel: 01563 576674
Fax: 01563 578321

Fitzpatrick, Eugene (Service Mgr CJ)

Criminal Justice; Services (North)
15 Strand Street
Kilmarnock KA1 1HU
Tel: 01563 539888
Fax: 01563 578321
Gaffney, Mark (Team Mgr, CJ Service)
Kane, Terry (Team Mgr, CJ Service)

Unpaid Work Unit
Block 13 Unit 1,
27 Glenfield Place, Glencairn Industrial Estate, Kilmarnock KA1 4AZ

Social Work Department
Criminal Justice Services (South),
Rothesay House, 1 Greenholm Road,
Cumnock
KA18 1LH
Tel: 01290 428379
Fax: 01290 428380
Haddow, Anita (Team Mgr, CJ Services)

Ayrshire Criminal Justice Partnership
Programme Delivery Team, Kiln Court,
East Road **Irvine** KA12 0BZ
Tel: 01294 318750
Fax: 01294 318799

MacKinnon, Fiona (Partnership Mgr)

Including the following teams

Constructs Team
Walkerdine, Sue (Constructs, PSSO, Women Offenders Team Mgr)

Programme Delivery Team
Jones, Ray (Community Sex Offender Groupwork Programme (CSOGP) and Caledonian System Mgr)

Training & Development
Westbrook, Andy (Coord)

Drug Testing & Treatment Order (DTTO) Team
1 Glebe Street, Stevenson KA20 3EN
TE: 01294 475800 Fax: 01294 475810
David, Andy (Team Manager CJ Services)

MAPPA Office
South West Scotland Community Justice Authority, Ayr Police Office
1 King Street AYR KA8 0BU
Tel: 01292 664069
Fax: 01292 664023

Penal Establishment
Social Work Unit, **HMP Kilmarnock,**
Mauchline Road
Kilmarnock KA1 5JH
Tel: 01563 548851 Fax: 01563 548869

Stevenson, Joanne (Team Mgr)

Courts
Ayr Sheriff Court & Justice of the Peace Court
Ayr KA7 1EE
Tel: 01292 268474 Fax: 01292 292249
Hall, Drew (Team Leader)

Kilmarnock Sheriff Court & Justice of the Peace Court
St Marnock Street Kilmarnock KA1 1ES
Tel: 01563 550024 Fax: 01563 543568
Hamilton, Jackie (Team Manager)

EAST DUNBARTONSHIRE COUNCIL

Out of hours standby service tel: 0800 811 505 (freephone)

Social Work Headquarters
Southbank House, Southbank Road,
Kirkintilloch, Glasgow
Tel: 0141 777 3000 Fax: 0141 777 6203

Keogh, Tony (Chief SW Off)
Simmons, John (Corp Dir, Community)

Criminal Justice Unit
Unit 23, Fraser House, Whitegates,
Kirkintilloch G66 3BQ
Tel: 0141 578 8320 Fax: 0141 578 0101

Garnder, Keith (Service Manager
Criminal Justice)
Email:
keith.gardner@eastdunbarton.gov.uk

Offender Services
Lynch, Tracy (SW Throughcare)
Cranston, Morven (SW)
Chiang, Belinda (SW)
Kier, Lynn (SW)
Shearer, Alison (SW)
Karpinski, Noel (CJ Asst)

**Community Service & Supervised
Attendance**
Sutherland, Neil (CS Off)
Nixon, Joseph (CS Asst)
Dickson, William (CS Supvr)
Coyne, Martin (CS Supvr)

Administration Section
Watt, Karen (Business Support Officer)
Young, Lynn (Clerical Off)

Penal Establishment
Social Work Unit
HMP Low Moss
Crosshill Road, Bishopbriggs
Glasgow G62 2QB
Tel: 0141 762 9591
Gardner Keith (Service Manager
Criminal Justice)

EAST LOTHIAN COUNCIL

**Out of hours emergency social work
service tel:** 0800 731 6969 (freephone)

Email: initiallastname@eastlothian.gov.uk

Dept of Community Services
John Muir House
Haddington EH41 3HA
Tel: 01620 827 827

Murray Leys (Adult Well Being)
Patricia Kaminski (Acting Criminal
Justice Service Manager)

Criminal Justice Team
Criminal Justice Services
Brunton Hall
Ladywell Way
Musselburgh EH21 6AF

Tel: 01620 827939 or 01620 827763 Fax:
0131 653 5277
Email: cjsupport@eastlothian.gsx.gov.uk

Harvey, Steven (Acting Team Ldr)
Steel, Audrey (Team Ldr)
Cairns, Helen (CJSW)
Douglas, George (CJSW)
McFadzean, Frances (CJSW)
Hammond, Lucy (CJSW)
Stuart Macdonald (CJSW-temporary)
Neil Cosnette (CJSW – temporary)
Carolyn Barbour (Caledonian Women's
Worker – temporary)
Eve Mullins (Caledonian Childrens
Worker – temporary/part time)
Ellis, Duncan (SW Asst Voluntary
Throughcare/
Throughcare Addiction Service – part
time)
Davy Rutherford CS/Unpaid Work
Manager
McAlpine, Owen (Depute CS Off)
Hicks, Gary (CS Asst)
Kevan, Neill (CS Asst)
Cairns, Lesley (Business Systems
Administrator)
Davis, Stephanie (Senior Business
Support Assistant)

Youth Justice Team
Dept of Children's Wellbeing
Randall House
Macmerry EH33 1RW
Tel: 01875 824090 Fax: 01875 612748

Coates, George (Team Ldr, Young
Peoples Team)

Courts
Haddington Sheriff Court & Justice of the
Peace Court
Haddington EH41 3HN
Tel: 01620 822325/822836 Fax: 01620
825350

EAST RENFREWSHIRE COUNCIL

Out of hours tel: 0800 811 505

Email:
firstname.lastname@eastrenfrewshire.gov.uk

**East Renfrewshire Community Health &
Care Partnership**
CHCP Headquarters
1 Burnfield Avenue
Giffnock G46 7TT

Tel: 0141 577 3844 Fax: 0141 577 3846

Murray, Julie (Director of CHCP)
Baxter, Safaa (Chief SW Officer/Head of Children's Services, Criminal Justice & Addictions)

St Andrew's House
113 Cross Arthurlie Street, **Barrhead** G78 1EE
Tel: 0141 577 8569/3370 Fax: 0141 577 3762

Hinds, Jonathan (Service Mgr, CJ Social Work Services)

Criminal Justice Team
Council Offices (1st Floor), 211 Main Street
Barrhead G78 1SY
Tel: 0141 577 8337/8 Fax: 0141 577 8342

Gaff, Les (Team Mg)
Craig, Dawn (Snr SW Pract)
Crichton, John (SW)
McDade, Karen (SW)
Smith, Colin (SW)
Downie, Eddie (CJ Support Worker)
Kerr, Peter (CS Supvr)
Bell, Shona (Admin Asst)
McQuade, Anne Marie (Admin Asst)

Drug Treatment and Testing Order Service
(East Renfrewshire, Inverclyde & Renfrewshire)
St Andrew's House, 113 Cross Arthurlie Street, **Barrhead** G78 1EE
(offices at Paisley and Greenock)
Paisley tel: 0141 577 8442 Fax: 0141 577 4135
Greenock tel: 01475 800975 Fax: 01475 800976

Mulholland, Róisín (Team Manager)
Findlay, Debbie (SW)
Murray, Patricia (SW)
Soper, Helen (SW)
Farrell, Denise (Support Wkr)
Galbraith, Wendy (Support Wkr)
Chellamuthu, Prabhu (Doctor)
Lough, Jennifer (Snr Addiction Nurse)
Nelis, Michael (Snr Addiction Nurse)
Corsar, Anne (Addiction Nurse)
Mordini, Shannon (Snr Clerical Asst: Greenock)
Vacant (Clerical Asst: Paisley)

Forensic Community Mental Health Team
(East Renfrewshire, Inverclyde & Renfrewshire)
Blythswood House, Fulbar Lane **Renfrew** PA4 8NT
Tel: 0141 314 9226/9227 Fax: 0141 314 9228
Email: firstname.lastname@ggc.scot.nhs.uk

Hendry, Shona (Forensic Community Services Manager)
MacDonald, Dr George (Consultant Forensic Psychiatrist)
Cameron, Dr Lisa (Consultant Clinical Psychologist)
O'Donovan, Roberta (SW)
Stewart, Karen (SW)
Beckwith, Alan (SW Assistant)
Lee, Shelley (Medical Secretary)
McIntosh, Pauline (Medical Secretary)
Grierson, Lesley (Forensic CPN)
Murphy, Andrew (Forensic CPN)
O'Brien, Chris (Forensic CPN)
O'Neill, Denise (Forensic CPN)
Willsone, Nicola (Forensic CPN)

Court
Paisley Sheriff Court and Justice of the Peace Court
St James' Street Paisley PA3 2HW
Tel: 0141 887 5291 Fax: 0141 887 6702/889 7664

CITY OF EDINBURGH COUNCIL

Social Care Direct Tel: 0131 200 2324

Out of hours contact tel: 0800 731 6969 (emergency social work service freephone)

Health and Social Care Headquarters
Level 1:8 Waverley Court, 4 East Market Street, **Edinburgh** EH8 8BG
Tel: 0131 553 8520 Fax: 0131 529 6218

Gabbitas, Peter (Director of Health and Social Care)
Miller, Michelle (Chief Social Work Officer)
Boyle, Monica (Head of Older People and Disability Services)

Criminal Justice Service
Tel. 0131 553 8200 Fax 0131 529 6218

Beck, Colin (Senior Manager, CJ, Mental Health, Substance Misuse and Homelessness)
Robertson, Harry (CJ Service Mgr)

Community Intervention Teams

Edinburgh North
Units C&D Newkirkgate Shopping Centre
Edinburgh EH6 6DJ
Tel: 0131 555 8959 Fax: 0131 443 6540

Lawrie, Val (Sector Mgr)

Edinburgh South
40 Captain's Road
Edinburgh EH17 8HN
Tel: 0131 529 5321 Fax: 0131 529 5384

Fuller, Carey (Sector Mgr)

City-wide Services
Services include: unpaid work, drug treatment and testing orders, bail and diversion
2–4 Grindlay Street Court, Edinburgh EH3 9AR
Tel: 0131 469 3408 Fax: 0131 229 8628

Fraser, Rona (Sector Mgr)

Re-integration
Services include: Crane (supported accom facility), MAPPA, sex and violent offender liaison staff and resettlement team.
24 Broughton Place Edinburgh EH1 3RT
Tel: 0131 556 9969

Peters, Jackie (Sector Mgr)

Penal Establishment

Social Work Unit
HMP Edinburgh
33 Stenhouse Road Edinburgh EH11 3LN
Tel: 0131 444 3080

Fraser, Dorothy (Practice Team Manager)

Courts
The High Court Edinburgh
Edinburgh Sheriff Court & Justice of the Peace Court
27 Chambers Street Edinburgh EH1 1LB
Tel: 0131 225 2525

FALKIRK COUNCIL

Social Work Headquarters
Denny Town House, Glasgow Road, **Denny** FK6 5DL
Tel: 01324 506400 Fax: 01324 506401

Anderson, Margaret (Director of Social Work)
McCarroll, Kathy (Head of Children & Families, & CJ)
Burgess, Nick (Acting Criminal Justice Service Mgr)

Criminal Justice Service
Brockville Hope Street **Falkirk** FK1 5RW
Tel: 01324 506464 Fax: 01324 506465

Duncan, Robin (Research, Info & Training Off)

Community Payback & Throughcare Team
Connelly, Kristine (Acting Team Mgr)
Parnell, Anne Marie (Team Mgr)
SWs
Andrews, Carol
Barnaby, Les
Bond, Michael
Boslem, Mary
Bowie, Iain
Brodie, Andrew
Brown, Jacqueline
Goodwin, Anne-Marie
Kent, Gill
Kostlin, Donna
McCartney, Lynn
McCormick, Jim
McLean, Rachel
Marshall, Kay
Melvin, Shirley
Millar, Alan
Rodger, Claire
Vacancy
Gardner, Melanie (Women's Wkr)
Boslem, Vicky (SW Asst)
Fotheringham, Brian (SW Asst)
Thomson, Stephen (SW Asst)

Unpaid Work Team
Hamilton, Mary (Team Mgr)
Howard, Fred (SW)
Armstrong, Donna (SW)
Unpaid Work Officers
Adams, Gordon
Brockie, Clem
Cooper, Dave
Glowacki, Louisa
Sharkey, Brian

Unpaid Work Supervisors
Amatller, Philippe
Dewar, Roy
Hogg, Doug
Lumsden, Irene
Rogerson, Tony
Smith, Andy

Accredited Programmes Team
(Also serving Clackmannanshire &
Stirling CJS)
Timpany, David (Team Mgr)
Feesey, Emma (Delivery Mgr)
McDonald, Scott (Snr Wkr)
Barr, Dominique (Group Wkr, Sacro)
Begen, Margaret (Group Wkr)
Ekebuisi, Eny (Group Wkr, Sacro)
Hubner, Pauline (Group Wkr)
Murray, Douglas (Group Wkr)
Chalmers, Jill (Group Wkr)
Winkley, Jonathan (Group Wkr, Sacro)
Kennedy, Janey (Women's Wkr)
Ferguson, Jen (Women's Wkr, Sacro)
Judson, Siobhan (Women's Wkr, Sacro)
Rae, Jackie (Women's Wkr, Sacro)
Spence, Eileen (Women's Wkr, Sacro)
Wilson, Yvonne (Women's Wkr)
Dickson, Chris (Children's Wkr, Sacro)
McKay Fletcher, Angela (Children's Wkr,
Sacro)
Sherlock, Jennifer (Children's Wkr,
Sacro)
Administration
Cartwright, Sandra (Supportive Services
Officer)

Voluntary Organisation

Sacro
c/o Unit 1 St John's Sawmill, Etna Road,
Falkirk FK2 9EG
Tel: 01324 501230 Fax: 01324 501061
Conway, Bill (Acting Service Mgr)
Robertson, Adele (Admin)

Restorative Justice Service
Horwood, Caroline (Youth Justice Wkr)
Emerson, Iain (Youth Justice Wkr)
Aitken, Shelley (Youth Justice Wkr)

**Groupwork Service (see Acc Prog Team
above) Accommodation Service**

Prison Housing Advice & Support
c/o Brockville Hope Street **Falkirk** FK1
5RW
Tel: 01324 506464 Fax: 01324 506465
Easton, Craig (Criminal Justice Worker)
Miller, Evelyn (Criminal Justice Wkr)

Youth Justice

Social Work Headquarters
Denny Town House, Glasgow Road,
Denny FK6 5DL
Tel: 01324 506400 Fax: 01324 506401
Davies, Matthew (Service Mgr)

Programme Providers
Connect Youth Justice Service
Kinglass Centre
Gauze Road, **Bo'ness** EH51 9UE
Tel: 01324 506400

Vacancy (SW)
Kelly, Janet (SW)
Mullen, Lindsay (Com Educ Wkr)
Vacancy (Admin)

Penal Establishment

Social Work Unit
HMYOI Polmont
Redding Road Brightons
Falkirk FK2 0AB
Tel: 01324 711708 Fax: 01324 722297

Whyte, Jackie (Team Mgr)
Vacancy (Snr Wkr)
SWs
Berry, Ruth
Vacancy
Irvine, Anne
Macfarlane, Bernadette
Paget, Sharon-Ann
Vacancy
Walker, Natalie
Baillie, Lesley (Snr Admin)
Moore, Elaine (Admin)

Courts
Falkirk Sheriff Court and Justice of the
Peace Court
Camelon Falkirk FK1 4AR
Tel: 01324 620822 Fax: 01324 678238

FIFE COUNCIL

Out of hours tel: 08451 550099

Social Work Headquarters
Rothesay House, Glenrothes
Fife KY7 5PQ
Tel: (08451) 555555 ext. 444112

Moore, Stephen (Executive Director
(Social Work) and Lead for Health)
Dunlop, Douglas (Head of Service
Children and Families and Criminal
Justice)

Dunfermline Sheriff Court
Carnegie Drive, Dunfermline KY12 7HJ
Tel: (01383) 480049 Fax: (01383) 602540

Bouglas, Dale (Business Supt)
Donald, Kimberley (Business Supt)

Kirkcaldy Sheriff Court
Whytescauseway
Kirkcaldy KY1 1XQ
Tel: (08451 555555) 470320 fax (01592)
583197

Robson, Angela (CJA)
Quipp, Jennifer (Business Supt)

Cupar Sheriff Court
21 St Catherine Street, Cupar KY15 4TA
Tel: (01334) 659356 Fax: (01334) 659316

Rose, Susan (Team Mgr)
Davidson, Collette (Business Supt)

Criminal Justice Offices

Cupar Base
21 St Catherine Street
Cupar KY15 4TA
Tel: (01334) 659356 Fax: (01334) 659316

Rose, Susan (Team Mgr)
Paterson, Carol (Business Officer,
Support Services)
Carroll Caroline (Business Supt)

Buckhaven Base
1 College Street
Buckhaven KY8 1AB
Tel: (01592) 583335 Fax: (01592) 583651

Bill Kinnear (Service Manager)

Collins, Margaret (Team Mgr)
Rattray, Fiona (Team Mgr)
Ralph, Karen (System Sup off)
Pattie, Cheryl Business (Supt)

Dunfermline Base
Rannoch House, 2 Comely Park
Dunfermline KY12 7HU
Tel: (01383) 602354

Thompson, Susan (Team Mgr)
Campbell, Zoe (Business Supt)

Kirkcaldy Base
7 East Fergus Place
Kirkcaldy KY1 1XT
Tel: (01592) 583657 Fax: (01592 583646)

MacArthur, Stuart(Team Mgr)
Simpson, Angela (Team Mgr)
Hopton, Gayle (Business Co-ordinator)
King, Dawn (Business Supt)

Glenrothes Base
390 South Street, Glenrothes KY7 5NL
Tel: (01592) 583321 Fax: (01592) 583262

Collins, Margaret (Team Mgr)
Thomson, Christine (Business Supt)

Kirkcaldy Base
Broomlea, 1 Swan Road
Kirkcaldy KY1 1UZ
Tel: (01592) 583336 Fax: (01592) 583198
Richley, Joanne (Team Mgr)
Melville, Archie (Snr Project Officer)
Ashraf, Arif (Business Supt)

GLASGOW CITY COUNCIL

Social Work Services
Wheatley House
25 Cochrane Street Glasgow G1 1HL
Tel: 0141 287 8847 Fax: 0141 287 4895

Williams, David (Exec Director Social of
Work Services)

Criminal Justice Unit
Centenary House 100 Morrison Street
Glasgow G5 8LN
Tel: 0141 420 5753
Fax: 0141 420 5957
Direct dial: 0141 420 + number

McKendrick, Sean Head of Service CJ
5756

McBride, Jim (Service Manager) 5854

Milne, Bruce (Assistant Service
Manager) 5699
McNulty, Mary (Principal Off CJ) 5899
Fraser, Serena (Resource Wkr) 5844
McAulay, Lesley (Resource Wkr) 274
6101

North East Area
Newlands Office
The Newlands Centre
871 Springfield Road
Parkhead
Glasgow G31 4HZ

Tel: 0141 565 0230 Fax: 0141 565 0164

McCullough, Janet (Service Mgr CJ)

Team Leaders CJ
Allan, Anne-Marie
McSherry, Liz
Lafferty, Caroline

Easterhouse Office
1250 Westerhouse Road
Easterhouse
Glasgow G34 9AE
Tel: 0141 276 4100 Fax: 0141 276 7113

Royston Office
15 Glenbarr Street
Royston
Glasgow G21 2NW
Tel: 0141 276 7050 Fax:
McAulay, Adrienne (Team Ldr CJ) Fast
Track Cover Only
McLaughlin, Linda (Team Ldr CJ)

CSO Project
Templeton Business Centre
White Studios Unit 4A3
62 Templeton Street Glasgow G40 1DA
Tel: 0141 276 1850 Fax: 0141 276 1851

McAulay, Adrienne (Team Ldr CJ)

Nairn, Stewart (Team Ldr CJ)

Fast Track CPO Team
80 Norfolk Street
Gorbals
Glasgow G5 9EJ
Tel: 0141 274 6000 Fax: 0141 274 6069
McDonald, Ann (Team Leader)

North West Area
The Quadrangle
59 Ruchill Street, Maryhill
Glasgow G20 9PY
Tel: 0141 276 4560 Fax: 0141 276 6222

Lynsey Smith (Service Mgr CJ)

Team Leaders CJ
Jenkins, Steve
Keogh, Mike
Boner, Patrica

South Area
187 Old Rutherglen Road, Twomax
Building, Gorbals
Glasgow G5 0RE
Tel: 0141 420 0070 Fax: 0141 420 8004

Johnstone, Yvonne (Service Mgr CJ)
Brittain, John (Team Ldr CJ)
Conkie, Maria (Team Ldr CJ)
Smith, Laura (Team Ldr)

South Area
130 Langton Road, Pollok
Glasgow G53 5DP
Tel: 0141 276 2960 Fax: 0141 276 2981

Team Leaders CJ
Ashworth, Mary
Munro, Jean

North West Area
Mercat House 31 Hecla Square
Drumchapel
Glasgow G15 8NH
Tel: 0141 276 4320 Fax: 0141 276 4331

Team Leaders CJ
Campbell, Susan
Coyle, Martin
Clarke, Dominic

Homeless Persons Team
180 Centre Street
Glasgow G5 8EE
Tel: 0141 287 1800 Fax: 0141 287 1887

Mearns, Gerry (Service Mgr)
McShane, Tony (Team Ldr CJ)

Clyde Quay Project (Sex Offenders)
85 Paisley Road, Glasgow G5 8LN
Tel: 0141 276 5410
Fax: 0141 420 5760

Brown, Angelene (Team Ldr)

MAPPA
Centenary House 100 Morrison Street
Glasgow G5 8LN
Tel: 0141 420 5765

Sex Offender Liaison Team (SOLO)
Centenary House 100 Morrison Street
Glasgow G5 8LN
Tel: 0141 276 5410

Gregson, Debbie (Snr Off)
Kennedy, Alison (Snr Off)
McDade, Bob (Snr Off)
Miller John (Snr Off)

DTTO/Drug Court Team
80 Norfolk Street Glasgow G5 9EJ
Tel: 0141 274 6000 Fax: 0141 274 6088

Gallagher, Tom (Team Ldr CJ)

Voluntary Organisations

SACRO
(inc supported accommodation)
2nd Floor, Central Chambers
93 Hope Street Glasgow G2 6LD
Tel: 0141 248 1763 Fax: 0141 248 1686

Glasgow Council on Alcohol
7th Floor Newton House
457 Sauchiehall Street Glasgow G2 3LG
Tel: 0141 353 1800 Fax: 0141 353 1030

Victim Support (Glasgow)
131–141 Saltmarket Glasgow G1 5LF
Tel: 0141 553 2415 Fax: 0141 553 2405

Victim Support (Scotland)
10 Jocelyn Square Glasgow G1 5JU
Tel: 0141 553 1726 Fax: 0141 552 3316

Dick Stewart Hostel (Crossreach)
40 Circus Drive Glasgow G31 2JE
Tel: 0141 554 0277 Fax: 0141 554 6646

The Wise Group
72 Charlotte Street Glasgow G1 5DW
Tel: 0141 303 3131 Fax: 0141 552 9673

218 Service (Turning Point)
218 Bath Street Glasgow G2 4HW
Tel: 0141 331 6200 Fax: 0141 331 6202

Penal Establishment

HMP Barlinnie
81 Lee Avenue
Riddrie
Glasgow G33 2QX
Tel: 0141 770 2000 Fax: 0141 770 2060

Social Work Unit
Tel: 0141 770 2123 Fax: 0141 770 9808
McDade, Alexis (Team Ldr CJ)

Courts

City of Glasgow Stipendiary/Justice of the Peace Court
1 Carlton Place Glasgow G5 9DA
Tel: 0141 429 8888 Fax: 0141 418 5185

Social Work Unit
Tel: 0141 276 1790/1791/1792 Fax: 0141 559 4528
McLaughlin, Sandra (Team Ldr)
Ross, Cath (Team Ldr)
Jamieson, Helen (Team Ldr)

Glasgow & Strathkelvin Sheriff Court
Social Work Unit 80 Norfolk Street
Glasgow G5 9EJ
Tel: 0141 274 6000 Fax: 0141 274 6088

McLaughlin, Sandra (Team Ldr)
Ross, Cath (Team Ldr)
Jamieson, Helen (Team Ldr)

Glasgow High Court
1 Mart Street Glasgow G1 5JT
Tel: 0141 552 3795 Fax: 0141 559 4519

Social Work Unit
Tel: 0141 276 1790/1791/1792 Fax: 0141 559 4528

Bail Services
80 Norfolk Street Glasgow G5 9EJ
Tel: 0141 274 6000 Fax: 0141 2741 6088

Jamieson, Helen (Team Ldr)

Structured Deferred Sentence (SDS)
80 Norfolk Street
Glasgow G5 9EJ
Tel: 0141 274 6000 Fax: 0141274 6088

McLaughlin, Sandra (Team Ldr)

Glasgow Community Justice Authority (CJA)
Community Justice Authorities are strategic partnership organisations. For all operational enquires about cases, please contact the relevant Criminal Justice Social Work Team.
Suite 4(a) 4th Floor
101 Portman Street
Glasgow G41 1EJ
Tel: 0141 287 0916
www.glasgowcja.org.uk

THE HIGHLAND COUNCIL

Out of hours tel: 08457 697284

The Highland Council Headquarters
Glenurquhart Road Inverness IV3 5NX
Tel: 01463 702874 Fax: 01463 702855

Alexander, Bill (Director of Health & Social Care)
Palin, Fiona (Head of Social Care)

Social Work Headquarters
Kinmylies Building Leachkin Road
Inverness IV3 8NN
Tel: 01463 703472 Fax: 01463 713237

HQ Team
Maybee, James (Principal Off, CJS)
Nicholls, Pat (Admin Asst, CJS)
McNab, Rachel (p, Clerical Asst)

O'Brien, Clare (p, Info/Research & QA Off, CJS)

MAPPA Team
Criminal Justice Services Police Headquarters
Perth Road Inverness IV2 3SY
Tel: 01463 720833 Fax: 01463 720858

Lyon, Ron (MAPPA Coord)
Brown, Alana (Admin Asst)
Davidson, Tracy (Clerical Asst)

Criminal Justice Services
Highland North Team

Caithness
Social Work Criminal Justice Services
Unit 27b
Airport Industrial Estate
Wick KW1 4QS
Tel: 01955 603161 Fax: 01955 603164

Rainnie, Bill (Team Mgr, North)
Easton, Alan (p, SW)
Meldrum, Sarah (p, SW)
McCormick, Cath (p,SW)
Keith, Tracey (Clerical Asst)

Sutherland
Criminal Justice Services
Drummuie **Golspie** KW10 6TA
Tel: 01408 635369 Fax: 01408 634041

Rainnie, Bill (Team Mgr, North)
MacPherson, Margaret (p, SW)
MacRae, Diane (p, Clerical Asst)

Ross-shire
Criminal Justice Services
Station Road **Dingwall** IV15 9JX
Tel: 01349 865600 Fax: 01349 865279

Rainnie, Bill (Team Mgr, North)
Forbes, Bill (p, SW)
Mackay, Hilary (p, SW)
Morrison, Gail (p, SW)
Church, Arlene (p,SW)
Nicolson, Don (SW)
MacKinnon, Mary (p, SW)
MacKay, Maureen, (CJO Bail & Courts)
Grigor, Brycie (Clerical Asst)
MacRae, Diane (p, Clerical Asst)

Highland South Team

Inverness
Criminal Justice Services
Ground Floor, North Tower, The Castle,
Castle Street,
Inverness IV2 3EE

Tel: 01463 255250 Fax: 01463 719740

Paulin, Jeremy (Team Mgr, South)
Barr, Bob (SW)
Botha, Mornay (SW)
Baxter, Stuart (SW)
Higgs, Caroline (p,SW)
MacKay, Claire (p, SW, SDS)
Horrobin, Derek (SW)
MacKenzie, Eileen (SW)
MacLennan, Aimee (p, SW)
MacRae, Margo (p,SW, Diversion)
Church, Arlene (p SW)
Vacant (SW)
Murdoch, Sara (CJO, Courts)
Fraser, Claire (Clerical Asst)
McNab, Rachel (p, Clerical Asst)

Lochaber
Criminal Justice Services Unit 4B1 Blar
Mhor Industrial Estate
Caol **Fort William** PH33 7NG
Tel: 01397 704668 Fax: 01463 700422

Paulin, Jeremy (Team Mgr, South)
Bell, Trevor (p, SW)
Finnimore, Andrew (SW)
Laing, Sara (Clerical Asst)

Skye
Criminal Justice Services Top Floor
Tigh na Drochaid Bridge Road
Portree Isle of Skye IV50 9ER
Tel: 01478 612943 Fax: 01478 613213
Rainnie, Bill (Team Mgr, North)
Henderson, Dianne (SW)
MacPherson, Ann (p, Clerical Asst)

Substance Misuse
Criminal Justice Services The Old
Schoolhouse 196 Culduthel Road
Inverness IV2 4BH
Tel: 01463 716324 Fax: 01463 712895

Millar, Lynn (Team Mgr, Substance
Misuse) (also at HMP Inverness)
MacKay, Claire (p, SW, DTTO)
Sangster, Agnes (SW, DTTO, CIU)
Lindsay, Ann Marie (p, DTTO Addictions
Wkr)
Urquhart, Shona (p, CPN)
Russell, Annette (p,CPN)
Edmiston, Linda (TAS Wkr)
Owen, Jennie (p, Alcohol Wkr)
Urquhart, Amanda (Alcohol Wkr)
Vacant (p, Clerical Asst)
Vacant (p,Clerical Asst)

HMP Inverness
Criminal Justice Services Porterfield
Duffy Drive Inverness IV2 3HH
Tel: 01463 223489 Fax: 01463 243361
Lynn Millar (Team Mgr)
Haughey, Mike (p, SW)
Macdonald, Luisa (p, SW)
Cameron, Mike (p, SW)
Watt, Claire, (SW Addictions)
McRobert, Patricia (p, Clerical Asst)

Unpaid Work

Inverness
Criminal Justice Services The Old
Schoolhouse
196 Culduthel Road Inverness IV2 4BH
Tel: 01463 242511 Fax: 01463 716187

Millar, Lynn (Team Mgr)
Boyd, David (UWO)
Vacant (UWO)
Mackay, David (p, UWO)
Relph, Erin (FWO)
MacKenzie, Claire (Clerical Asst)
Vacant (p, Clerical Asst)

Ross-shire
Criminal Justice Services Unit 5 River
Wynd
Teaninich Industrial Estate
Alness Ross-shire IV17 0PE
Tel: 01349 884118 Fax: 01349 884158

Rainnie, Bill (Team Mgr)

Stewart, Jim (UWO)
MacKay, David (p, UWO)
Vacant (Clerical Asst)

Lochaber
Criminal Justice Services, Units 4B2–4B3
Blar Mhor Industrial Estate
Caol Fort William PH33 7NG
Tel: 01397 704668 Fax: 01397 700422

Paulin, Jeremy (Team Mgr)
Haldenby, Mark (p, UWO)
Laing, Sara (Clerical Asst)

Caithness
Criminal Justice Services Unit 27b
Airport Industrial Estate
Wick KW1 4QS
Tel: 01955 603161 Fax: 01955 603164

Rainnie, Bill (Team Mgr)
Brass, Rodney (UWO)
Keith, Tracey (Clerical Asst)

Sutherland
Criminal Justice Services
Drummuie Golspie KW10 6TA
Tel: 01408 635369 Fax: 01408 634041

Rainnie, Bill (Team Mgr)
Sinclair, Jamie (p, UWO)
MacRae, Diane (p, Clerical Asst)

Skye
Criminal Justice Services Top Floor
Tigh na Drochaid, Bridge Road
Portree Isle of Skye IV50 9ER
Tel: 01478 612943 Fax: 01478 613213

Rainnie, Bill (Team Mgr)
MacPhee, Stewart (p, UWO)
MacPherson, Ann (p, Clerical Asst)

Voluntary Projects

APEX (Employment Guidance)
17 Lotland Street Inverness IV1 1ST
Tel/fax: 01463 717033

McDonald, Alistair (Service Dev Mgr)

**Action for Children (Gaelog
Probation)**
2nd Floor 46 Church Street Inverness IV1
1EH
Tel: 01463 717227 Fax: 01463 236335
Cooper, Grahame (Service Mgr)
Snedden, Iain (Practice Mgr)

Sacro (Supported Accommodation)
Ballantyne House Academy Street
Inverness IV1 1LU
Tel: 01463 716325 Fax: 01463 716326
Jennifer MacKay (Mgr)

Venture Trust
Applecross Strathcanon IV54 8ND
Tel: 01520 744332 Fax: 01520 744306

Bibbey, Mark (Chief Exec)

Pulteney People's Project
(HomeLink, Caithness)
Tel: 01955 606950

MacNab, Katrina (Chief Exec)

Lifestyles Housing Support
46 The High Street Fort William
Tel: 01397 700740

Powell, Bryan (Mgr)

Penal Establishment

HMP Inverness
Porterfield Duffy Drive Inverness IV2
3HH

Tel: 01463 223489 Fax: 01463 243361

See Substance Misuse Team and/or
HMP Inverness above
for CJS contacts

Courts

Dingwall Sheriff Court and Justice of the
Peace Court
Dingwall IV15 9QX
Tel/fax: 01349 863153

Dornoch Sheriff Court and Justice of the
Peace Court
Dornoch IV25 3SD
Tel/fax: 01862 810224

Fort William Sheriff Court and Justice of
the Peace Court
High Street Fort William PH33 6EE
Tel: 01397 702087 Fax: 01397 706214

Inverness Sheriff Court and Justice of the
Peace Court
Inverness IV2 3EG
Tel: 01463 230782 Fax: 01463 710602

Portree Sheriff Court and Justice of the
Peace Court
Portree IV51 9EH
Tel: 01478 612191 Fax: 01478 613203

Tain Sheriff Court and Justice of the
Peace Court
Tain IV19 1AB
Tel/fax: 01862 892518

Wick Sheriff Court and Justice of the
Peace Court
Wick KW1 4AJ
Tel/fax: 01955 602846

INVERCLYDE COUNCIL

Email: firstname.lastname@inverclyde.gov.uk

Social Work Services

Kim House
Ravenscraig Hospital
Inverkip Road
Greenock
PA16 9HA
Tel: 01475 715365 Fax: 01475 714060
McAlees, Sharon (Head of Service)

Criminal Justice Services

Court Liaison/Fieldwork
2nd Floor Right 99 Dalrymple Street
Greenock PA15 1HU

Tel: 01475 714500 Fax: 01475 714515

Howard, Audrey (Service Mgr)
Bradley, John (SSW)
Thomson, Sharon (SSW)

Greenock Sheriff Court
Social Work Office
1 Nelson Street Greenock PA15 1TR
Tel: 01475 715992 Fax: 01475 715993

Johnston, David (SW)
Stewart, Kimberley (Bail Info Worker)

Community Service
Unit 6 Kingston Business Park
Port Glasgow PA14 5DR
Tel: 01475 715791 Fax: 01475 715794
Chesnutt, Andrew (Unpaid Work
Manager)

Action For Children

Integrated Criminal Justice Service
Lyle House, Unit 31, Lynedoch Industrial
Estate
Greenock PA 15 4AX
Tel: 01475 723044 Fax: 01475 723045

Fergus, Iain (Mgr)

Supervised Attendance Order Scheme
Unit 6 Kingston Business Park
Port Glasgow PA14 5DR
Tel: 01475 715791 Fax: 01475 723405
McClafferty, Louise (Sup Att Off)

Throughcare Team
Criminal Justice Team
2nd Floor Right 99 Dalrymple Street
Greenock PA15 1HU
Tel: 01475 714500 Fax: 01475 714515

Aitken, Gordon (Throughcare Co-ord)
Area covered: Inverclyde, Renfrewshire &
East Renfrewshire

MAPPA
Greenock Police Station
160 Rue End Street
Greenock PA15 1HX
Mob: 07825 584634 (no land lines yet)

Booth, Gillian (Temp)

Penal Establishments

Social Work Unit
HMP Greenock
Gateside, Greenock PA16 9AJ

Tel: 01475 883323
McCue, Gillian (ASSW)
Caroline Cassidy (SW)
Paul Kersten (SW)
Yvette Millar (SW)
Gail Hughes (SW)

Courts
Greenock Sheriff Court & Justice of the Peace Court
1 Nelson Street Greenock PA15 1TR
Tel: 01475 787073 Fax: 01475 729746

MIDLOTHIAN COUNCIL

Out of hours contact:

Emergency social work service tel: 0800 731 6969 (freephone)

Email: enquiries@midlothian.gov.uk

Communities and Wellbeing
Fairfield House 8 Lothian Road
Dalkeith EH22 3ZH
Tel: 0131 270 7500 Fax: 0131 271 3624

Criminal Justice Team
Dalkeith Social Work Centre
11 St Andrew Street Dalkeith
Midlothian EH22 1AL
Tel: 0131 271 3860 Fax: 0131 660 6792

Brewer M (Service Mgr)
Email:
Margaret.brewer@midlothian.gov.uk

Pemble I (Team Leader)
Jessup, J (Team Leader)
Criminal Justice Social Workers
Borowski, M
Brewster, A
Fletcher, S
Kennedy, F
Scorgie, A
Cameron B
Docherty J
Mullins, E (Child Wkr Caledonian)
Stephen, D (Women's Wkr Caledonian)
Martin R (CSO)
Kane, F (CSO)
Vacancy
Hicks, B (CS Asst)
Beveridge M (CS Asst)

THE MORAY COUNCIL

Out of hours tel: 0845 756 5656

Community Services Department
Council Office
High Street Elgin IV30 1BX
Tel: 01343 543451 Fax: 01343 540183

Riddell, Sandy (Corporate Director, Education & Social Care)
Carney, John (Head of Children & Families & Criminal Justice Services)

Criminal Justice Team
11 North Guildry Street
Elgin IV30 1JR
Tel: 01343 557200 Fax: 01343 557201

Dempsie, Blair (Operations Mgr)
Kelly, Jane (Team Mgr) (JS)
Richford, Tish (Team Mgr) (JS)
Cambridge, Megan (SSW)
Anderson, Peter (SW)
Dufficy, Fran (SW)
Jamieson, Sean (SW Addictions)
Reid, Ron (SW)
Terry, Liz (p, SW)
Westmacott, Jane (SW)
Clark, Anne (Support Wkr)

Other Social Work Teams

1 Gordon Street
Elgin IV30 1JQ
Tel: 01343 557222 Fax: 01343 541125

Moray Central Child Care Team
Rizza, Graeme (Team Mgr)

Moray North Childcare Team
Harkins, Gerry (Team Mgr)

Moray West Child Care Team
Auchernack House, High Street
Forres IV36 1DX
Tel: 01309 694000 Fax: 01309 694001

Cotter, Mark (Team Mgr)

Moray East Child Care Team
13 Cluny Square Buckie AB56 1AH
Tel: 01542 837200 Fax: 01542 837201

Robertson, Judy (Team Mgr)
Leitch, Robert (SW CJ)

Courts
Elgin Sheriff Court & Justice of the Peace Court
Elgin IV30 1BU
Tel: 01343 542505 Fax: 01343 559517

NORTH AYRSHIRE COUNCIL

Social Services Headquarters
4th Floor West Wing
Cunninghame House, Friars Croft
Irvine KA12 8EE
Tel: 01294 317700 Fax: 01294 317701

Colvin, Iona (Corporate Director, Social Services)
Gault, Sheena (Head of Service, Children & Families & CJ)
McCrae, James (Mgr CJ Services)

Criminal Justice Services
157 New Street **Stevenston** KA20 3HL
Tel: 01294 463924 Fax: 01294 471283

Weaver, A (Team Manager CJ Services)
Hamilton, J (Team Manager CJ Services)

Community Service Team
Block 4 Unit 2 Moorpark Place Ind Est
Stevenston KA20 3JT
Tel: 01294 608900 Fax: 01294 608897

Watson, M (Team Manager CJ Services)

Ayrshire Criminal Justice Partnership
Kiln Court, East Road,**Irvine , KA12 0BZ**
Tel: 01294 318753 Fax: 01294 318799

Programme Delivery Team
Kiln Court, East Road, **Irvine**, KA12 0BZ
Walkerdine, Sue (Team Manager Constructs)
Tel: 01294 318750, Fax: 01294 318799

Jones, Ray (Team Manager, CSOGP)

DTTO Team
(Ayrshire CJ Services)
1 Glebe Street **Stevenston** KA20 3EN
Tel: 01294 475800 Fax: 01294 475810

Davie, Andy (Team Manager CJ services)

Social Work Unit
Kilmarnock Sheriff Court
St Marnock Street **Kilmarnock** KA1 1ED
Tel: 01563 570836 Fax: 01563 570837

Courts
Kilmarnock Sheriff Court & Justice of the Peace Court
St Marnock Street Kilmarnock KA1 1ED
Tel: 01563 550024 Fax: 01563 543568

Irvine Justice of the Peace Court
66 High Street Irvine KA12 0AZ
Tel: 0300 790 0075 Fax: 01294 274171

NORTH LANARKSHIRE COUNCIL

Housing & Social Work Services
Scott House 73/77 Merry Street
Motherwell ML1 1JE
Tel: 01698 332000 Fax: 01698 332097

Fegan, Mary (Head of Social Work Services & Chief Social Work Officer)

Cringles, Lillian (Mgr, Justice Services)
Coates, Liz (Service Mgr, Justice Services)
McAuley, Iain (Service Mgr, Youth Justice)
Rodger, Kay (Snr Officer, Justice Services)

Social Work Services
Coats House Gartlea Road
Airdrie ML6 9JA
Tel: 01236 757000

Airdrie Locality
Blair, Andy (SSW, Justice Services)

Baron Chambers, Bron Way, North Carbrain Road
Cumbernauld G67 1DZ
Tel: 01236 638700

Cumbernauld Locality
Juttlay, Rajinder (SSW, Justice Services)

303 Main Street
Bellshill ML4 1AW
Tel: 01698 346666

Bellshill Locality
Murdoch, Ann (SSW, Justice Services)

122 Bank Street
Coatbridge ML5 1ET
Tel: 01236 622100

Coatbridge Locality
Ewing, Anthea (SSW, Justice Services)

Kings Building, King Street
Wishaw ML2 8BS
Tel: 01698 348200

Wishaw Locality
Kelly, Mary Ann (SSW, Justice Services)

Scott House

73/77 Merry Street
Motherwell ML1 1JE

Tel: 01698 332100

Motherwell Locality
Nicol, Karen (SSW, Justice Services)

Throughcare
2 Hunter Street
Bellshill ML4 1RN
Tel: 01698 346873

Miller, Patricia (SSW)

Ranachan, Gerry (SSW)
Gilmartin, Jane (SSW)
McCord, Lynn (Admin Assistant)
Tel: 01698 346912

Restorative Justice
2 Hunter Street
Bellshill ML4 1RN
Tel: 01698 346873

Hughes, Maureen (Service Mgr, Restorative Justice)
Goode, Tina (SSW)
Reilly, Mary (SSW)
O'Neill, Terri (SSW)
Carroll, Elaine (Admin Assistant)
Tel: 01698 346879

Penal Establishment
Social Work Unit
HMP Shotts
Newmill Canthill Road
Shotts ML7 4LE
Tel: 01501 824100

Clark, Amanda (SSW)

Courts
Airdrie Sheriff Court
Graham Street Airdrie ML6 6EE
Tel: 01236 751121 Fax: 01236 747497

Coatbridge Justice of the Peace Court
Graham Street Airdrie ML6 6EE
Tel: 01236 751121 Fax: 01236 747497

Cumbernauld Justice of the Peace Court
Graham Street Airdrie ML6 6EE
Tel: 01236 439184 Fax: 01236 747497

Justice of the Peace Court at Motherwell
4 Beckford Street Hamilton ML3 DBT
Tel: 01698 282957 Fax: 01698 201365

ORKNEY ISLANDS COUNCIL

Out of hours emergency contact:
via Balfour Hospital Kirkwall tel: 01856 888000

Email: criminal.justice@orkney.gsx.gov.uk

Orkney Health and Care
School Place **Kirkwall** KW15 1NY
Tel: 01856 873535 Fax: 01856 886453
Cowan, Cathie (Executive Director of Orkney Health and Care)
Sinclair, Caroline (Chief Social Work Officer)
O'Sullivan, Marie (Head of Service, Children's and Criminal Justice Services)

Criminal Justice Section
Council Offices School Place
Kirkwall KW15 1NY
Tel: 01856 873535 Fax: 01856 886453

Humphreys, Jon (Service Mgr)
Mathieson, Fiona (SW)
Crawford, Caroline (SW)
Vacancy (YJSW)
Mathieson, Fiona (SW)
Hall, Lindsay (CPO)
Gray, Joyce (Clerical Asst)
Learmonth, Gillian (p Clerical Asst)

Court
Kirkwall Sheriff Court
Kirkwall KW15 1PD
Tel: 01856 872110 Fax: 01856 874835

PERTH & KINROSS COUNCIL

Housing & Community Care
Perth & Kinross Council
5 Whitefriars Crescent Perth PH2 OPA
Tel: 01738 476700 Fax: 01738 476822

Burke, David (Exec Director, Housing & Community Care)
Walker, John (Depute Director, Housing & Community Care)
Gilruth, John (Head of Community Care)

Criminal Justice Service
Unit 45 St Martin's House North
King Edward Street Perth PH1 5UT
Tel: 01738 444244 Fax: 01738 444250
Email: CJS@pkc.gsx.gov.uk
Email for Reports:
CJSCourtrequests@pkc.gsx.gov.uk

Newton, John (Service Manager)
Cranmer, Charlie (Research & Info Officer, CJ Services)
Paton, Mary (Snr Admin Asst) (JS)
Patterson, Gillian (Snr Admin Asst) (JS)

Unpaid Work & Youth Justice Teams
Brown, Bill (Team Leader)

Unpaid Work Team
Bryson, Colin (Projects Officer)
Gowans, Susan (Unpaid Work Co-ordinator)
Duncan, Brenda (Case Officer)
Pow, Barbara (Case Officer)
Swan, Tracy (Case Officer)
Moran, Audrey (Case Officer)
Christie, Ron (Project Supvr)
Spark, John (Project Supvr)
Whyte, Fraser (Project Officer)
Richards, Charlie (Project Officer

Youth Justice Team
Michie, Joy (Snr Practitioner)
Anton-Thomson, Gillian (CJ Asst, Right Track)
McClymont, Alastair (Social Care Off)
Matthewson, Emma (Social Care Off)
Saunders, Amy (Social Care Off)
McKean, Jenny (Social Care Off)
SWs
Garland, Tracy
Jones, Chris
Hope, Karlyn

Supervision & Throughcare Team
Banks, Pamela (Team Leader)
Gavin, Anne (Snr Practitioner)
Mortimer, Derek (Snr Practitioner)
Bonthrone, Steve (CJ Asst)
Geekie, Radley (CJ Asst)
Murray, Gill (CJ Asst – Resettlement)
Petrie, Nicola (CJ Asst)
SWs
Cassidy, Susan
Dickson, Alan
Duncan, Robbie
Duncan, Shona
Egan, Susan
Fraser, Gordon
Penman, Shirley
Thomson, Robert
Warren, Alasdair

Admin Support
Stevenson, Jacqueline (Admin Asst)
George, Cary (Snr Clerical Asst, MAPPA)
Aitken, Aimie (Snr Clerical Assistant)
Brand, Alison (Clerical Asst)
Johnson, Yvette (Clerical Asst)
MacKenzie, Rebecca (Clerical Asst DTTO)
Milne, Carol (Clerical Asst)

Hawksby, Laura (Clerical Asst)
Young, Pauline (Clerical Asst, Reception)
Bolam, Anne (Snr Clerical Asst, Service Manager Support)

Social Work Unit

HMP Perth
3 Edinburgh Road
Perth PH2 8AT
Tel: 01738 458172 Fax: 01738 625964

Ramage, Christina (Team Leader)
MacDonald, Flora (Snr Practitioner)
Geddes, Richard (SW)
Hewitt, Elizabeth (SW)
MacKay, Margaret (SW)
Halley, Sandy (SW)
Scott, Fiona (SW)
Bibby, Aileen (Snr Clerical Asst)
Ker, Alison (Snr Clerical Asst)

Social Work Unit
Scottish Prison Service Open Estate
Tel: 01382 319333

HMP Castle Huntly
Open Estate Castle Huntly
Longforgan near Dundee DD2 5HL
Fax: 01382 360510
Greig, Lex (Team Ldr)
Millar, Anna (Snr Pract)
MacDonald, Andrew (SW)
McGrath, Paula (SW)
Whyte, Steph (SW)
Minchin, Bronia (SW)
Vannart, Alex (SW)
Simmonds, Tom (SW)
Nicoll, Christine (Snr Clerical Asst)
Vannart, Ann (Snr Clerical Asst)

Courts
Perth Sheriff Court and Justice of the Peace Court
Perth PH2 8NL
Tel: 01738 620546 Fax: 01738 623601

RENFREWSHIRE COUNCIL

NB All CJSW/HBR requests should be sent to Social Work Services, Paisley Locality Team, Abbey House, not Social Work Headquarters.

Social Work Headquarters
3rd Floor Renfrewshire House
Cotton Street Paisley PA1 1TZ
Tel: 0300 300 1199 Fax: 0141 618 6436
Macleod, Peter (Director of SW)

Hawthorn, Dorothy (Head of Childcare & Criminal Justice)

Social Work Services Fieldwork Team
Social Work Services, Paisley Locality Team,
Abbey House, 8 Seedhill Road
Paisley PA1 1JT
Tel: 0141 618 2539 Fax: 0141 618 6440

Allison Scott (Criminal Justice Services Manager)

West, David (SSW)
Cloherty, Tom (SW)
Christie, Emma (SW)
Jamieson, Paula (SW)
Kane, Allison (SW)
McEwan, James (SW)
Matheson, Catriona (SW)
Tavendale, Juliette (SW)
Wright, Gill (SW)

Hamilton, Kirsten (SSW)
Bryce, Sandy (SW)
McAleer, Alice (SW)
McGlinchey, Paul (SW)
Nelson, John (SW)
O'Neil, Karen (SW)
Seager, Mandy (SW)

Community Service Team
Units 48 – 50, Greenlaw Industrial Estate,
Wallneuk Road, Paisley, PA3 4BT
Tel: 0141 840 1001 Fax: 0141 848 6469
Connelly, Mike (SSW)
Skouse, Jake (CSA)
and: Paisley Locality Office, Abbey House,
8 Seedhill Road, Paisley PA1 1JT
Tel: 0141 618 2539 Fax: 0141 618 6440
Goodwin, Irene (CSO)
Hendry, George (CSO)
McCallum, Joe (CSO)
O'Hara, Catherine (CSO)
Elizabeth Jeffrey (CSO)

Community Alternatives Unit
20 Backsneddon Street
Paisley PA3 2DF
Tel: 0141 842 3020 Fax: 0141 842 1078

Kelly, Julie (SSW)
McKenna, Barry (SW)
Neil, Lyndsay (SW)
Sheridan, Patricia (SW Asst)
Aitchison, Karen (SW Asst)
Boylan, John (SW Asst)

Pathways Partnership Project
20 Back Sneddon Street
Paisley PA3 2DJ
Tel: 0141 842 8060 Fax: 0141 842 1078

Wilson, Lorna (Project Leader)
Clabby, Jim (SW)
Marshall, Harry (SW)
Thomson, Duncan (SW)
Toland, Frances (SW)
Mackenzie, Barbara (SWA)

St James' Street
Paisley PA3 2HW
Tel: 0141 889 0617 Fax: 0141 848 9348

Paisley Sheriff Court
Anne Buchan (SSW)
McNamara, William (SW, Court Service)
Stewart, Mary (SW Bail Officer)
Brown, Jim (SW Asst, Diversion)

Supervised Attendance Order Team
Gillespie, Richard (Resource Officer)

Courts
Paisley Sheriff Court & Justice of the Peace Court
St James' Street Paisley PA3 2HW
Tel: 0141 276 1790/1791/1792 Fax: 0141 559 4581

SCOTTISH BORDERS COUNCIL

Social Work Headquarters
Newton St Boswells
Melrose TD6 0SA
Tel: 01835 825080 Fax: 01835 825081

Lowe, Andrew (Director of Social Work Services)
Cressey, David (Head of Service, Housing and Community Justice)
Gray, Marian (Group Manager, Criminal Justice)

Criminal Justice Team
Henderson, Sarah (Team Ldr)
McKenzie, Ishbel (Team Ldr)
Birse, Billy (Manager – Unpaid Work with Offenders)
Kelly, Danny (Case Manager – Unpaid Work with Offenders)
Nichol, Diane (Admin Asst)

Social Workers
Campbell, Morag
Cousin, Marilyn
Craig, Lorraine

Hawthorn, Hannah
Moore, Clare
Nicol, Keri
Thomson, Stephen
Criminal Justice Officers
Matthews, Angela
Renwick, Derek
Deacon, Fiona
Unpaid Work Supervisors
Beck, Stewart
Farrell, Kevin
Heatlie, John
White, Jimmy

13/14 Paton Street
Galashiels TD1 3AT
Tel: 01896 664140

Courts

Duns Sheriff Court and Justice of the Peace Court
Courthouse Castlegate Jedburgh TD8 6AR
Tel: 01835 863231 Fax: 01835 864110

Jedburgh Sheriff Court and Justice of the Peace Court
Courthouse Castlegate Jedburgh TD8 6AR
Tel: 01835 863231 Fax: 01835 864110

Peebles Sheriff Court and Justice of the Peace Court
Courthouse Ettrick Terrace Selkirk TD7 4LE
Tel: 01750 721269 Fax: 01750 722884

Selkirk Sheriff Court and Justice of the Peace Court
Courthouse Ettrick Terrace Selkirk TD7 4LE
Tel: 01750 721269 Fax: 01750 722884

SHETLAND ISLANDS COUNCIL

Out of hours tel: 01595 695611 (duty social worker)

Email: firstname.lastname@shetland.gov.uk

www.shetland.gov.uk

Department Community Care

Social Work Department
91–93 St Olaf Street
Lerwick Shetland ZE1 0ES
Tel: 01595 744400 Fax: 01595 744445

Criminal Justice Social Work Unit
Tel: 01595 744446 Fax: 01595 744445

Email:
criminaljustice@shetland.gsx.gov.uk

Morgan, Denise (Executive Manager)
McKay, Shirley (SSW)
Robertson, Adrienne (PT SW)
Prittie, Francis (PT SW)
Morton Cluness, Fiona (SW)
Alderman, Andy (CS Organiser)
Halcrow, Julie (CJ Asst)
Vacant (CS Supvr)
Gilfillan, Frank (CS Supvr)
Fullerton, Ann Marie (CJ Support Wkr)

Court

Lerwick Sheriff Court
Lerwick ZE1 0HD
Tel: 01595 693914 Fax: 01595 693340

SOUTH AYRSHIRE COUNCIL

Email: nancy.mcneil@south-ayrshire.gov.uk

County Buildings

Wellington Square
Ayr KA7 1DR
Tel: 0300 123 0900

Garland, Harry (Exec Dir Children & Community)

Tel: 01292 612419
Carswell, Hugh (Hd of Service Children & Community)
Tel: 01292 612224

Children and Community

Burns House, Burns Statue Square, Ayr

Tel: 01292 616200 Fax: 01292 616338

McNeil, Nancy (Criminal Justice Mgr)
01292 612783

Criminal Justice Team

MacAdam House
34 Charlotte Street, Ayr KA7 1EA
Tel: 01292 289749 Fax: 01292 260065
TEAM LEADERS

Court Services
Hall, Drew Tel: 01292 289749/610257

Fieldwork Services
Strachan, FionaTel 01292 289749
Taylor, William; Tel 01292 289749

Unpaid Work Scheme
Lavelle, Helen Tel: 01292 289749

Administration
McCartney, Rachelle (Snr Admin Officer)

Social Work Unit – Court
Wellington Square, Ayr KA7 1EE
Tel: 01292 610257 Fax: 01292 260065

Court
Ayr Sheriff Court and Justice of the
Peace Court
Ayr KA7 1EE
Tel: 01292 268474 Fax: 01292 292249

SOUTH LANARKSHIRE COUNCIL

Social Work Headquarters
Criminal Justice Services
Council Offices, Almada Street
Hamilton ML3 0AA
Tel: 01698 453700 Fax: 01698 453784

Stevenson, Harry (Exec Dir Social Work
Resources) 01698 453700
Swift, Robert (Hd of Children and
Families & Justice Services) 01698
454887
Sing, Arun (Children Services Manager)
01698 453764
McGregor, Hugh (Service Mgr, High
Risk Offenders) 01698 894022
Dade, Santosh (Service Mgr, DTTO &
Substance Misuse) 01698 452800 or
01698 453905
Tannahill, Andrea (Service Mgr, Local
Offices & Reception Services)
01698 453905

Local Offices

East Kilbride Local Office
1st Floor, Civic Centre
Andrew Street, East Kilbride G74 1AD
Tel: 01355 807000 Fax: 01355 264458

Earl, Joyce (Team Ldr)
SWs
Foster, Mary
Murdoch, Caroline
Skeffington, Brenda

Rutherglen & Cambuslang Local Office
380 King Street
Rutherglen G73 1DQ
Tel: 0141 613 5000 Fax: 0141 613 5075

English, Allan (Team Ldr)
SWs
Borden, Claire

Campbell, Pamela
Cocozza, Caroline
Durkin, Stephen
McVittie, Charlotte
Robertson, David
Stewart, Victoria
Guthrie, Lyndsey

Blantyre Local Office
45 John Street, Blantyre G72 0JG
Tel: 01698 527400 Fax: 01698 527428

O'Donnell, Alex (Team Ldr)
Yakubu, Abu
Bagley, Liz (SW)
McAvoy, Gill (SW)
McMullan, Margaret (Groupworker)

Hamilton Local Office
Brandongate, 1 Leechlee Road
Hamilton ML3 0XB
Tel: 01698 455400 Fax: (0698 283257

Finnegan, Hilary (Team Ldr)
SWs
Connachan, Gerry
Fleming, Sheena
Reid, Lennox
Shaw, Janice

Clydesdale Local Office
Council Offices, South Vennel
Lanark ML11 7JT
Tel: 01555 673000 Fax: 01555 673401

Potter, Kim (Team Ldr)
SWs
Dunnery, Theresa
Hutchison, Moira
Biggart, Heather
Brown, Steven
Tod, Coaster
MacGregor, Fulton
Mason, Ross

Larkhall Local Office
6 Claude Street, Larkhall ML9 2BU
Tel: 01698 884656 Fax: 01698 307504

Monaghan, Mary (Team Ldr)
McBride, Michael (SW)
Lockhart, Paul (SW)
McGinn, Norma (SW)

Unpaid Work Unit
Auchentibber, East Avenue
Blantyre G72 0JB
Tel: 01698 722150
Fax: 01698 722151
O'Neill, Colin (Team Ldr CS)
Docherty, Gerry (Team Ldr CS)

Canning, Tom (CS Officer)
McGuire, Mary (CS Officer)
McGeever, Mark (CS Officer)
Pirrie, Andrew (CS Resource Asst)
Inness, John (SAO Officer)
O'Shea, Tony (SAO Officer)
Soones, Carol Anne (Training & Dev)

Clydesdale Area
Council Offices, South Vennel
Lanark ML11 7JT
Tel: 01555 673000 Fax 01555 673401
Constable, Bill (CS Officer)

Lockhart, Brian (CS Resource Asst)

Court Units

Hamilton Sheriff Court and Justice of the Peace Court
Beckford Street, Hamilton ML3 6AA
Tel: 01698 282957 Fax: 01698 201365

Social Work Court Unit
101 Almada Street, Hamilton ML3 0EX
Tel: 01698 452050 Fax: 01698 457427

Johnson, Hazel (Team Ldr)
Brady, John (SW)
Green, David (SW)
MacTavish, Sarah (SW)
Lockhart, Paul (SW)
Hughes, Karen (SW Asst)
Loudon, Jackie (SW Asst)
Corrie, Elizabeth (Bail Officer)
Davidson, Angela (Bail Officer)
Gillespie, Clare (SWA)

Lanark Sheriff Court and Justice of the Peace Court
24 Hope Street, Lanark ML11 7NE
Tel: 01555 661531 Fax: 01555 664319

Social Work Unit
Council Offices, South Vennel
Lanark ML11 7JT
Tel: 01555 673000 Fax: 01555 673401

Brady, John (SW)

DTTO
9 High Patrick Street
Hamilton ML3 7ES
Tel: 01698 452800 Fax: 01698 452831

Johnstone, Jim (Team Ldr)
Glynn, Joe (SW)
McDade, Lisa (SW)
Adams, Janet (SW)

High Risk Offenders Team
Beckford Street Annex, Council Offices
Almada Street, Hamilton ML3 0AA

Dempsey, Robert (SW) 01698 494023
McCann, Marie Therese 01698 494027
Wilson, Sarah (SW) 01698 494024

Youth Justice Team
For Youth Justice matters contact the
Children & Families Team in appropriate
local office, or headquarters on 01698
453905.

STIRLING COUNCIL

Out of hours tel: Emergency Duty Team
01786 470500

Criminal Justice Services, Social Services
Drummond House, 1st Floor, Wellgreen
Stirling FK8 2EG
Tel: 01786 471177 Fax: 01786 443640

Criminal Justice Service
Val De Souza (Interim Head of Social
Services)
Landels, Stuart (Service Mgr)

Probation & Throughcare Team
Smillie, Alistair (Team Ldr)
Haney, John (Snr Pract)
Russell, Bobby (Snr Pract)
Casey, Carol (SW)
McDonald, Seona (SW)
McCartney, James (CJ Off) – Youth
Justice
Lee, Michelle (SW)

Court, Community Service & Supervised Attendance Orders
Grinly, Helen (Team Ldr)
Kay, Linda (Court SW)
Freck, Jane (CJ Off)
Armstrong, Adele (CJ Off)
Gilmour, Norman (Snr CJ Off)
Williamson, Jenny (SW)
Sanchez, Alexandra (Snr Pract)
Hillen, Robbie Ann (SW)

Forth Valley Criminal Justice Drug Treatment Services
Drummond House, 2nd Floor, Wellgreen
Place
Stirling FK8 2EG
Tel: 01786 443900 Fax: 01786 443901

DTTO Team
Mackie, Dot (Team Ldr)
Shillington, Aileen (SW)
O'Donnell, John (Snr Prac)
Stewart, Norma (Treatment Nurse)
Steele, Alan (Treatment Nurse)

Fast Track Team
Denholm, Anne (Treatment Nurse)
Neary, Denise (Care Mgr NHS)
Snell, Susan (Treatment Nurse)
Watson, Anne (SW Asst)

Penal Establishment

HMP Cornton Vale
Cornton Road, Stirling FK9 5NY
Tel: 01786 835359 Fax: 01786 833597
Walls, Alison (Team Leader)
Collins, Linsey (SW)
Sarah Simpson (SW)
Hoey, Carol Anne (SW)
Travers, Jane (SW)
Mitchell, Gillie (SW)

Courts

Stirling Sheriff Court and Justice of the
Peace Court
Stirling FK8 1NH
Tel: 01786 462191 Fax: 01786 470456

WEST DUNBARTONSHIRE COUNCIL

Out of hours tel: 0800 811 505

Social Work Headquarters

Community Health & Care Partnership
Council Offices, Garshake Road
Dumbarton G82 3PU
Tel: 01389 737000 Fax: 01389 737513

Redpath, Keith (Director)

Community Health & Care Partnership

Criminal Justice Services
Municipal Buildings, Station Road
Dumbarton G82 1NR
Tel: 01389 738484 Fax: 01389 738480

Firth, Norman (Partnership Mgr)

Steven, Craig (SSW)

Dady, Philip (SSW)
Steven, Craig (SSW)
SWs
McLaughlin, Mariclaine
Ferguson, Marianne

Robertson, Helen
Brown, Janice
Carruthers, Donna
Sellars, Connie
Bohill, Christine
McLean, Gordon
Currie, Anne (Bail Officer)
Rankine, Carol (SW Asst)
Wrigley, Lorraine (Woman's Support Off,
Domestic Abuse)
McVey, Grace (Woman's Support Wkr,
Domestic Abuse)
Colliingwood, Alisa (Hope Wkr)

Groupworkers
Gallagher, Michael
Haggerty, Eddie
Johnstone, Alex
Throughcare Team
Livingstone, Maureen (SSW)
SWs
McGroggan, Isobel
McGuire, John
Traynor, Petrina
McKechnie, Anne

Unpaid Work Team
Pryce, Ruth (Unpaid Work Team
Manager)
Unpaid Work Case Officer
Hamilton, Margaret
Monaghan, Seamus
O'Hara, Edward (Unpaid work organiser)
Freeland, Bill (Unpaid work organiser)
Kathleen, Sweeny
Taylor, Nicola
Glen, Anne (APPEX Wkr)

Turnaround
Douglas, Gary
Campbell, Heather

DTTO
Dowall, Joanna (SSW)
Boag, Chris (SW)
Keegan, Helen (SW)
Williams, Caroline (Support Worker)

Courts

Dumbarton Sheriff Court and Justice of
the Peace Court
Church Street, Dumbarton G82 1QR
Tel: 01389 763266 Fax: 01389 764085

WEST LOTHIAN COUNCIL

Out of hours tel: 01506 281028
Email: tim.ward@westlothian.gsx.gov.uk

Social Policy Headquarters
West Lothian Civic Centre
Howden South Road
Livingston EH54 6FF
Tel: 01506 282043

West Lothian Civic Centre
Howden South Road
Livingston EH54 6FF
Tel: 01506 280999 Fax: 01506 281243
Email:
Criminaljusticeteam@westlothian.gsx.gov.
uk

Criminal Justice Services
Tim Ward – Senior Manager, Young
People and Public Protection
Gillian Oghene – Group Manager,
Criminal Justice/Youth Justice
Fiona Muir – Administration Officer
Paul Streater – Service Development
Officer

Assessment and Early Intervention Team
Linda Probka (Team Manager)
John Cheighton (Senior Practitioner)
Lynne Foster (Senior Practitioner)
Edith Hogg (Senior Practitioner)
Patrick Kelly (Social Worker)
Margaret Smith (Admin Assistant)
Alison Aien, Social Worker
Chris Allan, Criminal Justice Assistant

Community Payback Team
Vivienne Murphy (Team Manager)
Richard Amos (Social Worker)
Daryl Chin (Social Worker)
Chris Paxton (Social Worker)
David Timpany (Social Worker)
Amy Johnston (Social Worker)
Geoff Pritchard (Project Worker)
Brian Hughson (Community Work Order
Officer)
David Young (Community Work Order
Officer)
Nik Graham (Criminal Justice Assistant)
Laura Mackie (Criminal Justice Assistant)
Kate Fleming (Social Worker)
Laura Reid (Admin Assistant)
Pamela Bestwick (Admin Assistant)
Nathan Strain, (Criminal Justice
Assistant)
Jan Scott, (Criminal Justice Assistant)
David Winning, (Criminal Justice
Assistant)

Throughcare Team
Robin Allen (Team Manager)
Stephen Holmes (Senior Practitioner)
Eilidh Cook (Social Worker)
Laura Murray (Social Worker)
Cameron Wilson (Social Worker)
David Walker (Criminal Justice Assistant)
Harry Cameron (Admin Assistant)

Drug Treatment & Testing Orders Team
Sharon Oxley (Team Manager)
Caroline Campbell (Social Worker)
Alison McInally, (Criminal Justice
Assistant)
Kelly Morrice (Criminal Justice Assistant)
Tom McGlone (Addiction Nurse)
Sarah Smillie (Admin Assistant)

Youth Justice Team
Kevin Carter (Team Manager)
Douglas Allan (Support Worker)
Heather Allan (Social Worker)
Jo Reynolds (Social Worker)
Margaret Smillie (Social Worker)
Sarah Longson (Support Worker)
Tam Hall (Support Worker)
Natalija Straiziene (Support Worker)
Kim Young (Clerical Officer)

Prison Based Social Work Team

HMP Addiewell
Station Road Addiewell West Lothian
EH55 8QA
Tel: 01506 874566 Fax: 01506 874563
Email:
addiewellprison/cjsteam@westlothian.
gsx.gov.uk
Mary Graham (Team Manager)
Annemarie McCheyne (Social Worker)
Ian Murray (Social Worker)
John White (Social Worker)
Selena Smith (Social Worker)
Claire Murray (Social Worker)
Grace Kirk (Admin Assistant)

Courts
Livingston Sheriff Court & Justice of the
Peace Court
Livingston EH54 6FF
Tel: 01506 402400 Fax: 01506 415262

COMMUNITY PROJECTS: NACRO – THE CRIME REDUCTION CHARITY

Head Office
Park Place 10–12 Lawn Lane
London SW8 1UD
Tel: 020 7840 7200 Fax: 020 7840 7240
www.nacro.org.uk

Registered charity no 226171
Email: (unless otherwise stated)
firstname.lastname@nacro.org.uk

Websites
Corporate: www.nacro.org.uk
Resettlement Service Finder:
www.rsfinder.info
Resettlement Advice Service Information &
advice for ex-offenders, their families &
people working with them.
Tel: 020 7840 6464
Prisoners only tel: 0800 0181 259 (freephone)
Email: helpline@nacro.org.uk

Leadership Team
Head Office, as above

Chief Executive: Paul McDowell Tel: 020 7840
7208 Fax: 020 7840 7240

Director Finance & Corporate Service:
Patrick Murphy Tel: 020 7840 7226 Fax: 020
7840 7240

Director Human Resources: Lucy Anderson
T: 020 7840 7209 Fax: 020 7840 7240

Director Strategic Development: Graham
Beech Tel: 020 7840 7209 Fax: 020 7840 7240

Policy and Public Affairs
Head Office, as above
Head of Policy and Public Affairs: Sally
Benton 020 7840 7215 / 07423 43403
Media Manager: Alex Dziedzan 020 7840 7214
/ 0797 418 9979
Press Officer: Amy Hanson 020 7840 7216 /
07423 434 038
Media out of hours: 07974 189979
Policy Officer: Rosie Miles 020 7840 7220
Online communications: Minuche Mazumdar
020 7840 7217
Brand and Marketing Team: 020 7840 7232 /
brandandmarketing@nacro.org.uk

Equality Strategy
Head office, as above
Head of Inclusion and Development Anis
Ghanti Tel: 0121 380 4856 M: 07423 43 40 09

Finance
Director: Patrick Murphy (head office)
Finance team: Challenge House 148–150 High
Street Aston Birmingham B6 4US
Tel: 0121 250 5250 Fax: 0121 359 3510

Health and Safety
Health and Safety Manager: Andrew Johnson
Challenge House, as above
Tel: 0121 380 4866 Fax: 0121 359 3510

Human Resources Directorate
Head Office and Challenge House
Tel: 0121 380 4884 Fax: 0121 359 1760)

Director: Lucy Anderson Tel: 020 7840 7209

IT
Challenge House, as above
Tel: 0121 250 5250 Fax: 0121 270 2324

Property & Contracts
Asst Director: Dave McCarthy
567a Barlow Moor Road Chorlton-cum-Hardy
Manchester M21 8AE
Tel: 0161 860 7444 Fax: 0161 860 7555

Nacro Services East
(Bedfordshire, Cambridgeshire, Essex,
Hertfordshire, Lincolnshire, Norfolk &
Suffolk)

Area Mgr: Claire Kirk Fenland House, as
above Tel: 01945 587898 Fax: 01945 582670

Area Mgr Essex: Donia Slyzuk
Suite 2, Unit 6, Challenge Way, Hythe Hill,
Colchester, Essex CO1 2LY
Tel: 01206 798954 Mobile: 07436 260983

Area Mgr East Midlands: Sara Jones
Nacro, The Crime Reduction Charity
12 Melville Street Lincoln LN5 7HW
Tel: 01522 525383 Mobile: 07866440059 Fax:
01522 870178

Nacro Services Midlands
*Area Mgr West Midlands, Shropshire,
Staffordshire and Warwickshire:* Charlie Duffin
Nacro, The Crime Reduction Charity
56–60 Church Street, Tamworth,
Staffordshire B79 7DF
Tel: 01827 57219 Fax: 01827 51587 Mobile:
07967 210381

Nacro Services North
(Cumbria, Newcastle, Humberside, Durham
Tees Valley, Yorkshire)

Area Mgr North East & Cumbria: Brian
Rowcroft
Nacro, The Crime Reduction Charity

Hutchinson St, Stockton on Tees TS18 1RW
Tel: 01642 615554 Fax: 020 7840 7240 Mobile:
07920189190

Nacro Services South
Acting Area Mgr Wales & Cheshire: Marsha
Allen
Nacro, The Crime Reduction Charity
Interim Area Manager (London & South)
14B Stowage, London SE8 3ED
Tel: 020 8469 3366 Mobile: 07815 842 875 Fax:
0208 469 2233

Nacro Services West & Wales
Area Mgr Wales & Cheshire: Anne M Newhall
Nacro, The Crime Reduction Charity
Unit 2a Chestnut Court, Menai Park, Bangor
LL57 4FH
Uned 2a Llys Castan, Parc Menai, Bangor
LL57 4FH

SACRO

National Office Services

National Office
29 Albany Street
Edinburgh EH1 3QN
info@national.sacro.org.uk
Tel: 0131 624 7270 Fax: 0131 624 7269

Administration
Finance & Payroll
Human Resources
Operations Support
IT Management & Support
Publicity & Media Services

Chief Executive: Tom Halpin
Email: info@ sacro.org.uk

Scottish Community Mediation Centre
29 Albany Street
Edinburgh EH1 3QN
Tel: 0131 624 9200 Fax: 0131 557 2102
Email: infoscmc@sacro.org.uk

Aberdeen & Aberdeenshire
110 Crown Street
Aberdeen AB11 6HJ
Tel: 01224 560560 Fax: 01224 560 551
Email: info@aberdeen.sacro.org.uk

Intensive support & monitoring

Supported tenancies
Supported accommodation
Tel: 01244 560550

Restorative justice services

Tel: 01244 560560

Community mediation
Street mediation
Tel: 01244 560570

Angus
Unit E, Market Mews
Market Street, Dundee DD5 4AA
Tel: 01382 459252 Fax: 01382 459318
Email: info@dundee.sacro.org.uk

Community mediation

Argyll & Bute
6/14 Bridge Street
Dumbarton, Glasgow G82 1NT
Tel: 01389 772031 Fax: 01389 772033
Email: info@argyllbute.sacro.org.uk

Restorative justice services

Ayrshire
Belford Mill, 16 Brewery Road,
Kilmarnock KA1 3HZ
Tel: 01563 525815 Fax: 01563 525328
Email: info@ayrshire.sacro.org.uk

Restorative justice services
Arrest referral service
Bail supervision

Dumfries & Galloway
Children's Services, Council Offices
Dryfe Road, Lockerbie DG11 2AP
Tel: 01576 205070 Fax: 01576 204411
Email: info@dumgal.gov.uk

Youth justice services (east)

Supporting people services

c/o Youth Justice, Dunbae House
Church Street, Stranraer DG9 7JG
Tel: 01776 702151 Fax: 01776 707282
Email: paulinebaxter@dumgal.gov.uk
Youth justice services (west)

Dundee
Suite E, Market Mews
Market Street, Dundee DD1 3LA
Tel: 01382 459252 Fax: 01382 459318
Email: info@dundee.sacro.org.uk

Community mediation

Suite F, Market Mews
Market Street, Dundee DD1 3LA
Tel: 01382 524758 Fax: 01382 524757
Email: info@dundee.sacro.org.uk
Restorative Justice

East Dunbartonshire
c/o East Dunbartonshire Council,
Southbank House
Strathkelvin Place, Glasgow G66 1XQ
Tel: 0141 777 3000 Fax: 0141 777 3010
Youth Justice Services

East Lothian
The Brunton Hall, Ladywell Way
Musselburgh EH21 6AF
Tel: 0131 653 5295 Fax: 0131 665 7643
Email: infoeastlothian @sacro.org.uk

Community mediation

Edinburgh
Community Justice Centre
23 Dalmeny Street
Edinburgh EH6 8PG
Tel: 0131 622 7500 Fax: 0131 622 7525
Email: info@lothiancjs.sacro.org.uk
Alcohol Groupwork service
Arrest referral
Throughcare
'Another Way' service for street sex
workers
Travel service
Restorative justice services
Edinburgh Community Mediation
29 Albany Street
Edinburgh EH1 3QN
Tel: 0131 624 9200 Fax: 0131 557 2102
Email: infoedincm@sacro.org.uk
Community Mediation

Falkirk Youth Services
c/o Unit 1, St John's Sawmill
Etna Road, Falkirk FK2 7EG
Tel: 01324 501230 Fax: 01324 501061
Email: sacro@falkirk.gov.uk

Youth Justice services

Fife
24 Hill Street
Kirkcaldy Fife KY1 IHX
Tel: 01592 593100 Fax: 01592 593133
Email: info@fife.sacro.org.uk

Youth Justice services
Community mediation
Peer mediation in schools
Transition to high school training
Fife Circles of Support & Accountability
Women's Mentoring Service

Forth Valley
c/o Falkirk Council, Brockville,
Hope Street, Falkirk FK1 5RW
Tel: 01324 506464 Fax: 01324 506465
Email: info@falkirk.sacro.org.uk

Groupwork service (domestic abuse)
Groupwork service (sexual offenders)
Email:
info@groupworkservices.sacro.org.uk

Supported accommodation

Housing Advice Service
Email: info@falkirksas.sacro.org.uk
Restorative justice services
Email: info@falkirk.sacro.org.uk

Glasgow
Central Chambers, 93 Hope Street
Glasgow G2 6LD
Tel: 0141 248 1763 Fax: 0141 248 1686
Email: info@glasgow.sacro.org.uk

Bail curfew service
Intensive support & monitoring
Supported accommodation
Throughcare service
Travel service
Community Payback Service
Women's Mentoring Service

Highland
Ballantyne House, 84 Academy Street
Inverness IV1 1LU
Tel: 01463 716325 Fax: 01463 716326
Email: info@highland.sacro.org.uk

Supported accommodation

North & South Lanarkshire
11 Merry Street
Motherwell ML1 1JJ
Tel: 01698 230433 Fax: 01698 230410
Email: info@nslanarkshire.sacro.org.uk

Restorative justice services
Arrest referral
Women's Mentoring Service

Moray
Guildry House, Hall Place, Elgin IV30 1JP
Tel: 01343 559737
Email: info@moray.sacro.org.uk

Supported Accommodation Service

14–20 Covesea Road,
Bishopmill, Elgin IV30 4JX

Young person's Supported
Accommodation Service
Community Mediation

Orkney
43 Junction Road
Kirkwall, Orkney KW15 1AR
Tel/fax: 01856 875815
Email: info@orkney.sacro.org.uk

Supported accommodation
Youth justice services
Community mediation

Perth & Kinross
24 Hill Street
Kirkcaldy Fife KY1 IHX
Tel: 01592 593100 Fax: 01592 593133
Email: info@fife.sacro.org.uk
Community mediation services
Youth Justice Services

West Dunbartonshire
6/14 Bridge Street
Dumbarton, Glasgow G82 1NT
Tel: 01389 772031 Fax: 01389 772033
Email: info@argyllbute.sacro.org.uk

Youth justice services

SOVA

Central Administration
SOVA Head Office & Southern Area Office
1st Floor, Chichester House
37 Brixton Road, London SW9 6DZ
Tel: 020–7793 0404 *Fax: 020–7735 4410*

Janet Crowe (Acting Chief Exec)
Val Abraham (Core Administrator, South)
David Barlow (Dir Ops, South)
Ineke Burke (Area Co-Ord, South)
Susan Cooper (Dir Learning & Quality)
Coral Evans (It Mgr)
Steve Lally (Learning & Quality Co-Ord)
Steve Mcpartland (IT Mgr)
Tony Savage (Head of ICT)
Jennie Spanton (Dev Mgr, South)

North Area Office (Sheffield)
St Silas House
18 Moore Street, Sheffield S3 7UW
Tel: 0114–270 3700 *Fax: 0114–270 3701*

Sharon Lowrie (Finance Director)
Keith Osborne (Financial Controller)
Anne Naylor (Finance Officer)

Lynne Spamer (Finance Officer)
Sam Briggs (Finance Officer)
Gary Kernaghan (Dir Dev & Ops)
Julia Stanley (Dir Ops, North)
Andy Whitehead (Dev Mgr, North)
Sam Dumoulin (Area Mgr, North)
Gina Carter (Area Mgr, North)
Kerry Halsall (Area Co-Ord, North)
June Graham (HR Mgr)
Heather Eyre (Core Administrator, North)

SOVA Midlands Area Office (Birmingham)
Scala House, Suites F6 F7 FS
5th Floor, Scala House, 36 Holloway Circus
Queensway, Birmingham, B1 1EQ
Tel: 0121–643 7400 *Fax: 0121–643 7454*

Sophie Wilson (Dir Ops, Midlands)
Gaynor Cartwright (Area Co-Ord, Midlands)

4. SOVA Wales Office (Newtown)
2nd Floor, Ladywell House
Newtown, Powys SY16 1JB
Tel: (01686) 623873 *Fax: (01686) 623875*

Chris Arnold (Dir Ops, Wales)
Martin Jones (Area Co-Ord, Wales)

Projects
FC Scott Foundation (Lancaster Farms)
HMP/YOI Lancaster Farms
SOVA Mentoring Link Building
Far Moor Lane, Stone Row Head
Off Quermore Road, Lancaster LA1 3QZ
Tel: (01524) 563828 *Fax: (01524) 563833*

Becky Bland (Co-Ord, Volunteers)

HMP Garth
Ulnes Walton Lane
Leyland, Preston PR26 8NE
Tel: (01772) 443585

Imraan Hussain (Housing Officer)
Emily Keogh (Housing Co-Ord)

HMP Kirkham
Freckleton Road, Preston
Lancashire PR4 2RN
Tel: (01772) 675677 *Fax: (01772) 675600*

Deborah Rossall (Housing Officer)
Tara Smallshaw (Housing Co-Ord)

Hull Independent Visitors
Stonefield House
Young Peoples Support Service
Stonefield House
16/20 King Edward's Street
Hull HU1 3SS
Tel: (01482) 331004 *Fax: (01482) 318356*

Louise Brown (Project Mgr)
Richard Mullins (Co-Ord, Volunteers)

London Offender Intensive Support Programme
SOVA, Chichester House, 37 Brixton Road
London, SW9 6DZ
Tel: (020) 7793 5879

Sarah Connor (Specialist Mgr)

Norfolk Probation Partnership
SOVA Norfolk
Centenary House, 2nd Floor
19 Palace Street, Norfolk NR3 1RT
Tel: (01603) 303018

Anna Haggith (Project Mgr)

Sheffield Mentoring Services
c/o SOVA Regional Office
3rd Floor, St Silas House
18 Moore Street, Sheffield, S3 7UW
Tel: 0114–270 3744 *Fax: 0114–270 3701*

Dennis Ward (Support Officer)
Rosie Chitty (Project Mgr)

SOVA Barnsley ETE
2nd Floor, Central Chambers
74–75 Eldon Street, Barnsley S70 2JN
Tel: (01226) 215257 *Fax: (01226) 215262*

Lorna Szkliniarz (Co-Ord)
Libby Wood (Admin & Monitoring Officer)
Helen Swift (Project Mgr)
John Parker (Admin Assistant)
Joan Bradley (Co-Ord)
Jonathan Ferguson (Support Officer)
Philip Clough (Support Officer)
Mark Willoughby (Support Officer)

SOVA Barnsley Youth Justice
BMBC Youth Offending Team
Crookes Street, Barnsley S70 6BX
Tel: (01226) 774986 *Fax: (01226) 774968*

Tim Hawkins (Project Mgr)

Rosemary Delderfield (Bail & Remand Officer)
Gillian Grainger (Bail & Remand Officer)

SOVA Bexley
c/o Leaving Care Team
Howbury Centre
Slade Green Road
Erith, Kent DA8 2HX
Tel: (01322) 356463 *Fax: (01322) 356473*

Chrissie Wild (Project Mgr)
Philip Erswell (Support Officer)
Jenny Hudson (Support Worker)

SOVA Camden YOT Mentoring
Third Floor, Crowndale Centre
218–220 Eversholt Street
London NW1 1BD
Tel: 0207–974 6173 *Fax: 0207–974 4163*

Danielle Thorn (Project Mgr)
Michael Sojirin (Support Officer)
Jennifer Winters (Support Officer)

SOVA Canolfan Dewi Sant
Clwyd Buildings, Clwyd Street
Rhyl, Wales LL18 3LA
Tel: (01745) 362429 *Fax: (01745) 362434*

Brian Davies (Support Officer)
Imogene Elie (Support Worker)
Wyn Roberts (Support Worker)
Heather Saunders (Admin Assistant)
Geoff Bainbridge (Project Mgr)
Dawn Tisdell-Melling (Support Worker)
Melanie Newport (Support Worker)
Sharon Gibbon (Support Worker)
Stephan Burke (Support Worker)

SOVA CAST
Leaving Care Team
92–98 Queen Street, Sheffield S1 1WU
Tel: 0114–293 0034 *Fax: 0114–275 2357*

Thelma Whittaker (Project Mgr)
Christian Dixon (Support Worker)

SOVA Croydon Young People
Cornerstone House, 14 Willis Road
Croydon CR0 2XX
Tel: 0208–665 5668 *Fax: 0208–665 1972*

Pauline Mcgrath (Senior Project Mgr)
Ally Mckinlay (Project Mgr)
Angela Pryce (Support Officer)
Angela Sinclair (Support Officer)
Grace Williams (Support Officer)

SOVA Derby Community Safety Partnership & Appropriate Adults
2nd Floor, St Peters House
Gower Street, Derby DE1 9BK
Tel: (01332) 256826 *Fax: (01332) 256830*

Kelly Buswell (Project Mgr)
Alan Keeton (Project Co-Ord)
Clive Topley (Support Officer)
Martin Cooper (Support Officer)
Helen Stretton (Victim Liaison Support Officer)
Katie Peirce (Admin Assistant)

SOVA Derby Engage
Suite 30, Beaufort Business Centre
Beaufort Street, Derby DE21 6AH
Tel: 07947 126189 *Fax: (01332) 256830*

Martin Cooper (Support Officer)

SOVA Ealing
2 Cheltenham Place
Acton, Ealing, London W3 8JS
Tel: 0208–896 0042 *Fax: 0208–752 2179*

Jean-Michel Jordan (Project Mgr)
Khurm Islam (Practical Skills Co-Ord)
Simone Hill (Support Officer)

SOVA Eastern Circles of Support and Accountability
Stevenage Probation Office
Argyle House, Argyle Way, Stevenage
Herts, SG1 2AD
Tel: (TBC)

Annabel Francis (Specialist Mgr)

SOVA Essex
The Probation Office
4th Floor, Ashby House
Brook Street, Chelmsford CM1 1UH
Tel: (01245) 287154 *Fax: (01245) 491321*

Peter Brown (Project Mgr)

SOVA Essex DAT Mentoring
54 New Street, Chelmsford
Essex, CM1 1NE
Tel: (01245) 345401

Alison Battersby (Project Mgr)
Brian Hunt (Support Officer)

SOVA Herts
25d Alma Road
St Albans, Herts AL1 3AR
Tel: (01727) 867 800

Anne Regan (Project Mgr)
Cathy Sanderson (Admin/Support Worker)
Sharon Ahmad (Support Officer)
Barbara Bathurst (Support Officer)

SOVA Humberside NPS Employment Project
Salters House, Salters Court
156 High Street
Hull HU1 1NQ
Tel: (01482) 480241

Hayley Cullen (Co-Ord ETE)
Kevin Carrick (Project Mgr)
Dennis Margerison (Administrator)
Kenny Ross (Support Worker)
Julie Lancaster (Support Worker)
Cheryl Carrick (Admin Assistant)
Paul Banyard (Support Worker)
Nanette Tuck (Support Officer)

SOVA Invest to Save Bail Support Scheme
Valley Mills Trading Estate
334 Meanwood, Leeds LS7 2JF
Tel: 0113 239 2674 *Fax: 0113–237 9499*

Debbie Harding (Project Mgr)

(07809) 587167
Daniel Priest (Volunteer Co-Ord)
Philip Marsham (Support Worker)

SOVA Lincolnshire IV and Befrienders
Lamb Gardens, Lincoln LN2 4EG
Tel: (01522) 567711 *Fax: (01522) 537490*

Helen Caskie (Support Officer)
Carrie Flint (Support Officer)
Jayne Watson (Admin Assistant)

SOVA Lincolnshire Mentoring
SOVA Volunteer Centre
Lamb Gardens, Lincoln LN2 4EG
Tel: (01522) 567711 *Fax: (01522) 537490*

Maureen Keddy (Project Mgr)
Carrie Flint (Support Officer)
Elaine Harwin (Volunteer Co-Ord)
Jane Buchanan (Admin Assistant)

SOVA London Probation Impact Project
SOVA, Chichester House,
37 Brixton Road
London SW9 6DZ
Tel: (020) 7793 5881

Beatrice Celotti (Project Mgr)

Jocelyn Bartlett-Mingle (Volunteer
Co-Ord)

SOVA Newham Mentoring Project
Newham DIP
2nd Floor, 409 High Street
Stratford, London E15 4QZ
Tel: (020) 8430 6633

Vacancy (Project Mgr)

SOVA NEWID
204 High Street
Bangor LL57 1NY
Tel: (01248) 352974 *Fax: (01248) 364755*

Soo Paul (Support Officer)

SOVA NEWID
Priory Offices, 8–10 Priory Street
Wrexham, Clwyd LL11 1SU
Tel: (01978) 262223 *Fax: (01978) 263332*

Sheree Davies (Support Officer)

SOVA P2 BME Employment for All
33 Heathfield, Swansea
SA1 6EJ
Tel: (01792) 463597 *Fax: (01792) 461884*

Tarig Sanousi (Project Mgr)
Susan Raddon (Admin Assistant)

SOVA Cardiff Refugee Services
Marine House
23 Mount Stuart Square
Cardiff, Wales CF10 5DP
Tel: 029–2049 5281 *Fax: 029–2049 2148*

Glyn Parry (Project Mgr)
Julia Alderman (Admin Assistant)

SOVA Cardiff REIS Project
Marine House
23 Mount Stuart Square
Cardiff, Wales CF10 5DP
Tel: (029) 2049 5281 *Fax: (029) 2049 2148*

Adil Shashaty (Project Mgr)

SOVA Rotherham
Bank Courtyard, 2a Wellgate
Rotherham S60 2NN
Tel: (01709) 839579 *Fax: (01709) 515111*

Aileen Housley (Co-Ord)
Janette Walker (Project Mgr)
Michelle Marshall (Co-Ord)
Margo Middleton (Support Worker)

Jenny Mattrick (Support Officer)
Paula Martin (Specialist Mgr)
Michelle Griffin (Support Worker)
Sally Sedgley (Admin & Monitoring
Officer)
Michelle Smith (Support Officer)

SOVA Sheffield Youth Justice Project
7 St Peters Close
Sheffield S1 2EJ
Tel: 0114–228 8545 *Fax: 0114–228 8500*

Darren Smith (Project Mgr)
Fahreen Khan (Support Worker)
Stephen Walker (Admin Assistant)
John Graham (Support Worker)

SOVA Staffordshire Leaving Care
Stafford Area Office
Madford Retail Park
Foregate Street
Stafford ST16 2PA
Tel: (01785) 276984

Margaret Collier (Support Officer)
Hannah Evans (Project Mgr)
Michelle Elliot (Support Officer)

SOVA Thames Valley Mentoring Project
Units C/D, Agora Centre
47–49 Church Street
Wolverton MK12 5LD
Tel: (07809) 587005

Kathleen Power (Project Mgr)

SOVA Transform
5th Floor, Scala House
36 Holloway Circus
Queensway, Birmingham B1 1EQ
Tel: 0121–643 7400 *Fax: 0121–643 7454*

John Leach (Area Mgr)
Stephen Ashton (Volunteer Support
Officer)
Tarah Inniss (Volunteer Support
Officer/Cover Support Worker)
Anesta Benjamin (Support Worker)
Leslie Rennocks (Employment Support
Worker)
Claire Evans (Employment Support
Worker)

SOVA Young London

London – Cornerstone House
Cornerstone House, 14 Willis Road
Croydon CR0 2XX

Tel: 0208–665 5668 *Fax: 0208–665 1972*

Adwoa Jeremiah (Project Mgr)

v involved

VAS, The Circle
33 Rockingham Lane, Sheffield S1 4FW
Tel: 0114–253 6755 *Fax: 0114–253 6756*

Fiona Ross (Youth Volunteer Dev Mgr)
Jonathan Tyrell (Youth Volunteer
Adviser)
Tamar Wharam (Youth Volunteer
Adviser)

CATCH22

Formerly Rainer and Crime Concern,
amalgamated from the two national charities
in 2008.

London head office
26 Seward Street
London EC1V 3PA
Tel: 020 7336 4800 *Fax: 020 7336 4801*

HR and Facilities
*Regional office for HR, Facilities, all support
services*
Rectory Lodge, High Street, Brasted
Westerham, Kent TN16 1JF
Tel: (01959) 578202 *Fax: (01959) 561891*

www.catch-22.org.uk

A forward looking social business, Catch22
has over two hundred years' experience of
providing services that help people in tough
situations to turn their lives around.

Our programmes help those we work with to
steer clear of crime or substance misuse, do
the best they can in school or college and
develop skills for work, live independently on
leaving care or custody, gain new skills and
confidence as parents, and play a full part in
their community.

SERVICES FOR OFFENDERS: ST MUNGO'S OFFENDER SERVICES

Housing Advice Service provides housing
advice for new prisoners with problems that
can arise from a prison sentence. Works with
prisoners to plan for their discharge, by
finding accommodation for the day of release.
Focuses on post-release needs so that young
clients have the best chance of sustaining a
crime-free life back in their community.

Includes support and information to the
families with concerns about the release of a
family member with accommodation issues.
Provides a mediation service to try to rebuild
relationships between clients and their
families to enable a return to the family home.
The team liaises with the Probation Service,
solicitors, social workers and court officials.
They will provide support at court hearings
when required

Assessment & Referral Service provides
an initial screening assessment of all new
prisoners within 4 days of entering the prison
to identify needs and make referrals to all of
the relevant agencies working within the
prison. The assessment identifies housing,
substance use, alcohol, health, children and
family, finance and debt, attitude and
behavioural needs.

Muslim Resettlement project at HMP
Pentonville for prisoners from a Muslim
background. Builds links with a range of
Muslim agencies and services in the prison
and the community to improve resettlement
prospects for these prisoners.

Floating Support dovetails with prison based
services and local probation and
homelessness agencies. It is developing best
practice in meeting the housing needs of
Probation clients, in the context of community
based orders and drug requirements.

Offender Work and Learning Service
provides support to male and female
ex-offenders over 18 who want training to
improve their work skills. Provides coaching
to help in finding employment. Helps people
who wish to set up their own businesses,
including support finding grants and specialist
business planning advice. It offers workshops
on personal development and skills training,
and a chance to develop business idea. Offers
personal one-to-one careers and job coaching,
supporting clients to obtain funding for
training and education, opportunities to
volunteer, advice on disclosure of convictions
and help with planning. Support is provided
with setting up bank accounts and applying
for passports or other ID. Access to
computers with internet access to job sites
and use of telephones, photocopier and fax.
Offers specific support to women, on issues
such as building self confidence,
assertiveness, and sharing experiences with
other women.

HM Prison & YOI Feltham

Housing Advice, Resettlement & Post-Release Floating Support Service
Sam Cowie, Manager
Tel: 020 8844 5374
Samantha.cowie@hmps.gov.gsi.uk
samc@mungos.org

Eligibility criteria
Serving or remand prisoners. Aged 18+
No geographic restrictions

HMP Pentonville

Housing Advice, Resettlement Service
Sam Cowie, Manager
Tel: 020 7023 7320
Samantha.cowie@hmps.gov.gsi.uk
samc@mungos.org

Eligibility criteria
Serving or remand prisoners. Aged 18+
No geographic restrictions

Muslim Resettlement Service
Ahmed Patel, Service Co-ordinator
Tel: 07791 7212781
ahmedpatel@mungos.org

Eligibility criteria
Serving or remand Muslim prisoners.
Aged 18+
No geographic restrictions, although the service focuses on Muslim prisoners from East London

HMP Wormwood Scrubs

Housing Advice, Resettlement Service
Eligibility criteria
Serving or remand prisoners. Aged 18+
No geographic restrictions

Assessment and Referral Service
Eligibility criteria
All new prisoners

Michael Kenny, Manager
Tel: 020 8588 3649
michael.kenny@hmps.gov.gsi.uk
samc@mungos.org

HMP Latchmere House

Housing Advice, Resettlement Service
Michael Kenny, Manager
Tel: 020 8588 3649

michael.kenny@hmps.gov.gsi.uk
samc@mungos.org

Eligibility criteria
Serving or remand prisoners. Aged 18+
No geographic restrictions

Tower Hamlets Resettlement Service
(The Looking Out Project)
Sam Cowie, Manager
Tel: 020 8844 5374
Samantha.cowie@hmps.gov.gsi.uk
samc@mungos.org

Eligibility criteria
Serving or remand prisoners preparing for
discharge to LB of Tower Hamlets. Aged 18+

Harrow Probation Housing Advice Service
Brian Stevenson, Manager
Tel: 020 8762 5500
BStevenson@mungos.org

Eligibility criteria
Clients of Harrow Probation or prisoners returning to the borough. Aged 18+

Hillingdon Offender Housing Floating Support
Brian Stevenson, Manager
Tel: 020 8762 5500
BStevenson@mungos.org

Eligibility criteria
Clients of Hillingdon Probation or prisoners returning to the borough. Aged 18+

Brent Probation Housing Advice and Floating Support
Rachel Kerr, Co-ordinator
Tel: 0208 451 7537
rkerr@mungos.org

Eligibility criteria
Offenders living in the LB of Brent. Aged 18+

Offender Work & Learning Services
Graham Burton, Manager
Tel: 020 7549 8200
grahamb@mungos.org

Eligibility criteria
Ex-offenders, particularly disabled and female

Accommodation

Larix Annexe
(London Borough of Brent)
The Manager
Tel: 020 8965 4763

Eligibility criteria
Offenders with complex needs in the LB of Brent

Referrals via
Probation Officer, Brent Council

7 bed supported housing project for clients with complex needs including mental health and substance misuse, (dual diagnosis). There is a multi-disciplinary team including a supported housing officer, activity worker, resettlement worker that facilitates access to drug, alcohol and mental health services.

Pound Lane
(London Borough of Hackney)
115 Pound Lane, London NW10 2HU
Tel: 020 8809 7241

Eligibility criteria
Male ex-offenders

Referrals via
Brent Probation

The hostel has 46 bed spaces that currently houses about 15 ex-offenders referred by the Probation Service, from our Brent ex-offender floating support service and from Wormwood Scrubs.

Accommodation in Haringey
188 Vartry Road, London N15 6HA
Tel: 020 8809 5742

Eligibility criteria
Mixed gender, no couples

Referrals via
Vulnerable Adults Team, Haringey Council

Mixed 23 bed first stage hostel where 30% of the residents are ex-offenders and live in self-contained flats. Has attached peripatetic mental health worker, substance use worker, and resettlement worker.

14 Weston Park, Crouch End
London N8 9TJ
Tel: 020 8341 0258
Eligibility criteria

Males only Persistent Prolific Offenders
Referrals via
Referrals strictly through PPO structures from Probation, the council, and Drug Intervention Partnerships.
8 beds, providing semi-independent accommodation. A substance use worker is attached to the project. A senior project worker with specialist knowledge of the criminal justice system is being recruited. Available at any point post release.

Accommodation in Islington
35 Tollington Road, London N7 6PB
Tel: 020 7700 2402
(or contact 155 Tufnell Park Road 020 7609 4773)

Eligibility criteria
Mixed gender, ex-offenders

Referrals via
Referrals from the Islington Supporting People Referral Coordinator

An 8 bed semi-independent accommodation project. Has self contained studio flats for clients with low to medium support needs. . A link worker will available to assist clients search for work. Has a health worker, a project worker and senior project worker with specialist knowledge of the criminal justice system. Available at any point post release.

127 Huddleston Road, London N7 0EH
Tel: 020 7281 4261
(or contact 155 Tufnell Park Road 020 7609 4773)

Eligibility criteria
Males only, ex-offenders.

Referrals via
Referrals from the Islington Supporting People Referral Coordinator

7 bed medium support semi independent accommodation project. Rooms are single occupancy with shared bathroom and kitchen. A link worker will available to assist clients search for work. Has a health worker, a project worker and senior project worker with specialist knowledge of the criminal justice system. Available at any point post release.

Accommodation in Hackney
178 Glyn Road, London E5 0JE
Tel: 020 8533 8305

Eligibility criteria
Ex-offenders, those at risk of offending, going through courts, on suspended sentence or probation order

Referrals via
Referrals through London Probation, the council or the Drug Intervention Programme or from ex-offenders previously referred into Mare Street hostel or directly from St Mungo's Prison Services Team.

5 bed semi-independent housing project, mixed gender. For progressively independent living prior to independent living. Links into local external services. Access available at any time post release. The project is being remodelled to support ex-offenders with complex needs. Specialist senior project workers and substance use workers with a knowledge of the criminal justice system will be recruited.

27 Kenworthy Road, London E9 5PB
Tel: 020 8533 8305

Eligibility criteria
Ex-offenders, those at risk of offending, going through courts, on suspended sentence or probation order

Referrals via
Referrals are through London probation, the council or the Drug Intervention Programme or directly from St Mungo's Prison Services Team.

5 bed semi-independent housing project for men. Access available at any time post release. The project is being remodelled to support ex-offenders with complex needs. Specialist senior project workers and substance use workers with a knowledge of the criminal justice system will be recruited.

Confidential address
Tel: 020 7249 5294

Eligibility criteria
Females only

Referrals via
Direct from prison, or from Hackney Probation and Drug Intervention Programmes.

First stage direct access 29 bed hostel. Access available at any time post release. There is a full time substance use worker, resettlement worker, and project workers, the latter having specialist knowledge of the criminal justice system.

Mental Health Team Services

Neighbourhood Link Worker Scheme
Tel: 020 7549 8236
neighbourhoodlink@mungos.org

Eligibility criteria
Clients must live in Islington, 18–65 with a mental health need (including needs that do not meet statutory services' criteria)

Referrals via
Self referral, SNTs and other agencies.

A pilot project that pioneers a partnership working with the Metropolitan Police's Safer Neighbourhood Teams in Islington. Aims to contact and provide support to vulnerable adults at the earliest point in the criminal justice system, and prevent an escalation of their mental health needs and offending. The experience from the Scheme will be used to produce a model suitable for national replication across the Neighbourhood Policing network.

Prison Link Worker Scheme

HMP Holloway
Tel: 07764 958 916

Eligibility criteria
Black and minority ethnic women with mental health needs (including needs that do not meet statutory services' criteria).

Referrals via
Self referral, Inreach Mental Health Team, Prison Resettlement Teams and St Mungo's.

Support for black and minority ethnic women who are in contact with the criminal justice system and have mental health needs that are not met by statutory mental health services. Offers emotional and practical support in helping women link into the community services and resources (including primary and secondary care, housing and benefits).

Outreach Service

Drug Intervention Programme
Assertive Outreach Programme
Great Guildford Business Square, 30
Great Guildford Street, London SE1 0HS
Tel: 020 7525 0830

Referral not needed

Provide assertive street-based outreach to
locate individuals who have disengaged
from Drug Intervention Programmes.
Undertakes intensive, time limited
interventions with ex-service users to
re-engage with them.

Drug & Alcohol Services

Cedar's Road Hostel
113–117 Cedar's Road, SW4 0PJ
Tel: 020 7720 7377

Eligibility criteria
Must be resident at the hostel

Referrals via
Hostel project workers, or self referral

This 120 bed first stage mixed gender
hostel has four substance use workers,
and links with local DIP and Probation
Services. Additionally. The service offers
a women's worker and a Portuguese
speaking worker. Provides in-house
methadone scripting services, moving
scripts from different boroughs, referrals
for detox, rehab and community day
programmes, individual sessions,
acupuncture and Women's Relaxation
Group as well as Blood Borne Virus
testing.

Pagnell Street Hostel
Exeter Way, New Cross, SE14 6LL
Tel: 020 8692 3454

Eligibility criteria
Must be resident at hostel

Referrals via
Hostel project workers, or self referral

At 43 bed first stage mixed gender hostel
there is access to one substance use
worker. The following services are
offered: one to one sessions, referrals to
detox, rehab, DIP, day programmes and
onsite Blood Borne Virus testing.

ARTS FOR OFFENDERS

Rideout (Creative Arts for Rehabilitation)
The Roslyn Works, Uttoxeter Road, Stoke on
Trent ST3 1PQ
(01782) 32555 admin@rideout.co.uk
www.rideout.org.uk

Rideout specialise in drama, theatre and
multi-artform projects in prisons. The aim of
the company's work is to aid prisoners'
rehabilitation through the provision of a range
of arts activities. These include both
long-term drama-based workshops exploring
multiple aspects of offending behaviour, and
theatre and multi-artform projects that allow
for the development of creativity and
self-expression, as well as a number of inter-
and intra-personal skills.

Art Alive Trust
Creative Centre for the Arts, Unit 6A,
Clapham North Arts Centre, 26–32 Voltaire
Road, Clapham, London, SW4 6DH
020 7622 0441 mobile 07944 476 459
fax 020 7622 0441
info@artalive.org.uk

Promotes rehabilitation of offenders and
ex-offenders, with particular but not exclusive
reference to young offenders from an ethnic
minority background. Art-Alive Arts Trust
offers arts education and mentoring, with the
aim of assisting (ex)offenders to re-integrate
into the community and to acquire creative
skills that will assist them in avoiding
re-offending, and gaining employment.

Burnbake Trust
29 North Street, Wilton, Wilts SP2 0HE
(01722) 744178 Weds & Fri, between
08.00–15.00 art@burnbaketrust.co.uk

The trust provides prisoners with art
materials, and invites them to return the work
produced in order that it can be sold for
them. Prisoners then receive the profits of the
sales and are encouraged to purchase new
materials with them.

Clean Break Theatre Company
2 Patshull Road London NW5 2LB
020 7482 8600 *fax 020 7482 8600*
general@cleanbreak.org.uk
www.cleanbreak.org.uk

The UK's only women's theatre education and new writing company for ex-offenders, prisoners, ex-prisoners and women at risk of offending due to drug or alcohol use or mental health issues. Clean Break produces theatre that engages audiences in the issues faced by women whose lives have been affected by the criminal justice system. Their belief is that engaging in theatre can create new opportunities for these women and develop their personal, social, artistic and professional skills.

The Comedy School

15 Gloucester Gate, London NW1 4HG
020 7486 1844 email@thecomedyschool.com
www.thecomedyschool.com

Practical and realistic approaches to stand-up comedy in prisons nationally. Believes that comedy is a powerful tool that can be used to help people gain the motivation to learn.

Dance United

One KX, 120 Cromer Street, London WC1H 8BS
Tel: 020 7713 7242 Fax: 020 7794 9989
lucy@dance-united.com
www.dance-united.com

Plays a part in helping marginalised or excluded people to transform the way they see themselves and the way they are viewed by society. Through the dance process offenders are able to research their identity as a community and as individuals.

Escape Artists

Studio 24, 7–15 Greatorex Street, London, E1 5NF and The Cambridge Resource Centre, 47–51 Norfolk Street, Cambridge, CB1 2LD
020 7655 0909 admin@escapeartists.co.uk
www.escapeartists.co.uk

Provides NOCN accredited arts based programmes and pre-employment training courses specifically designed for use within the criminal justice sector. Also offers a project management service providing a wide range of services from financial and administrative support to project delivery and funding advice.

Fine Cell Work

38 Buckingham Palace Road, London, SW1W ORE
020 7931 9998 enquiries@finecellwork.co.uk
www.finecellwork.co.uk

A registered charity that teaches needlework to inmates and pays them for their work so they can accumulate a nest egg and sells their products. The inmates are taught by volunteers from the Embroiderers Guild, the Royal School of Needlework and the world of professional design. The prisoners do the work in their cells and the earnings give them hope, skills and independence.

Geese Theatre Company

Woodbridge House, 9 Woodbridge Road, Birmingham B13 8EH |
0121 449 6222 *fax 0121 449 1333*
mailbox@geese.co.uk
www.geese.co.uk

A team of specialised theatre practitioners working within the criminal justice system. Geese design and deliver performances, workshops, groupwork programmes and creative residencies with offenders and young people at risk of offending both in a custodial and a community setting. Geese also provides staff training and consultancy with criminal justice system staff and bespoke performances at criminal justice conferences.

Good Vibrations

2–6 Cannon Street, London, EC4M 6YH
info@good-vibrations.org.uk
www.good-vibrations.org.uk
020 8673 5367

Since 2003, over 3000 prisoners, secure hospital patients, people on probation, ex-offenders and young people in the community have taken part in Good Vibrations projects, which last one or two weeks and culminate in an informal performance. Every participant receives a professionally-produced CD of the group's work. Prison staff have observed striking improvements in people's ability to work together, listen to each other, levels of concentration and sense of self-worth. They have found the workshops effective at engaging prisoners who have not previously participated in anything and who do not respond well to more 'traditional' forms of education. Most prisons use the workshops as a way of helping participants work towards basic and key skills qualifications. Good Vibrations use a specially-developed workbook to enable people to gain accreditation for Communications Skills Level 1 through the workshops and have now been formally recognised by the Open College Network in London to develop accredited courses. In December 2009 their one-week gamelan courses were awarded 'approved intervention' status by NOMS' Directorate of High Security Prisons. Good Vibrations is now officially recognised as an effective tool for high security prisons in their efforts to reduce reoffending.

Irene Taylor Trust
Music in Prisons, Unit 401, Bon Marche Centre, 241 Ferndale Road, London SW9 8BJ
020 7733 3222
info@musicinprisons.org.uk
www.musicinprisons.org.uk

Through music and high quality arts activities, the Trust aims to teach artistic and personal skills that participants will be able to draw on in everyday life. By working in conjunction with prison education departments, the Trust enables prisoners to achieve recognised accreditation in key skills. The Trust continues to raise the profile of music and arts in prisons through the evaluation and dissemination of its working practices

Koestler Trust Arts Centre
168a Du Cane Road, London W12 0TX
020 8740 0333
info@koestlertrust.org.uk
www.koestlertrust.org.uk

A prison arts charity, founded by Arthur Koestler in 1962. Its annual competition and exhibition, that has grown in recent years to be a high profile event, promotes and encourages the arts and creativity in UK prisons, YOIs, high security hospitals, secure units and probation.

Safe Ground Productions
PO Box 11525, London SW11 5ZW
020 7228 3831 *fax 020 7228 3885*
safeground@aol.com
www.safeground.org.uk

Produces projects and programmes of education using drama, design and film. Also focuses on peer education and parenting projects, and mapping key skills.

Synergy Theatre Project
Riverside Studios, Crisp Road, London W6 9RL
020 8237 1177
info@synergytheatreproject.co.uk
www.synergytheatreproject.co.uk

Runs theatre based projects in prisons and creates drama opportunities for ex-offenders on their release.

The Theatre in Prison and Probation Centre (TIPP)
The Martin Harris Building, University of Manchester, Oxford Road, Manchester M13 9PL
0161 275 3047 *fax 0161 275 3877*
admin@tipp.org.uk
www.tipp.org.uk

Uses theatre to explore issues (drugs, anger management, employment, etc) with socially excluded groups; particularly within the criminal justice system. Also provides specialist training.

Valley and Vale Community Arts
Sardis Media Centre, Heol Dewi Sant, Betws, Bridgend CF32 8SU
(01656) 729246 mail@valleyandvale.co.uk
www.valleyandvalecommunityarts.co.uk

Valley and Vale offer access to Community Arts and media workshops as well as projects in video, animation, dance, drama, forum theatre, photography, visual and digital arts, multimedia, music and design. They connect groups and communities through outreach, cross-generational projects and local and international cultural exchange.

The Writers in Prisons Network
PO Box 71, Welshpool SY21 0WB
(01938) 810402
wipn@btinternet.com
www.writersinprisonnetwork.org

Supports a wide range of prison-based projects (and in the wider Criminal Justice system) that use creative writing, oral storytelling, publishing, video, radio, theatre, reading and music to address issues such as adult literacy, parenting, journalism and personal development. Writers in residence are placed in prisons to work for 2.5 days a week for up to three years. The scheme is jointly funded by Arts Council England, the Learning & Skills Council and individual establishments. Lord Longford Prize Winner 2004.

EDUCATION FOR PRISONERS

Prisoners' Education Trust
Wandle House, Riverside Drive, Mitcham, Surrey CR4 4BU
020 8648 7760 *Fax: 020 8648 7762*
info@prisonerseducation.org.uk
www.prisonerseducation.org.uk

A national charity that aims to extend and enrich educational opportunities available to prisoners and promote debate about offender learning policy. It offers grants to prisoners with at least six months to serve (or a good chance of completing the course before release) to enable them to study by distance learning. Courses that have been studied range from GCSEs, A levels, Open University Degrees to subjects such as fitness, counselling, computing, navigating and horticulture. Prisoners are advised to discuss their plans with their prison's education department, complete an application form (the education department has copies), and write a short letter to the Trust outlining their aims and stating how the course they have chosen will help meet them. Applications are normally processed within 6 to 8 weeks. The Trust also runs projects that strengthen support for prisoner learning.

Haven Distribution—Books to Prisoners
Haven Distribution, 27 Old Gloucester Street, London WC1N 3XX
info2011@havendistribution.org.uk
www.havendistribution.org.uk

Haven Distribution is a small charity that provides free educational books to prisoners in the UK & Republic of Eire who are currently attending educational courses in prison, such as Open University, NVQ, etc. It also supplies dictionaries to prisoners in their chosen language. To apply for an application form, write to Haven Trust or download application form from the website.

RELIGIOUS ORGANISATIONS OFFERING SERVICES TO PRISONERS

Chaplain General of the Prison Service
William Noblett, Chaplaincy, HQ NOMS, Room 308, Abell House, John Islip Street, London SW1P 4LH.
020 7217 8201 (admin) *Fax: 020 7217 8664*

Angulimala
The Buddhist Prison Chaplaincy Organisation, The Forest Hermitage, Lower Fulbrook, Nr Sherbourne, Warwickshire CV35 8AS.
01926 624385
enquiries@angulimala.org.uk

Angulimala is the Buddhist Religious Consultative Service to HM Prison Service and provides visiting Buddhist prison chaplains and advises the Prison Service on Buddhist matters. Ven. Ajahn Khemadhammo O.B.E., the Spiritual Director, is the Buddhist Adviser to the Prison Service & NOMS – Ajahn.Khemadhammo@hmps.gsi.gov.uk

The Baptist Union of Great Britain
Baptist House, PO Box 44, 129 Broadway, Didcot, Oxon OX11 8RT
(01235) 517700.

Contact The Ministry Support Administrator, Ministry Department.

Churches Criminal Justice Forum
39 Eccleston Square, London SW1V 1BX
020 7901 4878 *Fax: 020 7901 4878*
ccjf@cbcew.org.uk
www.ccjf.org

A national, ecumenical group that seeks to raise awareness of criminal justice concerns among people of faith. It encourages people to get involved in the criminal justice system in ways that will improve it, and also urges politicians to address those aspects of social disadvantage that lie behind crime.

The Church of Jesus Christ of Latter Day Saints
Office of Area Presidency, 751 Warwick Road, Solihull, West Midlands B91 3DQ.
0121 712 1200.
www.lds.org

Members of the church are sometimes known as 'Mormons' or 'Latter Day Saints'.

IQRA Trust Prisoners' Welfare
3rd Floor, 20 East Churchfield Road, London W3 7LL
020 8354 4460 *Fax: 020 8354 4465*
www.iqratrust.com

Promotes better understanding of Islam in Britain. It supports prisoners through its Prisoners' Welfare Directorate by providing books, religious clothing and special foods. It can also train people who are working with Muslim inmates. For their publications phone 020 7838 7987 or email info@iqratrust.org.

The National Council for the Welfare of Muslim Prisoners
20 East Churchfield Road, London W3 7LL
020 8354 4460 *Fax: 020 8354 4465*.

Gen Secretary Salah El Hassan.

The Jewish Prison Chaplaincy
Rev Michael Binstock, United Synagogue,
8/10 Forty Avenue, Wembley, Middx HA9
8JW
020 8343 5669 *Fax: 020 8457 9707*
michael@aje.org.uk.

The Methodist and Free Churches Prison Ministry
Contact Rev Alan Ogier, Superintendent
Methodist Chaplain, NOMS, Horseferry
House, Dean Ryle Street, London SW1P 2AW
020 7217 8048 *Fax: 020 7217 8980*
alan.ogier@hmps.gsi.gov.uk

In collaboration with the Prison Service
Chaplaincy, is responsible for appointing,
training and giving pastoral support to
Methodist/Free Church chaplains in every
prison in England and Wales.

The Pagan Federation
BM Box 7097, London WC1N 3XX
secretary@pagonfield.org

Covers all areas of Paganism including Wicca,
Druidry and the Northern Tradition. Can
supply information and reading lists for
inmates as well as providing visiting
Ministers.

Prison Fellowship
England & Wales, PO Box 945, Maldon, Essex
CM9 4EW.
(01621) 843232 *Fax: 01621 843303*
info@prisonfellowship.org.uk
www.pfew.org.uk.

Northern Ireland, 39 University Street, Belfast
BT7 1FY
Tel: / *Fax: 028 9024 3691*
info@pfni.org.

Scotland, 110 St James Street, Glasgow G4
0PS
Tel: / *Fax: 0141 552 1288*
prisonfellowship@lineone.net.

A Christian ministry providing practical and
spiritual support to prisoners and their
families. Volunteer based organisation with
local groups throughout UK that work closely
with prison chaplaincy teams and local
churches.

The Prison Phoenix Trust
PO Box 328, Oxford OX2 7HF
01865 512 521
all@theppt.org.uk
www.theppt.org.uk

Supports prisoners of any faith or none in
their spiritual lives by teaching the disciplines
of meditation and yoga, working with silence
and the breath. It sends out free books *We're
All Doing Time, Freeing the Spirit, Becoming
Free Through Meditation and Yoga* etc. and
CDs, and supports prisoners by regular
correspondence, newsletters and by
establishing weekly prison yoga classes. The
trust also works with prison officers.

Religious Society of Friends (Quakers)
Quaker Prison Ministry Group, QPSW,
Friends House, 173 Euston Road, London
NW1 2BJ.
020 7663 1035 *Fax: 020 7663 100*
qpsw@quaker.org.uk
alisonp@quaker.org.uk
www.quaker.org.uk

The group supports about 100 Quaker prison
ministers throughout Britain.

Seventh-day Adventist Church
Search Prison Ministries, Stanborough Park,
Watford WD2 9JZ
(01923) 232728 *Fax: (01923) 250582.*

North England Conference of Seventh-day
Adventists, 22 Zulla Road, Mapperley Park,
Nottingham NG3 5DB

Welsh Mission, Ty Capel, Twyn Road, Ystrad
Mynach, Caerphilly CF82 7EU

Scottish Mission, Gwydyr Road, Crieff,
Perthshire PH7 4BS

Irish Mission Office, 9 Newry Road,
Bambridge, Co Down, N Ireland BT32 3HF

Provides spiritual help and counselling to
prisoners and their families. Teams of
volunteers in London and other large cities.

HIGH SECURITY HOSPITALS

Ashworth Hospital
Mersey Care NHS Trust
Parkbourn, Maghull, Liverpool L31 1HW
Tel: 0151 473 0303 *Fax: 0151 526 6603*

Social Care
Tel: 0151 471 2312/473 2713 *Fax: 0151 473
2720*
Email name@merseycare.nhs.uk

McLean, Robert (Head of Forensic Social
Care, nominated officer safeguarding
children)
Corbishley, Angela (pa)

0151 473 2808
Anson, Sue (Forensic Social Care Mgr)
Hicks, Douglas (Forensic Social Care Mgr)

SSWs
Appleton, Phil
Brown, Katharine
Caffrey, Karen
Carroll, Jane
Goodridge, Elizabeth
Heywood, Lynne
Hughes, Dennis
McBride, Amanda
O'Mara, Joyce
Shea, Nicholas
White, Lesley
Whittred, Stephanie
Warwick, Anne (Child Protection Liaison Mgr)
Tunstall, Neil (Vol Sector & Carers Liaison Mgr)
Francis, Irene (Admin Mgr)

Broadmoor Hospital
Crowthorne, Berks RG45 7EG
Tel: (01344) 773111 *Fax: (01344) 754625*

Social Work Services
Tel: (01344) 754523 *Fax: (01344) 754421*

Frost, Carol (Sw Mgr)
Townsend, Ruth (Acting Asst Mgr)
Allen, Martine
Barker, Denis
Chalk, Pat
White, Anne
Davies, Gareth
Hames, Carol
Heffernan, Susan
Hulin, Gillian
Kelly, Gareth
Kenworthy, Frances
Mukasa, Paul
Nijjar, Daljit
Pearce, Clive
Phillips, David
Ainsworth, Janice (locum)
Kruger, Arnold (locum)

Rampton Hospital
(Forensic Division, Nottinghamshire
Healthcare NHS Trust)
Retford, Notts DN22 0PD
Tel: (01777) 248321 *Fax: (01777) 248442*

Forensic Social Care Service
11/12 Galen Avenue, Rampton Hospital,
Retford, Notts DN22 0PD
Tel: (01777) 247354 *Fax: (01777) 247259*

Gardner, Julie (Trust Associate Director of
Social Care, Nominated Officer Children's
Safeguarding)
Wendy Cove (PA/Admin Manager)
Clayton, Amanda (Children's Safeguarding Mgr)
Jane Brown (Children's Safeguarding Admin)

Learning Disability Directorate
Clayton, Amanda (Sw Mgr)

SFSWPs
Bryson, Beverley
Cowling Stephen
McNeil, Kevin

Mental Health Directorate
Parkinson, John (Sw Mgr)

SFSWPs
Singh, Janga
Page, Clare
Johnson, Lynn
Wray, Corrina
Greenwood, Julie
Lanfranchi, Elizabeth (Natnl Deaf Service)

Peaks Unit
Corcoran, Lynne (Sw Mgr)

SFSWPs
Bryson, Beverley
Cochrane, David
Adamson, Lyn
Robertson, Kim

Personality Disorder Directorate
Corcoran, Lynne (Sw Mgr)

SFSWPs
Hahn, Gill
Humphries, Gail
Oliver, Sonia

Women Services Directorate
Cochrane, Sarah (Sw Mgr)

SFSWPs
Briggs, Myra
Garrib, Aasra

Volunteer Co-ordination
Phillips, Janet (Volco Mgr)
Strawson, Val (Volunteer Co-Ord)

Visitors Centre/Family Support
Christian, Carmel (family supt manager)
(Family Supt Wrkrs)
Bridge, Karen
Weaver, Helen

SPECIALIST ACCOMMODATION FOR OFFENDERS

Bromford Support
6 Hadley Mews, Donnithorne Avenue,
Nuneaton CV11 4SF
Tel/fax: 02476 373603

Housing related support for offenders aged 18 or over, under the supervision of the probation service and on a community order, licence condition or moving on from probation approved premises, or registered under MAPPA. Weekly floating support, covering Nuneaton and Bedworth, North Warwickshire and the Rugby area, for single people, couples and people with children. The scheme offers support for 10 adult offenders and aims to help reduce the risk of re-offending and to assist them in obtaining and/or sustaining their own accommodation within the community. The length of support generally ranges from six months to two years, depending on need. The service is funded by Supporting People and there is no charge for support.

To make a referral from the probation service via the Warwickshire Accommodation Referral service, contact Accommodation Officer, Warwickshire Probation, 2 Swan Street, Warwick CV34 4BJ. Tel: 01926 405805.

Referrals from MAPPA should contact Bromford Support direct.

Carr-Gomm
11 Harewood Road, Edinburgh EH16 4NT
0300 666 3030 info@carrgommscotland.org.uk
www.carrgommscotland.org.uk
A charitable housing association that provides supportive environments for single people with a range of needs, including physical and mental health, ex-alcohol, drug users, ex offenders and those who cannot live on their own without support, referred by social services or housing departments

To find out more about the services or the referral process email info@carr-gomm.org.uk

Gordon House Association
See section on services for problem gamblers

Langley House Trust
Central Services: PO Box 181, Witney,
Oxfordshire OX28 6WD
(01993) 774075 *fax (01993) 772425*
info@langleyhousetrust.org

www.langleyhousetrust.org

A national Christian charity and registered social landlord providing specialist resettlement accommodation for those who are hard to place (ex-offenders and those at risk of offending) 16 projects and associated move-on provision.

Referrals direct to the chosen project or via Witney office

Drug Rehabilitation Centres
(Registered Care Homes)
Chatterton Hey, Exchange Street, Edenfield, Ramsbottom, Lancashire BL0 0QH. (01706) 829895 fax (01706) 828761
Chatterton@langleyhousetrust.org

Fresh Start Projects
Ashdene Provision for adult ex-offenders and has some places for wheelchair users.
29 Peterson Road, Wakefield, West Yorkshire WF1 4DU
(01924) 291088 *fax (01924) 366529*
Ashdene@langleyhousetrust.org

Box Tree Cottage Provision for adult male ex-offenders including those with complex needs
110 Allerton Road, Bradford, West Yorkshire BD8 0AQ
(01274) 487626 *fax (01274) 543612*
BoxTree@langleyhousetrust.org

Langdon House Provision for male ex offenders age 25 and above.
66 Langdon Road, Parkstone, Dorset BH14 9EH
(01202) 747423 *fax (01202) 256718*
Langdon@langleyhousetrust.org

The Shrubbery Provision for male ex offenders age 18 and above.
35 Frindsbury Road, Strood, Rochester, Kent ME2 4TD
(01634) 717085 *fax (01634) 291049*
Shrubbery@langleyhousetrust.org

Park View Provision for male ex-offenders and homeless men aged 21 and over
85 Warrenhurst Road, Fleetwood, Lancashire FY7 6TP
(01253) 872162 *fax (01253) 879345*
ParkView@langleyhousetrust.org

Residential Training Centres
Elderfield Works with full range of male ex-offenders
Main Road, Otterbourne, Winchester, Hampshire S021 2EQ

(01962) 712163 *fax (01962) 711174*
Elderfield@langleyhousetrust.org

House of St Martin Provision for men and
women. Offers training leading to recognised
qualifications
1 Langford Lane, Norton Fitzwarren, Taunton,
Somerset TA2 6NU
(01823) 275662 *fax (01823) 352455*
StMartin@langleyhousetrust.org

Wing Grange Provision for male ex-offenders
aged 18 and over. Specialises in working with
those with mental health problems or
learning and behavioural difficulties.
Preston Road, Wing, Oakham, Rutland LE15
8SB
(01572) 737246 *fax (01572) 737510*
WingGrange@langleyhousetrust.org

Resettlement Projects
These projects cater for residents requiring a
high degree of support who might otherwise
reoffend, Training programmes form part of
the working week.

Bedford Project Provision for men and women
over 18.
PO Box 395, Bedford MK43 6AD
(01234) 855515 *fax (01234) 843137*
Bedford@langleyhousetrust.org

Rothera Women only over 18
PO Box 977, Bradford BD5 9YJ
(01274) 603664 *fax (01274) 605677*
Rothera@langleyhousetrust.org

Kent Resettlement Project Provision for men
and women over 18.
35 Frindsbury Road, Strood, Rochester, Kent
ME2 4TD
(01634) 723200 *fax (01634) 723244*
KentProject@langleyhousetrust.org

Homeless Project
The Torbay Project For individuals within the
Torbay area, referrals via The Housing
Support Referral Hub at Housing Services,
Pearl Assurance House, 101–107 Union Street,
Torquay TQ2 5LB
(01803) 208058
referralhub@torbay.gov.uk

Registered Care Homes
The Knole Provision for men over 30.
23 Griffiths Avenue, Cheltenham,
Gloucestershire GL51 7BE
(01242) 526978 *fax (01242) 237504*
Knole@langleyhousetrust.org

Longcroft Provision for men over 18. Can cater
for individuals with complex needs.
58 Westbourne Road, Lancaster LA1 5EF
(01524) 64950 *fax (01524) 844082*
Longcroft@langleyhousetrust.org

Nacro
Nacro has a number of specialist housing
projects. These are listed in the Nacro
section.

Penrose Housing Association
Head Office: 356 Holloway Road, London N7
6PA.
020 7697 4200 *fax 020 7700 8133*
enquiries@penrose.org.uk
www.penrose.org.uk

Specialist housing association providing
supported housing and resettlement service
for homeless male and female offenders in
the London area. All housing is shared
ranging from 2 bedroomed flats to 14 bed
hostel. Assured short hold tenancies are
issued. Move-on for most tenants through
public and private sector accommodation with
resettlement support.

Women: women only housing provided in
small shared flats and self-contained flats
using high care and floating support.

Priority: lifers and other long term prisoners.
Exclusions: Penrose operates no blanket
exclusions.

All enquiries to head office or the relevant
project. Applications can only be accepted
from probation officers in the London Area or
other approved referral sources.

Penrose also operates separate
accommodation for mentally disordered
offenders.

St Mungo's
Has a number of specialist housing projects,
listed in the St Mungo's section

Stepping Stones Trust
Referrals to: Suffolk House, George Street,
Croydon CR0 1PE
020 8253 0450 *fax 020 8680 8077*
info@steppingstonestrust.org.uk
referrals@steppingstonestrust.org.uk
www.steppingstonestrust.org.uk

Hope House, 14a St Augustine's Ave, South
Croydon CR2 6BS

Supported housing for ex-prisoners or referrals from probation services. No local connection necessary. Our focus is on helping residents find employment and move-on accommodation and providing spiritual support (from a Christian perspective) for people who feel this would help them stay clear of crime. Residents must be clean of drugs, accept a curfew (11 pm to 7 am) and want support.

Bridge House, PO Box 3209, London SW8

Accommodation and care for Christian male sex offenders. For the unemployed, rent covered by DSS and Housing Benefit. Residents will usually stay for up to two years and can receive psychiatric assessment and treatment through the NHS. NOTE: before making any referral please contact SPO, 217a Balham High Road, London SW17 020 8767 5905

Stonham
Head Office, 2 Gosforth Park Way, Gosforth Buiness Park, Gosforth, Newcastle upon Tyne NE12 8ET 0845 155 1234
stonham@homegroup.org.uk
www.stonham.org.uk

Stonham, a division of the Home Group, is England's largest specialist provider of housing with support for socially excluded people. It runs 545 directly managed services, working in partnership with local authorities, health care providers, probation services and others, delivering services to over 15,000 people each year. Stonham works with ex-offenders, including those with mental health problems, drug and/or alcohol addiction and basic skills needs. There are over 100 Stonham projects for ex-offenders around England.

Regional offices
North
Key contact: Sally Parsons (Operations Director)
Meridian House, Artist Street, Armley Road, Leeds LS12 2EW
0113–246 8660
sally.parsons@homegroup.org.uk

West
Key contact: Alan Ryan (Operations Director)
2nd Floor, High Point, Thomas Street, Taunton, Somerset TA2 6HB
01823 327388 alan.ryan@homegroup.org.uk

East

Key contact: Molly Newton (Operations Director)
Malt House, 281 Field End Road, Eastcote, Ruislip, Middlesex, HA4 9XQ.
020–8868 9000
molly.newton@homegroup.org.uk

SERVICES FOR DRUG & ALCOHOL USERS

HELPLINES
Alcoholics Anonymous 0845 769 7555

Drinkline 0800 917 8282 9am-11pm Mon-Fri

Frank (national drugs helpline) 0800 77 66 00

Narcotics Anonymous 0300 999 12 12

National AIDS Helpline 0800 012 322

Release 0845 4500 215
Advice on drug related legal problems

DrugScope 020 7520 7550
Online *Helpfinder* database accessed via *www.drugscope.org.uk*

National organisations & head offices

Addaction
67–69 Cowcross Street, London EC1M 6PU
020 7251 5860, *fax: 020 7251 5890*
info@addaction.org.uk

www.addaction.org.uk
With over 40 years' experience of working with people affected by drugs and alcohol we have designed a range of treatment services that helps people reduce and end their dependencies. All services are free and confidential to the people who use them, and we also offer support and information to friends and family.
In addition to treatment services, we also carry out research and offer professional training to people who work in the drugs field as well to ex-service users who are considering becoming drug or alcohol workers.

Adfam
25 Corsham Street, London N1 6DR
020 7553 7640 *Fax: 020 7253 7991*
www.adfam.org.uk
admin@adfam.org.uk

National charity supporting families and friends of drug users. Specialist support for prisoners' families.

Alcohol Concern
Suite B5, West Wing, New City Cloisters, 196 Old Street, London EC1V 9FR
020 7566 9800 *Fax: 020 7488 9213*
contact@alcoholconcern.org.uk
www.alcoholconcern.org.uk

Alcohol Concern Cymru
Sophia House, 28 Cathedral Road, Cardiff CF11 9LJ
029 2066 0248
acwales@alcoholconcern.org.uk

Voluntary agency working on alcohol misuse. Library, information service, can refer caller to local agencies, produces a variety of literature and directory of local services.

The Alliance
32 Bloomsbury Street, London WC1B 3QJ
020 7299 4304 helpline 0845 122 8608
(10am-5pm weekdays except bank holidays)
info@m-alliance.org.uk
www.m-alliance.org.uk

The Alliance is a user led organisation that provides advocacy, training and helpline services to those currently in drug treatment, those who have accessed drug treatment in the past and those who may access drug treatment in the future.

Aquarius
2nd Floor, 16 Kent Street, Birmingham B5 6RD
0121 622 6193 *Fax: 0121 622 8189*
headoffice@aquarius.org.uk
www.aquarius.org.uk

Drug, alcohol and gambling projects in the Midlands, providing information, training, counselling, residential and day services. Also delivers the Alcohol and Offending Programme in partnership with W Midlands Probation Area in Solihull, Wolverhampton, Walsall, Sandwell and Dudley; and alcohol arrest referral programmes in Dudley and Sandwell.

Compass—Services to tackle problem drug use
Langton House, 5 Priory Street, York YO1 6ET
(01904) 636374 *Fax: (01904) 632490*
info@compass-uk.org
www.compass-uk.org

Provides a range of community services in York and North Yorkshire, Hull, Nottingham and the East Midlands, and Milton Keynes. Services include structured day programmes, young people's services, throughcare aftercare and resettlement, progress2work, arrest referral, substitute prescribing, and tier 2 and 3 adult services.

Cranstoun Drug Services
1st Floor, St Andrew's House, St Andrew's Road, Surbiton, Surrey KT6 4DT
020 8335 1830 *Fax: 020 8399 4153*
info@cranstoun.org.uk
www.cranstoun.org

Major NGO provider of a range of services for substance misusers in the UK. Encompasses high care residential services, supported housing, community drug agencies and specific criminal justice services.

Crime Reduction Initiatives (CRI)
140–142, Kings Cross Road, London WC1X 9DS (Regional offices in Leeds and Brighton)
020 7833 7975 *Fax: 020 7833 0863*
www.cri.org.uk

Leading national charity focused on crime reduction, rehabilitation and community safety. Services include: DIP; prison drug treatment programmes (CARAT, P-ASRO etc); DRRs and ATRs; supported housing for ex-offenders; street outreach; domestic abuse services; parenting support services and interventions for young offenders.

DrugScope
4th Floor, Astra House, 1 Long Lane, London SE1 4PG
020 7234 9730 *Fax: 020 7520 7555*
info@drugscope.org.uk
www.drugscope.org.uk

UK's leading centre of expertise on drugs. Its aim is to inform policy and reduce drug related risk. Provides information, promotes effective responses to drug taking, undertakes research at local, national and international levels, advises on policy making, encourages informed debate and speaks for member bodies working on the ground.

Frank
0800 77 66 00 (24 hour national drugs helpline)
For the hearing impaired textphone FRANK on 0800 917 8765
frank@talktofrank.com

www.talktofrank.com

Drugs information and help service.

HIT
The Arts Village, 20–26 Henry Street,
Liverpool L1 5BS
0844 412 0972/0844 412 0972
stuff@hit.org.uk
www.hit.org.uk

Provide training and information on drug related issues. Provides a library and information service, training courses, publications and campaigns. The main distributor of DrugScope publications.

Langley House Trust
The Langley House Trust has two dry rehabs. See their entry under the Specialist Accommodation for Offenders Section.

Lifeline Project
101–103 Oldham Street, Manchester M4 1LA
0161 834 9118
www.lifeline.org.uk

Helps drug users and their families. Offices in the North East, North West, Yorkshire & Humberside and London providing a range of services for drug users and those affected by drug use.

Phoenix Futures
3rd Floor, ASRA House, 1 Long Lane, London
SE1 4PG
020 7234 9740 *Fax: 020 7234 9770*
info@phoenix-futures.org.uk
www.phoenix-futures.org.uk
National referral number for adult & family residential rehab services: 0845 600 7227
intake@phoenixfutures.org.uk

Offers structured rehabilitation services, designed around the needs of people with drug and alcohol problems. Largest UK provider of residential rehabilitation services for single adults and families and structured community day services. Extensively involved in resettlement, aftercare, supported housing, tenancy sustainment services and education and retraining services. Work in partnership with probation and prison services in England and Scotland delivering a full range of intervention services.

Phoenix Futures Approved Premises and Homeless Offenders Resettlement Unit Team
AP/HORU, Phoenix Futures, 2nd Floor
Ruskin Chambers, 191 Corporation Street
Birmingham B4 6RP

Tel: 0121 212 1122 *Fax: 0121 212 2777*
Team manager: Janet Bright
mobile (07817) 423 963

Provides drug interventions across Approved Premises and Homeless Offenders Resettlement Units within the West Midlands. Includes substance misuse assessment and care planning, access to substitute prescribing, harm reduction advice, relapse prevention, referral into subsidiary support services, acupuncture, crack cocaine specific programmes, group work and onward referrals. Referrals can be sent by West Midlands Probation staff. (Cannot accept referrals for individuals on a DRR or PPOs whose Offender Manager is located within the Birmingham area.)

RAPt (Rehabilitation for Addicted Prisoners Trust)
Riverside House, 27–29 Vauxhall Grove,
London SW8 1SY
020 7582 4677 *Fax: 020 7820 3716*
info@rapt.org.uk
www.rapt.org.uk
National charity with full accreditation from the joint Prisons and Probation Accreditation Board. Provides intensive abstinence based treatment and supportive counselling and CARAT services to substance users in the CJ system. Services include prison based 12 step treatment and CARAT services, a community based DIP team and community based residential and day treatment programmes.

Release
124–128 City Road, London EC1V 2NJ
020 7324 2989 (office) *Fax: 020 7324 2977*
helpline 0845 4500 215 Mon-Fri, 11am-1pm,
2pm-4pm.
ask@release.org.uk
www.release.org.uk

Advice on legal drug related problems.

Scottish Drugs Forum
Main Office: 91 Mitchell Street, Glasgow
G1 3LN
0141 221 1175 *Fax: 0141 248 6414*
enquiries@sdf.org.uk
www.sdf.org.uk

Scottish Drugs Forum is the national, voluntary sector and membership-based drugs policy and information agency with regional offices throughout Scotland. It work to reduce drugs harm through improving awareness and understanding of drugs use issues, and developing, promoting, and supporting improvements to the range and quality of services to all drug users. Provides an on-line directory of Scottish drug services.

Turning Point

Head Office: Standon House, 21 Mansell Street, London E1 8AA
020 7481 7600.
Helpline 020 7481 7600
info@turning-point.co.uk
www.turning-point.co.uk

Manchester Office: The Exchange, 3 New York Street, Manchester M1 4HN
0161 238 5100

Turning Point is a leading social care organisation. It provides services for people with complex needs, including those affected by drug and alcohol abuse, mental health problems and those with a learning disability.

Solvents

Re-Solv

Head Office: 30a High Street, Stone, Staffs ST15 8AW
(01785) 817885 *Fax: (01785) 813205*
free national helpline 01785 810762 (9am-5pm, Mon-Fri except bank holidays)
information@re-solv.org
www.re-solv.org
National charity with offices in the North East, East Midlands, Wales and Scotland. Deals with all aspects of solvent and volatile substance abuse (that currently kills an average of 6 young people a month). Research, educational materials, training and community projects.

Self help organisations

Narcotics Anonymous

UK Service Office, 202 City Road, London EC1V 2PH
Organisation for recovering adults
020 7251 4007 *Fax: 020 7251 4006*
ukso@ukna.org
www.ukna.org
Helpline 0300 999 12 12
NAHelpline@ukna.org. Public information pi@ukna.org

Alcoholics Anonymous

PO Box 1, 10 Toft Green, York YO1 7NJ
(01904) 644026 helpline 0845 769 7555
www.alcoholics-anonymous.org.uk

Cocaine Anonymous

PO Box 46920, London E2 9WF
0800 612 0225
info@cauk.org.uk
www.cauk.org.uk

A fellowship of men and women who share their experience, strength and hope so that they may solve their common problem and help others recover from addiction.

Al-Anon Family Groups (UK & Eire)

61 Great Dover Street, London SE1 4YF
020 7403 0888 (confidential helpline 10am-10pm daily) *Fax: 020 7378 9910*
enquiries@al-anonuk.org.uk
www.al-anonuk.org.uk
Scotland 0141 339 8884 (helpline 10am-10pm daily)
Republic of Ireland 01 873 2699 (helpline 10.30am-2.30pm, Mon-Fri)
Northern Ireland 028 9068 2368 (helpline 10am-1pm Mon-Fri, 6pm-11pm daily)

Al-Anon is worldwide and offers understanding and support for families and friends of problem drinkers, whether the alcoholic is still drinking or not. Alateen, a part of Al-Anon, is for young people aged 12–20 who have been affected by someone else's drinking, usually that of a parent. For details of meetings throughout UK and Eire, please contact the helpline.

Families Anonymous

Doddington & Rollo Community Association, Charlotte Despard Avenue, Battersea, London SW11 5HD
0845 1200 660 helpline (lo-call) *Fax: 020 7498 1990*
office@famanon.org.uk
www.famanon.org.uk

Free and confidential support groups for families and friends of drug users. Office and helpline staffed Mon–Fri 1pm-4pm and 6pm-10pm, weekends 2pm-10pm.

PADA (Parents Against Drug Abuse)

Ellergreen Community Centre, Ellergreen Road, Liverpool L11 2KY
0151 270 2108 *Fax: 0151 647 8050*
Helpline 08457 023 867 (confidential, staffed 24hrs 365 days calls charged at local rate)
admin@pada.org.uk
www.pada.merseyside.org
A national network of local support groups offering help and support to parents and families of drug users.

Campaigns

Transform Drug Policy Foundation
9–10 King Street, Bristol BS1 4EQ
0117 325 0295 *Fax: 0117 941 5809*
info@tdpf.org.uk
www.tdpf.org.uk

The leading drug policy reform charity in the UK aiming to create a just, humane and effective drug policy. It campaigns for an effective system of regulation and control to replace the failed policy of prohibition through advocating reform at national and international levels.

Health issues

HIV/AIDS
National AIDS Trust
NAT, New City Cloisters, 196 Old Street, London EC1V 9FR
020 7814 6767 *Fax: 020 7216 0111*
info@nat.org.uk
www.nat.org.uk

Strategic body campaigning for effective prevention, development of vaccines, quality treatment/care, and an end to discrimination against people with HIV and AIDS.

The Terrence Higgins Trust
314–320 Gray's Inn Road, London WC1X 8DP
020 7812 1600 (switchboard) 0845 1221 200 (adviser) *Fax: 020 7812 1623*
info@tht.org.uk
www.tht.org.uk

Offices and centres across England, Scotland and Wales. Offers a buddying service, information, advice and counselling on the law, welfare, housing and insurance for people affected by HIV/AIDS.

HEPATITIS C
UK Hepatitis C Resource Centre
Mansfield Traquair Centre, 15 Mansfield Place, Edinburgh EH3 6BB
0131 474 8044
helpline 0870 242 2467 10am-4pm, Mon-Fri
hepccentre@mainliners.org.uk
www.hepccentre.org.uk
195 New Kent Road, London SE1 4AG
020 7378 5495 *Fax: 020 7378 5489*
info@hepccentre.org.uk

Provide information to people living with hepatitis C, healthcare professionals, the public and media. Also provides a peer perspective on experiences of HCV positive individuals regarding day-to-day living, treatment, alternative therapies and support.

SERVICES FOR PROBLEM GAMBLERS

National organisations

GamCare
2nd Floor, 7–11 St Johns Hill, Clapham, London SE11 1TR
020 7801 7000 *Fax: 020 7801 7033*
Helpline 0808 8020 133 (8am-midnight daily)
info@gamcare.org.uk
www.gamcare.org.uk.

Provides free advice, information and counselling to problem gamblers, their family and friends. Offers a national helpline and on-line support services as well as free face to face counselling from the London office and via a network of national partner organizations. Also provides training and literature to organizations working with problem gamblers and their families.

Gamblers Anonymous
c/o CVS Building, 5 Trafford Court, off Trafford Way, Doncaster DN1 1PN

National and regional 24 hour helplines
National helpline 08700 50 88 80; London 020 7384 3040; Glasgow 0141 630 1033; Sheffield 0114 262 0026; Manchester 0161 976 5000; Birmingham 0121 233 1335; Ulster 0287 135 1329
info@gamblersanonymous.org.uk
Prison liaison
plo@gamblersanonymous.org.uk
www.gamblersanonymous.org.uk

GA is a self-help fellowship of men and women who have joined together to do something about their own gambling problem and to help other compulsive gamblers to do the same. Over 200 groups throughout the UK and in many prisons.

Gam-Anon
address as GA above
National helpline 08700 50 88 80
www.gamanon.org.uk

'Sister' organisation to GA, providing advice and support to the spouses and parents of compulsive gamblers.

Residential/rehabilitation

Gordon Moody Association

Central Office: 114 Wellington Road, Dudley, West Midlands, DY1 1UB
01384 241292
help@gordonhouse.org.uk
www.gordonmoody.org.uk
Midlands: 01384 241292 *Fax: 01384 251959*
South East: 020 8778 3331 *Fax: 020 8659 5036*

Counselling and discussion of gambling problems. Website also offers instant online chat

Also offers residential facility for men & women 18+, including offenders on court orders or ex-prison. Therapeutic environment, individual and group counselling and support whilst at hostel and after. Catchment area is national.

Groups & organisations with local projects

England
Cumbria Alcohol & Drug Advisory Service (CADAS)

17a West Tower St, Carlisle, CA3 8QT
01228 544140
info@cadas.co.uk
www.cadas.co.uk

Provides a telephone and one-to-one counselling service to problem gamblers and their relatives/friends.

Off The Record

Freephone support line 0808 80 10 724
Admin base: 138 Purbrook Way, Leigh Park, Havant PO9 3SU
023 9278 5999 *Fax: 0239243 3999* Client line 023 9247 4724
admin@off-the-record.org.uk
www.off-the-record.org.uk
Portsmouth base: 250 Fratton Road, Portsmouth PO1 5HH
023 9278 5111 *Fax: 023 9261 2111* Client line 023 9281 5322

Point of contact for young people, 11–25, who wish to receive counseling, support and information in Hampshire regarding problem gambling.

North East Council on Addiction (NECA)

Head Office: Derwent Point, Clasper Way, Swalwell, Newcastle upon Tyne N16 3BE
0191 414 6446
info@neca.co.uk

www.neca.co.uk

Centres in Newcastle, South Tyne, Gatehead, Durham, Consett, Peterlee, Hartlepool, Washington, Stanley, Mid Tyne, Chester le Street, Sunderland, Bishop Auckland, Seaham, Sedgefield, Darlington. All centres provide telephone and one-to-one counselling to problem gamblers and their relatives/friends. Addresses and phone numbers from head office.

Alcohol Problems Advisory Service (APAS)

36 Park Row, Nottingham NG1 6GR
0115 948 5570, Lo-call 0845 7626 316, text 0789 671 6260 *Fax: 0115 948 5571*
apas@apas.org.uk
www.apas.org.uk

Provides advice, information and counselling service to problem gamblers, drinkers and drug takers and for people affected by someone else's dependency on alcohol, drugs and gambling. Drop in service.

Options (Southampton)

147 Shirley Road, Southampton, SO15 3FH
023 8063 0219
southampton@optionscounselling.co.uk
www.optionscounselling.co.uk

Well established agency on the South coast provides one-to-one counselling, information and guidance for problem gamblers, their families and friends who are affected by gambling dependency.

Wales
Islwyn Drug & Alcohol Project

Bryn Road, Markham, Blackwood, Caerphilly, Gwent NP12 0QE
(01495) 229299

Provides information, advice and one-to-one counselling to problem gamblers and their relatives/ friends who are affected by a gambling dependency as part of a community project within South Wales and surrounding districts.

Scotland
Renfrew Council on Alcohol

Mirren House, Back Sneddon Street, Paisley PA3 2AF
0141 887 0880

In conjunction with other services, also offers information, advice, and one-to-one counselling to problem gamblers, their relatives and friends affected by gambling dependency as a part of a community project.

VOLUNTARY WORK

CSV (Community Service Volunteers)
237 Pentonville Road, London N1 9NJ
020 7278 6601, volunteers 0800 374 991
info@csv.org.uk
www.csv.org.uk

CSV Scotland
12 Torphichen Street, Edinburgh EH3 8JQ
0131 622 7766

CSV Wales
CSV House, Williams Way, Cardiff CF10 5DY
029 20 415717

CSV provides opportunities for people to volunteer in the community.

CSV offers full time volunteering opportunities to those aged 16 and over who are able to volunteer full time and away from home at hundreds of social care and community projects throughout Britain. Volunteers receive a weekly allowance plus free accommodation and food. CSV also works through service and contract agreements (e.g. with the probation services) to involve volunteers as mentors to young offenders and also places as volunteers in their local area young people at risk of offending.

Volunteering with CSV gives young people greater self-confidence and provides them with a range of workplace skills such as team working and decision making. Of special interest to probation officers based in YOIs, Cat C and Cat D prisons is CSVs partnership with HM Prison Service. CSV offers, as part of an effective resettlement process, one month full time away from home volunteering opportunities to young people usually in their last month prior to release.

Voluntary Service Overseas
Global Xchange, c/o VSO, Carlton House, 27a Carlton Drive, Putney, London SE15 2BS
020 8780 7500 and 020 8780 7670
enquiry@globalxchange.org.uk
www.globalxchange.org.uk

Runs many different programmes such as The Global Xchange Programme, a partnership between the British Council, Community Service Volunteers (CSV) and Voluntary Service Overseas (VSO). An international youth exchange programme aimed at building active global citizens. Nine young adults from the UK are paired with nine from an African/Asian country (all aged 18–25) to live and to carry out voluntary work in host communities, three months in the UK and three months in the exchange country. Global Xchange is open to all UK/EEA citizens who are resident in the UK, regardless of skills, experience and educational background. The Global Xchange Programme covers the costs of participation – all travel, food, accommodation, medical expenses and insurance, training and support.

INSURANCE SERVICES FOR EX-OFFENDERS

Fresh Start Insurance Services
Vinpenta House, 4 High Causeway,
Whittlesey, Peterborough, PE7 1AE
Freephone: 0800 0213029 Tel: 01733 208278
Fax: 01733 208610
johnc@culpeck.co.uk
www.freshstartinsuranceservices.co.uk
Fresh Start has been providing Home (Buildings &/or Contents), Let Property & Business Insurance Packages for people with unspent criminal convictions since 1999. A fully comprehensive, supportive and confidential service is provided by experienced staff offering the right products at competitive premiums.
For Home Insurance Fresh Start is able to offer online quotations & accept business via the above website. This scheme is underwritten by a large and well known insurer.
Fresh Start is supported and recommended by Nacro, the Probation Service, Unlock, CABs, BIBA, HM Prison Service & numerous Banks & Mortgage Lenders throughout the UK. Fresh Start is a trading name of Voyager Insurance Services Ltd, which is authorised and regulated by the Financial Services Authority.

Fairplay Insurance Services
Charter House, 43 St Leonards Road,
Bexhill-on-Sea, East Sussex TN40 1JA
01424 220110 *Fax: 01424 217107*
cover@bureauinsure.co.uk
www.fairplayhelp.com

Fairplay Insurance Services, part of the Bureau Insurance services Group, authorised and regulated by the FSA, was established solely to promote Household and Motor Insurance for proposers with criminal convictions. Fairplay guarantees that each applicant will be dealt with in a sensitive, non-judgmental and helpful way. Every proposer will be treated with respect and in total confidence, regardless of previous convictions. Fairplay has been in existence for several years and is confident in its ability to provide household and motor insurance for ex-offenders.

The Fairplay scheme is endorsed by the British Insurance Brokers' Association and is their officially appointed scheme provider. Fairplay works closely with the home office, Unlock, NACRO, the Probation Service etc. The Fairplay proposal form notes that spent convictions need not be declared and they provide information that will show when a conviction is spent.

MISCELLANEOUS SERVICES FOR OFFENDERS

The Aldo Trust
c/o NACRO, 169 Clapham Road, London SW9 0PU.
020 7582 6500.

Charitable small grants to prisoners in England and Wales only, no applications direct from prisoners.

Alternatives to Violence Project
contact AVP London, Grayston Centre, 28 Charles Square, London N1 6HT.
0207 324 4757
Email: info@avpbritain.org.uk
www.avpbritain.org.uk

Works to relieve those afflicted by violence or abuse, whether they are victims or aggressors or both. Provides group experiential workshops that develop people's ability to resolve difficult situations without resorting to violence. These are delivered across the UK in prisons, for charities and the public. AVP also trains prisoners, ex-offenders and members of the community to become workshop facilitators and volunteers for AVP.

Apex Trust
7th Floor, No.3 London Wall Buildings, London Wall, London EC2M 5PD.
020 7638 5931 *Fax: 020 7638 5977*
Email: jobcheck@apextrust.com
www.apextrust.com

Helps people with a criminal record obtain jobs, self employment, training or further education through its projects in England providing direct advice and guidance to ex-offenders. Provides employers with information about the best ways of recruiting and retraining people with a criminal record. National helpline 0870 608 4567 offers confidential information on issues relating to employment and having a criminal record.

Black Prisoners Support Groups
POPS, Valentine House, 1079 Rochdale Road, Blackley, Manchester M9 8AJ.
0161 740 3679 *Fax: 0161 740 3206*
Email: info@nbbpsg.org
www.nbbpsg.co.uk

Dyspel
88 Clapham Road, London SW9 0JR 020 7793 3722 *Fax: 020 7820 3577* email info@dyspel.org.uk *www.dyspel.org.uk* A project that helps dyslexic offenders and offers training in the screening of dyslexia to probation officers and partnership staff.

Fairbridge
The Prince's Trust, 18 Park Square East, London NW1 4LH
020 7543 1234 *Fax: 020 7928 6016.*
Email: info@fairbridge.org.uk
www.fairbridge.org.uk

National youth charity working with people aged 13–25 in 15 disadvantaged areas of UK. Many are ex-offenders or are at risk of offending. Using a combination of challenging activities and long term support, young people are encouraged to re-engage with mainstream opportunities in education training and employment.

Irish Council for Prisoners Overseas. ICPO (London)
50–52 Camden Square, London NW1 9XB.
020 7482 4148 *Fax: 020 7482 4815*
Email: prisoners@irishchaplaincy.org.uk
www.catholicbishops.ie/prisoner

ICPO is a subsection of the Bishops' Commission for Emigrants. It cares for all Irish prisoners abroad, regardless of faith, offence or prison status, and their families when requested. ICPO works to ensure that minimum levels of human rights for Irish migrants, refugees and prisoners abroad are respected and enforced. As an NGO, ICPO operates on a not for profit basis to represent the needs of Irish individuals imprisoned overseas.

Lincolnshire Action Trust
PO Box 985, Lincoln LN5 5GF
(01522) 806611 *Fax: (01522) 806610*
Email: admin@lincolnshire-action-trust.org.uk
www.lincolnshire-action-trust.org.uk

Employment, training and education advice
and guidance, etc for offenders in community
and prison Lincolnshire and surrounding
area. Also provides assistance to employers
considering recruitment of people with a
criminal record.

New Bridge
27a Medway Street, London SW1P 2BD.
020 7976 0779
Email: info@newbridgefoundation.org.uk

New Bridge runs a wide range of
resettlement advisory services in prisons;
covering housing, debt advice, education and
mentoring. The keynote service (which has
been running for over 50 years) is the
friendship and support given by 200+
volunteers. Every volunteer knows his or her
prisoner client as an individual with their own
personality, problems and potential and values
them as such. Also runs 'Family Matters'
parenting education courses in prisons and a
subsidiary company publishes *'Inside Time'*
the national newspaper for prisoners.

New Bridge Prison Liaison Project
4 & 5 Laurel Business Centre, 15 Laurel
Road, Liverpool L7 0LJ
0151 254 2558 *Fax: 0151 254 2559*
Email: info@prisonlisaisonproject.co.uk
www.prisonliaisonproject.co.uk

Provides services and information working
with offenders who will be settling in
Liverpool.

The POW Trust
295a Queenstown Road, Battersea, London
SW8 3NP.
020 7720 9767 *Fax: 020 7498 0477*
www.powtrust.org

Devoted to helping the socially excluded,
especially assisting inmates and ex-offenders,
to fit back into society with a 'second chance'.

Prison Dialogue
PO Box 44, Chipping Campden, Gloucs GL55
6YN
01386 849186 *Fax: 01386 840449*
Email: enquiries@prisondialogue.org.uk
www.prisondialogue.org

Relationship based approach to organisational
and therapeutic issues in the criminal justice
system. Work is targeted across the criminal
justice continuum from high security to local
prisons and into the community.

Prison Link Cymru (PLC)
Operated by Shelter Cymru and Trothwy Cyf,
delivering a national Prison Link service
throughout Wales. Shelter Cymru, 23 Abbot
Street, Wrexham, LL11 1TA.
01978 317914
Email: prisonlink@sheltercymru.org.uk

Provides information to local authorities in
Wales about homeless prisoners due to be
discharged to their area and to facilitate the
provision of appropriate housing and support.
The service operates across the four Welsh
prisons and Altcourse, Walton, Risley, Styal,
Stoke Heath, Eastwood Park and Ashfield
prisons in England.

Prisoners' Advice Service
PO Box 46199, London EC1M 4XA.
020 7253 3323 *Fax: 020 7253 8067*
helpline 0845 430 8923
www.prisonersadvice.org.uk

The PAS is an independent charity that offers
free confidential advice and information to
prisoners in England and Wales, particularly
concerning prisoners' rights and the
application of Prison Rules. Publishes a
quarterly bulletin "Prisoners' Rights".

**UNLOCK – the National Association of
Reformed Offenders**
35a High Street, Snodland, Kent ME6 5AG.
01634 247350 *Fax: 01634 24735*
Email: enquiries@unlock.org.uk
www.unlock.org.uk

Women in Prison
Unit 10, The Ivories, 6 Northampton Street,
London N1 2HY.
020 7359 6674
Helpline: 0800 953 0125
www.womeninprison.org.uk

Established as a support and campaigning
group for women prisoners, visits women
prisoners and offers practical advice on a
range of welfare issues, particularly
accommodation, education and training. WIP
has a mother and child grant fund for women
in mother and baby units or the carers of the
children of women prisoners. It produces a

national magazine for women in custody and co-ordinates volunteer mentors for women leaving prison.

SERVICES FOR FAMILIES OF OFFENDERS

Prisoners' Families Helpline 0808 808 2003
(9am–8pm Mon–Fri, Sun 10am–3pm)
www.prisonersfamilieshelpline.org.uk
Fax: 0845 862 4003
Email: info@prisonersfamilieshelpline.org.uk

Free confidential, national helpline that provides information and support for prisoners' families and friends.

Action for Prisoners' Families
Unit 21, Carlson Court, 116 Putney Bridge Road, London SW15 2NQ.
020 8812 3600 *Fax: 020 8871 0473*
Email: info@actionpf.org.uk
Email: info@actionpf.org.uk
www.prisonersfamilies.org.uk

National umbrella organisation speaking for, and encouraging the development of organisations that provide assistance for prisoners' families. Publishes a National Directory and other resource material including a series of children's books. Provides details of local support services.

Female Prisoners' Welfare Project / FPWP Hibiscus
Unit 3.2, Holloway Resource Centre, 356 Holloway Road, London N7 6PA
020 7697 4120 *Fax: 020 7837 3339*
Email: fpwphibiscus@aol.com
www.fpwphibiscus.org.uk

Charity providing advice and support to women in prison, their children and families. Visits and supports British and foreign national women also group sessions for foreign nationals including Spanish speaking women. Provides Home Circumstance Reports for the Courts via an office in Jamaica. Staff speak a wide range of languages.

Offenders' Families Helpline 0808 808 2003
Mon–Fri 9am–5pm, Sat 10am–3.pm Free confidential, national helpline providing information and support for prisoners' families and friends.
Email: info@prisonersfamilieshelpline.org.uk
www.prisonersfamilieshelpline.org.uk

Partners of Prisoners Families Support Group
POPS, Valentine House, 1079 Rochdale Road, Blackley, Manchester M9 8AJ.
Tel/Fax: 0161 702 1000
Email: mail@partnersofprisoners.co.uk
www.partnersofprisoners.co.uk

Offers a wide range of services to anyone who has a loved one in prison. Advice, information, emotional support is available to families from arrest to release. POPS is Manchester based but operates nationally. Manages the Black Prisoner Support Project that provides services to black offenders.

Prison Advice & Care Trust (PACT)
(Central Office) Park Place, 12 Lawn Lane, Vauxhall, London SW8 1UD,
020 7735 9535 helpline 0808 808 2003
Email: info@prisonadvice.org.uk
www.prisonadvice.org.uk

Provides services for families including information, advice and support. Visits Centres in London, South West and at HMP Woodhill. First night in custody schemes at HMP Holloway and HMP Exeter.

Prison Link
29 Trinity Road, Aston, Birmingham B6 6AJ.
0121 551 1207 *Fax: 0121 554 4894*
Email: PL@ueponline.co.uk

Specialist prisoners' families support service, Counselling/individual support.

Prisoners Abroad
89–93 Fonthill Road, Finsbury Park, London N4 3JH.
020 7561 6820
Helpline 0808 172 0098 *Fax: 020 7561 6821*
Email: info@prisonersabroad.org.uk
www.prisonersabroad.org.uk

The only UK charity providing information, advice and support to British citizens detained overseas, to their families and friends, and to released prisoners trying to re-establish themselves in society. Prisoners Abroad makes no moral judgement about its clients: it helps convicted and unconvicted, guilty or innocent, solely on the basis of need.

Prisoners' Families and Friends Service
20 Trinity Street, London SE1 1DB.
020 7403 4091 *Fax: 020 7403 9359.*
free helpline for families 0808 808 3444
Email: info@pffs.org.uk
www.pffs.org.uk

Advice and information service for prisoner's families. Other facilities available in the London area.

VICTIM SERVICES

NOMS Victim Helpline
PO Box 4278, Birmingham B15 1SA
Tel: 0845 7585 112
Victims of crime and their relatives who have received unwanted contact from a prisoner or are worried about their release from prison can call or write to the NOMS Victim Helpline.

Victim Support
National Office, Victim Support National Centre,
Hallam House, 56–60 Hallam Street, London W1W 6JL
020 7268 0200 *Fax: 020 7268 0210*
helpline 0845 30 30 900
contact@victimsupport.org.uk
www.victimsupport.org.uk

Co-ordinates the work of local community-based branches providing services to victims of crime and their families, also co-ordinates the Witness Service which supports witnesses in every criminal court in England and Wales.

Victims' Voice
PO Box 21, Fairford GL7 4WX
(07984) 078918
victimsvoice@hotmail.com
www.victimsvoice.co.uk

Victims' Voice is an umbrella charity which provides a 'voice' for its affiliated organisations and individual members. It raises issues that arise when people are bereaved by sudden and traumatic death and have to cope with the involvement of police, coroners, mortuaries, hospitals and the courts.

Witness Service
Central Criminal Court, Old Bailey, London EC4M 7EH
020 7192 2422 *Fax: 020 7192 2142*
CCWS.CentralCriminalCourt@vslondon.org

The Witness Service is a free and confidential service, available at every criminal court in London, which helps witnesses, victims and their families before, during and after a trial.

Bereavement support

Care for the Family
Garth House, Leon Avenue, Cardiff CF15 7RG
029 2081 0800
mail@cff.org.uk
www.careforthefamily.org.uk/adj

Offers support to those suffering bereavement or family breakdown, together with any children.

Bereaved Parents Support
Bereaved Parents Network, Care for the Family, Garth House, Leon Ave, Cardiff F15 7RG
029 2081 0800
mail@cff.org.uk
www.careforthefamily.org.uk/bps

Offers support to those who have been bereaved of a child (including adult children), together with siblings.

The Child Bereavement Charity
The Saunderton Estate, Wycombe Road, Saunderton, Buckinghamshire HP14 4BF
tel (01494) 568900 *fax (01494) 568920*
support@childbereavement.org.uk
www.childbereavement.org.uk

Support and information for bereaved children, young people and families and the professionals who work with them, both when a baby or child dies and when a child grieves. Offers telephone helpline and web service, resources (e.g. videos and books) and trains c5000 caring professionals annually.

Cruse Bereavement Care
PO Box 800, Richmond, Surrey TW9 1RG
020 8939 9530
helpline 0844 477 9400 helpline@cruse.org.uk
(for young people) 0870 167 1677
info@cruse.org.uk
www.crusebereavementcare.org.uk
www.rd4u.org.uk (for young people)

The only national organisation that helps and supports anyone who has been bereaved. It provides advice, bereavement support and information on practical matters for bereaved people entirely free of charge. Its support is delivered through a network of 180 branches across the UK. It also offers training, support, information and publications to those working to care for bereaved people.

The Candle Project
St Christopher's Hospice, 51–59 Lawrie Park Road, Sydenham, London SE26 6DZ

020 8768 4500
info@stchristophers.org.uk

The Candle Project provides one to one and group bereavement support for children, young people and families in the South East London area. It also offers a telephone advice service for parents, carers and professionals nationwide. This is a free service for those who need it.

The Child Death Helpline

York House, 37 Queen Square, London WC1N 3BH
020 7813 8416 (admin) 020 7813 8550 (volunteering) *fax 020 7813 8516*
contact@childdeathhelpline.org
www.childdeathhelpline.org.uk

Helpline 0800 282 986 open throughout the year every evening 7pm-10pm, Mon-Fri mornings 10am-1pm, Tue & Wed afternoons 1pm to 4pm. This is a lifelong freephone listening service of emotional support for anyone affected by the death of a child.

Liverpool Office: The Alder Centre, Alder Hey Children's NHS Foundation Trust, Eaton Road, Liverpool L12 2AP 0151 252 5391 (admin & volunteering) *fax 0151 252 5513*

The Compassionate Friends

14 New King Street, Deptford, London SE8 3HS
helpline 0845 123 2304
10am-4pm and 6.30pm-10.30pm (local rate), day/evening 365 days a year
info@tcf.org.uk helpline@tcf.org.uk
www.tcf.org.uk.
Northern Ireland helpline 028 8778 8016 10am-4pm and 7pm-9.30pm

The Compassionate Friends was founded in 1969 as an organisation of bereaved parents and their families helping each other through their grief.

Winston's Wish

Head Office: 3rd Floor, Cheltenham House, Clarence Street, Cheltenham, Gloucs GL50 3JR
(01242) 515157 *fax 01242 546187* helpline 08452 03 04 05 (open Mon-Fri, 9am-5pm)
info@winstonswish.org.uk
www.winstonswish.org.uk

West Sussex: Unit 6, The Colonnades, 17 London Road, Pulborough, West Sussex RH20 1AS 01798 874742 *fax 01798 875852*
westsussex@winstonswish.org.u

Winston's Wish provides support for bereaved children and young people up to the age of 18. They also support parents and carers. Whether the death was sudden or expected they work closely with children and families in a variety of practical and creative ways to create an atmosphere where they can share their thoughts and feelings and meet others.

Specialist trauma care

ASSIST Trauma Care

Assistance, Support & Self Help in Surviving Trauma, 11 Albert St, Rugby CV21 2RX (01788) 551919, helpline (01788) 560800 Mon-Fri 10am-4pm
www.assisttraumacare.org.uk

Provides therapeutic support and counselling to probationers, prisoners and all those involved in the prison system, who have been affected by trauma, including their friends and families. Specialist treatment for those suffering from Post-Traumatic Stress and Post-Traumatic Stress Disorder.

Disaster Action

No 4, 71 Upper Berkeley Street, London W1H 7DB
(01483) 799066 (office is open on a part-time answerphone outside office hours)
pameladix@disasteraction.org.uk
www.disasteraction.org.uk

Survivors and bereaved people from major UK and overseas disasters founded Disaster Action in 1991 as a British Based Charity. All their members have direct personal experience of surviving and or being bereaved in a wide variety of disasters of different origin including terrorist attacks, transport and natural disasters.

Support after murder or manslaughter

SAMM (Support After Murder and Manslaughter)

SAMM National L & DRC, Tally Ho!, Pershore Road, Edgbaston, Birmingham B5 7RN
helpline 0845 872 3440
info@samm.org.uk
www.samm.org.uk

An independent voluntary organisation offering help and support to families and friends bereaved as a result of murder or manslaughter. All their support volunteers have been similarly bereaved and can share what it feels like to have a loved one taken in this violent and tragic way. They are also involved in training, research, raising public awareness and increasing the understanding of organisations that work with bereaved families, particularly with the criminal justice system. Please contact the National Office for details of local groups.

SAMM Abroad
0845 123 2384 info@sammabroad.org
Support group for people who are bereaved through murder or manslaughter abroad.

MAMAA
support@mama.org
www.mamaa.org

Mothers Against Murder and Aggression is a national registered charity that provides support to families and friends of victims of murder, manslaughter and unlawful killing.

North of England Victims' Association
PO Box 111, Jarrow, Tyne & Wear NE32 5TE
0191–423 2210
n.e.v.a@blueyonder.co.uk
info@victimsfirst.co.uk
www.victimsfirst.co.uk

Helps those in the North East of England who are suffering or who have suffered, as a result of serious crimes, such as murder and manslaughter, by the provision of financial assistance, advice, counselling and support services.

Scotland
PETAL Support Group (People Experiencing Trauma and Loss)
8 Barrack Street, Hamilton ML3 0DG
(01698) 324502 office hours Mon-Thur 9am-5pm, Fri 9am-4pm
www.petalsupport.com

PETAL provides practical, emotional and confidential support, advocacy, group support and counselling for the families and friends of murder and suicide victims. The level of practical and emotional support provided by PETAL differs from the support available from other agencies since the membership consists of the families and friends of murder and suicide victims. The Support Provision by PETAL centres on practical and emotional support and assists people to come to terms with the implications of these traumatic events. Clients can attend Fortnightly Support Meetings at PETAL and use PETAL as a Drop-in Centre for Support or get One to One

Counselling. Telephone support and counselling can be provided to those families outwith a reasonable travelling distance.

Families of Murdered Children (F.o.M.C)
99 Wood Crescent, Motherwell ML1 1HQ
fomcuk@yahoo.co.uk or
www.groups.yahoo.com/group/fomcuk
helpline 01698 336646, 24 hour contact number 0777 562 6779

A non-religious, charitable organisation providing support, information, advice and advocacy to anyone who has lost a loved one as a result of murder, culpable homicide or unlawful killing regardless of age, sex, religion or sexual orientation. Services including a helpline, a 24 hour contact number, home visits, court support, weekly meetings and a secure internet group (by invitation only) including secure chat room facilities.

Support after a road death

BrakeCare
PO Box 548, Huddersfield HD1 2XZ
(01484) 559909 *Fax: (01484) 559983*
helpline 0845 603 8570
helpline@brake.org.uk
www.brake.org.uk

This division of Brake the national road safety charity supports people who have been bereaved and injured in road crashes and assists professionals working with road crash victims. It provides emotional support and practical information to road crash victims.

Campaign Against Drinking & Driving (C.A.D.D.)
PO Box 62, Brighouse, West Yorkshire HD6 3YY
0845 123 5541 helpline 0845 123 5542
(9am-9pm, 365 days)
cadd@scard.org.uk
www.cadd.org.uk

The Campaign Against Drinking and Driving (CADD) was set up in 1985 to support all victims of drunk or drugged drivers throughout the UK.

RoadPeace
Shakespeare Business Centre, 245a Cold Harbour Lane, Brixton, London SW9 8RR
helpline 0845 4500 355, open Mon-Fri, 9am-5pm
info@roadpeace.org &
helpline@roadpeace.org

www.roadpeace.org

RoadPeace is UK's specialist charity for road traffic victims with headquarters in London and 10 local groups throughout the country. RoadPeace offers dedicated support to people bereaved and injured through a road crash and represents their interests.

S.C.A.R.D. (Support & Care After Road Death & Injury)
PO Box 62, Brighouse HD6 3YY
0845 123 5541 helpline 0845 123 5542, open 7 days, 9am-9pm *Fax: 0845 123 5543*
info@scard.org.uk
www.scard.org.uk

Inspired by the tragic death of the founder's son at the hands of a drunk and illegal driver, S.C.A.R.D. is a registered charity, which exists to provide emotional and practical support to the people affected by road tragedies all over the United Kingdom.

Other organisations offering support

Criminal Injuries Compensation Authority
Tay House, 300 Bath Street, Glasgow G2 4LN.
0300 003 3601 (8.30am–8pm Mon–Fri, 9am–1pm Sat)
www.cica.gov.uk

Administers the government funded-scheme to provide compensation to innocent victims of violent crime in Great Britain.

DAMN (Deaths After Medical Negligence)
Mrs Litty Lewy 020 8205 4985
lhl005@londonmet.ac.uk

Formally RAID: Rigorous Analysis of Iatrogenic Death – when the cause of death is given as 'Natural Causes' yet the cause was through negligence.

Samaritans
Chris, PO Box 9090, Stirling, FK8 2SA
www.samaritans.org
UK 08457 90 90 90 or Text 07725 90 90 90
Republic of Ireland 1850 60 90 90 or Text 0872 60 90 90
For the deaf or hard of hearing there are minicom numbers: UK 08457 90 91 92
Republic of Ireland 1850 60 90 91
jo@samaritans.org
www.samaritans.org

Survivors UK
Ground Floor, 34 Gt James Street, London WC1N 3HB.

0207 404 6234 helpline 0845 122 1201(7pm–10pm Mon–Tue–Thur)
Email: info@survivorsuk.org
www.survivorsuk.org

Provides information, support and counselling to men who have experienced any form of sexual abuse, and to advance public education about all matters relating to the sexual abuse of men.

Women's Aid Federation of England Ltd
PO Box 391, Bristol BS99 7WS.
National co-ordinating office telephone: 0808 2000 247 *Fax: 0117 924 1703*
Email: info@womensaid.org.uk
www.womensaid.org.uk
Freephone 24hr national domestic violence helpline 0808 2000 247 (run in partnership between Women's Aid & Refuge)
Email: helpline@womensaid.org.uk

Public information, publications and training on domestic violence. National helpline for women and children experiencing domestic violence. Co-ordinates work of women's refuges in England.

OTHER SERVICES AND SUPPORT GROUPS

Descriptions of the organisations are their own; the publisher takes no responsibility for these statements. Any information about other organisations that might usefully be included will be welcomed. Please send to probation.directory@thomsonreuters.com

Advisory Service for Squatters
Angel Alley, 84b Whitechapel High Street, London E1 7QX.
020 3216 0099 (Phone first, Mon–Fri 2–6pm)
Fax: 020 3216 0098.
Email: advice@squatter.org.uk
www.squatter.org.uk

Legal and practical advice for squatters and homeless people.

ARC (Antenatal Results & Choices)
73 Charlotte Street, London W1T 4PN.
Tel/Fax: 020 7631 0280 helpline 0845 077 2290 (10am–5.30pm Mon–Fri)
Email: info@arc-uk.org
www.arc-uk.org

Offers non-directive, specialised support to parents who discover that their unborn baby may have an abnormality, gives support to parents making a decision about ante-natal testing and offers support regardless of the future of the pregnancy.

ARX (Advocacy Resource Exchange)
Portman House, 53 Millbrook Road East, Southampton SO15 1HN.
02380 234 904 (enquiries), 08451 22 86 33 (advocacy resource finder)
Email: enquiries@advocacyresource.org.uk
www.advocacyresource.org.uk

Maintains a national database of independent advocacy schemes and provides information, training and publications on advocacy.

Asian Family Counselling Service (AFCS)
Suite 51, Windmill Place, 2–4 Windmill Lane, Southall, Middx UB2 4NJ.
020 8571 3933 020 8813 9714 *Fax: 020 8571 3933*
Email: afcs@btconnect.com

Offers family, marital and individual counselling to the Asian community.

Association for Shared Parenting
The Association for Shared Parenting, Spring Cottage, Binton Hill, Stratford-upon-Avon CV37 9TN
0116 254 8453
Email: spring-cott@btopenworld.com
www.sharedparenting.org.uk

Seeks to promote the rights and needs of children following separation or divorce, through promoting view that children have the right to receive love and nurture from both parents. Offers support workshops for parents and a child contact centre for families.

Beating Eating Disorders
1st Floor, 103 Prince of Wales Road, Norwich, Norfolk NR1 1DW admin only.
0300 123 3355 *Fax: (01603) 664915.*
Helpline 0845 634 1414 (Mon–Fri 10.30am–8.30pm, Sat 1pm–4.30pm)
Email: info@b-eat.co.uk
Youth helpline 0845 634 7650 (up to 18yrs, Mon–Fri 4.30pm–8.30pm, Sat 1pm–4.30pm)
Email: fyp@b-eat.co.uk
www.b-eat.co.uk

Provides information, help and support for people affected by eating disorders and, in particular, anorexia and bulimia nervosa.

Brook
50 Featherstone Street, London EC1Y 8RT
020 7284 6040 (admin) *Fax: 020 7284 6050 (admin)*

0808 802 1234 (free, confidential helpline for under 25s 9am–5pm Mon–Fri)
Email: admin@brook.org.uk
www.brook.org.uk

Offers young people under 25 free confidential advice on health and contraception. For immediate information about contraception (inc emergency), pregnancy testing, abortion, sexually transmitted infections. Recorded 24 hour information 020 7950 7755 or 'Ask Brook' at *www.brook.org.uk* for a confidential response to an enquiry. Email brook@adc-uk.com for info on Brook publications.

The Butler Trust
Howard House, 32–34 High Street, Croydon CR0 1YB.
020 8688 6062 *Fax: 020 8688 6056*
Email: info@thebutlertrust.org.uk
www.thebutlertrust.org.uk

Independent charity, which aims to celebrate, support and share good practice in UK correctional settings. The Butler Trust Annual Awards recognise outstanding dedication, skill and creativity on the part of those working in correctional settings across the UK.

Cambridge Family Mediation Service
3rd Floor, Essex House, 71 Regent Street, Cambridge CB2 1AB.
(01223) 576308 (24 hour answerphone)
9.30am–5pm Mon–Thur, 9.30am–4pm Fri, *Fax: (01223) 576309*
Email: families@cambridgefms.co.uk
www.cambridgefms.co.uk

Specialist family mediation service for divorcing or separating couples. Has free counselling service for under 19s.

The Centre for Crime and Justice Studies
2 Langley Lane, Vauxhall, London SW8 1GB.
020 7840 6110
Email: info@crimeandjustice.org.uk
www.crimeandjustice.org.uk

An independent charity that informs and educates about all aspects of crime and criminal justice. Provides information, produces research and carries out policy analysis to encourage and facilitate an understanding of the complex nature of issues concerning crime. A membership organisation working with practitioners, policy makers, academics and students, the media and voluntary sector offering programmes of events, publications and online resources.

Child Poverty Action Group
94 White Lion Street, London N1 9PF.
020 7837 7979 *Fax: 020 7837 6414*
Email: info@cpag.org.uk *www.cpag.org.uk*

For details of CPAG and training courses and membership schemes contact above address. Welfare rights enquiries (advisors only): Citizens' Rights Office 020 7833 4627, 2pm–4pm Mon–Fri Promotes action for relief, directly or indirectly, of poverty among children and families with children. Works to ensure that those on low incomes get their full entitlement to welfare benefits. Aims to eradicate the injustice of poverty.

ChildLine
42 Curtain Road, London EC2A 3NH. Address for children Freepost NATN1111, London E1 6BR.
admin 020 7650 3200 *Fax: 020 7650 3201*
helpline 0800 1111 24 hr national telephone helpline for children and young people in trouble or danger.
Calls free from landlines or mobiles.
Informative website *www.childline.org.uk*

The service is free and confidential. Email info@childline.org.uk (cannot answer problems or offer counselling online).

Children's Legal Centre
University of Essex, Wivenhoe Park, Colchester, Essex CO4 3SQ.
(01206) 877 910 (admin + publications) *Fax: (01206) 877 963*
Email: clc@essex.ac.uk
www.childrenslegalcentre.com

Free and confidential advice and information service covering all aspects of law affecting young people including refugees. Publishes 'Childright' and other publications. Education law helpline 0845 456 6811.

Citizens Advice
Myddelton House, 115–123 Pentonville Road, London N1 9LZ.
020 7833 2181 (admin) *Fax: 020 7833 4371* (admin)
www.citizensadvice.org.uk

The independent national charity and membership organisation for Citizens Advice Bureaux, providing free, confidential, and impartial advice to anyone on all subjects. Citizens Advice monitors the problems that CAB clients are experiencing and reports

these findings to show where services and policies are failing both locally and nationally. The address and telephone number of local offices can be found in the telephone directory or on the website. For CAB information advice online see
www.adviceguide.org.uk

CLAPA
Cleft Lip & Palate Association, 1st Floor, Green Man Tower, 332B Goswell Road, London EC1V 7LQ.
020 7833 4883 *Fax: 020 7833 5999*
Email: info@clapa.com
www.clapa.com

Offers information and support to all people affected by cleft lip or palate. Bottles and teats available by mail order.

CoDA (Co-dependents Anonymous)
CoDA UK, PO Box 2365, Bristol BS6 9XJ.
www.coda-uk.org

An informal Twelve Step fellowship of men and women, whose common problem is an inability to maintain functional relationships with self and others as a result of co-dependency in their lives. CoDA uses the Twelve Steps, as a part of its suggested programme of recovery and for building healthy relationships, in a safe and confidential environment.

Criminal Cases Review Commission
5 St Philip's Place, Birmingham B3 2PW
0121 233 1473
Fax: 0121 232 0899
Email: info@ccrc.gov.uk
www.ccrc.gov.uk

An independent public body reviewing alleged miscarriages of justice with power to refer convictions and sentences to the appeal courts.

Depression UK
c/o Self Help Nottingham, Ormiston House, 32–36 Pelham Street, Nottingham NG1 2EG.
0870 774 4320 *Fax: 0870 774 4319*
Email: info@depressionuk.org
www.depressionuk.org

Self help organisation for people with depression (and relatives). Members receive 4 newsletters a year, can join penfriend/phonefriend schemes. Some local self help groups. Information line open to anyone at anytime

Down's Syndrome Association
Langdon Down Centre, 2a Langdon Park,
Teddington TW11 9PS.
0333 121 2300 (helpline 10am–4pm Mon–Fri)
Fax: 0845 230 0373.
Email: info@downs-syndrome.org.uk
www.downs-syndrome.org.uk

Exists to support parents and carers of people
with Down's Syndrome and to improve the
lives of those with the condition.

Epilepsy Action
New Anstey House, Gate Way Drive, Yeadon,
Leeds LS19 7XY.
0113 210 8800 *Fax: 0113 391 0300* helpline
0808 800 5050
Email: epilepsy@epilepsy.org.uk
www.epilepsy.org.uk

Advice and information on all aspects of living
with epilepsy.

Equality & Human Rights Commission
(offices in London, Manchester, Glasgow and
Cardiff)
Helplines Mon, Tues, Thurs, Fri 9am–5pm;
England 0845 604 6610, Scotland 0845 604
5510, Wales 0845 604 8810.
London 3 More London, Riverside Tooley
Street, London SE1 2RG.
020 3117 0235 (admin) *Fax: 020 7407 7557*
Email: info@equalityhumanrights.com
Manchester Arndale House, The Arndale
Centre, Manchester M4 3AQ.
0161 829 8100 (admin) *Fax: 0161 829 8110*
Email:info@equalityhumanrights.com
Glasgow The Optima Building, 58 Robertson
Street, Glasgow G2 8DU, 0141 228 5910
(admin), *Fax: 0141 228 5912*
scotland@equalityhumanrights.com
Cardiff 3rd Floor, 3 Callaghan Square, Cardiff
CF10 5BT.
029 2044 7710 (admin) 029 204 47713
(textphone) *Fax: 029 2044 7712*
Email:wales@equalityhumanrights.com
www.equalityhumanrights.com

The Commission took over the
responsibilities of the former Commission for
Racial Equality (CRE), Disability Rights
Commission (DRC) and Equal Opportunities
Commission (EOC), with new responsibilities
for sexual orientation, age, religion and belief,
and human rights.

Families Need Fathers
134 Curtain Road, London EC2A 3AR.
020 7613 5060 (admin). Helpline 0300 0300
110 (Mon–Fri 6pm–10pm)

Email: fnf@fnf.org.uk
www.fnf.org.uk

National network of voluntary contacts.
Keeping children and parents in contact after
separation or divorce. Regular meetings are
held around the country.

Family Action
501–505 Kingsland Road, London E8 4AU.
020 7254 6251
www.family-action.org.uk

Provides a range of social care services
including community mental health services,
activity based resource centres, family
centres, grants to people in need, and grants
advice for students undertaking vocational
courses.

Family Rights Group
2nd Floor, The Print House, 18 Ashwin Street,
London E8 3DL.
020 7923 2628 *Fax: 020 7923 2683.*
Email: office@frg.org.uk.
Advice line freephone 0808 801 0366
(Mon–Fri 10am–3.30pm)
Email: advice@frg.org.uk
www.frg.org.uk.

Provides a phone and written advice service
for parents, relatives and carers who have
children in care, on the child protection
register, or who are receiving services from
social services departments.

FPA (Family Planning Association)
London office: 50 Featherstone Street,
London EC1Y 8QU.
020 7608 5240 (admin) *Fax: 0845 123 2349*
Email: general@fpa.org.uk
www.fpa.org.uk.
Helpline England 0845 122 8690 (Mon–Fri
9am–6pm).
Helpline Northern Ireland 0845 122 8687
(Mon–Thur 9am–5pm, Fri 9am–4.30pm).
Publications 0845 122 8600 *Fax: 0845 123
2349*
Email: fpadirect@fpa.org.uk.

Providing information and advice on
contraception, sexual health, planning a
pregnancy and pregnancy choices, and family
planning and sexual services.

Gingerbread
520 Highgate Studios, 53–79 Highgate Road,
London NW5 1TL
Single parent helpline 0808 802 0925
(9am–5pm Mon–Fri, Wed till 8pm)
Email: info@gingerbread.org.uk

www.gingerbread.org.uk

Information service for lone parents, other organisations, local authorities and the media. Providing consultancy on employment initiatives for lone parents and rights based training for professionals working with lone parents. Campaigning and lobbying to change the law and improve provision for lone parents and their children.

Headway – the brain injury association
190 Bagnall Road, Old Basford, Nottingham NG6 8SF.
0115 924 0800 *Fax: 0115 958 4446* free helpline 0808 800 2244
Email: enquiries@headway.org.uk
www.headway.org.uk

Exists to promote the understanding of all aspects of brain injury and to provide information, support and services to people with brain injury, their family and carers.

Homeless Link
Gateway House, Milverton Street, London SE11 4AP
020 7840 4430 *Fax: 020 7840 4431*
Email: info@homelesslink.org.uk
www.homeless.org.uk

Membership body for local organisations and individuals providing services and support to homeless people. Also runs the Homeless Services Unit which brings together front line workers in the resettlement and emergency accommodation fields.

Howard League
1 Ardleigh Road, London N1 4HS.
020 7249 7373 *Fax: 020 7249 7788*
Email: info@howardleague.org
www.howardleague.org

Charity working for humane and effective reform of penal system.

Institute of Criminology
University of Cambridge, Sidgwick Avenue, Cambridge CB3 9DA.
(01223) 335360 *Fax: (01223) 335356*
Email: enquiries@crim.cam.ac.uk
www.crim.cam.ac.uk

A centre for teaching and research in criminology and criminal justice matters, a biennial senior course for practitioners in the criminal justice system, and a part-time masters degree course for senior corrections officials and police officers.

Joint Council for the Welfare of Immigrants
115 Old Street, London EC1V 9RT.
020 7251 8708 (admin) *Fax: 020 7251 8707*
Email: info@jcwi.org.uk *www.jcwi.org.uk*

An independent national organisation that exists to campaign for justice in immigration, nationality and refugee law and policy. It undertakes strategic casework and acts as an expert training resource for others who work in this field.

Justice
59 Carter Lane, London EC4V 5AQ.
020 7329 5100 *Fax: 020 7329 5055*
Email: admin@justice.org.uk
www.justice.org.uk

Justice is a law reform and human rights group. It cannot deal with individual cases, but has produced 'How to Appeal' a simple guide to the criminal appeal process. This is currently out of print but available from the website as a pdf file. When in print it is free to prisoners (send sae 9"x6" with 34p stamp). It is available to others at £2.50 inc p&p.

Kidscape
2 Grosvenor Gardens, London SW1W 0DH.
020 7730 3300 *Fax: 020 7730 7081*
Parents anti-bullying helpline 08451 205 204
www.kidscape.org.uk

Provides books, posters, videos, teaching materials and training about prevention of child sexual abuse and school bullying.

Law Society
The Law Society's Hall, 113 Chancery Lane, London WC2A 1PL
020 7242 1222 *Fax: 020 7831 0344*
Email: contact@lawsociety.org.uk
www.lawsociety.org.uk

The representative body and regulator of solicitors in England and Wales.

Men's Advice Line
freephone 0808 801 0327 (10am–1pm and 2pm–5pm Mon–Fri) a helpline for male victims of domestic violence.
Email: info@mensadviceline.org.uk or *www.mensadviceline.org.uk*

Mencap
123 Golden Lane, London EC1Y 0RT.
020 7454 0454 *Fax: 020 7608 3254,* helpline 0808 808 1111
Email: help@mencap.org.uk
www.mencap.org.uk

The largest charity for people with learning difficulties.

Message Home
freephone confidential, 24 hour helpline, 0800 700 740
Email: messagehome@missingpeople.org.uk
www.missingpeople.org.uk
Operated by National Missing Persons Helpline for missing adults allowing them to pass a message home.

Mind (Nat Assn for Mental Health)
Granta House, 15/19 Broadway, Stratford, London E15 4BQ
020 8519 2122 *Fax: 020 8522 1725*
Mind*info*Line 0845 766 0163
Email: contact@mind.org.uk
www.mind.org.uk

Mind is the leading mental health charity in England and Wales and works for a better life for everyone with experience of mental distress. There are over 220 local Mind associations.

Missing People
Roebuck House, 284 Upper Richmond Rd West, London SW14 7JE
020 8392 4590 *Fax: 020 8878 7752*
national helpline 0500 700 700
Email: info@missingpeople.org
www.missingpeople.org.uk

UK's only charity dedicated to finding missing people and supporting those left behind. Supports the work of police, Social Services. Works in partnership with other agencies. Registers all types of missing persons and can help to publicise medium-high risk cases and offers ID and reconstruction services. Missing people can send a message home Freefone 0800 700 740 or email messagehome@missingpeople.org.uk

Muslim Youth Helpline
18 Rosemont Road, London NW3 6NE
020 7435 8171 *Fax: 0870 774 3519*
Email: info@myh.org.uk (admin)
freephone helpline 0808 808 2008 (6pm–12am Mon–Fri and 12pm–12am Sat/Sun
Email: help@myh.org.uk
www.myh.org.uk

A free confidential counselling and befriending service for young Muslims in need.

National Association of Child Contact Centres
1 Heritage Mews, High Pavement, Nottingham NG1 1HN.
0845 4500 280 *Fax: 0845 4500 420*
Email: contact@naccc.org.uk
www.naccc.org.uk

Promotes safe child contact within a national framework of child contact centres. These exist to provide neutral meeting places where children of a separated family can enjoy contact with one or both parents, and sometimes other family members, in a comfortable and safe environment where there is no viable alternative.

National Association of Official Prison Visitors
32 Newham Avenue, Bedford MK41 9PT
Tel/Fax: (01234) 359763
Email: info@naopv.com
www.naopv.com

Napac (National Association for People Abused in Childhood)
NAPAC, 42 Curtain Road, London EC2A 3NH.
www.napac.org.uk
Support Line 0800 085 3330

National Children's Bureau
8 Wakley Street, London EC1V 7QE.
020 7843 6000 *Fax: 020 7278 9512*
Email: enquiries@ncb.org.uk
www.ncb.org.uk

Identifies and promotes the interests of children and young people through policy, research and practice development. The Bureau is multi disciplinary, working with professional across all sectors.

National Youth Agency
Eastgate House, 19–23 Humberstone Road, Leicester LE5 3GJ.
0116 242 7350 *Fax: 0116 242 7444*
General enquiries: dutydesk@nya.org.uk
www.nya.org.uk

Information, advice and support for those working with young people. Validates qualifying training for youth and community work.

NORCAP – supporting adults affected by adoption
AAA-NORCAP, 112 Church Road, Wheatley, Oxon OX33 1LU.
(01865) 875000 (9.30am–4.30pm Mon–Thur, 9.30am–4pm Fri)
Email: enquiries@norcap.org

www.norcap.org.uk

Provides support, guidance and sympathetic understanding to adult adopted people and their birth and adoptive relatives. Contact Register. For members: telephone helpline, intermediary role for those seeking renewed contact, advice on searching and research service, comprehensive research pack.

NSPCC
Weston House, 42 Curtain Road, London EC2A 3NH.
020 7825 2500 *Fax: 020 7825 2525.*
24hr child protection helpline 0808 800 5000
Email: help@nspcc.org.uk
www.nspcc.org.uk

The NSPCC is the UK's leading charity specialising in child protection and prevention of cruelty to children. It exists to prevent children from suffering significant harm as a result of ill treatment; to help protect children who are at risk from such harm; to help children who have suffered abuse overcome the effects of such harm; and to work to protect children from further harm.

Papyrus
67 Bewsey Street, Warrington, Cheshire WA2 7JQ
(01925) 240502 *Fax: (01282) 432777*
Email: admin@papyrus-uk.org
www.papyrus-uk.org
helpline HOPElineUK 0800 068 4141
(10am–5pm & 7pm–10pm Mon–Fri, 2pm–5pm Sat/Sun).

Aims to prevent young suicide by providing support to families, friends, carers and professionals, and helpline for them and for suicidal youngsters.

Parentline Plus
CAN Mezzanine, 49–51 East Road, London N1 6AH.
020 7284 5500 Helpline 0808 800 2222,
Textphone 0800 783 6783
Email: parentsupport@parentlineplus.org.uk
(for parents, not general enquiries)
www.parentlineplus.org.uk

National charity offering help and information for parents and families via a range of services including a free 24 hour confidential helpline, workshops, courses, leaflets and website. Works to recognise and to value the different types of families that exist and expand services available to them; understands that children's needs cannot be separated from the needs of parents/carers, believes that it is normal for all parents to have difficulties from time to time.

The Prince's Trust
18 Park Square East, London NW1 4LH.
020 7543 1234 *Fax: 020 7543 1200*
General enquiries freephone 0800 842 842
Email: webinfops@princes-trust.org.uk
www.princes-trust.org.uk

(12 national and regional offices) Helps 14–30 year olds to develop confidence, learn new skills, move into work and start businesses. It offers training, personal development opportunities, business start up support, mentoring and advice. The Trust has four priority target groups—unemployed, educational under achievers, offenders/ex-offenders, and those leaving care.

POA
The Professional Trades Union for Prison Correctional and Secure Psychiatric Workers, Cronin House, 245 Church Street, London N9 9HW. 020 8803 0255 email general@poauk.org.uk *www.poauk.org.uk*
Trade Union and professional staff association for workers in penal institutions and secure psychiatric units in England, Wales, Scotland and Northern Ireland.

Prison Reform Trust
15 Northburgh Street, London EC1V 0JR.
020 7251 5070 *Fax: 020 7251 5076*
Email: prt@prisonreformtrust.org.uk
www.prisonreformtrust.org.uk

Runs a research and publishing programme, and offers advice and information on all aspects of penal policy, publishes a quarterly magazine 'Prison Report'. Jointly (with HM Prison Service) publishes "Prisoners' Information Book".

Probation Managers' Association
PMA Office, Unite, Hayes Court, West Common Road, Hayes, Kent BR2 7AU.
020 8462 7755 *Fax: 020 8315 8234*
Email: info@probationmanagers.co.uk
www.unitetheunion.com

Repetitive Strain Injury Association
Has now ceased to exist, RSI advice is provided as a free service by Keytools Ltd, Abacus House, 1 Spring Crescent, Southampton SO17 2FZ.
023 8029 4500

Email: rsia@keytools.com
www.keytools.co.uk

Respect Phoneline 0808 802 4040
An information and advice line for domestic violence perpetrators, their (ex)partners as well as frontline workers.
Email: info@respectphoneline.org.uk
www.respectphoneline.org.uk

Rethink (formerly National Schizophrenia Fellowship)
89 Albert Embankment, Vauxhall, London SE1 7TP.
Adviceline 020 7840 3188 (10am–1pm Mon–Fri)
Email: advice@rethink.org
0300 5000 927 (enquiries)
Email: info@rethink.
www.rethink.org

A national voluntary organisation that helps people with a severe mental illness, their families and carers and provides training for professionals.

The Rights Shop
296 Bethnal Green Road, London E2 0AG.
020 7739 4173 *Fax: 020 7613 3758*

Open Mon & Wed 9am–1.30pm (drop-in service), Tues & Thurs 9am–2pm (appt only). Drop-in welfare rights/housing advice/money advice.

Royal National Institute of the Blind (RNIB)
105 Judd Street, London WC1H 9NE.
020 7388 1266 *Fax: 020 7388 2034*
Helpline 0303 123 9999
Email: helpline@rnib.org.uk
www.rnib.org.uk

General enquiries: RNIB Resource Centre, London; benefit rights; education; employment and leisure enquiries; services for local societies; health, social and environmental services; reference library; advice on wills and legacies; enquiries on multiple disability; physiotherapy support.

RNID —for the deaf and hard of hearing
19–23 Featherstone Street, London EC1Y 8SL.
0808 808 0123 (telephone helpline), 0808 808 9000 (textphone helpline), 020 7296 8000 (admin) 020 7296 8001 (admin textphone)
Fax: 020 7296 8199
Email: informationline@rnid.org.uk
www.rnid.org.uk

The RNID is the largest charity working to change the world for the 9 million deaf and hard of hearing people in the UK. As a membership charity it aims to achieve a radically better life for deaf and hard of hearing people. It does this by campaigning and lobbying, by raising awareness, by providing services and through social, medical and technical research.

Runaway Helpline 116 000
(or text 80234) operated by Missing People for young people under 18 and away from home or care.
Call 116 000
Text 116 000
Email 116000@missingpeople.org.uk
www.runawayhelpline.org.uk

Sands (Stillbirth and Neonatal Death Charity)
28 Portland Place, London W1B 1LY.
020 7436 7940, *Fax: 020 7436 3715*
Helpline 020 7436 5881 (Mon–Fri 9.30am–5.30pm, Tue & Thur 6pm–10pm)
Email: helpline@uk-sands.org or support@uk-sands.org
www.uk-sands.org

Support and advice for parents and families whose baby dies before, during or after birth.

SANE
1st Floor, Cityside House, 40 Adler Street, London E1 1EE.
020 7375 1002 *Fax: 020 7375 2162*
SANEline 0845 767 8000 (1pm–11pm everyday)
Email: info@sane.org.uk or sanemail@sane.org.uk
www.sane.org.uk

A national mental health helpline for anyone with a mental health problem, their friends, families, carers and interested professionals. Can offer emotional support and information on local and national services, illnesses, medications, therapies and mental health law.

Shelter (National campaign for homeless)
88 Old Street, London EC1V 9HU.
0844 515 2000 (Mon–Fri 9am–5.30pm)
eEmail: info@shelter.org.uk
www.shelter.org.uk
Freephone housing advice helpline 0808 800 4444 (8am–8pm Mon–Fri, 8am–5pm Sat/Sun).

Runs a network of housing aid centres providing advice and advocacy to people who are, or are threatened with, homelessness, and campaigns on their behalf.

SITRA
3rd Floor, 55 Bondway, London SW8 1SJ.
020 7793 4710 *Fax: 020 7793 4715*
Email: post@sitra.org
www.sitra.org.uk

Training, advice, policy information and consultancy on all supported housing and supporting people matters. Monthly journal 'SITRA Bulletin' goes to all SITRA members.

Together
12 Old Street, London EC1V 9BE.
020 7780 7300 *Fax: 020 7780 7301*
Email: contactus@together-uk.org
www.together-uk.org

A national charity providing a wide range of high quality community and hospital based services for people with mental health needs and their carers; including advocacy, assertive outreach schemes, community support, employment schemes, forensic services, helplines/information, respite for carers, social clubs, supported accommodation including 24 hour care.

Workaholics Anonymous
PO Box 394, Witney OX28 9BR.
www.workaholics-anonymous.org

12 step self help programme for compulsive workers. Free literature in return for an sae.

Working Links
freephone 0800 917 9262.

A public, private, voluntary company working across Great Britain with long-term unemployed people. Also working with local Learning and Skills Councils as well as supporting offenders in prisons.

PRISONS

HM Inspectorate of Prisons
1st Floor Ashley House 2 Monck Street
London SW1P 2BQ
Tel: 020 7035 2136
Fax: 020 7035 2141
Email:
hmiprisons.enquiries@hmiprisons.gsi.gov.uk

HM Chief Inspector of Prisons: Nick Hardwick
CBE
HM Deputy Inspector of Prisons: Martin Lomas

HM Chief Inspector of Prisons is appointed from outside the Prison Service, for a term of five years. The Chief Inspector reports directly to the government on the treatment and conditions for prisoners in England and Wales and other matters.

The Prisons Inspectorate also has statutory responsibility to inspect all immigration removal centres and holding facilities on behalf of the Immigration and Nationality Directorate and has recently been invited to regularly inspect the Military Corrective Training Centre in Colchester. In addition, HM Chief Inspector of Prisons is invited to inspect prisons in Northern Ireland, the Channel Islands, Isle of Man and some Commonwealth dependent territories.

PENAL INSTITUTIONS ENGLAND & WALES, WITH CATEGORIES

Key to prison categories:

ABCD	prisoner categories (see Prison Service Order 0900 Categorisation)
CL	closed
F	females
HC	holding centre
IRC	immigration removal centre
J	juveniles
L	local
M	males
O	open
RC	remand centre
RES	resettlement
S-O	semi-open
YOI	young offenders
*	privately run prison

HMP Acklington (M C CL)
Morpeth Northumberland NE65 9XF
Tel: 01670 762300 Fax: 01670 762301

HMP Altcourse* (M L)
Higher Lane Fazakerley Liverpool L9 7LH
Tel: 0151 522 2000 Fax: 0151 522 2121
Website: www.hmpaltcourse.co.uk

HMP/YOI Ashfield* (Serco) (CL J RC YOI)
Shortwood Road Pucklechurch Bristol BS16 9QJ
Tel: 0117 303 8000 Fax: 0117 303 8001

HMP/YOI Askham Grange (F O)
Askham Richard York YO23 3FT
Tel: 01904 772000 Fax: 01904 772001

HMYOI Aylesbury (YOI(M) A CL RES)
Bierton Road Aylesbury HP20 1EH
Tel: 01296 444000 Fax: 01296 444001

HMP Bedford (M L)
St Loyes Street Bedford MK40 1HG
Tel: 01234 373000 Fax: 01234 273568

HMP Belmarsh (M A CL)
Western Way Thamesmead London SE28 0EB
Tel: 020 8331 4400 Fax: 020 8331 4401

HMP Birmingham (M L)
Winson Green Road Birmingham B18 4AS
Tel: 0121 345 2500 Fax: 021 345 2501

HMP Blantyre House (M C S-O)
Goudhurst Cranbrook Kent TN17 2NH
Tel: 01580 213200 Fax: 01580 213201

HMP Blundeston (M C CL)
Lowestoft NR32 5BG
Tel: 01502 734500 Fax: 01502 734501

HMP/YOI Brinsford (YOI J CL RC)
New Road Featherstone Wolverhampton
WV10 7PY
Tel: 01902 533450 Fax: 01902 533451

HMP Bristol (M L)
19 Cambridge Road Bristol BS7 8PS
Tel: 0117 372 3100 Fax: 0117 372 3113

HMP Brixton (M B L)
PO Box 269 Jebb Avenue London SW2 5XF
Tel: 020 8588 6000 Fax: 020 8588 6191

HMP Bronzefield* (Kalyx) (F)
Woodthorpe Road Ashford Middlesex TW15
3JZ
Tel: 01784 425690 Fax: 01784 425691

HMP Buckley Hall (MC)
Buckley Road Rochdale OL12 9DP
Tel: 01706 514300 Fax: 01706 514399

HMP Bullingdon (M C CL L)
PO Box 50 Bicester OX25 1PZ
Tel: 01869 353100 Fax: 01869 353101

HMP/YOI Bullwood Hall (M C)
High Road Hockley Essex SS5 4TE
Tel: 01702 562800 Fax: 01702 562801

HMP Bure (M C)
Jaguar Drive Scottow Norwich NR10 5GB
Tel: 01603 326000 Fax: 01603 326001

HMP Canterbury (M L)
46 Longport Canterbury CT1 1PJ

Tel: 01227 862800 Fax: 01227 862801

HMP/RC Cardiff (M L RC)
Knox Road Cardiff CF24 0UG
Tel: 02020 923100 Fax: 02920 923318

HMP/YOI Castington (YOI J CL)
Morpeth Northumberland NE65 9XG
Tel: 01670 382100 Fax: 01670 382101

HMP Channings Wood (M C CL)
Denbury Newton Abbot TQ12 6DW
Tel: 01803 814600 Fax: 01803 814601

HMP/YOI Chelmsford (M L RC)
200 Springfield Road Chelmsford CM2 6LQ
Tel: 01245 552000 Fax: 01245 552001

HMP Coldingley (M C CL)
Shaftesbury Road Bisley Woking GU24 9EX
Tel: 01483 344300 Fax: 01483 344427

HMP Cookham Wood (F CL)
Sir Evelyn Road Rochester ME1 3LU
Tel: 01634 202500 Fax: 01634 202501

HMP Dartmoor (M C CL)
Princetown Yelverton PL20 6RR
Tel: 01822 322000 Fax: 01822 322001

HMYOI Deerbolt (YOI CL)
Bowes Road Barnard Castle Co Durham
DL12 9BG
Tel: 01833 633200 Fax: 01833 633201

HMP/YOI Doncaster* (Serco) (M L)
Off North Bridge Road Marshgate Doncaster
DN5 8UX
Tel: 01302 760870 Fax: 01302 760851

HMP Dorchester (M L RC)
North Square Dorchester DT1 1JD
Tel: 01305 714500 Fax: 01305 714501

HMP Dovegate* (Serco) (M B CL)
Uttoxeter Staffordshire ST14 8XR
Tel: 01283 829400 Fax: 01283 8200066

IRC Dover (CL IR C)
The Citadel Western Heights Dover CT17
9DR
Tel: 01304 246400 Fax: 01304 246401

HMP Downview (F C CL)
Sutton Lane Sutton Surrey SM2 5PD
Tel: 020 8196 6300 Fax: 020 8196 6301

HMP/YOI Drake Hall (F S-O YOI)
Eccleshall Staffordshire ST21 6LQ
Tel: 01785 774100 Fax: 01785 774010

HMP Durham (M RES)
Old Elvet Durham DH1 3HU
Tel: 0191 332 3400 Fax: 0191 332 3401

HMP/YOI East Sutton Park (F O)
Sutton Valence Maidstone ME17 3DF
Tel: 01622 785000 Fax: 01622 785001

HMP/YOI Eastwood Park (F L)
Falfield Wootton-under-Edge Gloucestershire
GL12 8DB
Tel: 01454 382100 Fax: 01454 382101

HMP Elmley (Sheppey Cluster) (M B CL L)
Church Road Eastchurch Sheerness ME12
4DZ
Tel: 01795 882000 Fax: 01795 882001

HMP Erlestoke (M C CL)
Devizes Wiltshire SN10 5TU
Tel: 01380 814250 Fax: 01380 814273

HMP Everthorpe (M C CL)
1a Beck Road Brough East Yorkshire HU15
1RB
Tel: 01430 426500 Fax: 01430 426501

HMP/YOI Exeter (M L RC)
New North Road Exeter EX4 4EX
Tel: 01392 415650 Fax: 01392 415691

HMP Featherstone (M C CL)
New Road Featherstone Wolverhampton
WV10 7PU
Tel: 01902 703000 Fax: 01902 703001

HMP/YOI Feltham (M CL RC)
Bedfont Road Feltham Middlesex TW13 4ND
Tel: 020 8844 5000 Fax: 020 8844 5001

HMP Ford (M D O)
Arundel West Sussex BN18 0BX
Tel: 01903 663000 Fax: 01903 663001

HMP/YOI Forest Bank* (Kalyx) (M L YOI)
Agecroft Road Pendlebury Salford M27 8FB
Tel: 0161 925 7000 Fax: 0161 925 7001

HMP/YOI Foston Hall (F CL)
Foston Derbyshire DE65 5DN
Tel: 01283 584300 Fax: 01283 584301

HMP Frankland (M A CL)
Brasside Durham DH1 5YD
Tel: 0191 376 5000 Fax: 0191 376 5001

HMP Full Sutton (M A CL)
Full Sutton York YO41 1PS
Tel: 01759 475100 Fax: 01759 371206

HMP Garth (M B CL)
Ulnes Walton Lane Leyland PR26 8NE
Tel: 01772 443300 Fax: 01772 443301

HMP Gartree (M B CL)
Gallow Field Road Market Harborough LE16
7RP
Tel: 01858 426600 Fax: 01858 426601

HMYOI & RC Glen Parva (CL RC YOI)
Tigers Road Wigston Leicester LE8 4TN
Tel: 0116 228 4100 Fax: 0116 228 4000

HMP/YOI Gloucester (M B L RC)
Barrack Square Gloucester GL1 2JN
Tel: 01452 453000 Fax: 01452 453001

HMP Grendon (M B CL)
Grendon Underwood Aylesbury HP18 0TL
Tel: 01296 445000 Fax: 01296 445001

HMP/YOI Guys Marsh (M C CL YOI)
Shaftesbury Dorset SP7 0AH
Tel: 01747 856400 Fax: 01747 856401

IRC Haslar (HC)
2 Dolphin Way Gosport PO12 2AW
Tel: 023 9260 4000 Fax: 023 9260 4001

HMP Haverigg (M C CL)
Millom Cumbria LA18 4NA
Tel: 01229 713000 Fax: 01229 713001

HMP Hewell (M B C D (*varied sites*))
Hewell Lane Redditch B97 6QS
Tel: 01527 785000 Fax: 01527 785001

HMP High Down (M L)
Sutton Lane Sutton Surrey SM2 5PJ
Tel: 020 7147 6300 Fax: 020 7147 6301

HMP Highpoint North (M C CL)
Stradishall Newmarket CB8 9YG
Tel: 01440 743100 Fax: 01440 743092

HMYOI Hindley (RC CL YOI)
Gibson Street Bickershaw Wigan WN2 5TH
Tel: 01942 663100 Fax: 01942 663101

HMP Hollesley Bay (M D O YOI(CL))
Woodbridge Suffolk IP12 3JW
Tel: 01394 412400 Fax: 01394 410115

HMP/YOI Holloway (F L)
Parkhurst Road London N7 0NU
Tel: 020 7979 4400 Fax: 020 7979 4401

HMP Holme House (M B CL L)
Holme House Road Stockton-on-Tees TS18
2QU
Tel: 01642 744000 Fax: 01642 744001

HMP Hull (M L YOI(CL))
Hedon Road Kingston-upon-Hull HU0 5LS
Tel: 01482 282200 Fax: 01482 282400

HMP Huntercombe (M C CL)
Huntercombe Place Nuffield
Henley-on-Thames RG9 5SB
Tel: 01491 643100 Fax: 01491 643101

HMP Isle of Wight (M B C)

Clissold Road Newport Isle of Wight PO30
5RS
Tel: 01983 556300 Fax: 01983 556362

HMP Kennet (M C)
Parkbourn Maghull Liverpool L31 1HX
Tel: 0151 213 3000 Fax: 0151 213 3103

HMP Kingston (M B C)
122 Milton Road Portsmouth PO3 6AS
Tel: 020 9295 3100 Fax: 023 9295 3181

HMP Kirkham (M D O)
Freckleton Road Kirkham Preston PR4 2RN
Tel: 01772 675400 Fax: 01772 675401

HMP Kirklevington Grange (M C D RES)
Yarm Cleveland TS15 9PA
Tel: 01642 792600 Fax: 01642 792601

HMP Lancaster Castle (M C CL)
The Castle Lancaster LA1 1YL
Tel: 01524 565100 Fax: 01524 565022

HMP/YOI Lancaster Farms (J YOI RC CL)
Stone Row Head off Quernmore Road
Lancaster LA1 3QZ
Tel: 01524563450 Fax: 01524 563451

HMP Leeds (M L)
Gloucester Terrace Armley Leeds LS12 9TJ
Tel: 0113 203 2600 Fax: 0113 203 2601

HMP Leicester (M L)
116 Welford Road Leicester LE2 7AJ
Tel: 0116 228 3000 Fax: 0116 228 3001

HMP/YOI Lewes (M L YOI(CL))
1 Brighton Road Lewes BN7 1EA
Tel: 01273 785100 Fax: 01273 785101

HMP Leyhill (M D O)
Wotton-under-Edge Gloucestershire GL12
8BT
Tel: 01454 264000 Fax: 01454 264001

HMP Lincoln (M L)
Greetwell Road Lincoln LN2 4BD
Tel: 01522 663000 Fax: 01522 663001

HMP IRC Lindholme (M C CL O IRC)
Bawtry Road Hatfield Woodhouse Doncaster
DN7 6EE
Tel: 01302 524700 Fax: 01302 524750

HMP Littlehey (M C CL)
Perry Huntingdon PE28 0SR
Tel: 01480 333000 Fax: 01480 333070

HMP Liverpool (M L)
68 Hornby Road Liverpool L9 3DF
Tel: 0151 530 4000 Fax: 0151 530 4001

HMP Long Lartin (M A CL)

South Littleton Evesham Worcestershire
WR11 8TZ
Tel: 01386 295100 Fax: 01386 295101

HMP Lowdhan Grange* (Serco) (M B CL)
Old Epperstone Road Lowdham Nottingham
NG14 7DA
Tel: 0115 966 9200 Fax: 0115 966 9220

HMYOI Low Newton (F L CL)
Brasside Durham DH1 5YA
Tel: 0191 376 4000 Fax: 0191 376 4001

HMP Maidstone (M C CL)
36 County Road Maidstone ME14 1UZ
Tel: 01622 775300 Fax: 01622 775301

HMP Manchester (M A CL)
Southall Street Manchester M60 9AH
Tel: 0161 817 5600 Fax: 0161 817 5601

HMP/YOI Moorland Closed (M C CL YOI)
Bawtry Road Hatfield Woodhouse Doncaster
DN7 6BW
Tel: 01302 523000 Fax: 01302 523001

HMP/YOI Moorland Open (M D O YOI)
Thorne Road Hatfield Doncaster DN7 6EL
Tel: 01405 746500 Fax: 01405 746501

HMP Morton Hall (F O)
Swinderby Lincoln LN6 9PT
Tel: 01522 666700 Fax: 01522 666750

HMP The Mount (M C CL)
Molyneaux Avenue Bovingdon Hemel
Hempstead HP3 0NZ
Tel: 01442 836300 Fax: 01442 836301

HMP/YOI New Hall (F CL YOI(CL))
Dial Wood Flockton Wakefield WF4 4XX
Tel: 01924 803000 Fax: 01924 803001

HMYOI Northallerton (YOI CL)
15A East Road Northallerton North Yorkshire
DL6 1NW
Tel: 01609 785100 Fax: 01609 785101

HMP North Sea Camp (M D O)
Freiston Boston PE22 0QX
Tel: 01205 769300 Fax: 01205 769301

HMP/YOI Norwich (M L YOI(CL))
Knox Road Norwich NR1 4LU
Tel: 01603 708600 Fax: 01603 708601

HMP Nottingham (M L)
Perry Road Sherwood Nottingham NG5 3AG
Tel: 0115 872 4000 Fax: 0115 872 4001

HMP Onley (M C CL)
Willoughby Rugby CV23 8AP
Tel: 01788 523400 Fax: 01788 523401

HMP/YOI Parc* (G4S) (M B L YOI(CL RC))
Heol Hopcyn John Bridgend CF35 6AP
Tel: 01656 300200 Fax: 01656 300201
Website: www.hmpparc.co.uk

HMP Pentonville (M L)
Caledonian Road London N7 8TT
Tel: 020 7023 7000 Fax: 020 7023 7001

HMP Peterborough* (Kalyx) (M F L RC)
Saville Road Westwood Peterborough PE3 7PD
Tel: 01733 217500 Fax: 01733 217501

HMYOI Portland (YOI CL)
104 Grove Road Portland Dorset DT5 1DL
Tel: 01305 715600 Fax: 01305 715601

HMP/YOI Prescoed (M C CL D O YOI(O))
Coed-y-Paen Pontypool NP4 0TB
Tel: 01291 675000 Fax: 01291 675158

HMP Preston (M L)
2 Ribbleton Lane Preston PR1 5AB
Tel: 01772 444550 Fax: 01772 444551

HMP Ranby (M C CL)
Retford Nottinghamshire DN22 8EU
Tel: 01777 862000 Fax: 01777 862001

HMP/YOI Reading (YOI RC)
Forbury Road Reading RG1 3HY
Tel: 0118 908 5000 Fax: 0118 908 5001

HMP Risley (M C CL)
Warrington Road Risley Warrington WA3 6BP
Tel: 01925 733000 Fax: 01925 733001

HMP Rochester (YOI)
1 Fort Road Rochester ME1 3QS
Tel: 01634 803100 Fax: 01634 803101

HMP Rye Hill* (G4S) (M B)
Willoughby Rugby CV23 8SZ
Tel: 01788 523300 Fax: 01788 523311
Website: www.hmpryehill.co.uk

HMP Send (F CL)
Ripley Road Send Woking GU23 7LJ
Tel: 01483 471000 Fax: 01483 471001

HMP Shepton Mallet (M C CL)
Cornhill Shepton Mallet Somerset BA4 5Lu
Tel: 01749 823300 Fax: 01749 823301

HMP Shrewsbury (M B L)
The Dana Shrewsbury SY1 2HR
Tel: 01743 273000 Fax: 01743 273001

HMP Spring Hill (M D O)
Grendon Underwood Aylesbury HP18 0TL
Tel: 01296 445000 Fax: 01296 445001

HMP Stafford (M C CL)
54 Gaol Road Stafford ST16 3AW
Tel: 01785 773000 Fax: 01785 773001

HMP Standford Hill (Sheppey Cluster) (M D O)
Church Road Eastchurch Sheerness ME12 4AA
Tel: 01795 884500 Fax: 01795 884638

HMP Stocken (M C CL)
Stocken Hall Road Stretton Oakham Rutland LE15 7RD
Tel: 01780 795100 Fax: 01780 410767

HMYOI Stoke Heath (J YOI CL)
Market Drayton Shropshire TF9 2JL
Tel: 01630 636000 Fax: 01630 636001

HMP/YOI Styal (F CL L)
Wilmslow Cheshire SK9 4HR
Tel: 01625 553000 Fax: 01625 553001

HMP Sudbury (M D O)
Ashbourne Derbyshire DE6 5HW
Tel: 01283 584000 Fax: 01283 584001

HMP Swaleside (Sheppey Cluster) (M B CL)
Brabazon Road Eastchurch Isle of Sheppey ME12 4AX
Tel: 01795 804100 Fax: 01795 804200

HMP Swansea (M L RC(YOI))
200 Oystermouth Road Swansea SA1 3SR
Tel: 01792 485300 Fax: 01792 485430

HMYOI Swinfen Hall (YOI CL)
Swinfen Lichfield Staffordshire WS14 9QS
Tel: 01543 484000 Fax: 01543 484001

HMYOI Thorn Cross (J YOI O)
Arley Road Appleton Thorn Warrington WA4 4RL
Tel: 01925 805100 Fax: 01925 805101

HMP Usk (M C CL)
47 Maryport Street Usk Monmouthshire NP15 1XP
Tel: 01291 671600 Fax: 01291 671752

HMP The Verne (M C CL)
The Verne Portland Dorset DT5 1EQ
Tel: 01305 825000 Fax: 01305 825001

HMP Wakefield (M A)
5 Love Lane Wakefield WF2 9AG
Tel: 01924 612000 Fax: 01924 612001

HMP Wandsworth (M L)
PO Box 757 Heathfield Road Wandsworth London SW18 3HS
Tel: 020 8588 4000 Fax: 020 8588 4001

HMYOI Warren Hill (YOI CL)
Hollesley Woodbridge Suffolk IP12 3JW
Tel: 01394 633400 Fax: 01394 633401

HMP Wayland (M C CL)
Griston Thetford Norfolk IP25 6RL
Tel: 01953 804100 Fax: 01953 804220

HMP Wealstun (M C CL D O)
Church Causeway Thorp Arch Wetherby LS23 7AZ
Tel: 01937 444400 Fax: 01937 444401

HMP Wellingborough (M C CL)
Millers Park Doddington Road
Wellingborough NN8 2NH
Tel: 01933 232700 Fax: 01933 232701

HMYOI Werrington (J)
Ash Bank Road Stoke-on-Trent ST9 0DX
Tel: 01782 463300 Fax: 01782 463301

HMYOI Wetherby (J CL)
York Road Wetherby LS22 5ED
Tel: 01937 544200 Fax: 01937 544201

HMP Whatton (M C CL)
New Lane Whatton Nottingham NG13 9FQ
Tel: 01949 803200 Fax: 01949 803201

HMP Whitemoor (M A)
Longhill Road March Cambridgeshire PE15 0PR
Tel: 01354 602350 Fax: 01354 602351

HMP Winchester (M B L)
Romsey Road Winchester SO22 5DF
Tel: 01962 723000 Fax: 01962 723001

HMP Wolds* (G4S) (M L)
Everthorpe Brough East Yorkshire HU15 2JZ
Tel: 01430 428000 Fax: 01430 428001
Website: www.hmpwolds.co.uk

HMP Woodhill (M A L)
Tattenhoe Street Milton Keynes MK4 4DA
Tel: 01908 722000 Fax: 01908 867063

HMP Wormwood Scrubs (M L)
PO Box 757 Du Cane Road London W12 0AE
Tel: 020 8588 3200 Fax: 020 8588 3201

HMP Wymott (M C CL)
Ulnes Walton Lane Leyland Preston PR26 8LW
Tel: 01772 442000 Fax: 01772 442001

*Further information can be found on the Prison Service website
www.justice.gov.uk/contacts/prison-finder

HIGH SECURITY PSYCHIATRIC HOSPITALS

Ashworth Hospital
Parkbourn Maghull Liverpool L31 1HW.
Tel: 0151 473 0303. Fax: 0151 526 6603

Broadmoor Hospital
Crowthorne Berkshire RG11 7EG.
Tel: 01344 773111. Fax: 01344 754848

Rampton Hospital
Retford Nottinghamshire DN22 0PD.
Tel: 01777 248321. Fax: 01777 248442

IMMIGRATION REMOVAL CENTRES

Brook House
Perimeter Road South Gatwick Airport
Gatwick West Sussex RH6 0PG.
Tel: 01293 566500 Fax: 01293 566590

Campsfield House
Langford Lane Kidlington Oxon OX5 1RE.
Tel: 01865 233600 Fax: 01865 233723

Colnbrook
Colnbrook Bypass Harmondsworth West
Drayton Middlesex UB7 0FX.
Tel: 020 8607 5200 Fax: 020 8607 5383

Dover
Dover Immigration Removal Centre The
Citadel Western Heights Dover Kent CT17 9DR.
Tel: 01304 246400. Fax: 01304 246401.

Dungavel
Strathaven South Lanarkshire ML10 6RF Tel:
01698 395000 Fax: 01698 395067

Harmondsworth
Colnbrook Bypass Harmondsworth West
Drayton UB7 0HB.
Tel: 020 8283 3850 Fax: 020 8283 3851

Haslar
Haslar Immigration Removal Centre 2
Dolphin Way Gosport Hampshire PO12 2AW.
Tel: 023 9260 4000 Fax: 023 9260 4001

Lindholme
HMP Lindholme Bawtry Road Hatfield
Woodhouse Doncaster DN7 6EE.
Tel: 01302 524700 Fax: 01302 524620

Morton Hall
Swinderby, Lincolnshire LN6 9PT
Tel: 01522 666700 Fax: 01522 666850

Tinsley House
Perimeter Road South Gatwick Airport
Gatwick West Sussex RH6 0PG.
Tel: 01293 434800 Fax: 01293 434846

Yarl's Wood
Twinwoods Road Clapham Bedfordshire
MK41 6HL.
Tel: 01234 821000 Fax: 01234 821096

HM PRISONS IN NORTHERN IRELAND

Prison Service Headquarters
Dundonald House Upper Newtownards Road
Belfast BT4 3SU.
Tel: 028 9052 2922. Fax: 028 9052 4330

HMYOI Hydebank Wood
Hospital Road Belfast BT8 8NA.
Tel: 028 9025 3666 Fax: 028 9025 3668

HMP Maghaberry
Old Road Ballinderry Upper Lisburn Co
Antrim BT28 2PT.
Tel: 028 9261 1888 Fax: 028 9261 9516

HMP Magilligan
Point Road Limavady Co Londonderry BT49
0LR.
Tel: 028 7776 3311 Fax: 028 7775 0819

Northern Ireland Prison Service College
Woburn House Millisle Co Down BT22 2HS.
Tel: 028 9186 3000 Fax: 028 9186 3022

SCOTTISH PRISON SERVICE

Headquarters
Calton House 5 Redheughs Rigg Edinburgh
EH12 9HW.
Tel: 0131 244 8745 Fax: 0131 244 8774

Chief Executive, Scottish Prison Service: Colin
McConnell
Director of Operations: Dan Gunn
Director of Human Resources: Stephen Swan
Director of Partnerships & Commissioning:
Eric Murch.
Director of Finance & Business Services: Willie
Pretswell
Director of Estates & Technical Services: Andy
Craig

HMP Aberdeen
Craiginches 4 Grampian Place Aberdeen
AB11 8FN.
Tel: 01224 238300 Fax: 01224 896209

HMP Addiewell
Station Road Addiewell West Lothian EH55
8QA.
Tel: 01506 874500 Fax: 01506 874501

HMP Barlinnie
Barlinnie Glasgow G33 2QX.
Tel: 0141 770 2000 Fax: 0141 770 2060

HMP Castle Huntly
Open Estate Castle Huntly Longforgan Nr
Dundee DD2 5HL.
Tel: 01382 319333 Fax: 01382 319350

HMP Cornton Vale
Cornton Road Stirling FK9 5NU.
Tel: 01786 832591 Fax: 01786 833597

HMP Dumfries
Terregles Street Dumfries DG2 9AX.
Tel: 01387 261218 Fax: 01387 264144

HMP Edinburgh
33 Stenhouse Road Edinburgh EH11 3LN.
Tel: 0131 444 3000 Fax: 0131 444 3045

HMP Glenochil
King O'Muir Road Tullibody
Clackmannanshire FK10 3AD.
Tel: 01259 760471 Fax: 01259 762003

HMP Greenock
85 Old Inverkip Road Gateside Greenock
Renfrewshire PA16 9AH.
Tel: 01475 787801 Fax: 01475 783154

HMP Inverness
Porterfield Duffy Drive Inverness IV2 3HH.
Tel: 01463 229000 Fax: 01463 229010

HMP Kilmarnock
Bowhouse Mauchline Road Kilmarnock KA1
5AA.
Tel: 01563 548800 Fax: 01563 548845

HMP Low Moss
Crosshill Road Bishopbriggs Glasgow.
Tel: 0141 762 4848 Fax: 0141 772 6903

HMP Perth
3 Edinburgh Road Perth PH2 8AT.
Tel: 01738 622293 Fax: 01738 630545

HMP Peterhead
Salthouse Head Peterhead Aberdeenshire
AB42 2YY.
Tel: 01779 479101 Fax: 01779 470529

HMYOI Polmont
Brightons Nr Falkirk Stirlingshire FK2 0AB.
Tel: 01324 711558 Fax: 01324 714919

HMP Shotts
Scott Drive Shotts Lanarkshire ML7 4LE.
Tel: 01501 824000 Fax: 01501 824001

Scottish Prison Service College
Newlands Road Brightons Falkirk
Stirlingshire FK2 0DE.
Tel: 01324 710400 Fax: 01324 710401

State Hospital
Carstairs Junction Lanark ML11 8RP.
Tel: 01555 840293 Fax: 01555 840024

SCOTTISH RESIDENTIAL ESTABLISHMENTS

Ballikinrain School
Balfron Glasgow G63 0LL.
Tel: 01360 440244/440645

Junior, intermediate school for 34 boys and girls. Head: Paul Gilroy. Correspondent: Chris McNaught, General Manager Children's Services, Crossreach, Church of Scotland, Charis House, 47 Milton Road East, Edinburgh EH15 2SR. Tel: 0131 657 2000.

Geilsland School
Beith Ayrshire KA15 1HD.
Tel: 01505 504044

Residential school for 35 senior boys. Head: Paul Gilroy. Correspondent: Chris McNaught, General Manager Children's Services.

Kibble Education & Care Centre
Goudie Street Paisley Renfrewshire PA2 3LG.
Tel: 0141 889 0044 Fax: 0141 887 6694
Email: mailbox@kibble.org

Provides residential care for 50 boys and day care for 40 boys aged 9–19. Chief Executive: Mr G. Bell. Correspondent: D. Nairn, Messrs Milne and Craig, 79 Renfrew Road, Paisley PA3 4DA.

Rossie Secure Accommodation Services
Montrose Angus DD10 9TW.
Tel: 01674 820204 Fax: 01674 820249

Secure accommodation service provides care and education for 28 boys and girls aged 12–18. Chief Executive & Official Correspondent: Mr Richard Murray.

St Mary's, Kenmure
Bishopbriggs Glasgow G64 2EH.
Tel: 0141 586 1200 Fax: 0141 586 1224
Email:
Administrator@stmaryskenmure.org.uk

Secure facility providing care and education for boys and girls. Correspondents: Messrs J. McSparran & McCormick, Waterloo Chambers, 19 Waterloo Street, Glasgow G2 6AH. Tel: 0141 248 7962/226 5203.

St Philip's School
Plains Airdrie Lanarkshire ML6 7SF.
Tel: 01236 765407

Junior/intermediate school for 36 boys with social, emotional and behavioural difficulties. A/Principal: Mr B. Harold. Correspondents: Messrs J. McSparran & McCormick.

Springboig St John's School
Glasgow G33 4EH.
Tel: 0141 774 9791

Senior school for boys. Head of Service: Ms Grace Fletcher. Correspondents: Messrs J. McSparran & McCormick.

Wellington School
Peebles Road Nr Penicuik Midlothian EH26 8PT.
Tel: 01968 672515

School for boys aged 13–16, any denomination. Up to 16 residents and 34 day places. Head & Official Correspondent: Mr R. Wells.

ISLE OF MAN, JERSEY, GUERNSEY

Isle of Man Prison
99 Victoria Road Douglas Isle of Man IM2 4RD.
Tel: 01624 621306 Fax: 01624 628119 special visits 01624 663813

HMP La Moye, Jersey
La Moye St Brelade Jersey Channel Islands JE3 8HQ.
Tel: 01534 441800 Fax: 01534 441880

Guernsey Prison
Les Nicolles Baubigny St Sampson Guernsey Channel Islands GY2 4YF.
Tel: 01481 248376 Fax: 01481 247837 Fax: 01481 200949

IRISH PRISON SERVICE

IDA Business Park Ballinalee Road
Longford Co Longford
Tel: 043 35100 Fax: 043 35101
Email: info@irishprisons.ie
Website: www.irishprisons.ie

Arbour Hill Prison
Arbour Hill Dublin 7
Tel: 01 6719333 Fax: 01 6799518

Castlerea Prison
Harristown Castlerea Co Roscommon
Tel: 094 962 5213 Fax: 094 962 6226

Cloverhill Remand Prison
Cloverhill Road Clondalkin Dublin 22
Tel: 01 6304530/01 6304531 Fax: 01 6304580

Cork Prison
Rathmore Road Cork City Cork
Tel: 021 4518800 Fax: 021 4518860

Dochas Centre
North Circular Road Dublin 7
Tel: 01 8858987 Fax: 01 8858910

Limerick Prison
Mulgrave Street Limerick
Tel: 061 204700 Fax: 061 415116

Loughan House Open Centre
Blacklion Co Cavan
Tel: 071 9853059 Fax: 071 9853234

Midlands Prison
Dublin Road Portlaoise Co Laois
Tel: 05786 72110/72100 Fax: 05786 72219

Mountjoy Prison
North Circular Road Dublin 7
Tel: 01 8062800 Fax: 01 8062824

Portlaoise Prison
Dublin Road Portlaoise Co Laois
Tel: 05786 21318 Fax: 05786 20997

Shelton Abbey
Arklow Co Wicklow
Tel: 0402 42300 Fax: 0402 42350

St Patrick's Institution
North Circular Road Dublin 7
Tel: 01 8062896 Fax: 01 8307705

Training Unit
Glengarriff Parade North Circular Road
Dublin 7
Tel: 01 8062890 Fax: 01 8307460

Wheatfield Prison
Cloverhill Road Clondalkin Dublin 22
Tel: 01 620 9400 Fax: 01 620 9430

Under development
Thornton Hall
Kilworth

INDEX